Lecture Notes in Computer Science 4326

Commenced Publication in 1973
Founding and Former Series Editors:
Gerhard Goos, Juris Hartmanis, and Jan van Leeuwen

Stefan Göbel Rainer Malkewitz
Ido Iurgel (Eds.)

Technologies for Interactive Digital Storytelling and Entertainment

Third International Conference, TIDSE 2006
Darmstadt, Germany, December 4-6, 2006
Proceedings

Springer

Volume Editors

Stefan Göbel
Rainer Malkewitz
Ido Iurgel

ZGDV e.V. - Computer Graphics Center
Digital Storytelling Department
Rundeturmstr. 10, 64283 Darmstadt, Germany
E-mail: Stefan.Goebel@zgdv.de

Library of Congress Control Number: 2006937264

CR Subject Classification (1998): H.5, H.4, I.2, I.3, I.4, I.7, J.5

LNCS Sublibrary: SL 2 – Programming and Software Engineering

ISSN 0302-9743
ISBN-10 3-540-49934-2 Springer Berlin Heidelberg New York
ISBN-13 978-3-540-49934-3 Springer Berlin Heidelberg New York

Springer is a part of Springer Science+Business Media

springer.com

Printed in Germany

Typesetting: Camera-ready by author, data conversion by Scientific Publishing Services, Chennai, India
Printed on acid-free paper SPIN: 11944577 06/3142 5 4 3 2 1 0

Preface

This textbook contains the proceedings from the 3rd International Conference on Technologies for Interactive Digital Storytelling and Entertainment (TIDSE 2006). The contributions are grouped into six sections, which include subjects like virtual characters, story authoring, narrative systems, and examples of their application.

During recent years, Interactive Digital Storytelling has evolved as a prospering research topic, banding together formerly disjoined disciplines stemming from the arts and humanities as well as computer science. The subject of this book is of course strongly related to the notion of 'storytelling', which has been used as an effective means for the communication of knowledge and social values, ever since the early history of humankind. It also tries to build a bridge between current academic trends, for example, by investigating and formalizing narrative aspects of computer games, and by its developments for the experience-based design of human–media interaction in general.

Starting with a scientific workshop at national level in 2000, the Digital Storytelling group at ZGDV Darmstadt originated TIDSE, the International Conference for Technologies in Interactive Digital Storytelling and Entertainment. TIDSE 2003, TIDSE 2004, and TIDSE 2006 continued this series, and provided the latest research outcomes and indications for its usage within entertainment applications. Further, TIDSE continued its collaboration with the International Conference on Virtual Storytelling, ICVS (conducted 2001, 2003 and 2005 in France): While ICVS focuses on virtual storytelling and VR environments, the focus of TIDSE is set on interactive storytelling, addressing the narrative paradox and the overall question of how to bring true interactivity into storytelling systems. Scientific contributions to TIDSE 2006 thus covered a broad spectrum, from conceptual ideas, theories, systems and technological questions, to best practice examples in the different storytelling application domains, with a focus on entertainment and games.

Apart from traditional conference talks and sessions, TIDSE 2006 provided specific workshops and round tables, mainly around the issue of 'story authoring'. In the pre-conference program, on December 3, a demo workshop titled "Little Red Cap: The Authoring Process in Interactive Storytelling" brought together creative persons to present their latest authoring tools and concepts. During the conference program, two round table/panel discussions in the context of the ongoing EU projects INSCAPE and U-CREATE provided deeper insight and mulitple perspectives brought to the audience by invited guests from research and industry. In addition, practical demonstrations of systems, tools and concepts, as well as best-practice examples from industry were presented in the demo and exhibition area.

TIDSE 2006 was organized by the Storytelling group at ZGDV Darmstadt. However, the conference only came about thanks to the financial, moral and pragmatic support of various institutions: ZGDV Darmstadt e.V. and the INI-GraphicsNet foundation hosted and sponsored the conference. The European Commission provided support for the round tables by way of the projects IN-SCAPE and U-CREATE, and Nintendo of Europe offered a prize for the best paper award.

The social program had its highlight in the first public presentation of the philosophical service installation Ludus Globi Digital. It combines new media, drama, and personal service, investigating new forms of presenting and experiencing themes from the humanities. Ludus Globi Digital could only be brought into being with the dedication and enthussiasm of students from several German universities.

December 2006

Stefan Göbel
Rainer Malkewitz
Ido Iurgel

Table of Contents

Story Authoring

Virtual Characters

Storytelling and Games

Applications

Believable Agents and Intelligent Story Adaptation for Interactive Storytelling

Mark O. Riedl[1] and Andrew Stern[2]

[1] University of Southern California, Institute for Creative Technologies, 13274 Fiji Way, Marina del Rey, California, USA
[2] Procedural Arts LLC, Portland, Oregon, USA
riedl@ict.usc.edu, andrew@proceduralarts.com

Abstract. Interactive Narrative is an approach to interactive entertainment that enables the player to make decisions that directly affect the direction and/or outcome of the narrative experience being delivered by the computer system. Interactive narrative requires two seemingly conflicting requirements: coherent narrative and user agency. We present an interactive narrative system that uses a combination of narrative control and autonomous believable character agents to augment a story world simulation in which the user has a high degree of agency with narrative plot control. A drama manager called the Automated Story Director gives plot-based guidance to believable agents. The believable agents are endowed with the autonomy necessary to carry out directives in the most believable fashion possible. Agents also handle interaction with the user. When the user performs actions that change the world in such a way that the Automated Story Director can no longer drive the intended narrative forward, it is able to adapt the plot to incorporate the user's changes and still achieve dramatic goals.

1 Introduction

Simulation has been, and continues to be, an important part of computer ente-Srtainment. Computer games such as *The Sims* and *SimCity* are simulations in the strictest sense. The initial parameters, a model of state change, and legal player moves are the forces that drive the user's experience. Real-time strategy games are simulations of combat and have been used effectively for entertainment and for military training. First- and third-person action/adventure games also rely on simulation to a lesser extent. Each mission can be considered a simulation of physics, weapon effects, opponent movements, etc. One difference between action/adventure games and other games such as *The Sims* or *SimCity* is the use of story to constrain the player's experience to a particular narrative path.

It is a commonly held belief that narrative and interactivity are diametrically opposed, meaning one can have story or one can have interactivity but not both simultaneously. The most common role of story in computer games is to provide "glue" between missions. Modern computer games consist of interleaved periods of interactive play and cut scenes – short non-interactive scenes that transition from one mission to the next, providing the player with goals and motivation for the next

S. Göbel, R. Malkewitz, and I. Iurgel (Eds.): TIDSE 2006, LNCS 4326, pp. 1 – 12, 2006.

segment of game play. In this mode of alternating between game play and cut scenes, story elements and simulation are kept strictly separate. This is one manifestation of the trade-off between control and coherence [10; 14]. On one hand, the player wants control to make decisions for the player's character. On the other hand, game designers want the player to experience a coherent narrative progression.

Interactive Narrative is an approach to interactive entertainment that enables the player to make decisions that directly affect the direction and/or outcome of the narrative experience being delivered by the computer system. We are building an Interactive Narrative System for training and entertainment that mixes story and simulation. But why use simulation? After all, it has been demonstrated that Interactive Narratives can be constructed out of branching story sequences such as those used by the Choose-Your-Own-Adventure books. The reason is that simulation provides a realistic, continuous, life-like modality for interaction that can result in a more immersive and compelling experience for players than simple branching stories. The realism of simulation is also beneficial to educational games that provide a realistic learning experience, in addition to a coherent narrative progression. Mateas and Stern [9] lay out a continuous spectrum of technical approaches to interactive narrative ranging from *strong autonomy* to *strong story*. The strong autonomy approach advocates that interactive narratives be generated procedurally by simulating a virtual environment populated by autonomous agents that play the roles of characters. The strong story approach advocates that a single decision-making process that operates as if it were a hypothetical author, choosing the activities of all story world characters in a centrally coordinated fashion, generate interactive narratives.

We present an interactive narrative system that uses a combination of strong story and strong autonomy techniques to provide a story-based experience in which the player also has a high degree of agency. A prototype called IN-TALE (the Interactive Narrative Tacit Adaptive Leader Experience) demonstrates the combination of declarative story planning and reactive agents in the context of a story-based military leader training scenario. In the scenario, the user plays the role of a military leader in a foreign peacekeeping mission. Computer-controlled agents play the roles of merchants in a volatile marketplace. The scenario is based on dramatic principles and is designed to expose the user to dramatic and pedagogical situations. While the prototype scenario has an emphasis on training, we believe that the techniques described here have broad applicability to interactive entertainment applications.

The system is built on top of a 3D graphical computer game engine. Agent-controlled characters are capable of managing their own behaviors and interacting with the user through limited natural language. The player has a wide repertoire of actions, including dialogue acts, that he or she can perform at any time resulting in the look and feel of a social simulation instead of a more conventional branching interactive media. An intelligent component called the Automated Story Director maintains a script of expected events that it uses to provide high-level direction to the character agents to cause the story to progress. Character agents carry out local autonomous behaviors as well as behaviors that satisfy directives. While the character agents are capable of handling a wide degree of variability due to player interactivity, it is possible that the player can perform actions that make it impossible for the Automated Story Director to continue the story. In these circumstances, the Automated Story Director is capable of adapting the story structure to find new ways to coherently achieve its dramatic and pedagogical goals.

2 Related Work

Interactive narrative systems attempt to tell a story in which the user is able to make decisions and perform actions that dynamically affect the direction and/or outcome of the story. We catalog some related work according to the strong-autonomy/strong-story spectrum of technical approaches described in [9]. *Strong autonomous* approaches to interactive narrative are those in which narrative emerges through simulated interactions between believable character agents. Strong autonomy systems include [1], [3], and [5]. *Strong story* approaches to interactive narrative are those in which some form of global story control is implemented. Often story control is achieved through the use of a drama manager [4], a special agent that attempts to coerce the experience of the user to conform to a pre-existing story structure by directing or influencing the story world characters. Strong story systems include [20], [14], [21], and [17].

The work we present here is an attempt to integrate strong story and strong autonomy approaches to achieve greater impact on the user in terms of coherent narrative experience and the perception of user-agency. Systems that rely on combinations of autonomous agents and drama management include [2], [7], and [10]. Particularly relevant work are the *Mimesis* system [14; 21] and the *Façade* interactive drama [10]. Our system merges the generative narrative drama management approach pioneered by the *Mimesis* system combined with the believable agent capabilities of the ABL behavior specification language [11] used to endow NPCs with reactivity and believability of characters in *Façade*.

Also relevant are research efforts to create interactive narrative systems for training and education (c.f. [8], [16], [5], and [12]).

3 Example Plot

To motivate the problem, we present the following simple example narrative in which the user plays the role of a Captain in the U.S. Army as part of a peacekeeping mission deployed to a foreign country. The user plays the role of a Captain in charge of maintaining the security of civilian merchants and buyers in a marketplace.

The narrative is expected to unfold as follows. While the player is engaged in daily procedures concerning the new marketplace, a heated argument breaks out between two merchants. One merchant, named Saleh, accuses the other, named Hassan, of luring away his customers. Afterwards, Saleh approaches the trainee and complains that the presence of the peacekeeping troops is impinging on his ability to do business in the marketplace. He makes a dire prognostication that violence could ensue. Hassan, in contrast appears to be nothing but friendly. Later that day, Hassan slips away from the marketplace and returns concealing an improvised explosive device (presumably acquired from an insurgent conspirator). When Saleh steps away from his place of business, Hassan plants the bomb there. Shortly afterwards, the bomb goes off. Fortunately for all involved, the bomb is a dud, but the marketplace is nonetheless left in a state of chaos, panic, and confusion.

Note that if the player succeeds in preventing the attack by catching Hassan with the explosive device then it will be impossible for Hassan to plant the bomb and therefore impossible for the bomb to go off and establish the primary dramatic outcome. In the remainder of the paper, we describe a novel technique for trainee experience management that is designed incorporate strong story aspects into a system that retains the look and feel of a simulation.

4 Believable Characters

Social simulation is achieved through a collection of non-player characters (NPCs) that are reactive and appear intelligent, motivated, and reactive. Our agents are partly composed of a broad, general collection of local autonomous behaviors that are designed to afford suspension of disbelief. Local autonomous behaviors (LABs) such as working, running errands, shopping, etc. supply agents with a "rich inner life." The objective is not to have agents that are competent reasoning agents, but agents that *appear* to be intelligent, motivated, emotional, and consequently believable. This emphasis on appearance is referred to as a "broad but shallow" approach to agents [2]. That is, agents can perform a wide repertoire of behaviors in a convincing manner but without performing "deep" reasoning.

It is important that NPCs are capable of acting to bring about a specific narrative. Narrative-specific interactive events such as confronting the player and acquiring, planting, and detonating an explosive device, are carried out by narrative directive behaviors (NDBs). Narrative directive behaviors are incorporated into the agents' behavior repertoires before run-time and triggered by high-level narrative direction from the Automated Scenario Director (see Section 5). These scenario-specific behaviors are designed to modulate, mix with, and/or override local autonomous behaviors.

4.1 Agent Architecture

To achieve the desired life-like qualities we implemented our agents using the reactive planning language ABL (A Behavior Language) [11] using a behavioral infrastructure licensed from the Procedural Arts Behavior Library (PABL). The ABL language and PABL infrastructure were initially created for the interactive drama, *Façade* [10] and are designed to support the detailed expression of artistically-chosen personality, automatic control of real-time interactive animation, and architectural support for many of the requirements of believable agents (see [6] for an enumeration of properties of believable agents).

In ABL, an activity (e.g., walking to the user, or speaking a line of dialog) is represented as a goal, and each goal is supplied with one or more behaviors to accomplish its task. An active goal chooses one of its behaviors to try. A behavior is a series of steps, that can occur sequentially or in parallel, that accomplish a goal. Preconditions are used to determine behavior applicability by matching against working memory elements (WMEs) that make up the agent's subjective knowledge about the world. A behavior may itself have one or more subgoals.

Further, to harness the dramatic power of multi-agent teams of characters, ABL supports authoring of joint goals and behaviors [11]. When a goal is marked as joint, ABL enforces coordinated entry into and exit from the team members' behaviors chosen to accomplish the goal. This coordination is transparent to the programmer and analogous to the STEAM multi-agent coordination framework [18]. The driving design goal of joint behaviors is to combine rich semantics for individual expressive behavior with support for the automatic synchronization of behavior across multiple agents.

4.2 Behavior Authoring

There are two broad categories of agent behaviors that must be authored: local autonomous behaviors and narrative directive behaviors. Local autonomous behaviors (LABs) are the somewhat generic, re-usable "inner life" activities such as working, running errands, shopping, etc. Narrative directive behaviors (NDBs) are scenario-specific and are triggered by the Automated Scenario Director.

Local Autonomous Behaviors. Local autonomous behaviors (LABs) are implemented as a loosely structured collections of sub-behaviors called "LAB goals", that depend on and assert simple events in episodic memory. For example, the *opening the store* LAB may involve the agent *unlocking the store*, *unpacking boxes*, *chatting with assistant*, and *displaying new goods*. Each of these parts is implemented as its own simple LAB goal with ordering constraints between goals. User interactions, should they occur, can easily be inserted during or in between the loosely organized LAB goals.

Each individual agent is responsible for selecting and sequencing their local autonomous behaviors. LABs manage their own sequencing. Whenever a new LAB needs to run, either upon start-up or once the previous LAB completes, each LAB may make a bid for how important it is to run next. A LAB chooses a bid strength depending upon current world conditions, such as time of day, and episodic memory as needed; if the LAB does not care to run, it does not bid at all. A simple arbitration behavior makes a weighted probability choice among the bids.

Narrative Directive Behaviors. By contrast, narrative directive behaviors (NDBs) are more tightly structured collections of sub-behaviors, intended to perform more important and more sophisticated parts of the scenario. NDBs are invoked when an agent is directed to adopt a goal by the Automated Story Director (as described in Section 5). Further, user interaction afforded in NDBs usually needs to be richer and more responsive than in LABs. The collection of sub-behaviors that constitute an NDB are organized around the dramatic beat [9; 10], a component of the PABL infrastructure. A beat is a ~60-second-long dramatic interaction between characters such as a shared experience (e.g., witnessing a bombing), or a brief conflict about a topic (e.g., the user questioning an agent), or the revelation of an important secret. Beats are organized around a collection of "beat goal" behaviors, the dramatic content that the beat is designed to communicate to the user through animated performance.

The PABL authoring strategy for handling user interaction within a beat is to specify the "canonical" beat goal behavior logic (i.e., what dramatic performance the author intends the beat to accomplish), as well as a collection of beat-specific handler behaviors that modify this default logic in response to user interaction. Each interaction handler behavior is a demon that waits for some particular type of user interaction and "handles" it accordingly. User interaction includes dialogue interaction (the user can speak to the characters at any time by entering discourse acts, e.g. "disagree Saleh") and physical interaction (e.g. the user takes action such as "arrest Saleh"). Every NDB specifies some beat-specific handlers; additionally, there are more generic LAB handlers for handling interactions for which there are no beat-specific responses supplied by the current beat.

5 The Automated Story Director

There is a trade-off between narrative coherence and the trainee's perception of self-agency [14]. On one hand, a storytelling system will want to ensure a coherent progression of scenario events that lead the trainee through a dramatic and pedagogically relevant sequence of events. On the other hand, in a training simulation, the player needs to observe a realistic, populated social environment best delivered by a simulation and be able to problem-solve – to perform actions and make decisions. In our system, the player is allowed to perform any of a wide repertoire of communicative and physical actions at any time. Simulation with social agents alone, however, is not enough to ensure that the trainee is exposed to dramatic and pedagogically relevant situations in an appropriate and contextual order.

To ensure that the player's experience is managed and that the appropriate sequence of dramatic situations occur, an agent called the Automated Story Director acts as an unseen over-mind to coerce the player's experience to conform to a given scenario. Specifically, the Automated Story Director maintains a representation of the expected sequence of events that make up the scenario. From this representation, the story director derives and distributes directives to the NPCs to achieve certain conditions necessary to drive the scenario forward. For example, the Automated Story Director would direct the agent representing the Saleh character (from the example in Section 3) to establish the condition that the player distrusts the character – something that that agent might not choose to do if left to it's own devices.

Consistent with the design decision that the trainee can perform any of a wide repertoire of actions at any time, the Automated Story Director has a second responsibility: to monitor the simulation environment, detect inconsistencies between the simulation state and the expected narrative, and to reconcile any inconsistencies. This is essential in balancing the trade-off between narrative coherence and trainee self-agency because the player may perform actions that make it impossible for the story director to progress towards the desired dramatic situations. For example, the player could decide to apprehend Hassan before he plants the improvised explosive device in the marketplace. In this instance, the player has created an inconsistency between the simulation state (e.g. Hassan is detained) and the expected narrative representation (e.g. it must not be the case that Hassan is detained for the bomb to be planted). When inconsistencies arise, the narrative is adapted to reconcile the inconsistencies.

5.1 Anticipating Necessary Narrative Adaptations

Following [14; 21], we represent narratives as partially-ordered plans. A plan contains steps – events that change the state of the world – and annotations that explicitly mark the temporal and causal relationships between all steps in the plan, defining a partial order indicating the steps' order of execution [19]. Plan steps, which in this application represent plot points, have preconditions are conditions in the world that must be true for the operator to be applicable. Effects are conditions in the world that become true after successful execution of the instantiated operator. Other annotations, called *causal links*, are used to mark all causal relationships between the steps in the plan. In a plan, a causal link relates the effect of one plan step to a precondition of another plan step that is temporally constrained to occur later than the first operator. A plan is not considered complete unless every precondition of every plan step is satisfied by a causal link.

Using planning structures to model scenarios is advantageous because a plan can be analyzed for points in which failure can occur due to unpredictable and interactive behaviors performed by the trainee. We use a technique similar to that described in [14] to analyze the causal structure of the scenario to determine all possible inconsistencies between plan and simulation state that can occur during the entire duration of the scenario. For every possible inconsistency that can arise that threatens a causal link in the plan, an alternative scenario plan is generated. We have modified the original algorithm to use a tiered replanning approach. For each potential inconsistency that can arise, first the system attempts to repair the causal link that is threatened by the inconsistency. Barring that, the system attempts to remove any events that were dependent on the threatened causal link and then repair the plan by filling in events required to restore causal coherence. Finally, if all else fails, the system attempts to select new goals and relevant learning situations and rebuild the scenario plan.

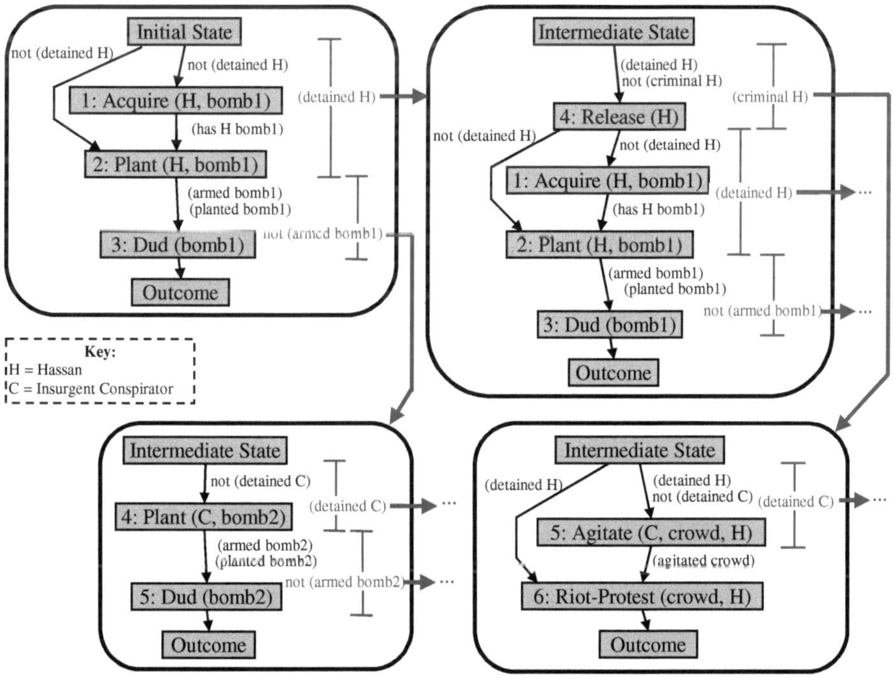

Fig. 1. Portion of the generated branching story

Narrative replanning can be performed offline to avoid delays due to computation [14]. The result of this process is a tree of contingency plans in which each plan represents a complete narrative starting at the initial world state or at the point in which an inconsistency can occur. If the user performs an action that causes an inconsistency that threatens the narrative plan, the system looks up the appropriate branch in the tree of contingencies and seamlessly begins directing the believable agents based on the new narrative plan. User actions that do not threaten causal links are considered by the Automated Story Director to be consistent with the current narrative structure [14]. We find that by separating the system into a drama manager and autonomous character agents, the drama manager can focus on plot-level details and that relatively few user actions threaten the plot. This allows for a larger repertoire of user actions – including dialogue acts – to be implemented. Autonomous character agents are capable of providing a large amount of variability in the user's experience, especially with dialogue, without requiring the plot to be regenerated. We believe this will invoke in the user a greater sense of agency.

5.2 Example of Narrative Adaptation

Continuing the example story from Section 3, suppose the system is instantiated with a pre-constructed plan (shown in the upper left-hand corner of Fig. 1). Except for the plan steps and causal links in the original narrative plan, everything in the tree of contingency plans is automatically generated, including the potential inconsistency annotations of the original narrative itself. For the purposes of this discussion we have simplified the narrative further into the following steps:

1. `Hassan` acquires `bomb1`
2. `Hassan` plants `bomb1` in the marketplace
3. `bomb1` goes off as a dud.

The directed connections between steps are causal links indicating what must be true for a step to be applicable and which preceding step establishes that condition. This plan represents the narrative that will execute if the trainee does not inadvertently (or intentionally) cause an inconsistency between the simulation state and the plan structure. The plan is annotated with two intervals in which inconsistencies will threaten the causal coherence of the plan:

– `Hassan` is detained before he completes the planting of `bomb1`
– `bomb1` is disarmed before it goes off.

The former can occur if the trainee has Hassan arrested. The latter can occur if the player finds the bomb and calls in a bomb squad.

Each potential inconsistency annotation links to a contingency plan that repairs the inconsistency, should it occur. The detainment of Hassan links to a plan (upper right of Fig. 1) that is repaired by the addition of a step that releases Hassan from custody, ostensibly because he has not committed a crime. If the player searches Hassan and Hassan in fact has `bomb1` in his possession, he will be marked as a criminal. This does not cause an inconsistency that threatens the original plan. But once detained, if Hassan is marked as a criminal, he cannot be released, instantly causing a second transition to the plan in the lower right of Fig. 1.

The plan in the lower left of Fig. 1 represents the narrative in which `bomb1` is found and disarmed by the trainee. In this case, the outcome of the original narrative cannot be achieved. This plan repairs the original narrative by having an insurgent conspirator step in and complete the attack on the marketplace with a second bomb.

The plan in the lower right of Fig. 1 represents the narrative in which Hassan is caught with a bomb and permanently detained. Like the previously described contingency, the outcome of the original narrative can still be achieved by having an insurgent conspirator complete the attack with a second bomb. However the planner can find a more appealing variation. The insurgent conspirator uses the detention of Hassan to agitate a crowd. The crowd then riots in protest of the player's actions.

6 Integrating Story Direction and Believable Character Agents

Believable character agents, the Automated Story Director, and a variant of the example scenario from Section 3 have been combined into a prototype called IN-TALE (the Interactive Narrative Tacit Adaptive Leader Experience). The system is built on top of a 3D computer game engine. The system is currently in prototype stage, implementing a version of the example scenario in Section 3 that can be automatically adapted in a large number of ways. The Automated Story Director generates a tree of contingency plans with over 1000 paths, although most are minor variations for maintaining narrative coherence. Fig. 2 shows a screenshot of the trainee (central avatar) being confronted by an NPC. A set of believable social agents are implemented as semi-autonomous, intelligent agents in ABL. Each ABL agent controls a single virtual avatar in the game engine. The Automated Story Director receives state updates from the game engine via an interface described in [13].

As in [1], the Automated Story Director is responsible for coercing the player's experience to conform to a high-level plot structure. A high-level plot is one that

Fig. 2. Screenshot of trainee (central) confronting a non-player character

describes the narrative progression in terms of a sequence of world states – or *plot points* – that describe situations or scenes that should occur without reference to the primitive character actions that have occurred to bring out each state or the primitive character actions that should occur once a situation occurs. The directives from the Automated Story Director to the NPCs are not detailed instructions. Directives are goals the NPC must adopt, in terms of declarative world state change. Character agents are left to determine the best way to achieve the directives, barring any behavior case world states explicitly prohibited by the Director. This gives the agents the leeway to engage in behaviors that are believable, achieve scenario goals, and take full advantage of the current world situation, e.g. executing one or more NDBs as described in Section 4.

The paradigm of high-level directives and low-level agent autonomy opens up the possibility of an agent selecting joint behaviors. A joint behavior is a method – one of many methods known to the agent for achieving a goal – that co-opts the participation of other NPCs in the world for close coordination of activity and/or dramatic effect. For example, if the agent representing the Hassan character is directed to acquire an explosive device (e.g. `(has Hassan bomb1)`), that character might not be able to do so while the trainee is in close proximity. Assume there is a directive that `(knows player (has Hassan bomb1))` should never become true. The agent may select a joint behavior – one of many known methods for acquiring an object – that in conjunction with another agent, possibly a bystander, creates a diversion. The joint behavior provides coordination so that Hassan knows to slip off while the player is distracted.

To avoid the appearance of agents that schizophrenically [15] switch between goals– in this case goals autonomously selected for believability and goals demanded by the Story Director – behaviors selected to achieve the appearance of believability (LABs) and behaviors that achieve narrative goals (NDBs) must mix seamlessly. Local autonomous behaviors can run in parallel and/or interleave with behaviors selected to achieve scenario goals. "Real life" behaviors can be modulated to believably blend with the high-level scenario behaviors imposed on them. Modulations of LABs include: timing alteration to accommodate the needs of the scenario; reducing the number of physical resources required to avoid conflicts with scenario-driven behaviors; and avoiding actions that would violate overall believability in any way.

Mixing NDBs with LABs involves annotating NDBs and LABs with the resources they require: location requirements, object requirements, emotional state requirements and so on. When an NDB prepares for execution in order to fulfill a directive from the Automated Story Director, the NDB announces its resource requirements. LABs are coded with behavior variations in order to gracefully degrade their performance to accommodate the needs of the more important NDBs, while still behaving believably. When a LAB is required to interrupt or even abort its execution to serve the NDB's needs, it selects from a variety of short transition-out sub-behaviors to believably "glue", i.e., explain why. For example, if a *cleaning the store* LAB needs to be truncated or aborted in order for the agent to participate in NDBs to acquire and plant a bomb, the agent may choose to insert some dialogue to the effect of, "Hmmm, the store is pretty clean today… I think sweeping can wait till tomorrow". Similarly, whatever LAB begins after the NDB ends can select from transition-in sub-behaviors similarly "gluing" the agent's behavior back into its daily routine.

7 Conclusions

Our approach draws heavily from previous research. A generative narrative approach is used by our drama manager, the Automated Story Director, modeled after the methods developed in [14; 21]. The believable agents are based on the ABL behavior specification language [11] originally developed for the *Façade* [10] interactive drama system. Our goal is to provide an interactive narrative experience that merges the benefits of the strong story approach with the benefits of the strong autonomy approach. Interactive narrative requires two seemingly conflicting requirements: coherent narrative and user agency. On one hand, we would like to ensure a coherent narrative experience for a player that always has a dramatic quality that leads to a recognizable outcome. One the other hand, we would like the player to be able to perform actions to effect change in the world in a non-superficial way – to be able to influence the direction and outcome of the narrative. Our system presents the user of the perception of a simulation-like experience to afford greater agency to the user. Meanwhile, plot-level drama management ensures that the simulation progresses in such a way as to provide the user with a narrative experience. Specifically, we provide for believable agents that can interact with the player in real-time and are autonomous enough to plan their own courses of action for increased believability. The agents are directed by the Automated Story Director at a high level of abstraction so that local situations can play out naturally. Most player interaction is handled by the believable agents. When the player performs actions that change the world in a way that makes it impossible for the Story Director to continue the plot, the Automated Story Director adapts the plot to incorporate the player's actions while still achieving the dramatic goals.

Acknowledgements

The project or effort described here has been sponsored by the U.S. Army Research, Development, and Engineering Command (RDECOM). Statements and opinions expressed do not necessarily reflect the position or the policy of the United States Government, and no official endorsement should be inferred.

References

[1] Aylet,, R.: Emergent narrative, social immersion and "storification." *Proc. of the 1st International Workshop on Narrative and Interactive Learning Environments* (2000).

[2] Bates, J.: Virtual Reality, Art, and Entertainment. *Presence: The Journal of Teleoperators and Virtual Environments*, 1, (1992).

[3] Cavazza, M., Charles, F., & Mead, S.: Planning Characters' Behaviour in Interactive Storytelling. *Journal of Visualization and Computer Animation*, 13 (2002) 121-131.

[4] Kelso, M., Weyhrauch, P., Bates, J.: Dramatic Presence. *Presence: The Journal of Teleoperators and Virtual Environments*, 2 (2005).

[5] Louchart, S., Aylett, R., Dias J., & Paiva, A.: Unscripted narrative for affectively driven characters. *Proc. of the 1st National Conf. on Artificial Intelligence and Interactive Digital Entertainment* (2005).

[6] Loyall, A.B.: *Believable Agents: Building Interactive Personalities*. Ph.D. Dissertation, Carnegie Mellon University (1997).
[7] Magerko, B. Story Representation and Interactive Drama. *Proc. of the 1st Conf. on Artificial Intelligence and Interactive Digital Entertainment* (2005).
[8] Marsella, S., Johnson, W.L., LaBore, K.: Interactive Pedagogical Drama. *Proc. of the 4th Int. Conf. on Autonomous Agents* (2000).
[9] Mateas, M., & Stern, A.: Towards Integrating Plot and Character for Interactive Drama. *AAAI Spring Symposium on Social Intelligent Agents: The Human in the Loop* (2000).
[10] Mateas, M, & Stern, A.: *Architecture, Authorial Idioms and Early Observations of the Interactive Drama* Façade (Technical Report CMU-CS-02-198). School of Computer Science, Carnegie Mellon University (2002).
[11] Mateas, M. & Stern, A.: A Behavior Language: Joint Action and Behavior Idioms. In: H. Prendinger & M. Ishizuka (eds.): *Life-like Characters: Tools, Affective Functions and Applications*. Springer (2004).
[12] Mott, B.W., Lester, J.C.: U-Director: A Decision-Theoretic Narrative Planning Architecture for Storytelling Environments. *Proc. of the 5th Int. Joint Conf. on Autonomous Agents and Multi Agent Systems* (2006).
[13] Riedl, M.O.: Towards Integrating AI Story Controllers and Game Engines: Reconciling World State Representations. *Proc. of the IJCAI Workshop on Reasoning, Representation and Learning in Computer Games* (2005).
[14] Riedl, M.O, Saretto, C.J., and Young, R.M.: Managing Interaction Between Users and Agents in a Multi-Agent Storytelling Environment. *Proc. of the 2nd Int. Conf. on Autonomous Agents and Multi Agent Systems* (2003).
[15] Sengers, P.: Schizophrenia and Narrative in Artificial Agents. In: M. Mateas & P. Sengers (eds.): *Narrative Intelligence*. John Benjamins (2003).
[16] Si, M., Marsella, S., & Pynadath, D.V.: Thespian: Using multi-agent fitting to craft interactive drama. *Proc. of the 4th Int. Joint Conf. on Autonomous Agents and Multi Agent Systems* (2005).
[17] Szilas, N.: IDtension: a narrative engine for interactive drama. *Proc. of the 1st Int. Conf. on Technologies for Interactive Digital Storytelling and Entertainment* (2003).
[18] Tambe, M.: Towards Flexible Teamwork. *Journal of Artificial Intelligence Research*, 7 (2003).
[19] Weld, D.: An Introduction to Least Commitment Planning. *AI Magazine*, 15 (1994).
[20] Weyhrauch, P.: *Guiding Interactive Fiction.* Ph.D. Dissertation, School of Computer Science, Carnegie Mellon University (1997).
[21] Young, R.M., Riedl, M.O., Branly, M., Jhala, A., Martin, R.J., and Saretto, C.J.: An Architecture for Integrating Plan-Based Behavior Generation with Interactive Game Environments. *Journal of Game Development*, 1 (2004) 51-70.

An Event-Driven, Stochastic, Undirected Narrative (EDSUN) Framework for Interactive Contents

Adam Barclay and Hannes Kaufmann

Institute of Software Technology and Interactive Systems, Vienna University of Technology, Favoritenstr. 9-11/188/2,
A-1040 Vienna, Austria
kaufmann@ims.tuwien.ac.at, adam.br@gmx.at

Abstract. In this paper, we present an extensible framework for interactive multimodal contents, with emphasis on augmented reality applications. The proposed framework, EDSUN, enables concurrent and variable narrative structures as well as content reusability and dynamic yet natural experience generation. EDSUN's main components include a canonical specification of 5-state lexical syntax and grammar, stochastic state transitions, and extensions for hierarchical grammars to represent complex behavioral and multimodal interactions. The benefits of EDSUN in enabling classical contents to support the affordances of AR environments and in complementing recent published works are also discussed.

Keywords: augmented reality, event driven, stochastic transitions, undirected narrative, content, framework, grammar, story telling.

1 Introduction

Interactive environments pose several challenges for multimodal contents. One challenge is the lack of pre-existing rich interactive contents to draw upon, whereas new content creation is expensive and time consuming [5]. Despite the availability of rich classical contents, as found in film and drama, their suitability in matching the corresponding affordances of interactive environments is another challenge. Early storytelling systems and history-centric applications, for instance, often put the user in a passive audience role [6],[7]. This is due to the monolithic non-event driven nature of classical contents. Recent interactive story telling environments [10],[11] rely on hierarchical task networks to support emergent narrative and balance user's needs of both interactivity and realism. A third challenge is multimodal content reusability, where no common format exists to enable cross application content reuse. Furthermore, the interplay between the content author's objectives, choice of narrative, and the user's tendencies to drift off the main path envisioned by the content author, form the basis for the opposing attributes of interactive environment affordances.

In this paper, an extensible framework for interactive multimodal contents is presented, where the mentioned challenges are addressed. In the course of our treatment of the challenges in interactive multimodal contents, the focus is on

S. Göbel, R. Malkewitz, and I. Iurgel (Eds.): TIDSE 2006, LNCS 4326, pp. 13–24, 2006.

augmented reality environments, due to the additional constrains present. Table 1 illustrates the relevant affordances in augmented reality environments and EDSUN's approach in supporting them.

Table 1. A taxonomy of relevant AR affordances and the proposed enabling techniques

AR Environment Attributes	Supported Technique	Section
Unconstrained user interactions	Infinitesimal undirected narrative elements.	2
Real-time event driven environment	5-state lexical syntax, canonical form for content presentation.	2.1
Task oriented within an undirected narrative	State coupling through stochastic state transitions.	2.2
New experience generation, complex interaction representation, specialized narrative support	Hierarchical grammars	2.3
Rich content and multiplicity support.	Structured and unstructured variations	2.4

The first component of EDSUN, as detailed in Section 2.1, is an undirected narrative-based canonical form for content representation with a 5-state lexical syntax and grammar. The proposed canonical form enforces the separation between narrative structure and narrative content, and enables content classification and segmentation to support event-driven environments, as well as cross-application reusability. The lexical syntax and grammar model the set of possible user experiences within the AR environment, and script actual user experiences that result from his interactions. The second component of EDSUN, Section 2.2, forms stochastic state transitions that provide the content author with flexibility in incorporating variety of user experiences ranging from exploratory style navigation to task-oriented step-by-step interactions. The third component, hierarchical grammars in Section 2.3, is an extensibility mechanism to support author-specific interaction methodologies such as support for the Branigan cinematic narrative model [1] as implemented in DINAH[4]. Section 2.4 presents structured and unstructured variations, which enable support for variable tone experiences. An example is then presented to illustrate EDSUN's support for variety of experiences from a single source script, and we conclude with a summary of what has been accomplished.

1.2 Related Work

Traditionally, interactive media has adopted a classical narrative approach to content presentation due to the pre-programmed nature of contents within a given environment. The interactive media environment is then viewed as the narrator, and the user is encouraged to participate through dramatic enactment as an avatar of himself or others in the environment as in GEIST[6] or in MacIntyre *et al* [5]. The contents are usually borrowed from film, books, and drama along with their linear and non-linear narrative formats. In this section, several relevant published works, in the area of interactive narrative are reviewed and examined including: Mad Tea-Party[5], GEIST[6], Three Angry Men[7], DINHA[4], CrossTalk[10], Goldfinger[12], and Façade[8],[9].

MacIntyre *et al* [5] applies new media theory and media remediation techniques to propose solutions for AR-based interactive narrative, and in the process, explores the creation of unconstrained story telling systems in Mad Tea-Party. One of the key problems facing interactivity in the AR world as pointed out by MacIntyre *et al* [5] is the need for an unconstrained narrative to bring the story-world to reality. The paper asserts that an unconstrained narrative defines a contradiction: if the user is unconstrained, there is no guarantee that he'll experience the narrative or reach the pre-scripted ending - as a result of not being in the right location at the right time. Consequently, the paper proposes using the affordances of the objects in the virtual and physical world as well as symmetric activities of the interactive objects involved to encourage the user to stay within the limitations of the predefined narrative. The techniques used are based on conventions borrowed from both film and drama – in defining the interaction and in directing the participant. To facilitate subplot branching, the author breaks user interaction up into primitives or basic building blocks that the story can respond to. Procedural nodes along with corresponding procedural rules that match pre-scriptesd subplots are utilized to enhance the variety of user's experiences.

GEIST [6] is a history-based digital story telling system, where the non-linear interactive narrative encourages the user to influence the flow of the story. The digital story telling system in GEIST educates the user about historical aspects of the locations the user encounters. Although the user is allowed to explore the AR environment, interacting with the virtual world is pre-scripted and directed where a story is told based on the participant's proximity to a location of a historical relevance. The act of story telling itself is immotive as the participant assumes a passive audience's role.

Three Angry Men, TAM [7], explores interactive content presentation of multiple points of view. The user can experience one of three jurors' point of view by sitting in a given juror's seat, and listening to the other two jurors "deliver their dialogue". The dialogue stops when the participant decides to switch seats in order to get the point of view of other jurors. Similar to GEIST, dialogue delivery expects the user to assume a passive audience role, which could be envisioned as suitable for a court setting.

Digital storytelling with DINAH[4] addresses the challenge of multiple subplot generation through digital narrative composition. In DINAH, Ventura *et al* [4] uses a metalinear narrative approach, and applies a Branigan cinematic narrative model [1] to auto-compose stories from a database of story clips. The narrative engine in DINAH is constrained through preconditions and post-conditions that obey the Branigan model embodied within each story clip, as well as narrative state vectors that determine the user's progress towards one of the pre-scripted endings. Despite the similarity to Mad Tea-Party [5] in breaking up the story up into primitives or basic building blocks, content segmentation is narrative-specific and subplot-specific. In other words, specific to the story or application with no support for content reusability or new experience generation.

CrossTalk[10] is a virtual character exhibition for public spaces, where interaction between the virtual characters and the user is based on a combination of pre-scripted scenes as well as an hierarchical task network (HTN) plan-based dialog generation. Similarly, Goldfinger [12], which is a multimodal mixed reality role-playing interactive environment, relies on HTN to handle the frequent yet unexpected user interactions by requesting a new action plan to achieve the current task, which in turn, leads the story into a new direction based on user's actions. Both of these examples strive to create a balance between task-oriented environments and free-play through HTN replanning. Despite the flexibility of HTN, it is not possible to implement in each character all possible responses for the permutations of possible interactions [11].

Façade [9] is an interactive first person drama that relies on dialogue generation to maintain the desired interactive narrative. Dialogue generation in Façade is text based, and defines a many-to-few mapping of surface text to discourse acts [8]. Façade's natural language processing (NLP) mechanism defines a set of 24 discourse acts, against which user input is mapped. The response of Façade's characters is the product of an HTN plan that defines a particular narrative path, and the NLP environment that determines the output text.

Although the mentioned works reflect the rich possibilities within interactive multimodal contents, common challenges as has been shown, become apparent, namely: classical contents are (a) application/story specific, (b) monolithic, (c) with limited number of subplots, and (d) support for one type of narrative. As shown in [9], [11],[10], dynamic dialog and scene generation are becoming popular in addressing the affordances of interactive environments, and in enabling a rich user experience. In this paper, a framework is proposed to compliment the mentioned works by defining infinitesimal undirected narrative elements, along with associated lexical syntax, and stochastic state transitions to enable the embodiment of interactive environment affordances and reusability into classical contents.

2 A Framework for Event-Driven AR Content

In formulating a framework for interactive multimodal contents in AR environments, the affordances of AR environments need to be considered, and be embodied within the attributes of AR geared content. As shown in table 1, AR affordances include real-time interactivity, event driven environment updates, and synchronized multi-modality for audio and visual content, as well as geophysical location and orientation.

The challenge in simultaneously satisfying the mentioned affordances for a rich and immersive user experience lies in developing a balance between contradictory attributes. For example, the proposed approach of infinitesimal undirected narrative elements to enable unconstrained user interactions, may not help the user accomplish any given task [5], and may result in plot discontinuity. Similarly, event driven environments are, by definition, a hindrance to narrative continuity. Legacy contents, such as film and classical drama that are often the focus of story telling systems and history-based tourist guide applications, do not lend themselves easily to real-time event driven environments.

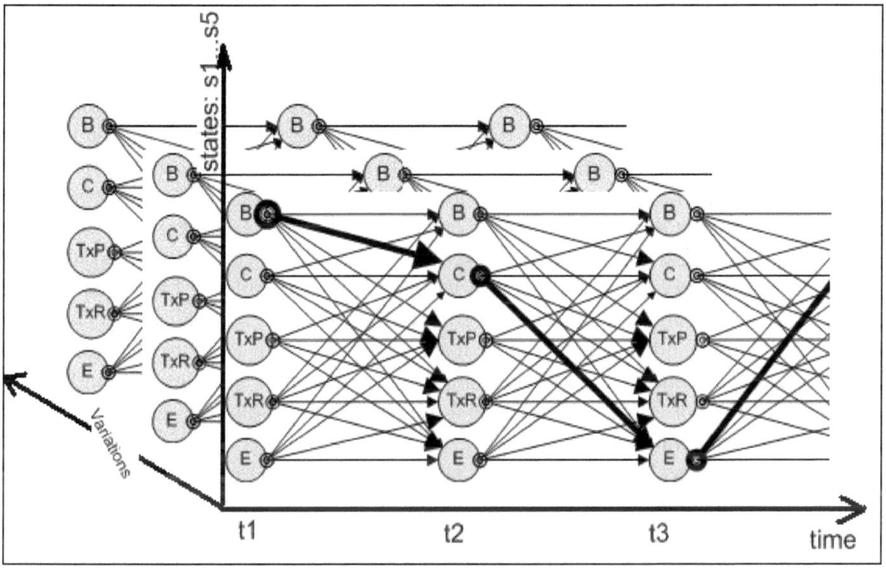

Fig. 1. An illustrative diagram of the universe of infinitesimal undirected narrative elements, mapped to the 5-state canonical form. The user's experience is highlighted by blue arrows, representing the path of stochastic state transitions.

If the present tense could be viewed as an engine that transforms unstructured future events into a structured past tense, an AR environment could be viewed as an engine that transforms a subset of the universe of infinitesimal undirected narrative elements that represent future events into a past represented by a linear narrative. With this in mind, we model the possible set of interactions in the AR environment with a set of infinitesimal undirected narrative elements S, a subset of which, s, forms the user experience and becomes his past, scripted by his own interactions within the AR environment, and is represented by a linear narrative. Therefore, our choice for basing EDSUN on infinitesimal undirected narrative elements lies in its suitability for event driven environments, and flexibility in modeling linear and non-linear narratives, as well as random real-world events.

Despite its flexibility, basing EDSUN on infinitesimal undirected narrative elements poses two challenges. The first is in formulating a methodology for classifying and segmenting contents into basic elements that could be mapped onto the desired set of infinitesimal undirected narrative elements. The second lies in task-oriented applications, where an undirected narrative approach may not guarantee that the user experiences what the content author has in mind. To address the first challenge, a 5-state canonical content representation is introduced in Section 2.1, along with the required lexical syntax and grammar. The second challenge is addressed through stochastic state transitions, in Section 2.2, as an extensible mechanism to control the order and degree of coupling within the corpus of infinitesimal undirected narrative elements.

2.1 Undirected Narrative, Canonical Representation, and Lexical Syntax

The choice of infinitesimal undirected narrative elements lies in both their flexibility to model classical content segments and real world events, which are often unrelated or loosely coupled, and in the fact that a directed narrative, in its linear and non-linear forms, could be built from a set of tightly coupled, ordered, infinitesimal undirected narrative elements. To maintain separation between narrative structure and content, and to support content reusability within and across applications, the segmented multimodal contents need to be mapped onto the set of undirected narrative elements that are in a canonical form. Although variety of published works attempted to break contents up into story clips, behavioral elements, or basic building blocks as in Mad Tea-Party [5], and DINAH [4], the identified building blocks and behavioral elements are story specific, and not in a standardized canonical form to facilitate reusability. In this section, a canonical form defining cross-application infinitesimal undirected narrative model for generic multimodal contents, including the required lexical syntax, states, and grammar are specified.

The proposed lexical syntax specifies 5 states against which multimodal contents need to be segmented and classified, and is shown below in extended Backus-Naur form:

(1) A begin element: an infinitesimal undirected narrative element representing the start of a story line or task subset. The begin element could be used by the content author to determine which stage the user is in, within the AR environment, and is specified as follows:

```
<B>::= {begin-element}|{intro-element}
```

(2) A transaction start element: an infinitesimal undirected narrative element representing the start of an interaction, a story element, or a sub-task, that requires a response. Transaction elements need to be time limited as not to interfere with user's experience, and may be associated with a time-out.

```
<TxP>::= {<tx-initiation-element>}
```

(3) A transaction response element: an infinitesimal undirected narrative element representing the response to an interaction, a story element, or a sub-task, that was initiated with a TxP element. This element could be utilized by the content author to determine success or failure of the user in accomplishing a given task.

```
<TxR>::= { <tx-response-element> }
```

(4) A continuity element: an infinitesimal undirected narrative element that represents any generic interaction that can not be classified as one of the

other 4 states. This element could also be a no-op or a time-wait, and could be used by the content author to maintain continuity of the user's experience across objects and across variations.

```
<C> ::= { <space-filler> }                |
        { <redirection-element> }  |
        { <suggestion-element>  }  |
        { <surprise-element> }        |
        { <interruption-element> }
```

(5) An end element: an infinitesimal undirected narrative element that represents the end of a story line or task subset. The end element could be used by the content author to determine user's progress within the AR environment, as well as success or failure in accomplishing a given task, and is specified as follows: <E> ::= { <end-element> }

With the total set of interactions within an AR environment modeled by a set of infinitesimal undirected narrative elements, as specified above, a given user's interactions within such an environment capture his own unique experience, and is modeled by a linear narrative whose context free grammar, CFG, is specified as follows:

```
<user-interaction-element>::= [<B>]*[<C>]*
                              [[<TxP>]*[<C>]*[<TxR>]*]*
                              [<C>]*[<E>]*
<user-experience> ::=  { <user-interaction-element> }
```

Conversely, the AR environment creates an experience for the user by transforming a subset of infinitesimal undirected narrative elements representing future events into a past represented by a linear narrative, which could be stated as follows:

```
<linear-narrative> ::= [<undirected-narrative-element>]*
```

2.2 Stochastic State Transitions

Transforming a set of unrelated or loosely coupled infinitesimal undirected narrative elements that represent the set of possible user interactions into a past - represented by a linear narrative - requires attribute-based association, or state transitions, between the elements that represent states, of the mentioned set. One extreme would be to organize the infinitesimal elements into an ordered directed linear narrative, where unrestricted user interactions within the interactive environment would be sacrificed. Another extreme would be to assign the state transitions between all the infinitesimal elements equal probabilities, resulting in a random environment, often referred to as a universe of chaos. The proposed framework supports both extremes, reflecting EDSUN's flexibility and extensibility.

Mathematically, the universe of segmented and classified contents S, are divided into subsets s_i, where each subset embodies a given objective or an element of a story line, and is assigned a temporal position relative to other subsets, as illustrated by the time line $(t_1..t_n)$ in Figure 1. State transition probabilities are then assigned to each

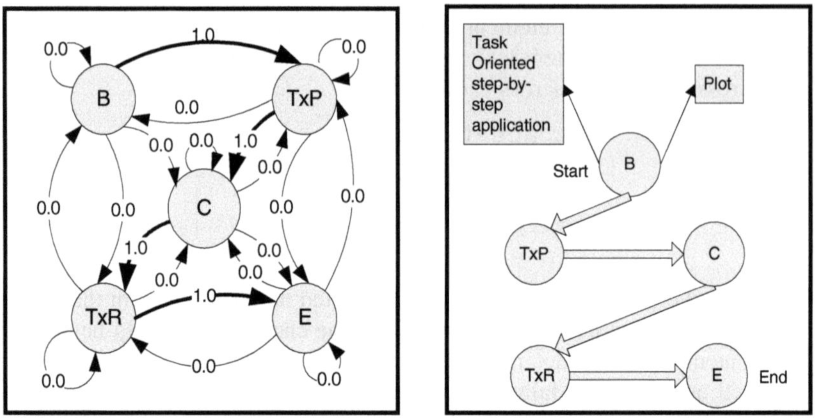

Fig. 2. On the right: an illustration of a classical linear directed narrative. On the left, EDSUN's support for an equivalent linear directed narrative.

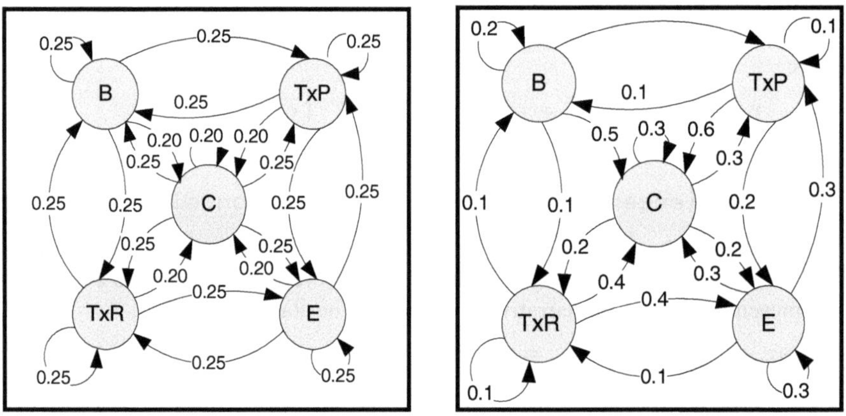

Fig. 3. On the left: EDSUN's support for the universe of chaos, and fora sample model of event-driven AR contents on the right

state transition within a given subset as shown in Figures 2 and 3, as well as to those that connect two subsets based on their temporal positions. The state transition probabilistic values allow for the desired degrees of freedom of a user's interactions, whereas additional external weights can be added, and adjusted externally based on the interactive environment or user's profile to provide for additional fine tuning and enhanced realism of user's experience.

The lexical syntax of section 2.1 specifies 5 states as follows:

$$S = \{ B, C, TxP, TxR, E \}. \tag{1}$$

To form the user's experience from the set of infinitesimal undirected narrative elements, the likelihood of each state transition is specified as follows:

$A = \{ a_{ij} \}, \quad 1 \le i,j \le N;$ where A is the set of state transitions between each of the states in S, and (2)

$$\sum_{j=1}^{N} a_{ij} = 1; \text{ where } a_{ij} \text{ is the state transition probability from } s_i \rightarrow s_j \qquad (3)$$

Therefore, the maximum number of possible unique user experiences in proposed model per content sequence is: $g = (N)^t$ (4)

where N = 5 as the number of states in the proposed lexical syntax, and t is the number of time slice increments that forms the subset of infinitesimal undirected narrative elements for a given user's experience. This provides for a quantifiable measurement of percent coverage of a given AR environment implementation compared with the real world, or the maximum possible set of experiences the user may have.

2.3 Hierarchical Grammars

The output of stochastic state transitions of Section 2.1 forms the input set for one or more optional layers of experience specific grammars, such as that of Branigan's cinematic narrative[1] that was implemented in DINAH[4], natural language processing of Façade[8], or plan-based multimodal interaction processing of Goldfinger[12]. Hierarchical grammars enable concurrent support for multiple narratives, complex interactions [2], and languages [3], as well as specialized new experience generation from existing contents [9],[10],[12], all while enforcing the corresponding preconditions, post conditions, and experience continuity requirements. Consequently, EDSUN extensions may maintain and enhance story coherency, or ensure a specific level of dramaturgy. For example, the metalinear narrative approach of DINAH[4], and its auto-generation of story-clip based experiences can be supported here as an extension.

2.4 Structured and Unstructured Variations

To represent environments with rich contents and variety of tones, support for structured and unstructured variations is introduced. Variations are structured when variable contents representing each of the 5 states in equation (1) exist for the lifetime of a given experience, and is represented along the variations axis in Figure 1. Variations are unstructured when variable contents exist for a subset of the 5-states in equation (1) and not for the full duration of a given experience. Unstructured variations are modeled through sub state transitions within each state where variety of contents exist. Both structured and unstructured variations enable recreating environments with varying tones for a given experience, such as polite, rude, reckless, or insane environments to name a few, as well as representation of historical versus fictional and mythological environments.

2.5 Content Reusability and New Experience Generation – An Example

The example introduced here illustrates content reusability and new experience generation once contents are segmented, and classified according to the 5-state lexical syntax of Section 2.1. Figure 4 contains the original text of a dialog from one of Austin Power's movies titled "International Man of Mystery". Figure 5 contains

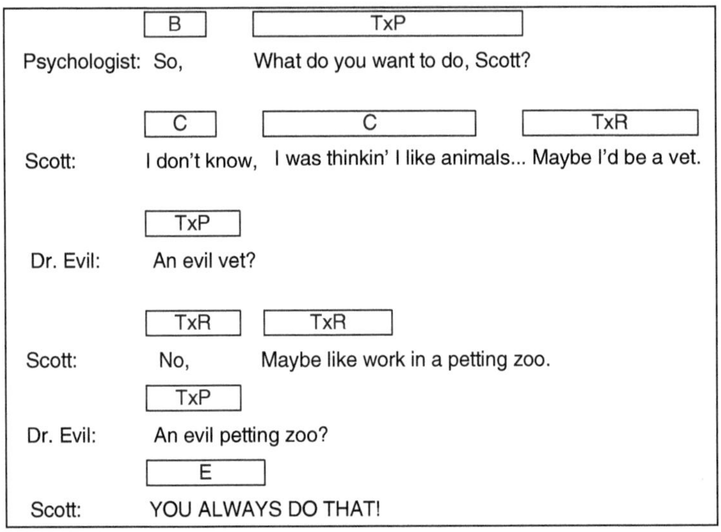

Fig. 4. A sample classification of an original dialog from Austin Powers "Inter-national Man of Mystery" – as mapped to the proposed 5-state canonical repre-sentation described in Section 2.1

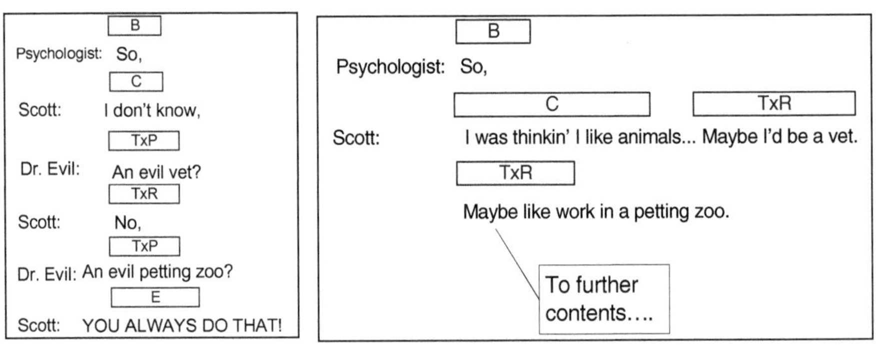

Fig. 5. An illustration of grammar and state transition compliant variants of original text of Figure 4. (a) On the left, a typical teenager-parent talk emphasizing impatience and lack of context. (b) On the right, a thoughtful detailed dialog with no references to Dr. Evil.

two new experiences generated from the original text, while complying with the grammar and state transitions of Sections 2.1 and 2.2. The left side of Figure 5 presents the experience of a typical teenager-parent's talk, emphasizing impatience and lack of context. The right side of Figure 5 presents a more thoughtful experience with no references to "evil". This example illustrates the extensibility of EDSUN, and its ability to support different narratives concurrently as well as to generate new experiences from existing contents.

3 Conclusion

In this paper, an extensible framework for interactive multimodal content representation is introduced and examined. The proposed framework, EDSUN, enforces separation between narrative structure and content. EDSUN is based on infinitesimal undirected narrative structure to support unconstrained user interactions, and to enable event-driven interactivity with multimodal contents. EDSUN's canonical format along with the proposed lexical syntax and grammar enable cross-application content reusability and new experience generation as shown in Section 2.5. The associated stochastic state transitions enable concurrent support for different types of narratives, and provide the content author with flexibility in coupling content elements. Extensibility through the proposed hierarchical grammars enable complex behavioral representation and user-defined narrative structures, whereas structured and unstructured variations facilitate the management of rich contents. Based on early conceptual experimentation with EDSUN, the potential it provides as an enabler for rich interactive multimodal contents as well as cross-application reusability is rather promising.

References

1. Branigan, E. "Narrative Comprehension and Film", Sightlines,ed. E. Buscombe. Vol. 1. Routledge, New York, New York, 1992.
2. Oliver, N. Horvitz, E., and Garg, A. "Layered representations for human activity recognition", In Fourth IEEE Int. Conf. on Multimodal Interfaces, pages 3-8, 2002.
3. Ivanov, Y., Bobick A., "Recognition of visual activities and interactions by stochastic parsing", IEEE Trans. PAMI, vol. 22(8), pp. 852-872, 2002.
4. Ventura D., Brogan D., "Digital Storytelling with DINAH: dynamic, interactive, narrative authoring heuristic.", IFIP First International Workshop on Entertainment Computing, May 2002.
5. MacIntyre, B., Bolter J.D., Moreno E., Hannigan B., "Augmented Reality as a New Media Experience", IEEE and ACM International Symposium on Augmented Reality (ISAR'01), pp. 197-206, 2001.
6. Schneider, H., "GEIST: Mobile outdoor AR-Information System for Historical Education with Digital Story Telling", CeBIT 2003, and Intergeo 2003.
7. MacIntyre, B., Bolter, J. D., "Single-narrative, multiple point-of-view dramatic experiences in augmented reality", Virtual Reality, Vol. 7, pp. 10-16, 2003.
8. Mateas, M., Stern A., "Natural Language Understanding in Façade: Surface-text Processing". In Proceedings of the 2nd Technologies for Interactive Digital Storytelling and Entertainment (TIDSE'04), Darmstadt, Germany.

9. Mateas, M., Stern A., “A Behaviour Language: Joint Action and Behavioural Idioms”. In Predinger, H. and Ishiuka, M. (Eds), Life-like Characters: Tools, Affective Functions and Applications, Springer 2004.
10. Klesen, M., Kipp, M., Gebhard, P., Rist, T., “Staging exhibitions: methods and tools for modelling narrative structure to produce interactive performances with virtual actors.”, Virtual Reality, Vol. 7, pp. 17-29, 2003.
11. Cavazza, M., Charles, F. and Mead S.J., ”Developing Re-usable Interactive Storytelling Technologies”. IFIP World Computer Congress 2004, Toulouse, France.
12. Cavazza, M., Martin O., Charles, F. and Mead S.J., Marichal X. and Nandi A., “Multi-modal Acting in Mixed Reality Interactive Storytelling”, IEEE Multimedia, July-September 2004, Vol. 11, Issue 3.

A Simple Story: Using an Agents' Based Context-Aware Architecture for Storytelling

Fabio Pittarello

Università Ca' Foscari di Venezia - Dipartimento di Informatica,
Via Torino 155, 30172 Mestre (VE) Italy
pitt@dsi.unive.it

Abstract. Context-aware systems are conceived for diminishing the cognitive load of users that perform tasks such as retrieving information or accessing services. A wide range of applications is available, with emphasis on tourism, cultural heritage and e-commerce. This work explores the possibility of using an agents based context-aware architecture for controlling the evolution of a story on the basis of different types of context, including the user profile, the location, the user history and time. In order to prove the suitability of such architecture to the domain of storytelling, a real novel by a famous Italian writer was rewritten in the form of an interactive 3D world where users play the roles of the different characters of the story.

Keywords: agents, context-awareness, storytelling, virtual environments.

1 Introduction

Context-awareness is one of the keywords that nowadays characterize different areas of the computer science and it is usually referred to the ability of a system to recognize the features of the context and to take it into account for the computation. More specifically, the interest of the human-computer interaction area for the context is related to the possibility to use such information for improving the quality of the interaction, presenting to the user only appropriate information and diminishing her/his cognitive load.

The dimensions of the context examined so far by the researchers are different and include the location, the user profile and history, time, devices and network. Different systems have been built to take advantage of its knowledge, including realizations for e-commerce, cultural heritage and tourism.

This work is focused on a less explored application area, the one of interactive storytelling, and explores the possibility to use a context-aware architecture (in particular the one developed in [16, 17]) for the narration of a story. Such architecture is based on the adoption of a set of software agents for managing the presentation of a set of multimedia documents in 3D navigational environments, including different segments of mixed reality [13].

In order to prove the expressivity of the architecture in the domain of storytelling we considered a real novel, *A Simple Story*, written by the famous Italian novelist Leonardo Sciascia.

S. Göbel, R. Malkewitz, and I. Iurgel (Eds.): TIDSE 2006, LNCS 4326, pp. 25–36, 2006.

The rest of the paper is organized as follows: Section 2 describes related work in the area of context awareness, 3D environments, storytelling theories and software agents; Section 3 summarizes the main features of the data structures and of the context-aware architecture that will be used in this work; the section evidences also some modifications to the original proposal derived from the application to the narrative domain; Section 4 is focused on the application to storytelling and on the case study related to the Sciascia's novel; Section 5 will draw the final conclusions.

2 Related Work

The notion of context has been explored by a number of authors [5, 11] that have focused on different dimensions of it, including the user profile and history, the location, time, devices and network. Context-aware applications drive the user's experience in relation to the context and its modifications. The adaptation of the user experience, including both interaction and information fruition, characterizes many proposals in the area of the hypermedia and the web [2, 7, 15].

Concerning 3D navigational environments, the location was considered at first as the only relevant type of context [23]; later on other dimensions of the context, including the user profile and history, have been considered. The knowledge of the context has been used by the authors of 3D navigational worlds to influence several aspects of the user's experience, including the structure of the 3D world [6], the navigation [9] and other types of interaction [4].

While in most of the previous research work the knowledge of the context was applied to diminish the cognitive load of the users, in this work such knowledge is used for directing the user experience. Context-awareness is used here primarily for building a system of constraints that guides the users through the experience, yet giving them the chance to make significant choices at the crucial points of the story.

Concerning storytelling, studies related to the formalization of the narration have gradually developed from theories centered on linear narration (see Gustav Freytag's theory, described in [12]) that explain the different informational and emotional phases of a novel, up to non-linear narration that has gradually developed in the computers era.

While in linear narration the sequence of events gradually develops towards the unique end of the novel, non-linear storytelling is characterized by a more active role of the reader. According to [22], different approaches characterizes non-linear storytelling: some of them focus on characters and on their evolution inside the environment; others focus on the identification of macro-elements named scenes whose order can be predefined or can follow certain rules; finally other studies are centered on the identification of the minimal narrative structures that can be aggregated to build a story [21].

The approach that characterizes this work is similar to the second one: in fact, the novel has been split in a number of macro-elements characterized by predefined time-intervals. The sequence of such macro-elements, as will be explained in Section 4, is not predefined but is guided by the action of the characters inside the system of constraints controlled by the agents and can lead to very different endings.

3D environments for narration have been considered in several works, experimenting solutions both for virtual reality [8, 20] and for real environments [14].

They have been often coupled with the definition of software agents; different approaches take advantage of them for simulating human characters that are part of the story [3, 10, 18, 19] or for introducing a virtual narrator [1]. In this work agents, rather than simulating humans visible in the scene, are a sort of invisible entities that take care of the development of the story and are associated both to the locations and to the real user.

3 Data Structure and Implementation Architecture for Context-Awareness

The specific background on which this work is based includes the definition of the implementation architecture and of the data structure for storing the different narrative elements of the plot. While both elements have already been described in previous research work to which the author contributed [16, 17], the novelty of this work lays on their application to a realm completely different from that one for which they were conceived.

3.1 The Experience Layer

The data structure named *experience layer* derives from the analysis of the authors' habits in relation to the production of content for a navigational environment. We define it as a layer superimposed to a virtual or real scene that collects all the data, including multimedia information presented to the user, related to a specific experience authored for such environment. Generally speaking, we may have one or more experience layers for the same environment (e.g., the *Carnival experience* and the *Renaissance architecture experience*, for the environment *city of Venice*). Besides, the experience layer is typically authored for a specific user profile (e.g., *a tour through an art museum* for the user profile *student* or *a visit to the city center* for the user profile *tourist*).

The navigational environment is structured in a set of hierarchically organized locations that are semantically relevant for the user both in terms of morphology and use of space. Such locations are named *Interaction Loci* [16] and are pointed by the main components of the experience layer. Each component associated to an Interaction Locus has different features, including a description of the physical volume that defines the limits of the location, multimedia content organized in a hierarchical structure and a description of the conditions for accessing content and objects inside the location itself.

3.2 The Implementation Architecture

The architecture has been defined to control the evolution of an experience, characterized by the data contained in a specific experience layer and developing in a 3D environment, in relation to context changes. While the case study considered in this work is related to the so-called desktop virtual reality, the architecture applies to different segments of mixed reality. The following description gives a hint about the activities performed by the cooperating agents, acting as components of the context-aware architecture, inside the 3D environment. A detailed explanation can be found in [16].

The agents associated to the user (the *numen* agent) and to the locations (the *genii loci* agents) log and analyze the changes of context; such analysis guides the presentation of the multimedia information and the management of the behavior of the interactive objects.

Each genius loci accesses the data structure associated to its location and logs the changes of the different types of context, including the user history, time, device and network. Such information is used by the genius loci for managing the presentation of the multimedia chunks associated to the location and the interactive objects that are relevant for the experience; the genius loci may also activate certain components of the location: for example, an agent may trigger the opening of a door as a consequence of a specific change of context.

The action of the genii loci is mediated by the numen that receives the data logged by them, performs some processing and passes the result back to the genius loci of the current location as an input for its action. In such a way the numen maintains the knowledge about the previous part of the experience of the user and transmits it to the genii loci that have only a local knowledge.

The knowledge about the past user activity is stored in a data structure named *experience process*, a sequence of tuple $<s_t, a_t, s_{t+1}, content_{t+1}>$, where s_t is the state of the control finite state machine (CFSM) mapping the 3D environment at the time t, a_t is the action performed by the user at the time t, s_{t+1} is the state of the CFSM at the time $t+1$ determined by the action a_t, $content_{t+1}$ is an indexed version of the multimedia content presented to the user as a consequence of his/her activity a_t.

In the previous research work, which was characterized by a keen attention on lowering the cognitive load of the user, the definition of the experience process was accompanied also by the definition of the *experience pattern*, a sub-sequence of the experience process that identifies a recurring behavior. Such knowledge was used in a number of scenarios related to cultural heritage and e-commerce to diminish the interaction steps for performing a recurring task or for browsing recurring categories of multimedia content. More information about the experience process and the experience pattern can be found in [17].

In this work the role of the experience pattern is less relevant because the goal of the agents is guiding the development of the narration rather than helping the user interaction. For reaching such goal the agents will use the experience process in a different way, to collaboratively build a map of the visited states of the CFSM. Such map is the representation of the user history, one of the most important dimensions of the contexts considered in this work, and an important component for the evolution of the story.

4 Case Study: A Simple Story

As stated in the Introduction, the main goal of this work is to experiment the flexibility of the data structures and of the context-aware architecture described above to guide the user through a narration.

In order to test the expressivity of the system we considered a real novel by a famous Italian writer, Leonardo Sciascia, and mapped the different narrative components to a set of experience layers, defined for the different characters of the story (e.g., the diplomat Giorgio Rocella killed inside his villa, the good policeman Antonio Lagandara that tries to solve the mystery related to the death of the diplomat, etc.); in parallel, the complex 3D world representing the environment of the novel was modeled using as sources the description found in the original novel and the iconography that characterized the movie derived from the novel itself, *A Simple Story*, directed by Emidio Greco in 1991 (Figure 1).

Fig. 1. The 3D environment

In spite of the title, the novel by Leonardo Sciascia is a complicated story, whose theme is a murder investigation. An eminent diplomat, Giorgio Rocella comes back unexpectedly to his remote villa near a small Sicilian town to look for some correspondence between his family members and the famous Italian historical figures Luigi Pirandello and Giuseppe Garibaldi. While there, he calls the police, but before they can get around to seeing him, he's killed. One of the policemen, Antonio Lagandara, suspects a murder and unveils intricate illegal activities performed in the villa during the absence of Giorgio Rocella.

To add a further level of complexity, the original linear structure of the novel was considered as the starting point for building a non-linear narration where the actions of the characters participating to the different phases of the story can lead to very different endings.

At the end of the process the original sequence of the events is therefore transformed in a set of macro-elements characterized by specific time-intervals for the action. The sequence of macro-elements is not predefined but is guided by the actions of the characters and by the system of constraints controlled by the context-aware agents.

Each macro-element is defined as a narrative graph with linear sub-sequences and special nodes characterized by the user chance to change the route of the events. In Figure 2 the arcs represent the actions of the user that are relevant for the continuation of the narration (e.g., entering/exiting locations, touching objects, etc.). The nodes of the graph represent the states of the narration and are labeled with the names of the locations and the objects that are affected by the user action.

The user interaction is logged by the set of agents that control the 3D world. The log is then compared both with the current values of the different dimensions of the context and with the conditions that characterize each location and each interactive object.

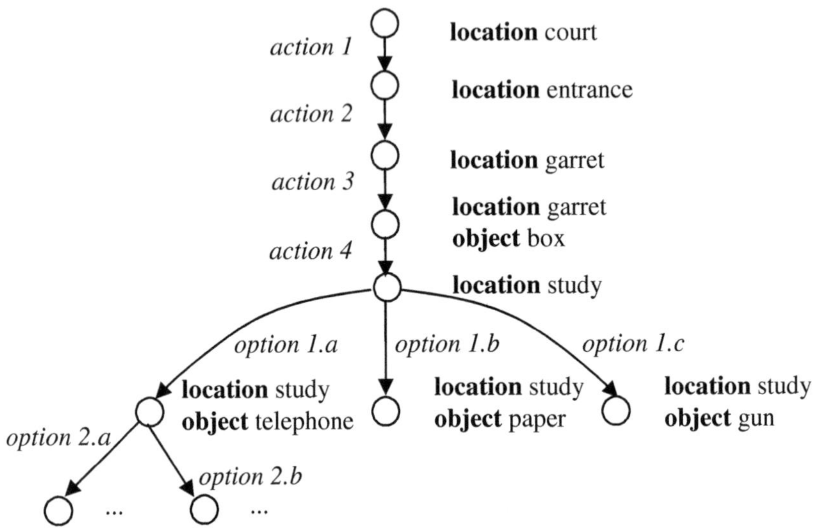

Fig. 2. A part of the narrative graph related to one of the macro-elements of the story

Such activity leads to the presentation of a specific chunk of multimedia content or to the activation of a particular object behavior, chosen among the ones defined in the authoring phase and stored in the experience layers.

In order to reduce the complexity of the interaction and to speed the action development the transitions between the different nodes of the linear subsequences are encouraged by appropriate messages that direct the user towards the next location or object to examine (see the fragment of the novel described below).

When the user reaches the special nodes that can determine significant modifications of the narration s/he's typically required to make a choice. The user's choice, elaborated by the system of agents, determines the selection of a specific route along the graph.

In some particular cases the choice can lead to dramatic modifications, including the voiding of the current user profile and the shift to another macro-element of the narration. For example, the choice of Giorgio Rocella of calling the police after discovering some strange activities inside his house causes his death because one of the policemen was corrupt. A different choice, like calling one of his old friends would produce a different, less cruel, ending of the story.

Let us consider a possible evolution of the story that represents a path through the narrative graph described in Figure 2:

Giorgio Rocella, while looking for the correspondence between his family members and the famous Italian historical figures, Pirandello and Garibaldi, discovers a work of art hidden inside a box in the garret; Guido Rocella suspects that the work of art might have been stolen somewhere and brought to his villa during his absence.
At this point:

- ***option 1.a**: Giorgio Rocella decides to pick up the phone and ask for help;*
- ***option 1.b**: Giorgio Rocella is frightened; he looks for his gun before calling for help;*
- ***option 1.c**: Giorgio Rocella writes on a piece of paper "I have found a work of art hidden in a box" before calling for help.*

Then Giorgio Rocella picks up the phone and decides to:

- ***option 2.a**: call the police;*
- ***option 2.b**: call one of his old friends.*

The behaviors of different locations and objects belonging to the 3D world have been associated to specific context instances. For example the object *box* in the location *garret* has been associated with the messages:

- "There is a work of art inside this box", presented to the user for the following context instance: user profile *Rocella*, user history *null*, time $0 < t < t_1$ that corresponds to the night hours of the first part of the story, when Guido Rocella comes back home.
- "This box contains only old stuff", presented to the user for the values of the context instance user profile *Lagandara*, user history *null* and time $t_1 < t < t_2$.

During the time interval $0 < t < t_0 < t_1$ the box contained inside the garret is the only active object of the house; all the other locations and objects are programmed for giving no information to the user profile Guido Rocella, in order to permit him to discover the box by himself. When the time t_0 is reached without any finding all the locations are programmed for giving to the user the hint "Look for the box in the garret" as soon as the user enters inside of them. The action of touching the box determines an advance along the narrative graph (*action 3*, Figure 2) and activates other objects useful for the continuation of the story.

The network of agents takes care of managing the presentation of information, on the basis of the analysis of the context and of the user interaction.

A fragment of the communication protocol between the different components of the story, corresponding to the sequence *action 2*, *action 3*, *action 4*, *option 1.a* and *option 2.a* of the narrative graph is described in Figure 3:

1. The user Rocella enters in the garret (*action 2*) at the time t, where $t_0 < t < t_1$; therefore the genius loci that controls the location and the objects contained inside it asks information about the contexts user profile and history to the numen and checks the current time exchanging messages with the time controller component. Then the genius loci examines the conditions related to the multimedia chunks associated to the location and, as a result, presents the message "Look for the box inside the garret".

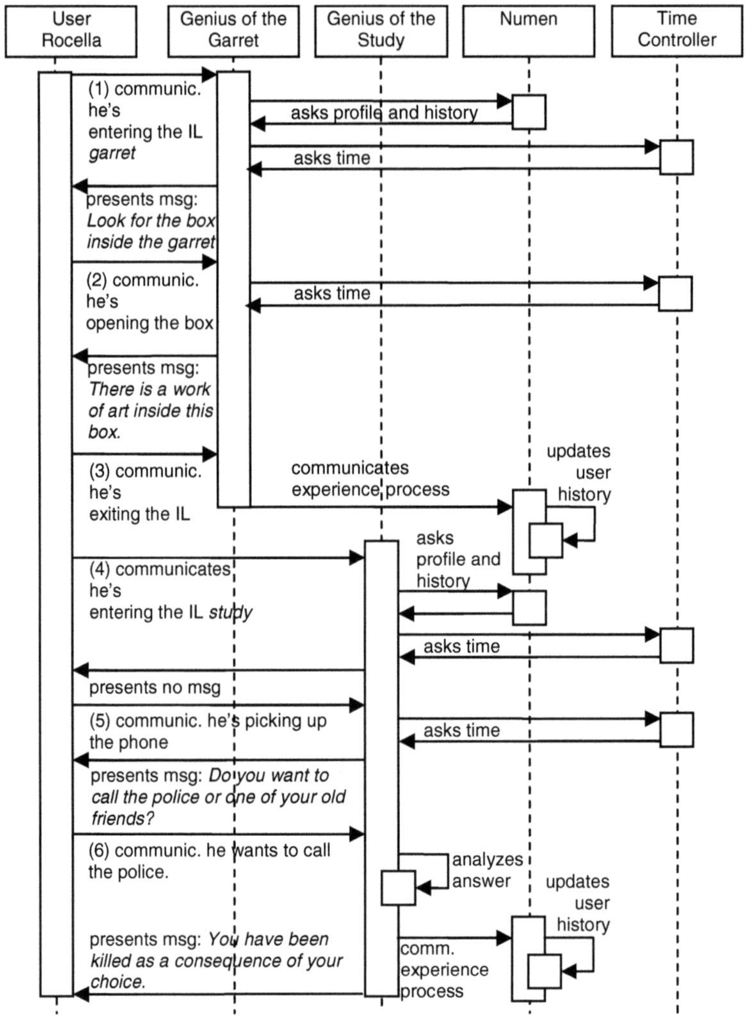

Fig. 3. A fragment of the communication protocol between the user Giorgio Rocella and the software agents during the first phases of the interactive story

2. The user Rocella, after some wandering inside the room, clicks over the box (*action 3*); the genius loci of the garret, on the basis of its knowledge of the contexts and of the conditions associated to the multimedia data associated to the object, presents the message "There is a work of art inside this box".
3. The user exits the garret; such information is passed to the genius loci that sends to the numen the logged tuples of the experience process for further elaboration. After the elaboration the numen updates the user history.
4. The user chooses to enter the location study (*action 4*). The genius loci of this location, on the basis of the context information and of the data contained in the structure associated to the study, doesn't present any message to the user.

5. The study contains several objects, including a telephone, a sheet of paper and a gun. The user decides to pick up the phone (*option 1.a*). As a result, the genius presents the message "Do you want to call the police or one of your old friends?"
6. The user decides to call the police (*option 2.a*), causing a dramatic event: his assassination. In terms of the communication protocol the choice is communicated to the genius loci of the study that sends such information to the numen together with the other tuples of the experience process. The death of Giorgio Rocella corresponds to the end of the narrative macro-element described by the Figure 2, to the unloading of the experience layer corresponding to the diplomat and to the loading and initialization of the experience layer associated to the policeman Lagandara that will begin his investigation. Before starting the procedures for the unloading of the current experience layer the genius loci of the study communicates to the user Rocella the message "You have been killed as a consequence of your choice".

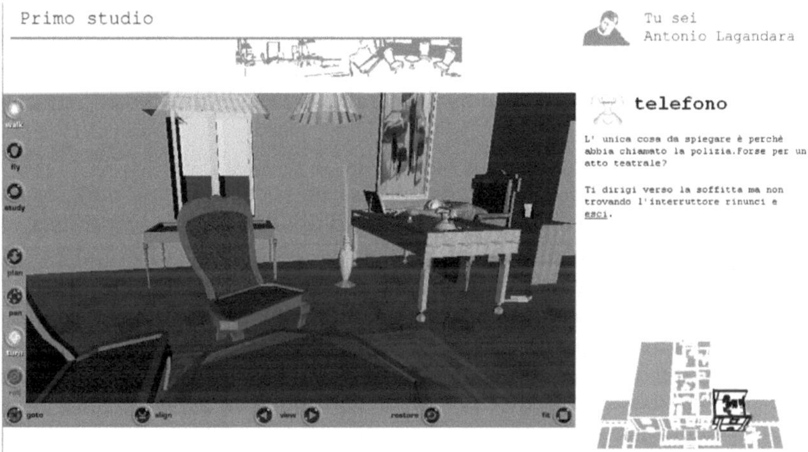

Fig. 4. The interface

Figure 4 shows a snapshot of the user interface developed for the interactive version of *A Simple Story*. The main part of the screen is occupied by the 3D scene that can be navigated by the user with the mouse or the keyboard arrows. In Figure 4 you can see the Giorgio Rocella's study with the body of the diplomat reclined over the table.

For improving the navigation, each location is identified by a label shown in the upper part of the screen and by a miniature map shown at the screen bottom that identifies the location of the room in the villa.

The label on the upper right part of the screen identifies the profile of the user which is currently experiencing the 3D world. In Figure 4 the user interprets the role of Antonio Lagandara, the policeman that tries to solve the mystery behind the death of Giorgio Rocella.

The right part of the screen is reserved to the multimedia content associated to the locations and to the interactive objects; content presentation is managed by the set of agents in relation to the values of the different dimensions of the context and to the conditions assigned in the authoring phase of the story. The user's choices that determine different routes along the narrative graph are usually made clicking over alternative links available in this area.

5 Conclusion

The work done so far represents a first encouraging confirmation of the possibility of using a context-aware architecture for guiding the development of an interactive story.

The architecture has proved to be flexible enough to control complex non-linear narrative structures, as demonstrated by the case study.

The experimentation with the novel *A Simple Story* was also a good test to improve the existing architectural solution and led to extend the association of the components of the experience layers, originally anchored only to locations, also to the interactive objects contained inside the environment, in order to improve the expressivity of the system.

A current limitation of the control capabilities demonstrated in this work is the application to the domain of the murder stories, where the characters' action is often mediated by objects. An interesting development may include the experimentation of more dynamic stories, characterized by the parallel presence of different characters to interact with.

While the presence of software agents in the domain of storytelling is not new, some features that characterize such components are peculiar to this work, including their definition as backend components associated to locations and related to a multi-purpose context-aware implementation architecture. As a matter of fact, the possibility of using the implementation architecture in several application areas is one of the findings of this work, opposed to specialized solutions targeted to storytelling, cultural heritage or to other specific realms.

While the results obtained so far are comparable to those resulting from alternative approaches for branching narrative, the additional features of our context-aware architecture such as the ability to recognize recurring sequences of actions and/or content browsed may grant additional benefits for the users. For example, the application of proactive behaviors to narration might contribute to lower the cognitive loads and/or the number of boring situations that are one of the unwanted features of the interactive storytelling.

Such proactive features were not exploited in this work, but the future development of the research will focus on them, permitting, for example, the recognition of sequences of interaction that are recurrent or not useful for the advancement of the narration. Of course the possibility to use all the different capabilities of our architecture at the same time will be considered.

The proposed architecture has been evaluated, and the benefits demonstrated, in other domains. In particular the results in the domain of e-commerce [24] show that users benefit from the application of a proactive engine that alleviates repetitive tasks. Besides, the results evidence also the importance of informing the users about the existence of adaptation mechanisms, for avoiding disorientation and loss of control.

A full evaluation of the approach in the domain of storytelling will be an important part of the future development.

Acknowledgements

I gratefully acknowledge Alessandra Florian that modeled the graphical components of the prototype as part of her thesis at the Accademia di Belle Arti di Venezia.

References

1. Braun, N., Rieger, T: Evaluation of a Virtual Narrator's Expressiveness in Terms of Suspense Signaling. Proc. of TIDSE '04. Lecture Notes in Computer Science 3105, Springer Verlag, 2004, pp. 89 - 94
2. Brusilovsky, P.: Adaptive hypermedia, User Modeling and User Adapted Interaction, 11(1-2) (2001) 87-110
3. Cavazza, M., Charles, F., Mead, S. J., Characters in Search of an author: AI-based Virtual Storytelling. Proc. of the First International Conference on Virtual Storytelling (ICVS 2001). Lecture Notes in Computer Science 2197, Springer Verlag, 2001, pp. 145-154
4. Celentano, A., Pittarello, F.: Observing and Adapting User Behavior in Navigational 3D Interfaces. Proc. of AVI 2004, Gallipoli, Italia, May 25-28, 2004, pp. 275-282
5. Chen, G., Kotz, D.: A Survey of Context-Aware Mobile Computing, Technical Report TR2000-381, Dartmouth College, Department of Computer Science, 2000
6. Chittaro, L., Ranon, R.: Dynamic Generation of Personalized VRML Content: a General Approach and its application to 3D E-commerce. Proc. of the 7th International Conference on 3D Web Technology, Tempe, Arizona, 2002, pp. 145-154
7. Garzotto, F., Paolini, P., Speroni, M., Pröll, B., Retschitzegger, W., Schwinger, W.: Ubiquitous Access to Cultural Tourism Portals. Proc. of DEXA'04, Zaragoza, Spain, September 2004, pp. 67-72
8. Geigel, J., Schweppe, M.: Theatrical Storytelling in a Virtual Space. Proc. of ACM Workshop on Story Representation, Mechanism and Context, New York, NY, October 2004, pp. 39-46
9. Hughes, S., Brusilovsky, P., Lewis, M.: Adaptive navigation support in 3D e-commerce activities. Proc. of Workshop on Recommendation and Personalization in eCommerce at AH'2002, Malaga, Spain, 2002, pp. 132-139
10. Iurgel, I.: From Another Point of View: Art-E-Fact. Proc. of TIDSE '04. Lecture Notes in Computer Science 3105, Springer Verlag, 2004, pp. 26-35
11. Kappel, G., Retschitzegger, W., Kimmerstorfer, E., Schwinger, W., Hofer, Th., Pröll, B.: Towards a Generic Customisation Model for Ubiquitous Web Applications. Proc. of the 2nd Int. Workshop on Web Oriented Software Technology (IWWOST), Spain, June, 2002, pp. 79-104
12. Laurel, B., Computer as Theatre, Addison-Wesley, Reading, MA, 1993
13. Milgram, P., Kishino, F.: A Taxonomy of Mixed Reality Visual Displays. IEICE Transactions on Information Systems, Vol. E77-D No. 12 (1994) 1321-1329
14. Nisi, V., Wood, A., Davenport, G., Oakley, I.: Hopstory: An Interactive, Location-Based Narrative Distributed in Space and Time. Proc. of TIDSE '04. Lecture Notes in Computer Science 3105, Springer Verlag, 2004, pp. 132-141
15. Perkowitz, M., Etzioni O.: Adaptive Web Sites. Communications of the ACM, 43(8) (2000) 152-158
16. Pittarello, F.: Context-Based Management of Multimedia Documents in 3D Navigational Environments. Proc. of the 11th International Workshop on Multimedia Information Systems (MIS 2005). Lecture Notes in Computer Science 3665, Springer Verlag, 2005, pp. 146-162

17. Pittarello, F., Fogli, D.: Modelling Complex User Experiences in Distributed Interaction Environments. Proc. of the 11th International Conference on Distributed Multimedia Systems (DMS 2005), Banff, Canada, 5-7 Settembre 2005, pp. 184-189
18. Riedl, M., Saretto, C.J., Young, R.M.: Managing interaction between users and agents in a multi-agent storytelling environment. Proc. of the second international joint conference on Autonomous agents and multiagent systems (AAMAS '03), Melbourne, Australia, 2003, pp. 741-748
19. Sanchez, S., Balet, O., Lugal, H., Duthen, Y.: Autonomous Virtual Actors. Lecture Notes in Computer Science 3105, Springer Verlag, 2004, pp. 68-78
20. Seif El-Nasr, M.: A user-centric adaptive story architecture: borrowing from acting theories. Proc. of the ACM SIGCHI International Conference on Advances in computer entertainment technology, Singapore, 2004, pp. 109-116
21. Szilas, N.: IDtension: a narrative engine for Interactive Drama. In Proc. of TIDSE'03, Frauenhofer IRB Verlag, 2003, pp. 187-203
22. Szilas, N., Rety, J.-H., Minimal structure for stories. Proc. of the First ACM Workshop on Story Representation, Mechanism, and Context, 12th ACM International Conference on Multimedia, New York, NY, USA, 2002, pp. 25-32
23. Want, R., Hopper, A., Falcao, V., Gibbons, J.: The Active Badges Location System. Tech. Rep., Olivetti Research Ltd, 1992. http://www.uk.research.att.com/pub/docs/att/tr.92.1.pdf
24. Zucconi, P.: Usabilità e Accessibilità nel Web 3D. Master Thesis, Università Ca' Foscari di Venezia, 2005 (in Italian)

Hypervideo vs. Storytelling Integrating Narrative Intelligence into Hypervideo

Peter Hoffmann and Michael Herczeg

University of Luebeck
Institute for Multimedia and Interactive Systems
Ratzeburger Allee 160, 23538 Luebeck, Germany
{hoffmann, herczeg}@imis.uni-luebeck.de
http://www.imis.uni-luebeck.de

Abstract. Hypervideo is one of several possible ways for interactive non-linear media. In its characteristics it is closely related to the purposes of digital narratives. The techniques of hypervideo could be used for the presentation of digitally told stories and vice versa. Many projects in both fields of work show the impressive possibilities each. But there seems to be a lack of using narrative intelligence in hypervideo. This paper shows how both fields of work could benefit from each other. Therefore two projects are introduced and their combination is discussed. The hypervideo environment HyPE includes an authoring tool, a stand-alone player for hypervideos and offers an API for the use in higher-ranking applications. Secondly the storytelling system called Jeherazade is introduced, which bases on the idea to enhance the classical theory of Aristotle to the new form of digital narrative. It is primarily developed for the use in presentations in distributed exhibitions but it is planned to be used for e-leraning as well.

Keywords: Hypervideo, non-linear media, interactive media, digital storytelling, narrative intelligence.

1 Introduction

As hypervideo has two basic roots, the conventional video and hypermedia, there are several different definitions for it. One kind of definitions has its origins in hypermedia. Therefore it emphasises the aspect of augmenting information into digital video as for example Hesse does [9]. The user activates hyperlinks in the video and gets access to additional information to the actual scene in form of texts, images or even other videos. Another kind of definitions on the other hand emphasises the influence of the audience on the storyline [8]. This definition has its origins in storytelling. In this case the activation of a hyperlink by the viewer means that the viewer changes from one scene to another or from one perspective to another. So the audience does not follow the content in a linear but in a non-linear way; the audience creates an individual story-plot. None of both types of definitions is wrong, but in an ideal case hypervideo should include both: the usual interaction options like watching a video, fast-forward and fast-backward, stopping and the like, which derive from the

S. Göbel, R. Malkewitz, and I. Iurgel (Eds.): TIDSE 2006, LNCS 4326, pp. 37–48, 2006.

medium “video”, are combined by the possibilities of hypermedia and storytelling. So the surplus of hypervideo consists in the chance to break up the linearity of traditional video into a non-linear but still time-based medium. Furthermore the audience is no longer limited to the primary medium. The individual viewer is able to follow connections in the same video as well as connections to entirely different documents and media. So there is the chance of getting additional information to the basic video. Those connections are defined in form of hyperlinks as in any other hypermedia too.

As mentioned above, hypervideo offers the possibility to change from the linear order in a video to a non-linear order. The changing of the order is controlled by the viewer. The viewer has the opportunity to influence the course of the video on defined points-in-time. So the viewer can switch to another point-in-time than the actually presented point-in-time in the video or even to utterly different documents. Those documents can be other video-clips as well as other media-clips which are presented additionally to the actual video-clip.

Where hypervideo presents a movie with the embedded opportunity of the viewers interaction, digital storytelling goes on one step further. Braun [1] defines digital storytelling as “the telling of a story with an audience impact on the storyline, but without an impact on the story goal”. This means that the audience has influence on the order in which the content is presented. All chosen and presented parts are conductive for reaching the goal, which is to be informed and/ or to acquire knowledge about a specific field in an entertaining and motivating manner.

The new form of “digital” or “virtual” storytelling follows the same well-known strategies similar to classical storytelling. The strategy most frequently used is the one which follows the course of suspense in a poetic story as Aristotle described it long ago. Following his ideas and theories, most narratives are divided in the four phases exposition, ascension, climax and conclusion [10, 11].

This more than 2000 years old concept is actually still in use and the basis for most plot in modern entertainment. One prominent example for the use of this theory gives Syd Field in his work [4]. Field follows strictly the ideas of Aristotle to include suspense to story plots even if gives the phases of the plot new names.

Digital storytelling offers another dimension which is not available in classical storytelling. A freedom of movement and a wider range of decisions is available in digital storytelling [9]. The new kind of narrative offers the choice between different narrative paths to the audience. The two dimensional story line does not longer exist in this method. It is expanded with at least one more dimension so that it can no longer be called a (story) line. So it is more precise to say, that the story told by using digital storytelling methods take place in a “story site” than to say it follows a single story line [14]. For supporting the viewer with a good guidance the storytelling system has to be intelligent in the narrative aspect [15]. The narrative intelligence decides which next parts of a story-site would fit best to the story experienced so far by the audience and gives the audience hints and clues how to get there.

Including a narrative intelligence into hypervideo should offer a big surplus to both, the viewer as well as to the author of hypervideos. The author is less limited in designing a content structure to the hypervideo. The viewer receives a presentation in form of a hypervideo which is adapted in its dramaturgy to the individual expectations.

Fig. 1. Augmented additional information and interaction options to change the order of points-in-time

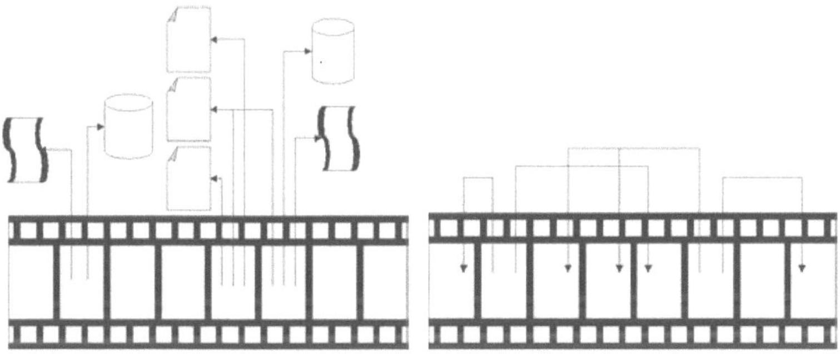

Fig. 2. Different kinds of hypervideo definitions of:left: access to additional information right: access to other points-in-time or scenes

2 Problems in Design and Use of Hypervideo

During designing and authoring hypervideo there are several different problems to be considered. The most important problem is the field of the interaction design. This includes both, placing additional information as well as providing information of the content structure.

With the option of augmenting additional media to the basic video the viewer of a hypervideo is able to reach more information as with a classical video. This is what hypervideo reaches for. But it is easily possible to overwhelm the visitor with too much augmented information or with information augmented at a badly chosen location on the screen. Furthermore the necessarily needed video links, the hotspots, appear and disappear during the time the video is presented. This might lead to a demotivation of the viewer. The viewer is possibly surprised by the appearing and disappearing signs which do not belong to the video itself. This detract the viewer from the context of the video and from experiencing it. It is mostly the task of the author of a hypervideo to avoid such problematic designs.

An even bigger problem is the design of the content structure and how to inform the audience about it. Usually in hypervideo it is possible for a viewer to jump between defined points-in-time in the basic video. With that option for example the opportunity is supported to view single scenes or even the whole video from different perspectives. An extensive problem comprises in the task to offer the information of the content structure to the viewer. So the viewer knos which point-in-time can be reached from the actual position or point-in-time. Actual two different ways to present this kind of information are commonly adopted.

The first one is to give a hint about the possible option to change to another scene or perspective. The viewer now has the opportunity to stop the video and to go back to a main menu. This shows the reachable scenes which can be jumped to. This is the way which most of the actual DVDs support. The big disadvantage of this kind of access to the content structure is that the immersion into the video is massively disturbed. The viewer has to stop the video for the interaction and therefore is distracted from the story line of the video.

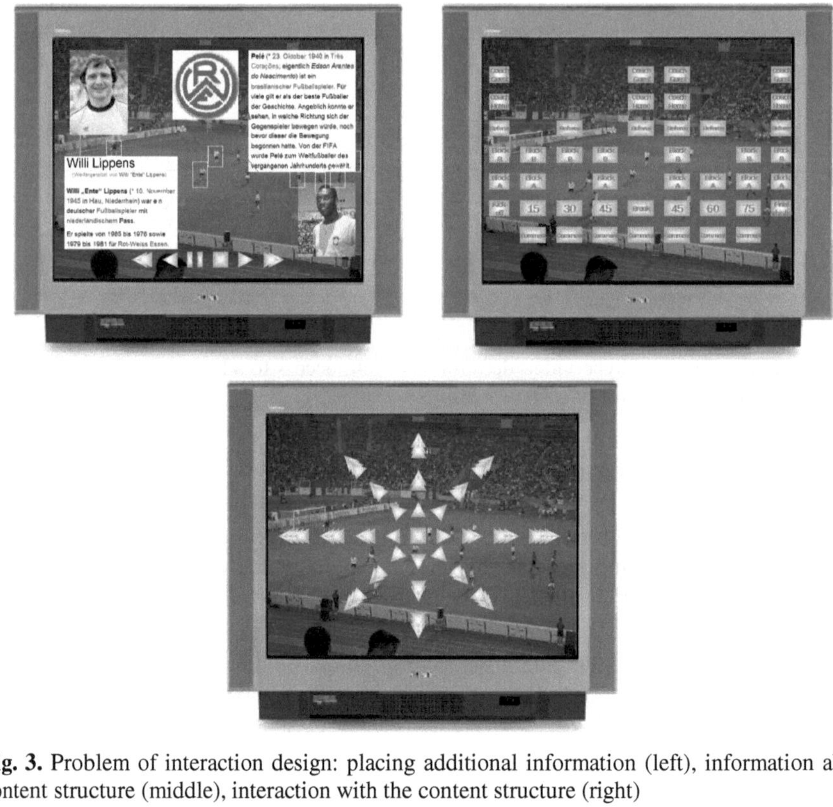

Fig. 3. Problem of interaction design: placing additional information (left), information about content structure (middle), interaction with the content structure (right)

The second way of providing information commonly is to superpose a menu with all reachable scenes over the basic video. The video keeps running while the menu is shown as long as the interaction is possible. The story plot is not disturbed even the immersion into the video is affected by a possibly bothering menu. This is even more important when the menu is not really necessarily needed. In case the viewer does not want to switch to another scene or another perspective or does not want to get additional information, the menu is dispensable.

Such problems appear because most hypervideo systems do not consider the user and his interaction history. So the navigation structure is mostly realised in a static way which is designed by an author for all users. For the individual user this can lead into getting lost in hyperspace. The user has an cognitive overflow while he does not know which information hides behind the number of possible links and hotspots [16, 18].

For considering the question if superposing a menu is necessary at a special point-in-time of the hypervideo it is furthermore essential that a hypervideo player has knowledge about the viewer. Only if the hypervideo player knows about the viewers target group, age, preferences, previous knowledge and most important about the viewers history in he hypervideo it can adapt the presentation individually. This means that not all defined hotspots make sense at any time of the presentation. So for example if a viewers' history leads to the conclusion, that the viewers most favoured topic is "architecture" it does not seem to be really reasonable to offer him a hotspot which leads to "philosophy". With fading in this hotspot the individual immersion of the viewers is again disturbed.

It would be a big advantage if hypervideo environments would support such a flexible way of access to additional media and to the content structure. The more adjusted the presentation is to the individual needs and preferences, the more entertaining and motivating is the hypervideo itself and its experience..

3 Integrating Narrative Intelligence

One way to reach a flexible access to hotspots respectively to the additional media and the content structure would be to connect a kind of „narrative intelligence" to a hypervideo environment. A problem to be solved for that way is, that most hypervideo players are not really open to be used by external applications. The hypervideo environment or at least the hypervideo player needs to understand messages the narrative intelligence sends to it and vice versa.

At the Institute for Multimedia and Interactive Systems at the University of Luebeck two applications are in the deployment which fulfil the needs to reach an individual and a narrative supported hypervideo presentation.

3.1 The Jeherazade Storytelling System

The Jeherazade system is an interactive digital storytelling system which is based on the idea that audiences become story chasers [11, 12]. Analog to the classical reader the audience in this new role of the chaser experiences a narrative by choosing an individual story path in a story site. The audience adopts an active role in the narrative: the audience chooses an individual story path and meets abstract and real characters who tell the information, give hints, and clues where to go and what to see next. The given information allows the audience to interact with the story line by making individual decisions.

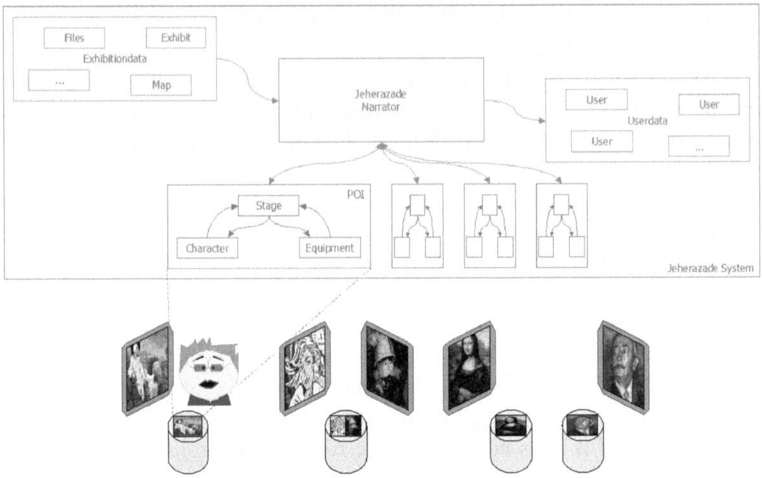

Fig. 4. The Jeherazade storytelling Application

Characters in the Jeherazade system have the task to present the information stored in the story site. This is the way Jeherazade presents the story and gives hints and clues for the forthcoming story path. The Jeherazade system provides two kinds of characters. The first kind is called the story chaser. This character represents the audience and is therefore totally free to follow own individual paths through the story site. It does not present the stored information but informs the Jeherazade system about the audience's actions and choices. The other kind of characters in the Jeherazade system are called actors. Their special task is to present the narrative's content. Actors can appear in a wide range of different kinds. So an actor can be a personalized character like a 2D or a 3D avatar as well as an abstract character like a video or an audio player, a text or an image windows and so on [12].

The Jeherazade system uses equipment for the task of providing the interaction between the audience and the narrative. This is the way the audience "tells" the story site which story path he wants to choose or what kind of information he needs before he continues his story experience. As the characters too, the equipment in the Jeherazade system is also divided in two categories. The first kind of equipment builds the environment in which the story takes place, comparable to the scene or the stage in theatre or film. The other category of equipment supports the interaction especially the user's input. Analog to the characters the equipment also appears in a wide range of different kinds. So simple interaction devices like e.g. keyboard, mouse and joystick are supported as well as complex ones like speech input. As the Jeherazade system has a modular software architecture, it is easily possible to connect new and other kinds of characters and equipment to the system [12].

One possible application area of the Jeherazade system is the narrative support of presentations in distributed exhibitions. The visitor of a museum or the like can use the Jeherazade system as a guide through the exhibition. Therefore the system has several POIs where a Jeherazade stage is located. On the stages information to neighbouring exhibits are presented. The content and design of the local presentation depends on the visitors preferences, previous knowledge and the history in the exhibition. On the base of the information about the visitor and combined with the stored information about the exhibits the Jeherazade system calculates the best fitting exhibits for the further tour through the exhibition. The goal is to maintain a tour which follows an appealing and motivating dramaturgy in the order of the visited exhibits.

Other possible application areas are e-learning and edutainment. Here a flexible and even more an individually adapted order leads to a higher motivation for the user to follow a lecture. The goal is that the knowledge about his individual level gives information about his needs so that the best individual learning results can be reached. This is furthermore supported by the adaption of the presentation style to the users' target group.

3.2 The HyPE Hypermovie Application

The Hypervideo Environment HyPE is a hypervideo application, which supports both, the use as a stand-alone application as well as the simple integration into other projects. Therefore an environment with

- a stand-alone hypervideo player,
- an authoring tool
- and an open API to support the use of HyPE in external applications

was planned and realized. The first of those external applications which should use HyPE as an output device is Jeherazade. Because the Jeherazade system is implemented in Java it was obvious to start the realization of HyPE as well in Java, with all its supported interaction and media APIs for an easy connection of both.

A HyPE hypermovie consists of two parts, the video itself and the additional meta-data file where the interaction possibilities are defined. The meta-data contains the annotation of the linkage to other time sequences and to other media. Therefore it was decided to be describe the meta-data in XML. This supports both, the readability and editability by (human) users as well as the automatically generation by appropriate editor applications.

```
. . .
<hotspot active="true"
    begintime="31.78"
    endtime="42.99"
    fillcolor="Color(255,255,255,255)" id="0" hotkey=""
    linecolor="Color(255,0,0,255)"
    name="Hotspot 1"
    visible="true">
    <action>
        gotoAndPlay("Label 2");
    </action>
    <nodes>
        <node x="256" y="28"/>
        . . .
        <node x="319" y="73"/>
    </nodes>
</hotspot>
. . .
```

Fig. 5. Source-Code example for the HyPE-API and the hotspot definition

The user's interaction in HyPE takes place via hotspots. An HyPE hotspot is an area the viewer can activate. This usually happens by a mouse click but can also take place by using keyboard shortcuts or the like. The hotspots can be defined in any way the author wants. So the author has influence

- on the geometry of the hotspot,
- on the visibility,
- on the time in the video, the hotspots appears and disappears,
- and on the actions which are activated with the hotspot.

Via the HyPE API it is possible to control all defined hotspots by an external application like the Jeherazade system. So it is possible for such external applications to set hotspots visible or active while the (hyper-) video is presented and to react on the activation of hotspots by the visitor individually.

3.3 Hypervideo Meets Storytelling: Connecting Jeherazade and HyPE

Even hypervideo is more flexible than usual video though it is still more or less static:

- The author of a hypervideo defines an ambient structure for a basic video. In this structure the additional media are embedded by hotspots which link to this additional media.
- Furthermore the content structure is described by hotspots which link to points-in-time of the basic video which are related to the actual scene.

In general each time the hypervideo is started, the defined hotspots appear and disappear strictly at the defined time. This behaviour is independent of the viewers former choices. If for example the viewer followed in scene "A" a link to the point-of-time "B", this interaction is usually not stored. So it is not possible in the later presentation to react on this interaction. The history of the visitor, which could offer much information about his preferences, is lost.

By connecting an external "intelligence" like a storytelling application to the hypervideo environment the hypervideo gets a highly flexible structure in the content. After it is started the external storytelling application loads the meta-data information which describes the structure of the hypervideo and uses it in relation to the story parameters and audience parameters for the decisions of

- which hot spot has to be shown,
- which links to other points-in-time make sense for the actual audience and
- which additional media make sense for the actual audience .

The hypervideo player loads and starts the basic video and the meta data information. Even if the hypervideo player is driven by any external application the player needs to have the meta data information of the visdual parameters of the hotspots like their location on the screen, their collor and appearance. When reaching a point-in-time where the author had defined a hotspot, the player sends a message to the storytelling application. This decides whether the hotspot should be set visible and acitve or not and thus answers to the message. The knowledge about the hotspot and its target is described in the meta-data, the storytelling application loaded at the start.

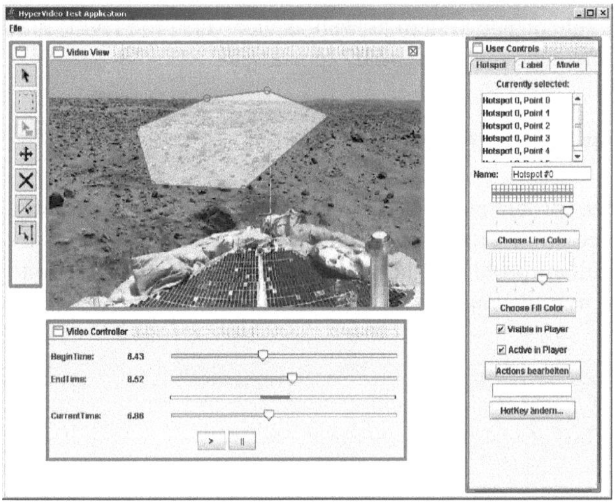

Fig. 6. The HyPE-Application (Authoring tool including the hypervideo player)

Only if a hotspot is active an interaction by the viewer is possible. Is a hotspot activated by the viewer, the hypervideo player sends the message about the interaction also to the external storytelling application which starts the defined action for the activated hotspot.

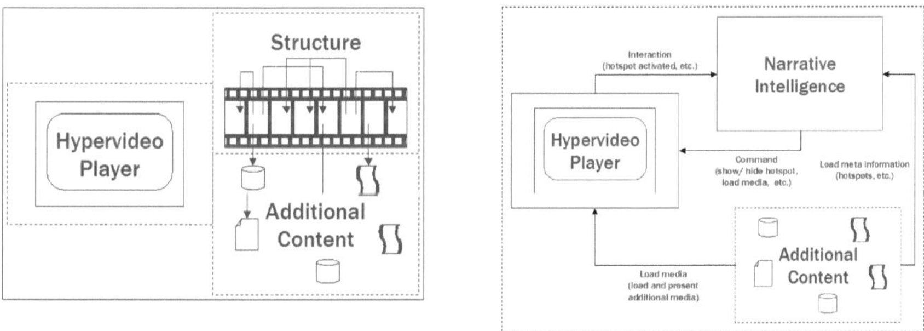

Fig. 7. Hypervideo meets Storytellingleft: usual static linkage of content and scenes to a basic videoright: an open API of the hypervideo player supports flexible linkage

Thus the hypervideo system (in this case: the hypervideo player plus the external narrative intelligence) has the opportunity to respond on the users behaviour. The presentation including the possible interactions is adapted to the history of the viewer. Furthermore the viewers preferences and previous knowledge, which is possibly known, can be considered for the actual presentation.

With the open API of the HyPE Hypervideo Environment the above mentioned idea of connecting external storytelling applications like the Jeherazade system is easily possible. The message objects send by the HyPE player can be received and processed in the Jeherazade system as well as vice versa the HyPE player can receive and process the message objects send by Jeherazade.

4 Conclusion and Future Prospects

In this paper the problems of design and use of hypervideo was discussed. In particular the interaction with the content structure of a hypervideo was contemplated. To solve the resultant problems the possibility of connecting a narrative intelligence to a hypervideo environment was examined.

Fig. 8. The HyPE stand alone player with a demo presentation of Luebeck

With the Jeherazade storytelling system an application was available which fulfilled two aspects. On the one hand the Jeherazade systems offers a kind of narrative intelligence, on the other hand the Jeherazade system can use the HyPE player as a stage for itself. A presentation supported by Jeherazade follows in its order an dramaturgy which is individually adapted to the viewer. While both, Jeherazade and HyPE, support the usage of the same amount of different media and different media formats it was obvious to try to use the HyPE player as a possible stage for the Jeherazade system.

The deployment of the hypervideo environment HyPE was started for answering technical questions like the feasibility and capability of a Java based hypervideo application. In the further development of the HyPE environment aspects like the flexible and dynamic support of links and hotspots in the basic video was also considered. One special answer which resulted from the discussion about flexibility and dynamically shown hotspot was, that there should be an open API which can also be used by other applications.

Therefore a demo hypervideo was produced. It introduces the viewer to the city of Luebeck, Germany and leads to several different places of interest. The viewer has the opportunity to choose his way in a totally free order. Furthermore the viewer can choose to receive additional information for each place.

The combination of the hypervideo environment and the external storytelling application in the demo movie offers good results. Hotspots are only shown when they are necessary and when they fit in the history of the viewer. So it is possible to support a dramaturgy into a hypervideo as originally mentioned.

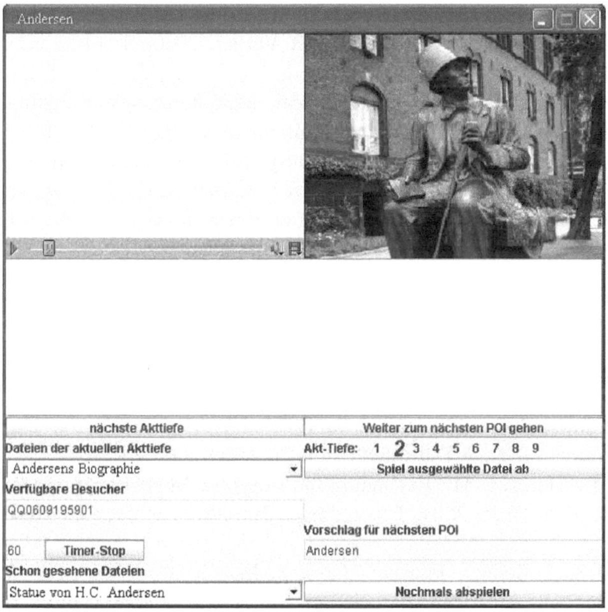

Fig. 9. Prototypical stage of the Jeherazade system

References

1. Braun, N.. Kontrolliertes Erzählen von Geschichten mit integrierten, Videobasierenden Hyperstories. In: R. Keil-Slawik, H. Selke, G. Szwillus (Hrsg.): Mensch & Computer 2004: Allgegenwärtige Interaktion. München: Oldenbourg Verlag. 2004, S. 157–167 (2004).
2. Braun, Norbert: Interaction Approach for Digital Video Based Storytelling. 9-th International Conference in Central Europe on Computer Graphics, Visualization and Computer Vision'2001, WSCG 2001, University of West Bohemia, Campus Bory, Plzen-Bory, Czech Republic, February 5-9, 2001
3. Doherty, J & Girgensohn, A. & Helfman J. & Shipman F. & Wilcox L. (2003). Detailon-Demand Hypervideo. Palo Alto: FX Palo Alto Laboratory.
4. Field, Syd: Screenplay: The Foundation of Screenwriting (2005). Dell Publishing co. Inc. New York.

5. Finke, M. & Wichert, R. (2003). Augmented Reality and Hypervideo Supporting Distributed Communities for Education & Training. Darmstadt: Zentrum für Graphische Datenverarbeitung e.V.
6. Francisco-Revilla, L. (1998). A Picture of Hypervideo Today. Texas A&M University. (www. csdl.tamu.edu/ ~l0f0954/ academic/ cpsc610/ p-1.htm 20.03.2006).
7. Fransecky, R. & Debes, J. (1972). Visual Literacy: A way to learn - A Way to Teach. Washington: Association for Educational Communications and Technology.
8. Girgensohn, A. & Shipman, F. & Wilcox, L. (2003). Hypervideo Summaries. Palo Alto: FX Palo Alto Laboratory
9. Heintze, J. v., Bode, C.: Emergent Stories - Eine neue Herangehensweise zum Erleben und zum Authoring interaktiver Geschichten. In: Spierling, Ulrike (Hrsg.): Digital Storytelling - Tagungsband. Stuttgart : Fraunhofer IRB Verlag, 2000, S. 13-28 (Computer Graphik Edition 02).
10. Hesse, W. (2005). Didaktisches Design, Mediengestaltung, Visualisierung. (http://www.e-teaching.org/didaktik/gestaltung/visualisierung/hypervideo, 20.03.2006).
11. Hoffmann, P., Herczeg, M.: Distributed Storytelling for Narrative in Spacious Areas. In Göbel, St., Braun, N., Spierling, U., Dechau J. & Diener, H. (Eds.) Proceedings of Technologies for Interactive Digital Storytelling an Entertainment, Computer Graphik Edition, Band 9.Stuttgart: Fraunhofer IRB Verlag. pp. 346-350.
12. Hoffmann, P., Herczeg, M.: Expanding the storyline. In Bearman, D. & Trant, J. (Eds.), Museums and the Web 2004, Proceedings. Toronto: Archives & Museum Informatics.1. Baldonado, M., Chang, C.-C.K., Gravano, L., Paepcke, A.: The Stanford Digital Library Metadata Architecture. Int. J. Digit. Libr. 1 (1997) 108–121
13. Hoffmann, P.; Herczeg, M.: Distributed Storytelling for Narrative in Spacious Areas. In: TIDSE, 1st International Conference on Technologies for Interactive Digital Storytelling and Entertainment (Hrsg.). Darmstadt, 24. – 26. März 2003
14. Hoffmann, P.; Herczeg, M.: Expanding the storyline. In Bearman, D. & Trant, J. (Eds.), Museums and the Web 2004, Proceedings. Toronto: Archives & Museum Informatics (2004).
15. Mateas, Michael, Senger, Phoebe: Narrative Intelligence (Advances in Consciousness Research Series). American Association for Artificial Intelligence. Benjamins, John Publishing Company (1998).
16. Ransom, S., Wu, X., Schmidt, H. (1996): Disorientation and cognitive overhead in hypertext systems, TR96-13, Department of Software Development Technical Report, Department of Software Development, Monash University, Melbourne, 1-21, 21pp. Technical report SD TR96-13 (1996).
17. Sawhney, N. & Balcon, D. & Smith, I (1996). HyperCafe: Narrative and Aesthtetic Properties of Hypervideo. Atlanta: Hypertext '96. (www. cs.unc.edu/ ~barman/ HT96/P24/ HyperCafe.html) [31.08.05].
18. Zahn, Carmen (2003). Wissenskommunikation mit Hypervideos. Untersuchungen zum Design nichtlinearer Informationsstrukturen für audiovisuelle Medien (Knowledge Communication with Hypervideo). Waxmann Verlag, Berlin (2003).

A Fabula Model for Emergent Narrative

Ivo Swartjes and Mariët Theune

University of Twente, Human Media Interaction group
Enschede, The Netherlands
{i.m.t.swartjes, m.theune}@ewi.utwente.nl

Abstract. In this paper we present our continuing efforts to generate narrative using a character-centric approach. In particular we discuss the advantages of explicitly representing the emergent event sequence in order to be able to exert influence on it and generate stories that 'retell' the emergent narrative. Based on a narrative distinction between fabula, plot and presentation, we make a first step by presenting a model based on story comprehension that can capture the fabula, and show how it can be used for the automatic creation of stories.

1 Introduction

In the Virtual Storyteller project [1] we investigate how stories can emerge through simulation of a virtual world inhabited by virtual characters, an approach that is often referred to as *Emergent Narrative* [2]. We are currently investigating the possibility to explicitly represent narrative based on the emerging event sequence, so that it can feed a story generation process. We believe that such a formal representation will allow the system not only to *express* the event sequence that it produces in e.g. natural language, but also to *comprehend*, and as such, *manipulate* the event sequence. For this representation, a narratological distinction is made between three layers of information that together constitute narrative. Mieke Bal calls these layers fabula, story and narrative text [3]. The fabula consists of a series of logically and chronologically related events that are caused or experienced by characters in a story world. A story is a fabula that is looked at from a certain angle. A narrative text is an expression of the story in language signs (e.g. words, pictures). Our distinction is similar but more aimed at formalization:

1. The *fabula* layer is an account of what happens in the story world and why. It is a causal network of all events that took place in the story world.
2. The *plot* layer is based on a relevant selection of the fabula layer that forms a consistent and coherent whole, adhering to an Aristotelian understanding of these concepts similar to Sgouros [4]. One can say that many plots coexist within one fabula.
3. The *presentation* layer represents the information needed for the actual presentation of the plot in a certain medium. The medium of choice for the Virtual Storyteller is natural language, both written [5] and spoken [6]. In the future, we also intend to investigate graphical presentations.

S. Göbel, R. Malkewitz, and I. Iurgel (Eds.): TIDSE 2006, LNCS 4326, pp. 49–60, 2006.

In this paper we focus on the fabula layer, how it can be modeled and what it can be used for. The paper is structured as follows. In section 2, we discuss why we need an explicit fabula structure for story generation, and how we intend to use it. In section 3, we present our model of fabula structure and show how it can be generated. Guided by an example, section 4 shows how such a structure can be transformed into a written story. Finally, in Section 5 we provide some conclusions and discuss how we intend to use the fabula model in the future to support plot guidance and creativity.

2 The Need for a Formal Narrative Structure

Our approach to automated story generation is to first generate a fabula layer, then apply selections and transformations in order to form plot and presentation layers. The fabula layer is generated by observing what happens in a Multi-Agent simulation where autonomous, intelligent Character Agents are situated within a virtual story world in which they pursue their goals [1]. A risk factor for such an approach is the fact that an interesting plot is not guaranteed. Characters follow their individual goals which are different from the goals of the plot. As a consequence, the stories produced by such an approach may not be very interesting. Therefore, a Plot Agent (similar to the Drama Manager introduced in the OZ project [7]) exerts influence on the emerging event sequence, motivated from a goal to stimulate the occurrence of 'interesting things' from a plot point of view. A prerequisite for the pursuit of plot goals is that the system has some understanding of the plots that are generated. Developing a model of fabula contributes to this by making the causal and temporal relationships between fabula elements explicit, allowing them to be analyzed for 'plot potential'. The system does not commit to any particular plot during the simulation; all story world events, relevant for a plot or not, are captured in the fabula.

Generating stories like this has many advantages. First, consistency and coherence of the fabula underlying any generated story can be ensured by the simulation and is not a plot concern. Second, by making the fabula explicit we have an objective account of events at our disposal which is independent of stylistic concerns such as viewpoints, author opinions, time lapses and couleur locale, and therefore has the potential to be shaped into any form of presentation desired. This makes it possible to tell different stories based on the same fabula. It also makes plot generation independent of presentation; the same plot can form the input for the production of a narrative text, an animation or picture story.

Much research has focused on understanding and formalizing event structures appearing in stories, from both the perspective of narratology (e.g., Propp's seminal work [8]), and story comprehension (e.g., [9]). Given the advantages of having an explicit narrative structure for story generation, it is surprising that — as also noted by [10] and [11] — story generation systems often lack a formalization of such structures. This was also the case for previous versions of the Virtual Storyteller, where the lack of a formal fabula representation resulted in a rather boring, literal account of the events occurring in our story world [1]. When representations are used in other systems, they are often rather ad-hoc (e.g., the representation used in MINSTREL [12]) or biased towards action planning (e.g., the definition of fabula in the story generation system Fabulist [13]).

A recent attempt in formalizing drama structures is the Drammar ontology [10], a high-level ontology for the representation of drama on which our fabula structure can be said to elaborate. The ontology considers drama on two levels: the actional and the directional level, comparable to our idea of fabula and plot layers. Another recent attempt at formalizing fabula, albeit more focused on annotation, is the OntoMedia project [11].

3 A Formal Model of Fabula

We base our fabula model on story comprehension research, since we believe that the use of story comprehension models brings the way the story generation system understands the stories it develops closer to the way humans think about them. In [14], Trabasso et al. presented a story comprehension model, which was later applied to experiments in the narration of picture stories [15]. Children and adults were asked to narrate the events that they inferred to be happening in a sequence of pictures, and the clauses that these children used were categorized using the model to expose the underlying narrative structure. This revealed three stages in the development of story comprehension. Very young children comprehend a story as a sequence of isolated states and actions, whereas at a later age, they can identify a temporal ordering.[1] Eventually, children learn to identify and express causal relationships between goals, actions and outcomes, developing into a full hierarchical ordering of episodes that comprise coherent stories.

The result of Trabasso's research is the General Transition Network (GTN) model, which forms the basis for our fabula structure for story generation. The GTN model identifies a causal network of six story elements (Setting, Event, Internal Response, Goal, Attempt and Outcome) connected by causal relationships: physical (ϕ) and psychological (ψ) causality, motivation (m) and enablement (e). These story elements and their relationships form an implicit hierarchical structure of one or more episodes, which together form a story. The basis for each episode is formed by a causally related Goal, Attempt, and Outcome. Goals set expectations, Outcomes affirm or deny them.

The GTN model is a model of story *analysis*, which is not useful for story *generation* unless we succeed to formalize the way in which the different elements and their connections can be created, and subsequently narrated. We propose a model that is based on the GTN model but differs in important aspects. One of the main differences with the GTN model is that the fabula model we propose attempts to capture the fabula in a single (objective) network, whereas in the GTN model a separate network is constructed from the (subjective) viewpoint of

[1] This can be witnessed when these children tell about their experiences: "And then this happened and then that happened and then...". A similar, simple temporal ordering can be seen in stories generated by previous versions of the Virtual Storyteller and other generation systems.

each character in the story. In the GTN model, something that is an Action for one character can be an Event for another. Our model, however, is independent of viewpoints and therefore offers a global perspective on the fabula.

The fabula model we propose can be seen in Figure 1, showing all possible causal relations between fabula elements. Networks generated using this model do not form a complete account of everything that happened in the course of the story, but only of those fabula elements that have either a cause or an effect on other elements. Unlike Trabasso, we leave the Setting of the story (characters, locations) out of this model. We consider it to be the background against which the story unfolds. The fabula elements are however linked to representations of the characters and objects in the story world via their arguments (e.g., agens and patiens of an Action). At a later point in the story generation process, i.e., when forming the plot or presentation layer, decisions can be made which parts of the setting are conveyed.

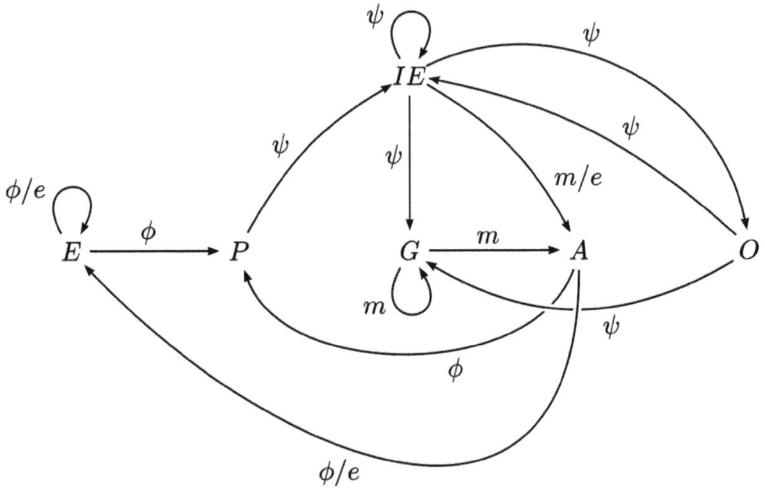

Fig. 1. Fabula model for story generation. The arrows represent possible causal relationships between the elements of the fabula.

3.1 Fabula Elements

Our fabula model defines causal relationships between six types of elements: Goals, Actions, Outcomes, Events, Perceptions and Internal Elements. Before we discuss these causal relationships, let us first take a look at the elements themselves, and discuss their differences with the GTN model.

Goal (G). A Goal is the main drive for a character to act. We adopt Trabasso's definition used in the GTN model; a Goal in this context describes a desire to attain, maintain, leave or avoid certain states, activities or objects [14].

Action (A). The term Action is used to indicate a goal-driven, intentional world change brought about by a character. The GTN model uses the term

Attempt, which from a planning perspective can be seen as a series of Actions that constitute a plan. We use Actions directly since the individual Actions in an Attempt can have separate effects (e.g., an Action can be perceived or cause an Event).

Outcome (*O*). Every Goal has an Outcome. In the GTN model this Outcome is the real world result of an Attempt. In our fabula model it is a mental concept: when a character believes that its Goal is fulfilled, the Goal has a positive Outcome, but if the character believes that the performed Actions did not succeed in fulfilling the Goal, the Outcome is negative. The Outcome is thus closely tied to the world as the character believes it to be, not necessarily to the world as it actually is.[2]

Event (*E*). From the personal viewpoint of the GTN model, an Event is anything that evokes a response for a character, and in this sense an action of one character can be an event for another. From the global perspective of our fabula model, however, an Event is defined as any change in the world that is not the direct and planned result of *any* character action, e.g. a tree that falls down, or a twig that breaks.

Perception (*P*). Perceptions are understandably lacking in the GTN model since the presence of an element in the character's personal network implies that it has been perceived by that character. However, when adopting a global fabula perspective, the explicit notion of Perception is important because the Character Agents do not necessarily perceive all that happens in the story world.

Internal Element (*IE*). Anything that happens within a character, such as cognitions, emotions, feelings and beliefs, is considered to be an Internal Element. We prefer to use the term 'Internal Element' instead of 'Internal Response' as used in the GTN model, because the word 'response' suggests that there is a cause even though there isn't always one, at least not at the level of abstraction we intend to use.[3]

The model has been implemented as an OWL ontology; the aforementioned elements are only the top elements of a more extensive subsumption hierarchy. For instance, Goal subsumes AttainGoal and AvoidGoal, Internal Element subsumes BeliefElement and Emotion, and Perception subsumes See and Hear. Furthermore, properties are available for each element that allow for the expression of knowledge about which Character Agent originated or experienced the fabula element, and the time at which the element occurred (in terms of discrete, virtual time steps in the story world). This enables a temporal ordering of the elements.

---

[2] This enables some interesting dramatic situations. For instance in the story of Romeo and Juliet, Juliet pretends to be dead. Romeo however thinks Juliet is *really* dead, which is a very negative Outcome for his Goal to be together with her.

[3] Consider for instance the Internal Element "hunger". This element could be seen as caused by complicated biophysical processes, but this seems overly specific for most story generation domains.

3.2 Causally Connecting the Fabula Elements

Following [14], we distinguish four types of causality that are used to connect the fabula elements: physical causality, psychological causality, motivation and enablement. These types differ in causal strength [16], physical causality being the strongest, followed by motivation, psychological causation and enablement. This difference in causal strength can be reflected in the generated presentation, i.e., stronger causal relationships might need less explicit wording. Note that these causal relationships only *reflect* what is happening in the simulated story world; they have no generative power themselves.

We realize that any attempt to formalize a layer of causality is unavoidably connected to assumptions about the generative processes of the underlying narrative simulation. We will therefore make these assumptions explicit where necessary. Let's consider the possible causal relationships between the six elements of the fabula, from strong to weak.

Physical causality (ϕ). When an Event or Action happens in the story world and causes something else to happen, this causality is physical. This is the strongest form of causality and might not need to be made explicit in the presentation of the story.[4]

1. Actions physically cause Events. For instance, when a knight stabs a dragon with a sword, this can physically cause the dragon to die. This can also be used as a way to model the occurrence of non-standard results: when the knight crosses a small bridge, it can cause the bridge to break.
2. Events physically cause other Events. For instance, a tree that falls on a bridge causes the bridge to collapse. Or Sleeping Beauty pricking herself on the spinning wheel (an unintended action, thus an Event) causes her to fall asleep.
3. Events and Actions physically cause Perceptions. When a character perceives either the Events or Actions themselves, or their results, such Perceptions are caused by the Events and Actions.

Motivation (m). Motivation (m) is an intentional causality, originating within the Character Agents' minds. Wanting to kill the monster can motivate the knight to stab it with a sword. Motivation relates to Riedl's definition of character believability [13], i.e., that the events in a story are reasonably motivated by the beliefs, desires and goals of the characters that participate in the events.

1. Goals motivate other Goals. A Goal G_1 motivates another Goal G_2 when G_2 is a subgoal of G_1. For instance, the Goal of a knight to kill a dragon could motivate a subgoal of finding the dragon.

[4] In fact, this causality is often so strong that it is difficult for a reader to *not* infer it, even when unstated. Take for instance the two Actions *John fired his gun* and *Peter died.* Most readers presented with these successive actions would infer that John shot Peter, but this is not stated explicitly and other explanations are very well possible.

2. Goals motivate Actions. Using a planning algorithm ensures that the planned Actions are driven by one or more (motivating) Goals. Each Action from a generated plan will be motivated by the Goal for which the plan was made.
3. Internal Elements motivate Actions. Actions that are causally connected to Internal Elements are reflex-like Actions like crying and screaming, that are directly caused by an Internal Element and not by a strategic attempt to fulfill a Goal.

Psychological causality (ψ). Psychological causality (ψ) takes place within the mind of the characters. For instance, if a knight believes that a dragon is going to kill him, this psychologically causes fear within him. It is causality on the level of the cognitive processes of the Character agents. The difference with motivation is that psychological causality is not intentional. A causal chain of event appraisal, as described in [1], can be identified where perceptions lead to Goals: (1) Perceptions psychologically cause Internal Elements, i.e., beliefs; (2) Internal Elements (beliefs) psychologically cause other Internal Elements (emotions); (3) Internal Elements psychologically cause Goals. The Character Agents need a way to determine Goals based on their beliefs, desires and emotions, which are then seen as psychologically causing the Goal.

Psychological causality also applies to Outcomes, since the Outcome is a mental concept. Internal Elements psychologically cause Outcomes when a Character Agent believes that a plan for his Goal failed or succeeded: a positive Outcome when a plan succeeds and a negative one when the plan failed. When a character stops wanting to achieve the Goal, this will lead to a neutral Outcome. These Outcomes can in turn psychologically cause Goals or Internal Elements. Positive Outcomes lead to positive emotions; negative Outcomes lead to negative emotions and possibly the reinstatement of the failed Goal.

Enablement (e). Enablement (e) is the weakest form of causality. If a fabula element A enables another fabula element B, this means that B is possible because of A, but no more than that. An obvious formalization of enablement is that the effects of A satisfy preconditions of B. In the case of an Internal Element enabling an Action, the requirement would be that the Internal Element is a belief and the contents of that belief satisfy preconditions of the Action.

Note that the model does not include Actions enabling other Actions; because Actions are consciously planned by the characters (except if they are directly caused by emotions, without any deliberation) they can only be enabled by beliefs. E.g., killing a rabbit does not enable eating the rabbit until the character sees and believes that the rabbit is indeed dead. Since Events are not planned, this restriction does not apply to them. Note also that as a consequence, Events can only occur if their preconditions are truly met by the Story World, whereas a Character may be mistaken about meeting the preconditions of an Action.

4 Example: Generating a Story from a Fabula

One of the main reasons for making the fabula structure explicit is to be able to generate coherent stories based on it. In this section we show how a (written) story can be generated from a simple fabula. As an example we use the fabula of a fragment from "Princess Lovely", a story written by Katri Oinonen. The story is about Princess Lovely, who lives alone with her father in a big castle. She wants to play with some children she sees outside, but her father, King Mikura, does not allow it. Instead he gives her a little lamb to play with. Princess Lovely loves the lamb very much, but one day it runs away. Lovely searches for the lamb, only to discover that the children she wanted to play with have slaughtered the lamb because they were hungry. Figure 2 shows the elements of the fabula network we have (manually) reconstructed for the final part of the story, starting from the moment that Princess Lovely hears that the lamb has run away. Figure 3 shows this fabula network.[5]

From this fabula, first we select those elements we want to include in the plot. Presenting the entire fabula is possible, but, as argued earlier, this generally does not result in a very interesting story. An example method to form a plot layer based on the fabula layer is to select one goal to form the core of the plot (Sgouros calls this the *Storyline Goal* [4]), necessarily turning the character having the goal into the protagonist. The selection process can then be based on this goal by including everything that is affiliated to this goal, nothing more, nothing less.[6] Another, simpler way of creating a plot from a fabula is to focus on one character, and include only elements directly pertaining to this character in the plot structure. (A more advanced selection method is presented by [17], who describe how to construct a plot from a fabula so as to maximize suspense.) In our example, we choose Princess Lovely as the protagonist and select the bold-faced elements from Figure 2 for inclusion in the plot structure. Note that besides Lovely's Goals, Actions, etc. we also include one Action performed by the children (slaughtering the lamb) in the plot, because it directly causes one of Lovely's Perceptions.

The resulting plot structure forms the input for the Narrator component of the Virtual Storyteller, which generates a natural language text in three steps. The first step is the creation of a 'document plan': a binary branching tree containing selected elements from the plot structure, connected by rhetorical relations that are suitable for expression in natural language. Constructing the document plan involves removing those plot elements that will not be explicitly expressed in the story, e.g., beliefs caused by Perceptions, which are considered to be inferable by the reader. It also involves adding new elements that represent background information about the story world or properties of the characters, e.g., Lovely

[5] To save space, we have only included elements pertaining to Lovely and the children, not other characters such as King Mikura. As a further simplification, we have left out some elements that are not essential for understanding the course of the fabula, e.g., many other Perceptions that have occurred as a consequence of Actions and Events.

[6] It remains to be investigated what it means for fabula elements to be affiliated with a goal.

$IE_{c(1)}$: The children are hungry.
$G_{c(1)}$: The children want to stop being hungry.
$P_{L(1)}$: **Lovely hears that the lamb has fled.**
$IE_{L(1)}$: **Lovely believes the lamb is gone.**
$IE_{L(2)}$: **Lovely is sad.**
$G_{L(1)}$: **Lovely wants the lamb back.**
$G_{L(2)}$: **Lovely wants to find the lamb.**
A_L: **Lovely runs out of the castle.**
E_1: The lamb appears on the children's location.
$P_{c(1)}$: The children see the lamb.
$IE_{c(2)}$: The children believe the lamb is there.
$G_{c(2)}$: The children want to eat the lamb.
$A_{c(1)}$: **The children slaughter the lamb.**
$P_{L(2)}$: **Lovely sees the lamb.**
$IE_{L(3)}$: **Lovely believes the lamb is there.**
$IE_{L(4)}$: **Lovely believes the lamb is dead.**
$O^+_{L(2)}$: **(Lovely has found the lamb)**
$O^-_{L(1)}$: **(Lovely cannot have the lamb back)**
$IE_{L(5)}$: **Lovely is sad and hurt.**
$A_{c(2)}$: The children cook the lamb.
$A_{c(2)}$: The children eat the lamb.
$P_{c(2)}$: The lamb is eaten.
$IE_{c(4)}$: The children believe they have eaten the lamb.
$O^+_{c(2)}$: (The children have eaten the lamb)
$IE_{c(3)}$: The children are not hungry.
$O^+_{c(1)}$: (The children are no longer hungry)

Fig. 2. Fabula elements of a selection of the Princess Lovely story. Bold-faced elements are included in the plot structure underlying the presentation in Figure 4.

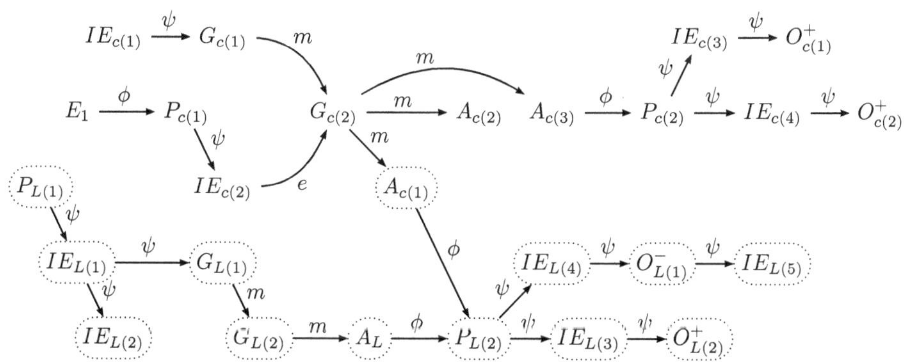

Fig. 3. Network showing the fabula elements of Figure 2 and their causal relationships. From left to right, the elements are chronologically ordered. Encircled elements are included in the plot structure underlying the text in Figure 4.

Because Princess Lovely heard that the lamb had fled, she was sad. She wanted the lamb back, so she wanted to find it and ran out of the castle. Meanwhile, the hungry children slaughtered the lamb. Because Lovely saw the dead lamb, she was sad and hurt.

Fig. 4. Example outcome of generation for the Princess Lovely story

being a princess and the lamb being dead after having been slaughtered. In the second step, the leaf nodes (plot elements) of the document plan are replaced with abstract sentence structures called Dependency Trees. In the third step, these Dependency Trees are combined to form complex sentences, in which the clauses are connected with appropriate cue words (*because, then, but, ...*) to express the rhetorical relations between them. Recurring elements in these complex sentences are deleted where possible; e.g., *Lovely cried and Lovely screamed* becomes *Lovely cried and screamed.* Next, appropriate referring expressions such as pronouns are generated for all references to characters and objects that have not been deleted, and the abstract sentence structures are made concrete by applying rules for word order and morphology. A possible result of all these processes for our input plot structure is shown in Figure 4 (translated into English).

Not all parts of the generation process described here have been implemented; most notably we do not have automated conversion from fabula to plot yet. Transforming plot information into a presentation involves making a further selection of what is to be expressed explicitly and what is to be left to be inferred by the reader, but also involves processes like adding relevant background information, applying stylistic ordering and adding couleur locale. The Narrator component, however, has been fully implemented. The construction of complex sentences with appropriate cue words by the Narrator is discussed in detail in [5]; all other parts of the Narrator are described in [18].

5 Conclusions and Future Work

In this paper, we have discussed a model that can be used to capture the fabula of Emergent Narrative. We have described the fundamental elements of the model and four types of causal relationships between these elements, as identified by story comprehension theory. Furthermore, we have shown how these causal relationships can arise using a character-based approach to automated story generation.

Due to our use of the formal fabula model, in combination with a sophisticated Narration component that can make the most of the information specified in the fabula, we can generate stories that are more coherent than those generated by previous versions of the Virtual Storyteller, although by no means of the quality achievable by a human author. In contrast to systems that only produce a list or plan sequence of actions or events, expressed by means of simple sentences (e.g., [13,17,19]), the Virtual Storyteller also mentions the underlying emotions and goals, and expresses them in fluent text using complex sentences connected by suitable cue words.

Further work on improving the Narrator is still necessary. More importantly, we still need good methods to transform fabula structures into plot structures. We will use the work of [4] and [17] as a starting point for this.

Finally, we would like to continue investigating the use of our fabula model for guiding plot development using creative problem solving. Fabula structures as identified in this paper can be used to represent cases and problems as input for Case Based Reasoning (CBR), similar to MINSTREL [12]. CBR can support the Plot Agent in making authorial decisions to guide the fabula development on different levels of control [20]. On the environmental level, Events can be generated to influence the plans of characters, perceptions of the characters can be influenced, and changes in the setting of the story world can be made in the course of the generation (initial state revision, as in [21]). On the behavioral/motor skill level, the characters can be directed by suggesting Goals or Actions[7]. Such problems can be expressed using partially uninstantiated fabula fragments. Based on a case base of fabula fragments, novel solutions can be found using creativity heuristics. For instance, the problem "what Event can be caused by the children eating the lamb?" can be solved using a stored fabula fragment expressing for instance that Snow White fell asleep after eating an apple, leading to the creative solution that eating the lamb causes the children to fall asleep. To this end, we are currently in the process of defining problem space requirements and creativity heuristics. We believe that the Character Agents can also benefit from CBR by using it to aid their deliberation processes (i.e., to interpret Perceptions or to reason about possible consequences of their planned Actions).

References

1. Theune, M., Rensen, S., op den Akker, R., Heylen, D., Nijholt, A.: Emotional characters for automatic plot creation. In Göbel, S., et al., eds.: Technologies for Interactive Digital Storytelling and Entertainment (TIDSE). Lecture Notes in Computer Science 3105, Springer-Verlag (2004) 95–100
2. Louchart, S., Aylett, R.: Narrative theory and emergent interactive narrative. Int. J. Continuing Engineering Education and Lifelong Learning **14** (2004) 506–518
3. Bal, M.: Narratology: Introduction to the Theory of Narrative. 2nd edn. University of Toronto Press (1997)
4. Sgouros, N.M.: Dynamic generation, management and resolution of interactive plots. Artificial Intelligence **107** (1998) 29–62
5. Theune, M., Hielkema, F., Hendriks, P.: Performing aggregation and ellipsis using discourse structures. Research on Language and Computation, Special Issue on Cross-Modular Approaches to Ellipsis (2007) to appear.
6. Theune, M., Meijs, K., Heylen, D., Ordelman, R.: Generating expressive speech for storytelling applications. IEEE Transactions on Audio, Speech and Language Processing **14** (2006) 1137–1144

[7] We consider suggestion to be a weak form of prescriptive control aimed at keeping the Character Agents autonomous, basically telling them: make your own goals and plan your own actions, but if any of those contain the suggested goals or actions, give preference to intentions that contain the suggestions.

7. Kelso, M.T., Weyhrauch, P., Bates, J.: Dramatic presence. PRESENCE: The Journal of Teleoperators and Virtual Environments **2** (1993) 1–15
8. Propp, V.: De morfologie van het toversprookje: vormleer van een genre. Spectrum, Utrecht (1997)
9. Van Dijk, T.A.: Story comprehension: An introduction. Poetics **9** (1980) 1–21
10. Damiano, R., Lombardo, V., Pizzo, A.: Formal encoding of drama ontology. Lecture Notes in Computer Science **3805** (2005) 95–104
11. Tuffield, M.M., Millard, D.E., Shadbolt, N.R.: Ontological approaches to modelling narrative. In: Proceedings of 2nd AKT DTA Symposium. (2006)
12. Turner, S.R.: The creative process: a computer model of storytelling. Lawrence Erlbaum Associates, Hillsdale, NJ (1994)
13. Riedl, M.O.: Narrative Generation: Balancing Plot and Character. PhD thesis, North Carolina State University (2004)
14. Trabasso, T., Van den Broek, P., Suh, S.Y.: Logical necessity and transitivity of causal relations in stories. Discourse Processes **12** (1989) 1–25
15. Trabasso, T., Nickels, M.: The development of goal plans of action in the narration of a picture story. Discourse Processes **15** (1992) 249–275
16. Tapiero, I., Van den Broek, P., Quintana, M.P.: The mental representation of narrative texts as networks: The role of necessity and sufficiency in the detection of different types of causal relations. Discourse Processes **34** (2002) 237–258
17. Cheong, Y.G., Young, R.M.: A computational model of narrative generation for suspense. In: Proceedings of the Twenty-First National Conference on Artificial Intelligence (AAAI06). (2006)
18. Slabbers, N.: Narration for virtual storytelling. Master's thesis, University of Twente (2006)
19. Meehan, J.: TALE-SPIN. In Schank, R., Riesbeck, K., eds.: Inside computer understanding - five programs plus miniatures. Lawrence Erlbaum Associates (1981) 197–226
20. Blumberg, B., Gaylean, T.: Multi-level control for animated autonomous agents: Do the right thing... oh, not that... In Trappl, R., Petta, P., eds.: Creating Personalities for Synthetic Actors: Towards Autonomous Personality Agents. Springer-Verlag (1997) 74–82
21. Riedl, M.O., Young, R.M.: Open-world planning for story generation. In: International Joint Conference on Artificial Intelligence (IJCAI). (2005) 1719–1720

Telling Stories Through Space: The Mindstage Project

Michael Nitsche[1] and Paul Richens[2]

[1] School of Literature, Communication & Culture, Georgia Institute of Technology
686 Cherry Str., Atlanta, GA 30332-065, USA
michael.nitsche@lcc.gatech.edu
[2] Paul Richens, Department of Architecture and Civil Engineering, University of Bath
Bath BA2 7AY, UK
P.N.Richens@bath.ac.uk

Abstract. *Mindstage* is a real-time multi-user 3D virtual environment used to explore the relationships between a linear story and the virtual world in which it unfolds. The prototype uses as its narrative spine an illustrated lecture on film design by Christopher Hobbs. It provides a stage for interaction featuring a customized 3D environment based on this material, with the necessary actors and objects in it. The main design issues were mapping the linear talk onto the virtual space, and the implementation of various interactive features within it. We argue that a careful use of spatial design supports a degree of non-linear story-telling without compromising the core linear content.

Keywords: virtual space, narrative, educational, architecture.

1 Introduction

Interactive real-time 3 dimensional virtual environments (RT 3D VE) operate as virtual stages that provide certain options to visiting users, who enact events within the given framework [25]. The action itself depends on those users, who realize the events through ergodic participation [2]. We argue that the spatial design of the stage heavily influences the event realization so that story-telling and re-telling can be shaped by the architectural design of virtual spaces.

The range of possibilities opened up by the RT 3D VE allows for flexible interaction between user and virtual world. ‘Possibility space’ defines the options a player has open to him within a certain situation in a video game world. The depth of a ‘possibility space’ describes the richness of these possibilities. Many video games (prime examples of the commercial RT 3D VE) implement them to enhance a player’s game experience. They are a feature mentioned and applied by many leading game designers (e.g. Warren Spector [18]; [33] and Will Wright [41]). In games, they are often manifested through the complexity of computer-controlled characters’ artificial intelligence, player-player interaction, combinations of virtual objects, visualization, and spatial design – among other conditions. Ultimately, ‘possibility spaces’ profit from their openness and flexibility, which raises the question of how linear content (a story) can ever fit into such a matrix? This tension is a central issue in adapting linear material, whether it is story, film or music, for presentation in a RT 3D VE.

S. Göbel, R. Malkewitz, and I. Iurgel (Eds.): TIDSE 2006, LNCS 4326, pp. 61 – 71, 2006.

1.1 Linking Nodes

Addressing this challenge, some design guidelines suggest the application of a linear dramatic form through a set path of pre-defined events [40] or via the adaptation of dramatic act structures from film and television [32]. The problem with such pre-set structures is their rigid format. In contrast, hypertextual approaches operate with nodes and links forming branching networks – termed 'linkmeshes' by Crawford [9] – of varying sizes and levels of complexity from a basic branching tree to the monstrous rhizome of the Internet [7] where innumerable interconnections between different pages are made available by a shared protocol. The linking process and access replaces the fixed work. Finally, randomizing linking and access leads to Weinbren's proclaimed 'revolution of random access' [39], where tracing any specific content becomes optional – the reading surpasses the story. The structure stays conditional and often unpredictable. A user cannot predict where a certain link leads and remains dependent on the designer's expertise in setting up the linkmesh. Set dramatic structures might be too narrow, but these forms of linkmeshes can be too unpredictable and/ or to arbitrary to allow for a significant shape.

1.2 Character AI

Research in artificial intelligence (AI) re-establishes a form of intentionality, logic, and predictability through certain rules and behaviors within operational entities – agents. Agents are digital entities with an AI driven behavior, that can participate in a dramatic event involving the user, and can contribute an underlying narrative setting or form to it [22, 35]. A pioneering project for dramatic story-structuring through AI has been the *Oz* Project at CMU [4, 5, 20]. It influenced Mateas and Sengers to research the use of AI for dramatic characters [23] and had further impact on the work on agents at Stanford University [14]. In comparison, the MIT MediaLab's *Synthetic Characters Group* concentrated on a basic emotional behavioral model of agents (from [6] to [37]). Implementing such a complex behavior in an RT 3D VE is difficult, but has been undertaken notably by Mateas and Stern in *Façade* [24] and Young, Saretto & Riedl in the *Mimesis* system [29]. These projects address the question of the narrative and dramatic structure but due to their concentration on AI agent behavior they have made little use of the virtual stage itself. Although these AI systems have some form of spatial awareness, their focus is on the actors and their performance, rather than the virtual stage on which they perform. They exclude a prime structuring principle.

1.3 Stepping into Space

Space as a narrative structuring principle has been acknowledged in new media studies for some time (e.g. [7, 30]). Much work deals with social elements – often connected to the question of body and identity in virtual worlds [31, 34, 36]. But only recently has visually represented space (as opposed to textual descriptions of space) entered the academic debate. Jenkins suggested parallels between game explorations and travel logs [12] and – influenced by de Certeau and LeFebvre – developed his approach into the concept of games as 'spatial art' [17, 18]. His notion of the 'narrative architect' informed our approach significantly. A parallel view is carried further by Friedman who argues ultimately that virtual geography itself can become the 'primary narrative agent' [11]. In contrast, Aarseth argues against a focus on the representational aspect and for an understanding of spatial representation in virtual worlds as symbolic and rule-based [1]. Yet, a player's experience of virtual spaces often takes the shape of a quest. A player can realize the quest as a string of events that unfold in a given virtual world but whose precise spatio-temporal conditions depend on the interaction.

While some see a quest mainly as discourse[3, 38], we agree with Jenkins and others and maintain a certain narrative direction within such a discourse (for a form of spatial understanding see also Herman's principle of 'story maps' [15]). Our project encourages the interactor to generate a unique path through the virtual world and explore its ingredients at a convenient pace. At the same time it has clear goals to structure this process: acquisition of specific knowledge, reaching the end of the lecture, finding and solving a given sub-problem. The interactor is channelled in his or her spatial progress by our world design. *Mindstage* is mainly concerned with the design of the spatial elements of RT 3D VEs that on the one hand provide structure to such a quest and on the other allow for divergence from it. Users can see where they are going and where they come from; they can literally create their own perspective to the elements implemented in the virtual world. The focus on space allows for a more directed interaction from the user's side as well as a wide range of freedom to realize this interaction in a quest-like form. Insofar, the *Mindstage* prototype provides one possible answer to the question of how to spatialize a narrative in a virtual world.

2 Mindstage Project

The *Mindstage* project grew out of earlier work on the integration of narrative and mediated virtual architecture [26, 27]. The basic research question was whether a RT 3D VE can be effective as a learning environment. How could the architectural design of virtual space reinforce the piece's impact, and promote engagement, exploration and legibility? The research focused on the design of an effective spatial arrangement of knowledge and the implementation of the means to explore it interactively.

Virtual learning environments have become a wide-spread research area usually with a focus on networks and e-learning. For 3D learning environments one can trace a trend from early experiments such as the *Active Worlds Educational Universe* (http://www.activeworlds.com/edu/index.asp) that contains some educational material just like the more recent Massive Multiplayer Online world of *Second Life* (http://secondlife.com/) to the increasing use of video game technology exemplified in MIT's *Games to Teach* project (http://www.educationarcade.org/). In part, this is a result of the technological development and accessibility of games. As games and their development platforms become more accessible to universities and individuals they get more easily adapted into educational programs. Many current games ship with special editors that support custom-generated content and encourage users to create their own variants. *Mindstage* is an example of this trend in that it uses a game-prototyping development platform: *Virtools*.

Technically, *Mindstage* was delivered as a free standing proof-of-concept prototype running on consumer level personal computers. It needs 650Mb disk space, a 3GHz PC with 1Gb of RAM and a good 64Mb graphic card. Its multi-user functionality needs Internet access and targets seminar-sized groups of up to 7 students. Production limitations allowed us to include about 75 % of the intended material. We have described the production workflow and further design process elsewhere in more detail [28].

2.1 Design Philosophy

The underlying content of *Mindstage* is a talk on film design by the acclaimed British Art Director Christopher Hobbs whose credits include *Long Day Closes*, *Caravaggio*, *Edward II*, and the BBC *Gormenghast* trilogy. The prototype aims at graduate students of film and media studies. These students often come from different backgrounds with different levels of knowledge and computer literacy. To optimize the educational impact *Mindstage* allows for individual exploration of the content at any speed convenient to the individual student, exploration in a group during a multi-user session, and guided navigation led by a pre-coded avatar. But unlike commercial video games, *Mindstage* could not alter the underlying material. Hobbs' lecture had to be adapted without any changes to its length or material in order to preserve the expertise of the lecturer. Any change would jeopardize exactly the unique scholarly qualities of Hobbs that the project aimed to document. In contrast, games can adjust their underlying narrative heavily if the circumstances of the production demand it. Levels can be excluded or changed to meet a release deadline, stories adjusted to the necessities of the game production, characters added or removed to support the flow of the title.

Mindstage's fundamental design approach reversed the idea of the 'memory palace' by mapping the pre-conceived academic lecture onto a navigable multi-user RT 3D VE. A virtual space was generated around the given lecture and the movement through the space referred to the argument of the talk. The computer-controlled avatar represents the lecturer and guides students through the virtual world, moving from one object of interest to another while delivering the pre-recorded talk. Students can follow the lecturer-guide or explore the space by themselves or in groups.

After a linear video introduction, students have to select an avatar representation in a *robing-room*. Once they have selected a representation for themselves, they enter into the main lecture space, a transition that could be understood as step from a 'prolog' to the main content. Occasional path markings indicate the flow of the virtual lecture in the main space and support the guiding lecturer visually. At the same time the free exploration, interactive access and multi-user features provide the necessary variety for a functional 'possibility space'.

In addition to the lecture, *Mindstage* includes interactive puzzles and illustrative material set in a shared multi-user world to support group-based learning and the students' active involvement with the topic. This meant we had to combine linear story elements and non-linear exploration which lead to a number of challenging clashes for the overall design.

Linear	**Non-linear**
pre-recorded lecture audio	free multi-user text chat
predefined movement path of lecturer-avatar	free movement of student avatars
avatar selection	free-form exploration of illustrative material during own exploration
linear introduction and summary	logging in and out at any time

The resulting overall design had to incorporate both elements: highly non-linear free exploration with the unpredictable state of a multi-user environment as well as the linear and pre-defined lecture. As a result we concentrated on two main issues and their combination during the development of the *Mindstage* prototype: *spatial design* of the virtual environment and *interaction design* for the user's interaction with the system. Both of them had to support the linear guided tour as well as non-linear exploration. In comparison to the other narrative models outlined above, our AI level was basic and only present in the lecturer avatar's behavior. We avoided any kind of conditional hyper-linking, replacing it with a form of spatial arrangement.

2.2 Spatial Design

Mindstage's virtual world had somehow to map the narrative structure of the lecture to make it accessible in 3D virtual space. A number of architectural theories indirectly informed our design process. Hillier and Hanson's 'space syntax' [16] and especially Lynch's work on cognitive maps [21] stand out as relevant approaches. But our main reference point was Christopher Hobbs' lecture itself.

In a first step, we divided the lecture into chapters that relate to central themes of Hobbs' talk: 'Perspective Illusion', 'Gothic Tendencies' and 'Textural Depth'. Where necessary we defined sub-chapters within these main topics. This structure was translated into designated locations: *zones* signify chapters and *rooms* sub-topics of a chapter. *Rooms* and *zones* were assembled so that any student could follow the lecture seamlessly through space. The central theme, thus, provided the spatial design with a core path to which we added freely navigable planes to allow for short-cuts. *Zones* are defined by themes and consist of *rooms*, which contain specific sub-topics. *Paths* mirror a linear logic and connect these locations. Users are free to use the pathways or leave them and follow their own interest. Each room features a range of *nodes*, visual references to precise points of the lecture. Locations can be explored in any order but are aligned along a principal path with the wider context of the *zones* following the argument of the lecture.

The main direction of the exploration is upwards. The central interconnecting spine consists of a four-layered construction that references the principle of a tree of knowledge and branches out into more specific *zones* and *rooms*. Unlike many games such as *Quake* or *Diablo* that lead the player deeper into the dungeons, away from light and into darker interiors, closer to the core of all evil, *Mindstage* provides an ascending movement path along which the knowledge elements are grouped.

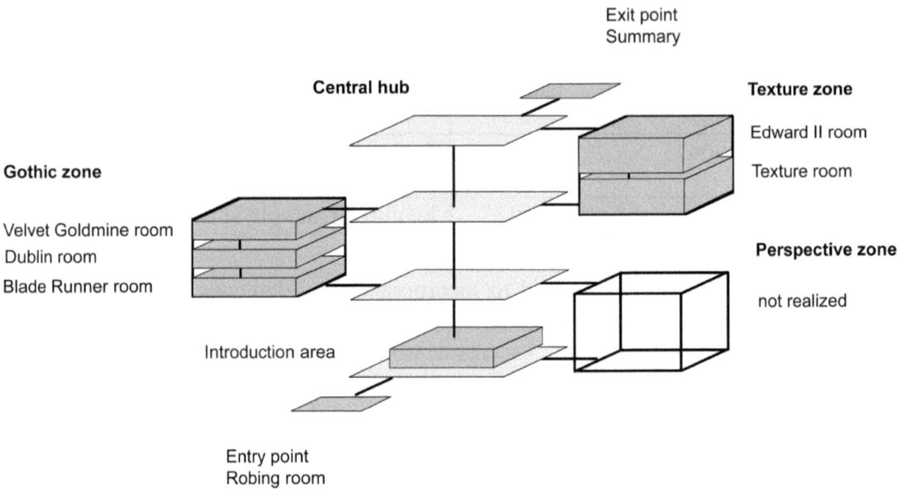

Fig. 1. Schema of the lecture break-down into *zones* and *rooms*

Each *room* contains a certain part of Christopher Hobbs' argument in the form of local *nodes*. *Nodes* stand out as visual attractors that are clearly distinguishable from a less detailed background. Most *nodes* present illustrative material that supports a particular point of the argument, for example: film clips, stills, and 3D models.

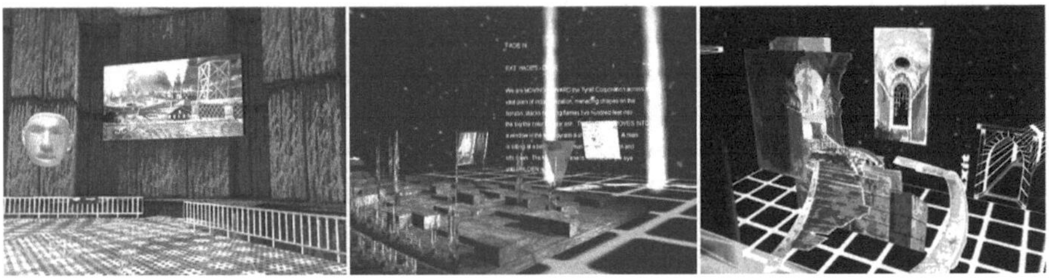

Fig. 2. *Mindstage* screenshots; Lecture avatar next to a film clip in the *Introduction Area* (left); display screens and objects in the *Blade Runner room* (middle); interactive spatial puzzle in the *Velvet Goldmine room* (right)

Like most lectures, Hobbs' talk included main points and chapters, digressions, footnotes, illustrations and examples, with glimpses ahead to upcoming parts of the lecture as well as back references to established points. All of these rhetorical devices are suggestive of spatial equivalents and we tried to map them onto the virtual stage for the lecture. For example, the spatial design in most *rooms* allowed us to keep various elements visible at the same time. Thus it generated a visual reference between different items of the lecture. Students can see schematic 3D models referring to Scott's *Blade Runner* in combination with production stills, movie clips, screenplay excerpts and storyboard sketches (see figure 2; screenshot in the middle), thanks to the depth of the spatial presentation and the avatar's position within the arrangement of the individual nodes. Users are invited to create their own perspective towards the various *nodes*, their own visual content assembly.

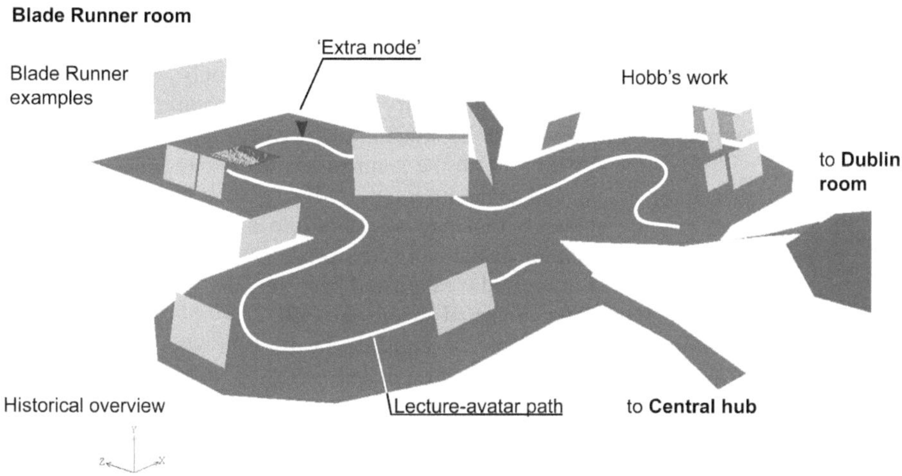

Fig. 3. Schema of the *Blade Runner room* within the *Gothic zone*

Spatial arrangement and exploration replaced conditional linking. The *Blade Runner* room exemplifies this approach. The room has a pre-defined linear lecture path along which various *nodes* are aligned but as one enters the *room* the end of this lecture part is as visible and accessible as any other part of Hobbs' talk on *Blade Runner*. The first and the last page of the chapter are visible at the same time – open for exploration through spatial movement through the arranged elements.

Virtual space literally becomes a basic narrative element and the basis for the flexibility of our 'possibility spaces'.

2.3 Interaction Design

On the conceptual level, most of our problems centered on spatial and temporal issues arising from the multi-player feature, which demanded a more fundamental re-interpretation of the linear lecture form. How could individual lecture elements stay available to different students at the same time and keep as many students engaged as possible? How to incorporate the multi-player functionality in the virtual world? In order to provide different parts of the lecture simultaneously each room included an instance of the lecturer-avatar that operated independently from those in other rooms. Such a multiplication of the lecturer avatar made different parts of the lecture accessible to different groups of students at the same time. While one student might explore the *Texture zone*, another group might visit the introductory part. Different parts of the lecture-story are being told simultaneously. But to maintain a consistent view of the lecturer as a unified character, it was then necessary to visually isolate the spaces controlled by the individual avatars.

The initial design included a voice-chat feature that would allow students to communicate via audio-link and discuss topics arising from the lecture. The feature was modified to a text-chat – in part because of technical difficulties but also due to design issues. In contrast to text-chat-rooms, and drawing from online game environments, we chose to display the chat as 'speech bubbles' above the student's avatar. Localized chat supported our focus on spatial design as students have to be in the same room and to face each other to chat effectively. Thus the interactive design forces a certain spatial behavior onto the students in contrast to the often confusing disembodied communication encountered in multi-user text-only chat-rooms. In addition, text-chat sidesteps any acoustic rivalry between the lecturer, who delivers his talk as an audible presentation, and the students, who might have interrupted this audio stream with their own chatter. With the soundspace uncluttered the spatialized audio from the lecturer avatar and other interactive objects such as film projection screens operate as guiding elements that lure students into a close proximity to the source. Students follow the lecturer avatar not only to see how he interacts with the next node but also to stay within his audio range and hear the talk. For more examples of the value of acoustic landmarks in virtual spaces see [19].

Competition for interactive elements is regulated in the following way. Students can freely experiment with the content in the virtual world by starting and stopping film clips, starting 3D animations, and moving objects such as movable screens and elevators. But control of any object is taken over by the lecturer avatar whenever this special object is needed for his talk. Such an 'override' function guarantees the consistency of the linear lecture without restricting the students' access to the objects too much. The most complex interaction is implemented in a spatial puzzle that lets users re-arrange cut-out scenery (fig. 2 right); mimicking the approach Hobbs' took in the set design for one of his films. Two users can re-arrange the set up at the same time, taking control over the pieces depending on the moment of access. A puzzle like this could only be realized in a 3D space and supports the project's overall approach.

To further support our spatial design most of the students' interactions are dependent on proximity to certain objects. For example, film clips can be started, stopped, and re-started by standing close to the relevant button, thereby selecting it, and then activating it. Visibility of some objects depends on collision with trigger objects, and moving architectural elements such as elevators depend on avatar positioning and orientation.

Spatial restrictions and arrangement were our prime content assembly method, while the definition of the interactive access shaped how students could encounter this content. The assembly in representational and functional space allowed us to use a different access method from the conditional linking available in web-based lecture forms. The spatial logic of the assembly and the conditional logic that structured the access combined for a flexible prototype where strict linear elements can be combined with free play. This might evoke the criticism that our design was too single-minded, forcing the interactor too much into a given direction. While *Mindstage* includes a pre-fabricated path, we would argue that spatial design and our basic interaction design allowed us to include a freer approach to our initially very linear content. *Mindstage* accepted the challenge of adapting a linear story without any change of the material whatsoever. In this context spatial design was not limiting the 'possibility space' but opening it up.

3 Value of Space for Digital Story-Telling

The focus on spatial design and a multi-user interactive setting came at a price. It allowed us to experiment successfully with the spatial arrangements but excluded some features such as an internal assessment of student work. *Mindstage* offers its contents – it does not force them onto the student. It avoids any directing 'challenge' that would drive the visitor to interact with the virtual world in a certain way (suggested e.g. in [8]). However, *Mindstage*'s multi-user functionality (basic as it is) allows it to become a 'social space' - key to virtual learning environments [10] - as well as being essential to the creation of the quality of 'place' in virtual space [13].

The narrative elements – sections of the lecture – are weaved into the virtual space and as a result the virtual space gains significance. The lecture and the argument only come to life through the user's exploration of and interaction with this virtual stage. It is the interconnection of the interactor's quest and the pre-set staging for this exploration that carries the 'story-ness' in *Mindstage*. Thus the 'possibility space' of *Mindstage* provides freedom *and* structure through spatial design that guides users without forcing a single pathway onto them. Interaction is not an added feature but interactive and unique exploration is essential for the realization of the piece. The options become concrete for each user through his or her own spatial navigation. Each user creates an own story based on the narrative set up weaved into the space.

One element that was merely touched on by *Mindstage* and that deserves further examination is the design and implementation of user-defined elements in a shared virtual space. *Mindstage* experiments peripherally with shared versus locally controlled add-on elements to the main lecture. Students were able to activate *extra nodes* that materialized additional elements within the shared multi-user space visible only to themselves. These *extra nodes* worked like spatialized footnotes or cross-references that point beyond the main text and into other research. Combining this feature with the uploading of user-defined content offers promising possibilities for the design of a richer and more flexible version of *Mindstage*.

Acknowledgements

Mindstage was conceived by Michael Nitsche, and implemented by the authors and Jonathan Mackenzie. Christopher Hobbs enthusiastically donated the content for the prototype. We were supported by the staff of the Cambridge University Moving Image Studio (CUMIS), especially Maureen Thomas. The project was funded from a generous grant from Informatix Inc of Tokyo.

References

1. Aarseth, E.J. Allegorien des Raums: Räumlichkeit in Computerspielen *Zeitschrift für Semiotik*, 2001, 301-318.
2. Aarseth, E.J. *Cybertext: Perspectives on Ergodic Literature*. The John Hopkins University Press, Baltimore, London, 1997.
3. Aarseth, E.J. Quest Games as Post-Narrative Discourse. in Ryan, M.-L. ed. *Narrative Across Media: The Languages of Storytelling*, University of Nebraska Press, Lincoln, NE, 2004, 361-377.
4. Bates, J. The Role of Emotion in Believable Agents. *Communications of the ACM*, *37* (7). 122-125.
5. Bates, J., Loyall, B.A. and Reilly, W.S. An Architecture for Action, Emotion, and Social Behaviour. in Castelfranchi, C. and Wemer, E. eds. *Artificial Social Systems Selected Papers from the Fourth European Workshop on Modelling Autonomous Agents in a Multi-Agent World (MAAMAW) '92*, Springer, Heidelberg, 1994, 55-68.

6. Blumberg, B. Old Tricks, New Dogs: Ethology and Interactive Creatures, Massachusetts Institute of Technology, 1997.
7. Bolter, J.D. *Writing Space. Computers, Hypertext, and the Remediation of Print.* Lawrence Erlbaum Assoc., Mahwah, New Jersey; London, 2001.
8. Brophy, S.P. Constructing Shareable Learning Materials in Bioengineering Education. *IEEE Engineering in Medicine and Biology Magazine*, *22* (4). 39-46.
9. Crawford, C. *Understanding Interactivity (draft 7.0).* n.n., n.n., 2000.
10. Dillenbourg, P. Virtual Learning Environments *EUN Conference '00*, Brussels, 2000.
11. Friedman, T. Civilization and Its Discontents: Simulation, Subjectivity, and Space. in Smith, G. ed. *Discovering Discs: Transforming Space and Genre on CD-ROM*, New York University Press, New York, 1999, 132-150.
12. Fuller, M. and Jenkins, H. Nintendo® and New World Travel Writing: A Dialogue. in Jones, S.G. ed. *Cybersociety: Computer-Mediated Communication and Community*, Sage Publications, Thousand Oaks, 1995, 57-72.
13. Harrison, S. and Dourish, P. *Re-place-ing Space: The Roles of Place and Space in Collaborative Systems.* ACM Press, New York, 1996.
14. Hayes-Roth, B. and van Gent, R. *Improvisational Puppets, Actors, and Avatars.* Miller Freeman, San Francisco, 1996.
15. Herman, D. *Story Logic: Problems and Possibilities of Narrative.* University of Nebraska Press, Lincoln; London, 2002.
16. Hillier, B. and Hanson, J. *The Social Logic of Space.* Cambridge University Press, Cambridge, 1984.
17. Jenkins, H. Game Design as Narrative Architecture. in Harrington, P. and Wardrup-Fruin, N. eds. *First Person: New Media as Story, Performance, and Game*, MIT Press, Cambridge, MA, 2004.
18. Jenkins, H. and Squire, K. The Art of Contested Spaces. in King, L. ed. *Game On: The History and Culture of Video Games*, Universe, New York, 2002, 64-75.
19. Loomis, J.M., Lippa, Y., Klatzky, R.L. and Golledge, R.G. Spatial Updating of Locations Specified by 3-D Sound and Spatial Language. *Journal of Experimental Psychology: Learning, Memory, and Cognition*, *28* (2). 335-345.
20. Loyall, A.B. Believable Agents: Building Interactive Personalities, Carnegie Mellon University, Pittsburgh, 1997.
21. Lynch, K. *The Image of the City.* MIT Press, Cambridge, MA, 1960.
22. Mateas, M. Interactive Drama, Art and Artificial Intelligence, Carnegie Mellon University, 2002.
23. Mateas, M. and Sengers, P. *Narrative Intelligence.* John Benjamins Publ. Co., Amsterdam, 2002.
24. Mateas, M. and Stern, A. *Integrating Plot, Character and Natural Language Processing in the Interactive Drama Façade.* Fraunhofer IRB Verlag, Darmstadt, 2003.
25. Murray, J.H. *Hamlet on the Holodeck. The Future of Narrative in Cyberspace.* MIT Press, Cambridge, MA, 1997.
26. Nitsche, M., Roudavski, S., Thomas, M. and Penz, F. Building Cuthbert Hall Virtual College As a Dramatically Engaging Environment. Binder, T., Gregory, J. and Wagner, I. eds. *Proceedings of the Participatory Design Conference 2002*, CPSR, Malmoe, 2002, 386-390.
27. Nitsche, M., Roudavski, S., Thomas, M. and Penz, F. Drama and Context in Real-Time Virtual Environments: Use of Pre-Scripted Events as a Part of an Interactive Spatial Mediation Framework. Göbel, S., Braun, N., Spierling, U., Dechau, J. and Diener, H. eds., Fraunhofer IRB Verlag, Darmstadt, 2003, 296-310.

28. Richens, P. and Nitsche, M. Mindstage: Towards a Functional Virtual Architecture. Martens, B. and Brown, A. eds. *11th International CAAD Futures Conference*, Springer, Vienna, 2005, 331-340.
29. Riedl, M., Saretto, C.J. and Young, M.R. *Managing Interaction between Users and Agents in a Multi-agent Storytelling Environment*. ACM Press, New York, 2003.
30. Ryan, M.-L. *Narrative As Virtual Reality. Immersion and Interactivity in Literature and Electronic Media*. The John Hopkins University Press, Baltimore; London, 2001.
31. Schroeder, R. *The Social Life of Avatars: Presence and Interaction in Shared Virtual Environments*. Springer, London, 2002.
32. Siegel, D. The Nine Act Story Structure *Proceedings of the Computer Game Developers Conference 1996*, Miller Freeman, San Francisco, 1996, 421-431.
33. Smith, H. The Future of Game Design: Moving beyond Deus Ex and other dated Paradigms *Multimedia International Market*, Montreal, 2001.
34. Stone, A.R. Cyberdaemmerung at Wellspring Systems. in Moser, A.M. ed. *Immersed in Technology. Art and Virtual Environments*, MIT Press, Cambridge, MA, 1996, 103-118.
35. Szilas, N. *Interactive Drama on Computer: Beyond Linear Narrative*. AAAI Press, Menlo Park, 1999.
36. Taylor, T.L. *Play between Worlds. Exploring Online Game Culture.* MIT Press, Cambridge, MA, London, 2006.
37. Tomlinson, W.M., Jr. Synthetic Social Relationships for Computational Entities, Massachusetts Institute of Technology, 2002.
38. Tosca, S. The Quest Problem in Computer Games. Gőbel, S., Braun, N., Spierling, U., Dechau, J. and Diener, H. eds. *Technologies for Interactive Digital Storytelling TIDSE*, Fraunhofer IRB Verlag, Darmstadt, GE, 2003, 69-82.
39. Weinbren, G. The Digital Revolution is a Revolution of random Access. *Telepolis*. (online magazine) Heise, 17 Feb 1997
40. Wimberley, D. and Samsel, J. *Interactive Writer´s Handbook*. The Carronade Group, Los Angeles; San Francisco, 1995.
41. Wright, W. Content, Compression, and Creativity *Living Game Worlds Symposium*, Atlanta, GA, 2005.

Narratology for Interactive Storytelling: A Critical Introduction

Marc Cavazza and David Pizzi

School of Computing, University of Teesside, TS1 3BA Middlesbrough, United Kingdom
{m.o.cavazza, d.pizzi}@tees.ac.uk

Abstract. Most research in Interactive Storytelling (IS) has sought inspiration in narrative theories issued from contemporary narratology to either identify fundamental concepts or derive formalisms for their implementation. In the former case, the theoretical approach gives raise to empirical solutions, while the latter develops Interactive Storytelling as some form of "computational narratology", modelled on computational linguistics. In this paper, we review the most frequently cited theories from the perspective of IS research. We discuss in particular the extent to which they can actually inspire IS technologies and highlight key issues for the effective use of narratology in IS.

Keywords: Interactive Storytelling, Narrative Theory, Virtual Actors.

1 Introduction

Since the early descriptions of Swartout et al. [19] and Young [26], most Interactive Storytelling systems have integrated Artificial Intelligence (AI) techniques, which generate narrative actions sequences, with 3D graphics and animations, staging these narrative actions to produce the actual interactive story. However, AI formalisms can only succeed with appropriate processes for knowledge acquisition. When investigating which domain knowledge could best support the IS endeavour, most researchers turned to narratology as the main discipline that could support narrative analysis and formalisation.

In this paper, we review the main narrative theories that have inspired IS research and provide a critical insight into how these theories can support further developments of our discipline[1]. One key question here would be to which extent narrative formalisms facilitate computational description [25]; as we shall see, many IS researchers have already embraced them with some success, although much remains to be done to take full benefit of these theories. Our goal is not to judge on the appropriateness of past use of narrative theories by IS colleagues; rather, it is to provide a perspective and some critical comments, which hopefully should prove helpful when considering the use of narratology to support research in IS.

[1] We have restricted ourselves to the most often cited, "traditional", narrative theories, most of which have been developed in the course of the XXth century.

S. Göbel, R. Malkewitz, and I. Iurgel (Eds.): TIDSE 2006, LNCS 4326, pp. 72–83, 2006.

2 Aristotle and the Foundations of Drama Theory

Aristotle provided the earliest analysis of what (throughout later centuries) became known as traditional drama, insisting in particular on its progression through climax and the final resolution (denouement). It is the strength of the classical model to have imposed itself virtually unchallenged almost until the 20th century, and as such its descriptive power has been considerable. This has led IS researchers such as Mateas, in his early work [15], to subscribe to a neo-aristetolian vision of Interactive Drama (also following [12]). However, Mateas acutely identified the lack of emphasis on agency as a limitation of the Aristotelian model, and consequently proposed an extension to the Aristotelian model precisely incorporating user interaction. Although Aristotle's Poetics is often cited in IS work for its description of narrative evolution (see e.g. "narrative arcs" in [27]), only Tomaszewski and Binsted [22] have proposed an IS model based on its principles.

To which extent can Aristotelian theory assist in the development of IS systems? As its discussion in previous IS work suggests, it does provide a model for story progression that encompasses important aesthetic properties of the story. Aristotle also introduced the important concept of *proairesis* (or "deliberate choice", which we will see developed in Barthes' work) as a central aspect of narratives. On the other hand, the Aristotelian model's descriptive power is not sufficient to be considered as a narrative formalism *sui generis*. The main reason is that it does not include a fine-grained description, or even a proper formalisation, of narrative actions. In IS, the Aristotelian model seems to have been primarily used as an inspiration, a theoretical framework in which to describe narrative concepts, rather than a source of narrative formalisms, let alone their implementations in IS systems.

3 Propp and the Formalist Turn

Morphology of the folktale [17] is probably the best known essay in narratology, and is certainly the most cited amongst researchers in IS. Propp was the first to uncover stable structures underlying Russian folktales and to describe these structures using the first ever formalism in narratology, together with a symbolic notation. Propp introduced *narrative functions* as the basic representational unit of a narrative. These constitute narrative primitives, describing prototypic narrative events encountered in all (Russian) folktales, such as *Transgression*, *Deception*, *Struggle*, *Punishment*, *Wedding*, etc. For Propp, all Russian folktales follow a common structure and can be described through a sequence of narrative functions, of which he has identified 31 in the corpus he studied.

Propp's approach can be summarised into four major points:

- narrative functions are the basic primitives of folktales; as such, they are stable and invariant elements; they are independent from the characters that executes them, as well as from the modalities of their execution.
- there exists a limited number of narrative functions describing Russian folktales (narrative functions thus behave as primitives; the canonical description identifies 31 such functions).

- functions always occur in the same order (Fig. 1), although each given tale only comprises a subset of functions. This means that if functions in general (across all folktales) are described in the order A→B→C→D→E→F, only subsequences of the type A→D→E→F and B→C→D→F would be "well-formed" folktales (the order of functions is unalterable, and no "backtracking" is allowed).

$$\alpha\beta^3 d^1 A^1 B^1 C \uparrow H^1\text{-}J^1 K^4 \downarrow w^3$$

Fig. 1. A typical sequence in Propp's formalism. Each basic function is associated a symbol [B^1: Abduction; J^1: Antagonist killed during fight]. The up and down arrows correspond to the Hero's departure and return.

It is worth citing here Bremond's criticism of Proppian hypotheses, especially from the perspective of IS [4]. Because of the fixed nature of the functions sequence, Propp's approach inherently prohibits any kind of "branching functions" that could alter the course of the folktale to provide alternative paths. In other words, we would say that narrative functions prevent all forms of *proairesis*, and that functions have fixed conditions for their applications and always produce similar outcomes.

Provided that the narrative genre considered is isomorphic to folktales, Propp's narrative functions can be adopted almost as a ready-to-use formalism, and there have been good examples of such use in IS by Grasbon and Braun [8], Machado et al., [13][14] and Peinado and Gervas [16]. On the other hand, Hartmann et al. [11] have extended Propp's formalism to describe "branching points", trying the address the above limitations of the original approach.

Yet, fundamental limitations, such as the lack of character perspective, the lack of a psychological level of representation (for emotions, feelings or self-appraisal) would make it unsuitable to other forms of interactive drama.

4 Greimas: A Linguistic Perspective on Narrative Analysis

Greimas developed his contribution to narratology as an extension of his work in (natural language) semantics. The two keys for accessing his work are indeed its preoccupation with semantics and his strong structuralist stance; hence the emphasis on paradigms, oppositions and semantic roles. He introduced what can be described as the first role-based analysis of narratives. More specifically, he used the concept of *actant* [21] to formalise the roles of Propp's *dramatis personae*. In Barthes' terms, Greimas proposed to define and categorise characters, "not for who they are, but for what they do" [2].

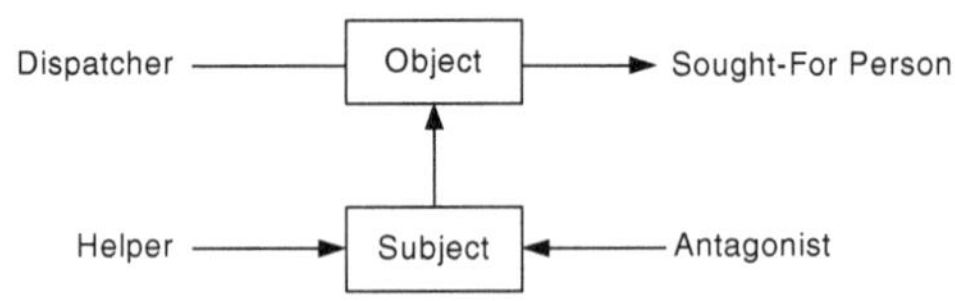

Fig. 2. Greimas' generic actant model. The basic roles described above are instantiated to the specific domains of the "narrative" considered.

Greimas' hypothesis is that a small number of formulas organised around actors could account for the organisation of the narrative universe [9, p.176]. He starts by considering Propp's 31 narrative functions from the perspective of the characters enacting these functions, to conclude, with Propp, that Russian folktales are based on a 7-actants model. He then takes a first step towards formalising a system of oppositions between narrative actants, which is freely based on generic syntactic roles such as *subject vs. object*[2]. Through the definition of oppositions such as *Hero vs. Sought-for Person* and *Helper vs. Opponent* he proposes a generic model of mythical roles[3], which is summarised on Figure 2. Now, where this model really acquires descriptive power, is through the notion of *thematic investment*, which posits that each element of that model can be instantiated by a specific semantic field. He shows that this model can be instantiated by such diverse semantic fields as Philosophy, to describe the quest for knowledge as a narrative, or even Marxist politics to describe class struggle and revolutionary processes.

Greimas further identifies several such semantic fields, whose relevance to storytelling requires no justification: *love, political or religious fanaticism, greed/ambition, jealousy, patriotism, frustration with one's life*… (with a potential to describe narrative topics from *Romeo and Juliet* to *Madame Bovary*).

Greimas contribution was not limited to actors, as he also revisited Propp's functions themselves from a paradigmatic perspective, analysing the opposition between narrative functions to propose a more systematic classification. One of his findings is the "crescendo" of functional oppositions throughout the story progression [10, p. 200]. This, however, falls short of providing a self-contained formalism for analysing story progression in general, and only constitutes an analysis of story progression within the fixed framework of the Proppian description of fairytales.

Again, despite being often cited in IS work, few implementations have really sought their inspiration in his work, to the exception of [23].

5 Barthes and the Interpretative Codes

Roland Barthes was a celebrated semiotician and one of the most prolific authors in the field of narratology during the seventies. Most remarkable is the fact that he has produced comprehensive narrative analyses of classical novels, such as Balzac's *Sarrasine* [3] as well as of popular literature, such as Ian Fleming's *Goldfinger* [2]. His paper on structural analysis of narratives [2] remains still today one of the best and most accessible introductions to narratology for the IS researcher. In the structuralist tradition, Barthes studied both syntagmatic and paradigmatic aspects of narratives. His syntagmatic approach extends the linear sequencing of Propp to give the story an actual structure, possibly opening space for choice points. His first attempt consists of the stemmatic[4] description of a scene of *Goldfinger*, which identifies the structure of

---

[2] Greimas explicitly states that his model is "an extrapolation of syntactic structures" [10, p. 185].

[3] Greimas has generalised the Proppian opposition between Hero and Sought-for Person into sender and recipient.

[4] In Tesniere's grammar [21] the *stemma* is a graph-like dependency structure formalising the syntax of a sentence or an utterance. This use of stemma by Barthes probably emphasises structure, although from the example itself, the relations appear rather trivial.

the scene in terms of action ramifications. This kind of analysis has been further refined in *S/Z* to produce a tree-like structure organising narrative actions from the explicit perspective of *proairesis* [3, p.135], which corresponds to the choice of actions and their possible consequences (Fig. 3).

Barthes has introduced a paradigmatic organisation of narrative functions which Propp's approach was certainly lacking (despite paving the way for such a description when he associated narrative functions to character categories). Barthes' notion of action goes significantly beyond the elementary narrative function that describes a specific action taking place at a given stage of the story. Barthes' actions have the dimension of semantic field, and as such are not constrained to a specific occurrence.

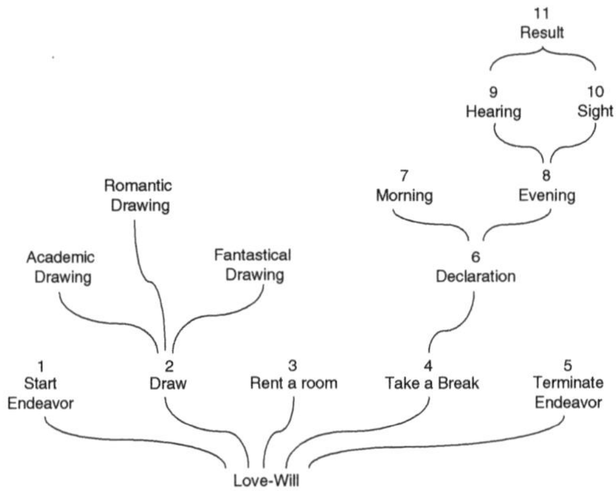

Fig. 3. A Tree-like structure for actions in Sarrasine, according to Barthes. The emphasis is on the proairetic aspects related to a choice of actions, e.g. the type of drawing in (2) or the time for the declaration in (6).

For instance his MURDER action [3, p. 261] subsumes different narrative events such as the warning, the act of murder itself (Sarrasine killed by the Cardinal's men) and even the explanation of the murder's reasons. These events are semantically related but most importantly do not constitute a continuous sequence (a significant departure from Propp's syntagmatic approach). One such illustration lies in the 48 action categories described in *S/Z*. Barthes posits in particular that actions constitute the real basis for *proairesis* [3, p. 259] and that applies to the whole set of 48 actions identified. On closer examination, these actions play the same role that narrative functions did in Propp's theory, but without the limitations imposed by a strict temporal sequence and with a broader semantic coverage (as illustrated by the above MURDER example).

Barthes' narrative theory is based on five "codes", each of which indicating how to interpret the current text segment (*Sarrasine* being broken down into text segments each corresponding to a basic narrative unit). The ACT (for ACTion) code corresponds to the actions discussed above and can be considered a generalisation of narrative functions [3, p. 267]: it also addresses the issue of action sequences, whose canonical form is the tree rather than the list [3, p. 67] (Fig. 3). The REF (for REFerence) code indexes a narrative event into background knowledge required for its interpretation; most often this knowledge is prototypical (with prototypes describing feelings, women or social situations). These provide contextual knowledge for the narrative, improving the understandability of actions in context. The SYM (for SYMbolic) code, on the other hand, captures major cultural objects that are heavily symbolic (e.g. money and fortune, the human body, etc)[5]. The SEM (for SEMantic) code appears specific to the textual aspect of the written narrative: it relates the choice of words to the narrative events (hence is of moderate relevance to IS as it does not extend to dialogue). Finally, the HER (for HERmeneutic) code signals those items that should trigger interpretation (from the reader); in other words, important narrative events which contain cues for future events, or elements of mystery whose solution is an important part of the narrative. In Barthes' words, "to defer truth helps reassembling it at a later stage", which would be the motto for a progressive resolution of the narrative. The HER code is invoked by Barthes to explain how narrative cues can be interpreted by the reader (and need to be interpreted for the story to produce proper effects). In *Sarrasine*, these cues will refer to the femininity of the Zambinella[6], a central topic of the novel.

Of particular relevance to IS is the fact that two of these codes, HER and ACT, are described as determinants of suspense in storytelling: the former because it forces interpretation to "fill the gaps", the latter because the perplexity associated with an action possible outcomes[7] (*proairesis*) will generate expectations, tension and surprise. A related notion is Barthes' description of *dispatchers*[8], as being narrative objects which constitute affordances for key narrative actions. These implicitly introduce branching points corresponding to the potential use of the object and the subsequent outcomes of that use. This offers interesting perspectives in IS for the role of virtual objects, which has been used, to some extent, in [5]. Zagalo et al. [26] have based their approach in part on Barthes' early work [2] using nuclei and catalyses to distinguish between *proairetic* actions which can alter the course of the story (nuclei or cardinal functions) and those whose main role is to support story presentation/staging (catalyses).

6 Bremond and the Reintroduction of Characters

Bremond developed a narrative theory centred on the description of character's roles. Not unlike Greimas, his theory starts with an opposition between *Agent* and *Patient*.

[5] This code also includes famous metaphors, and is not exempt from psychoanalytic influences as it sometimes happens with Barthes' writings.

[6] The plot of Sarrasine is that of a French sculptor falling in love with an Italian singer, the Zambinella, unaware that he is actually a *castrato*, according to the codes of theatrical interpretation in Italy at that time. Sarrasine will end up murdered by the henchmen of Cardinal Cicognara, his protector.

[7] It is also important to realise that the example so often associated with the proairetic code, which describes a character drawing a gun, is most likely to be taken from Tomachevski's analysis of the Russian novel "The girl without dowry" by Ostrovsky. The object (handgun) associated with the proairetic action is termed a *dispatcher*.

[8] Once again this should not be confused with the term "dispatcher" as used by Greimas, following Propp, which represents the character who sends off the hero to accomplish his quest. This potential confusion is a consequence of translation (Barthes uses the English word in the original French text).

A Patient is any character that will be influenced by the narrative actions to occur, while an Agent is responsible for changes in the narrative universe (which can also affect other characters as Patients, in which case there are "psychological" changes rather than "physical" changes to the world).

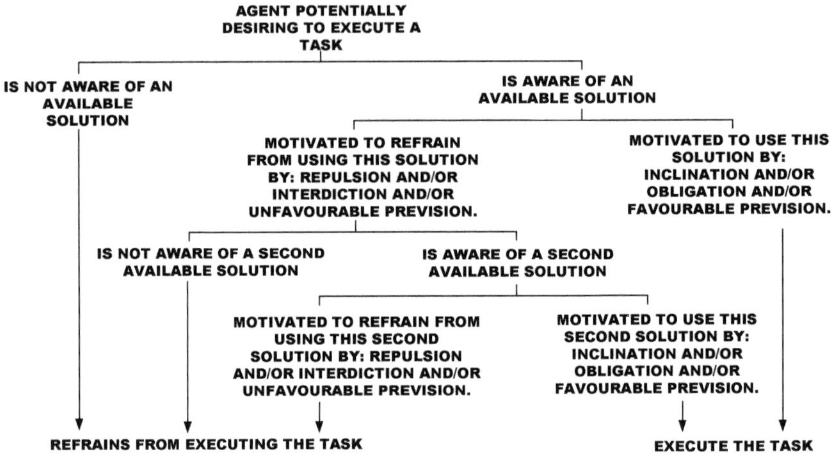

Fig. 4. Action deliberation in Bremond's model addresses the Agent's beliefs, motivations as well as the anticipation of possible consequences / appraisal of his own situation. Importantly, it also includes potential contradictory influences.

Yet, the important difference is that the status of Agent or Patient is a transient one, and that most characters can alternate between the two roles, i.e. the Patient being prompted into taking action subsequently assumes an Agent's position. A comprehensive, sophisticated framework unfolds from that dichotomy through the progressive description of sub-types of agents and patients, how they are affected by narrative processes, and how they perceive and experience their situation. Patients can be the object of two different kinds of narrative processes: i) those influencing their awareness of their situation, which are information-transmitting processes, generating, as a consequence of increased knowledge in the Patient, satisfaction or frustration, hope or fear, and ii) those objectively altering the patient situation, improving it, worsening it, or preserving it (although preservation can mean both absence of deterioration and absence of improvement). Each of these processes is mediated by a corresponding agent type, such as (in Bremond's original terminology) the *influencer*, the *improver*, the *protector* (Fig. 5), the *frustrator* ...

As far as Agents are concerned, Bremond distinguishes the *voluntary* Agent, who purposefully initiates a goal-oriented process (Fig. 4), from the *involuntary* Agent, whose narrative impact derives from some unintended side-effects of his intentional actions. Voluntary agents are defined by a set of motivations (which can themselves result from influences by other Agents or actions affecting them as Patients), and by their actions' goals (e.g. overcome an obstacle, obtain favours, etc.). Involuntary Agents, on the other hand, are better defined par those circumstances that impair their understanding of the actual consequences of his actions, and by the logical relations between intended and actual consequences of the actions they undertake. One example of the latter is Kriemhild revealing Hagen which part of Siegfried's body is vulnerable: while trying to protect Siegfried, she is actually causing his demise (she becomes the involuntary Agent of his death).

A central aspect of Bremond's model is that it re-introduces character's psychology in a quite sophisticated manner, with characters having beliefs (which may turn out to be accurate or inaccurate), motivations (see below) and goals. Of particular importance is the fact that some of these beliefs relate to an appraisal of their own situation, leading to a narrative recognition of the character's psychology. As an example of this, let us consider the possibilities for a Patient who is affected by property X (where X could be as diverse as: *bankruptcy*, *progressive illness*, *being of noble descent*):

A. The Patient has no information about X
B. The Patient has information about X and:
- believes s/he actually has property X
- believes s/he has property not X
- is unsure about whether s/he is X or not X

These correspond to various states of mind such as: lack of awareness, (right or wrong) belief, open doubt, etc. This can be further complexified by introducing a truth value for the information given to the Patient by another character, who may deceive him etc. One instantiation of this situation would be in *The Matrix* film, the successive beliefs that Neo is "The One", going from lack of information (early stages), to information he doubts (Morpheus), to false information he believes (the oracle), etc.

Another important aspect corresponds to the appraisal that a Patient makes of her situation, meaning that she can be satisfied (that the situation changes or on the contrary is stable), dissatisfied or neutral. These states of minds are explicitly termed affects by Bremond and, like other psychological properties, they are subject to various influences that the Patient can be exposed to. And these can be further extended to the anticipation of future satisfaction or disappointment, serving as a basis for generating hope or, conversely, fear.

Now is the time to illustrate (for Patients) the influencing processes through which the Patient's state of mind is altered. Bremond exemplifies this using the Odyssey [4, p. 159]: Ulysses and his crew are potentially Patients of an influence process (seduction) by the Sirens: his crew evade that influence altogether (by plugging their ears with beeswax), while Ulysses who has instructed his crew to tie him to the mast, is actually under that influence, which alters his state of mind but is prevented from any hazardous action by his being tied.

A refined description of influences relies on a categorisation of a character's motives. These are defined by considering the temporal relations between an action and its reward. Pragmatic motivations correspond to actions that will result in a subsequent reward (Socrates drinking a remedy to be cured of an illness). Hedonistic motivations refer to actions whose reward is concomitant to their execution (Socrates drinking wine at a banquet). Finally, Ethical motivations are those for which the reward actually precedes the undertaking of the action (Socrates drinking hemlock rather than going into exile).

It is possible to define an influence matrix considering that for each motivation, influences can be positive (incentives) or negatives (inhibition). The table below illustrate this:

Table 1. Influence matrix

Motivation	Incentives	Inhibition
Hedonistic	Seduction	Intimidation
Ethical	Obligation	Interdiction
Pragmatic	Advice	Negative Advice

The above model has been used, for its communicative aspects, by Cavazza and Charles [6] to generate dialogue acts in IS, representing influences from one character to another. In recent years there has been a growing interest in Bremond's theory for IS: Szilas et al. [20] have proposed to use it to support their narrative logic, and Schaefer et al. [18] have adopted Bremond's model, although mostly as a direct translation of some of Bremond's patterns (see Fig. 5 for an illustration) into decision trees, somehow losing the expressive power of the formalism. Finally, Donikian and Portugal [7] have shown how extensive drama maps could be constructed from logical formulas derived from Bremond's action description.

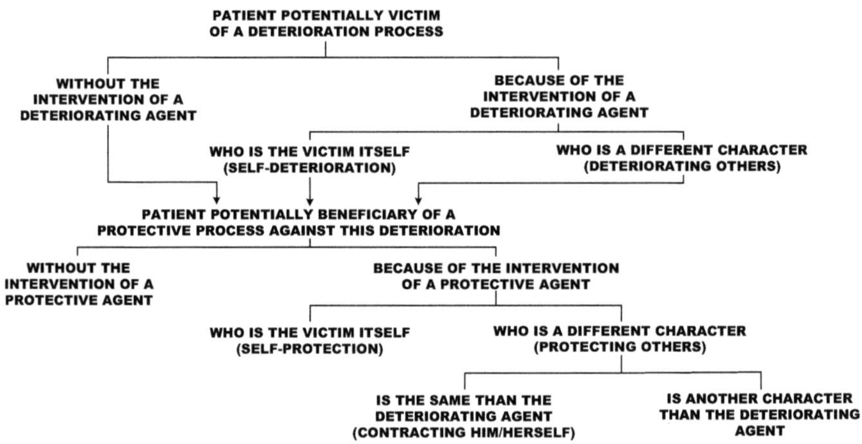

Fig. 5. The role of "Protector" according to Bremond illustrates the complexity of the formalism. On one hand, the intervention of a Protector assumes that the Patient is first the object of a deterioration process, which is a necessary context for this role to occur. On the other hand, there are multiple possible instantiations of the "Protector" role, summarised on the above figure. The original formalisation is probably excessively procedural and lacks compositionality to serve as a direct inspiration for computer formalisations.

Table 2. Use of Selected Narrative Theories by Previous Work in Interactive Storytelling

Narrative Theory	IS Approach
Aristotle	[22]
Propp	[8] [11] [13] [14] [16]
Greimas	[23]
Barthes	[5] [27]
Bremond	[6] [7] [18] [20]

7 Conclusions

Throughout IS research, there are constant references to narratology. These references range from illustrations of fundamental problems to the theoretical underpinning of narrative formalisms used in the research described.

In the field of Computational Linguistics, Wilks [24] cautioned long ago that "systems do not always work by means of the formalisms that decorate them". This makes it even more important to assess the actual rationale for the proper use of narratological theories. Further, the problem of narrative formalisms cannot be dissociated from the narrative genres considered.

This point has not often been discussed, to the exception of Anstey [1] who has identified genres (implicitly) through representative authors, namely Aristotle, Brecht, etc. This is worth emphasising, as there has been no extensive discussion of the genres actually targeted by various works in IS. Even leaving aside the too obvious criticism that Propp's narrative functions constitute an attempt to generalise across genres a description developed for folktales, the narrative's genre constrains the type of narrative formalism that can be used to represent it.

Acknowledgments. David Pizzi is funded through the DTI Technology Programme "BARDS" Project, in collaboration with Eidos Interactive Ltd.

References

1. Anstey, J.: Agency and the Emotion Machine In: Gérard Subsol (ed.): Virtual Storytelling, Using Virtual Reality Technologies for Storytelling, Third International Conference, ICVS 2005, Lecture Notes in Computer Science 3805 Springer (2005) 125-128
2. Barthes R.: Introduction à l'analyse structurale des récits, In: L'analyse structurale du récit, Communications, n° 8, Paris, Seuil, (1966) 7-33 (in French)
3. Barthes, R., In: S/Z, Paris: Editions du Seuil, (1970) (in French)
4. Bremond, C., In: Logique du Recit, Paris: Editions du Seuil,(1973) (in French)
5. Cavazza, M., Charles, F. and Mead, S.J.: Characters in Search of an Author: AI-Based Virtual Storytelling. In: Olivier Balet, Gérard Subsol, Patrice Torguet (Eds.): Virtual Storytelling: Using Virtual Reality Technologies for Storytelling, Lecture Notes in Computer Science 2197, Springer, (2001) 145-154
6. Cavazza, M. and Charles, F.: Dialogue Generation in Character-based Interactive Storytelling. AAAI First Annual Artificial Intelligence and Interactive Digital Entertainment Conference, Marina del Rey, California, USA, (2005)
7. Donikian, S. and Portugal, J.-N.: Writing Interactive Fiction Scenarii with DraMachina. In: Stefan Göbel, Ulrike Spierling, Anja Hoffmann, Ido Iurgel, Oliver Schneider, J. Dechau, Axel Feix (Eds.): Technologies for Interactive Digital Storytelling and Entertainment, Second International Conference, TIDSE 2004, Lecture Notes in Computer Science 3105 Springer, (2004) 101-112
8. Grasbon, D. and Braun, N.: A Morphological Approach to Interactive Storytelling, In Proceedings of on Artificial Intelligence and Interactive Entertainment, Cast'01, Living in Mixed Realities, Sankt Augustin, Germany, (2001)
9. Greimas, A.J., In: Sémantique structurale, Larousse, (1966) (in French)
10. Greimas, A.J., In: Du Sens, In: Essais sémiotiques. Le Seuil, (1970) (in French)

11. Hartmann, K., Hartmann, S. and Feustel, M.: Motif Definition and Classification to Structure Non-linear Plots and to Control the Narrative Flow in Interactive Dramas. In: Gérard Subsol (Ed.): Virtual Storytelling, Using Virtual Reality Technologies for Storytelling, Third International Conference, ICVS 2005, Lecture Notes in Computer Science 3805 Springer, (2005) 158-167
12. Laurel, B.: Computers as Theatre, Reading, MA, Addison-Wesley, (1991)
13. Machado, I., Paiva, A. and Prada, R.: Is the Wolf Angry or ... Just Hungry? In: Proceedings. of the Fifth Conference on Autonomous Agents,. New York: ACM Press, (2001) 370–376
14. Machado, I, Brna, P. and Paiva, A.: 1, 2, 3 .... Action! Directing Real Actors and Virtual Characters. In: Stefan Göbel, Ulrike Spierling, Anja Hoffmann, Ido Iurgel, Oliver Schneider, J. Dechau, Axel Feix (Eds.): Technologies for Interactive Digital Storytelling and Entertainment, Second International Conference, TIDSE 2004, Lecture Notes in Computer Science 3105 Springer, (2004) 36-41
15. Mateas, M.: A Neo-Aristotelian Theory of Interactive Drama", Working Notes of the AAAI Spring Symposium on Artificial Intelligence and Interactive Entertainment, AAAI Press (2000)
16. Peinado, F. and Gervás, P.: Transferring Game Mastering Laws to Interactive Digital Storytelling. In: Stefan Göbel, Ulrike Spierling, Anja Hoffmann, Ido Iurgel, Oliver Schneider, J. Dechau, Axel Feix (Eds.): Technologies for Interactive Digital Storytelling and Entertainment, Second International Conference, TIDSE 2004, Lecture Notes in Computer Science 3105 Springer, (2004) 48-54
17. Propp, Vladimir., In: Morphology of the Folktale. 1928. 2nd ed. Trans. Lawrence Scott. Austin: U of Texas P, (1968)
18. Schäfer, L., Stauber, A. and Bokan, B.: StoryNet: An Educational Game for Social Skills. In: Stefan Göbel, Ulrike Spierling, Anja Hoffmann, Ido Iurgel, Oliver Schneider, J. Dechau, Axel Feix (Eds.): Technologies for Interactive Digital Storytelling and Entertainment, Second International Conference, TIDSE 2004, Lecture Notes in Computer Science 3105 Springer, (2004) 148-157
19. W. Swartout, R. Hill, J. Gratch, W.L. Johnson, C. Kyriakakis, C. LaBore, R., Lindheim, S. Marsella, D. Miraglia, B. Moore, J. Morie, J. Rickel, M. Thiebaux, L., Tuch, R. Whitney, and J. Douglas: "Toward the Holodeck: Integrating Graphics, Sound, Character and Story", in Proceedings of the Autonomous Agents Conference, (2001)
20. Szilas, N., Rety, J.-H., and Marty, O.: Authoring highly generative Interactive Drama, In: Olivier Balet, Gérard Subsol, Patrice Torguet (Eds.): Virtual Storytelling; Using Virtual Reality Technologies for Storytelling, Second International Conference, ICVS 2003, Lecture Notes in Computer Science n. 2897,(2003) 37-46
21. Tesnière, L.: Eléments de syntaxe structurale, C. Klinksieck, Paris, (1959) (in French)
22. Tomaszewski, Z., and Binsted, K.: A Reconstructed Neo-Aristotelian Theory of Interactive Drama. Workshop on Computational Aesthetics: Artificial Intelligence Approaches to Beauty and Happiness, National Conference on Artificial Intelligence (AAAI), Boston, Massachusetts, (2006)
23. Theune, M., Rensen, S., op den Akker, R., Heylen, D., and Nijholt, A.: Emotional Characters for Automatic Plot Creation. In: Stefan Göbel, Ulrike Spierling, Anja Hoffmann, Ido Iurgel, Oliver Schneider, J. Dechau, Axel Feix (ed.): Technologies for Interactive Digital Storytelling and Entertainment, Second International Conference, TIDSE 2004, Lecture Notes in Computer Science 3105, Springer, (2004) 95-100

24. Wilks, Y.: Form and Content in Semantics, in: R. Johnson and M. Rosner, (eds.), Computational Linguistics and Formal Semantics. Cambridge: Cambridge University Press, (1992)
25. Young, R.M.: Cognitive and Computational Models in Interactive Narratives In: Chris Forsythe, Michael L. Bernard & Timothy E. Goldsmith (Eds.), Cognitive Systems: Human Cognitive Models in Systems Design, Lawrence Erlbaum, (2005)
26. Young R.M.: Creating Interactive Narrative Structures: The Potential for AI Approaches. AAAI Spring Symposium in Artificial Intelligence and Interactive Entertainment, AAAI Press, (2000)
27. Zagalo, N., Barker, A., Branco, V.: Story Reaction Structures to Emotion Detection, in Proceedings of the SRMC'04, ACM Multimedia 2004 Workshop on Story Representation, Mechanism and Context - New York, (2004) 33-38

Insights into the Design of Computer Entertainment from Schemas in Film

Gregory Hale

Centre for Usable Home Technologies (CUHTec), Department of Psychology,
University of York, York YO10 5DD, United Kingdom
g.hale@psychology.york.ac.uk

Abstract. After offering reasons why film can offer insights into computer entertainment and reviewing the concept of 'schemas', the results of a qualitative investigation of viewer's talk about a short film, Ice Cream Dream, are reported, related to genre, character relationships, use of props, schematic sequences, locations and sound. This material is extended and deepened by drawing on an ongoing cognitive analysis of another short film, The Wrong Trousers.

Keywords: Schemas, entertainment psychology, user reactions.

1 Introduction

This section firstly reviews changes in the context of entertainment. Then it examines film as a paradigm case of entertainment, before concluding by arguing that the study of film can provide many insights into computer entertainment. The paper then gives a final report on a study of viewer's talk on a British short film, *Ice Cream Dream* [17] (investigation one of an ongoing programme of research). This material is supplemented by material from investigation two, a cognitive analysis of the Oscar ™ winning *The Wrong Trousers* [13], which is moving into its closing stages. The extension of the results from investigation one with a comparison of some preliminary results from investigation two deepens the insights about effective and less effective use of schemas in entertainment.

Entertainment content and delivery are profoundly changing. People are making increased use of interactive entertainment, mobile delivery is becoming a key delivery mechanism, movies (both the making and the delivery) are going digital and advances in software together with lower costs have meant that consumers are increasingly empowered to become creators and changers of content [10].

Film is a paradigmatic case of entertainment, in which carefully designed sonic and visual events take place in a story context, to prompt strong cognitive and emotional reactions in viewers. Film also comes with a ready-made grammar that is readily transposable to other entertainment experiences where narrative is important [9]. Methods and materials in film often have explicit overlap with computer games [12,14].

Despite the similarities between film and games, there are also obvious differences such as overt interactivity (user input affects system state) and the element of

S. Göbel, R. Malkewitz, and I. Iurgel (Eds.): TIDSE 2006, LNCS 4326, pp. 84–92, 2006.

'addiction' that game designers seek to build into their games [12,14], as compared to filmmakers who generally seek to create a holistic self-contained and satisfying viewer experience (e.g.[3]). The issue of interactivity is represented as one key difference between film and computer games, yet the similarities between film and computer games are profound (overt interactivity notwithstanding) and studying film with reference to cognitive structures such as schemas has great benefit to designers of computer games content. Indeed, an approach based on schemas would seem to be a very useful addition to the range of games research and design methodologies currently on offer (see for example, [1,6,7]).

1.1 Schemas and Entertainment

As a basic mechanism of human cognition, schemas cover all things recognizable and nameable to human beings. Schemas were originally propounded by Bartlett [2] as a structuring mechanism in his studies of perception and memory. In Bartlett's account, schemas refer to active organization of past reactions and experiences, facilitated by the "effort after meaning" and are built up by repetition. Schemas serve to adaptively facilitate and organize perception and memory by minimizing cognitive load and facilitating speed and accuracy of response. Central to the notion of schemas (and related terms such as 'scripts' and 'mental models') is the attempt to gain purchase on the patterning of mental representations and how these patterned mental representations facilitate cognition in different contexts.

Structurally, schemas are conceived of as consisting of a fixed part and a variable part. The fixed part of the schema maps the unvarying elements. The variable parts consist of those elements where the specific problem is different from the initial schema, requiring changes to that schema.

There are many types of schema. For instance, the universal story is prototypical and generic (e.g. [4,8,11]). The universal story is a high-level prototype schema, which facilitates the generation of powerful stories because it references culturally widespread schemas built up in individuals through long exposure. There are also prototypical schemas linked to genre, specifying elements that should be in a film or computer game, though genre can be a slippery concept. Genre refers to the category of text under consideration [8] and its identifying characteristics, though there are also social aspects to the construction of genre ([16] review different ways in which the term is used). Genre schemas convey meaning and shape viewer's and listener's responses to artifacts and texts [16] and also provide a set of expectations (slots) against which one film may be assessed against others of the same genre that the viewer has seen. Finally, as a film is watched, viewers develop a situation model (a progressively constructed schema) of the film [8], a run-time schema of the film in the viewer's mind which functions as a 'mental microworld' containing characters, actions goals, obstacles, conflict, resolutions and consequences [8].

2 Method

The material from this section was presented in a similar form, in an interim paper [9].

2.1 Design and Participants

The design was a qualitative grounded theory investigation using post-film semi-structured interviewing, which facilitates theory building. The interviews focused on participants' reactions to a short film (*Ice Cream Dream* [17]), exploring these experiences methodically by working through the film in its scenes. Three male and seven female students were interviewed (all students were either undergraduate, Master's, PhD students or graduates of the University of York). The age range of 22 to 26 fits the prime demographic for frequent cinemagoers.

2.2 Materials and Procedure

The short film is of ten minutes duration. The investigator prepared a factual summary of the content of the film, a segmentation [5], an authoritative template of the film (see [9] for details). The film is about a little girl who overcomes her fear of making friends.

The film was shown using a DVD player on a 23-inch flat plasma screen television, in a residentially styled living room in the CUHTec Responsive Home at the University of York, United Kingdom. A copy of the *Independent Television Commission - Sense of Presence Inventory*, a cross media questionnaire developed to measure immersion and general media habits was filled out for each session (Part A and the Background Information section only) and additional questions drawing on commercial surveys and other sources was used to investigate media use and related issues.

Participants took part singly. Participants watched the ten-minute short film in the living room of the responsive home, seated on a two-person sofa, which was about three meters from the screen. After the film had finished the investigator interviewed the participants. First, the participants were asked to summarize the film. Then the investigator used the remote control to 'step-through' the film, using the scene-by-scene segmentation (analysis) of the film, which was prepared by the researcher beforehand. Participants were asked to reflect on their reactions to each scene of the film from the first viewing. Checks were made throughout the interview by the interviewer to ensure that these reactions were from the first viewing, not the viewing of the film in its scenes i.e. the second viewing. It was recognized early on that in fact reactions to the second viewing would also constitute information of interest (not analyzed here) since people often watch films more than once. Particular attention was paid to exploring the qualitative aspects of the experience as they related to specific scenes or elements of the film. Participants were then questioned using Part A (six questions) from the ITC-SOPI, which was filled in by the investigator to preserve the informal conversational tone of the session. After this the ITC-SOPI section *Background Information* was filled in, with the investigator asking the questions and recording the responses on the pre-prepared field notes proforma. There was a post-session de-brief, which also investigated the participants views of the session and provided the opportunity for feedback. For data analysis, the interviews were recorded on audiocassette.

3 Results and Discussion

3.1 Entertainment Scores

Enjoyment scores are scored on a 1-5 Likert scale (to match ITC-SOPI items), with 3 representing a neutral point. Five participants were neutral to the film (score of 3), with three liking it (two scores of 4, one of 5). Two participants mildly disliked the film (score of 2).

3.2 Nomenclature

In reporting the Results for viewer's talk, a specific nomenclature was developed. The term 'segment' is used to refer to a coded section of participant's speech. The term 'category' is used to refer to the code level, which is at the start of each section detailing the results. The term 'cluster' or, less usually, 'grouping' refers to thematically similar segments which are collected together into a named group within a code category, with a requirement that there be a minimum of three segments and two participants to be so classified. The term 'viewer' is used to denote someone who is watching a film in a future and non-experimental setting i.e. generic viewers.

Segments are coded for positive, neutral and negative response pattern. A segment coded as neutral will usually consist of an observational piece of talk by a participant, with no indication of their emotional or cognitive reaction. An example of a neutral coded segment is

> *...the music just represented that sort of mood like quiet* PC 8.8

In the above segment the participant is merely observing or commenting on the film content, without indicating a personal emotional reaction.

Positively coded segments are coded on explicit positive comment by the participant and are so coded either because a participant likes a particular sequence in a film or because they are reacting in a way intended by the filmmaker. The emotion may normally be considered negative but in the context of the film it is positive. The case of the negative emotion of fear in horror films is the clearest example of this. Where a participant's comments contain a suggestive inference of a positive emotion but no explicit statement of this, the segment is coded as neutral. An illustration of a positively coded segment where a participant expressed a liking of an element of the film is,

> *Nice music...* PI 17.2

An example of where a segment is coded positively because the emotion (in this case a negative emotion) corresponds to what is intended by the film-maker is,

> *I remembered the first time round being annoyed, that's right, that um she hadn't reprimanded him immediately for being rude...* PE 12.2

Segments coded as negative in response consist of segments where participants are puzzled by content (content is unclear to them), to content which they regard as unreal and content where they explicitly say they do not like a particular film sequence or element.

An example of a negatively coded segment where a participant is puzzled by content that is unclear to them is as follows,

> *You know, when he looked over at the red [money] box, that sort of puzzled me a bit, why was he looking at that, why had they shown that for so long, why was that significant.* PH 16.2

An example of a negatively coded segment where a participant regards the content as unreal is as follows,

> *The kids being unrealistically crowd, an unrealistic crowd again.* PL 11.3

An example of a negatively coded segment where a participant expresses a dislike to an element or sequence in the film is as follows,

> *Um, and I didn't like the way the bank manager picked the ice cream up with his hands, I thought that was gross [laughs].* PJ 6.7

Only overtly stated personal response comments by participants are response coded. Inferences that could be made in the analysis are left coded as 'neutral', because of the difficulties of attempting to code them as positive or negative. Cases where participants were laughing at the film rather than its content would be coded negatively (i.e. this would be the case where someone had a positive reaction such as laughter when the film would seem to be seeking to promote fear).

Sample extracts, grouped under headings, which are coding categories, are now discussed. These selected codings from *Ice Cream Dream* have been supplemented by commentary from an ongoing analysis of *The Wrong Trousers* [13], which is an internationally popular short film, which won an Oscar ™.

3.3 General Film Experience Category

This schematic category refers to film genre. The schema is prompted in viewers by elements such as specific music and visual effects. When genre expectations are not met, this can have an adverse effect on the experience of viewers.

This category is defined by participants speaking of the film in relation to other types (genres) of film they are familiar with. In *Ice Cream Dream* (sixteen segments, six participants) the two main clusters referred to films and television programmes for children (twelve segments) and horror films (four segments), with both clusters referencing typical elements in films for children and horror films. So in the horror cluster, sinister music and slow motion blinking in a hostile gaze were mentioned (see *ICD 7:50*), contrasting with the opening cheerful song of this film. Here, horror and children's elements were presented at different times, with viewers unable to resolve the serious horror cues (slow motion, very sinister music that reminded participants of death) with cues relating to children's programmes (bright cheerful graphics and happy music).

The analysis of *The Wrong Trousers* also revealed that a mix of horror and children's programme is present, but here the horror elements are done in spoof 'B' movies horror style (the opening sequence has a canted camera angle, jagged 'B' movie text for the film's title and stereotypical horror 'shriek' music, *TWT 0.00-00.26*), with the presentation of horror and comedy cues together, giving a clear set of pre-blended expectations to the viewer. Additionally, viewers have expectations from the first Wallace and Gromit film which would preclude any later films being considered as genuine horror movies. By contrast, viewers of *Ice Cream Dream* have only the cues provided in the film to help them interpret it, since the film has no preceding films and lacks well known characters.

Design implications are that schemas are important: it is good to have novelty but players need to be cued if mixed schemas are used. It is noteworthy that *The Wrong Trousers* has a major tone of comedy and only a minor thrill/horror tone. This balance between different schematic tones needs to be managed particularly carefully in developing mixed genre computer entertainment.

3.4 Character Relationships

Relationship schemas are prompted by seeing characters interacting closely with each other, in contexts such as the home environment. This category is defined by participants speculating about the biological and marriage/co-habitation relationships of characters (the father wears a wedding ring but this is only seen clearly towards the end of the film). The largest cluster of responses in this category for *Ice Cream Dream* focused on uncertainly about the relationship of the girl (the main character) to the woman at home (eight segments, seven participants), based primarily on the fact that the girl didn't look like the daughter of the woman. This prompted speculation amongst participants as to the relationships of the woman, the girl and her father (*ICD 2:03-2:18*). In *The Wrong Trousers*, in contrast, Wallace and Gromit are in the schematic and therefore immediately understandable relationship of owner and pet dog. This schema is prompted as soon as the viewer sees Gromit the dog inside the house (see also the prototypical pet dog actions, such as Gromit waiting for the newspaper to take it to Wallace in his mouth *TWT 9:36-9:42*). The owner-pet schema is readily extensible to 'the friendship between a human being and their pet dog' and this extension is a key part of *The Wrong Trousers*, with Wallace explicitly reaffirming his friendship with Gromit at the end of the film, calling him, "friend", "old friend" (*TWT 26:48*). This friendship dimension mimics the experiential feeling of a pet owner for his or her pet, as one child commented, "Gromit is loyal. I'd like a dog like that. He'd be the best friend you'd ever have" [15]. The film consciously plays with the owner-pet-friends schema at one point by having Wallace say to Gromit after having given him a dog collar, whilst putting it on too tight, "You look like someone owns you, now!".

Design implications are that relationships need to be cued for players, if not understanding them is going to take viewers away from the story world of the entertainment experience.

3.5 Specific Film Aspects - Properties

This category is defined by participants commenting on physical items within the film world. The technical term from theatre and film, 'properties' ('props') is used for this cluster of responses (forty-six responses, thirty of these from the first viewing coded as negative). In *Ice Cream Dream* many props either in use by characters or in the visual field (such as the mobile hanging in the bedroom, *ICD 2:59*) generated negative responses, being perceived as unreal, bizarre or puzzling: all negative experiences which disrupt the story world experience. In contrast, in *The Wrong Trousers,* all props are clear in the visual field when they need to be and the use of props is always in the context of 'normal' use or abnormal use that is nevertheless visually clear (such as firing jam onto toast with a spring loaded spoon, *TWT 1:52-1:57*). The film also makes referential use of props, so in the opening credits sequence there is a visual joke where, instead of three porcelain flying geese on the wall there are three porcelain flying rockets in the style of the rocket used in the first film (*TWT 0:00-0:26*).

Design implications are that use of props needs to be visually clear at the point where the viewer needs to understand them (props may be obscured till then, as is often the case in The Wrong Trousers, which is a technique that adds interest to the content). Symbolism in films and games is very difficult to implement successfully, unless the player is cued from the outset to look for it.

3.6 Specific Film Aspects – Dreams Category

In *Ice Cream Dream* there is a schematic dream sequence. Elements within this cluster relate to altered reality, visual effects such as blurred colours and dream like music (*ICD 4:29-6:37*). Many films have sequences that are schematic in nature i.e. similar elements would be found in a schematic sequence, across a range of films. In *The Wrong Trousers*, there is no dream sequence, though there are schematic sequences such as the chase sequence at the end of the film (*TWT 24:09-26:18*). The generic features of a chase sequence are by definition: speed (often in machines such as cars, planes and trains), a pursuer and a pursued. Additionally, chase sequences often have little victories and reversal events within the chase sequence, ever increasing danger to the hero or heroine and a culmination (if the chase is the final action sequence in the film) involving a successful and extreme effort to snatch victory from the adversary at the last moment. The dream sequence in *Ice Cream Dream* evoked mixed reactions as some viewers felt it was too obviously schematic i.e. not novel.

Design implications are to follow the schemas for sequences but to consider carefully how to preserve the physical dynamics of the sequence whilst changing the elements (such as the machinery involved) to add novelty and therefore interest and viewer/user engagement.

3.7 Specific Film Aspects- Location

This category is defined by participants commenting on the locations in the film, within the story world of the film. In *Ice Cream Dream* (a low budget movie, which may have limited the choice and use of locations), there were eight codes in the first viewing, with four neutral and four negatively coded responses, with no clear patterning to the responses. Because the film is live action, the locations are real and seem to be presented as they are in real life, without changes and with no special characteristics. In *The Wrong Trousers* (a film with a much higher budget), the realization of locations is very detailed and specific to the characters and the needs of the dramatic moment, with some of the locations forming the known environment of two beloved characters, whereas in *Ice Cream Dream* the location are places which have little in the way of personal character and are visually bland. In addition, particular locations, such as the dining room in Wallace and Gromit's house, are made interesting because various machines invented by Wallace operate to supply and mis-supply food, providing an ongoing stream of visually interesting information (compare *ICD 2:43-2:59* with *TWT 1:50-2:17*).

Design implications are that locations should be schematic in the sense of matching the characters and the needs of the moment. The texture of these locations in terms of detail and personalization should be higher than real locations, since the objective is to keep the viewer or player involved.

3.8 Sound Category

This category consists of utterances where participants specifically mentioned the use of sound effects, where these sounds are non-storyworld sounds used by the filmmaker to cue viewer response to a particular scene. In *Ice Cream Dream*, the filmmakers used what participants described as a 'ching' effect to introduce a sequence where the main character imagines a literal fulfillment of a comment made in fun to her by her mother (three responses from participants, one each of positive, neutral and negative, *ICD* 2:18). This represents a symbolic use of sound, which the viewers are consciously aware of. By contrast, sound in *The Wrong Trousers* is not symbolic in this way but rather is often intensified sound i.e. the sound is perceived by viewers as coming from real objects and characters in the film, but is created by the film makers in such a way that it is more intense than it would be in real life, such as the qualitatively exaggerated (and humorous) sound of the stopper in the bottom of the piggy bank being pulled out (*TWT 2:58*). Investigation three, viewer's talk on *The Wrong Trousers* may offer the opportunity to examine this issue more closely.

Design implications are unclear since no trend exists in the three responses. It may be that sound should follow an intensified schema trajectory, not a symbolic usage, an issue that requires further investigation.

4 Conclusion

Designers and researchers of computer games and other entertainment experiences need to understand the power of schemas and how to adequately deploy this power. The second and following investigations in this research project will involve a complete analysis of *The Wrong Trousers*, as well as viewer's talk on this film. In addition, a handheld game will be investigated in two further investigations.

Acknowledgments

PhD supervisor Andrew Monk, funded by Microsoft Research Cambridge (U.K.).

References

1. Aarseth, E. Playing Research: Methodological Approaches to Game Analysis. DAC2003, Melbourne. (2003)
2. Bartlett, F. C. *Remembering: A Study in Experimental and Social Psychology.* Cambridge University Press (1932)
3. Boorstin, J. *Making movies work.* Silman-James (1995)
4. Bordwell, D. *Narration in the Fiction Film.* Methuen (1985)
5. Bordwell, D. *The McGraw-Hill film viewer's guide.* McGraw-Hill. (2001)
6. Davis, J.P., Steury, K. and Pagulayan, R. A survey method for assessing perceptions of a game: The consumer playtest in game design. *Games Studies*, 5-1 (2005)
7. Desurvire, H., Caplan, M., Toth, J.A. Using Heuristics to Evaluate the Playability of Games, *Proc. CHI 2004,* ACM (2004)
8. Graesser, A.C., Olde, B., Klettke, B., How does the mind construct and represent stories. In Green, M., Strange, J., and Brock, T. *Narrative Impact.* Erlbaum (2002)
9. Hale, G.G. A Qualitative Exploration of Entertainment Experiences. *ACE 2005.* ACM Siggchi (2005)
10. Hale, G.G. Re-conceptualising 'fun' through viewer's experiences to build new home system interfaces. In *Home-Orientated Informatics and Telematics*, (2005), pp.193-207, Proceedings of HOIT 2005 (York, April 13-15, 2005). Springer. (2005)11. Lessiter, J., Freeman, J., Keogh, E., & Davidoff, J.D. (2001). A Cross-Media Presence Questionnaire: The ITC Sense of Presence Inventory. Presence: Teleoperators and Virtual Environments, 10(3)
11. Mandler, J.M., *Stories, Scripts, and Scenes; Aspects of Schema Theory.* Erlbaum (1984)
12. McGann, N. Watching Games and Playing Movies: The Influence of Cinema on Computer Games. Masters Thesis, Dublin Institute of Technology (2003)
13. Park, N. The Wrong Trousers. Aardman Animations/ Wallace and Gromit Ltd. (1993)
14. Rouse, R. Computer Games, Not Computer Movies. *Computer Graphics* 34/4 (2000)
15. Shoard, C. Gromit has a Day Out. *Seven Magazine, The Sunday Telegraph* (2006)
16. Vaughan, M.W. and Dillon, A. The Role of Genre in Shaping Our Understanding of Digital Documents. *Proc. 61st. Annual Meeting of the American Society for Information Science.*, 559-566. (1998)
17. Walia, E. *Ice Cream Dream.* UK Film Council. (2003)

Minstrel Reloaded: From the Magic of Lisp to the Formal Semantics of OWL

Federico Peinado and Pablo Gervás

Departamento de Ingeniería del Software e Inteligencia Artificial
Universidad Complutense de Madrid
Profesor José García Santesmases s/n, 28040 Madrid, Spain
email@federicopeinado.com, pgervas@sip.ucm.es

Abstract. This paper is a review of a story generation system called Minstrel. It uses complex but hand crafted Lisp knowledge structures to generate short computer-generated stories within the King Arthur domain. The knowledge representation model of Minstrel is reimplemented using a W3C standard language to analyze the pros and cons of technology updates over this kind of classic AI projects.

Keywords: Story Generation, Story Representation, Computational Narratology, Semantic Technologies.

1 Introduction

There are many reasons for revisiting the classics. One is to learn from them, another one is to revive them bringing their old ideas face to face with new trends and technologies. The last one considered in this paper is to open a discussion for fair comparisons between their achievements and the results of our up-to-date –technologically speaking– research projects.

As a first step to these goals, Minstrel, the classic story generator, has been partially reimplemented in order to transfer the original Lisp-based knowledge representation of the application to a more accurate and interoperable framework based on W3C formal semantics. The purpose of this experiment is to give insight into the issues of updating frame-based projects to formal semantics of OWL and the specific problems arising for Minstrel as a specific computational narrative model.

2 Minstrel Overview

Minstrel was developed in the late 1980s by Scott R. Turner. It is a stand-alone application for the automatic generation of short tales (around 200 words in English) set in the universe of King Arthur and the Knights of the Round Table. Focusing on creative heuristics and well known problem-solving methods, Turner presents exciting results claiming that simple but powerful reasoning mechanisms manipulating big amounts of knowledge will lead us to more intelligent systems.

S. Göbel, R. Malkewitz, and I. Iurgel (Eds.): TIDSE 2006, LNCS 4326, pp. 93–97, 2006.

Unfortunately, there is no working version of Minstrel on the web, but the available documentation is meticulous enough to deeply study many details of the implementation.

The knowledge representation is an extension of a Lisp library called Rhapsody. It uses frames, schemas with slots and facets which represent story themes or morals, dramatic effects (suspense, foreshadowing, pacing, dialogue...), world states, character's beliefs and affects, etc.

Minstrel uses a Case-Based Reasoning approach to create new stories reusing parts of old stories taken from an episodic memory. The main goals of the systems are divided in four categories: story theme, plot consistency, dramatic narration and linguistic presentation. Planning Advice Themes (PATs) are more specific goals designed for generalize, specialize, mutate and recombine story themes while the system is running.

The fictional world of the characters is modeled using three concepts: Goal, Act and State. Goals and Acts are divided in two categories: Character-Level and Author-Level, this last one oriented to high-level task concerning the narrative structure of the result. Goals have priority numbers (from 0 to 100) for the planner to put them in order.

Transform-Recall-Adapt Methods (TRAMs) are used to mutate the story in order to obtain creative results.

To sum up[1], the winding network of linked individuals belonging to different knowledge domains is rich, but it is ruled by a constellation of untyped semantic operators and empirically-defined processing algorithms. There are also "ghost individuals" as Planner, Other, Someone or Elsewhere, that Minstrel uses for their internal planning operations.

The assumption is that, from the point of view of Knowledge Engineering, such a knowledge base is hard to maintain, evolve and reuse, even for the same engineer who took all decisions during the development of the system. That is the main reason for recoding a new version using a formal methodology.

3 OWL Overview

The proposal of the W3C to formalize ontologies for interoperability on the web is OWL (Ontology Web Language [1]). The goal of this standard is to formalize the semantics that was created *ad hoc* in old frame systems and semantic networks.

OWL has three increasingly-expressive sublanguages: OWL Lite, OWL DL, and OWL Full. OWL Full is powerful for representing complex statements but not useful for reasoning with them due to their computational properties. OWL DL is the subset of OWL designed for applications that need the maximum expressiveness without losing computational completeness and decidability. It is based on Description Logics, a particular fragment of first order logic, in which concepts, roles, individuals and axioms that related them (using universal and existential restrictions, negation, etc.) are defined.

[1] Readers can find more theoretical and technical details in Turner's PhD thesis [4].

OWL DL has support for polihierarchical reasoning and automatic classification what means knowledge engineers can develop an ontology in a more natural way (e.g. creating a simple taxonomy in which concepts one parent as maximum) and after that let the system put things in order automatically.

Minstrel Reloaded aims for intensive reasoning capabilities and that is the reason why OWL DL is chosen.

4 A List of Knowledge Reengineering Incidents

This section presents a list of incidents detected when transferring Turner's annotation to the new ontology and knowledge base implementation.

- *Lack of canonical nomenclature.* Identifiers of schemas in Minstrel vary between adjectives and names. Singular and plural names both are used to represent concepts. Lowercase and uppercase letters are used with no clear criteria in the nomenclature, because there are inconsistences along the identifiers used in the examples of Turner's thesis.
- *Lack of modularization.* Schemas of totally different domains are put all together at the same level, due to unexisting prefixes, suffixes, namespaces or separated files to identify each domain.
- *Reification of types/Proprietary "is-a" relationship.* Instead of assigning a primitive concept to an individual to represent its type, Minstrel does an extensive use of reification, creating an individual for each type of goal, act or state. A different interpretation of this phenomenon is to consider that Minstrel is using a proprietary "is-a" relationship to assign concepts to individuals, which is usually an embedded relationship in any formal knowledge representation system (e.g. John –individual– "is-a" Male –concept–). Indeed OWL DL does not allow any relation between concepts and individuals apart from the built-in "is-a" relationship. Minstrel has to manage some "backlinks". These are called "inverse roles" in the terminology of OWL and they are included as a standard feature in the W3C language. "Connections" in Minstrel are special roles which establish a link between *another roles.* This kind of "metaroles" is not allowed in DL.
- *Consistency checking.* DL reasoners can check consistency of any DL model with restrictions automatically. On the other hand Minstrel requires a specific library and a set of plans exclusively developed for that task. Both systems can check consistency automatically but in Minstrel this is application-specific and handcrafted whereas using DL ensures that this does not have to be implemented.
- *Untyped roles.* Because of the Lisp features, relationships in Minstrel have no types, additional semantics, domain or range. By default DL roles can link any individuals of role domain with any individual of the role range, but designers can define roles as functional, symmetric, transitive, etc. There is also no taxonomy of roles (e.g. goalType, actType and stateType should be classified under a more generic "type" role). This presents serious difficulties

for visualization and organization due to the number of current roles: 56. Untyped roles make the system more error prone and more difficult to debug.
- *Overridden concepts.* "The values and meanings of the slot fillers for state schemas vary depending upon the sub-type of states" [4] (p. 30). In Minstrel a specialization of a concept can have a different structure from its parent, and it can also change the meaning of inherited slots according to the values found in other slots, as it happens in the "Decision" slot of a Plan Advise Theme, for instance. This behaviour is not tolerated in OWL.
- *Unclear polihierarchy.* It is not clear if there is a polihierarchy of concepts in Minstrel or not. According to the different taxonomies presented in the documentation, there are some special cases of individuals belonging to more than one concept. Goals and Acts are divided in Author-Level Goals/Acts and Character-Level Goals/Acts. Due to the polihierarchical reasoning, there is no need for artificial duplication of concepts in the OWL taxonomy.
- *Anonymous individuals.* Planner, Other, Someone or Elsewhere are individuals that Minstrel uses for their planning operations. Thanks to the Open World Assumption in OWL DL, it is not necessary to put a name to these individuals for their existence to be inferred by the system.
- *Defined concepts.* Minstrel's concepts are not defined with axioms or restrictions. Talking about violent Goals, Turner gives a definition like this: "a violent Goal is a Goal that has a violent Act as part of its plan". This informal definition matches quite well with the idea of "defined concepts" in OWL DL, the definitions of which are used by DL reasoners to classify automatically concepts or individuals according to their relationships.

5 Discussion

Minstrel Reloaded is just a reimplementation of the main knowledge schemas of the original system in a modern ontology and knowledge base. Every concept of the original system and some basic individuals of the King Arthur domain have been implemented. The rest of scenes, stories, plans and other individuals of the knowledge base are not implemented because they are not listed exhaustively in the book of Turner. To evaluate the whole system is not possible yet because the processes that deals with this knowledge have not been developed, so in this section it follows a discussion on knowledge representation and the practical results.

The OWL DL files for the basic ontology[2] includes 65 concepts and 56 roles, the knowledge base[3] has 99 individuals.

Minimum indispensable changes have been required for implementing the new version of Minstrel's knowledge base. Concepts and individuals have been separated. Concepts are put together in the ontology (what we have called *MinstrelOnto*) and individuals have been placed in the knowledge base (*MinstrelKB*). The "minstrel" namespace has been created. The priority of goals is represented

[2] http://federicopeinado.com/projects/minstrel/onto/MinstrelOnto.owl
[3] http://federicopeinado.com/projects/minstrel/onto/MinstrelKB.owl

as a datatype property, indeed a simple integer because its value cannot be trivially restricted to an interval in OWL DL, as it was in the original system.

The advantages of standard semantics are revealed when creating and editing the ontology and the knowledge base with powerful tools as Protégé-OWL[2], sharing them on the Internet or validating and classifying the model using a DL reasoner as Pellet [3].

6 Conclusions

A partial reimplementation of the knowledge structures of Minstrel, the classic story generator, has been created, focusing on knowledge representation. Several problems have been found during the process, most of them concerning lack of reusability related to the lack of formal semantics of complex applications written in Lisp. There are also problems related to the artificial restrictions of OWL DL, which are justified by theoretical requirements for efficient and sound DL reasoning.

One of the design problems that Turner found as a knowledge engineer was the construction of extensible taxonomies of concepts. Discipline and methodology are still requirements for this task, but with the help of automatic validators, classifiers and ontology engineering tools it is reasonable to envisage a future in which systems like Minstrel can be developed by a heterogeneous team of domain experts without the need of such an enormous effort and sacrifice.

Next steps go through the improvement of this resource (currently shared on the web) for being explored and used for a wider audience, developers of narrative applications and even research communities working in the field of interactive storytelling.

Acknowledgements

This research is funded by the Spanish Ministry of Education and Science (TIN2005-09382-C02-01 and TIN2006-14433-C02-01 projects), Complutense University of Madrid and the G.D. of Universities and Research of the Community of Madrid (UCM-CAM-910494 research group grant).

References

1. S. Bechhofer, F. van Harmelen, J. Hendler, I. Horrocks, D. L. McGuinness, P. F. Patel-Schneider, and A. Stein. OWL web ontology language reference. `http://www.w3.org/TR/2004/REC-owl-ref-20040210/`.
2. M. Crubézy, O. Dameron, R. W. Fergerson, H. Knublauch, M. A. Musen, N. F. Noy, D. Rubin, S. W. Tu, and J. Vendetti. Protégé project. `http://protege.stanford.edu/`.
3. Mindswap. Pellet OWL reasoner. `http://www.mindswap.org/2003/pellet/index.shtml`.
4. S. R. Turner. Minstrel: A computer model of creativity and storytelling. Technical Report UCLA-AI-92-04, Computer Science Department, University of California, 1992.

Structuring Hypermedia Novels

Wolfgang Heiden[1] and Arjang Ostovar[2]

[1] University of Applied Sciences, 53754 Sankt Augustin, Germany,
Wolfgang.Heiden@fh-brs.de
http://www.inf.fh-bonn-rhein-sieg.de/Heiden.html
[2] Arjang.Ostovar@smail.inf.fh-brs.de

Abstract. A generic structure for media-oriented modular storytelling is presented. The concept is based on a simple container and content model. We also show how various paths along a continuous storyline and branching threads can be organized. An initial implementation is compared with a second, more general and flexible structuring approach.

1 Introduction

Interaction in digital storytelling can take place in various ways. A major distinction is whether or not user activities have any influence on the plot. If so, narration has either some gaming aspect (i.e. in order to continue the recipient as an acting character has to fulfill tasks whose outcome may change what happens further) or a branching aspect where user decisions represent the choice between one continuing story path or another, which may or may not lead to a different end. In case of a more directed narrative the recipient is enabled, but not forced, to make decisions regarding the presentation of a particular story, but usually has no influence on what actually happens in the plot. A somehow related (although not identical) distinction is that of linear and non-linear storytelling [1]. The Hypermedia Novel (HyMN) approach as introduced earlier [2],[3] focuses more on the primarily receptive meaning of narrative interactivity, although it can also cover the more active aspects as well.

A third interpretation of the term "interaction" in storytelling is a contribution of creative content to an existing narrative, e.g. by suggesting (or creating) follow-up stories. This aspect is in the particular focus of the HyMN paradigm by supporting distributed authoring, not only of successor stories but also with contributions that enhance the original story itself.

2 Hymn Structure

Interactive digital storytelling usually requires a modular representation of narrative content.

2.1 Narration Modules

Virtually any story can be segmented into some distinct modules that transport narrative content. In classical drama there is the typical 3-act structure, for written text

S. Göbel, R. Malkewitz, and I. Iurgel (Eds.): TIDSE 2006, LNCS 4326, pp. 98–103, 2006.

a subdivision into chapters and paragraphs is usual, in movies there is the concept of scenes, etc. A more general definition of such narrative units has been given as "movement" [4] or "narration module" (*NarMo*) [2],[3]. These narrative building blocks can sometimes be further decomposed into smaller units, which may – at the technical level – go down to "frames" in audio-visual data formats or single characters in written text. On the semantic level, however, such distinction does not make sense. Here we have larger elementary units that are generally defined by dramaturgy. Actually a piece of narrative information that can not be broken up further to segments that allow non-linear access without losing track of the story line, defines such an atomic narrative unit (ANU).

In the Hypermedia Novel context, each ANU is related to a particular media, because the information they carry can often be brought to the recipient in different ways, e.g. as written or read text, as a movie scene, an interactive 3D environment, etc. Some of these media may be more suited for transporting a particular content module than others, or the choice may just be up to the recipient's particular taste or current mood. The NarMo granularity may vary between different media, e.g. the content of a single movie scene might be told alternatively by a sequence of text blocks and images.

2.2 Containers and Content

The sub-structuring of Narration Modules produces a hierarchy of modules ordered in a linear sequence (representing the dramatic structure), or in parallel (representing choices between different media with identical informational content). Each module can either contain a sub-hierarchy or actually tell a part of the story as an ANU. Therefore, a generic structure for modular storytelling should distinguish between container and content elements [5].

A Hypermedia Novel requires only three different types of structural elements: serial containers *(SC)*, parallel containers *(PC)*, and content modules *(CM)* (see Fig. 1) [3].

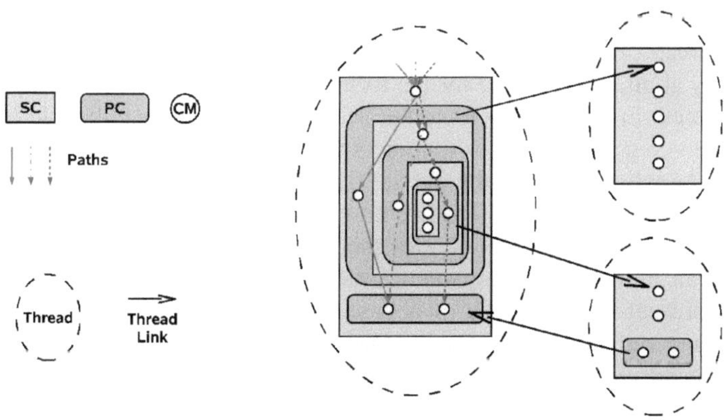

Fig. 1. Hierarchical structure of a Hypermedia Novel (including separate threads plus some paths and thread links): SC = Serial Container (sequential scenes, vertical); PC = Parallel Container (alternatives, horizontal); CM = Content Module (atomic narrative unit)

2.3 Connecting Modules

The container representation, despite its benefit for intuitive understanding of the story structure, lacks some aspects of flexibility usually associated with non-linear storytelling, such as rearrangement of module sequences due to active path changes, branching, or circular relationships. These aspects require an (at least internal) organization of Content Modules as a linked list whose links would be associated with paths through the story. Links to potential successors of a CM should be activated or deactivated according to the CMs visited before. Visualizing a complex structure with all potentially possible links between CMs, however, would rather irritate most recipients than support navigation. Therefore the recipient sees only the sequential arrangement of the current story path, possibly with some links to branching threads that may or may not lead back to the current narrative. The choice of a different path may result in a rearrangement of NarMos, though, which then again can be displayed in a sequential/parralel container structure.

The general concept of paths and threads in a Hypermedia Novel has been described in detail earlier [3]. It is important to mention that there should always be a default path leading the recipient through the complete story in a consistent way without requiring any decisive interaction. Subject of (possible) user interaction is a choice of path from an offered list (e.g. rather text- or video-oriented, short or detailed, etc.) or hopping from NarMo to NarMo via the navigation interface. Branching or supplemental threads (see also in Fig. 1) can contain varying story lines, background information (i.e. facts related to the fictional content) or different, but somehow related, stories.

3 Distributed Authoring

Many stories – in particular multi-sequel narratives (with or without an a-priori end) – create a vast story universe with lots of open knots. These often trigger the idea to follow story paths that may either support the understanding of the major intention of the actual thread or open completely different stories which do not lead back to the original story at all. An example for the former could be background information that had to be present in the author's mind but needs not necessarily to be told in detail for the final plot – e.g. also outtakes that are sometimes used for a "director's cut". An example of the latter might be the movie "The Scorpion King" [6], which was based on a character that appeared in "The Mummy Returns"[7].

Another example of separate stories that are interlinked by a common fictional world are "Fan fiction" websites, where fans of widely known large-scale fiction like Star Trek® present stories of their own, based on characters or events in the movies or series that inspired their imagination. Star Trek itself also provides examples for presenting background information to well-known episodes or scenes in later sequels (e.g. episode "Divergence"[1] giving an explanation for the existence of more human-like Klingons as first appearing in "Errand of Mercy"[2] which was produced almost 40 years earlier).

[1] Star Trek® – Enterprise – season 4, Paramount Pictures Corp., 2005.
[2] Star Trek® – The Original Series – season 2, Paramount Pictures Corp., 1967.

User interaction by content creation may vary from adding single NarMos in a Parallel Container to the contribution of complete separate threads branching from a particular NarMo in the original story.

4 Implementation

A prototype implementation of a HyMN Player has been realized with Macromedia Flash™, based on a first hierarchical structure of Narration Modules [2] with limited hierarchical depth. A new HyMN Player with enhanced features and an SVG-based interface represents the full scale of the generic container structure. Fig. 2 illustrates both structures in comparison.

Both players are based on plugins to current Web browsers in order to simplify access for everyone. Display of multimedia content in a central frame is directed via a navigation frame including the plugin that reads all structural information from an XML file. So it is easy to use the slim player for a broad variety of hypermedia novels through the XML interface.

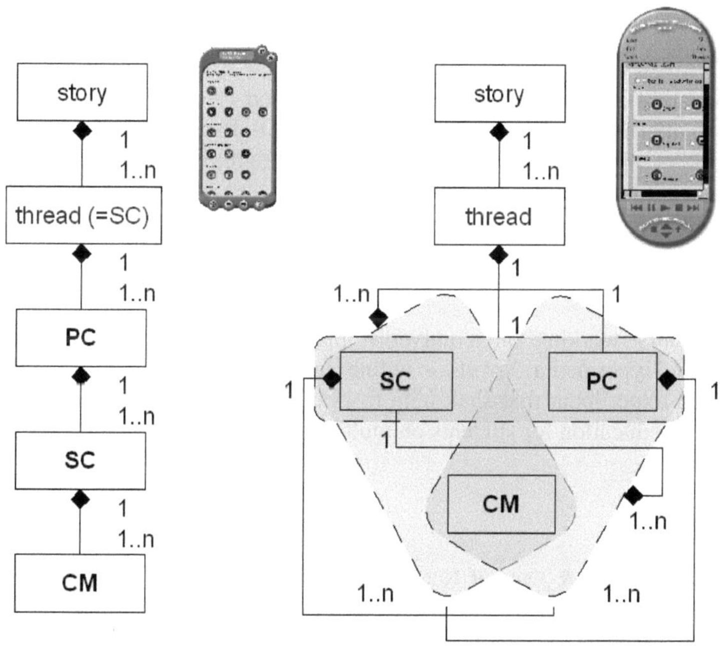

Fig. 2. Old (left) and new (right) HyMN hierarchy in (pseudo) UML notation. Dashed boxes (filled grey) represent an "XOR" relationship. Screenshots of navigation interfaces are included, respectively.

4.1 First Generation HyMN

The first player, which has been built using Macromedia Flash™ with Action Script™, offers a stable platform for the reception of Hypermedia Novels. Apart from storytelling, it can serve as a navigation interface for any complex multimedia content and has in fact been used for the organization and interactive (with respect to the audience) presentation of lecture material. To support distributed authoring a server platform was provided for NarMo upload.

An attempt to integrate player and (local as well as net-based) editor functions with Macromedia Director™ posed problems, due to Internet security restrictions of this platform.

4.2 Second Generation HyMN

The new implementation of a HyMN Player makes full use of the potentially unlimited depth of NarMo hierarchy. In addition to this, it offers a variety of new features:

- The recipient can record the current path and save it for further use.
- There is an autoplay mode, where no mouseclick is required. NarMos are played according to the currently chosen path. While continuous media have a pre-determined duration, static media are displayed for an according time span. Texts are scrolled automatically.
- There is a print function for static content (which is distinguished from dynamic content via XML attributes).

The navigation interface of the new player is based on SVG[3] as an (XML-based) OpenSource alternative to the scommercial Flash™ format [8]. As the currently available Browser plugins for SVG are yet still immature, not all features of this very potent format could actually be used.

5 Outlook

We are currently working on a universal platform for reception, authoring, and publication of Hypermedia Novels – online as well as offline. We are in parallel conducting an experiment that shall help to evaluate how HyMN storytelling can be integrated with education for students on multiple edutainment levels.

References

[1] Pearce, C.: The Ins & Outs of Non-Linear Storytelling. SIGGRAPH Comput. Graph., 28(2) (1994) 100-101
[2] Heiden, W., Frühling, C., Deuer, H.: Hypermedia Novel HYMN - A New Storytelling Paradigm. Proceedings cast01, St. Augustin, D (2001)
[3] Heiden, W.: Edutainment Aspects in Hypermedia Storytelling. LNCS 3942 (2006) 389-398
[4] Sharda, N.: Movement Oriented Design: A New Paradigm for Multimedia Design. International Journal of Lateral Computing (IJLC), 1 (1) (2005) 7-14
[5] Spaniol, M.: Enhancing MECCA for Movement Inspired Story-Telling (MIST): Conceptualization and Realization of an MPEG-7 based Story-Telling Environment. 3rd MPEG-7/21 Community Workshop, Aachen, D, Nov. 25 (2005)

[3] Scalable Vector Grafics, W3C.

[6] The Scorpion King. Universal Pictures (2002)
[7] The Mummy Returns. Universal Pictures (2001)
[8] Held, G., Ullrich, T., Neumann, A., Winter, A.: Comparing .SWF (ShockWave Flash) and .SVG (Scalable Vector Graphics) file format specifications. http://www.carto.net/papers/svg/comparison_flash_svg/index.shtml, accessed Sep. 05, 2006.

The Hacker: New Mythical Content of Narrative Games

Joris Dormans

Hogeschool van Amsterdam, Weesperzijde 190,
1090 DZ Amsterdam, The Netherlands
jd@jorisdormans.nl

Abstract. Mythology and its general relevance for popular culture is is a framework of growing importance for understanding the way narrative games function as cultural artefacts within society. Myths are better compatible than conventional stories with the key characteristics of games: interactivity, (world)simulation and gameplay. Furthermore, games as a technologically advanced medium, open up new mythological perspectives on contemporary society and technology, a perspective where the hacker is proposed as the new hero of this day and age.

Keywords: Computer Games, Interactive Storytelling, Mythology.

1 Introduction

For what had Prometheus done in the first place? He had given men a power-up.
- Steven Pool [1]

Storytelling has a long history and over the years many media were devised to relate tales. Games are one of the most recent additions to the possible narrative canvasses. Although there has been a long an heated debate on the subject, most scholars would agree that storytelling is a factor in some games. For some games story is just providing colour to the central gaming action. Others have higher narrative aspirations and are trying to carve out new paths to the ever illusive holy grail of interactive storytelling, more often than not with only limited success.

Up until this point games are not really known for the quality of the tales they spin. When compared to traditional (linear) forms of storytelling such as the printed novel or feature film games are lacking. Game characters are often flat and stereotypical, plots are considered weak and predictable. Although it may not be fair to compare a medium as young as games to the more mature cinema or the venerable printed word, some insist that games will never be able to catch up. Games' celebrated quality of interactivity goes against the authorial control required to create a narrative masterpiece. Several scholars, including myself, work hard to find ways to resolve the paradox between freedom of the player and control of author, but so far no definite strategies have emerged. One might start to believe those critics who say successful strategies that lead to the creation of narrative games on par with most important works of linear fiction might never be found.

S. Göbel, R. Malkewitz, and I. Iurgel (Eds.): TIDSE 2006, LNCS 4326, pp. 104 – 115, 2006.

At the same time, mythology is gaining ground in the study of narrative games as relevant framework to approach game stories. The mythological sources and aspirations of many fantasy games are obvious, and the 'Frontier myth' is a popular template applied to popular science-fiction or action cinema and games alike. If the mythological interpretation of games reveals one thing, it is that most myths are relative technophobic and conservative. As someone who does not particularly identifies himself with those notions, but also as someone who also enjoys science-fiction in general, this does not seem satisfactory. How come I enjoy that particular type of storytelling while I oppose its typical message?

To resolve this paradox I will investigate the the mythological nature and meaning of games from the perspective of media theory, ludology and social mythology. In particular I will investigate the way media and mythology shape society in general and in narrative games in particular.

2 Storytelling Media

Marshall McLuhan is notorious for the power he attributed to media to shape human society. His history is divided in four eras that coincide with development of dominant media: the eras of the spoken word, script, printed word and electronic media (perhaps best interpreted as our current computer age). Of these, McLuhan resented the era of printed word the most. Although he admits the printing-press improved education and literacy, it also inspired nationalism and the accumulation of power by military and commercial corporations. Instead of liberating the individual it took away his power to express and react. "Perhaps the most significant of gifts of typography to man," he writes, "is that of detachment and noninvolvement." [2]

Although, his observations have been nuanced by later media scholars (most notably by Raymond Williams) the relevance of these for storytelling are evident. In most literary circles the printed novel is still regarded as the most superior medium for storytelling, with theatre and certain types of cinema playing second and third fiddle respectively. Other media such as face-to-face storytelling, graphic novels, television and computer games compare poorly to the standards set by the printed novel.

A closer inspection of common ways to define stories and storytelling reveals that these have been shaped much by the medium of the printed word and its particular traits. At the heart of most definitions is that a story relates a series of chronological and causally related events, with beginning, a middle and closure at the end. No wonder that media that are sequential and authored in advance are good at telling tales like this. McLuhan might comment that such media shaped the way we tell stories so that it reflects their sequential and pre-authored nature and has little to do with the most superior shape of stories themselves (if such a thing can be said to exists).

To better understand and appreciate the stories told by other media than the traditional media of the era of the printed word, we need to resort to theories devised for these media. A well-known example from the world of comics is the work of Scott McCloud. In search of the elementary structure of comics he proposes the panel and the way it functions in relation to other panels on the page. The magic of comics, he says, is found in the space between the panels. The reader fills in the blanks herself and relates the depicted events in the panels. She provides her own closure based on a visual and verbal interpretation of the frames. This a pivotal point made by McCloud, as he states that: "If visual iconography is the vocabulary of comics, closure is its grammar. And since our definition of comics hinges on the arrangement of elements then, in a very real sense, comics is closure!" [3, my typesetting]. Interestingly, the type of closure McClouds talks about does not depend on pre-authored causal relations in a text, but is constructed in the mind of the reader, cued by the visual layout. Association, juxtaposition and similarity are far more important for this type of closure than the sequences and differences of printed word.

In a later work McCloud travels further down this alternative narrative path when he considers how comics are best adapted to digital forms. The computer screen, he observes, makes only for a poor substitution of the page in a comic book, and when single screen panels are use much power of the comic is lost. Instead, he proposes to use the screen as a window onto an infinite page where the panels are laid out unconstricted, where panel interrelation is free and expressive [4]. McCloud manages to use the move of comics to the computer to play up the strengths of the first, which shows insight into the particular attributes of his chosen medium and how these relate to the expressive art of telling stories.

His work led McCloud to a very different perspective on stories than the one advocated by traditional literature. Stories are not about the relation of events, they are not *his*tories, rather he states that: "Storytellers in all media and all cultures are, at least partially, in the business of creating worlds." [5]. This perspective on stories seems to be much more suited to games as well. Games are very good at creating worlds and many scholars have reflected on this ability. For example, Henry Jenkins [6] makes a strong case for architectural approach to designing game stories. In addition the larger interpretative freedom McClouds grants the reader of comics might be a welcome step away from a theory of narrative that makes creativity the province of the genius of the author only.

3 Games as a Medium for Storytelling

When we shift our attention to computer games as a medium a few characteristics particular to games that shape the way we tell stories come in to sharp focus. These characteristics are interactivity, simulation and gameplay. In this article I wish to address these terms in the most generic possible way. This is partly because different games implement these aspects in very different ways, and partly because there is not much consensus on these terms among scholars of games. In addition I hope the reader agrees that a generic approach to these characteristics suffices for this article. I am trying to comment on the narrative potential of games in general. The exact implementation of narrative in games is best left to the individual craftsmanship of game designers and interactive storytellers.

Interactivity is heralded as one of the hallmarks of new computerised media, and computer games are often placed at the pinnacle as the one of most interactive media to date. Although there are many ways to understand interactivity, with games interactivity is generally understood as the power of the user to interact with the game in such way that the game 'text' (the sounds and images it produces) itself is changed so that it in some way reflects the players choices (see for example [7]; or [8]). This type of interactivity is far beyond the interpretative freedom of a reader of a linear, non-interactive text. Interactivity grants some control over the game to the player to the extent that the game designer no longer produces a text, as the author of a novel does, rather the player produces one within the framework provided by the game designer. The job of the game designer is to create a tool, a semiotic space or machine for the player to use and craft her own stories. Unfortunately, giving up authorial control seems to be a rather hard thing to do. Few writers are prepared to vest enough confidence in the storytelling abilities of their audience, while the audience also seems reluctant to pick up the challenge to entertain themselves. As Steven Poole expresses the sentiment: "we don't want to have to make crucial narrative decisions that might, in effect, spoil the story for us. We want to have our cake and eat it." [9]

The perspective of games as interactive machines ties in nicely with games as simulations. The logic that is embedded in the machine can be described as a system of rules that model in game-world. The game-world might be taken quite literary as a fictional playground for the player but some worlds are more abstract and have no real-world counter part or consists only in mathematical relations of the various game elements. Most game-worlds are somewhere in between these two extremes. The old game of chess is a good example. This game metaphorically represents two opposing armies at a field of battle, but the abstract rules that make up the game are more important than any reference to a real historical place or battle. Simulation in computer games has a long history (long as far as computer games goes that is). In his early work Chris Crawford already drew the same parallel between simulations and games as between technical drawing and a work of art [10]. More recently, Gonzalo Frasca worked on the notion of simulation as an alternative to narrative or textual representation. An alternative that takes into account the status of a game not as a text but as a machine for the production of texts [11]. It is important to see that most approaches to games simulations scholars stress the importance expressive power of the simulation itself over the direct representation of a (fictional or non-fictional) reality. As Steven Poole argues: "Videogames will become more interesting artistically if they abandon thoughts of recreating something that looks like the 'real' world and try instead to invent utterly novel ones that work in amazing but consistent ways – because [...] a 'realistic' simulation is always built on a foundation of compromise anyway." [12].

Gameplay, finally, is probably the most fluid of these three aspects. Although every gamer has an intuitive grasp of what gameplay she likes and what gameplay she dislikes, finding a solid definition of gameplay is difficult. Most people will acknowledge that gameplay is the thing the player does while playing, and good gameplay amounts to a certain enjoyable quality of this activity. It is not uncommon to link gameplay to the notion of flow. A state of mind described by psychologist Mihaly Csikszentmihalyi [13] in which the player looses track of time, becomes unaware of her surroundings and is totally immersed in the game. To achieve flow the player needs to feel challenged, but not too much: she must also feel in control. Furthermore she needs clear goals and some sort of feedback. A well designed game delivers all these experiences and is easy to see that good interactivity design and a coherent simulation contribute to flow and gameplay.

These three aspects are of course not the only aspects crucial to gaming. For example, one might point out that games involve some sort of conflict and its resolution (winning or loosing). However, most stories also involve conflict and some sort of resolution (closure). If anything, the conflict in games is often represented in the most primitive form (violence) whereas other media have found more sophisticated ways of depicting conflict. Considering the relative young age of computer games this should not come as a surprise. What is surprising is that games already show the first signs of expanding their palette beyond violence alone [14].

In considering these aspects of games and how these relate to story telling a common mistake is encountered. The games industry has a tendency to focus on realism and transparency in order to create immersion. They seem to think that the player will only suspend her disbelieve when the simulated world is realistic enough, this requires the controls to be as transparent and intuitive as possible and rules out anything that might break the spell. Game scholars too, often retain that games as expressive media are less sophisticated than other media. For example, in his account of game time, Jesper Juul argues that chronologically discontinuous games work against immersion because they call attention to themselves as games [15]. In his view it something that might work in film or a book but goes against the ideal experience of a game. I disagree, games lack an established and expressive grammar to communicate discontinuous time, not the potential to express it effectively. Books and cinema were not invented with structures to represent discontinuous time from the start, and when the necessary grammar evolved it took time for the audience to adjust. It might very well be that most current games are always played in the 'now', as Juul insists, but that is not their necessary condition. David Jay Bolter and Diane Gromala argue against transparent interface design: "the most successful digital consumer products are not merely transparent, but instead make the interface part of the experience" [16]. It seems like a viable strategy for designing games as well. Gameplay consists of interacting with the game, and to think about the presses of the button and to integrate that experience into the game will give the player a great sense of control. Control will lead to flow, through which immersion can be reached. This is much closer to the transcendental cyborg consciousness famously described by Ted Friedman [17], which quite literary recall Marshall McLuhan's notion of media as the extensions of man. More expressive grammar and structures in games will only enhance the power at the command of the player, and deepen her experience.

What, then, are the types of stories games are suited to relate? For one thing games are part of popular culture and should appeal to a wide audience (often by economic necessity). They are good at delivering worlds and should be able to let the player roam free inside them. This makes games in many ways a closer cousin to television, episodic comics and cross-media events than to literature or cinema. They are part of a folk tradition of storytelling rather than they should aspire to storm the vestibules of high art and literature. To put it simple games are excellent vehicles for modern myths.

4 A Mythological Approach to Storytelling

The emergence of interactive storytelling, in games and outside games, have inspired a renewed interest in mythology. Myths are among the oldest forms of storytelling and stem from an age before written records existed. These days we like to imagine ways in which the shamans told their stories around the camp-fire interactively. Most of this is, of course, guesswork. Although the ritual re-enactment of certain myth are indeed ancient examples of interactive storytelling. But games copy more than the structure of myths alone. It is not enough to assume that the mythological content of many games only offers shallow, escapist entertainment, for the there is more power in myths than that.

Myths have long served a very particular role in society, they teach us how to live. It is a perspective on myth that has been popularised by Joseph Campbell. In his key work *The Hero with a Thousand Faces* [18] he presents his theory of the monomyth. Campbell shows that many stories from around the world and from many different sources all deal with life, death and the rites of passage. It is as if one single story, the monomyth (The Adventure of The Hero), underlies all these other stories, although they might focus on different parts of the monomyth. Basically the monomyth teaches us to overcome life's obstacles and to step into the footsteps of our parents; they show us how to live and experience life. Towards the end of his work, Campbell observes that today too much has changed for the monomyth to retain much relevance. Scientific progress and liberal democratic ideals have transformed society too much. No longer is it necessary to become as your parents, and people are more free to choose their own path in life. The symbols of the past seem to have lost their value [19]. Still, narrative works that follow the monomyth closely, or are directly inspired by it, are still created, and are still hugely successful. Two of the best known examples are the *Star Wars* series and *The Lord of the Rings*. The myths Campbell described keep emerging in popular culture; Campbell's work has found its way into many storyteller's handbook.

Another mythological take at popular fiction can be found in the work of film scholar Geoff King [20]. He recounts the frontier myth that inspired many popular films since the heyday of the Western, especially in the big action flicks of Hollywood. In King's account, the frontier myth also serves to help its audience to make sense of the world. Its basic premise is that of the strong male hero, purified by a hard and simple life on the frontier, who fights the technological and bureaucratic forces of modern, hedonistic society and restores the family unit or small community because he puts more trust in his wits and intuition than in technology. The frontier can take many guises, from its American frontier original, via any wild and untouched stretch of nature, to the vast unexplored stretches of deep space. The frontier myth pits mankind against technology and condemns a society that relies to much on the latter. The frontier myth can be easily identified in many action films and works of fantasy and science-fiction, including the aforementioned *Star Wars* and *The Lord of the Rings*. Both stories antagonise the industrial perfection of Saruman and the Empire, while contrasting it with nature loving heroes or the ramshackle technology of the Rebels. Games frequently use the frontier myth, a clear cut example can be found in *Half-Life* where the government turns out to be the real enemy after they failed to contain the aliens and to harness their own technology. In this case the frontier comes to our hero Gordon Freeman, and his perilous trek through the alien invested complex prepares him for the real encounter with the enemy. The fact that the government ends up using Freeman to eliminate the alien threat is a common twist that mostly serves to underlines the their inability despite their technological advantage.

As all proper myths, the frontier myth holds some relevance in real life. In this case technology is seen as a factor that is changing society, and not for the good. It reflects a conservative almost Luddite sentiment that apparently strikes a chord with a large part of the audience. Finding meaning in a increasingly anonymous society is difficult and many people do recognise the feeling of being enslaved by the technology that was supposed to make life easier. Ironically, the fact that these stories are often mediated by the very same technologies and are controlled by similar large companies the myth antagonises, seems to escape the general public.

5 The Success of Interactive Myth

Our appetite for mythical content is not the only reason of the success a mythological approach to storytelling in games might have. I find that as a strategy for *interactive* storytelling it holds some promise, at the same time it seems to go well with some recent trends and practices within the industry. The mythical form of stories simply seems to fit the media form of games rather well.

Games – or, according to Scott McCloud, any form of story – aim at delivering worlds. Most myths, too, concern themselves with the creation of a mythical universe. Despite the relevance myths might hold for their public, few people mistake the fictional character of the myths for facts. Or at least they should distinguish between myth and reality. Joseph Campbell, states that people sometimes do well to refer to the myths outside their own religion, for he feels when they do not take them for facts their message comes across more clearly [21]. Various myths often combined into a mythology, a collection of myths of a culture that deal with the same characters or locations. The cycle of Norse Myths are a well known example. These tales relate the dealings of the old gods of Scandinavia. Although some myths should be clearly placed at the beginning of the cycle and others towards the end, the tales in the middle are largely interchangeable. In the middle the characters are well established and do not change much as each has their own role to play at reflects their own part of life or the populace. Each new iteration of the same metaphorical conflict offers a new perspective on the represented themes. In this regard John Fiske draws a parallel between mythology and television series, where every show is often a similar reiteration of the same conflict. Within an episode "[t]he syntagmatic chain of events may reach closure, but the paradigmatic oppositions of character and situation never can" [22]. A similar observation could be made for video games, as most seem to reiterate the same paradigmatic oppositions over and over again, even when the cast and set change more frequently.

At the same time the recent trend in many cultural industries is to make repeated use of the same intellectual properties. It is expensive and considerably risky to keep investing in new fictional characters and worlds when the audience displays an unquenchable thirst for the same heroes. As a result there are more sequels and more adaptations from one media to another. These days a fictional character might start out as a minor comic book character that is ported to the silver screen before she stars in her own television series or computer game (see [23, 24]). This fictional universes that span many media texts and artefacts are build around a coherent core that function much like a ancient mythology: it represents a particular outlook on life. Interestingly such a fictional universe is inherently much more interactive than the content of a linear story, as fans can more freely explore or even contribute to this world. Many minor additions to these cross-media constructs are designed facilitate such visits. In his discussion of the frontier myth, Geoff King includes examples from film themed theme park rides. He argues that these rarely aim at delivering the same story as the main cinematic source, rather they are designed to make the visitor feel part of the same fictional universe [25]. Curiously, many of such theme park rides seem to include a moment where, apparently, something goes wrong. These moments help the audience to suspend their disbelieve and cross the boundary into fictional world. It helps them forget for a moment that they are safely strapped into a cart; it can be regarded as a form of media transparency. Although, I do not think it is fully transparent and it takes a little bit more to really make the audience forget that what they are seeing is only a show. In fact, as I argued above, I doubt these attractions should aim for full transparency or risk to stop being enjoyable. If anything, this common strategy of going off the beaten track illustrates better the willingness of the audience to buy into the fantasy. To some extent, we want these stories to be true; we welcome the chance to be able to participate and enjoy them as if they are real, in the safe knowledge that nothing really bad can happen.

This willingness of the audience to play their part in the communal fantasy is one of the foundations of an interesting structure for interactive storytelling discussed by Marie-Laure Ryan called fractal storytelling [26]. She takes the idea from Neal Stephenson's science-fiction novel *The Diamond Age* in which an interactive storybook plays a prominent role. Fractal storytelling resolves around the idea that people enjoy stories that to some extent are predictable. There are only so many stories and we are pretty good at recognising them: start with the words 'once upon a time' and we all know we are dealing with a fairy tale and easily predict the way the tale will develop. Horror films and action films are also notorious for reusing the same narrative developments and devices over and over again. Satirical takes on these genres such as *Scary Movie* or *Last Action Hero* are good examples where these mechanisms are clearly foregrounded.

Contrary to appeals to originality and creative genius, more often than not the audience wants the same action spiked stories, at best with some minor variations. Interactive storytellers can make use of this appetite of the audience by delivering what people want to hear and see. Authors should not struggle with the player for narrative control, rather the author and the player should cooperate. The author can expect that when the player buys a violent game she does not expect pacifist solutions to be part of it, and therefore the player should not be disappointed when these are indeed not part of the game. Games have already been described as a restrictive language where rules govern a world where we are challenged pursue goals in indirect or inefficient ways (see [27]). Likewise, stories also often rely on a restricted language, classical, traditional and modern myths in particular. Aristotle's theory of the drama is good example of such a restrictive language that is still applied to this day. In all likelyhood, these languages correspond to different genres while at the same time they might share a common, universal core. The interplay between stories, games and these genre-languages strongly resembles the way languages function in the social linguistic theories of popular and 'high' culture of Mikhail Bakhtin [28].

The idea of the fractal story helps the interactive storytelling to focus on giving the player freedom where it matters. To accommodate for all possible actions of the player is not very efficient when the goal of the story is more or less fixated by its initial premise. The abduction of a princess by a dragon leaves little doubt as to how the plot will end. However, the eventual demise of the dragon can take on several different meanings depending on the trajectory of the player. As Barry Atkins puts it: "The satisfaction of such stories, at least at the level of discrete plot fragment, rests not in matter of plot sophistication, but in matters of sophistication of telling. The question is never *will* the prince overcome the dragon but *how* will the prince overcome the dragon?" [29]. This still leaves a lot room for different stories. The interactive plot is not an end in it self, rather it is a means to create interactive stories that are the result of the creative collaboration between storyteller and player. In the end, it is not about the structure of the game but about the experience of the player. The best way to give the player an experience she likes is to establish a symbolical playground rife with dramatic, paradigmatic oppositions and leave it to the player to explore at her own leisure. When the symbolical oppositions are interesting enough, and when she has enough freedom to explore and experiment with these, the player will want to return over and over again. That way the interactive story can grow with the player: the game creates stories that within certain parameters also reflect back to the player.

6 Stories Games Might Tell

Closer inspection of the stories presented in games reveals that myths are indeed already popular content for games. Campbell's journey of the hero and King's frontier myth are both useful templates for analysis of games (as is the case for many science-fiction, fantasy or action stories). Most of these instances of these myths are not really known for their progressive message. We already have seen that a lot of films produced within the Hollywood studio model, with its reliance on technology and scale, advocate a sentiment that goes against their own mode of production. At a first glance games do not appear very different. Which is strange, because in so far, with games too, the medium is the message one would expect that these technologically advanced artefacts communicate a message that is more progressive and less technophobic.

However, there are alternative avenues to interpret the mythological content of games. Ian Bogosts [30] holds the view that video-games in fact represent a new mode of thinking and organising that he associates with complex systems. It is a way of thinking that favours 'unit operations' over top-down system thinking or 'system operations':

> Unit operations are modes of meaning-making that privilege discrete, disconnected actions over deterministic, progressive systems. It is a term loosely amalgamated from several fields, including software technology, physics, and cybernetics, but it could be equally well at home in the world of literary theory. I contend that unit operations represent a shift away from system operations, although neither strategy is permanently detached from the other." [31]

System operations refer the old practices of sciences and society to organise everything in large systems that are understood top-down. These days, our society and or knowledge has grown so much in scope that a top-down approach seizes to be effective. Most sciences have moved beyond system operations towards unit operations. The emergence of the computer game as a medium with social and cultural significance is a clear indication that culture will follow suit. For what is computer game but a complex and open system? Bogost proposes a comparative computer game criticism that interprets games among similar lines I have outlined here. Above all, it "would seek to understand how videogames reveal what it means to be human." [32] Interpreting games in this way, they might have to teach us a few lessons that go beyond technological and bureaucratic angst, despite the fact that still seems to be the most dominant theme in many game stories. The popularity in games of one particular character arch-type, the hacker, is particularly promising for the future of game myths.

Hackers have become common heroes of many science-fiction stories found in games and elsewhere. They are very prominent in the subgenre of cyberpunk where they are often encountered in their most pure form: computer wiz-kids that use their skills to enter the computers of mega corporations and governments in order to free information and to expose the evil intent of those organisations. Games like *System Shock* and *Deus Ex* make extensive use of this theme. William Gibson, one of the genre's classic authors, frequently uses the term console-cowboy to refer to these future criminals, data terrorist or freedom fighters. A term that recalls the frontier myth, and indeed that myth provides us with a meaningful interpretative framework to approach many works of cyberpunk. The new frontier is now the electronic frontier in cyberspace. We can also encounter the hacker in other stories. Geoff King briefly discusses the hacker nature of the girl Lex in the film *Jurassic Park* and contrasts her different, more intuitive approach with that of computer-nerd and villian Nedry. [33]. This whole film, like the book it is based upon, can be interpreted as a clean-cut example of the frontier myth, but also serves to illustrate the difference between unit operations and system operations (and represents the former as the more superior of the two).

Still, there is a important difference between the hacker and cowboy as the more typical frontier hero. Cowboys seem to live more in the past than hackers do. Cowboys invariably want to restore the country side, and human society, to a pure, unspoiled state, untouched by technology. Hackers, on the other hand, usually live by their technological skills, they cannot live without their technology. The hackers differ from their adversaries in their more intuitive, bottom-up, approach to technology, which allows them to control the technology rather than being controlled by it. In a sense the hacker represents a sort of synthesis between the old frontier heroes and the way our world has evolved. the hacker does not try to escape modern society, rather the hacker shows us how to embrace technology and without giving up our individuality. In this way the significance of the hacker exceeds the world of games and fiction. For example hackers would excel in Bogost's unit operations, and McKenzie Wark uses the hacker and the hack to describe modern information workers in his political *A Hacker Manifesto.* [34].

The difference between hackers and cowboys is clearly illustrated when one compares the films *The Matrix* to *Johnny Mnemonic*, which both star Keanu Reaves in the role of the 'hacker'. In *The Matrix* hacker Neo finds power within to fight the system, but although this leads to his personal transcendence, the film's main antagonist is clearly the technology itself. The sequels make a point in celebrating a more primitive tribal society over the world as we know it today. In the matrix Neo is more of a cowboy than a hacker. In contrast, *Johnny Mnemonic* does not really antagonise technology. One of its main heroes is the cyberdolphin Jones, an interesting mix between nature and technology. The antagonist is not technology itself, instead the bad guys are with the pharmaceutical corporation that are controlling the technological advances and withhold the cure for the disease that is caused by cyberware. Of course, in the end they prove to be no match for hacker Johnny and his friends who with their superior understanding and bottom-up control manage to save the day.

It should become clear that games are excellent vehicles for the figure of the hacker and the hacker myth. For what is gaming but a bottom-up approach to understanding complex systems? Control, so vital to gameplay, corresponds well to the performance of the hack. Last but not least, the hacker myth points the way forward instead of celebrating ages past. If we are in need of new road signs for life (as Joseph Campbell repeatedly stated), than the hacker myth holds much more relevance for contemporary, complex society than the way of the cowboy. The hacker, in its many guises, is the newest incarnation of the mythological trickster, and as the trickster has done for ages, the hacker shows us how to harness technology and how to incorporate it into our lives and society.

7 Conclusion

Every medium for storytelling favours its own type of story. We cannot and should not compare the stories of games to standards set by the 'high' culture of literature or art-house cinema. If games are to evolve as a storytelling medium a form of storytelling should be found that matches the characteristics of games. Mythological storytelling, which shapes many stories in popular media, seems to be very well suited to interactive storytelling in general and games in particular. The structural form of the myth with its own restrictive formal rules can be easily incorporated by games. The general audience relishes this type of story as they know what to expect and because it holds relevance to their everyday life, even when the narrative theme is anything but ordinary.

The mythological content of popular media, however, shows a serious conservative and technophobic streak. However, society advances and we need our stories to reflect that change, or at least to help us cope with it. To this end games, as one of the technologically most advanced media to date, seem to hold the key. They are more accommodating to the emerging myth of the hacker; a new and more progressive incarnation of the classic hero. In this way, games constitute an invaluable platform that can teach us how to deal with modern life in new ways. In this way, games give shape to new mythological content that will shape our lives.

References

1. Poole, S.: Trigger Happy, The Inner Life of Videogames. Fourth Estate, London. (2000) p. 216
2. McLuhan, M.: Understanding Media, The extensions of man. Routledge Classics, London (1964/2001) p. 188
3. McCloud, S. Understanding Comics, The Invisible Art. HarperCollins Publishers, New York. (1993) p. 67
4. McCloud, S. Reinventing Comics, How Imagination and Technology Are Revolutionaizing an Art Form. New York, HarperCollins Publsihers, New York (2000) p. 222
5. Ibid. p. 211

6. Jenkins, H.: Game Design as Narrative Architecture. In Harrington, P. and Frup-Waldrop, N. (eds.) First Person. The MIT Press, Cambridge. (2004) 117-130
7. Poole (2000) p. 105
8. Aarseth, E.J.: Cybertext, Perspectives on Ergodic Literature. The Johns Hopkins University Press, Baltimore. (1997) p. 3
9. Poole (2000) p. 123
10. Crawford, C.: The Art of Computer Game Design. (1983) p. 9
11. Frasca, G.: Simulation versus Narrative. In Wolf M.J.P. & Perron, B. (eds.) The Video Game Theory Reader. Routledge, New York. (2003) p. 221-235
12. Poole (2000) p. 240
13. Csikszentmihalyi, M.: Flow, The Psychology of the Optimal Experience. HarperPerennial (1990)
14. Meadows, M.S.: Pause & Effect, The art of interactive narrative. New Riders, Indianapolis. (2003) p. 20
15. Juul J.: Introduction to Game Time. In Harrington, P. and Frup-Waldrop, N. (eds.) First Person. The MIT Press, Cambridge. (2004) p. 131-142
16. Bolter, D.J. & Gomala, D. Windows and Mirrors, Interaction Design, Digital Art and the Myth of Transparency. The MIT Press, Cambridge. (2003) p. 149
17. Friedman, T.: Making Sense of Software, Computer Games and Interactive Textuality. Available at: <http://ww.duke.edu/~tlove/simcity.htm> (1999)
18. Campbell, J.: The Hero With A Thousand Faces. Princeton University Press, Princeton (1949)
19. Ibid. p. 387
20. King, G.: Spectacular Narratives, Hollywood in the Age of the Blockbuster. I.B. Tauris Publishers, London. (2000)
21. Campbell, J.: The Power of Myth. Ancher Books, New York. (1988/1991) p. 5
22. Fiske, J. Television Culture. Routledge, London. (1987) p. 145
23. Aarseth, E.J.: Waiting for Death Jr.: The culture and business of crossmedia productions. Paper presented at the IGDA conference. (2005)
24. Kerr, A.: The Business and Culture of Digital Games, Gameswork/Gameplay. SAGE Publication, London. (2006) p. 69-73
25. King (2000) p. 176-184
26. Ryan, M. Narrative as Virtual Reality, Immersion and Interactivity in Literature and Electronic Media. The Johns Hopkins University Press, Baltimore. (2001) p. 337
27. Carr, D., Buckingham, D., Burn, A., & Schott, G. Computer Games: Text, Narrative and Play. Polity Press, Cambridge. (2006)
28. Bakhtin, M.: Discourse of the Novel. In Holquist M. (ed.) The Dialogic Imagination: Four Essays. University of Texas Press, Austin. (1981) p. 259-422
29. Atkins, B.: More than a Game, The Computer Game as Fictional Form. Manchester University Press, Manchester. (2003) p. 43
30. Bogost, I.: Unit Operations: An Approach to Videogame Criticism. The MIT Press, Cambridge. (2006)
31. Ibid. p. 3
32. Ibid. p. 53
33. Poole (2000) p. 65-66
34. Wark, M.: A Hacker Manifesto. Harvard University Press, Cambridge. (2004)

The Interactive Artwork as the Aesthetic Object: Aesthetic Technology Converging Technological Applications and Aesthetic Discourses

Joonsung Yoon and Jaehwa Kim

Dept. of Digital Media, Soongsil Univ., 511 Sangdo-dong,
Dongjak-gu, 156-743 Seoul, Korea
{jsy, art801}@ssu.ac.kr

Abstract. Today the concept of art is studied in the term of aesthetic object. On the one hand, it is noticed that the aesthetic object has changed its form from material into interpretive and semantic entity. On the other hand, the aesthetic experience is shifting its site to the center of aesthetic object. Contemporary computer-based media art works are composed of physical bodies such as computer CPU, monitor, projector, camera and speaker including technologies of computer vision, computer graphics, virtual reality, artificial intelligence, augmented reality, etc. In particular, interactive art not only embodies characteristics of already changed aesthetic object, but also reveals contexts of returning the problem of aesthetic object into the aesthetic perception for the reconsideration. Therefore interactive art is the triggering and motivating point to discuss new aesthetic object in terms of art and science.

Keywords: aesthetic object, technolsogy, interactive art, art and science.

1 Introduction

De-viewer (Zerseher), 1991-1992 looks like a framed painting that is hanging on the wall, Giovanni Fransesco Caroto's *Boy with a Child-Drawing in His Hand*, 1520 but on closer inspection the viewer notices that the painting changes at the precise spot where he fixes his gaze (Fig. 1 and Fig. 2). This artwork was developed with the intention of encouraging interaction.

As a traditional aesthetic object, a framed painting hanging on the wall of a gallery has been the traditional form of installation over 500 years. The painting reveals us it's meaning denotatively, and we, the viewers try to find out its connotative meanings. The painting does not change at all, and whether the viewer moves his body or eyes, it does not respond. The viewer has just dug for its formal and semantic aspects through books, research papers and lectures. That is, the viewer has been eager to know about the painting, while it stands there silently. The aesthetic object has located in the simple web of the artist, the artwork and the viewer for a long time. Art historical researches are full of questions and answers what the painting tells us, how the painting is composed of, and who the artist is. Simply put, the painting does not care what the viewer sees, how the painting is understood, and who the viewer is.

S. Göbel, R. Malkewitz, and I. Iurgel (Eds.): TIDSE 2006, LNCS 4326, pp. 116 – 126, 2006.

Fig. 1. Joachim Sauter, *De-viewer (Zerseher),* 1991-1992

Fig. 2. Giovanni Francesco Caroto, *Boy with a Child-Drawing in His Hand (Ritratto di fanciullo con disegno)*, 1520, 37 x 29 cm, oil on wood, Museo di Catelvecchio, Verona

Last century, artworks have kept changing their forms continuously, and they seemed to overcome the limit of materiality as aesthetic objects. Through so called, conceptual art and minimal art, artworks minimized their hidden meanings and connotations, pronouncing the viewers' experience of an artwork. For an instance, minimalism's flag is based on the maximization of the viewer's experience of the artwork, rather than the artist's intention or message. Now the major field of an artwork is full of viewers' experiences, and the aesthetic object loses its traditional material territory.

The viewer's experience, however, has not been prominent in the visual art until the computer-based interactive artwork came into the art world. In the interactive art, 'to-see' becomes 'to-be-seen,' and then becomes 'given-to-be-seen' for the viewer. Responding to the viewer and following the viewer, the picture is now semantically and physically interactive and participatory for the viewer. That is, beyond the artist's intention, the viewer creates meanings and experiences in the artwork. This situation induces unconventional discourses on art and deconstructs the traditional notion of artwork as aesthetic object. In the interactive artwork, there are only computers with various accessories which are not just for art but for everyday life and for engineers. How can be the new aesthetic object located in the traditional aesthetic discourses? How can be the aesthetic discourse related to technological applications? To answer the questions, the interactive art is discussed in terms of modern art and its consideration. Also, technological properties are considered to create new visualized connection between aesthetic discourses and technological applications for the interactive art.

2 Intangible Pronunciation: Changing Locus of Aesthetic Object

The artwork of avant-garde in the early 20th century reveals prominent examples for changing aesthetic object.[1] The representative of avant-garde might be Marcel Duchamp's work, so called ready-made that does not use traditional art media, shifts the function of an artist, and alters the process of creating artworks. For example, photo-collage and montage are made from already published printing materials such as photographs of newspapers and magazines. Furthermore the space to show the artwork was not a traditional gallery space, but street sides or mass media.

Minimalism in the mid 20th century is closely related to the avant-garde. "Primary Structure" is an exhibition held in the Jewish museum, 1966. Extremely simplified sculptures were prominent, and the show is known to trigger minimalism. "The Art of the Real" in the museum of modern art, New York, 1968 is also an attempt to deviate the traditional way of exhibition. The exhibition highlighted "the brutally unframed character of the work in its abandonment of any sculptural pedestal in order to share the real space of its viewer."[2] The viewer can walk through objects and structures of the work, and even can sit on the artwork. The fundamental function of minimal artwork is to make the viewer experience the space and the artwork, and finally complete the work by the presence of the viewer. The artwork is not anymore an aesthetic object that the viewer beholds.

Although minimalism began with sculpture, these artworks are made of industrial products such as standard wood or acryl panels, and can be made indefinitely by anyone. Dan Flavin's work is composed of fluorescent light bulbs that can be purchased in any hardware store (Fig. 3). At this point, minimalists seem to shout, "if you like it, make it. If you want to invest it, buy it." Minimalists' slogan wakes us up, and they reconsider the art world including artist, gallery, museum and even art school. Reconfiguring art-ecosystem, minimalist moves aesthetic object to the center of the viewer's experience.

'Meaning-as-context' came out from this environment, and is theorized by Maurice Merleau-Ponty's thesis related to Ludwig Wittgenstein's text.[3] Denotative meanings are considered as limited usage like language, and connotative meanings produced in

---

[1] Avant-garde is different from modernist. The former deviates traditional ways of exhibition in space and media, while the latter takes unique themes and expressions keeping the traditional ways of exhibition and media.

[2] Hal Foster, Rosalind R. Krauss, Yve-Alain Bois, Benjamin Buchloh, Art since 1900 (New York: Thames & Hudson, 2005) 493.

[3] Maurice Merleau-Ponty, Phenomenology of Perception, trans. Colin Smith (New York: Humanities, 1974) 175.

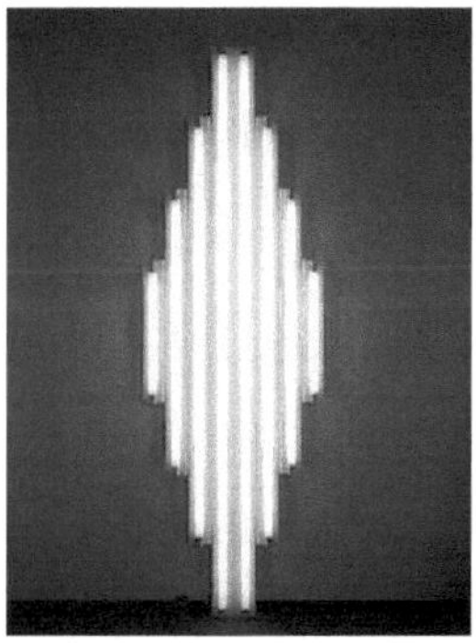

Fig. 3. Dan Flavin, *Monument for V. Tatlin*, 1968

the process of exchanging with others are practiced. Robert Morris's work is composed of three L-shape structures (Fig. 4). All structures are L-shape, but they are all recognized and communicated differently when they are put in the space differently. Meaning-as-context provides an opportunity for the artwork to take off the traditional function of an artist in the work, who suggests his intention and expresses it. The location of an aesthetic object is shifting.

Fig. 4. Robert Morris, *Untitled (Three L-Beams)*, 1965-1966

Roland Barthes's concept of text is closely related to this shifting. Birth of meaning based on difference, and play between signifier that has meaning and another signifiers are Barthes's point. He points out that text is not physical object, is subversive in the traditional classification, is experienced in the relation to sign, has multilateral plurality, is like a network, is an object through playing, and is jouissance.[4] Even though Barthes's view is focused on the changing process from literature work to text, visual artwork can be applied to the process. Barthes's discussion on text removes the distance between writing and reading, and this removal is closely related to the meaning-as-context of minimalists. It is a new way to communicate the reader or viewer to a text or an artwork.

Through the minimalist's attempts and discussions, the moved and moving locus of aesthetic object is revealed. Freeing a work from the maker and its materiality, the aesthetic object keeps changing its form and disengaging the artist's intention and the

[4] Roland Barthes, Image, Music, Text, trans. Stephen Heath (New York: Noonday, 1977) 155-164.

limited space. Intangible aesthetic object is floating over a book, a painting, a sculpture, or a structure. This aesthetic object must lose its materiality, and take its own name. Thus, many scholars call and postpone its name with 'new' in design, media and philosophy until aesthetic object finds another aesthetic 'something.'

3 New Aesthetic Object: Interactive Art and Technological Applications

After computer-based artworks came out, they have been called various name such as computer art, digital art, net art, etc. Media art can be the inclusive name including video art and later computer-based arts. Specifically, interactive art is to mean an artwork that the viewer becomes a user participating in the work itself, rather than simply interacting with a work physically or semantically. Participation indicates two sides of interactive art. Firstly, it indicates the viewer becomes an artist. The artist is not an individual, but a part of the collaborating entity. Secondly, it indicates the artwork is completed by the viewer's participation. The artwork does not produce any meaning without the viewer's experience of the work. In those two sides, the artist and the artwork, interactive art induces new aesthetic object.

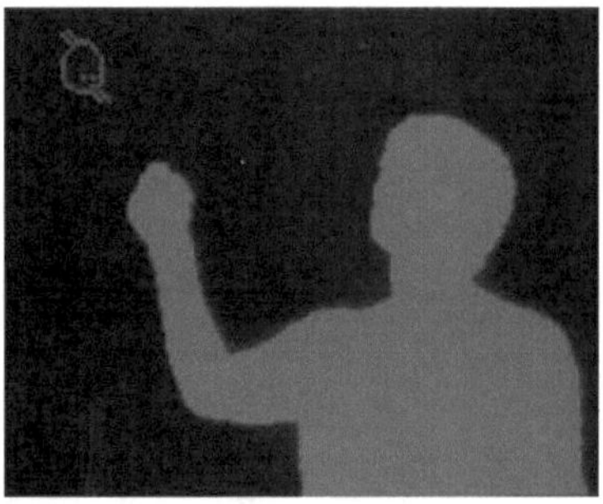

Fig. 5. Myron Krueger, Videoplace, 1969

In the interactive art, interaction between the viewer and the work is processed in real-time. PC camera recognizes the viewer and offers an interface which can transform the input image. A computer vision system provides the resolution which interactivity media system constructs.[5] The computer vision system offers the interface for the first time to the interactive artwork, Myron Krueger's *Videoplace System, 1969* (Fig. 5).[6] The system is not for simple image syntheses, but for inducing the viewer's participation and revealing the viewer's intention. It has been used for many early public performances, and the system is an early example of augmented reality art.[7]

[5] Ronald Azuma, Mark Billinghurst, Tobias Höllerer, Hirokazu Kato, Ivan Poupyrev, Dieter Schmalstieg. "Augmented Reality: The interface is everywhere," SIGGRAPH course note, vol. 27. Los Angeles, USA. (2001) 3, 26.

[6] Myron Krueger. Artificial Reality II (Reading, MA.:Addison-Wesley, 1991) 44.

[7] Ryotaro Suzuki, Yuichi Iwadate, Masayuki Inoue, Woontack Woo. "MIDAS: MIC Interactive Dance System," Proc. IEEE SMC, Oct. (Kyoto-fu, JP. 2000) 751-756.

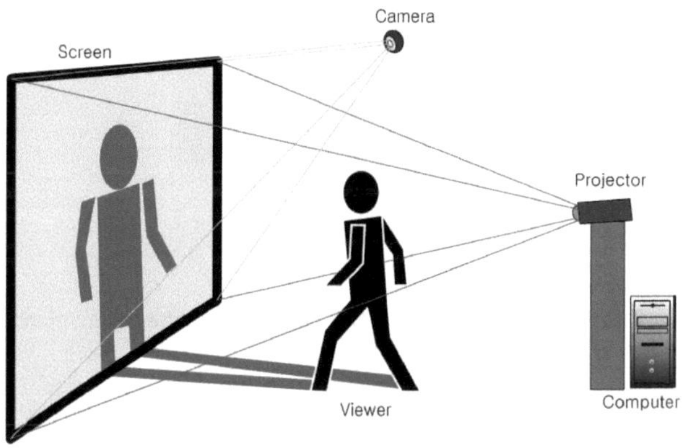

Fig. 6. The basic installation of the computer vision system for the real-time digital processing

The installation features computer projection that interacts with viewer's physical shadow (Fig. 6). The interactive artwork provides the viewer with actual feeling of reality and interaction without inconvenient tracing equipment for virtual reality such as data gloves or head-mount displays. Furthermore, the viewer can change the content of a series of images.

3.1 The Artist: Input by Vision System

In the first point, the artist in interactive artworks does not exist in terms of traditional definitions. As the relationship between the artist and the artwork has shifted through minimalism, in the process of art making, installation and exhibition, the formal and material aspect of interactive art looks different from the traditional aesthetic object. There are computer system often hidden behind the wall, big projected screen, and unknown interactive software to the viewer. There are engineers who program the software and manage the hardware. The artist's task is obscure because he does not make the work, but maybe orders it, and simply he seems to be a provider for the playground. For example, the real-time processing is composed of the following principles and practices.

The computer vision system is a part of artificial intelligence that is related to analyses of an image. In the vision system, the information is given to the computer by the camera instead of the human. The camera captures the viewer without physical contacts. The input data are classified as distinguishable elements by the system extracting characteristics or properties of the data. The fundamental application of the inverted image is used for the projection and for avoiding mirror-image (Fig. 7 and 8).

The pattern system is a recognition system that an optical signal of an object is input as data. As if we can find a friend who is talking in the crowd, or recognize his voice or face, the recognition is an important key in the pattern system. The computer pattern system can be applied easily to interactivity art by using camera. The computer pattern system offers recognition for the viewer's gesture by analyzing the image information delivered from the vision system by noticing the viewer's entering the exhibition space and touching or manipulating something in the space. The viewer's behaviors are input values when performing algorithms of new data in a

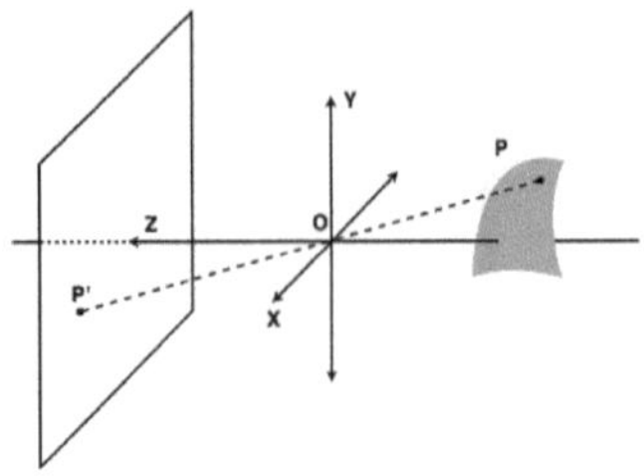

Fig. 7. The far and near projection to use the image plane

Fig. 8. A video image which supports in the CAMSHIFT

particular pattern. These series of algorithms can be realized easily by input through USB or IEEE1394 camera with software, such as OpenCV (Open Source Computer Vision Libraries) provided by Intel®. [8] The overall process of recognition is accomplished by the system, not the artist.

This process is used for understanding the viewer's motion and for providing the center location with various graphic effects. In the phase of initialization, the system finds the area of the window using CAMSHIFT algorithms that is specifically offered from open CV, and solves the operation. By choosing the center location of the window, the center of image is calculated using mean location. Then it finds the center value easily.

$$x_c = \frac{\sum_x \sum_y xI(x,y)}{\sum_x \sum_y I(x,y)}, \quad y_c = \frac{\sum_x \sum_y yI(x,y)}{\sum_x \sum_y I(x,y)} \tag{1}$$

In the above equation, the intensity value of the center location in the chosen window image can be found from the intensity value of *Xc* and *Yc* in the location of image (*x*, *y*). The center location is found using the pattern system that separates moving object as binary image from the stationary background scene.

The method that finds facial boundary or the center of abstracted binary image after separating background by difference-keying of sequential images come from PC camera, is used in the process of making the work. The system is essential for producing various interactivity artworks by using background sceneries or artistic effects recognizing the viewer. To trace motion and analyze gesture of the viewer, the system follows a process of separating the viewer from his background. The process

[8] OpenCV library, http://www.intel.com/research/mrl/research/opencv/

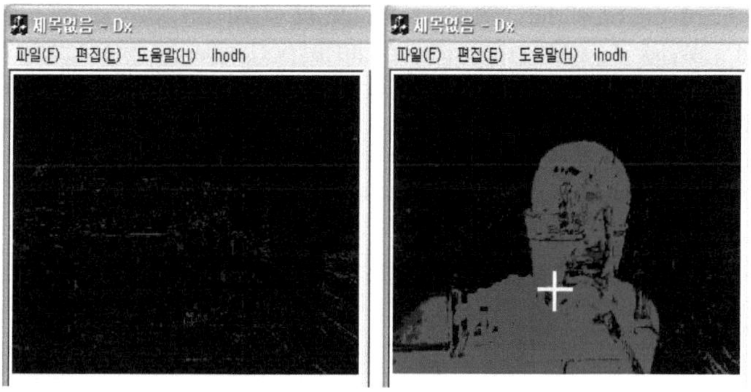

Fig. 9. The example we use the binary image, and find the center in A CAMSHIFT

is done by the viewer estimation of N(m, σ) without the background that bases confirmation from average m and standard deviation σ. Those binary images can be used for the information of distance and motion as well as color, accomplishing complete separation of the viewer from the background without blue-screen or special equipment such as chroma-key. Thus it is possible to produce natural interaction between the viewer and an object in the virtual space. The camera can be used for the invisible sensor, because the image separated from its background using the system has its own calculated information. The brightness must be considered when the viewer is separated from the background by comparing pixels in RGB system, because the camera is more sensitive to brightness than to color. Because the computer vision system is not much affected by color, the standardized color $I^k_{\{r,g,b\}}$ is defined, as k means pixel index in the below equation.

$$I^k_{\{r,g,b\}} = I \frac{I^k_{\{r,g,b\}}}{I^k_R + I^k_G + I^k_B} \tag{2}$$

In this work, the artist does not exist, but equations and their executions in the system. The interactive artwork recognizes the viewer's presence, motion, location and behaviors. This new aesthetic object cannot fit in the notion of traditional aesthetic object. In particular, the major role in an artwork is not the artist anymore. The center of an artwork is shifting from the artist to the system. Through those technical elements, recognition of the viewer is accomplished, and various responses of the viewer are input, executed and understood.

3.2 The Viewer: Image Control

In the second point, the viewer's role in the interactive artwork is essential. Without the viewer, the artwork does not exist. The viewer's presence and response are major component of the work. Furthermore, the viewer can participate in the manipulation of the image, which is totally different from the point of traditional aesthetic object. "Do not touch, but only see" would be an old fashioned sentence in our contemporary exhibition space, and today, there is a sentence in front of the space, "Please do touch."

Image control enables the viewer to interact with the image on the screen. In Jaehwa Kim's *Work-4*, 2005, the viewer can experience an interaction between his body and virtual images on the screen (Fig. 10). When the viewer moves, many floating heads are following him and gathering in his contour. Technically, images on the screen are clustered after confirming the center of image recorded by camera. The viewer experiences that many heads gather around his own body.

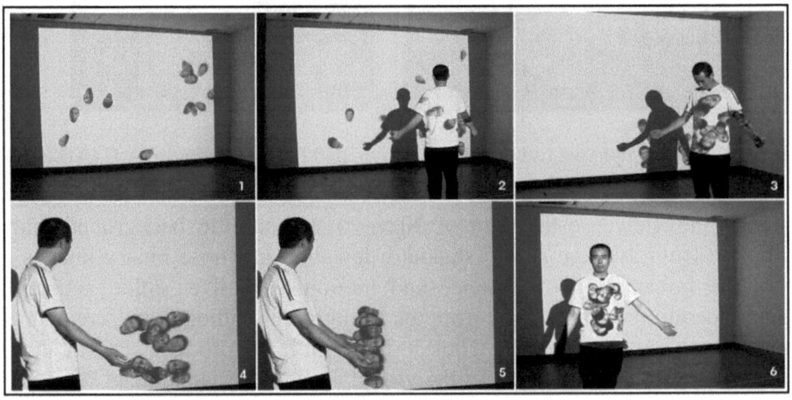

Fig. 10. Jaehwa Kim, *Work - 4*, 2005

The coordination of real and virtual space must be congruous to the interaction of the viewer. Virtual reality based on real-time processing can be constructed when the image variables that are input by the viewer's shadow, are obtained through calibration, and graphic objects for interaction are congruent with those variables. The image on screen is made by 24 frames per second using a single-computer-based system to drive the viewer's immersion considering his gesture and collision and composition of images (Fig. 11).

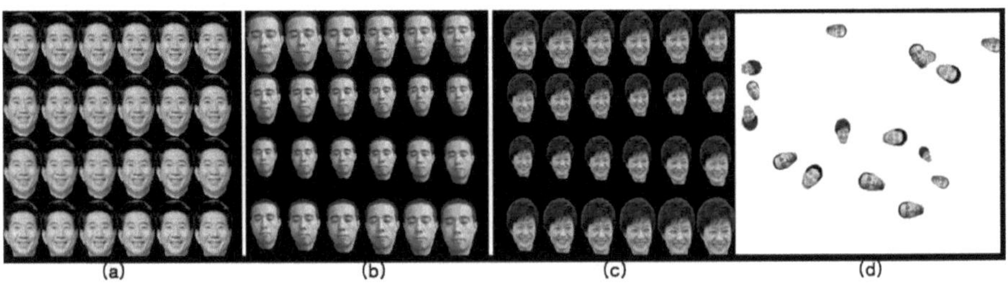

Fig. 11. (a), (b), (c) are made of virtual images, and then, (d) is shown and floating on the screen

Those images are just wandering meaninglessly on the screen before the viewer enters the space. The images respond only when the viewer enters the space, and the images gather around the center of an area that is calculated after recognizing the viewer's shadow image. The response of computer is to gather images in the center of viewer's image, but the viewer feels as if those images are gathered on his body and mixed with the body. The border line always provides an obscure interface, even though it seems to be dichotomizing cut between inside and outside, black and white, or semantically, the conscious and the unconscious. This surrealistic boundary provokes conflicts within the structure of our current society in it meaning.

Through the interactive technology, problems and discourses on real and virtual, in and out, individual and society and so on are come out. It seemed that interactive art as a genre using technologies. It, however, is that technology induces interactive art, provides environment and themes, adopts art, utilizes art, changes the artist and the artwork. Technology now becomes a mirror for aesthetic themes, and induces reciprocal influences on art. Interactive technologies convert the technology itself to an aesthetic form.

4 Conclusion: Aesthetic Technology

The new aesthetic object in interactive art should be called aesthetic technology. Using the new term, aesthetic technology, aesthetic object has to get a new and expanding formal structure. If it is recalled that the history of art has been progressed by subversive or revolutionary attempts, the aesthetic technology would be a necessary field of discourse in these days.[9]

First, the aesthetic technology reconsiders technology and art. It does not mean that the artist is the programmer himself. John Lee questions "can the computer be an artist?" And he answers that as Duchamp did "the role of the artist is entirely in implementation, since the execution is foregone," while he says, "of course, in many cases the artist is the programmer."[10] Whether the artist is the programmer, it does not matter at all in aesthetic technology. Lee keeps the traditional role of the artist, and applies Nelson Goodman's philosophical approach to art to the new media by assimilating language to computing.[11] As it has already mentioned at the beginning of this article, the avant-garde and the modernist are different. Lee, however, regards the interactive art as an art form like the modernist's work. Thus, artistic or humanistic vision comes first, and then technological matters come later. At this point, aesthetic technology does not work enough for a new art. Rather, the aesthetic technology should take the position of avant-garde, because it creates new venues (real and virtual spaces), new methods (technologies), new media (computers with accessories) and new discourses. Furthermore, it begins to include art and technology together, not as separated fields of study or collaborating (one is main and the other is sub) structures. It provides us to reconsider on art and technology equally.

Second, the aesthetic technology makes technology and art stimulate each other. From an equation, themes come out, and from a camera, gaze comes out. The real-time processing in computer vision provides multilateral views on concepts of center, margin, background, foreground, time, space, media, etc. Jay Bolter and Diane

[9] Aesthetic computing is referred by the recent book, Aesthetic Computing edited by Paul A. Fishwick from MIT Press, 2006.

[10] John Lee, "Goodman's Aesthetics and the Languages of Computing," Aesthetic Computing, ed. Paul A. Fishwick (Cambridge: MIT P, 2006) 39.

[11] Nelson Goodman, Language of Art (Indianapolis: Hackett, 1976) 255-264.

Gromala suspect the new media's transparency. They, however, consider the new media as invisible and intangible, and try to connect it to visible things and the tangibles. Then, they say, "The desire for transparency is a cultural and historical choice."[12] If it is reminded that an individual is unique, while a culture is for uniting individual's uniqueness to form a unity, the transparency is just a generalized phenomenon in an era and a space. That is, the tense for the analysis is the past, while the tense for discussing new media should be the future. Also, the aesthetic technology is not uni-directional, but undirectional. Nobody has predicted the current corruption in art. Early experimenting media artists' attempts did not have a goal, but have individual experimenting spirits. They have been stimulated by leading edged technologies at that time, and simultaneously, they sometimes influenced development of technologies, as we have already watched in E. A. T. (Experiments in Art and Technology) 1966.[13]

Technology has stimulated the artist par excellence in the age of digital media. Because of the reason that the stimulating subject is technology, for the future, aesthetic technology should be discussed in focusing technology more in depth in terms of art and technology converging each other.

Acknowledgments. This work was supported by Soongsil University Research Fund.

References

1. Azuma, R., Billinghurst, M., Hölerer, T., Kato, H., Poupyrev, I., Schmalstieg, D.: Augmented Reality- The interface is everywhere. SIGGRAPH course note, vol. 27. Los Angeles (2001)
2. Barthes, R.: Image, Music, Text. Trans. Stephen Heath. Noonday, New York (1977)
3. Bolter Jay, D., Gromala, D.: Windows and Mirrors: Interaction Design, Digital Art, and the Myth of Transparency. MIT P, Cambridge (2003)
4. Foster, H., Krauss, R., Bois, Y., Buchloh, B.: Art since 1900. Thames & Hudson, New York (2005)
5. Goodman, N.: Language of Art. Hackett, Indianapolis (1976)
6. Krueger, M.: Artificial Reality II. Addison, Wesley Publishing, Reading, MA. (1991)
7. A. Fishwick, P. (ed.): Aesthetic Computing. MIT P, Cambridge (2006)
8. Merleau-Ponty, M.: Phenomenology of Perception. Trans. Colin Smith. Humanities Press, New York (1974)
9. Suzuki, R., Iwadate, Y., Inoue, M., Woo, W.: MIDAS- MIC Interactive Dance System. Proc. IEEE SMC, Oct. Kyoto-fu, Japan. (2000)
10. http://www.intel.com/research/mrl/research/opencv/

---

[12] Jay David Bolter and Diane Gromala, Windows and Mirrors: Interaction Design, Digital Art, and the Myth of Transparency (Cambridge: MIT P, 2003) 35.

[13] Artist Robert Rauschenberg and engineer Billy Klüver established E.A.T. for the collaboration between artists and engineers, and they had a show, "Nine Evenings" in the Judson Church, New York.

SRST: A Storytelling Model Using Rhetorical Relations

Arturo Nakasone and Mitsuru Ishizuka

Dept. of Information and Communication Engineering, University of Tokyo, 7-3-1 Hongo, Bunkyo Ku, Tokyo 113-8656, Japan
arturo@mi.ci.i.u-tokyo.ac.jp, ishizuka@i.u-tokyo.ac.jp

Abstract. Storytelling models are usually constrained to the applications they are implemented in because of the particular characteristics of the data used to define story events and the way those events are linked. In order to develop a more generic model to create storytelling applications, we need to focus the solution not on the data itself, but on the manner this data, in the form of events, is organized and conveyed to the user. In this paper, we present SRST (Storytelling RST), our proposal for a generic storytelling ontology model based on the organization of events using the relations proposed by the Rhetorical Structure Theory (RST) and how narrative principles are applied to these RST relations to generate coherent stories.

Keywords: Storytelling, Ontology Model, RST, Rhetorical Relations.

1 Introduction

In a broad sense, stories are defined as "unique sequences of events, mental states, or happenings involving human beings as characters or actors" [4]. The notion of story event is defined in several ways, each one to suit a particular way to deliver the intended message to the audience. Events can be represented as plain text [8,26,28], scripted individual character actions [9], story world states [14,15,18,30], or multimedia content [5,23,31]. A storytelling model is usually constrained to a particular application due to the nature of these events and the way they are linked to one another. Most applications rely on the content of the event to describe a story, and its inherent temporal property to construct it. Nevertheless, this tight coupling between content and temporality makes it very difficult to use or even adapt the model to other domains. In addition, most applications rely on the implicit temporal relation of events to convey a narrative experience, but in most cases, this experience is predetermined, either by defining event by event sequences or by grouping events with similar space and temporal attributes and defining group by group sequences. In order to develop a more generic model to create storytelling applications, we need to focus the solution not on the content itself, but on the manner this content, in the form of events, is organized and how this organization can be conveyed to the user in the context of a narrative experience.

In this paper, we present SRST (Storytelling RST), our proposal for a generic storytelling ontology model based on the organization of events using the relations proposed by the Rhetorical Structure Theory (RST) [16] and narrative principles

S. Göbel, R. Malkewitz, and I. Iurgel (Eds.): TIDSE 2006, LNCS 4326, pp. 127 – 138, 2006.

applied to these RST relations. This model was developed as an extension to our web presentation system [20].

The rest of the paper is organized as follows. The next section will present related work on storytelling applications from the point of view of events. Section 3 discusses our approach to a generic storytelling model based on ontology classes and narrative rules. Section 4 presents the current implementation of our web based application that uses annotated data from the ontology. Finally, our plans for future research topics and a summary will conclude the paper.

2 Related Work

Even though storytelling applications were mostly oriented to text generation in the beginning, the range of applicability of storytelling has increased due to the ubiquitous presence of communication networks such as the Internet, and the availability of multimedia content. Most researchers assume a concept of "event" in order to organize the content of their applications, and, therefore, have developed storytelling engines to deliver such events using narrative techniques. Nevertheless, the algorithms implemented in those engines were selected because of the event definition they implied and vice versa.

State Transition based applications [9,14,18,26,29] define events as states that specify the current situation in a particular point of the story. Bayesian Networks, Finite State Machines, and their variations are commonly used as storytelling engines. Therefore, events must be annotated to fit the requirements for nodes in the network or machine.

In Goal based applications [6,22,32], a goal event or events are established as the final outcome of the story. From a set of initial conditions, a story is unfolded by the sequence of events that are needed to reach such goal event or events. Planners and their variations are commonly used for these applications. Due to the nature of planners, events have to be annotated with a set of pre and/or post conditions. Nevertheless, some applications make use of special narrative functions that enforce narrative principles in the context of the whole story [17,30]. Therefore, event sequencing is constrained not only by direct event links, but also by each event contribution to the overall storytelling experience.

In Template based applications [10,27,31], events are selected to fit story templates and permutated to create new narrative experiences based on those templates. Since the story template constrains which and how events are presented, these events must be annotated to determine their role in the context of the whole template. Script based applications [1,23,25,28] are a particular case in which stories are described using a high level language. The application, then, present the events in the way specified by such scripts. In some cases, narrative or dramatic effects are applied during the event transitions.

Semantically organized events using primarily RST have been used in applications that present multimedia content [5,11,13], but most of them use only a very limited set of relations. Since rhetorically structured content was mainly used for organizational purposes, these applications do not deal with the narrative implications that rhetorical relations have in storytelling-like presentations.

Even though the results obtained in these applications are impressive from the storytelling point of view, the cohesion between event definition and storytelling engine makes the task of adapting these models to other domains extremely difficult. Therefore, a model in which event definition and sequencing are separated is necessary to guarantee its generic attribute.

3 A Semantic Approach to Storytelling

Events in the world are not isolated but interconnected through some kind of relation. Even though each event itself is meaningful in its content, the relations between them are what make them meaningful in the context of a story. Semantic organization gives us not only a relationship of meaning, but also a relationship of temporality through the use of rhetorical extrapolations. This organization gives us enough flexibility to create stories, regardless of the kinds of events used.

In this section, we will present our approach to define a general ontology model for storytelling based on semantic RST relations. We will define not only how RST relations are referenced in the context of stories, but also how narrative properties are enforced by the proper use of these relations.

3.1 Story Concepts – Defining What a Story Is About

Even though stories are commonly referred to as "sequences of events", they are always developed in some particular context or around a particular concept. When we talk about stories, we need to convey to the user not only a general sequence of isolated events, but also a series of interconnected ideas that will evolve as a knowledge pattern inside our memories. Using storytelling to convey this complex mesh of ideas is what gives storytelling methods and properties their true value [7]. Therefore, to properly address this issue, our generic ontology must support a concept representation model that can reflect not only this complex organization of ideas but also a way to convey them through narrative channels.

In our model, a Concept Ontology is defined as a networked organization of nodes, which are connected through directed links. Each node is defined as a Concept or "a particular theme a story or part of it may talk about", and each link is defined as "a directed relation that defines the dependency between the two connected concepts".

When a story is fully constrained to talk about one particular topic, only one node in the Concept Ontology is referred; but when a story spans several topics, a smooth transition through the use of links between concepts ensures a fluid narrative experience. Even though links only specify a requirement relation between two concepts (i.e. the telling of one concept must precede the telling of the other), it also gives a pseudo-temporal relation since concepts are conveyed through linear narrative channels.

The main advantage of this model is that this sequenced organization of issues allows users to construct fluid and coherent stories based on the selection of a few key concepts. When a user specifies the key issues of the story, the storytelling model engine automatically selects other concepts that must be included in order to have a fluid experience.

3.2 Rhetorical Relations – Defining How a Story Is Organized

Events are related to one another with some kind of relation. From the very definition of story, we can extract the most common one: diachronicity [4], which means that events have a temporal relation between them (i.e. one event happens before, at the same time, or after another). In most cases, this attribute is taken for granted in any storytelling application and researchers have tried to enrich this temporal synchronization of events by modifying the mechanisms by which events are put one after the other.

Nevertheless, temporal relations are only one aspect in storytelling. Event temporization refers to the fact that narrative channels of communication are linear and, therefore, the only way to transmit these events is through the use of a time-sequenced pattern. In fact, stories in our minds are much more than a linear definition of events. Stories are "complete patterns that communicate a special kind of knowledge to our pattern recognizing mental module" [7]. Since these patterns are present in our minds as a web of interconnected events, it is clear that such connections deal with much more complex relations than temporal ones.

Natural text is one of the oldest ways to transmit a story and has been extensively analyzed in order to discover which rules govern its generation not only in terms of text organization, but also in terms of narrative characteristics. From a semantic point of view, rhetorical theories have provided us with the most useful analysis on which kinds of relations can be defined between pieces of text in a narrative. Moreover, it can be stated that rhetorical relations reflect not only semantic relations between pieces of text, but also between ideas, concepts, and events in a broader sense. Relations such as CAUSE (i.e. one event is the cause of another) or BACKGROUND (i.e. one event serves as background information for the other) that can be inferred from a text reflects not only the organization of those pieces of information in the text, but also the meaning that those events have in the mental story pattern of the author of such text.

In order to accurately reflect this story pattern in our model, we defined the relations between events as rhetorical. By defining only the relations between events and not the events themselves, we were able to enforce the generic attribute of the storytelling ontology model.

3.3 SRST: The Storytelling Ontology Model

Taking into consideration the conceptual and semantic aspects described above, we propose an ontology model implemented using OWL [21] that deals with the generic aspects of the storytelling construction process. The classes in this model were defined considering the many different definitions that researchers gave to their story components, but associating each class with a more general meaning that encompasses all those different definitions. Each class has a purpose in the context of story pattern organization, either to define a specific story component or a property of such component. The classes defined for the present version of SRST are:

- *Concept:* A Concept defines a specific topic that a story or part of it may refer to.
- *Event:* An Event is defined as a single piece of meaningful information worthy of being shown. Due to the generic property of SRST, an Event can specify a reference to piece of text, video clip, image, game scene, character scripts, etc.

- *Relation:* A Relation is a rhetorical binding between two entities, which states a specific rhetorical function. As specified in RST, entities in a Relation can be both Nucleuses (which is defined as a Multinuclear Relation Type), or a Nucleus – Satellite pair (which is defined as a Nucleus-Satellite Relation Type)
- *Act:* An Act is defined as a hierarchical structure composed of Nucleus and Satellite entities, joined by Relations. This class describes the minimum level of story organization in which a story may arise. An Act is a recursive structure, which means that Nucleus and/or Satellite entities can represent an Event or another Act object.
- *Scene:* A Scene is defined as a set of Acts, which are grouped in the context of a single Concept.
- *Agent:* An Agent is an actor that takes part in a Scene by executing or being part of one or more Events.
- *Role:* A Role is a part that an Agent plays during a Scene.

In the next subsections, we will explain the relations among the SRST classes and how these relations contribute to the overall story organization. The complete ontology model diagram is shown in Figure 1.

Scenes and Acts. In SRST, we made a clear distinction between semantically organized events (Acts) and conceptually organized events (Scenes). Even though they are indivisible properties for any story, this separation has been established to emphasize the fact that conceptually organized events can have different semantic organization to express, either the same content or a different content related to the same concept. For instance, if we were to define the Concept "ARRIVING LATE TO WORK", we could express the idea of this concept by using these two different semantic organizations of events:

- It was raining, THEREFORE, I missed the train (CONSEQUENCE relation)
- I missed the train, BECAUSE it was raining (CAUSE relation)

Even though we used the same set of events in this case, the relations used to join them are different and, therefore, the emphasis on which event is more important from a user's perspective changes accordingly.

Acts, Nucleuses, and Satellites. An Act represents a basic structure in which nucleus and satellite components are connected through relations. Even though SRST is flexible enough to allow an unlimited number or nucleus and satellite components connected to each other, in our current implementation, this structure is constrained to allow the definition of: (a) purely multinuclear relations of the same type, or (b) a single nucleus with one or more satellites with the same or different types or relations. This is due to the fact that we are primarily dealing with events in the form of texts to be uttered by an Agent. As more narrative domains are analyzed, other combinations in the Act structure will be implemented.

Scenes, Agents, and Roles. In every Scene, Agents are defined as character entities that either present the content of Events or take part during the execution of Events as actors. Since not every Agent can be part of every Event inside a Scene/Act, the Role

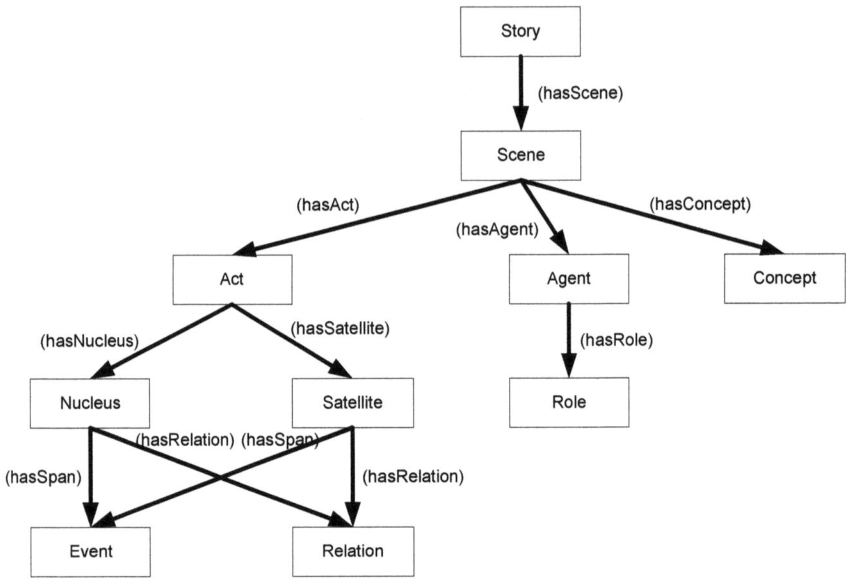

Fig. 1. The Complete Storytelling Ontology Model (SRST) based on RST relations

object is associated with every Agent and defines in which kind and on which side of relations it may intervene. Although Roleobjects depend on the kind of application in which the ontology is used, we have predefined five roles that identify and group the main characteristics of our RST relation set:

- *Questioning Role:* The Agent represents the character to which the information contained in the relation will be conveyed to. (e.g. Nucleus of SOLUTIONHOOD)
- *Informing Role:* The Agent represents the character that will convey the information contained in the relation (e.g. Satellite of SOLUTIONHOOD)
- *Contrasting Role:* The Agent represents a character that contrast information of one side of the relation with another (e.g. Satellite in CONTRAST)
- *Convincing Role:* The Agent represents a character that tries to gives a convincing explanation about the information contained in a relation (e.g. CAUSE)
- *Evaluating Role:* The Agent represents a character that states a final conclusion or assessment in a relation (e.g. EVALUATION)

We have defined the most important elements and their relations for any storytelling application. In the next section, we will define the rules by which these elements interact in order to assess narrative quality.

3.4 Adding the Narrative Component to SRST

The narrative rules defined in SRST are based on Jerome Bruner's work on narrative and its characteristics [4]. Even though SRST deals with the majority of Bruner's narrative principles to some extent, we will concentrate on the most important aspect of narrative: how events shall be put together in order to constitute a narrative, which is known as the principle of Hermeneutic Composability. The concepts and formulas proposed for SRST express the point of view of the authors on how Bruner's principles can be implemented in a computer model using RST, and should not be taken as a definite implementation guide. In future versions of the model, we will refine our assumptions using more accurate empirical information.

To address this principle, we have identified three stages in which story construction takes place: (a) Event Selection inside an Act, (b) Act Selection inside a Scene/Concept, and (c) Scene/Concept Selection in a Story.

Event Selection inside an Act. This is the lowest level of the SRST event organization scheme in which a story arises. In this level, our definition of story construction was centered in the concept of Conflict [3], defined as an imminent change on the current state of affairs. Based on this concept of Conflict, we classified our set of RST relations in:

(a) Relations that may introduce a Conflict or Conflict Relations (CONTRAST, SOLUTIONHOOD, ELABORATION, CONSEQUENCE, and SEQUENCE). Since not every Conflict Relation has the same potential to arise a Conflict, a numerical value known as the Conflict Weight Value (CWV) was assigned to each of these relations to show their importance in terms of conflict potential. The range of the CWV goes from 0 to 1, with higher values indicating higher conflict potential.

(b) Relations that provide the events to successfully resolve the conflicts or Resolution Relations.

Even though a general story is constructed around a Conflict and its resolution [3], a proper order of Conflict and Resolution relations must be defined in order to create narrative tension [17]. In SRST, we defined this order based on the assumptions that:

- Relations with low CWV build less narrative tension than relations with high CWV.
- Context and content explanations should precede results and user belief alterations to build up narrative tension.

Therefore, for each story constructed inside the scope of an Act, the following relations are to be considered in this specific order when available:

- Background Information
- Conflict Presentation. According to the CWV for Conflict Relations, conflicts will be created in a way that weaker conflict relations will be presented first.
- Resolution of Conflict, which is achieved when the information on the other side of the relation is stated. In order to build up narrative tension, relations are to be chosen following this pattern:
    - Context Explaining Nodes: Circumstance, Purpose
    - Multinuclear / Temporal Nodes (Content Explaining Nodes): List, Temporal_Before, Temporal_SameTime, Temporal_After

  - Result Nodes: Result, Cause
  - Presentational Nodes (User's belief alteration nodes): Evidence, Enablement
- Restatement or Evaluation. If both are available, the Evaluation relation will come first, since it is assumed to contain more narrative tension that the Restatement relation

Act Selection inside a Scene/Concept. Similar to the Event Selection case, Acts inside a Scene are selected in a way that they build narrative tension through the presentation of all the Acts in the Scene. To determine the narrative tension degree for an Act, we have defined two parameters that measure its tension level:

- *Conflict Resolution Value (CRV):* The CRV value is calculated based on the number of possible conflicts in the different levels of the Act structure. Conflicts that arise in higher levels of the Act structure have greater value than those that arise in lower levels. Therefore, the CRV for an Act is defined as a measure of conflict potentiality and is calculated through the following formulas:

$$CRV(A) = C_0(A) + \sum_{j=1}^{n-1} \frac{C_j(A)}{2j} \ . \tag{1}$$

$$C_j(A) = \sum_{k=1}^{5} CWV_k \times N_k(j) \ . \tag{2}$$

Where:

  - CRV(A) is the CRV for the Act
  - $C_0(A)$ is the number of conflict relations in the first level of the Act structure[1]
  - $C_j(A)$ defines a weighed value based on the total number of conflict relations in the jth level. In this formula, the total number of conflicts in each conflict relation (five in total) is multiplied by its corresponding CWV.
  - n is the maximum number of levels in the Act structure
  - CWV_k is the Conflict Weight Value for a particular type of Conflict k.
  - $N_k(j)$ is the number of conflicts of type k in the jth level

- *Multinuclear Relations Value (MRV):* The MRV value is calculated based on the number of multinuclear relations in several levels of the Act structure. Multinuclear relations in higher levels have greater value than those deeper in the hierarchy. Therefore, the MRV for an Act is calculated through the following formula:

---

[1] Given the recursive nature of the Act structure, the level value was defined to specify how deep an Act structure goes into such recursion. A zero level Act structure indicates that it is not contained in any other Act structure. Likewise, a jth level Act structure indicates that it is contained in j Act structures.

$$MRV(A) = N_0(A) + \sum_{j=1}^{n-1} \frac{N_j(A)}{2j} . \tag{3}$$

Where:

- MRV(A) is the MRV for the Act
- $N_0(A)$ is the number of nucleuses in the first level of the Act
- $N_j(A)$ is the total number of nucleuses in the jth level
- n is the maximum number of levels in the Act structure

To create narrative tension during the Act Selection process, it was assumed that multinuclear relations (e.g. SEQUENCE, LIST) inside an Act have more conflict potential due to the possibility of contrast between their components. Therefore, the order in which Acts are to be selected inside a Scene was defined by the following criteria:

- Acts with Background Information must be selected first when available. This criterion was set to satisfy Bruner's Referentiality principle [4].
- Acts with low MRV are selected before Acts with higher MRV. This ensure a narrative tension build up inside the Scene.
- If two Acts have the same MRV, the Act with the lowest CRV is selected first.

Scene/Concept Selection inside a Story. In SRST, a Story is constructed by selecting which Concepts from the Concept Ontology are to be included in it. Once the Concepts are selected, SRST calculates the optimum path through the ontology that guarantees a smooth transition between all the selected Concepts.

In extreme cases, if no path is found, selected Concepts are treated as individual stories. Therefore, it will depend on the author of the story to ensure a good narrative experience to his or her audience by providing a well defined concept ontology.

4 Current Implementation

The application to test our ontology model was implemented using .NET technology, Visual C#, and Java. It consists of 3 main modules:

Text Services: The Text Services Module is the module in charge of dealing with text processing and format conversions into the input needed by the system. Since creating the OWL text data can be a cumbersome process, this module facilitates the work of creating these files by processing LISP formatted files obtained with the RSTTool [24]. Even though the RST annotation process must still be done with this tool, the conversion process into OWL files is greatly simplified with this module.

Visual Services: This module deals with the presentation of the OWL annotated content and acts as the interface of the application.

OWL Services: This module acts as a proxy between the OWL Reasoner module (in this version of the application, a reasoner called Kaon2 [12] has been used due to its simple interface) and the Visual Services module. The OWL Services module is in charge of loading the ontology definitions and data into the reasoner, calculate the CRV and MRV values for the ontology data, and retrieve events based on the narrative rules specified by the ontology. Since this module maintains the whole status of the story at any moment, it can be deployed using any visual interface with which can establish a socket connection.

The complete application design diagram is shown in Figure 2.

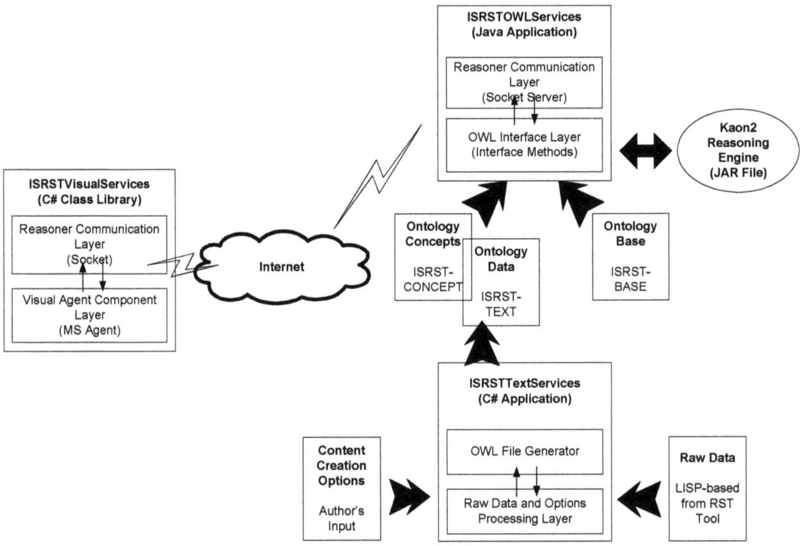

Fig. 2. Application Design Diagram

5 Conclusion and Future Work

In this paper, we have presented our proposal for a generic storytelling ontology model based on the organization of events using the relations proposed by the Rhetorical Structure Theory (RST). Even though the model was designed as generic as possible and taking into account all the different contributions from other works, there are some other elements that are part of stories that were not considered for this first version. Elements such as Location or Stage (see [10]), and Props (see [7]) will be analyzed to see how their contribution affects the narrative properties of the model.

Aside from making a complete ontology model for storytelling, our research is also focused on the interactive aspect of it. Therefore, our most immediate concern is to improve this model by analyzing how a user model can be implemented into this generic framework. Although most user model information depends on direct input received by the storytelling applications, our analysis will concentrate mostly on interaction that is non intrusive, namely, emotion recognition [19] and visual attention processing [2].

References

1. André, E., Concepcion, K., Mani, I., van Guilder, L. Autobriefer: A System for Authoring Narrated Briefings. Multimodal Intelligent Information Presentation , Oliviero Stock and Massimo Zancanaro , 143-158, Springer, 2005
2. Bee, N., Prendinger, H., Nakasone, A., André, E., and Ishizuka, M. AutoSelect: What You Want Is What You Get. Real-time processing of visual attention and affect. Proceedings International Tutorial and Research Workshop on Perception and Interactive Technologies (PIT-06), Springer LNAI 4021, Kloster Irsee, Germany, 2006, 40-52.
3. Bordwell, D. Narration in the Fiction Film. London Routledge, 1986
4. Bruner J. Acts of Meaning, Cambridge, Harvard University Press, 1991.
5. Callaway, C., Not, E., Novello, A., Rocchi, C., Stock, O., Zancanaro, M. Automatic Cinematography and Multilingual NLG for Generating Video Documentaries. In Artificial Intelligence, vol. 165, June 2005, 57-89
6. Cavazza M., Charles F., and Mead S.J. Interacting with virtual characters in interactive storytelling. In Proceedings First Conference on Autonomous Agents and Multiagent Systems (AAMAS-02), New York, 2002. ACM Press, 318-325
7. Crawford, C. Chris Crawford on Interactive Storytelling. New Riders 2005.
8. Figa, E. and Tarau, P. Story Traces and Projections: Exploring the Patterns of Storytelling. In N. Braun and U. Spierling, editors. First International Conference on Technologies for Interactive Digital Storytelling and Entertainment (TIDSE 2003), Darmstadt, Germany, March 2003.
9. Gebhard, P., Kipp, M., Klesen, M., Rist, T.: Authoring scenes for adaptive, interactive performances. The Second International Conference on Autonomous Agents and Multiagent Systems (AAMAS-03). 725-732
10. Gervas P., Diaz-Agudo B., Peinado F, and Hervas R. Story plot generation based on CBR. Journal of Knowledge Based Systems 18 (2-3), 2005, 235-242.
11. Geurts J., Bocconi S., van Ossenbruggen J., and Hardman L. Towards Ontology-Driven Discourse: From Semantic Graphs to Multimedia Presentations. In Proceedings of the International Semantic Web Conference 2003, 597-612.
12. Kaon2 Reasoning Engine. http://kaon2.semanticweb.org/
13. Little, S., Geurts, J., Hunter, J. Dynamic Generation of Intelligent Multimedia Presentations through Semantic Inferencing, In Proceedings of the 6th European Conference on Research and Advanced Technology for Digital Libraries, September 2002.
14. Magerko, B. and Laird, J.E. Building an Interactive Drama Architecture. First International Conference on Technologies for Interactive Digital Storytelling and Entertainment, 2003. Darmstadt, Germany, 226-237.
15. Magerko, B. and Laird, J.E. Mediating the Tension Between Plot and Interaction. AAAI Workshop Series: Challenges in Game Artificial Intelligence, 2004. San Jose, California, pp. 108-112.
16. Mann, W., and Thompson S. Rhetorical structure theory: A theory of text organization. Marina del Rey, CA: Information Sciences Institute, 1987.
17. Mateas, M., Stern, A. Façade: An Experiment in Building a Fully-Realized Interactive Drama; Game Developers Conference, Game Design Track, March 2003
18. Mott, B., Lester, J. U-DIRECTOR: A Decision-Theoretic Narrative Planning Architecture for Storytelling Environments. In Proceedings of the 5th International Joint Conference on Autonomous Agents and Multiagent Systems (AAMAS-2006), Hakodate, Japan, 2006

19. Nakasone A., Prendinger H., and Ishizuka M. Emotion recognition from electromyography and skin conductance. The Fifth International Workshop on Biosignal Interpretation (BSI-05), Tokyo, Japan, 2005, 219-222.
20. Nakasone A., Prendinger H., and Ishizuka M. Web Presentation System using RST Events. The Fifth International Conference on Autonomous Agents and Multiagent Systems (AAMAS-06), Hakodate, Japan, 2006, 995-997.
21. OWL - Web Ontology Language http://www.w3.org/TR/2004/REC-owl-features-20040210/
22. Riedl, M.O., Saretto, C.J., Young, R.M. Managing interaction between users and agents in a multi-agent storytelling environment. The Second International Joint Conference on Autonomous Agents & Multiagent Systems, AAMAS 2003, July 14-18, 2003, Melbourne, Victoria, Australia, Proceedings. ACM 2003. 741-748
23. Rocchi, C., Zancanaro, M. Rhetorical Patterns for Adaptive Video Documentaries. In Proceedings of Adaptive Hypermedia and Adaptive Web-Based Systems AH 2004, Eindhoven, August 2004.
24. RST Annotation Tool. http://www.isi.edu/~marcu/
25. Sgouros, N.M., Papakonstantinou, G., Tsanakas, P. Dynamic Dramatization of Multimedia Story Presentations. ACM International Conference on Intelligent User Interfaces (IUI-97), Orlando, FL, USA
26. Silva A., Guilherme R., and Paiva A. Tell me that bit again… Bringing Interactivity to a Virtual Storyteller. In Proceedings of the 2nd International Conference on Virtual Storytelling - ICVS 2003, 146-154.
27. Sobral, D., Machado, I., Paiva, A. Managing authorship in plot conduction. In Virtual Storytelling: Using Virtual Reality Technologies for Storytelling. Springer 2003.
28. Sumi, K., Tanaka, K. Automatic Conversion from E-content into Animated Storytelling, Entertainment Computing-ICEC2005, Springer Lecture Note in Computer Science, 24-35 (September, 2005).
29. Swartout, W., Hill, R., Gratch, J., Johnson, W.L., Kyriakakis, C., Labore, K., Lindheim, R., Marsella, S., Miraglia, D., Moore, B., Morie, J., Rickel, J., Thiebaux, M., Tuch, L., Whitney, R. Toward the Holodeck: Integrating Graphics, Sound, Caracter and Story in Proceedings of the 5th International Conference on Autonomous Agents, 2001
30. Szilas, N. IDtension: a narrative engine for Interactive Drama; 1st International Conference on Technologies for Interactive Digital Storytelling and Entertainment (TIDSE 2003), Germany, March 24–26 2003.
31. Wolff A., Mulholland P., and Zdrahal Z. Scene-Driver: A Narrative-Driven Game Architecture Reusing Broadcast Animation Content. In Proceedings of the Working Conference on Advanced Visual Interfaces, AVI 2004, Italy, 94-97.
32. Young, R.M. An Overview of the Mimesis Architecture: Integrating Intelligent Narrative Control into an Existing Gaming Environment. Working Notes of the AAAI Spring Symposium on Artificial Intelligence and Interactive Entertainment, Stanford, CA, March 2001

Scribe: A Tool for Authoring Event Driven Interactive Drama

Ben Medler and Brian Magerko

Games for Entertainment and Learning (GEL) Lab
Michigan State University
253 Comm. Arts Bldg., East Lansing, MI, USA 48824
{medlerbe, magerko}@msu.edu
http://gel.msu.edu

Abstract. Creating an interactive drama requires authors to produce large quantities of story content. A programmer or knowledge expert typically creates this content because they have experience with the story environment. By using an authoring tool someone with less experience with the story environment can organize and create story content. The Scribe Authoring Tool is an authoring tool that will be used to create interactive dramas. The tool will follow certain requirements to make it relevant to any story environment and will be usable enough for someone not familiar with the environment to author story content for interactive dramas.

Keywords: interactive drama, authoring tool, story representation.

1 Introduction

Authoring an interactive drama requires the author to generate a large amount of story content [9, 13]. However, the creative process of authoring content for an interactive drama typically requires an author that is both an artist (to generate the creative content) and a programmer (to encode that content in the logical representation being used, such as a partial-order plan [19], ABL [12], or plot points [9]). The creation of tools to aid in the authoring process is a necessity to make this task both more efficient and easier for authors who may not be computer programmers. Other authoring tools have been made for interactive dramas such as DraMachine [6], Art-E-Fact [8], and Scenejo [18]. These tools are lacking in encompassing everything needed for an interactive drama. Authoring tools must be robust and usable enough for them to encode their creative vision. It is for this purpose that we are creating a new authoring tool that will be independent of both game environments and story content and increase the scope of the available authoring functions for an interactive drama creator.

The Scribe Authoring Tool is the new authoring tool being used for the Interactive Storytelling Architecture for Training (ISAT). ISAT is a training architecture that combines elements of the interactive drama architecture IDA [10] and intelligent tutoring within a game environment [11]. The current instantiation of ISAT is being developed to train field knowledge for combat medic students. ISAT uses a 3D game

S. Göbel, R. Malkewitz, and I. Iurgel (Eds.): TIDSE 2006, LNCS 4326, pp. 139 – 150, 2006.

environment and takes the trainees through a story that requires them to perform soldier and medical duties while on active duty. Scribe will give subject matter experts (SMEs), who typically have no programming experience, the means of authoring relevant, meaningful interactive dramas that trainees will experience in this 3D game environment. We define requirements that are necessary for Scribe and discuss how this new authoring tool will function.

2 Requirements for an Interactive Drama Authoring Tool

To avoid creating a limited tool, we examined what makes a good authoring tool and how we could produce one that was more robust. We reviewed other authoring tools and programs to define a set of further requirements, in addition to content creation, that would have to be fulfilled.

2.1 Generality

Most authoring tools are made for a specific game environment or story setting [1, 2, 4, 5, and 15]. While these tools are efficient in their specific domain, they are not well suited for the varying and dynamic storytelling environments that are needed for interactive drama. A more *general* tool could be re-used across environments and story contexts rather than reinventing a new tool.

2.2 Enables Debugging

Debugging becomes extremely difficult when dealing with interactive dramas due to the large amount of content that they use. Interactive drama users are able to play through many different possible storylines [9, 13]. Content must be produced in large quantities with complex relationships between the various parts to allow for these variable storylines. With this larger structure comes an increase in the number of possible problems in both the system behavior and the authored content, such as poor decision making by the intelligent agent coordinating the story, redundancy in the storyline, continuity problems, or dead-ends that could affect the user experience.

It is difficult for the author to play through a large interactive drama fixing errors as they play each storyline possibility [9, 13]. Debugging of this content is typically done through playtesting the experience and observing if the correct behavior occurs. An authoring tool could help facilitate this process by decoupling the real-time experience of an interactive drama from the authored story content and agent behavior. By allowing debugging inside of an authoring tool, the author will save time by not having to switch into the story environment, and will be able to play through the story quicker, with various story navigation options.

2.3 Usability

Authoring tools are used to make creating stories easier. If the tool is hard to use and is not intuitive for a prospective author, then the tool becomes more of a hindrance than an aid. *Usability* includes ease of learning, efficient to use, tasks are easy to remember, and users make few errors while being overall pleased with using the tool [14]. An authoring tool's functions must allow the author to know what is happening by not having complex feature sets or mislabeled functions.

2.4 Environment Representation

Each story that is written for one type of environment can be similar to the others in many ways, but in different environments two stories can highly vary in game mechanics, narrative devices, or user interaction abilities. To protect against these varying environment definitions, an authoring tool will need an infrastructure to understand these definitions and have a relative representation of any environment defining these definitions. Examples of this representation include displaying map data, providing relative variables to manipulate, determining Non-Player Characters (NPCs) behaviors, etc.

2.5 Pacing and Timing

The *pacing and timing* of a story helps create dramatic feelings and allows the story to have a greater appeal to the reader by timing when information is given to them [17]. *Pacing and timing* can be crucial to dramatic development and encoding these effects is important to story representation. An authoring tool should allow an author to create timelines that bring captivating effects to their stories, which as been done in other narrative media, such as computer games, film, and literature. The tool should provide the author with ways in which to specify their stories *pacing and timing* that also adheres to the requirement of *usability*.

2.6 Scope

Interactive drama content includes: character behavior, story representation definitions, dialogue scripts, etc. and an authoring tool must cover this wide *scope* with authoring functions. This ensures that the pieces of an interactive drama can be manipulated and understood by the author. This gives one centralized tool in which these authoring functions take place.

3 Related Work

Authoring tools are used in many software developing situations as a means to generalize the software building process to make building applications easier. Authoring tools are found in PC game titles as a way for users to make their own content for the game with little or no coding [1, 2, 4]. Game genres such as Real Time Strategy (RTS) and Role Playing Game (RPG) generally have authoring tools that accompany them. There have also been tools, such as Redux [15], that show how authoring story content can be achieved for an environment such as the one in ISAT. Besides related tools, other interactive drama architectures such as Façade [13], MIMESIS [18] and IN-TALE [16] would benefit from using an authoring tool such as Scribe.

Authoring tools used for RTS and RPG games are fine examples of how typical authoring tools work in the game industry. Games like Starcraft [2], Warcraft 3 [4], or Neverwinter Nights [1] have functional authoring tools that allow users to build maps/levels, design gameplay effects, and create storylines. However, these tools are domain specific and do not have the *generality*, or *enables debugging*, for environment actions and story creation abilities that are needed for interactive drama.

Another authoring tool, ScriptEase [5], was made for a commercial game but was produced from an academic perspective. ScriptEase is used to build gameplay and storylines for an RPG called Neverwinter Nights (NWN). Again, this tool is domain specific, but ScriptEase fulfills two of the requirements discussed above, *generality* and *usability*, by generalizing actions and commands while using a simple interface.

Redux [15], an authoring tool that has influenced the design of Scribe, is used to create Human Behavior Models (HBMs) and helps SMEs create annotated diagrams that represent close quarter combat inside buildings. These models are then displayed inside a 3D environment for trainees to study. Redux however only presents linear diagrams of various tactics and models them. Scribe allows the creation of story content that will be presented to the trainee in a nonlinear way, based on the director agent's decisions (described in the following section) and trainee interaction.

Other interactive drama authoring tools, DraMachine [6], Art-E-Fact 8], and Scenejo [18], look into representing different parts of interactive dramas. DraMachine separates different story parts so that authors can work a story piece by piece. Art-E-Fact uses a directed graph approach to its stories and focuses on an NPC dialogue system. Scenejo uses a similar dialogue system, which allows the author to set different variables related to NPC actors. These variables use a dialogue database to communicate with other NPC actors. While each of these authoring tools help with certain pieces of interactive dramas, none of them bring together all of the requirements for an interactive drama authoring tool.

A current interactive drama architecture used for training, IN-TALE [16], is attempting interactive drama goals similar to our ISAT project. IN-TALE is an architecture that, like ISAT, allows the story and environment to change accordingly to how the trainee is acting. How ISAT differs from IN-TALE is that IN-TALE focuses more on the behaviors of intelligent agents and how these behaviors will make the story dynamic. ISAT focuses more on story representation and the trainee's specific action in the environment to influence a relevant storyline for that trainee. ISAT is also including Scribe as the key to help produce this story representation and manipulate how a trainee's actions will affect the story. Currently IN-TALE lacks an authoring tool for its architecture.

The field of interactive drama is sorely lacking in authoring tools for the myriad of approaches out there, much less a tool that is *general* enough to be used with different approaches. Other interactive drama works [13, 16, and 18] have architectures that would greatly benefit from an authoring tool such as Scribe. Programmers, or other knowledge experts, add time and cost to these other architectures. Having an authoring tool that adheres to the above stated requirements will work well for all of these story representation programs.

4 Overview of Scribe

Scribe is being created at the Games for Entertainment and Learning (GEL) Lab. Scribe's design is an attempt to fulfill the necessary requirements that are stated in Section 2. It is being built in parallel with ISAT and will be using a simulation environment called the Tactical Combat Casualty Care (TC3) trainer [7]; however, Scribe is designed with the intent of being more *general* than use only within ISAT. TC3 is a 3D game environment where Army medic trainees will be able to experience and interact with the content that is created in Scribe. The TC3 environment allows trainees to perform duties that will correspond to actions that a medic must perform out in the field. Work has been completed on an interface prototype of Scribe using Adobe Director. We are currently working on the core Java development of the tool for integration with ISAT and the TC3 trainer.

The hypothesis behind the ISAT approach is that interactive drama techniques can be used to provide more effective and engaging training experiences. ISAT's main component is an intelligent director agent that employs story-mediation techniques to manage the story world in response to authored story content and trainee actions. The director makes decisions based on the trainee's actions in the world and the state of the trainee skill model, which is the director's hypothesis of the trainee's aptitude in the set of skills being trained. The director can alter the environment and selects plot content to maximize the trainee's learning experience. The author can create story content and will provide information for the director to use and follow as it gives each trainee their own experience in the environment.

5 Authoring Modes

The structure of Scribe is split into three different authoring modes, each with its own functionality for producing story content:

- **Element Placement** will allow the author to view a 2.5D (shows a 2D figure but annotates height similar to a topographic view) version of the environment map. Here the author will place element pieces (defined below) on the map. These element pieces will be the dynamic content that will interact with the trainee.
- **Story Creation** is where the Author will create the storyline structure of what will occur as the trainee plays through the story. Varying levels of story detail allow the author to control different aspects of the story and its elements. Story Creation makes use of the configuration of the element pieces created by the author during Element Placement to create logical story statements from the visual map representation.
- **Debugging** will allow the author to interact with the director agent inside of Scribe. Here, the storyline can be easily navigated by the author and will be allowed to query the director as to how it will handle various storyline situations, which serves to both ensure that the story content and the director's behavior is correct.

Though this structure is comprised of three parts, Scribe allows the author to flip between these parts freely, providing a larger *scope* for an iterative design and debugging process. Changes to the story content areas are global in nature, giving the Author the ability to change the content and have it reflected in all of the areas.

6 Scribe Authoring Example

6.1 Element Placement

This example illustrates the features of Scribe and how they relate to the overall requirements described in section 2. The example involves three plot points (i.e. scenes from the story) to explain the story modes. The first plot point gives the trainee four wounded soldiers to treat. The plot point also requires eight friendly NPC soldiers (the trainee's squad) to be placed on the map as well. The plot point will have the friendly soldiers standing guard while the trainee treats the wounded soldiers.

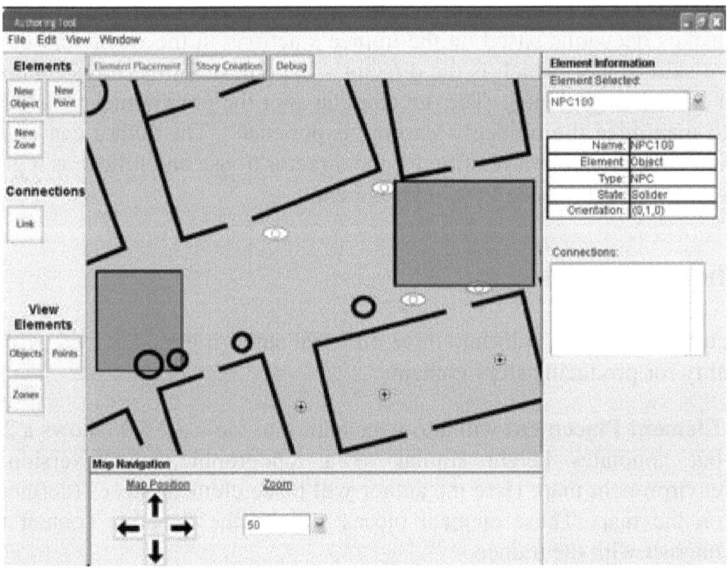

Fig. 1. Screen shot of the Element Placement window for the Scribe prototype

In this example, the author starts by creating a new project in Scribe and chooses a map where the author would like their story to take place. In terms of the ISAT project, a map is a large 3D model that is designed to look like realistic places a military medic could find out in the field. The author chooses a map and a representation of it is shown in Element Placement mode [Figure 1]. As part of the *generality* requirement, we created a XML protocol that can be used to represent 3D maps. This allows Scribe to understand any other map (necessarily ISAT specific) that is encoded in the same XML protocol. Scribe can read a map's XML file and create a 2.5D representation that will show an overhead shot of the map along with some height information, allowing the author to set elements on the map.

A Scribe element is anything tangible in the game environment that interacts with the trainee (e.g. NPCs, environment objects, or invisible elements like spawn points, which are described below). The goal of the Element Placement is to place these elements and configure them for the plot point(s) with which they are associated.

There are three types of elements: objects, points, and zones. Objects are anything that is visible to the trainee (e.g. NPCs, cars, buildings, trees, etc.). Points are invisible coordinates that exist in the game environment that can be annotated for reference by the director agent or for some use in the story. For example, a point can be used to spawn enemy soldiers at its location or to denote a point of interest to the synthetic characters. Zones are invisible rectangular prisms with dimensions that can be referenced by the director agent or used in the story. For instance, an event could be triggered when the player walks through a certain zone.

These element types fulfill part of the *generality* and *environment representation* requirements. We find that many stories taking place in a 3D environment will be able to use these three types of elements. Points and zones will allow the author to organize sections and specific locations in a 3D world. Objects will represent the tangible items that are seen in the environment. Examples of these element types have been used before in 3D game engines such as the Unreal Engine, so these representations have been generalized to fit most 3D environments [3, 9].

With the map now chosen and displayed, the author can start placing elements. For this story example eight friendly soldiers and four injured soldiers must be placed on the map according to the first plot point. Scribe allows the author to specify which type of element is being placed. To place the 12 NPCs the author turns on "object elements" and clicks on the map in the 12 spots they wish to place the NPCs. Each time an element is placed, a temporary element is created, allowing the author to annotate it with relevant information.

The author places 12 temporary object elements to represent the other NPCs on the map. By clicking on any of the temporary objects a list of variables is displayed in the Element Placement window. Each element has a set of variables that are associated with it and are set by the author. These variables are determined outside of the tool by encoding the list of variables, which the director agent understands, into a XML protocol that Scribe uses, allowing for *generality*. This *environment representation* ensures that the content is relevant to the environment.

Having set the 12 objects to eight soldiers and four casualties, the author has now completed the setup for the first plot points. As explained in the next section, each plot point has a start and end states that the elements of that plot point should be in for the plot point to begin. To set these states, the author selects a plot point and designates the current configuration as one of the plot point's states. At this stage, there are no plot points and the author must create one in Story Creation mode.

6.2 Story Creation

This section describes the design of the Story Creation mode [Figure 2], which was implemented in our interface prototype and is part of our current implementation efforts. Scribe uses plot points to describe major parts of the overall storyline, similar to scenes in a play [10]. Each plot point consists of three parts: preconditions, events, and actions, which were inspired by work done on IDA's story representation [9]. These three parts help with the *generality* of plot points because the statements in each of these parts can be relative to whatever environment Scribe is used for, as shown below.

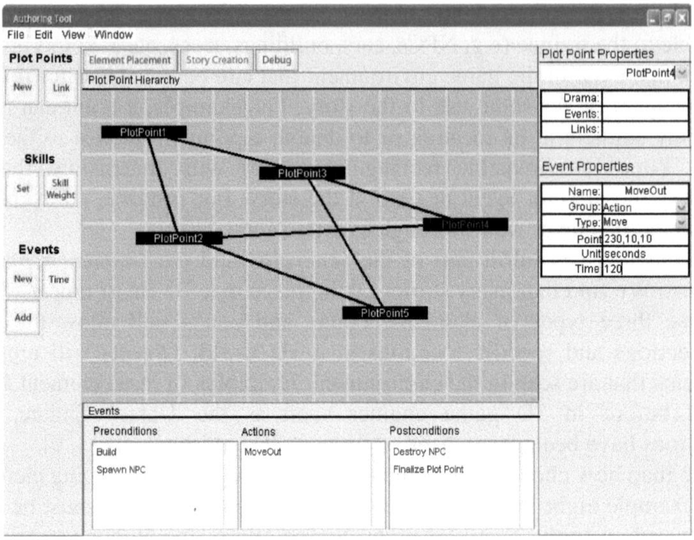

Fig. 2. Screen shot of the prototype Story Creation window for Scribe

Preconditions are logical statements that must be true for the plot point to occur. For example, a plot point precondition may state that the trainee must be in the marketplace (i.e. Location(User, Marketplace)). If the trainee is in the market place, then that precondition is fulfilled. With the preconditions and other ordering constraints fulfilled, the plot point can occur. Actions are logical statements that describe the changes in the world caused by a plot point's completion. For example, if a plot point had the trainee meet a NPC, an action could state that they have met. Finally, events are a set of statements that dictate what changes in the world occur during a given plot point. This is similar to systems such as Façade and IN-TALE that use dramatic beats [12, 16] which represent important occurrences that happen through out a story and happen over a fairly short period of time (about a minute).

Scribe events are used to temporally describe scripted, possibly temporally overlapping, changes in the environment. An event could call for an NPC to move to a new location, spawn a new enemy unit down the road, or start a dialogue that involves the trainee. Scribe allows for events to overlap one another, something IDA's story representation lacked [9], and intermixes NPC behaviors or goals in with environment commands. This is different from using ABL, such as in Façade and IN-TALE, as it focuses on NPC behavior to achieve story goals [12, 16]. However, Scribe currently assumes that NPCs are goal-based and directable. Note that Scribe has the ability to work with NPC behaviors but does not create them. The ABL language or Redux could be used to create NPC behaviors and could be imported into Scribe.

When the author switches to Story Creation mode, the map is taken away and a graph area to lay out plot points replaces it. The plot point graph area allows for the visual organization of plot points and events. Plot points can then be created or selected by the author and annotated (i.e. adding preconditions, events, and actions). For this example, the author creates a plot point and it appears on the graph area. The author then flips back to Element Placement mode and sets the initial position for the elements appearing in this plot point.

Scribe is capable of making use of a planning algorithm or relying on the author to causally connect each plot point to form a story plan. When the author sets a plot point's preconditions and actions for use in the story plan ordering and casual links are created to connect plot points. Ordering links restrict plot points from occurring until all order connected plot points occur. Casual links connect the actions of plot points to the preconditions they fulfill. This representation allows for the possibility of replanning when threats to the plan occur, as IN-TALE [16] or MIMESIS [19] would do, but will also allow the author to create the plan by hand. The representation also differs from typical narrative planning languages by incorporating the overlapping temporal events within in plot point. The representation will be evaluated after the completion of the tool for *usability*. Another option that could represent the story graph would be to use a representation similar to ABL or IDA's that has no explicit causal representation [12, 10].

All statements (preconditions, events or actions) can be set in the Story Creation window. Like elements, statements are defined outside of the tool, using a XML protocol, and are defined to how the director agent will be able to understand them. For this example the author creates two event statements, a dialogue and a conditional statement. The author can then set the variables of each event, with each event having its variables listed as part of the XML protocol.

The author adds a condition stating that after 300 seconds a new plot point will be triggered to run. The trainee may be in the middle of treating a casualty, and a new plot point could start. This does not mean that whatever the trainee was doing immediately stops, what this means is that now a new set of events will start running and may change the environment, forcing the trainee to react to these events. The author then adds the dialogue event to the example plot point, which occurs after the plot point starts and before the condition event starts. In this example an event is placed that has a soldier telling the trainee to treat the wounded soldiers.

Events need a start and end time to facilitate the *pacing and timing* requirement. There are three different types of time functions: fixed, random, and relative. Fixed time is any static amount of time, for example, 300 seconds. Random time allows an author to set a time range, zero to given number, in which a number will be randomly selected at runtime. The last type is relative time, or time relative to other events. An event could be set to start after another event ends, for example. These types provide *generality* to how time functions for events. For *usability*, each event's start and end time are placed on a linear layered timeline that is shown in a similar way to how movie editing software displays video clips.

The last thing that the author can use in Story Creation mode is the skill model. ISAT is currently used for training medic skills, such as how to apply a tourniquet. Performing skills correctly means that the trainee has a higher score in the corresponding skills. Story statements can take this skill information into account, such as setting how high a trainee's skill has to be before a certain plot point can begin. Again, skills are part of a XML protocol, for *generality*, that is read in by Scribe. In this example the author does not deal with the skill values.

So the author now has a functional plot point in this example. The trainee will be asked to treat the four casualties and after 300 seconds, a new plot point will begin. As the complexity of the story increases, the possibility of more errors occurring increases (e.g. director error, content error, etc.). In order to protect against these errors, functionality for debugging the story is included in Scribe.

6.3 Debugging Story Content

Debugging the story in Scribe will be able to save a large amount of time that would have been spent inside the environment going over the many different ways of working through the storyline [15]. What Debugging mode will allow is a direct communication link to the director, simulating how the environment will act for the trainee. The director can be queried with a given situation in the tool and gives an answer, with an explanation of why this decision was made. This allows the author to determine both the correctness of the story content and the director's behavior.

The example thus far has had only one plot point. Adding two more plot points will give a better example of how debugging will potentially work inside of Scribe. These next two plot points will introduce enemy units, requiring the trainee to react to their presence. The difference between these plot points will be based on how well the trainee is performing. If the trainee is easily treating the injuries then plot point 2 will be chosen, otherwise plot point 3 will be selected.

In Debugging mode, the map is once again presented to the author. The map will be used to display a rough version of how the elements on the map will look throughout the plot points. The trainee is also simulated, both as a unit on the map and as a skill model. This allows the author to move the trainee around on the map and manipulate the skill variables to test how different positions and skill values affects the director's decisions. The author selects a plot point to test and then queries the director about the story's events. When the director makes story decisions it will take into account: element setup on the map, the trainee's location, the trainee's skill model, etc. The author may also query the director to choose the next plot point.

For this example, the author wishes to test which new plot point will be selected next based on the trainee's skill model. The author sets the simulated skill model to show high percentages. The director should decide on plot point 2. The director, however, chooses plot point 3 stating the trainee's Apply Tourniquet skill was too low (this explanation feature is still under consideration). This could mean the author needs to set the apply tourniquet's skill value even higher, or the director may be interpreting the previous plot point's events wrong. With the director's actions known the author can go back and make the changes needed to get the desired results.

Enables debugging is one of the harder requirements to fulfill because of all the storyline possibilities that are part of interactive dramas. Debugging is scheduled to be included in Scribe but currently is still being designed. However, this feature of Scribe's design is a novel one in the field of authoring tools and is potentially an extremely useful one.

7 Discussion and Future Work

As stated before, Scribe has existed as a user interface prototype and is currently under Java development. Currently, Scribe works with one environment and one director agent. Additional environments should be easier to connect with by using the various XML protocols to allow for *generality* and relevant *environment representation*. Other representation abilities such as dialogue generation, which depend more on the architecture used with Scribe, are included in the design but how they will affect the tool is still being discussed. *Usability* of the tool has undergone internal user testing, with future external usability tests to come further into development. Events have the ability to have their *pace and timing* set so the story can be controlled to a higher degree and Scribe is scheduled to *enable debugging*. Scribe does a good job of fulfilling the above requirements and providing the *scope* needed for an authoring tool that will be used to produce interactive dramas.

The director and Scribe interactions are still being finalized. How much power the author will have over what the director can do with the story content must be determined. Also, how the director uses the story content is still under development. One example of this is whether a planner will be the best option to create the story graph that will then be used by the director at run-time.

Debugging is currently low priority on the project schedule since it is not part of the final project deliverables but it is a feature we want to add to Scribe. It is our goal to at least get test cases and a prototype interaction with the director by the end of next year. In the future, expanding on any work that is completed on Scribe's debugger, or testing other debugging methods, will be the best way to further the abilities of this authoring tool.

The ISAT project is looking at whether interactive drama could be more effective for training than by using other interactive or physical means. Scribe will help non-programmers, the real users of these tools, create superior story content. Through the definition of key areas of storyline creation, placing elements, creating the plot, and debugging interactions, Scribe will ease the pressures of creating interactive drama.

References

1. Neverwinter Nights, Atari, 2002.
2. Starcraft, Blizzard Entertainment, 1998.
3. Unreal Engine, Epic Games Inc., 1998-2006.
4. Warcraft 3, Blizzard Entertainment, 2002.
5. Carbonaro, M., Cutumisu, M., McNaughton, M., Onuczko, C., Roy, T., Schaeffer, J., Szafron, D., Gillis, S. and Kratchmer, S.: Interactive Story Writing in the Classroom: Using Computer Games. *International Digital Games Research Conference*, Vancouver, CA, 2005.
6. Donikian, S. and Portugal, J.-N.: Writing Interactive Fiction Scenarii with DraMachina. *In the Proceedings of the Technologies for Interactive Digital Storytelling and Entertainment: Second International Conference*, pages 101-112, Darmstadt, Germany, 2004. Springer Berlin / Heidelberg.
7. Fowler, S., Smith, B. and Litteral, C.D.J.: A TC3 Game-based Simulation for Combat Medic Training. *The Interservice/Industry Training, Simulation & Education Conference*, 2005.
8. Iurgel, I.: From Another Point of View: Art-E-Fact. *In the Proceeding of the Technologies for Interactive Digital Storytelling and Entertainment: Second International Conference*, pages 26-35, Darmstadt, Germany, 2004. Springer Berlin / Heidelberg.
9. Magerko, B.: Building an Interactive Drama Architecture. *In the Proceedings of the 1st International Conference on Technologies for Interactive Digital Storytelling and Entertainment*, pages 226-237, Darmstadt, Germany, 2003. Springer Berlin / Heidelberg.
10. Magerko, B. and Laird, J.E.: Mediating the Tension Between Plot and Interaction. *In AAAI Workshop Series: Challenges in Game Artificial Intelligence*, pages 108-112, San Jose, CA, 2004.

11. Magerko, B., Wray, R.E., Holt, L. and Stensrud, B.: Improving Interactive Training through Individualized Content and Increased Engagement. *Interservice / Industry Training, Simulation, and Education Conference*, Orlando, FL, 2005.
12. Mateas, M. and Stern, A.: A Behavior Language for Story-Based Believable Agents. *AAAI Spring Symposium Series: Artificial Intelligence and Interactive Entertainment*, Palo Alto, CA, 2002.
13. Mateas, M. and Stern, A.: Facade: An Experiment in Building a Fully-Realized Interactive Drama. *Game Developer's Conference*, San Francisco, CA, 2003.
14. Nielsen, J.: Usability Engineering. Morgan Kaufmann, 1994.
15. Pearson, D.J. and Laird, J.E.: Redux: Example-Driven Diagrammatic Tools for Rapid Knowledge Acquisition. *Behavior Representation in Modeling and Simulation Conference*, Arlington, VA, 2004.
16. Riedl, M.O. and Stern, A.: Believable Agents and Intelligent Scenario Direction for Social and Cultural Leadership Training. *Behavior Representation in Modeling and Simulation Conference*, Baltimore, Maryland, 2006.
17. Rimmon-Kenan, S.: Narrative Fiction. Methuen & Co. , 1983.
18. Weiss, S., Muller, W., Spierling, U. and Steimle, F.: Scenejo - An Interactive Storytelling Platform. *In the Proceeding of the Virtual Storytelling: Using Virtual Reality Technologies for Storytelling, Third International Conference*, pages 77-80, Strasbourg, France, 2005. Springer Berlin / Heidelberg.
19. Young, R.M., Riedl, M., Branly, M., Jhala, A., Martin, R.J. and Saretto, C.J.: An Architecture for Integrating Plan-based Behavior Generation with Interactive Game Environments. *Journal of Game Development*, pages 51-70, 2004.

Integrating VR-Authoring and Context Sensing: Towards the Creation of Context-Aware Stories

Dennis Erdmann, Klaus Dorfmueller-Ulhaas, and Elisabeth André

University of Augsburg, Multimedia Concepts and Applications, Eichleitnerstr. 30, 86159 Augsburg, Germany
{erdmann, dorfmueller-ulhaas, andre}@informatik.uni-augsburg.de

Abstract. Recent progress in the area of sensor technology has enabled the development of context-aware systems that are able to dynamically adapt their behaviours to the current situation and the individual user. In this paper, we present a framework for a new generation of context-sensitive stories that dynamically adapt to changing environmental conditions and user states. The framework combines approaches to interactive storytelling with work on context toolkits that foster the rapid prototyping of context-aware applications.

1 Introduction

Recently, a growing number of story telling environments are emerging that are embedded in the user's physical world and thus require more sophisticated mechanisms for acquiring context data. Unfortunately, the acquisition of context information is still cumbersome and requires a significant amount of technical expertise. Hardly any support is provided for the human author to specify context constraints in a declarative manner while abstracting from the details of the underlying context sensing mechanism. As a consequence, existing story telling systems that are embedded in the user's physical world usually rely on a limited set of dedicated context devices, such as a camera for tracking the user's motions.

In this paper, we present a framework that allows the author to specify context-sensitive stories at various levels of abstraction while providing specific support for the integration of context data that are not explicitly communicated by the user during the interaction. In this way, the author is able to specify at a high level of abstraction how a story changes considering user states and environmental information. For instance, a story may develop differently depending on where the user moves in the physical space, which objects he is grasping, the noise level of the environment, the time of the day etc.

In order to accomplish this goal, we need to provide the author with tools for the easy creation of audio-visual story elements. For instance, we may specify a story element that includes playing a complex animation sequence for presenting information to a user. In addition, tools have to be provided to specify how the flow of a story changes according to explicit user input and implicit contextual constraints. For instance, a different story element may be triggered

S. Göbel, R. Malkewitz, and I. Iurgel (Eds.): TIDSE 2006, LNCS 4326, pp. 151–162, 2006.

depending on where the user is looking. Finally, we need to account for an easy way to integrate heterogeneous context devices that gather information on the environmental conditions as well as user states.

2 Related Work

Our work combines approaches from the area of interactive storytelling with work on frameworks for the rapid prototyping of context-aware systems. In the following, we will first review work done in the two areas and then report on first attempts to enhance interactive story telling by limited forms of context awareness.

2.1 Authoring Paradigms for Interactive Storytelling

Hardman and Bulterman [Bulterman2005] distinguish between four paradigms of authoring: *structure-based*, *timeline-based*, *graph-based*, and *script-based* authoring.

Structure-based authoring is based on an abstract representation of the story. Media elements are structured in the manner they get activated. Commonly a presentation or a story is subdivided into substories and usually administrated using a document hierarchy or a document tree. An example of a structure-based authoring approach includes the narrative prose generator by Callaway and Lester [Callaway2002].

The *timeline-based* paradigm is based on an explicit ordering of media assets along a time axis. An example of a timeline-based approach includes the work by Pinhanez and Bobick [Pinhanez1998]. The basic idea is to associate actions and states of the user as well as of the system with temporal intervals. Programming interactive environments is then accomplished by establishing temporal constraints between these intervals.

The *graph-based* approach relies on directed graphs to describe the flow of an interactive multimedia presentation. An example for a graph-based approach includes the work by Gebhard and colleagues [Gebhard2003] who presented a toolkit called SceneMaker for authoring interactive performances with embodied conversational agents. First, the scene flow is modelled by means of a cascaded finite state machine in which states refer to scenes with characters. Second, the content is provided which has been either pre-scripted by a author or is generated automatically on-the-fly using a plan-based approach.

Finally, *script-based* approaches allow the user to specify multimedia presentations in a procedural manner. A prominent example includes the scripting language Lingo included in Macromedia Director or the authoring language LUA which has been used in a number of commercial game applications (such as World of Warcraft). Furthermore, a number of dedicated mark-up language have been developed to direct the verbal and non-verbal behaviour of animated agents. Usually, the approaches focus on the specification of the behaviours of single agents or a group of agents. There is hardly any approach that explicitly deals with reactive behaviours. An exception is the work by Nischt and colleagues [Nischt2006] who present a new mark-up language that relies on a reactive model which is able to handle interaction-rich scenarios with highly realistic 3D characters. Based on the reactive model, a scenario has been implemented that relies on eye tracking technology to monitor the user's focus of attention and adapt presentations accordingly. While their approach facilitates the creation of interactive stories, no mechanism is provided to easily integrate context information, however.

2.2 Context Aware Systems

The approaches discussed above allow the author to specify interactive stories at a high level of abstraction. However, they do not provide the author with the possibility to easily access context information. Context factors may refer to user states, for example his or her emotions, but also to environmental factors, such as temperature or luminosity. Context aware systems are able to dynamically adapt their behaviour to changing circumstances without explicit user interaction by continuously sensing and interpreting data from the user's environmental context.

Work done in the area of context-sensitive systems aims at the development of tools to foster rapid prototyping of context-aware applications. A prominent example includes the context toolkit by Dey [Salber1999] which is based on the widget principle. On the analogy of GUI widgets, context widgets provide a declarative interface for sensor hardware by abstracting from the details of context sensing. The context widget principle enables the easy exchange of widgets that provide the same kind of context information. For instance, we may exchange an RFID widget with a camera widget to get information on the position of objects in the physical environment. Furthermore, there is support for interpreting and aggregating context data.

2.3 Storytelling in Mixed Reality

There are also first approaches to create stories within a physical space which are of high interest to our own work because of the need to integrate context information. An example includes the approach by Romero and colleagues [Romero2004] who presented a hypermedia model that includes references to media elements, objects and relations between locations in physical and virtual worlds. Cavazza and colleagues [Charles2004] developed a mixed reality story telling environment which puts the user both in the role of an actor and a spectator by inserting the users video image in a virtual world that is populated by synthetic agents. The user interacts via natural language and gestures that are mirrored in the user's video image. The DART system of MacIntyre et al. [MacIntyre2004] has been developed to enable designers to work with Augmented Reality (AR). Many additional behaviours and actions are incorporated into Macromedia Director in order to access sensor data for Augmented and Virtual Reality, and to easily set up a new AR application. As a result, designers can work in the way they are accustomed to by using the timeline paradigm of Macromedia Director and predefined AR functionality provided by the DART framework. Unfortunately, the DART framework is limited to the performance and to interfaces of Macromedia's Director. Additionally, context is only provided by tracking sensors whereas a general concept for processing context information is not given.

2.4 Concluding Remarks

It is important to note that many approaches do not just rely on one authoring paradigm. For example, the graph-based approach by [Gebhard2003] may be combined with a planning approach that includes elements of structure-based authoring. For our purpose, the combination of a graph-based approach with a scripting approach seems most appropriate since it allows for a flexible way of integrating context information.

No authoring support is provided that enables both the specification of the content and flow of an interactive story as well as the easy integration of heterogeneous context devices. Our work aims at closing this gap by combining work done in the area of interactive story telling and work done in the area of context toolkits.

3 Overview of the ACOSAS System

The development of ACOSAS (**A** **CO**ntext **S**ensing **A**uthoring **S**ystem) was driven by our plans to focus on interactive story telling in highly dynamic and unpredictable articifical and natural environments. ACOSAS was designed to access context information from the user's physical environment and to fuse real with virtual context. The bulk of ACOSAS functionality comes from a collection of context data provided by different sensors in the environment which can be accessed at any time. Additionally, since authors often do not have working sensors in physical environments or alternatively want to simulate future sensor technology during the prototype stages, ACOSAS enables "Wizard of Oz" simulation similar to Dow et al. [Dow2005]. In order to provide informal content, ACOSAS enables us to import 3D content from commercial design tools, such as 3D Studio Max and Blender, and provides methods to access this data. Most of ACOSAS is implemented in an interpreted scripting language (LUA), and can be modified by authors and storytellers to suit their needs, e.g., to support a new sensor device. Due to performance improvements needed, we decided to develop ACOSAS instead of using Macromedia Director, the defacto standard for multimedia content creation. Additionally, we are not limited to the restrictive programming interface of Director. As a consequence, we gain higher flexibility when integrating novel research ideas using a low level programming language such as C++. Furthermore, we can easily support a manifold of sensors and new output devices with stereoscopic rendering and asymmetric viewing frustums. Advantages in regard to latency of transmitted sensor and tracking data can be measured. With respect to augmented reality applications, the ACOSAS system should allow authors to specify complex relationships between the physical and the real world.

3.1 System Design

The ACOSAS framework as depicted in Figure 1 contains a story engine executing an authoring file, a library with predefined actions, and a server collecting the data of real and simulated sensors. Client modules implemented in JAVA and

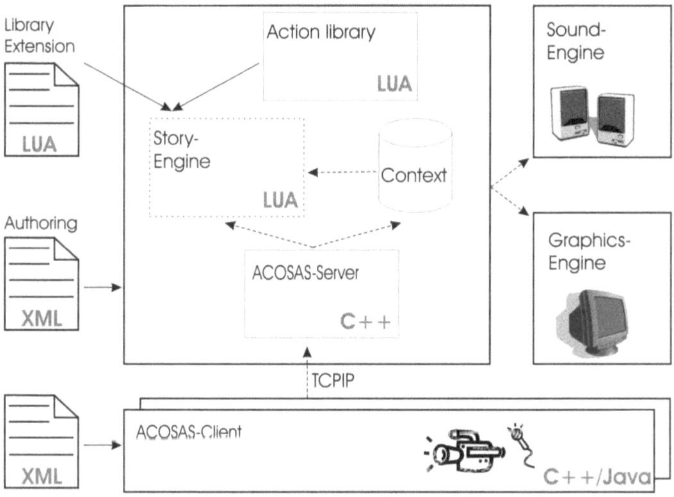

Fig. 1. Overview of the ACOSAS system. The core of ACOSAS is given by the interpretation of a graph-based authoring *XML*-file. The story engine converts this story content into a queue of invoked actions. Actions as defined by the action library are used to retrieve context data or to apply dynamic changes of the scene. In case, provided actions do not satisfy the needs of the author, additional scripted LUA functions can extend the functionality of ACOSAS. Last but not least, supporting a new sensor device requires the implementation of a client and the specification of client and event properties.

C++ are available and can be adjusted to easily support new sensor devices. Furthermore, the ACOSAS framework includes a sound and a graphics engine for rendering the audio-visual scene while the story engine is responsible for the synchronisation of the graphical animations and sound replay. The ACOSAS system additionally includes a database to store context information deliverable on request during runtime. Alternatively, for immediate and continuous requests the ACOSAS server is able to invoke a callback function defined by the author.

3.2 Context Modules

We make use of a client-server architecture in order to permit multiple clients to access sensor data concurrently that are gathered by a context server. This approach fosters not only the re-use of sensors, but also relieves the basic ACOSAS system from time-consuming operations.

ACOSAS-Client: ACOSAS clients collect contextual information recognized by specific sensor hardware and forward it to the context server using the local area network (TCP-protocol). To enable access to heterogeneous context devices, ACOSAS includes three basic modules to acquire context information: (1) a Java module to connect Java-based or Java-prepared hardware to the system, (2) a

C++ module with analogous functions and (3) a standalone client mainly used for non-changeable console programs, debugging, and Wizard of Oz simulation.

ACOSAS-Server: The counterpart of the clients, the server, waits for context registration on the pre-specified TCP-port. When noticing that a new context client tries to connect to the system, the server checks all parameters and verifies the data type. In case no error has occurred, the client will receive an acknowledgement. Context data transmitted by several context clients are processed by the server following the context widget principle introduced by Dey [Salber1999]. After receiving data from the context clients, the context server updates the information in the corresponding context widget. Information stored in context widgets may be further interpreted and aggregated. For instance, temperature and luminosity data may be transformed into higher level weather descriptions, such as "sunny hot day".

4 Authoring Context-Sensitive Stories

Following Gebhard and colleagues [Gebhard2003], we model the flow of a reactive story by means of cascaded finite state machines. The nodes of the finite state machines correspond to story elements while the edges represent transitions between story elements. We distinguish between the following kinds of transition:

- *Spontaneous transitions* do not underlie any constraints and may always be performed. They have the lowest priority of all transitions.
- *Conditional transitions* are performed only if the corresponding conditions are satisfied. In case the condition is not satisfied or information to verify the condition is missing, no transition is performed.
- *Context-sensitive transitions* are performed only if the corresponding context conditions are satisfied. In case the required sensory information is missing, no transition is made. Context-sensitive transitions have the highest priority.

In order to illustrate our concepts, we first present a single story node with a conditional transition, and then give an example of a small story including all three transition types.

Figure 2 shows a graphical representation of a single story node specified by the author in XML notation. To categorize the story node, the declaration includes a name. The name of a story node and its parameters define the type of the story node. A unique identifier id enables references to the story node. Using the sub-level identifier sub, we may group story nodes and thus define modules for a part of a story. The action tag is used to denote a function either specified in the action library or given by an additional LUA file, written by the author of the story (compare file Library Extension shown in Fig. 1). Parameters of this function are specified by the param tag while parameters are named references to geometry, sound or animation data referred in the header of the authoring XML file. A type tag is introduced to specify the type of transition tracing. In case of single, the story node is visited only once, in contrast to the statement multiple.

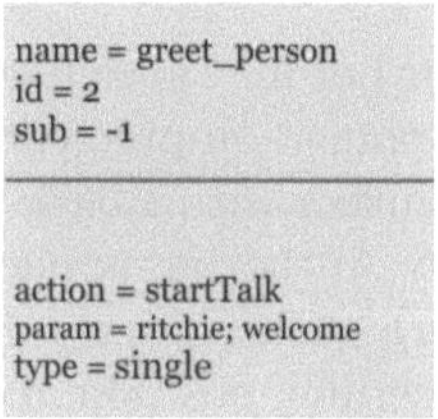


```
<storynode name="greet_person"
    id="2" sub="-1"
    action="startTalk"
    type="single">
    <param>ritchie</param>
    <param>welcome</param>
    <transition destination="3"
                type="condition"
                name="none"
                condition="end"
                value="none"/>
</storynode>
```

Fig. 2. A story node in the ACOSAS-System contains properties for naming and grouping story nodes, a story action to invoke, and transitions defined in child tags of the XML-node. Left: Graphical representation of a story node. Right: The corresponding XML file.

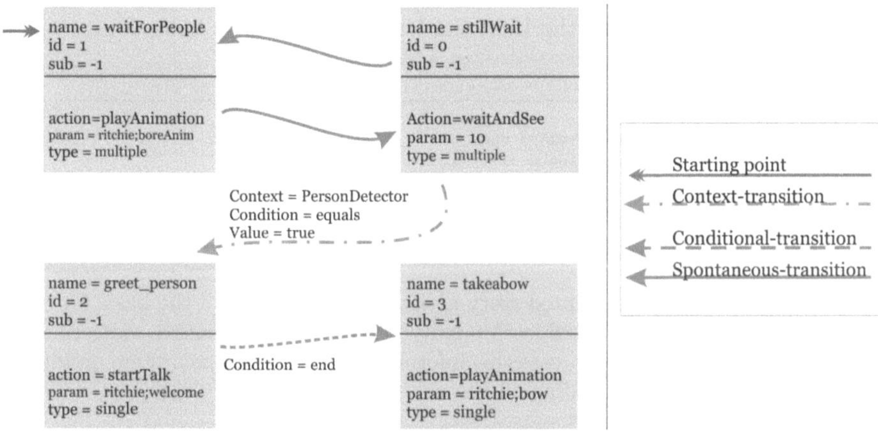

Fig. 3. Story scheme - example of a valid story flow using the three available transitions. (Orange/lined arrow = spontaneous transitions; blue/dotted arrow = conditional transitions; green/dotted-lined arrow = context transitions).

Figure 3 shows the representation of an XML defined story which illustrates the categories of valid transitions. This story begins with a character (compare parameter reference ritchie) who appears to be bored because nobody is close to the screen. After playing the corresponding animation file, the virtual character performs a "wait and see"-action for ten seconds. After looking around, it falls back to the "being bored"-state if still no person to interact with it is close to the setup. In case a sensor (e.g. an optical sensor) detects a person in front of the screen, the specified condition is activated and the character welcomes the detected person. In case of an end flag which is emitted if a story node and each of its sub nodes is processed, the character takes a bow.

5 Flexibility of the ACOSAS System

In the following, we briefly sketch how an experienced author may specify a story by enhancing the basic repertoire of story actions and transition predicates. To facilitate the creation of a story, ACOSAS provides the author with a basic repertoire of VR actions, which can be found in nearly every Authoring application. It includes methods for manipulating the virtual camera position and rotation, methods for modifying objects included in the VR, concerning position, rotation and animation, and methods for modifying global scene properties (e.g. light position). To create a new story, the author has the possibility to define a new LUA scripted method using the library extension file (cf. Fig. 1).

For illustration, let us have a look at a simple LUA script. Let us assume that we have access to a sensor which detects the environmental noise level. In case the environmental noise is high, the user may have problems to understand a pure verbal presentation. Therefore, the system would give a higher preference to graphics. Figure 4 shows the LUA-implementation of this behaviour.

```
function chooseModality()
if(contextPresent("NoiseLevel")) then
  noiseLevel = context["NoiseLevel"].value
  if(noiseLevel == "high") then
    preferModality("Graphics")
endif
end function
```

Fig. 4. Example of a LUA scripted story action in order to extend the basic functionality of the ACOSAS-system. chooseModality() verifies if the context, detecting the noise level, is present or not. In case this information is present, the system decides on a presentation modality depending on the noise level.

Furthermore, we have the option of defining new context-related actions that are triggered by sensor data (Callback functions). For example, an action `setVirtualUserPosition` as shown in Fig. 5 is triggered whenever the specified sensor detects a movement of the user and adjusts the position of the camera in the VR scene.

```
function setVirtualUserPosition(parameter)
    local userPosX = parameter[1]
    local userPosY = parameter[2]
    -- knowing that the tracking system provides the real position of the user
    -- with origin centred to the screen the story engine calculates the
    -- camera movement directly from the retrieved tracking values.
    Cam.Pos.x = Cam.Pos.x + (scale * userPosX)
    Cam.Pos.y = Cam.Pos.y + (scale * userPosY)
end
```

Fig. 5. Example of context triggered action. Using a context module specifying `setVirtualUserPosition` as their *context method* this code is executed each time new context data is available. Keeping the example simple no rotation is integrated.

6 Application Scenarios

In order to evaluate the ACOSAS approach, we have designed and implemented a couple of application scenarios relying on different kinds of sensor hardware. For the purpose of this paper, we only describe simplified versions of the applications to demonstrate how context information influences the flow of a story.

6.1 VR Tourist Guide

The VR Tourist Guide Ritchie provides the user with information on the city of Augsburg as a preparation for a real visit on the same day. As soon as a user has approached the screen, Ritchie engages in small talk before starting with the actual tour. The first stop is the Mayor's Hall. Ritchie adapts his presentation to the number of persons, the gender distribution as well as the current weather conditions. For example, if the weather is unpleasant, he keeps the presentation of the architectural features rather short and suggests to move inside the building instead. This application is realized using the following context modules:

- *person recognition:* A system which recognizes whether a person is standing in front of the screen using a camera positioned at the ceiling.
- *gender recognition:* This module finds out the gender distribution of the audience by employing techniques from [Vogt2006].
- *temperature module:* A system that acquires the present temperature value. In case a hardware temperature sensor is not available, the temperature is taken from an internet web service.

Fig. 6. A screen shot of the VR-Tourist guide application showing the guide Ritchie standing on the town hall square of Augsburg

Fig. 7. The constellation of the second application showing two displays with different characters and the head tracker. Depending on which display the user is focusing the story continues differently.

6.2 Guiding Presentations by Tracking the User's Attention

The second application serves to demonstrate how the user's head movements may be used to influence the continuation of a story.

The setup of this application (cf. Fig. 7) consists of two displays and one head tracker to recognize the head position and rotation of a person sitting in front of the monitors [Morency2002]. In this application the head tracker is the only context provider.

The character Ritchie who appears on the left screen aims at informing the user about the newest developments in information technologies while Tina who is displayed on the right screen is rather interested in informing the user about the latest gossip. Depending on which screen the user is looking at, the corresponding character starts talking. If the user shifts her attention to the other screen, the presenter will have to give the turn to the other character.

6.3 Augsburg City Run

Augsburg City Run is an immersive game which enables the user to navigate through a crowd via movements of his head. While the user moves in front of a 3D projection screen, he is wearing shutter glasses enabling a 3D impression (cf. Fig. 8). Virtual characters autonomously move through the inner city of Augsburg. The user's task in this game is to catch a specific pedestrian, but to avoid hitting others in a crowd within a close time limit. The player controls the continuation of his journey only by moving his upper body.

An optical tracking system recognizes markers attached to the player's shutter-glasses and is thus able to capture the player's movements. Context data in this

Fig. 8. The application Augsburg City Run. The user interacts with the VR-Environment only by head movement.

application include information on the user's head position. The system transmits positional changes in order to perform an adaption of the viewing perspective.

The impression of immersion is achieved by combining the optical tracking system with the navigation control and a special 3D projection system that adapts itself dynamically to the viewpoint of the user in front of the projection screen. This feeling is enhanced by 3D sound effects.

7 Conclusion

In this paper, we have presented a framework that allows an author to easily integrate context constraints that may relate both user states as well as environmental information into a story. In this way, contextual circumstances continuously influence a story at runtime. ACOSAS fosters the development of a new generation of story telling systems that allow for richer user interactions by taking into account the user's environmental context. Our approach bears many similarities with Gebhard's scene maker, but enhances it by mechanisms to easily access context information. Finally, we have presented a number of applications that have been developed using the ACOSAS framework.

References

[Bulterman2005] D. Bulterman, L. Hardman, *Structured Multimedia Authoring*, ACM Trans. Multimedia Comput. Commun. Appl. (2005) 89 - 109

[Charles2004] F. Charles, M. Cavazza, S. J. Mead, O. Martin, A. Nandi, X. Marichal, *Compelling experiences in mixed reality interactive storytelling*, Proceedings of the 2004 ACM SIGCHI International Conference on Advances in computer entertainment technology (2004) 32 - 40

[Dow2005] S. Dow, J. Lee, C. Oezbek, B. MacIntyre, J. D. Bolter, M. Gandy, *Wizard of Oz interfaces for mixed reality applications*, CHI '05: CHI '05 extended abstracts on Human factors in computing systems, ACM Press, New York, USA, 2005, 1339 - 1342

[Gebhard2003] P. Gebhard, M. Kipp, M. Klesen, T. Rist, *Authoring scenes for adaptive, interactive performances*, AAMAS '03: Proceedings of the second international joint conference on Autonomous agents and multiagent systems (2003) 725 - 732

[Callaway2002] C. B. Callaway, J. C. Lester, *Narrative prose generation*, Artif. Intell., 139(2), Elsevier Science Publishers Ltd., 2002, 213 - 252

[MacIntyre2004] B. MacIntyre,M. Gandy,S. Dow, J. D. Bolter, *DART: a toolkit for rapid design exploration of augmented reality experiences* In Proceedings of the 17th Annual ACM Symposium on User interface Software and Technology (Santa Fe, NM, USA, October 24 - 27, 2004). UIST '04. ACM Press, New York, NY, 197 - 206

[Morency2002] L.-P. Morency, T. Darrell, *Stereo Tracking using ICP and Normal Flow*, Proceedings Int. Conf. on Pattern Recognition, 2002.

[Nischt2006] M. Nischt, H. Prendinger, E. André and M. Ishizuka, *MPML3D: a Reactive Framework for the Multimodal Presentation Markup Language*, Intelligent Virtual Agents: 6th International Working Conference, IVA 2006, 2006.

[Pinhanez1998] C. Pinhanez and A. Bobick, *Human Action Detection Using PNF Propagation of Temporal Constraints*, Proceedings of IEEE Conference on Computer Vision and Pattern Recognition , Santa Barbara, CA, June 1998.

[Romero2004] L. Romero, J. Santiago, N. Correia, *Contextual information access and storytelling in mixed reality using hypermedia*, Comput. Entertain. (2004) 12 - 12

[Salber1999] D. Salber, A. K. Dey, G. D. Abowd, *The context toolkit: aiding the development of context-enabled applications*, CHI '99: Proceedings of the SIGCHI conference on Human factors in computing systems (1999) 434 - 441

[Vogt2006] T. Vogt, E. André, *Improving Automatic Emotion Recognition from Speech via Gender Differentiaion*, Proc. Language Resources and Evaluation Conference (LREC 2006) , 2006

U-Create:
Creative Authoring Tools for Edutainment Applications

Sebastian Sauer[1], Kerstin Osswald[1], Xavier Wielemans[2], and Matthias Stifter[3]

[1] ion2s – buero fuer interaction, Ober Ramstädter Straße 96b,
64367 Darmstadt – Mühltal, Germany
{sebastian.sauer, kerstin.osswald}@ion2s.com
[2] Alterface, 8 chemin des étoiles, 1348 Louvain-la-Neuve, Belgium
xavier.wielemans@alterface.com
[3] Vienna University of Technology, Karlsplatz 13, 1040 Wien, Austria
stifter@matthias.as

Abstract. The U-CREATE project aims at efficient content creation for new technologies, in particular interactive setups, Mixed Reality experiences and location-based services. A graphical authoring tool is developed to allow one to create elaborated contents in a fast and easy way. The present paper introduces the tool and elaborates on its main components, which allow the user to author an interactive story and also to manage the connected interaction devices.

Keywords: Authoring, Content Creation, Digital Storytelling, Edutainment, Mixed Reality, Mobile Learning, Location based Services, Editors.

1 Introduction

Not many content creation platforms are simultaneously targeting Augmented Reality (AR) and Mixed Reality (MR) applications, as well as conventional multimedia authoring. The predominant approach for authoring applications is time based (Dart [1]) and fewer are based on hierarchical (concurrent) state machines, like the prototype implementation of the U-CREATE[1] project, which allows the author to realize the applications with much less effort than conventional approaches.

Comparison and analysis of different approaches have shown, that the need for describing and creating interactive multimedia and AR/MR applications could not be covered be either the UML 2.0 standard [2,3] or others [4]. Especially the need for a general description language, which works at the base for the different target runtime platforms with their different scripting dialects, is a central issue of the described authoring and content creation system.

In the scope of the U-CREATE project, the goal is to provide an authoring tool for existing interactive technologies, which nowadays still require programming at

[1] U-CREATE is a CRAFT project funded by the European Commission under reference COOP-CT-2005-017683. For more details, one can consult http://www.u-create.org

S. Göbel, R. Malkewitz, and I. Iurgel (Eds.): TIDSE 2006, LNCS 4326, pp. 163 – 168, 2006.

code level. The authoring therefore pursues two goals: first, to increase competitiveness by significantly shortening production time (50% reduction of integration time) and effort (creation process affordable to non-specialists) for content development; and second to enable non-programmers to create contents for the intended systems.

Far from the latest considerations in interactive storytelling such as emergent simulated dialogues, the project aims at developing an authoring system that will allow anyone to create interactive stories that are experienced through mobile devices, VR trackers or gesture-based camera interfaces. In contradiction with [5], it intends to do so for anyone, not only people with "ability to program".

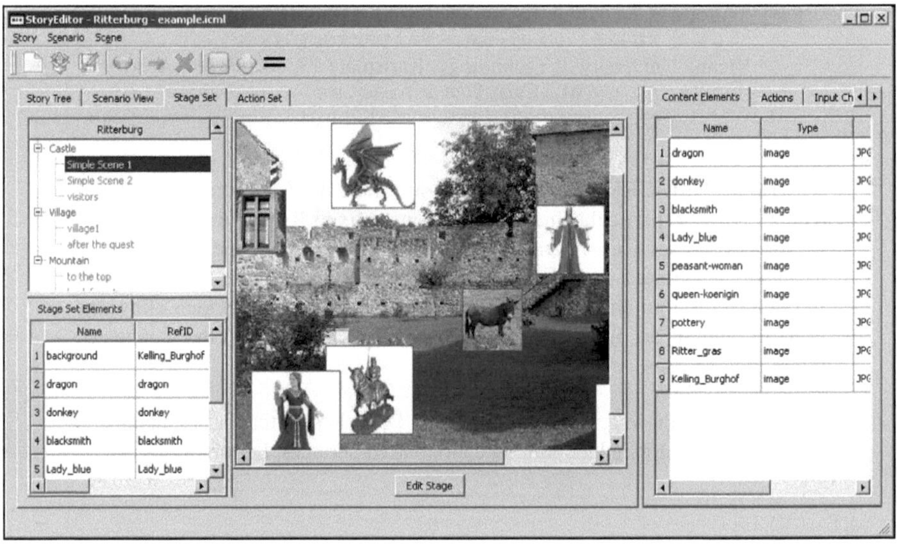

Fig. 1. Story Editor (Preview)

For the present purpose, the need is to create elements (e.g. content, actors, artifacts, stages or objects), arrange them into relations and embed them together in the scenes of a user-controlled interactive story. The authoring process has therefore been organized around four editors, which are linked together in a unified interface:

- The interactive story itself is managed as a hierarchical stage graph edited in the S*tory Editor.*
- The various scenes, which constitute the story, are edited within the S*tage* E*ditor*, which provides a layout representation of these.
- The transition conditions between the story scenes and the actions that take place in the scene are defined in the A*ction Editor.*
- Finally, the *Input Wiring Editor* allows the user to define the exact use of the external devices to experience the story and how these are linked to the defined actions.

The following sections elaborate on the two major interfaces, the Story and Stage Editors while presenting the concepts on which the developed prototype relies.

2 Story Editor

The Story Editor is the authoring interface for the structural model of the story: it organizes its structural elements and presents them in different views.

2.1 Structural Elements

Story. It is the root node of each story space, including the whole installation that has to be realized. The entire story structure, all media elements, input channels (i.e. devices), and actions are parts of it. A Story includes one story tree, composed of all scenes, but can have more than one scenario.

Scene. It is logical part of the story, a state of the story graph, an entity that encapsulates certain media elements and actions and defines a chapter of the story. Complex scenes may contain other scenes, while simple scenes do not.

Scenario. A scenario defines a specific way to perform a story. It is an executable version of the story graph, typically defining a constrained path through the scene space. Examples could be "short version", "guided tour for 1st floor", or "directors cut". Scenarios are a useful concept to design different variants of a story, and support concepts like shortcuts in the story flow.

Transition. This is a state change of the story, a switch from one scene to another. The transition is always related to some kind of condition, including an "empty" default condition that applies when the scene is at its end (all actions finished).

Action. The "atomic" performing primitive within a story is an action. It describes what a content element "does", or where and how it is presented in the performance. If actions are combined with some media element, it can mean for instance to start or stop the element (e.g. play video clip XYZ). Additional non-media action types can be switches, bifurcations, synchronizers, and transition triggers.

Action Set. A group of actions and their connections (sequencing and/or conditional jumps) is called action set. It is enabled within the same state (scene), and working on the same set of media elements (stageSet) within a scene. It describes a set of performance primitives and their temporal and conditional relationships. Action sets include a description of possible (valid) user input events.

StageSet. A stageSet is the configuration of content elements for a specific scene. StageSets are defined hierarchical, inheriting all content elements from ancestor scenes. Size and dimension of stageSets (2D or 3D graphics, mono, stereo, 5+1, 3D-sound) depend on the media elements and on the physical input and output facilities available in the targeted performance setting.

Asset. The lowest level primitive of the story structure are assets. These are typically pictures, text, sound, animation, AV-clips, or virtual characters. Assets are referenced by the actions. Named assets may be pre-arranged into stageSets, which is very useful to generate a preview of the scene.

2.2 Views

Because of the various tasks involved when authoring an interactive story, different views of the same story are offered to the author.

The scene-tree view shows the static structure of the story, composed of scenes, which are grouped into so-called complex scenes, comparable to the act vs. scene structure of a stage play (drama-like structure). This view gives the most administrational view, comparable to the File-Explorer in Windows Systems.

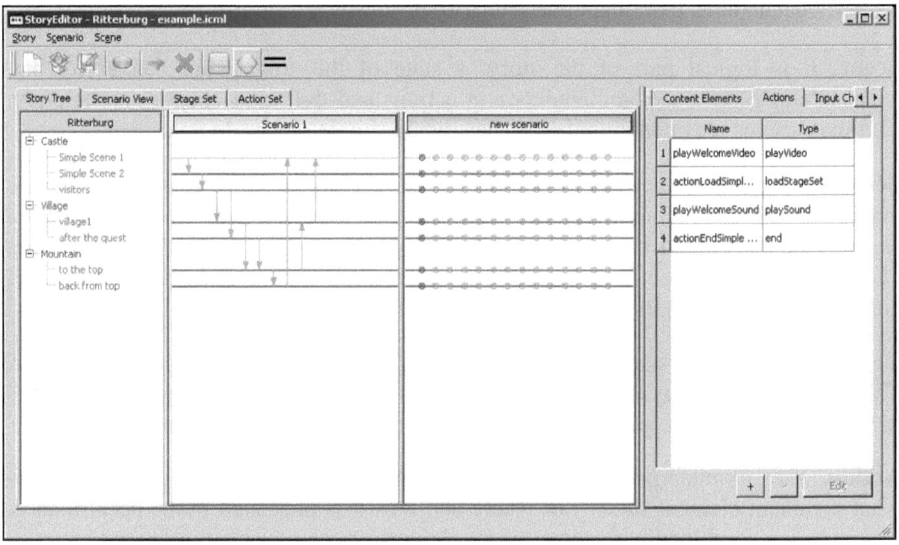

Fig. 2. Story-Tree View (Comparing different Scenarios)

The scene graph view (see figure 3) shows the possible transitions between all scenes. Transitions are grouped into scenarios, where each scenario is one possible navigation structure for the story. This interface shows the same transition network as the scenario preview in the tree-view, but here with scenes represented as elliptical symbols instead of swim-lane lines.

Scene symbols can be freely positioned by drag-and-drop moves, and Transitions are built as dynamic connectors, which can be labeled with a text. The lower right area provides a magnifying rectangle. The content inside the rectangle is shown in the main view. A background image (wallpaper) can be loaded (e.g. a floor plan of an exhibition), and the size of the work area is automatically adjusted to the image size.

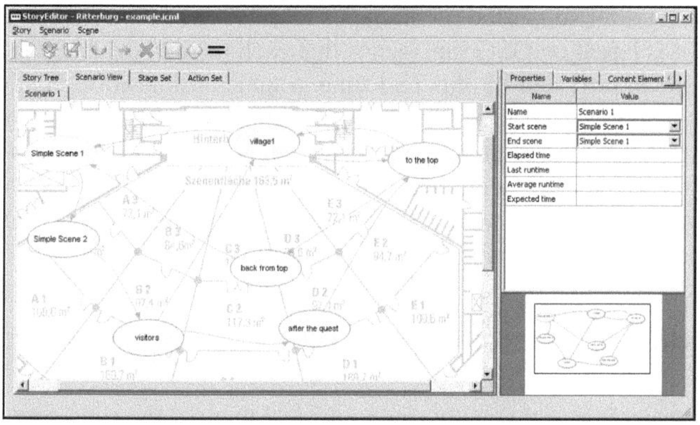

Fig. 3. The Scene Graph View shows all the scenes and transitions of one scenario, freely arranged on the canvas, in front of an optional background image (in this example, the floor plan of some building)

3 Stage Editor

The stage editor has the purpose to do the layout or setting of each scene of the story. It supports 2D and 3D scenes and also a mix of both. The latter are scenes where a 2D overlay is shown on top of a 3D scene. When navigating through the 3D scene the overlay stays unchanged, it is fixed to the virtual camera.

When editing a 2D scene the 3D space stays empty and all media objects are fixed to the overlay plain. For the author this will look and feel like a conventional 2D editor. With standard graphic accelerators it is more efficient to render everything in 3D.

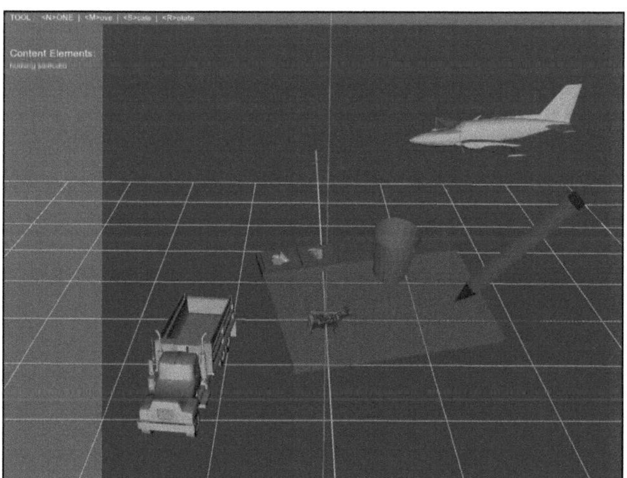

Fig. 4. 2D and 3D Rendering is available in the Stage Editor

The goal is that all supported media types (assets) can be viewed within the stage editor. Since it is based on OSG this means that each media type has to be rendered in 3D using methods provided by this real time graphics framework. While 3D objects are naturally supported, 2D media types need special solutions. Supported 2D media types are: texts, HTML data, images, vector graphics, sounds and movies.

Each imported media element is put into a container class, which provides methods to react on **user interaction**, which will be linked in the *Input Wiring Editor* with the interaction that are possible thanks to the various devices available.

4 Conclusion

Contrarily to many interactive authoring tools, which build the authoring part first and then progressively extend its experiencing capabilities, the U-CREATE prototype is aiming at building a tool to assist the creation of interactive contents for advanced experiencing systems that do already exist. Doing so, its challenge is to cope with all the already existing features of these systems and to come up with a solution that conceptualizes them all into one unique framework.

References

1. Maribeth Gandy, Steven Dow and Blair MacIntyre. "Prototyping Applications with Tangible User Interfaces in DART,The Designer's Augmented Reality Toolkit." Positional paper at: Toolkit Support for Interaction in the Physical World Workshop, held at: IEEE Pervasive Computing 2004, April 20, 2004.
2. S. Sauer and G. Engels, Extending UML for modeling of multimedia applications, Proc. IEEE Symposium on Visual Languages, Tokyo, September 13-16, 1999.
3. S. Sauer and G. Engels. UML-based behavior specification of interactive multimedia applications. In: Proc. IEEE Symposia on Human-Centric Computing Languages and Environments (HCC'01), pages 248--255, 2001.
4. F. Ledermann, An Authoring Framework for Augmented Reality Presentations, TU Wien, 2004
5. Mateas, M. & Stern, A.: Procedural Authorship: A Case-Study Of the Interactive Drama Façade. In: Proceedings of Digital Arts and Culture (DAC), Copenhagen (2005)

Towards Accessible Authoring Tools for Interactive Storytelling

Ulrike Spierling[1], Sebastian A. Weiß[2], and Wolfgang Müller[2]

[1] FH Erfurt, University of Applied Sciences, Erfurt, Germany
[2] PH Weingarten, University of Education, Weingarten, Germany
spierling@fh-erfurt.de, weiss@ph-weingarten.de, muellerw@ph-weingarten.de

Abstract. This contribution presents and discusses *Scenejo* as an experimental platform for Interactive Digital Storytelling, focusing on the authoring process as initial viewpoint for its development. Special emphasis is on the construction of conversational threads for virtual actors using pattern matching, employing transition graph representations as the main interface for authoring. In the conclusion, the opportunities and challenges of graph structures are discussed.

Keywords: Interactive digital storytelling, authoring, transition graph, conversational storytelling, visualization of dialogues.

1 Introduction

Interactive Digital Storytelling (IDS) provides opportunities for the future creation of rich media applicable in entertainment and education, combining aspects of story, simulation and games. In current IDS research and applications, however, there are many open issues and unsolved problems. This is especially the case with applications that support conversational interaction styles with digital agents, providing text input style in natural language, instead of using the artificial game vocabulary most established in contemporary computer games. Examples of open research issues are (from a creator's point of view):

- **Authoring:** How do authors / writers access tools and methods for the creation of dialogues with digital agents, without programming?
- **Emergence:** How do authors get a grip on the course of an agent-based conversation, while allowing emergent behaviour resulting from an interaction style with few constraints?
- **Visualization:** How can variations of verbal conversations be represented visually for creators and planners of the dialogue?

In this contribution, we focus on these questions and present *Scenejo*, an experimental platform allowing practical experiences with agent conversations for non-programming authors. *Scenejo* uses the simplest of technologies for the control of the verbal dialogues, employing the public licence chatbot technology A.L.I.C.E. [1], which supports accessibility for authors who enter the field as novices in dialogue

S. Göbel, R. Malkewitz, and I. Iurgel (Eds.): TIDSE 2006, LNCS 4326, pp. 169 – 180, 2006.

programming. *Scenejo* allows authors to either use plain AIML[1] to define a so-called knowledge base as written dialogue lines for each virtual actor, or to create more structured conversations using transition graphs in a graphical interface. The *Scenejo* platform is then capable of immediately playing the created dialogues between several agents, rendering them in real time as talking heads (compare Fig. 1) using TTS, and allowing users to participate in the conversation by typing text.[2]

In this contribution, we present the authoring tools conceived in *Scenejo*, including a discussion of the usefulness of specific visualizations for several steps of creation in an interactive storytelling project.

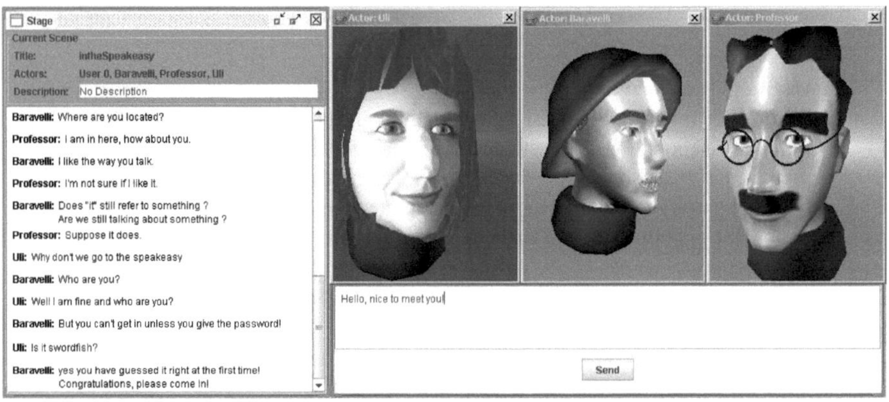

Fig. 1. Conversation in *Scenejo*, mixing emergent small talk and directed scene transitions

2 Related Work

With the concept of *Scenejo*, we follow an approach towards creation possibilities in a middle ground between predefined and emergent simulated dialogues, while thinking radically author-centred. This does not mean that we obtain a viewpoint in IDS that prefers author-driven plot to character-based story development. Rather, it indicates that authors should be able to define the way a conversation develops at any given time – including the occasional event of emergent conversation. Evidently, there are natural borderlines in complexity that are difficult to cross for any human author, which will be stressed again in the conclusion of this article. Having said that, we disagree with a generalized viewpoint that makes the "ability to program" a prerequisite for potential authors to enter the field of IDS, as supposed by Mateas and Stern in [10].

Examples of existing systems with a similar performance goal as *Scenejo* are Façade [11], art-E-fact [13] and CrossTalk [6].

Façade is well known in the IDS community, being the first - and so far only - working system of its kind that enables natural language interaction, based on keyboard

[1] AIML: Artificial Intelligence Markup Language [1].

[2] The *Scenejo* use concept has been explained in [18], and the operation of the drama manager being responsible for the control of the interlocutors' turn taking is described in [12].

input, with virtual characters. It enables complex structures for virtual character behaviour, employing rules that reduce user utterances to context-based semantic units and for the selection of so-called "beats" as the next performed action. The downside of its complexity is the huge obstacle that an author would have to overcome should she wish to create a new and different story than the provided one with Façade's programming language ABL. There is no concept as of yet for an authoring tool, which would be an interesting next step according to the creators of Façade.

The project art-E-fact [7] was a foundation for developments aiming at a similar goal as Façade, but focusing on the authoring aspect from the start. With art-E-fact's authoring tool Cyranus [8], from the outset, a visualization of transition networks is offered. It consists of nodes containing dialogue moves of several characters, and edges defining the pre- and post-conditions for their execution. In the beginning, the problem with this approach was the likelihood that authors would come up with rather linear plots, supported by the affordance of the transition graph tool as the only means of creation. Cyranus is currently being enhanced by rule-based possibilities, which, in the first instance, demand that authors program these rules in Jess[3].

CrossTalk [6] is described as a dialogue system for animated presentation agents using plan-based dialogue generation, as well as a corpus of pre-scripted scenes. The generative part is based on automatic presentation agents [3]. For the development of pre-scripted scenes, the tool SceneMaker has been developed, working with cascaded finite state machines. A scene is any reusable module that can be referred to in a conversation, carrying meta-information to maintain context. A dialogue compiler transfers pre-scripted scenes into plans. While non-programmers are addressed by the system, currently, the tool is mainly a script language to be written with a common text editor, involving some programming expertise.

In a wider context, existing creation tools for building human-computer speech dialogue systems, using transition graphs [9], are also relevant, as well as editors for chatbot applications, supporting the definition of huge dialogue bases, e.g. for AIML [2]. These methods do not involve conversations between several digital agents, but can be adopted to solve subtasks within the *Scenejo* concept.

We conclude that while the beginnings of *Scenejo* do not yet achieve the complexity in calculated emotional depth that is accomplished in Façade, nor the contextual meta information that is followed in Crosstalk, continuing research is justified by its initial viewpoint and main focus on accessibility for writers and authors, similar to that found in art-E-fact. In contrast to art-E-fact, AIML authoring of a single chatbot's knowledge base is the first access to the creation of a conversational scene, providing at least chatbot emergence from the outset, instead of at first constraining the dialogue into the corset of a transition network. The latter, however, is introduced later as a visualization tool and to provide structure.

The next section explains the details of the concept, showing where overall plot management and character-based dialogue creation meet in the interface. A result of the work with the experimental platform, we discuss the opportunities and challenges of transition network visualizations for Interactive Digital Storytelling.

[3] Jess rule system: http://herzberg.ca.sandia.gov/jess

3 Transition Graphs and Pattern Matching for Creation and Representation

In this section, details of the conceived *Scenejo* authoring concept are explained. Special emphasis is placed on the use of transition graphs as a means for structuring content – on several levels of abstraction in interactive storytelling.

3.1 Story vs. Plot

Story

Structural principles of classic stories focus on interesting characters with traits and goals, in constellations with antagonistic forces. Basic abstract functions are sketched in Figure 2 (right) as an adaptation of Frank Daniels' character-driven drama model suggested by Struck [16].

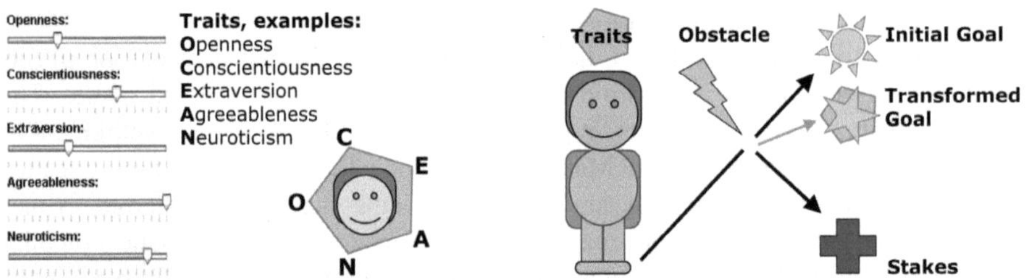

Fig. 2. Left: Trait tuning as currently arranged in the interface. Right: Abstract functions of character-based story, before plot generation.

In *Scenejo*, these structures are currently only implicitly supported. That is to say, if authors have an ambition to structure a story in a dramatic way, they define characters with trait parameters and emotional states. At the current stage of development, states can be set and evaluated as conditions within the dialogue, influencing the further development of a plot line. More sophisticated calculation models are planned for future work, as *Scenejo* currently mainly supports plot generation.

Plot

Character transformation forms the story, while telling over time forms the plot. The task of a storyteller is to restructure the story into a plot line, forming smaller elements, such as acts and scenes (compare Figure 3, Left). For interactive storytelling, there have been debates as to whether a predefined plot line is a desirable goal at all, since the interactive plot rather unfolds according to interactions of participants / players. In our project, we follow the hybrid concept suggested by Spierling [14], using several levels of semi-autonomy at which authors can define a balance between predefined and user-centric courses of action. Accordingly, in *Scenejo,* it's up to the author to either decide to arrange a prestructured plot line, or, to let conversations emerge based on previous utterances and state changes. Figure 3 (right) shows an example plot graph in *Scenejo* containing five scenes, while two of the scenes are apparently alternatives depending on user interaction. Within a scene, authors can define more detailed dialogue structures or just AIML dialogue bases for each actor (see section 3.3).

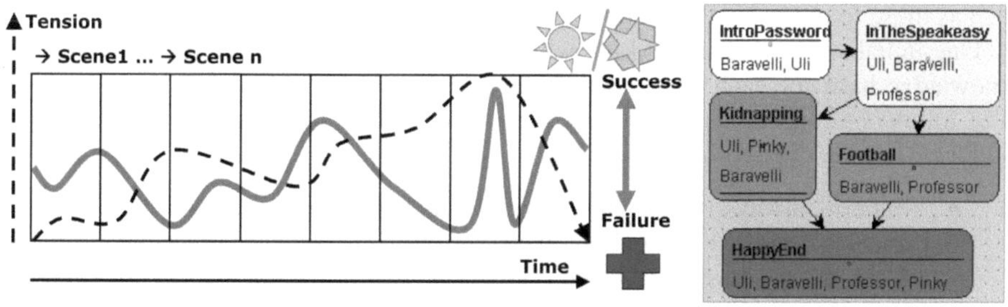

Fig. 3. Left: Telling over time, including scenes, separated by important plot points. Right: Plot graph in *Scenejo*, containing scene elements connected by scene transitions.

A "scene" element in *Scenejo* is a means to separate potential dialogues and different reactions to users according to a timed order. Put simply, it is a visualization of making potential utterances state-dependent. To achieve the same result technically, authors can also use only one scene and instead define conditions based on AIML predicates for structuring. This, however, increases conceptual thinking in terms of programming. The arrangement of several scenes, each working towards or against the character goals to provide tension, serves rather as a metaphor for cinematic story structure. Whenever more than one successive scene is defined, it is necessary to also define the transition conditions between them. Currently, these conditions can be the elapsed time, certain user utterances or state changes of a character predicate. Plot points, therefore, can be modelled as states to be reached through conversation. In the example in Figure 1, guessing the right password was the trigger to change the scene.

Technically, a scene is a sample of AIML knowledge bases available at a certain stage, building the search space for a pattern matching process. AIML is always attached to one particular actor represented by a specific chatbot. Therefore, the definition of a scene initially means to specify its cast and associated AIML. Categories of each actor's knowledge base can be either permanent or scene-dependent, and therefore loaded or discharged during a transition between the scenes.

3.2 Chatbot Knowledge Base vs. Structured Dialogues

Stimulus-Response Principle

A chatbot with a knowledge base as mentioned above works through pattern matching following a simple "stimulus response" principle. The simplest AIML element is a category, containing a pattern and a template. For each chatbot, a pattern defines a searchable word structure (receiving a matching "stimulus"), drawing a straight line to an attached answer template (the "response"). Further, more complex templates can be written that, for example, redirect stimuli to other patterns to allow synonym definitions, or that provide a random list of possible responses to support flexibility. Also, so-called "predicates" can be filled with values stemming from user utterances (or from internal state changes) to be used later during the conversation. Minimal dialogue context can be provided with AIML by defining the last utterance to get an answer for, or by setting a topic to mark a list of tagged categories with higher contextual priority. In summary, the language processing capabilities are far from being as rich as those found in NLP systems supporting grammar and semantic models.

One initial way to begin working with *Scenejo* as an author is to write AIML as a knowledge base for each actor using a text editor or available AIML creation tool. The following conceptual issues were discovered during the first authoring attempts and have been addressed in *Scenejo*:

- Patterns always represent concrete wording, while the possibilities of utterances (stimuli) in natural language appear to be endless. Therefore, an intermediate structure is introduced, serving as a pseudo-semantic level, herein called "dialogue acts" or "abstract input/output". This is summarized in a "stimulus-response" element in the authoring interface (compare Figure 4).
- Changing initiative between actors in a dialogue is difficult to handle, due to the stimulus-response nature of AIML, making every possible utterance an "answer" dependent on a "question". Therefore, in addition to a "stimulus-response" element, an "initiative" element is introduced that is independent of a stimulus.
- Each written category represents a one-directional view of one chatbot towards any interlocutor, originally a human user. Modelling a dialogue between two actors / bots means also mirroring the opposite side, turning templates into patterns. A first interface has been conceived to support writing bot-bot dialogues, resulting in interlocked patterns and templates providing the right "hot words" for the other bot.

The Stimulus-Response Element (SRE) in the *Scenejo* Interface

In addition to writing AIML directly (which is always possible), the Stimulus-Response Element (SRE) supports the planning of dialogue lines by an intermediate abstract structure. Metaphorically, this is comparable to using reported speech in a story treatment and fixing concrete utterances later in the refinement stage of the script.

Figure 4 shows a graphical editor for the SRE, as well as a concept as to how this fits into a level structure for dialogue planning. Authors can conceive a conversational turn on the dialogue act level (as abstract input and output in the upper level of the editor) and provide concrete utterances in the lower level of the editor. Each abstract stimulus defined on the left has to be answered with at least one abstract response on the right. By using conditions for distinction, more than one alternative abstract response can be defined, which can eventually lead to different follow-up SREs in a dialogue graph, or to a scene change defined here by the author. Conditions may depend on property states from memory, emotional and other "predicate" states, as well as values from user utterances. In section 4, the mapping of this structure to AIML is explained technically (compare Figure 7).

The SRE is the start to structuring many SREs into a dialogue graph, while it actually defines the content of one node in the transition network, as well as some of the transition rules. This is explained in the next subsection.

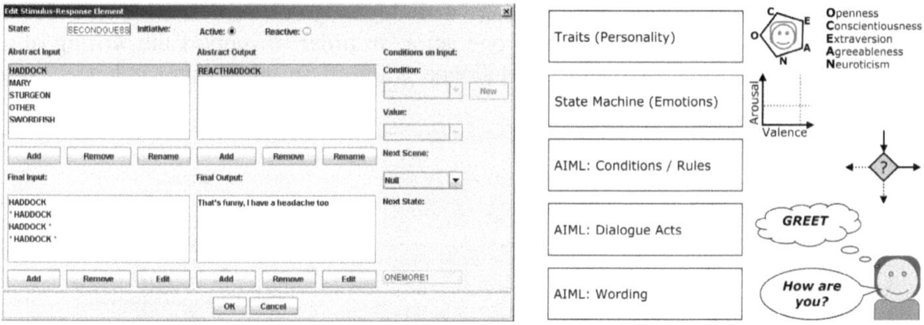

Fig. 4. Left: SRE-Editor for a Stimulus-Response Element: Abstract utterances (upper levels of input / output) can be used to plan the dialogue. Right: Interdependences of dialogue acts with other levels of parameters in *Scenejo*. The three lowest levels are contained in the SRE.

3.3 Dialogue Graphs

The *Scenejo* dialogue graph editor can be used to "draw" conversational threads, simply by combining several SREs with arrows. Through connecting certain SREs to one graph, a situational context constriction is generated, resulting in situational preferences for verbal pattern matching of one actor. A scene can contain multiple conversational threads (each represented by a dialogue graph; compare Figure 5). In total, three kinds of matching AIML patterns can determine the next utterance of an actor: the patterns within the AIML base associated with the actor (e.g. for general small talk), the patterns associated only with the current scene (scene context knowledge), and the patterns within a dialogue graph (situational within a specific thread of conversation). The search priority, quite naturally, puts the most specific (here: one dialogue graph) first.

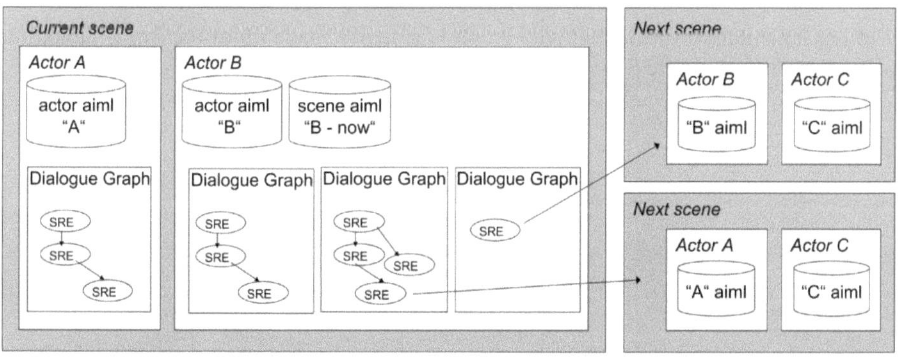

Fig. 5. The hierarchical concept: Dialogue graphs show one actor's potential conversational threads within a scene. Together with associated plain AIML, they form the knowledge base.

Figure 6 shows the graphical user interface. The dialogue graph also allows combinations of SREs that are not dependent on any matched pattern, by turning its mode to "initiative". This is an opportunity to give an actor the initiative in a dialogue, unlike original AIML concepts. Further, a dialogue graph represents one conversational thread from the viewpoint of one actor. In order to support the writing of a fixed dialogue between two actors, a dialogue graph of an interlocutor is loaded into the editor in reversed structure.

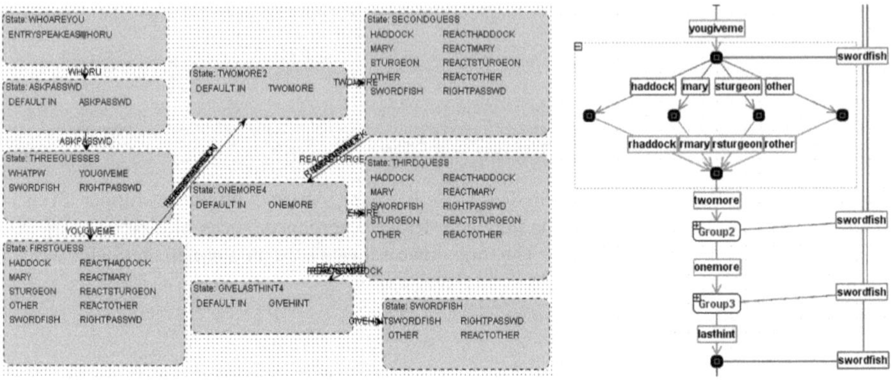

Fig. 6. Two versions of the dialogue graphs in *Scenejo*. The version on the right shows the option of visually collapsing nodes during editing for better clarity.

4 Implementation

There are two main tasks of implementing editable dialogue graphs. First, such graphs have to be represented by a data structure (in this case, primarily AIML), and second, a graphical tool for editing such structures has to be provided to authors as an alternative to simple text editing, letting them manage complexity more easily.

4.1 Mapping Dialogue Graphs to AIML

The implementation of the dialogue graph is actually made up of the implementation of its elements. A single SRE can be understood as one <topic> in AIML.

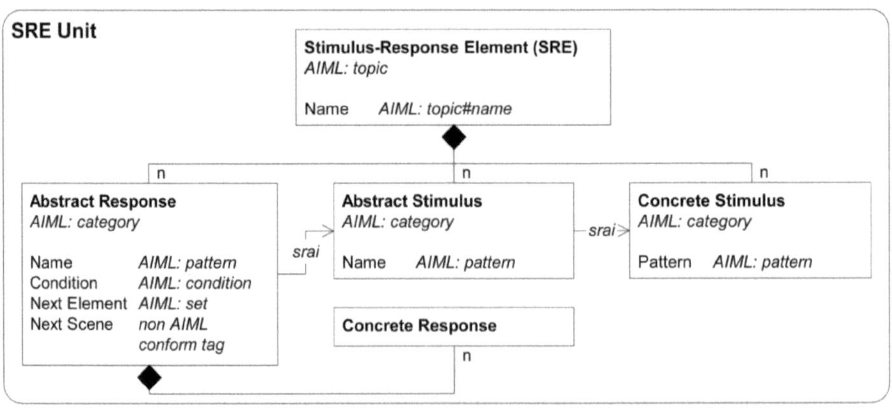

Fig. 7. Schematic view of a SRE and its AIML components

As shown in Figure 7, abstract stimuli, concrete stimuli and abstract responses are implemented by the <category> tag. By combining all categories of one SRE into one unique topic name, these categories in the overall knowledge base of an actor are marked off from others imported from further plain AIML files.

4.2 Visual Authoring of Plot Lines and Dialogues

As explained in section 3.3, a conversational thread can be modelled visually in the form of a dialogue graph that is made up of several SREs. At this level of granularity, authors can also define possible state changes of an actor. In other words, one can define the influencing rules, based on set AIML predicates of an actor, that determine the selection of an explicit response. Further, for incremental changes of any memory and emotional states (AIML or other predicates) of an actor, additional non-AIML constructions have to be implemented that support the state machine. For example, this is currently the case with scene changes.

Figure 8 shows in more detail how these dependencies are implemented.

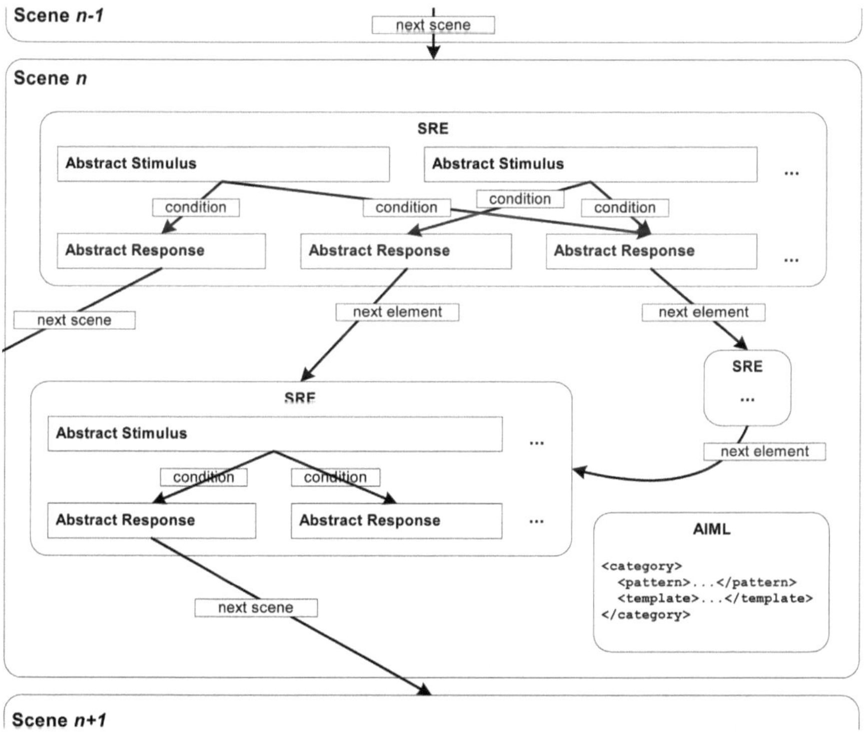

Fig. 8. Detailed view of scene transitions triggered from a SRE in a dialogue graph

This concept represents the conversation as a collection of transition graphs of conversational threads. States are represented by nodes, transitions by edges. A transition within the dialogue graph connects one particular abstract response in a SRE with one successive single SRE.

5 Conclusion

5.1 Authoring and Emergence

Scenejo serves as an experimental platform to experience authoring processes. As such, during the creation of initial demonstrators and content with the prototype, more open issues for the development of authoring tools have been recognized.

First, the visual plot line of scenes appears to be a reasonable way to start structuring on the highest abstraction level. In general, the affordance of a directed graph as a tool very often results in linear structuring – which is not as much of a problem on the highest abstraction level. On the lower levels, such as those of the dialogue acts, however, the experience of emergence is much more important. For example, more emergence can be experienced when a huge pattern base outside of a few constrained dialogue graphs is provided. So far, the experiments have shown that typical chatbot principles of redirecting sentences back to the interlocutor result in entertaining small talk, which can enhance the impression of a dynamic dialogue construction. On the other hand, this is less goal-directed than when more structured threads are involved. Authors depend a lot on tuning and testing when emergence is introduced, so including immediate playback facility in the tool is essential.

For first time users, the graph tools provide accessibility. Frequent users, by contrast, may experience usability problems in terms of low efficiency. Especially the - authoring of a two-directed conversation requires an extension of the dialogue graph tool, resulting in additional views that need to be rather text-based for better facility of inspection. In the future, text interfaces shall be mixed with graphical interfaces for that reason.

Graph representations have the advantage of building recognizable visual patterns. Authors are able to build primitives of reusable patterns of conversational threads. Their visual structure allows for identifying them among others as a unique iconic form.

The SRE editor allows to summarize and structure possible utterances into more abstract meaning, and to plan a dialogue based on this abstract level. As a consequence, if an author would like to reduce all possible stimuli to only a limited set of "artificial language" verbs, this is possible with the system.

5.2 Future Work: Visualizing Large Transition Graphs

While the plot and dialogue graphs implemented so far are still of limited complexity, their size has already made a visualization of these graphs difficult. The limited display area hardly allows for a depiction of the complete graph on the screen. Also, the manual layout of larger story and dialogue graphs is cumbersome and time-consuming. A partial representation of story graphs, however, makes it difficult for a user to grasp the story line and to edit the story graph. Similar, an ineffective representation of a dialogue graph hampers the understanding of possible alternatives and developments in a dialogue of an actor. It is apparent that more complex story lines and dialogues will only add to this problem in the near future.

The method for modelling plot and dialogue in *Scenejo* can be understood as an approach of visual programming. Consequently, the visualization of transition graphs can be related to the problem of visualizing flow graphs in software visualization. In terms of modelling, the sequence of actions corresponding to the Unified Modeling Language, this corresponds to a representation of a UML state chart.

There have been several approaches to the visualization of transition graphs using automated layout algorithms. Algorithms can be distinguished into those considering aesthetic criteria only (e.g. edge crossings) and those allowing for additional constraints. Algorithms are typically either force-based or apply layered layout strategies algorithmically [17]. While most of these techniques are limited to represent directed acyclic graphs, they can be adapted to visualize cyclic structures by cutting cycles appropriately. Layered strategies are in general more appropriate to present directed graphs[4]. Follow-up experiments in *Scenejo* include the application of different layouters.

For the display of larger graphs on limited display areas, Focus & Context techniques, such as "Fisheye Views" [5], have been applied, which render those nodes and transitions that are currently in focus in more detail [15]. In general, an effective application of Focus & Context techniques demands a careful and in-depth analysis of the application context to exploit the additional space of detail information effectively. We are currently analyzing the user requirements on information detail during the authoring process based on *Scenejo* user surveys.

Further, the graph complexity can be reduced by mechanisms for graph abstraction. A pattern library of conversational threads can provide reusable collections of dialogue acts, either stored and reused by authors or provided as primitives. In the resulting transition graph, patterns can be represented by a single abstracted node element, thus simplifying the graph.

Acknowledgements

Thanks to Florian Steimle for many fruitful discussions on authoring concepts during his Diploma thesis, and for his contributions to the existing prototype of *Scenejo*.

References

1. ALICE. Homepage of the A.L.I.C.E. Artificial Intelligence Foundation. Online: http://www.alicebot.org (Last accessed: 07.31.2006)
2. ALICE. News Archive of the A.L.I.C.E. Artificial Intelligence Foundation. Online: http://www.alicebot.org/oldnews2006.html (Last accessed: 07.31.2006)
3. André, E., Rist, T.: Presenting through performing: On the use of multiple animated characters in knowledge-based presentation systems. In: Proceedings of IUI'00, ACM Press (2000) 1-8
4. Di Battista, G., Eades, P., Tamassia, R., Tollis, I.G.: Graph Drawing: Algorithms for the Visualization of Graphs. Pearsons Pub. (1998)
5. Furnas, G.: Generalized Fisheye Views. In: Proc. CHI'86, (1986) 16-23
6. Gebhard, P., Klipp, M., Klesen, M., Rist, T.: Authoring scenes for adaptive, interactive performances. In: Proceedings of the Second International Joint Conference on Autonomous Agents and Multi-Agent Systems. Melbourne, Australia, ACM Press (2003)
7. Iurgel, I.: From another point of view: Art-E-fact. In: Proceedings of Technologies for Interactive Storytelling and Entertainment, Darmstadt (2004) 26-35

[4] For more details on graph drawing see [4].

8. Iurgel, I.: Cyranus – An Authoring Tool for Interactive Edutainment Applications. In: Proceedings of Edutainment 2006, International Conference on E-learning and Games, Zhejiang, China (2006)
9. Klemmer, S.R. et. al.: SUEDE: A Wizard of Oz Prototyping Tool for Speech User Interfaces. In: Proceedings of UIST (2000)
10. Mateas, M., Stern, A.: Procedural Authorship: A Case-Study Of the Interactive Drama Façade. In: Proceedings of Digital Arts and Culture (DAC), Copenhagen (2005)
11. Mateas, M., Stern, A.: A Behavior Language: Joint Action and Behavioral Idioms. In: H. Prendinger and M. Ishizuka (eds.): Life-like Characters. Tools, Affective Functions and Applications, Springer (2004)
12. Müller, W., Spierling, U., Weiß, S.: Synchronizing Natural Language Conversation Between Users And Multiple Agents In Interactive Storytelling Applications. In: Proceedings TESI 2005, Maastricht, The Netherlands. (2005)
13. Spierling, U., Iurgel, I.: "Just Talking About Art" – Creating Virtual Storytelling Experiences in Mixed Reality. In: Virtual Storytelling, Proceedings ICVS 2003, Springer Berlin-Heidelberg (2003)
14. Spierling, U.: Interactive Digital Storytelling: Towards a Hybrid Conceptual Approach. In: Proceedings of Digital Games Research Association's 2nd International Conference "Changing Views: Worlds in Play", Vancouver (2005)
15. Storey, M.-A.D., Müller, H.A., Wong, K.: Manipulating and Documenting Software Structures using SHriMP Views. In: Proceedings of the 1995 International Conference on Software Maintenance ICSM'95. Opio (Nice), France, October 16-20 (1995)
16. Struck, H.G.: Telling Stories Knowing Nothing: Tackling the Lack of Common Sense Knowledge in Story Generation Systems. In: Virtual Storytelling, Using Virtual Reality Technologies for Storytelling, Third International Conference, Proceedings, Strasbourg, France (2005) 189-198
17. Sugiyama, K., Tagawa, S., Toda, M.: Methods for Visual Understanding of Hierarchical Systems. IEEE Trans. Systems, Man, and Cybernetics Vol. 21(2), (1981) 109-125
18. Weiß, S., Müller, W., Spierling, U., Steimle, F.: Scenejo – An Interactive Storytelling Platform. In: Virtual Storytelling, Using Virtual Reality Technologies for Storytelling, Third International Conference, Proceedings, Strasbourg, France (2005) 77-80

Mixed Reality Based Interactive 3D Story Composition Tool

Jun Park and CheolSu Lim

[1] Computer Science Department, Hong-ik University
jpark@cs.hongik.ac.kr
http://iml.hongik.ac.kr
[2] Computer Engineering Department, Seokyeong University
cslim@skuniv.ac.kr

Abstract. For 3D story composition, interactive controls such as scene composition, character actions, and camera placement are important processes. In this paper, a Mixed Reality based interactive tool for 3D story composition is introduced. Using the proposed tool, non-experienced users composed 3D scenes through interfaces in his/her real environments. Preliminary studies showed that proposed 3D story composition tool was convenient and useful by interactively updating scenes through user's control over the stage items and camera viewpoints.

Keywords: Mixed Reality, story composition, interactive interface.

1 Introduction

As computer graphics and interaction technologies advanced, interactive storytelling or story composition in 3D graphics environments became feasible. For example, Donikian et al. developed an authoring tool for interactive fictions, results of which were simulated in virtual environments [1]. Other researchers focused on creating virtual actors [2, 3] and emotions of the characters [4, 5]. However, most of the interactions were performed in the virtual environments, which is isolated from the user's real environments.

For interactive control over the graphical elements, Mixed Reality technologies can be used. Romero et al. used marker-based Mixed Reality (MR) in order to link a painting to the virtual environment where the associated story continued [6]. However, MR technologies were not used for interactive controls in their system. Abawi et al. provided a toolkit for authoring MR-based storytelling environments [7]. The toolkit was used for calibration of real objects and specification of the relationship between virtual and real objects. Although their toolkit provided the capability to toggle between author's view and user's view, it did not seem to provide other interactions. In this paper, we present how MR technologies can be used for interactions in story compositions.

In many scene images of 3D storytelling, placement of items (characters, stage items, and the camera) is one of the most important factors for efficient story scene production. Functionalities and interfaces for scene composition and camera motion control are either lacking or insufficient in the previous tools. The goal of this research is to develop a 3D story composition tool that provides intuitive interface for

S. Göbel, R. Malkewitz, and I. Iurgel (Eds.): TIDSE 2006, LNCS 4326, pp. 181 – 186, 2006.

scene composition and camera pose/motion control. The proposed MR-based interactive 3D story composition tool is based on marker-based Augmented Reality technologies. Using this tool, non-experienced users composed 3D scenes for a story using interfaces in his/her real environments.

2 MR-Based Story Composition System

Proposed MR-based story composition tool is composed of a computing system, a video camera installed on a swing-arm base, and an MR stage (rotatable plate) with a set of "Building blocks" (Fig. 1). Building blocks represent characters, stages, or other stage items. As building blocks are placed within the camera view, the composed scene of the corresponding 3D models is rendered in the Mixed Reality view. Then the author may capture, store, and edit the scene images to create scenes of a story (Fig. 2). The author may also add texts related to the scenes. As user's desktop space replaces the stage, and building blocks replace characters and stage items, the proposed tool may be used to create a story in a simulated screen-filming environment.

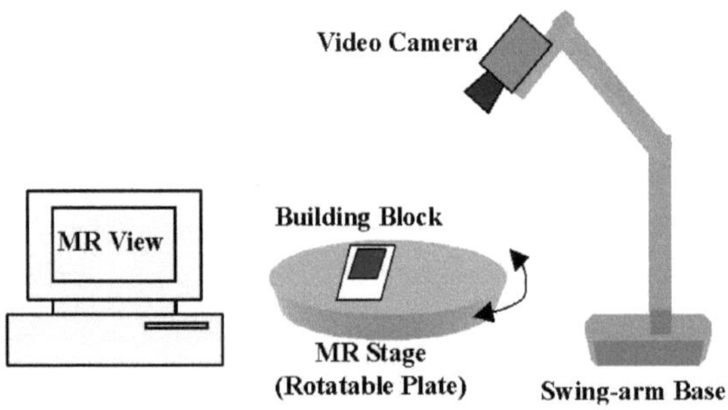

Fig. 1. Components of the MR-based Story Composition Tool

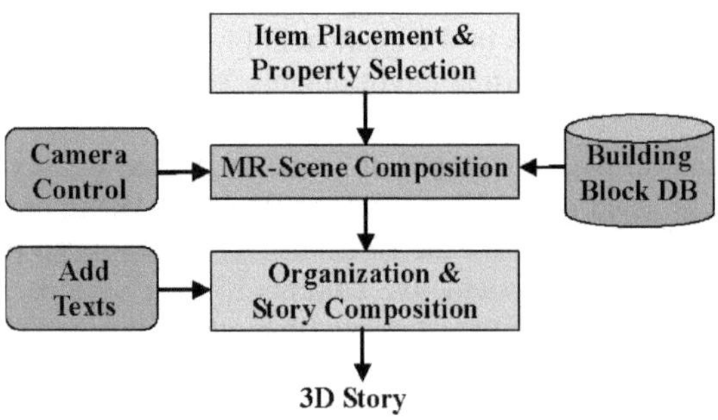

Fig. 2. Overview of the MR-based Story Composition Tool

2.1 Building Blocks

Given a story, we pre-defined characters, stages, stage items, and other properties. For Mixed Reality based authoring, we used building blocks, which are thick paper blocks, where visual information was printed. Building blocks are categorized into two types: item blocks and property blocks. Item blocks represent substantial objects including characters, stages(backgrounds), and other stage items, while property blocks are used to change properties of the existing items (e.g., actions, and facial expressions of an existing character).

The positions of the item blocks on the MR stage (rotatable plate) are used to represent the positions and orientations of the corresponding 3D items relatively from the virtual camera. Meanwhile, property blocks just alter the properties of the existing items. We used Cosmo World [8] to create 3D models and properties for the items. After creation they were stored in "vrml" format and rendered using OpenGL.

To reduce the number of building blocks, we allowed for multiple choices of items in a single block. For example, one character block was used for male, female, aged man, or baby character: users could select one of the four characters. Our novel magnetic selector (in a circular shape) was used for convenient selection. As the magnetic selector was placed at a proper position on the building block (magnets are also installed under the blocks in order to guide selector positioning), the corresponding item was recognized and rendered by the system.

The number of required building blocks depends on the story. We assume that less than 20 building blocks will be enough for short fairy tales (for example, Aesop's fables): 4 character blocks, 4 action blocks, 4 facial expression blocks, 2 background blocks, and 4 stage item blocks. Because we use separate action and facial expression blocks for different characters, the number of building blocks per each character is three. Figure 3 shows some examples of building blocks and the corresponding 3D models.

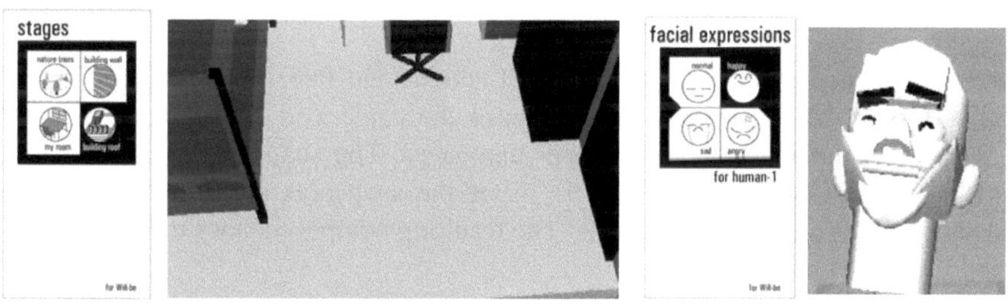

Fig. 3. Examples of Building Blocks: left - a background stage (room), right – a facial expression (happy face) with default male character

2.2 Camera Control

To control the position and orientation of the virtual camera, we used a real video camera and marker-based tracking. The camera position and orientation was calculated relatively from the building blocks in real-time. For marker detection and camera tracking, ARToolKit library was used [9].

For convenient control of the virtual camera, we placed the camera on the top of a swing-arm. The swing arm was composed of three limbs and five hinges. Using this method, users could fix as well as move the camera pose.

2.3 Scene Composition

A scene is composed, first, by preparing building blocks for the scene components. After scene components are determined, corresponding building blocks are placed on the MR stage (rotatable plate) within the camera view. The position and orientation of the item blocks determine the pose of the corresponding 3D models in the scene. However, property blocks can be placed anywhere within the camera-viewable region. Several combinations of building blocks may compose complex scenes and behaviors: for example, combination of a male character, a sitting action, and happy-face expression compose a happily sitting man (Fig. 4).

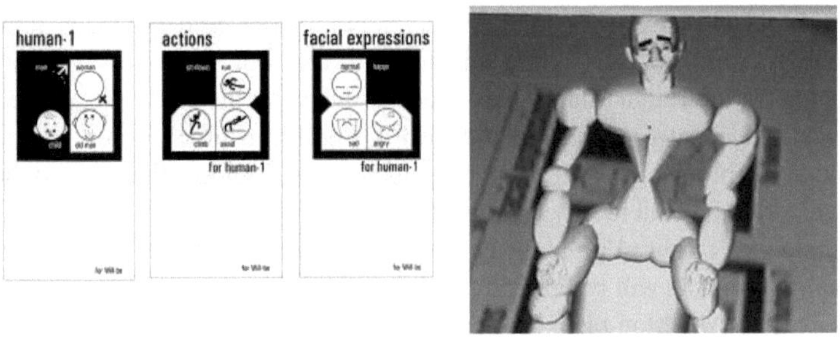

Fig. 4. Example of a character action / facial expression composition: left – three building blocks (a male character, sitting action, happy-face expression), right – the resulting scene (a happily sitting man)

2.4 Story Composition and Editing

After the scene is composed, animation of actions and facial expressions is replayed over and over. The user may, then, control the camera to determine the desirable viewpoint and take snapshots at proper time-steps. The snapshots are stored and selected using the editing tool (Fig. 5). After the snapshots are organized, texts are added on the corresponding columns. The resulting composed story may be printed or saved for further editing.

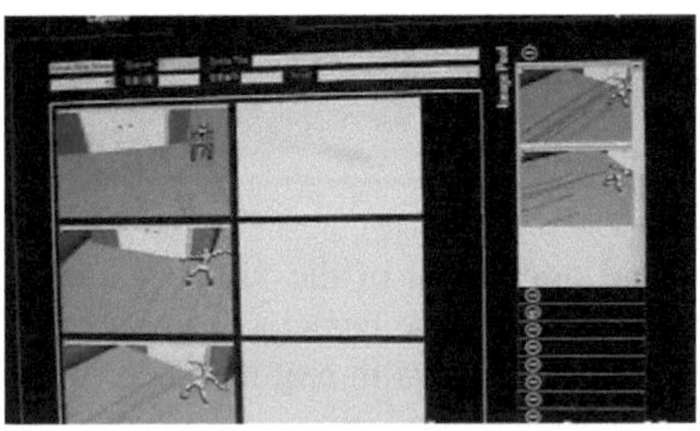

Fig. 5. Story Editing: organize the snapshots and add texts

3 Experiments and Results

As an example, we composed a scene from the film "Matrix". We prepared and placed building blocks for a building roof, a male character, a bullet-avoiding action, and a bullet item (Fig. 6-left). Composed animation was rendered repeatedly in the user's MR view. The user captured desired snapshots, simultaneously controlling the camera pose (Fig. 6-middle). After taking snapshots, the captured images were organized, and the composed story was printed out (Fig. 6-right).

We performed user tests with ten engineering students and staffs. Preliminary studies showed that the proposed tool was convenient and useful by interactively updating scenes through user's control over the stage items and camera viewpoints.

Fig. 6. Story Composition Example: A Scene from the film "Matrix"

4 Conclusions

MR-based interactive 3D story composition tool was introduced. The proposed tool provides interface for scene composition, camera pose/motion control, and story composition. Character postures and stage items could be composed in the MR view. By simulating virtual screen filming environment, the proposed tool provides an easy-to-use and intuitive interface.

The tracking range of ARToolKit is limited: especially, it is not stable when the camera position is low. To allow freedom of camera motion, advanced tracking technology is required. We also plan to provide a variety of building blocks and a set of building blocks for a whole story.

Acknowledgement

This work was supported by the Ministry of Culture & Tourism and KOCCA under the Culture and Content Technology Research Center (CTRC) Support Program.

References

1. Stéphane Donikian and Jean-Noël Portugal, "Writing Interactive Fiction Scenarii with DraMachina," Technologies for Interactive Digital Storytelling and Entertainment: Second International Conference, TIDSE 2004, June 24-26, 2004, LNCS 3105, pp. 101-112
2. Stéphane Sanchez, Olivier Balet, Hervé Luga, Yves Duthen, "Autonomous Virtual Actors," Technologies for Interactive Digital Storytelling and Entertainment: Second International Conference, TIDSE 2004, June 24-26, 2004, LNCS 3105, pp. 68-78

3. Stefan Göbel, Oliver Schneider, Ido Iurgel, Axel Feix, Christian Knöpfle, Alexander Rettig, "Virtual Human: Storytelling and Computer Graphics for a Virtual Human Platform," Technologies for Interactive Digital Storytelling and Entertainment: Second International Conference, TIDSE 2004, June 24-26, 2004, LNCS 3105, pp. 79-88
4. Mariët Theune, Sander Rensen, Rieks op den Akker, Dirk Heylen, Anton Nijholt, "Emotional Characters for Automatic Plot Creation," Technologies for Interactive Digital Storytelling and Entertainment: Second International Conference, TIDSE 2004, June 24-26, 2004, LNCS 3105, pp. 95-100
5. Norman I. Badler, "Embodied Agents and Meaningful Motion," Technologies for Interactive Digital Storytelling and Entertainment: Second International Conference, TIDSE 2004, June 24-26, 2004, LNCS 3105, pp. 1-2
6. Luis Romero, Jorge Santiago, Nuno Correia, "Wireless game and game story: Contextual information access and storytelling in mixed reality using hypermedia," ACM Computers in Entertainment (CIE), Volume 2 Issue 3, July 2004
7. Daniel F. Abawi, Silvan Reinhold, Ralf Dörner, "A Toolkit for Authoring Non-linear Storytelling Environments Using Mixed Reality," Technologies for Interactive Digital Storytelling and Entertainment: Second International Conference, TIDSE 2004, June 24-26, 2004, LNCS 3105, pp. 113-118
8. http://www.web3d-fr.com/outils/Download-Cosmoworlds.php
9. http://www.hitl.washington.edu/artoolkit/

Sharing Knowledge in Virtual Environments

Elsa Pecourt

DFKI GmbH, Stuhlsatzenhausweg 3, 66123 Saarbrücken, Germany
pecourt@dfki.de

Abstract. We report on an effort to ease authoring of XML-based knowledge sources for interactive Virtual Reality (VR) environments by generating them semi-automatically from a common ontology. The generation process is done using XSL Transformations. The automatic generation of knowledge sources ensures consistency and completeness of the modeled entities, by avoiding typical errors that result from hand-crafting knowledge sources for big domains.

1 Introduction

In recent years believable virtual characters have become common in desktop utilities, gaming and entertainment applications, and e-commerce, among others. In order to make a virtual character come to life multiple behavioral and presentation modules are needed, that model different aspects of the virtual entities and that interact producing the illusion of a single *living* entity (e.g. action planner, dialogue engine, emotion engine, cognitive model, sensors, rendering) These components may greatly differ in their semantics, data formats, or programming language, and require the tight collaboration of a team of experts. On the other hand, the development of knowledge sources needed in these environments is an arduous task normally done manually, which is a time consuming and error prone method.

To reduce the effort of implementing such an environment and to ensure the consistency between components, we propose the semi-automatic generation of knowledge sources, from a shared information model based on Semantic Web technologies. By providing explicit semantics in a unified view of the system knowledge, we support reusability and scalability of system components. The separation of abstract semantic concepts from their device-specific realization also enables portability and content customization.

To test our concept we use the Clue System (see fig. 1), which is a game environment that is being developed within the frame of a project at DFKI. It uses the multi-agent framework developed at DFKI within the Virtual Human project[1] as a base architecture and incorporates new components to fulfill the requirements of the game environment, i.e. a *Narration Engine*, and an *XML Player* for 3D rendering. To illustrate our approach we will briefly describe the components of the Clue system and how they interact. This will show how important it is to ensure

[1] http://www.virtual-human.org (last accessed September 2006).

S. Göbel, R. Malkewitz, and I. Iurgel (Eds.): TIDSE 2006, LNCS 4326, pp. 187–192, 2006.

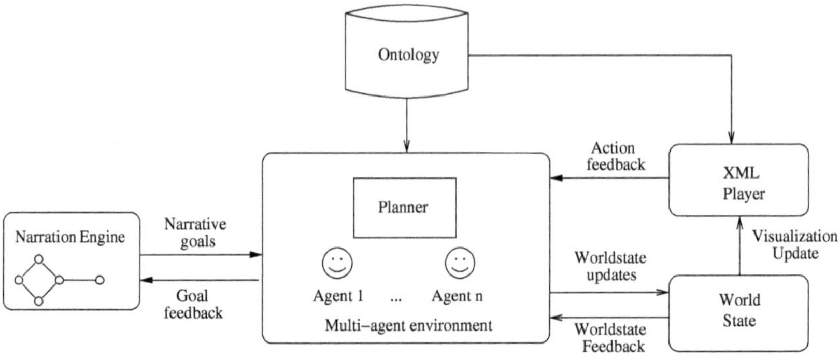

Fig. 1. Clue architecture

consistency between the modeled state of the world, the planning process, the execution process and the final rendering; and the need of methods that alleviate the modeling tasks, by providing reusability and scalability of components.

2 Related Work

The creation of interactive virtual environments is an arduous and time-consuming task. Therefore many attempts have been made to alleviate it. Most of these approaches allow the creation of *virtual stories* using hand-crafted scripts [3] or a combination of scripts with Finite State Machines (FSMs) [1].

However the modeling of interactive stories with manually written scripts or FMSs is only applicable to simple scenarios with limited interactions, as the number of required nodes/rules explodes combinatorially with the increase of complexity and interactivity of the scenes. The use of ontologies has proven useful to tackle this problem, by enabling the definition of rules in an abstract manner, that are applicable to the different concrete instances (see [4]). A further application of ontologies in interactive systems is the generation of the interface specification framework of the application, e.g. XMLS or DTD from the ontology [2]. This approach ensures the consistency of the generated structures with the system knowledge model.

We follow a similar approach by automatically generating the needed knowledge sources, from the ontological instances, rather than just defining constraints on their syntax and structure. For that purpose we use the principle of separating content from presentation and we use XSL Transformations to generate device-specific XML structures from the abstract world modeling.

3 Generation of Knowledge Sources for the Ontological Model

The world model of the Clue system is an ontological representation of the objects and relations of the domain. This representation is based on the upper ontology introduced in [6]. It represents all physical and representational objects known to the system. The ontology is written in RDF [2] using the ontology editing tool Protégé [5].

The building blocks of the ontology are classes (the concepts), instances of these classes, and slots (the relations). Classes represent all physical and abstract entities existing in the domain, both diegetic elements (i.e. characters, objects, and actions occurring in the story) and system internal concepts or *meta-concepts* (e.g. narrative goals, 3D visualization, or dialogue games). Slots specify the attributes of the instances and the relations between them. Figure 2 shows the physical actions in the Clue ontology, which are all subsumed by the top-level class *Process*. Each action has slots specifying action parameters, preconditions, postconditions, and what set of agents is aware of the action when executed (e.g. subject agent, agents in the same room).

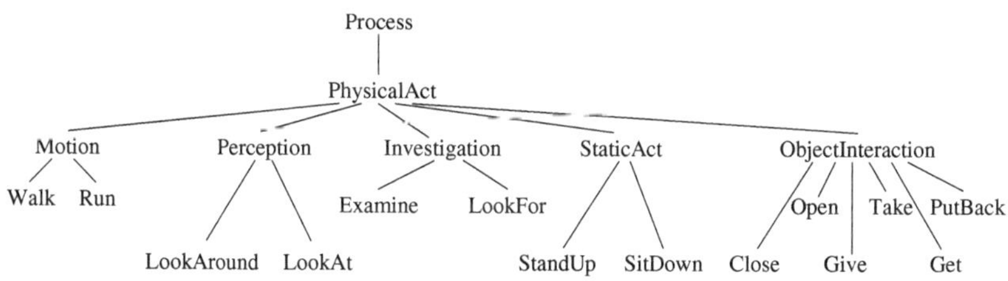

Fig. 2. Clue physical acts

The extension of the domain to include e.g. one new action requires editing several knowledge sources: the action with its preconditions and postconditions has to be added to the ontology to specify the world updates triggered by action execution; a corresponding plan operator has to be defined with its effects, as well as a plan method with preconditions and task decomposition; and a new action has to be provided to the 3D Player, specifying the action visualization in terms of translations and rotations of 3D polygons. In order to minimize the need for manual editing of the knowledge sources, which is time consuming and error-prone, we have developed a facility that automatically generates the needed sources from the shared ontological model.

In order to define our requirements, we studied the information coded in the ontological model, and the other knowledge sources that were not integrated in the ontology, for example because of their use of other formats. The inspection of these knowledge sources revealed many redundancies, errors, and discrepancies. Such problems are usual in manually written sources, when the domain starts growing.

To generate these knowledge sources automatically from the ontological instances, we decided to use XSLT [3], a W3C standard language for XML transformations that is widely used to separate content from presentation in web

[2] http://www.w3c.org/RDF (Last accessed September 2006).

[3] http://www.w3.org/TR/xslt (Last accessed September 2006).

and multimedia presentations. As all our internal knowledge sources are written in some XML-based representation, the use of XSLT fits perfectly our requirements. The use of XSLT also enables the explicit separation of abstract content from its realization in the specific application. The following sections describe the needed knowledge sources, their related ontology concepts, and how we tried to generate the former using the latter. Figure 3 shows the workflow for our generation process.

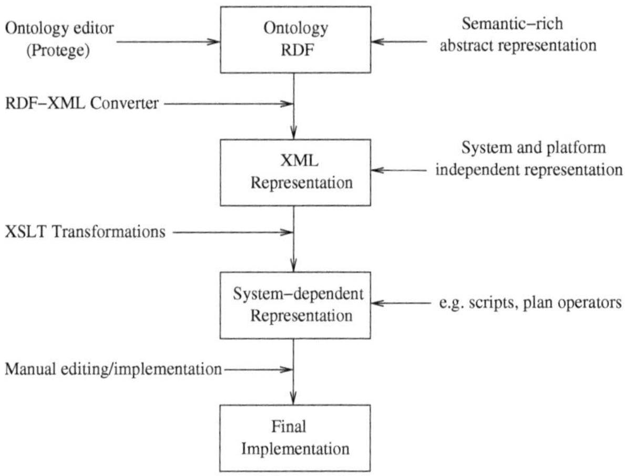

Fig. 3. Generation process

3.1 Planner Operators

The ontology contains classes that model all possible acts in the domain, both physical and communicative ones. Each act defines a set of parameters, a set of preconditions and postconditions, and which characters are aware of the act and its postconditions. This information is used for the *execution* of actions. On the other hand the planner operators have to be defined, including preconditions, postconditions, and action parameters, for *planning*. The transformations generate a plan operator for each act in the ontology. This plan operator contains the parameters and postconditions specified in the ontological object. As the planner operates with an incomplete knowledge of the world, i.e. the knowledge and perception of the agent executing the action, the transformation tool only considers postconditions that are labeled in the ontology as being perceived by the subject agent.

3.2 World State

At initialization time the set of objects and characters inhabiting the world and the relations between them, i.e. the initial world state, has to be loaded. The needed XML sources are generated from existing ontological instances as the one shown in figure 4.

```
Door1
   has_id: door
   has_name: Door
   has_geometry: Door3D
   has_relation: open(door), connects(door, bathroom, livingroom)

Door3D
   has_absolutePosition (0,0,2.55)
   has_source Media/Meshes/Door.x
   has_rotation 90
```

Fig. 4. Ontological instances of a character and a door

3.3 3D Player Scripts

Some of the abstract concepts coded in the ontology have different realizations at different components, e.g. two rooms connected by a door. This relation has to be defined not only in the *state of the world* specification, but also in the scene definition for the visualization. Our tool extracts this information from the ontology instances (see fig. 5) and uses it to generate both structures.

In order to explicitly associate abstract concepts with their realization, i.e. 3D objects, 3D animations, or sound files, we extended our ontological world model to include these presentation concepts and the needed links (e.g. the slot *has_geometry* in Fig. 4). These concepts are used to generate the scripts that communicate the 3D Player what objects and characters to load for visualization.

4 Testing

In order to test the generated knowledge sources and support an iterative development cycle, we have integrated the generation tool with the Clue testing environment. Thus the newly created knowledge sources can be readily tested in the real system. The testing environment consists of two main windows each containing a Graphical User Interface (GUI): the *Generation GUI*, and the *Testing GUI*. The Generation GUI enables the generation of initialization files, planner operators, and high level goals, from the ontological instances created using the Protégé tool. The generated files can be sent to the running system online using the Testing GUI. The tool enables the use of a combination of automatically generated files with hand-crafted ones. Generated files can also be manually edited and retested, thus enabling iteration in the authoring cycle.

Being our tool still *work in progress* we do not have numerical measures about time saving and improvement of consistency and completeness of the modeled concepts. Nevertheless the tool has already helped to discover hidden inconsistencies when comparing the generated knowledge sources with the hand-crafted ones, and thus saved debugging time.

5 Conclusions

This work was done in the framework of the EU-supported integrated project INSCAPE[4] (FP6 IST ref. 4150). The INSCAPE projects aims at enabling ordinary people to use and master the latest Information Society Technologies for interactively authoring and experiencing interactive stories, whatever their form. The presented work addresses these two main issues, user-friendliness and application-independence, by providing an approach to ease the authoring of interactive virtual environments by separating the abstract semantic specification of domain concepts from their application-dependent realizations.

References

1. Gebhard, P., Kipp, M., Klesen, M., and Rist. T., Authoring Scenes for Adaptive, Interactie Performances, Proceedings of the Second International Joint Conference on Autonomous Agents and Multiagent Systems (AAMAS'03), Melbourne, 2003
2. Gurevych, I., Porzel, R., Slinko, E., Pfleger, N., Alexandersson, J., and Merten, S., Less is More: Using a Single Knowledge Representation in Dialogue Systems, Proceedings of the HLT-NAACL 2003 workshop on Text meaning, Morristown (NJ), 2003.
3. Perlin, K. and Goldberg, A., Improv: A System for Scripting Interactive Actors in Virtual Worlds, Proceedings of the Siggraph 96, New York, 1996
4. Porzel, R., Pfleger, N. Merten, S., Löckelt, M., Gurevych, I., Engel, R., and Alexandersson, J., More on Less: Further Applications of Ontologies in Multi-Modal Dialogue Systems, Proceedings of the 3rd Workshop on Knowledge and Reasoning in Practical Dialogue Systems, an IJCAI Workshop, Acapulco, 2003.
5. Noy, N. F et al., Creating Semantic Web Contents with Protege-2000, IEEE Intelligent Systems, 16(2):60-71, 2001
6. Russell, S. J and Norvig P.: Artificial Intelligence: A Modern Approach, Prentice-Hall, Upper Saddle River, 1995

[4] http://www.inscapers.com (last accessed September 2006).

Pre-conference Demo Workshop "Little Red Cap": The Authoring Process in Interactive Storytelling

Ulrike Spierling[1] and Ido Iurgel[2]

[1] FH Erfurt, University of Applied Sciences, Altonaerstr. 25, 99085 Erfurt, Germany
spierling@fh-erfurt.de
[2] Zentrum für Graphische Datenverarbeitung, Rundeturmstr. 12, 64283 Darmstadt, Germany
ido.iurgel@zgdv.de

Workshop Abstract

Over the last several years, conferences in the field of interactive entertainment have showcased numerous presentations concerning concepts and technology for Interactive Digital Storytelling: runtime systems, such as story engines, intelligent / autonomous agents, drama managers and conversational systems. They focus on solutions to the problem of combining dramatic storytelling with user interactivity. In contrast to the many technical contributions concerning runtime performance, few discussions have been initiated about the question of how a new breed of "interactive storytellers" would create concrete original artefacts with the proposed systems. In our opinion, the authoring process is likely to be a serious bottleneck for generating innovative products in the future.

This workshop takes a detailed and applied look at the creative process currently associated with state-of-the-art technology. Creators, researchers and tool developers present authoring approaches, show hands-on examples of creation and discuss with each other the prospects of a shared understanding of the future production process in Interactive Digital Storytelling. Demonstrations cover the principles and usage of visual editors for non-programmers, as well as the detailed steps of using script languages in an explained design process.

In order to better compare different creative approaches and philosophies, a reference story is used, serving as a shared theme for short demonstrations: the widely

S. Göbel, R. Malkewitz, and I. Iurgel (Eds.): TIDSE 2006, LNCS 4326, pp. 193 – 194, 2006.

known Grimm's tale of "Little Red Cap" (German original: "Rotkäppchen"), sometimes also known as "Little Red Riding Hood". Each contributor presents a brief treatment showing his/her particular adaptation of "Little Red Cap" to the philosophy of the respective interactive storytelling system. Then, the associated authoring steps and tools are demonstrated and illustrated by means of a short piece of content prepared in advance.

Following up, plenary discussions in the context of the creative process include questions, such as:

- What is interactive storytelling, anyway?
- What is the scope of an author's work; who or what controls the resulting plot, and how?
- What constitutes the production chain in Interactive Digital Storytelling, which steps does it involve, and which cycles?
- What kind of editors and tools exist? What aspects can or could be handled by visual authoring tools, and where is programming really required?
- How does collaboration between experts of different domains work?
- Which aspect causes the biggest work load?
- How much of the process is intuition and creativity, and how much is software engineering or simply assiduity?

Participants take away valuable insight into the interactive story "factories" of others, as well as important feedback for their own work. Workshop results are subsequently reported on the Web.

Failing Believably: Toward Drama Management with Autonomous Actors in Interactive Narratives

Mark O. Riedl[1] and Andrew Stern[2]

[1] University of Southern California, Institute for Creative Technologies, 13274 Fiji Way, Marina del Rey, California, USA
riedl@ict.usc.edu
[2] Procedural Arts LLC, Portland, Oregon, USA
andrew@proceduralarts.com

Abstract. Interactive Narrative is an approach to interactive entertainment that enables the player to make decisions that directly affect the direction and/or outcome of the narrative experience being delivered by the computer system. One common interactive narrative technique is to use a drama manager to achieve a specific narrative experience. To achieve character believability, autonomous character agents can be used in conjunction with drama management. In this paper, we describe the problem of *failing believably* in which character believability and drama management come into conflict and character agents must intelligently produce behaviors that explain away schizophrenic behavior. We describe technologies for implementing semi-autonomous believable agents that can fail believably.

1 Introduction

Storytelling in one form or another is a central component in a vast majority of modern computer games. *Interactive Narrative* is an approach to interactive entertainment that enables the player to make decisions that directly affect the direction and/or outcome of the narrative experience being delivered by the computer system. Often this means the player assumes the role of a story world character, possibly the protagonist. Story and character are intertwined; story cannot exist without character, and character alone often implies narrative. Consequently, computational storytelling researchers have long placed emphasis on creating believable agents (c.f. [2], [13], [5], [11], and [8]). A believable agent [2; 13] is an autonomous agent that enacts the role of a story world character by manifesting through its behavior personality, emotion, beliefs, desires, intentionality, and a host of other traits that lead to the "illusion of life." Believability is an ill-defined concept. Within the context of the paper, we shall define believability as not performing actions that break the user's suspension of disbelief that a character is not an automaton.

Autonomous embodied agents are commonly used for achieving believable characters in interactive systems because autonomy affords reactivity, interactivity, and local grounding of agent decisions in observable behavior. Aylett [1] notes that interactive narratives that rely on autonomous agents alone do not always produce narrative experiences with recognizable structure or coherent, meaningful outcomes. Interactive narrative researchers often turn to the concept of drama management to

S. Göbel, R. Malkewitz, and I. Iurgel (Eds.): TIDSE 2006, LNCS 4326, pp. 195 – 206, 2006.

ensure coherent, recognizable narrative experiences in their systems (c.f. [18], [14], [24], [22], [16], [21], and [8]). A drama manager [12] is an intelligent, disembodied agent that manages the virtual world in order to bring about a narrative experience for the user. Typically, this is achieved is by providing the drama manager with some sort of pre-specified branching or non-branching storyline.

In our research, we adopt the use of both autonomous character agents and drama management. We believe the careful combination of these technologies affords a richer, more interactive narrative experience. Believable agents, through dialogue and reactivity, help immerse the user and invoke the sense of user self-agency. The drama manager provides a coherent narrative structure to the user's experience in the virtual world. We adopt a *generative* technique of drama management pioneered by [18; 25]. The generative approach affords a drama manager more flexibility to accommodate the user by dynamically re-generating narrative content to incorporate user actions into the plot representation. That is, the drama manager adapts its narrative automatically – changing the direction, in terms of future plot points, and/or outcome – to the actions of the user. The trade-off for using this approach is that narrative content cannot be known a priori, the consequence of which is that special attention must be paid to the coordination between the drama manager and believable agents. Specifically, one cannot design believable agents to avoid performing actions that conflict with the drama manager's storytelling goals because the narrative structure is not known at design time.

In this paper, we propose an approach to coordination between drama managers and autonomous believable agents that avoids or mitigates the effects of the inherent tension between believable agents and the drama manager. In the following sections, we describe circumstances where coordination between believable agents and a drama manager can result in character agent abandoning or abruptly changing its goals or inexplicably contradicting its previous actions, all of which may be perceived by a user as schizophrenic [20] behavior. Traditionally, agent goal failure is a topic addressed in artificial intelligence literature by techniques for avoiding failure or by re-planning when failure occurs. But agent goal failure that can be explained in the context of the narrative and virtual world may actually be desirable; for example, [5] uses goal failure to create comedic and/or dramatic situations. However, *inexplicable* goal failure results in a loss of agent believability. Explainability of the behavior of an agent is an integral component in user comprehension of autonomous agent performance [23].

The problem we are addressing is the realization that sometimes a believable agent under drama management is required to fail to achieve a goal, in the interest of preserving the drama manager's plotline. We use the term *failing believably* to refer to a technique whereby a believable agent can given an a priori unknown plotline (a) intelligently and believably avoid situations where the agent and drama manager come into conflict, and (b) enact a plausible and believable explanation for goal failure when conflict with the drama manager is unavoidable.

2 A Generative Drama Manager for Directing Autonomous Characters

In our research, we adopt a generative technique of drama management pioneered by [18; 25]. The generative approach allows a drama manager to accommodate user actions by incorporating user actions into the plot representation. When the user – knowingly or unknowingly – performs actions that change the story world in a way that makes it impossible or nonsensical to achieve future plot points, the drama manager adapts or repairs the plotline by re-generating part or all of the remaining plot structure. One restriction we enforce is that computer-controlled characters are disallowed from performing actions that cause the drama manager to adapt or repair the plot. This restriction is based on the assumption that the original plot is considered ideal and that every alteration to the plot degrades its effectiveness [18].

Scenario adaptation requires that the drama manager's plot be represented computationally so it can be reasoned over by an artificial intelligence system. Following [18], we represent plots as partially-ordered plans. A plan contains steps – events that change the state of the world – and annotations that explicitly mark the temporal and causal relationships between all steps in the plan, defining a partial order indicating the steps' order of execution. Causal annotations, called *causal links*, specifically are used to denote causal relationships between the steps in the plan. A causal link relates the effect of one plan step to a precondition of another plan step that is temporally constrained to occur later than the first step. Fig. 1 shows part of a plot plan taken from [19], used to train situation awareness to military leaders. Plan steps (boxes) represent a sequence of partially ordered plot points to be achieved in the story world if no branching occurs. The arcs represent causal links denoting conditions in the virtual world that are established by the successful achievement of the temporally earlier plot point and required for successful achievement of the temporally later plot point. For example, many plot points require that certain characters are not detained and not incapacitated.

The scenario is expected to progress as follows. Two characters, Hassan and Saleh, are merchants and sectarian rivals. Hassan is to act friendly towards the player while Saleh is to act hostilely towards the player. Later, Hassan acquires a bomb and plants it. However, Hassan is observed planting the bomb by a third character, Ali. The bomb goes off but it is a dud and no one gets hurt. Once the event takes place, Hassan falsely accuses Saleh of being the villain while Ali righteously accuses Hassan. The objective of the scenario is to challenge the user to develop more sophisticated situational understanding in order to peacefully resolve conflicts.

If the user performs an action in the virtual world that changes the world state in such a way that a causal link condition is negated, the drama manager re-generates the plot plan to reestablish the negated world condition or to remove jeopardized future plot points and find a new plot sequence. For example, suppose the trainee finds the planted bomb disarms it. Were this to occur the causal link specifying that the bomb must be armed before it can go off (as a dud) is negated. The drama manager, detecting the threat to the plot, re-generates the remaining plot. One simple adaptation is to have another character plant a second bomb, although the current state of the drama manager is capable of significantly more complex adaptations (see [19] for additional plot adaptations). Only actions that threaten causal links require adaptation of the plot. All other user actions are considered consistent with the plot as currently structured. Interactions with autonomous character agents that do not threaten the plot account for most of the variability in the user's experience.

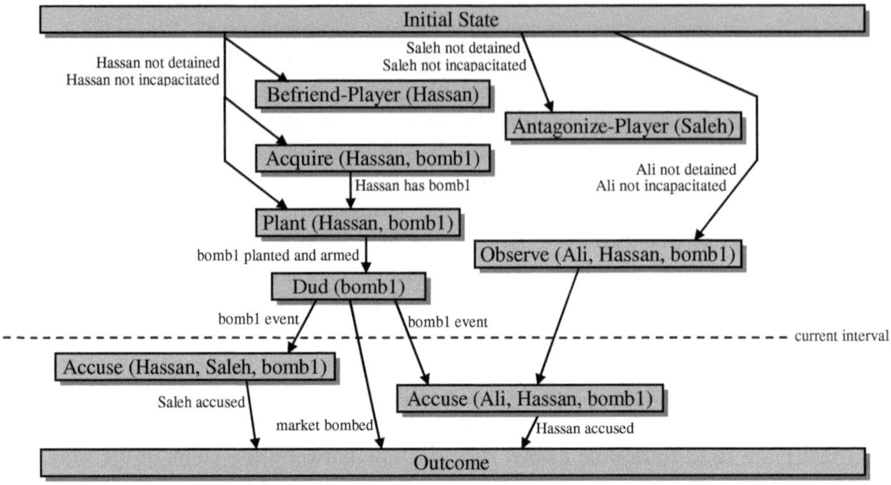

Fig. 1. A causally connected graph of plot points

By representing narrative as a plan, the narrative can be regenerated using specialized narrative planners such as [17]. This approach has been successfully applied to entertainment and educational applications (e.g. [18; 25]) and to interactive narrative-based training (e.g. [19]). For more information on the drama manager and the application, see [19].

2.1 Directing Autonomous Character Agents

Drama management techniques for interactive storytelling systems are often used to direct the behaviors of character agents so that they do the things that are required to drive a plot forward. But one aspect of drama management that has been largely overlooked is directing character agents to prevent undesirable world states. The issue at hand is that character agents with any degree of autonomy may make decisions to perform actions that change the state of the virtual world in such a way that the drama manager's intentions for future plot become hampered. A character agent acting autonomously may choose to perform an action that makes future plot progression impossible or nonsensical. For example, a character agent may destroy or make inaccessible an essential resource or in some other way change the state of the world so that it is incompatible with the plot sequence.

Drama managers do not always have to act proscriptively against autonomous character agents. In game-like systems where the drama manager's linear or branching storyline is known in advance by system designers, autonomous agents can be designed to perform behaviors that are guaranteed never to cause world state changes that will violate the drama manager's plotline. However, if the drama manager's story is not known before hand, can be dynamically adapted (c.f. [19]), or is generated automatically by the system on a per-session basis (c.f. [18; 25]), then it is impossible to design autonomous believable agents that are guaranteed never to conflict with the drama manager's storytelling goals.

Blumberg and Galyean [4] describe a way of controlling the behaviors of autonomous virtual agents through weighted preferences. Not only can control of agents be *prescriptive* – "do X" – but also *proscriptive* – "I don't care what you do as long as you don't do Y." One system, Virtual Storyteller, [22] produces stories using autonomous agents and a drama manager that applies prescriptive and proscriptive techniques; each autonomous character agent must ask permission of the drama manager before performing an action. Likewise, Szilas [21] proposes a model where the drama manager participates in the agent's intelligent action selection process.

Proscriptive control of autonomous believable agents presents the following challenge: How does one proscribe a believable agent without adversely impacting that character believability? At the heart of the issue is that an autonomous believable agent – designed to make local decisions in order to appear believable – can determine at any given moment that the most believable action to perform is one that will change the world in a way that negatively impacts the drama manager's ability to progress through the desired plot structure.

For example, in the context of the narrative plan shown in Fig. 1, suppose that Hassan and Saleh are bitter rivals and Saleh forms the goal to incapacitate Hassan. This may be seen as reasonable given the relationship between the two characters. Unlike the user, character agents are prohibited from performing actions that negate causal links – in this case the condition that Hassan is not incapacitated. Causal links extend over a period of time. If Saleh acts during an interval in which the condition that Hassan not be incapacitated is proscribed, then Saleh should not be able to execute any plan to incapacitate Hassan and may be forced to abandon the goal immediately. Suppose however, that the character agents have been operating for some amount of time before the drama manager begins managing the world and that Saleh has formed the goal before the drama manager proscribes against the condition. Further suppose that the Saleh agent has already gone through the motions of picking up a weapon and heading over to Hassan. When the drama manager proscribes against incapacitating Hassan, the Saleh agent will be forced to abandon the goal, in effect *failing*. The concept of failing believably is to append the aborted sequence of actions – the menacing of Hassan – with a continuing sequence of actions that is not inconsistent with past actions and also justifies to the user why Saleh did not attempt to complete the goal. In the simplest form, failing believably could mean (possibly pretending) to be called away on a more important issue. A more sophisticated variation on failing believably could involve a joint performance (for a discussion of joint behaviors in interactive drama systems, see [15; 16]) in which Hassan pleads with and convinces Saleh to leave him unharmed.

2.2 Generating Directives

Plot points and their causal relationships are used to generate directives to believable, autonomous agents. Directives take the following forms:

- *Prescriptive directive:* Direction to achieve some world state that is desirable to the drama manager and moves the plot forward. Prescriptive directives should be of sufficiently high level that character agents are free to achieve the directive in a way that best suites the believability of that character.
- *Proscriptive directive:* Direction to avoid particular states in the virtual world that are contradictory to the intermediate requirements of the drama manager's plot representation.

The drama manager must derive directives from its internal plot representation. Prescriptive directives are derived directly from plot points. That is, a plot point specifies a world state that must be achieved. The drama manager determines which story character is responsible for achieving this world state and formats the plot point as a goal for the character agent to achieve. It is often the case that the character responsible for a plot point is encoded directly into the plot point as the entity that is changed or creates the change.

Proscriptive directives are more problematic because they do not correspond to any particular plot point. Instead, proscriptive directives are derived from the causal relationships between plot points. Specifically, for every plot point in the drama manager's representation of expected user experience, there are certain world state conditions that must be maintained. These conditions are established by plot points that occur earlier in the plot structure or by the initial world state. If an autonomous agent were to perform an action that negates such a condition, future plot points would become impossible or, at the very least, cease to make sense.

Fig. 1 shows a hypothetical plot plan. The dashed line delineates a point in time in the plot plan where plot points above have been achieved and plot points below have yet to be achieved. The causal links that cross the current interval line are the conditions that must be maintained for the plot to continue. In the example, character agents will be directed to avoid actions that negate the truth values of conditions *(planted bomb1)* and *(armed bomb1)*. This is especially important as the agent playing the role of Ali, having seen the bomb being planted, may believably want to choose to do something about it. As character agents receive positive directives, achieve plot points, and report back successes, the current interval shifts downward and the set of world state conditions that must be maintained changes, further constraining or freeing up the actions available to character agents.

3 Believable, Directable Semi-autonomous Character Agents

Agents that must operate in dynamic environments often rely on robust teleo-reactive [3] plan execution systems such as RAPS [9], PRS [10], Soar (when not used to model psychomotor skills), and ABL [15] (used by the *Façade* [16] interactive drama) that take advantage of hierarchical representations of behavior. The advantage of these systems is that they can readily re-plan behaviors when circumstances change by failing the currently operating plan (also referred to in agent literature as methods, productions, task networks, or behaviors) and choosing a different decomposition of an abstract high-level goal.

One can represent the space of possible agent behaviors of a hierarchically-based plan execution system as an AND/OR graph [5]. Nodes are plans that, unless they are leaf nodes, have one or more child nodes. If a node is an AND-node, then the child nodes are ordered and must all be achieved in the specified order for the parent node to succeed. If a node is an OR-node, then the child nodes represent alternative methods for achieving the parent node and only one must be chosen. Preconditions on the children of OR-nodes determine which alternative methods of achieving the parent plan are legal

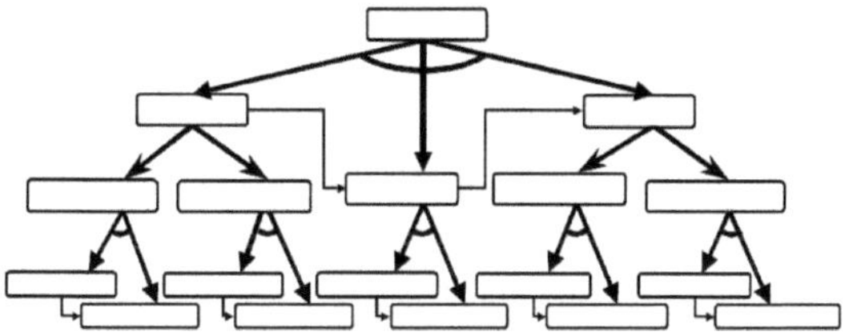

Fig. 2. Hierarchical AND/OR plan tree

given the current executing environment. Fig. 2 shows a conceptual hierarchical arrangement of goals. The boxes denote goals at different degrees of abstraction. Downward arrows show how plans are decomposed. If the arrows are joined by an arc, then that node is an AND-node. Otherwise, it is an OR-node. Horizontal arrows denote ordering constraints among children of an AND-node.

Agent behavior is determined in real-time by taking the current executing abstract plan and decomposing it. If the plan is represented by an OR-node, decomposition is a process of selecting one of the alternative sub-plans. When a chosen node is a leaf, a corresponding primitive action is executed by the agent in the world. Because of OR-nodes, it is impossible in many circumstances to predict what primitive actions an agent will perform from moment to moment. Key to believable agents in general, and those that must fail believably in specific, is for agents to have a lot of alternative OR-nodes to select from every time in needs to decompose a top-level goal into primitive actions.

3.1 Handling Prescription: Mixing Autonomy and Narrative Direction

Because of our high-level approach to drama management plot representation, positive directives are of the form of goals for a character agent to bring about a particular world state. Prescriptive directives may come infrequently, however. Character agents must fill up the duration between prescriptive directives by autonomously choosing goals and acting to achieve them. When a character agent receives a prescriptive directive from the drama manager, the agent must incorporate that new goal into it's reasoning in a way that does not violate believability, e.g. avoid schizophrenically [20] switching from one goal to another seemingly unrelated goal.

There are many intelligent design tricks that can be used to seamlessly integrate autonomous goals and directed goals. Our character agents use tables of resource requirements to determine whether a currently pursued autonomous behavior is compatible with a direction from the drama manager. These tables are compiled at agent design time. From this information and prioritization information, a character agent can determine if it can:

- Merge its current autonomous goal and the goal of the prescriptive directive, achieving both simultaneously through clever selection of decompositions;
- Complete the current autonomous goal and then switch to the task of achieving the prescriptive directive; or
- Abort or suspend the autonomous behavior to pursue the goal of the prescriptive direction.

In the last case, to avoid the appearance of the agent schizophrenically abandoning a goal without reason, we provide our character agents with transition behaviors. A transition behavior is a sequence of believable primitive actions that an agent can perform to justify or explain why it would stop doing one thing and start doing something else. This satisfies the requirement of explainable behavior.

For example suppose agent Hassan is performing the role of a merchant, enacting the types of behaviors one would expect a merchant to perform – autonomously interacting with customers and keeping shop – when it receives a prescriptive direction to acquire a bomb. The agent aborts its current behavior with a transition behavior in which the agent (possibly pretends to or not) receive an urgent phone call and closes the shop. The agent then begins executing actions to complete the directive.

3.2 Handling Proscription: Plan Coordination with Restoration Modes

The logic for avoiding certain world states is potentially more complicated than achieving particular world states; avoidance of world states requires autonomous agents to be aware of the implications and side effects of their actions. For an autonomous agent without the ability to perform sophisticated look-ahead it also means that the agent might encounter situations where it needs to adjust its course of action and do so without creating the appearance of schizophrenically changing goals. However, the standard agent architecture does not lend itself to sophisticated look-ahead because at any given moment, a teleo-reactive agent cannot predict which OR-decomposition the agent might pick when decomposing a behavior plan.

Handling proscriptive directives involves addressing two issues:

1. Given alternative plan decompositions, an agent must decompose plans in such a way that it never performs a primitive action that has effects that conflict with the drama manager's desired plot; and
2. Failing believably in the case that and agent's performing of a primitive action that conflicts with the drama manager's desired plot is imminent and inevitable.

The solution we have adopted is to treat the problem as one of plan coordination. That is, the drama manager has a plan for how the user's experience should progress, and the character agents have reactive plans for how to behave believably in the world. Because of the particular arrangement between the drama manager and the character agents, the drama manager's plan takes precedence and the agents must adapt their behavior selection to coordinate with the drama manager's plot plan. This must be done without sacrificing believability. That is, character agents must reactively plan without appearing schizophrenic. The next two sections respectively describe (a) how techniques for plan coordination can address the first issue, and (b) how the plan coordination algorithms can be adapted to support believability, addressing the second issue.

Plan Coordination. There is an existing body of research on the coordination of hierarchical plans of multiple agents. We base our approach on the plan synergy algorithm [6; 7] because it directly supports multiple teleo-reactive agents with hierarchical plans expressed as AND/OR trees of goals.

In the plan synergy approach [6; 7], the plans of the agents at run-time must be coordinated and that coordination should occur as close to the leaves of the plan trees as possible for the crispest coordination possible. The approach assumes that nodes are plans that achieve goals and that they have pre-conditions, post-conditions, and in-conditions. Pre-conditions are conditions that must hold before an agent can execute a plan. Post-conditions are conditions that must hold after an agent completes the execution of a plan. In-conditions are conditions that will be true at some point during the execution of a plan. The synergy approach uses a two phase process. The first phase is an offline process that preprocesses the AND/OR trees of plans for each agents. Each node is annotated with summary information that describe the pre-conditions, post-conditions, and in-conditions of that node plus the pre-, post-, and in-conditions of all sub-plans. Conditions are marked *must* or *may*. A *must* annotation denotes that a pre/post/in-condition will definitely be true during the execution of a plan and all sub-plans. A *may* annotation denotes that a pre/post/in-condition could be true during the execution of a plan and some sub-plans. The preprocessing algorithm is described in [6]. The second phase uses the annotated AND/OR trees of multiple agents to constrain each agent so that they avoid acting in a conflicting manner.

In our work on integrating reactive believable agents and high-level plot plans, we use the synergy preprocessing phase to annotate agent behavior libraries with *must* and *may* condition annotations. We discard all but *must* condition annotations because in our case the drama manager's plot plan is assumed to be static and character agents are constrained to enact behaviors that do not conflict with the plot plan. If a plan is annotated with a *may* condition, then the agent can find an OR sub-plan that does not cause/require that condition to become true. We use the *must* annotations to restrict certain sub-plans from executing if there is a proscriptive directive from the drama manager and that sub-plan is annotated to indicate that it conflicts with the directive. That is, if a proscriptive directive matches a *must* condition on a sub-plan, the sub-plan cannot be chosen for decomposition and the agent must select an alternative decomposition. Character agents trying to achieve a particular top-level goal will only pick methods for achieving that goal that do not conflict with any negative directive. If all methods of achieving a particular top-level goal conflict with a negative directive, the character agent will be forced to choose a different but equally plausible and believable top-level goal before execution begins.

It should be noted that many agent behavior specification languages such as ABL [15] do not encode information about post-conditions or in-conditions. To compensate, we maintain a dual STRIPS-like representation of all ABL behaviors that are part of a plan to achieve a top-level goal. We run the annotation process on this alternative representation and merge the *must* condition annotations derived from this process with agent behavior libraries to produce new behavior libraries that support failing believably. The input to this process is a vocabulary of predicates used by the drama manager to represent the state of the story world. The new behavior libraries contain modified behaviors with additional preconditions and context conditions that cause any particular behavior to (a) not be able to execute or (b) immediately fail if certain negative directives are being enforced by the drama manager.

Restoration Modes. There exists the possibility that an agent has already begun a behavior plan that already has or will cause some world state condition to become true in direct contradiction of the drama manager's plot plan. This situation can happen under two circumstances. First, the condition is not prohibited by the Story Director at the time the agent selects the behavior plan because the drama manager had not yet transitioned into an interval of the plot plan in which a particular condition must be maintained. Second, a user action forces the drama manager to branch to an alternative plot plan that has different protected conditions. We do not use look ahead to prevent character agents from performing actions that will conflict with future directives because agents will have to look down all possible branches of the plot regardless of plausibility. In either event, the agent can be executing a plan that has caused or will inevitably conflict with the drama manager's plot plan.

When a top-level goal is forced to fail after execution has begun because the character agent cannot continue to pursue that goal without conflicting with the drama manager's plot plan, we encounter the potential for character believability to falter. That is, a character has suddenly stopped pursuing one goal and has switched to another goal without apparent reason. To avoid the appearance of such schizophrenic behavior we provide our character agents with special goal handler daemons that note when a goal fails. If the goal fails because of a proscriptive directive, the goal hander daemon triggers a *restoration mode*. A restoration mode is a hierarchically organized behavior that is ordinarily inaccessible to the character agent and provides an enacted behavior that visibly explains why the agent would cease one plan and adopt a new plan. If the agent has already negated the condition at the time that the proscriptive directive is given, the failure mode also re-establishes the condition.

For example, suppose there is a proscription against any characters besides Hassan and Ali to be in a particular area when Hassan plants the bomb. If Ṡaleh is already in the area, the agent must produce actions that explain why it can no longer be in the area. At a minimum, the agent may suddenly remember that he forgot something, or coordinate with another agent that asks it to run an errand. To invoke less of a sense of *deus ex machina*, the agent deliberates and generates a plausible explanation for why he'd suddenly prefer to avoid this region or do something else somewhere else; this may be related to some specific personality quirk of the agent.

It should be noted that restoration modes are not immune from further proscriptive directives (the exception is the negative directive for which the restoration mode was invoked in the first place; it can disregard that particular directive since the mode exists to protect and restore the world in accordance with that directive). When the restoration mode is complete, the story world will be restored to a state that conforms to the drama manager's plot plan. Thus restoration modes are necessarily more sophisticated than the transition behaviors used to handle prescriptive directives. When the restoration mode completes, the character agent activates its goal arbitration process to autonomously choose a new top-level goal.

4 Conclusions

Failing believably is a term we use to describe the notion that autonomous agents should be designed to believably avoid inexplicable goal failures caused by the complex coordination of agents and a proscriptive drama manager. We present techniques for endowing actor agents with the ability to fail believably, that is, to generate believable behavior to explain to an observing player a reason why an agent must not proceed with, abort, or undo previous behavior plans. Our approach provides a framework in which teleo-reactive [3], believable agents can invoke believability-preserving behaviors in the face of goal failure. Although the agent framework automates the process, creative design of behaviors, transitions, and restoration modes is still in the hands of agent designers.

Failing believably becomes important when proscription by a drama manager can have an impact on agent believability. A drama manager must be able to proscribe agents from taking particular actions that make it impossible for the drama manager to drive the narrative forward. For systems such as [25] and [19] in which the desired narrative experience is a priori unknown, or can be adapted over time, or generated from scratch, it is impossible to design autonomous believable characters that can be guaranteed never to choose behaviors that will not conflict with the drama manager's global narrative plot specification. It is inherent to such systems that believable character goals may produce conflict with a drama manager's storytelling goals. However, both are important. Drama management affords a coherent narrative structure to the user's experience that can be adapted to the user's actions. The use of autonomous agents affords interactivity and believability and helps immerse the user in a world where he or she has the perception of minute-to-minute self-agency.

Acknowledgements

The project or effort described here has been sponsored by the U.S. Army Research, Development, and Engineering Command (RDECOM). Statements and opinions expressed do not necessarily reflect the position or the policy of the United States Government, and no official endorsement should be inferred.

References

[1] Aylett, R.: Emergent Narrative, Social Immersion and "Storification." *Proc. of the 1st Int. Workshop on Narrative and Interactive Learning Environments* (2000).

[2] Bates, J.: Virtual Reality, Art, and Entertainment. *Presence: The Journal of Teleoperators and Virtual Environments*, 1 (1992), 133-138.

[3] Benson, S. Nilsson, N.: Reacting, Planning, and Learning in an Autonomous Agent. In Furukawa, Michie, Muggleton (eds.): *Machine Intelligence*, 14. Clarendon (1995).

[4] Blumberg, B., Galyean, T.: Multi-Level Control for Animated Autonomous Agents: Do the Right Thing... Oh, not that... In: R. Trappl, P. Petta (eds.): *Creating Personalities for Synthetic Actors*. Springer (1997).

[5] Cavazza, M., Charles, F., Meade, S.J.: Planning Characters' Behaviour in Interactive Storytelling. *Journal of Visualization and Computer Animation*, 13 (2002), 121-131.

[6] Clement, B.J., Durfee, E.H.: Top-Down Search for Coordinating the Hierarchical Plans of Multiple Agents. *Proc. of the 3rd Int. Conf. on Autonomous Agents* (1999).

[7] Cox, J.S., Durfee, E.H.: Discovering and Exploiting Synergy between Hierarchical Planning Agents. *Proc. of the 2nd Int. Joint Conf. on Autonomous Agents and Multi Agent Systems* (2003).

[8] Figueiredo, R., Dias, J., Aylett, R., Paiva, A.: Shaping Emergent Narratives for a Pedagogical Application. *Proc. of the 4th Int. Conf. on Narrative and Interactive Learning Environments* (2006).

[9] Firby, J.: *Adaptive Execution in Complex Dynamic Domains*. Ph.D. Dissertation, Yale University (1989).

[10] Georgeff, M, Lansky, A.: Procedural Knowledge. *Proc. of IEEE Special Issue on Knowledge Representation*, 74 (1986), 1383-1398.

[11] Gratch, J., Marsella, S.: Tears and Fears: Modeling Emotions and Emotional Behaviors in Synthetic Agents. *Proc. of the 5th Int. Conf. on Autonomous Agents* (2001).

[12] Kelso, M., Weyhrauch, P., Bates, J.: Dramatic Presence. *Presence: The Journal of Teleoperators and Virtual Environments*, 2 (2005).

[13] Loyall, A.B.: *Believable Agents: Building Interactive Personalities*. Ph.D. Dissertation, School of Computer Science, Carnegie Mellon University (1997).

[14] Magerko, B., Laird, J.E., Assanie, M., Kerfoot, A., Stokes, D.: AI characters and directors for intereactive computer games. *Proc. of the 16th Innovative Applications of Artificial Intelligence Conference* (2004).

[15] Mateas, M., Stern, A.: A Behavior Language: Joint Action and Behavior Idioms. In: H. Prendinger & M. Ishizuka (eds.): *Life-like Characters: Tools, Affective Functions and Applications*. Springer (2004).

[16] Mateas, M., Stern, A.: Structuring Content in the Façade Interactive Drama Architecture. *Proc. of the 1st Conf. on AI and Interactive Digital Entertainment* (2005).

[17] Riedl, M.O. *Narrative Generation: Balancing Plot and Character*. Ph.D. Dissertation, North Carolina State University.

[18] Riedl, M.O, Saretto, C.J., Young, R.M.: Managing Interaction Between Users and Agents in a Multi-Agent Storytelling Environment. *Proc. of the 2nd Int. Conf. on Autonomous Agents and Multi Agent Systems* (2003).

[19] Riedl, M.O., Stern, A.: Believable Agents and Intelligent Story Adaptation for Interactive Storytelling. *Proc. of the 3rd Int. Conf. on Technologies for Interactive Digital Storytelling and Entertainment* (2006).

[20] Sengers, P.: Schizophrenia and Narrative in Artificial Agents. In: M. Mateas and P. Sengers (eds.): *Narrative Intelligence*. John Benjamins (2003).

[21] Szilas, N.: The Future of Interactive Drama. *Proc. of the 2nd Australasian Conf. on Interactive Entertainment* (2005).

[22] Theune, M., Faas, S., Nijholt, A., Heylen, D.: The Virtual Storyteller: Story Creation by Intelligent Agents. *Proc. of the 1st Int. Conf. for Interactive Digital Storytelling and Entertainment* (2003).

[23] van Lent, M., Fisher, W., Mancuso, M.: An Explainable Artificial Intelligence System for Small-Unit Tactical Behavior. *Proc. of the 16th Innovative Applications of Artificial Intelligence Conference* (2004).

[24] Weyhrauch, P.: *Guiding Interactive Fiction*. Ph.D. Dissertation, School of Computer Science, Carnegie Mellon University (1997).

[25] Young, R.M., Riedl, M.O., Branly, M., Jhala, A., Martin, R.J., & Saretto, C.J.: An architecture for integrating plan-based behavior generation with interactive game environments. *Journal of Game Development*, 1 (2004), 51-70.

Personality Templates and Social Hierarchies Using Stereotypes

Robert Mosher and Brian Magerko

253 Comm Arts Bldg.
Michigan State University
East Lansing, MI 48824
{mosherr2, magerko}@msu.edu
http://gel.msu.edu/

Abstract. In order for interactive agents to be believable, they will need to respond to any likely situation in a manner that is consistent with their personality, as well as their position within social hierarchies. Thus believable agents will need to have a clearly defined personality, social role, and other traits that will govern their actions in a virtual world. The goal of this paper is to present a template that can be used to define such traits of a character in order to maintain consistency. The template will be dominated by a model that defines aspects of personality typically used to define persons across cultures, aiding both intuitive creation by authors, and acceptance by users. It will also be able to take advantage of character stereotypes to ease the authoring process. In addition to this, a social hierarchy framework is given.

Keywords: interactive drama, synthetic characters, personality, social-hierarchy, stereotypes.

1 Introduction

Over the past decades there has been much work toward creating believable agents in static and interactive computer-generated works. Prior works used static templates to give agents a consistent foundation to base their behavior on [12] [8]. A template specifies a set of traits key to defining an agent's character, such as personality and knowledge areas. This paper presents a templating system that defines a set of traits for synthetic characters, a social hierarchy model that templates tie into, and a procedure for utilizing stereotype templates. The choice of personality traits for this system are taken from the five-factor model (FFM) of personality, augmented by the NEO personality inventory. This system differs from prior work by allowing for complex social hierarchies by using directed acyclic graphs as models rather than the simplistic linear power scales of previous work. This template system is intended to ease character creation by structuring the process and directing synthetic character authors toward key aspects of character. It is initial research intended to inform future prototypes.

One aspect necessary for making characters believable is giving them realistic personalities. Previous works [12] [8] have included a set of personality traits in

S. Göbel, R. Malkewitz, and I. Iurgel (Eds.): TIDSE 2006, LNCS 4326, pp. 207–218, 2006.

their templates. These traits keep characters consistent by defining a "disposition to act in a similar way in a wide range of situations" [7]. The set of traits used in this work are taken from the FFM, following previous work [1] [13].

To be believable, synthetic characters must also use social roles and the hierarchies associated with them to guide their interactions as people do. Prior work has looked at this, but it has been relatively simplistic, assuming a single linear hierarchy[15] . Here a more complex hierarchy that more accurately models real world hierarchies is specified, which can be utilized by the character templates

Conforming synthetic characters to a set of stereotypes also aids believability. Stereotypes are used by people to categorize others, helping them limit the complexity level of their world model. Thus, it is believed, by placing characters into stereotypes, users will have an easier time accepting them. Further, it simplifies the character author's task, allowing characters to be quickly defined in a broad sense. Stereotypes are also useful for systems like OPIATE [6], which places characters into predefined roles. "Stereotype" in this sense should not carry the connotation of prejudice. Rather it defines a set of traits that could realistically be expected of a person given their social role or background.

There are several criteria that should be met by a character template that will ease the creation of believable agents. First, it should *facilitate the creation of consistent and coherent characters* [12]. If both the inherent properties of agents and their world are not subject to drastic changes without some reasonable cause, consistency is maintained. Coherence is maintained if there is a logical explanation for events given the information available to the user.

A broader criteria is that the template should *model reality as closely as is practical.* For instance, if the template takes into account social relationships between agents, it should be able to model all probable relationships. In regard to personality, the template should be able to represent all aspects of personality, or at least those aspects that are necessary to govern observable behavior.

The template should also *strive for universality.* Freeing the template of chauvinism will likely result in a template that focuses on the core aspects of character. As this template is intended to be used in character creation, the *correspondence between what is defined in a template and how it is manifested in characters* should be apparent to authors. One aspect of this is that what is in the template should have a clear connection to a real world counterpart.

In the following section, previous work in this area is discussed in more depth. In section 3 the template framework is discussed in detail, with a short example of defining a character using this framework following in section 4. Section 5 describes future work that will be needed to utilize and test the effectiveness of the framework, with a conclusion in section 6.

2 Related Work

2.1 Character Templates

There have been prior attempts to create a standard template to be used in defining synthetic characters. Most notably are the "person frames" detailed in [12]. Lebowitz's "person frame" template for the UNIVERSE system was designed in order to maintain consistency and coherence in the story-telling world. That is any action an agent makes should be understandable given their history, personality, emotions, etc.

In order to maintain consistency and coherence, Lebowitz specifies information from three categories in his "person frames": personality traits, interpersonal relationships, and goals. His set of personality traits includes information such as age, sex, intelligence, guile, niceness, and other such broadly defined aspects of personality. In order to simplify the assignment of these traits, UNIVERSE uses stereotypes to provide default trait values. These stereotypes include traits associated with occupations, social groups, or backgrounds.

Goldberg also defined a similar template for personality traits focused on use for character animation [8]. Like UNIVERSE's "person frames" it defined traits that govern how physical activities would be performed, such as strength and coordination, as well as traits that govern interactions with other characters, such as amiability and intelligence. Along with these very general traits, very specific traits relating to a single task, character, or knowledge area can also be specified. These traits are used to give specifics to such broadly defined traits as *intelligent* or *strong*.

2.2 Stereotyping

It has been mentioned that stereotyping will aid authors in creating believable agents. Agents that conform to stereotypes will also be easier for users to size up. Rich states that:

> [P]eople use stereotypes as a means for dealing with the fact that the world is far more complex than they can deal with without some form of simplification and categorization. One of the ways in which stereotypes help to simplify the world is that they have a strong effect on what characteristics of a person are attended to and remembered. As a result, they will tend to be confined by experience since potentially disconfirmatory evidence will be ignored [16].

Though Rich's [16] system applied stereotypes to users, he gives evidence that users will attempt to stereotype agents. Thus, by creating agents that conform to a stereotype, authors can take advantage of conventions already used by users, perhaps even with the advantage that some errors that could detract from believability will be overlooked.

Both Rich [16] and Kobsa [11] point out that one person will need to fall into multiple stereotypes so as to flesh out all of their traits. This leads to conflicting traits that need to be resolved by selecting the one that is more fitting. Both also recognize the need for specific subgroups within a stereotype. Rich uses a directed acyclic graph (DAG) with a partial ordering relation of "generalization of" for the stereotypes. For example, at the top of the graph would be *any-person*, which may have a node *teacher*, which may have a node *high-school-math-teacher*, etc.

2.3 Personality

Prior use of templates to define agents has assumed that personality or psychological traits are the best means of creating such a definition. Rousseau & Hayes-Roth based their look at personality in synthetic agents on psychological trait theories [17]. In their work the claim is made that psychological traits (lazy, confident, friendly, etc.) are commonly used to describe people and are psychologically adequate to define the traits that influence a person's behavior. These traits are assumed to dispose people to exhibit consistent behavior across different situations, agreeing with Lebowitz's [12] requirement of coherence across an agent's actions.

Table 1. Factors and Facets of the Five-Factor Model

Factor	Facets
Neuroticism	Anxiety, Angry Hostility, Depression, Self-Consciousness, Impulsiveness, Vulnerability
Extroversion	Warmth, Gregariousness, Assertiveness, Activity, Excitement-Seeking, Positive Emotions
Openness	Fantasy, Aesthetics, Feelings, Actions, Ideas, Values
Agreeableness	Trust, Straightforwardness, Altruism, Compliance, Modesty, Tender-mindedness
Conscientiousness	Competence, Order, Dutifulness, Achievement Striving, Self-Discipline, Deliberation

Though it is held that traits are adequate to describe personality, what set of traits covers the full range of personality has been left open. One model of describing personality that is widely accepted by psychologists is the five-factor model (FFM). The FFM is well suited to creating personality representations that improve agent believability [1]. Further, evidence indicates the FFM is sufficient for describing the full range of personality. In tests where people were asked to describe themselves given a large list of adjectives, people tended to choose five, and rarely more than six [5]. Further, the adjectives selected repeatedly fell into the same five categories (see Table 1). Personalities tend to be very stable, having few changes over the years, and personality profiles using the FFM reflect this [5]. More importantly, the FFM is found to be free of chauvinism. Both males and females can be described by the FFM. McCrae & Costa shows research indicating that the FFM is also universal across cultures, though there may be differences in what is perceived as the norm, or in how different traits are expressed[14].

2.4 Social Roles

Agent awareness of social roles is another important factor in achieving believability. Prendinger & Ishizuka [15] have observed that synthetic agents do not modify their behavior with regard to their and others' social roles, and the social setting in which they find themselves. Yet humans do this with ease, and thus so must believable agents. One of the key aspects of social roles are power levels. An example of how power levels are important to agent behavior is given by Prendinger & Ishizuka where a secretary brushes off an aspirant's request to make copies but complies when a manager makes the same request. The two different responses are believable because of the difference in power level relative to the secretary. Prendinger & Ishizuka suggest modeling these power levels with a linear power scale, with each agent having a different place along the scale. However, this ignores the fact that a manager's high power level may be meaningless at another company, or even in another department within the company. Thus, the situation or setting is also a key aspect of social roles.

3 Template Framework

In the following section a template is given for defining a character's personality, physical, and other traits. A set of stereotype templates and a social hierarchy that work with the character templates is also described. It should be noted that this is an initial step intended to inform future prototypes, and thus may require further revisions.

3.1 Consistency and Coherence

The first aspect of this template is that it will primarily focus on things that are unchanging about a character. Lebowitz [12] makes a case for the importance of consistency and coherence. By focusing on those aspects that are static, a good foundation will be provided for character creation. This stability is expected to make characters more believable; as Digman [5] points out, people's personalities change very little over time. That is not to say that it is expected that an agent's template will remain unchanged throughout the course of their virtual life, but that there should be a strong basis for change in order to maintain believability.

3.2 Traits

The core of the whole template is the set of traits. Personality underlies much of the behavior of an agent. Though agent's goals, social roles, and emotions play an important part, these really only refine how the personality is exhibited. Physical traits are more important to how other agents and users view an agent. Traits concerning appearance cannot be left only to art directors as there must be a representation that is understandable by other agents. Along with these traits, more unique traits, such as specific skills or knowledge areas, can be defined.

Personality Traits. Selecting a set of personality traits without backing motivation can result in a set that is incomplete or redundant. To avoid these issues the FFM of personality is utilized as it covers the full range of personalities, it is universal, and, most importantly, it is made up of terms actually used by people to describe personality [5][14]. Though it is not known whether the FFM truly covers the depth and range of the core of personalities, it is adequate for both the average person's and the psychologist's description of personality, and thus, for character designers in defining personalities.

The five-factors of personality are listed in Table 1. Though there is strong agreement on the number of factors, there is not a strong consensus as to their meaning [5]. Even for traits like extroversion, whose meaning seem apparent, it may be difficult to translate into behavior. Still, the evidence that this model is well suited to describing personalities is strong, fulfilling the purpose of the defined template. The burden of how the personalities play out falls within the domain of programmatic implementations.

Fortunately, some of the ambiguity is cleared up in the NEO Personality Inventory, which splits each factor into six facets (an example report is seen in [3]). Agreeableness, for example, has facets such as trust, altruism, and modesty (Table 1). These facets clarify which aspects of personality agreeableness dictates, and allow finer control of character design. For this reason, the personality definition will consist of both the five factors, and their six facets as defined in the NEO Personality Inventory. Any facet that is left unspecified will inherit its value from its parent factor.

Physical and other Traits. The physical traits require a little less forethought, as they are more obvious. However, as stated, it is necessary to describe all physical traits that affect how an agent interacts with the world, and with how other agents view them. Some example traits are *name, sex, weight, age, height, hair color, hair style, voice, clothing style,* etc. Though *clothing style* and *hair style* may not fit the focus on aspects that are more static, it would be likely that a character's style choices (suits, trendy, utilitarian) would largely be static even though the clothes choices may not. The associated value type for a given trait is dictated by what that trait represents. *Height* and *age* would have real world units. *Clothing style* will use descriptive terms dictated by the agent's world.

Unique Traits. Unique traits include anything that does not fit into previous trait categories; the things that may not be necessary for every agent, or desired by every author. These include things like skill sets (expert sailor, average pool player), and knowledge areas (expert on Egyptology, novice of celebrity trivia). This specificity is necessary as general traits like *intelligent* mean little when a character does not have that intelligence applied to specific areas, and a character that has high intelligence in all areas would be unbelievable. Both the traits and their values are author defined, with the expectation that things like knowledge areas will tie into a related database containing the knowledge. Thus, the scale that defines the level of skill or knowledge should be such that it fits with the related database and will not be specified here.

3.3 Stereotypes

Stereotypes will be used to ease the creation of synthetic characters. Stereotypes provide default values for character templates based on what is expected of their social role or background. For instance, a construction worker would be expected to be skilled with tools and physically fit. A college graduate would be expected to have knowledge in certain areas. By having a set of stereotypes, an author can select one for a character to fill in some basic information, with the author needing only to tweak some values to make the character unique. Along with aiding author creation, stereotypes will help conform agents to user expectations. It is known that people use social roles to categorize people [10], and that these stereotype categories make it easier for people to deal with information in the world [16]. As long as the observed stereotype fits with the user's expectations, they can help users quickly appraise an agent, making them more believable to the users.

Though it may be acceptable for peripheral characters to only fall into one stereotype, when a major character is so tightly pigeon-holed they will likely appear, and in reality be, one-dimensional. As Rich [16] and Kobsa [11] suggest, characters should have multiple overlapping stereotypes. Dahlgren [4] indicates that richness, vividness, and distinction arise in characters when given multiple stereotypes.

One difficulty of combining stereotypes is deciding which stereotype wins out when two traits conflict. Automatic resolution of conflicting traits will not be addressed in this paper as it is expected authors will not choose multiple stereotypes with a large number of conflicting traits. Thus, resolving conflicts by hand should be manageable.

These stereotypes, following Rich's [16] model, will fall into a DAG with a single root stereotype, *any-person* (Fig. 1). Each stereotype will inherit trait values from its parents, and specify certain trait values in which it differs and overrides its parent's values. Stereotypes will be painted with broad strokes when high within the graph, and gain specificity deeper within the graph. An example path down the stereotype graph could go from *any-person*, to *medical-professional*, to *doctor*, to *pediatrician*. Having multiple parents is also acceptable, as, if a stereotype was given for a doctor at St. Jude's, it would be desired to have it inherit traits from *pediatrician* and *oncologist*.

The root stereotype, *any-person*, will likely be a challenge to define. Even something as simple as height will have to take into account cultural considerations to choose the norm. Some aspects of the norm may be best left to authors so they can select defaults suitable for their virtual world.

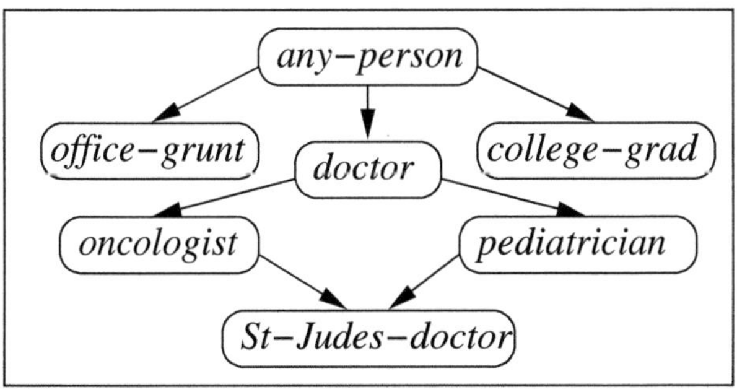

Fig. 1. Sparse Stereotype DAG

3.4 Social Hierarchies

Prendinger & Ishizuka [15] give evidence to the importance of social roles and the power levels associated with them. Certainly, if someone knows that someone else has control over their job or freedom, they will treat that person differently than if there were no power differential, or if the differential were reversed. Yet the application of social roles can be rather complex as they are situational and cannot be defined by a rigid power scale. For example, a bartender has a higher power level than the average person when at his bar, but not when on the street (yet if the man on the street is also a patron of his bar, the social relationship may still influence interactions). A proper model of social hierarchies will need to take this scope into account.

Prendinger & Ishizuka [15] suggests indicating power levels with a linear power scale. However, power levels are not universal. A CEO does not have authority over employees in every company, and a manager does not have authority over every department. Having one universal power scale will create very unrealistic interactions between agents.

To handle these complex relations, a directed graph that includes scope indicators will be used (Fig. 2). The graph can be separated into several sub-graphs, allowing for certain power relationships to have no meaning against others. Each node in the graph will have a title (e.g. "store manager") that can be referenced from an agent template or stereotype. Each node can have multiple scopes, one for each edge. The scopes dictate in what context the power relation is relevant (i.e. for the "store manger" it is in the store). It is imaginable that authority roles may change with situations. For instance, a manager would typically have authority over someone in tech support, but if there is a virus outbreak in the office their relationship could be temporarily reversed.

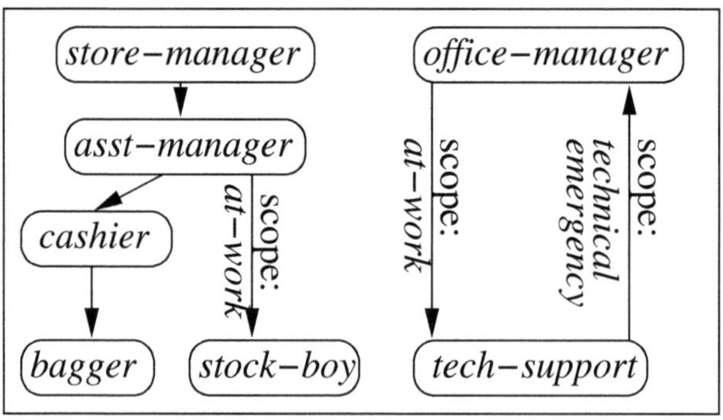

Fig. 2. Two Disconnected Social Hierarchies

3.5 Unspecified

A few notes on things that are not specified by this template: relationships, emotions, the nature of social hierarchy relationships, and gender differences.

Relationships. Marriages, friendships, feuds, and other relationships are important aspects of characters. If an agent does not act fittingly in regard to their relationships it will cause confusion. However, we believe that which relationships occur between people are affected by their personalities and social roles. Thus, the relationships can be generated after an agent's profile is created and should be separate from this template. In fact, Lebowitz [12] did something similar by simulating "past lives."

Emotions. Bates [2] states that "If the character does not react emotionally to events, if it does not care, then neither will we." Though emotions are critical for agents to be engaging, they change quickly whereas this project's intent is to focus on the static aspects of characters. Other research focused on computational emotion examines how emotional models can be used to influence synthetic character behavior [9]. This framework could plausibly augment such work, though that is beyond the scope of our current research.

Nature of Social Hierarchy Relationships. It may appear that the particular nature of the social relationships are not conveyed by this system. Can it differentiate between an evil tyrant's relationship with their subjects and a sweet mother's relationship with her children? Though not specified by the hierarchy, these differences will arise out of the agents involved in the relationship, i.e., a benevolent relationship would have an altruistic ruler.

Gender Differences. One area that may need more attention is that of gender differences. In the interest of maintaining a relatively narrow view, gender was for the most part ignored.

4 Example

In this section a character, Doug, will be specified. Doug is a *cardiologist*, so this will be one stereotype assigned to him. From this he inherits the unique trait *expert-knowledge: cardiology.* In this virtual world cardiologists are fairly straightforward, so he also inherits a *straightforwardness* (an *agreeableness* facet) of 0.75. It is expected cardiologists have to spend a good deal of time in medical school, and have practiced for several years, so he inherits an age of *40. Cardiologist* is a sub-stereotype of *doctor*, so traits are also inherited from this. Doctors are very straightforward in this world, having a value of 0.9, but this is not inherited as this trait is already specified by the more specific sub-stereotype. Doctors also have a high level of *conscientiousness*, 0.8. Since this is not specified for cardiologists, it is inherited. This is the same value used for all the facets of *conscientiousness* (*competence, dutifulness, self-discipline* . . .) as they are not specified. The unique traits of *high-knowledge: biology* and *high-knowledge: medical-procedures* are also inherited.

The next level above *doctor* is *any-person,* from which Doug inherits all personality traits not otherwise specified. He also inherits the average *height, weight,*

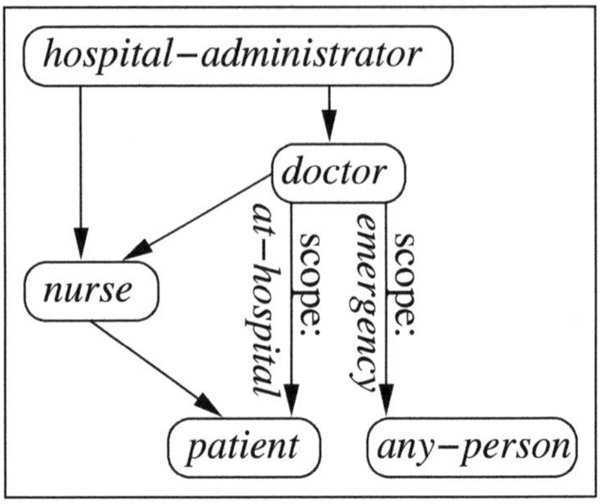

Fig. 3. Example Hierarchy

etc. for this world. So far Doug is rather bland, so we also assign him the stereotype of *Bostonian* to give him more character and some background. From this he inherits *Boston-accent* in regards to his voice, and *high-knowledge: Boston-area.*

Along with the stereotype of *doctor* comes the social role of *doctor* (note: using the same name is not necessary). This can be used to reference Doug's position in the social hierarchy. As a *doctor*, Doug must answer to *hospital administrators*, and has authority over *nurses* and *patients* (Fig. 3). All of these relations have a scope of *at-hospital-of-employment.* The author can define his hospital of employment directly in Doug's profile by giving his social role of *doctor* the trait of *at-city-hospital.* As a *doctor*, Doug also has an elevated social role in regards to *any-person* in the scope of *emergency.*

Once the author has assigned Doug a number of stereotypes to fill in most of his personality, they can start tweaking some more of the details to make him more unique. Say Doug is a cardiologist on a prime-time medical drama, so he is given high impulsiveness, and low warmth. His hair color is blond, his eye color blue, he is of a gaunt build, and so on.

5 Discussion

In this paper a framework for specifying character traits was proposed. The framework provides a template for defining a character's personality, physical and other non-personality traits, as well as placing them within a social hierarchy. The personality template differs from previous work in that the traits are based on the FFM, a widely accepted set of factors and facets for describing personality. Evidence that people's natural descriptions of personality conform to the FFM indicate that it will be well suited to aid designers in defining personalities, and guiding them towards characters that will meet user's expectations for believable agents.

Previous work has been seen to implement social hierarchies; however, they have been limited to power differentials. In this approach, the context in which the social hierarchy is relevant is taken into account. This is closer to how hierarchies manifest themselves in the real world, and is expected to give believable results in the virtual world.

The template meets the requirement of assisting the creation of consistent and coherent agents by focusing the character definition process on static aspects of character. An adequate job has been done to keep the template in-line with reality. The social hierarchy accounts for more aspects of real world social relationships than have been in the past. The FFM uses a set of personality traits that are adequate for psychologists to describe personality. The FFM model also meets with the condition for universality of the template. As people naturally use the FFM to describe personality, this partly meets the criteria of the template having a clear connection to its eventual manifestation. Yet exactly how trait values map to personality is still vague.

Given this template, the bulk of an author's work lies in filling out trait values, and creating hierarchies. If a set of stereotypes is defined, authors will be able to quickly define new characters, with prominent characters requiring more effort to make them unique. This speed of character creation is a significant advantage of a template system. Though defining a set of stereotypes is in itself a daunting task, once it has been defined it can be reused.

6 Future Work

The basic framework for the template system has now been presented, but remains to be implemented. A skeleton template will be defined in XML. This will then be connected to a DAG defined for the social hierarchy. Once these two basic building blocks are created, much work will need to go into creating a default set of stereotypes and social hierarchy. It is expected this will be time consuming and perhaps difficult. As Isbister & Hayes-Roth [10] found, expected stereotypes do not necessarily meet with what is found by psychological codifications.

The next important task is making the traits come to life. There needs to be a programmatic implementation that translates trait values into behavior for synthetic agent. Some questions that will need to be looked at are "what is the behavioral difference between an *extroversion* value of 0.5 and 0.6?" and "how should the social hierarchy be considered between two friends versus two acquaintances?" Once this is completed, and the system in integrated with a storytelling system, the choices made will need to be evaluated as to their efficacy.

References

1. André, E., Klesen, M., Gebhard, P., Allen, S., Rist, T.. Integrating models of personality and emotions into lifelike characters. In: Proceedings International Workshop on Affect in Interactions. Towards a New Generation of Interfaces. Siena, Italy (1999) 136-149
2. Bates, J.: The role of emotion in believable agents. In: Communications of the ACM, Vol. 37 (1997) 122-125
3. Costa, P., McCrae, R.: Revised NEO Personality Inventory Interpretive Report. http://www.testgrid.com/docs/NEO_PIR_Long.pdf (2000)

4. Dahlgren, K.: The Cognitive Structure of Social Categories. In: Cognitive Science, Vol. 9 (1985) 379-398
5. Digman, J.: Personality Structure: Emergence of the Five-Factor Model. In: Annual Review of Psychology, Vol. 41 (1990) 417-440
6. Fairclough, R., Cunningham, P.: AI Structuralist Storytelling in Computer Games. https://www.cs.tcd.ie/publications/tech-reports/reports.04/TCD-CS-2004-43.pdf (2004)
7. Frick, W.: Personality: Selected Readings in Theory. F.E. Peacock Publishing, Itasca, Illinois (1995) 230-255
8. Goldberg, A.: Improv. A system for real-time animation of behavior-based interactive synthetic actors. In: Trappl, R., Petta, P. (eds.): Creating personalities for synthetic actors, Vol. 1195. Springer, Berlin (1997)
9. Gratch, J., Marsella, S.: Tears and Fears: Modeling emotions and emotional behaviors in synthetic agents. In: Proceedings of the 5th International Conference on Autonomous Agents, Montreal (2001)
10. Isbister, K., Hayes-Roth, B.: Social Implications of Using Synthetic Characters: An Examination of a Role-Specific Intelligent Agent. In: Proc. of the IJCAI-97 Workshop on Animated Interface Agents: Making them Intelligent. Standford University, Standford (1998)
11. Kobsa, A.: Generic User Modeling Systems. In: User Modeling and User-Adapted Interaction Journal, Vol. 11 (2001) 49-63
12. Lebowitz, M.: Creating Characters in a Story-Telling Universe. In: Poetics, Vol. 13 (1984) 171-194
13. Martinho, C., Pavia, A.: Developing Pathematic Agents. In: Velasquez, J. D. (Ed.): Emotion-Based Agent Architectures. Seattle (1999) 79-83
14. McCrae, R., Costa, P.: Personality Trait Structure as a Human Universal. In: American Psychologist, Vol. 52 (1997) 509-516
15. Prendinger, H., Ishizuka, M.: Social Role Awareness in Animated Agents. In: Proceedings 5th International Conference on Autonomous Agents. ACM Press, Montreal, Canada (2001) 270-277
16. Rich, E.: User Modeling via Stereotypes. In: Cognitive Science, Vol. 3 (1979) 329-354
17. Rousseau, D., Hayes-Roth, B.: Personality in Synthetic Agents. Technical Report KSL-96-21. Knowledge Systems Laboratory, Standford University, Stanford (1996)

INSCAPE: Emotion Expression and Experience in an Authoring Environment

Nelson Zagalo[1], Stefan Göbel[2], Ana Torres[1], Rainer Malkewitz[2], and Vasco Branco[1]

[1] Department of Communication and Art, University of Aveiro, 3810-193 Aveiro, Portugal
{ntz, atorres, vab}@ca.ua.pt
[2] ZGDV e.V., Digital Storytelling Dept., Rundeturmstr. 10, 64283 Darmstadt, Germany
{stefan.goebel, rainer.malkewitz}@zgdv.de

Abstract. Human emotions are known to play an important role in the users' engagement, namely by activating their attention, perception and memory skills, which in turn will help to understand the story – and hopefully perceive, or rather "feel" it as an entertaining experience. Despite the more and more realistic and immersive use of 3D computer graphics, multi-channel sound and sophisticated input devices – mainly forced by game applications – the emotional participation of users still seems a weak point in most interactive games and narrative systems. This paper describes methods and concepts on how to bring emotional experiencing and emotional expression into interactive storytelling systems. In particular, the Emotional Wizard is introduced, as an emerging module for authoring emotional expression and experiencing. Within the INSCAPE framework, this module is meant to improve elicited emotions as elements of style, which are used deliberately by an author within an integrated storytelling environment.

Keywords: Virtual characters, emotion, emotional expression, author tools.

1 Introduction

The emotion modules are being developed as part of a complete authoring tool of interactive storytelling - INSCAPE. The INSCAPE tool aims at enabling ordinary people to use and master the latest Information Society Technologies for interactively conceiving, authoring, publishing and experiencing interactive stories whatever their form, be it theatre, movie, cartoon, puppet show, video-games, interactive manuals, training simulators, etc. INSCAPE will generate and develop the knowledge in the emerging domain of Interactive Storytelling by researching, implementing, demonstrating and disseminating a complete suite of innovative concepts, tools and working methods tightly integrated in a homogeneous web-based framework and offering a full chain to people with no particular computer skills, from content acquisition and creation, organising, processing, sharing, and using all the way to publishing, from creators to "viewers".

To accomplish these goals, INSCAPE depends of a suite of applications (plug-ins) that provides the necessary authoring innovations. Thus, we started assuming that in the virtual interactive storytelling of the future, virtual characters will play an increasingly important role, mainly because they represent the storytelling backbone in

S. Göbel, R. Malkewitz, and I. Iurgel (Eds.): TIDSE 2006, LNCS 4326, pp. 219–230, 2006.

emotional terms. We also believe that to help raising characters emotionality and believability in interactive storytelling we'll need to start by the behaviour modelling, not only expressively trough physicality or behavioural expression but also in the modelling of the characters experiencing of the artificial worlds. It is the modelling of characters emotion experience that will help in making stories more believable, increasing drama and so the user emotion experiencing.

2 State of the Art

The current cognitive theory of emotion defends the emotional experiencing as an appraisal activity. Emotions do have adaptive functions [1, 2, 3, 4, 5], for instance Izard argues that "induced emotion guides perception, increases the selectivity of attention, helps determine the content of working memory, in sum, it motivate, organize and sustain particular sets of behaviors" [1].

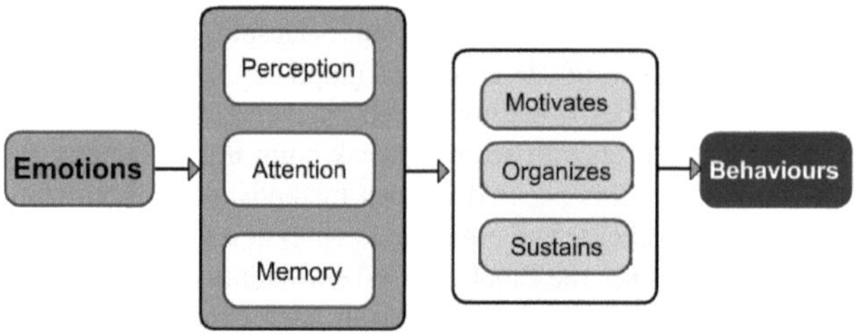

Fig. 1. Emotions get experienced and take adaptive functions that influence human behavior

This model of emotion can support not only our view of the characters experiencing construction but also delineates users activity to really engage with a story. In that way, Interactive Storytelling needs to induce emotion to engage users, in order to guarantee that they pay attention, understand and interact with the story.

We can see the double pathway of this model in a review made by Stern [6] about virtual digital pets - Catz and Dogz, Babyz, Tamagotchi, Furby, Aibo etc., where he argues that "Users can feed, clothe and give medicine to the characters. Petz express the need to be nurtured by acting excited when food is brought out, begging, acting satisfied and grateful after eating, or disgusted when they don't like the food.". All of them try then to establish an emotional relation with their human 'observer' by exchanging behaviour in both ways. To the user interaction virtual character develops behaviours of emotion expression in response, catching the user perception and attention. Once user recognizes and believes in character emotion expressions he reacts emotionally "recording" in his memory the event. The memory of the character performing these behaviours will lead him in demanding for more.

As we've acknowledged we defend characters as key for user emotion creation. However, also Environment and Events can lead to the emotion creation. We've divided interactive storytelling in three possible authoring levels. These levels encompasses only Form and Style and doesn't take into account the theme or story idea. We pursued this trail because we believe that an authoring tool should not be too intrusive of the author work. Thus the goal is to create tools that act at the levels of form and style and not the message or theme the author wants to portray.

In this paper we'll summarize parts of the current state of the research and concentrate more in detail in the characters.

2.1 Example Tools

In the last 6 years, research has been done in terms of applications that can help users in the design of emotions, e.g.: Emotion Cinematography [7], Emotion demos [8], and FacePoser[1]. Emotion Cinematography is a methodology developed by Tomlinson and Blumberg, with the purpose of transforming in real time the classes: lighting and camera according to when an environment needed emotions. This work delivers an interesting approach to the very difficult task of the class "editing" to be employed in interactive environments. However the work reaches very few of the initial objectives and so this represents work to be improved, also it's not sufficiently schematized foundationally to be used by any commercial machine, it is still a crude and incomplete system but in our view a possibility to be enhanced.

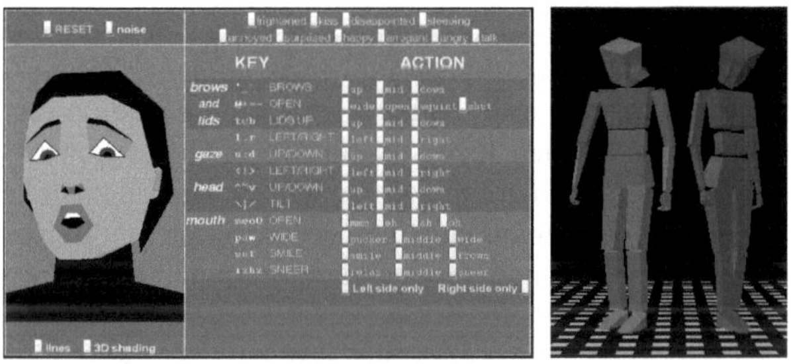

Fig. 2. Face and Emotive Actors (live demos may be found at http://mrl.nyu.edu/~perlin/)

Perlin [8] has developed various emotion demos for characters. The Face we can see in Fig. 2 above on the left was grounded in Ekman studies around thc world on facial expression [9]. This module is so strong in believability that it has been adapted by Valve in the creation of the wide known Half-Life 2 [10] computer game, being the face used in this model the same used for a main character (Alyx) in the game. On the right, we can see the demo on Emotive Actors, two interactive characters that seem to have a life of their own albeit the user being in control, because they behave accordingly to each other.

Finally about the Face Poser, as we said above, Perlin work has been of great support for the construction of the authoring SDK of Half-Life 2. Valve used all that knowledge to develop two interesting tools: Face Poser and Choreography[2]. Face Poser is very similar to the research work done by Perlin and Choreography is a tool that permits the manipulation of characters emotions in a regular time-based manner.

Also, in terms of example artefacts that are able to deal with emotions – Façade [11], Virtual Petz [12], and Nintendogs[3], Façade seems the most complete; it makes use of dramatic language to control the structure of Events, in emotional ways. Façade

[1] For more information about the tool, http://developer.valvesoftware.com/wiki/FacePoser
[2] For more information, see http://developer.valvesoftware.com/wiki/Choreography_Tool
[3] Videogame for the Nintendo DS platform - http://www.nintendogs.com/

provides a very efficient methodology for the story beats control, maintaining the common tension and interest in story terms, even when the user disrupts the events completely. Albeit failing in the creation of Emotion Environments, it delivers strong character emotion expression and experience behaviours.

Virtual Petz developed by Stern presents the problematic of emergence, putting the story fate in the agent's hands to build mini-stories without explicitly building narrative into the system. Recently the Game Industry presented a very successful product in terms of critique and popularity - Nintendogs – making use of Stern concept. The main problem with all these artefacts examples are not the emotional expressiveness, but the lack of standardization and consequent impossibility to use these models outside their proprietary closed systems.

2.2 Agents and Computer Emotion Models

The interest in general computational models of emotion and emotional behavior have been steadily growing, mainly in the 'agent' research community. The development of computational models of emotion facilitates advances in a large array of computational systems that model, interpret or influence human behavior[4]. Computational work on emotion can be roughly divided into "communication-driven" approaches our "emotion expression" which focus on surface manifestation of emotion and its potential for influencing human-computer interaction, and on the other hand "simulation-driven" approaches our "emotion experience" that attempt to model the cognitive mechanisms underlying real emotions, including its potential for influencing several cognitive processes [13].

In communication-driven approaches, the system chooses emotional behaviors on the basis of its desired impact on the user (in our case as a choice of the human story designer). Catherine Pelachaud and her colleagues for instance use facial expressions to convey the performative of a speech act [14]. Pelachaud presents a semantics-driven system to generate believable gaze behaviors between two 3D synthetic agents conversing with each other [15]. Klesen uses stylized animations of body language and facial expression to convey a character's emotions and intentions [16]. Biswas et al. have implemented human-like traits to promote empathy and intrinsic motivation in a learning-by-teaching system. [17]. Along the lines of Catherine Pelachaud, other authors concentrate more on the interaction between two virtual characters, rather than on the interaction between virtual character and human. Usually, when modeling a virtual character's behavioral characteristics, both aspects ought to be considered.

In simulation-driven approaches, the character system interprets the world and interactions accordingly to the emotion model he has and also the phase or mood being used in that moment like an human being facing a challenge it will reacts in accordance with its own personality plus the mood of that moment. For instance, Mao and Gratch [18] research concentrates on creating a model of an underlying process, and inferences of social causality are used to enrich the cognitive and social functionality of intelligent agents. Such a model can help one agent to explain the observed social behavior of others, which is crucial for successful interactions among social entities.

[4] For overview, see website of the HUMAINE (Human-Machine Interaction Network on Emotion) - Network of Excellence (FP6 - IST-2002-507422 - http://emotion-research.net).

It can enrich the design components of human-like agents, guide strategies of natural language conversation and model social emotions. Eladhari and Lindley [19] developed a model they called "the prosthetic Mind" taking into account among other theories, the Personality Traits model called the Big Five (see fig. 3).

Factor:	Facet
Extraversion	Friendliness, Gregariousness, Assertiveness, Activity Level, Excitement-Seeking, Cheerfulness
Agreeableness	Trust, Morality, Altruism, Cooperation, Modesty, Sympathy
Conscientiousness	Self-Efficacy, Orderliness, Dutifulness, Achievement-Striving, Self-Discipline Cautiousness
Neuroticism	Anxiety, Anger, Depression, Self-Consciousness, Immoderation, Vulnerability
Openness	Imagination, Artistic Interests, Emotionality, Adventurousness, Intellect, Liberalism

Fig. 3. Personality Traits, as used by Eladhari and Lindley [19]

3 Emotion Wizard

Emotion Wizard (EW) it's an authoring module in INSCAPE that will enable authors to easily and quickly "emotionally" change the environment and characters. The Emotion Wizard will be made of audiovisual templates and character behaviours models that the author can use to speed up work or to aid in finding the right emotional tone for the scene he or she is creating.

The objectives of the tool are, in a first approach, to develop a tool for inexperienced people, to help them to communicate expressively through interactive stories. From another perspective, the goal is to enhance INSCAPE with enough knowledge to help in the diversifying of interactive emotional representations.

With this in mind, we need to define here the main view of EW, describing it as more related to Form than to Theme or Content (see Fig. 4). And even in Form terms we're pursuing Form Style more than Narrative Form, even when we use characters we try to manage them in stylistics definitions. There's a great concern about avoiding entering in possible areas controlled by theme or context leaving these story qualities completely on the shoulders of the story author.

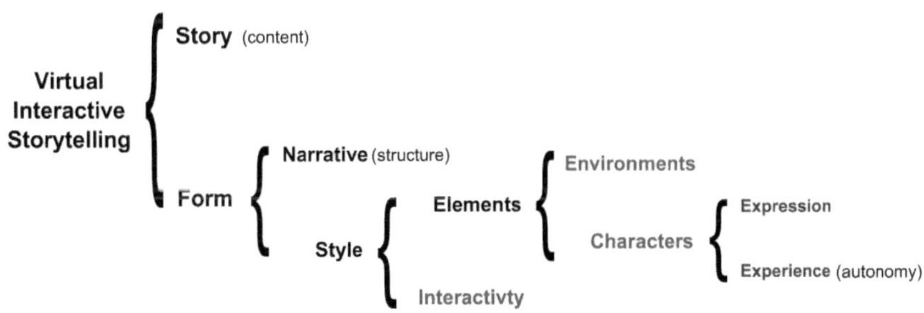

Fig. 4. EW is grounded in storytelling form, more specifically the stylistics

From a philosophical trend "mood" is seen as more consonant label for aspects related with emotional effects in film [20], [21], people approaching film from a cognitive psychologist view, know that mood is a much more complex state to manage than emotion [22], [23]. Taking into account these two views and mainly film structures of film interest defined by[24] we believe in Smith [25] words:

> "Film use emotion cues to prompt us [the viewer] toward mood, a predisposition toward experiencing emotion. Moods are reinforced by coordinated bursts of emotion cues, providing payoffs for the viewer.... Emotion cues of narrative situation, facial and body information, music, sound, *mise en scene*, lighting ... are the building blocks used to create narrational structures to appeal to the emotions. Mood is sustained by a succession of cues..." [25]

Following these views, we have designed an Affective diagram of film (see Fig.5) to demonstrate visually how EW affects the *experiencer* trough an overall story. The Time axis represent the duration of a movie artefact, where the Affectivity axis represents the intensity of the emotional stimulus produced by that movie. "Emotion cues", are developed in single bursts through simple events and environment or characters single characteristics. "Mood" is developed trough the entire presentation and depends of the entire causality of events of the way story gets represented.

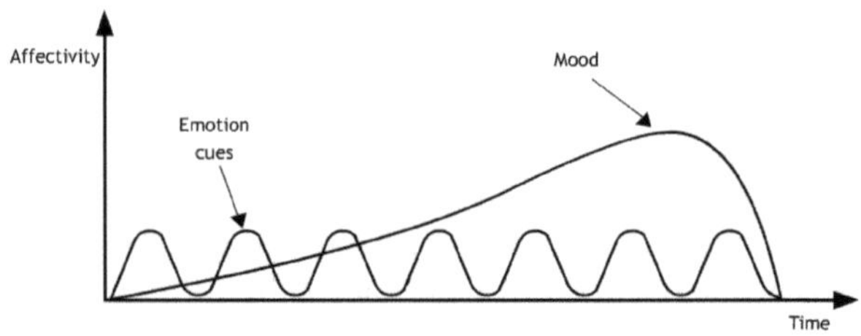

Fig. 5. Affective Film Diagram

Thus, EW is then looking for helping interactive storytelling authors only in the building of emotion cues and not to provide an entire mood frame of a story world. The story mood will only show if the author's idea and talent plus the receptivity and participativity of the *experiencers* work together. Thus, we will need to implement a first phase version of EW, in order to start receiving feedback, not only from *experiencers,* but also from practitioners (authors). In practical terms, EW consists of a software module for the story design of "emotion cues" in real time for environments and characters focused on their dramatical impact.

These "emotion cues" have been studied from existent films and videogames previously validated [26, 27, 28, 29]. Through the literature, we've developed aesthetic and emotional categories to assess each film and game sequence. The categories were chosen and parameterized, grounded in film, new media and psychology's theoretical foundations, in order to maximize the objectivity of each criterion. We've defined eleven categories for environments (Camera, Editing, Time, Frame Composition, Frame Shape, Screen Direction, Music, Sound, Lighting, Colour and Design Effects) and seven for characters (Character's Space; Physical - Clothes, Skin, Hair, Weight; Body Movement - Posture and Gestures; Face and Eyes; Vocal Tone; *Touchability* and Personality).

3.1 Characters Psychology

In the field social psychology, the importance of characters' qualities is well recognized. Therefore, if we pay attention to the forming impression phenomenon, we can notice that we don't need much information to form an impression about another person [30]. We usually shape impressions of others through the observation of quite little samples of their behaviour (verbal and non-verbal). We presume that this phenomenon is similar to character's perception in storytelling situations.

The dimensions that we purpose to analyse characters' qualities (Character's Space, Physical - Clothes, Skin, Hair, Weight, Body Movement - Posture and Gestures, Face and Eyes, Vocal Tone, *Touchability* and Personality) were collected attaining to their potential emotional perception value, as described in the literature. Next we will report findings, which lead us to each character's dimension attained.

Regarding the dimension of Characters' Space its importance has already been defined long ago by Halls' studies [31]. He established four distance levels, which consist on the intimate, personal, social and public and its objective measures (15-45 cm / 6-18 inches; 45-120 cm / 1,5-4 feet; 1,2-3,5 m / 4-12 feet and over 3,5 m / 12 feet, respectively). Accordingly, Argyle (1975) defends that the variations of spatial behaviour "is one of the main ways of expressing friendly-hostile attitudes to other people". He explains that a majority of people seeks a certain degree of proximity and feel uncomfortable if they cannot reach it. On the other hand if a person comes too close this will arouse stronger avoidance. He argues that the dominance is expressed through spatial behaviour too because greater distances are chosen between people of unequal status and a high status person is able to choose degrees of proximity with greater freedom than low status people are. He also postulates that greater distance indicates the desire for greater formality. But he adverts that greater distance can be explained through the presence of expectations of embarrassment. This fact is in agreement with Pickersgill's meta-analysis study [32], which states that one of our most common fears is about interpersonal situations. It includes fears of criticism, rejection and conflicts, i.e., embarrassment situations. These findings suggest that the characters' distance is potential important on emotion perception even on an Interactive Storytelling setting.

We take into account the dimension of costume too because it is known that sexual attractiveness depends partly on clothes, partly on hair, skin, grooming and physique [33]. This author refers that there is a lot of evidence that people choose their clothes in order to manipulate the impressions formed by others. Beyond this idea the clothes' colourfulness expresses people's personality and mood too. These findings suggest that the costume can predict the emotion perception so we take it also into account.

Body language seems very relevant to us too because it "takes place whenever one person influences another by means of facial expression, tone of voice or any other channels" and it expresses emotion [33]. If we also take in to account the eetymologically origin of the word emotion, we can observe that it is composed by the prefix "ex" (that means out, outward) and the word "motio" (that means movement, action, gesture). Therefore emotion can be perceptible through the characters movements and gestures and we pay attention to it too. The Facial Expression is the most important non-verbal channel for expressing emotions, and attitudes to other people, Ekman [9] is the major authority on this subject. He stated that there are universal emotions, which are recognized and experienced globally in a similar way. Another channel of expression of emotion is the voice. Johnstone & Scherer [34] are wide known for their studies on the expression of emotion through voice. They consider that voice is a motor expression of emotion, which can be perceived.

We think that it is also very important the way touch presented too. Because it is known that it has two main meanings: warmth and dominance [33]. In order to understand it, hit or kick someone is different of hug or embrace someone. Therefore different kind of touch has different meaning, and the viewer perceives it differently. The importance of this dimension can be highlighted if we pay attention to some knowledge acquired such as the fact that infants seek bodily contact with their mothers in strange situations [35] and the fact that its main meaning is a bond establishment. These two aspects can be applied into interactive behaviours.

The way that people react and their behaviour patterns also have effects on the way that others feel. People patterns behaviours are predictable trough personality traits. Similar to the social interaction can be seen the characters' interaction. We consider that at the end of a movie or game scene we have a general perception of characters' personality based on their actions, movements and interactivity. So we take in consideration the dimension of personality too. We opted for use the widely known "Big Five Factors Model" [36] because there is a general consensus that this model is the most unified, and parsimonious conceptual framework for personality [37].

4 Emotional Expression and Experience in INSCAPE

Moving to the more practical and forward aspects of emotion modelling, we now take a look at the implementations planned for the INSCAPE project. The intended GUI concept for the INSCAPE authoring tool, as well as the underlying data model, describe interactive stories in such structural terms as used in the INSCAPE story format ICML (Inscape Communication mark-up language), namely trees and graphs of connected objects and their diverse attributed properties.

The GUI design provides four main areas, or functional blocks, to define an interactive story. In a first step, authors can use one part of the interface in a top-down fashion to describe a story in a "story-board like" manner: A common-style text editing environment is used, including the possibility to insert sketches, icons etc. In contrast to that, there is another part following more the bottom-up approach: This part of the GUI provides visible library of all story assets (objects, props), in a symbolic form, e.g. by showing icons for each library item.

In the central part of the GUI, we will find the interfaces used for editing the stages (assemblies of objects, and their positions within the stage), for defining interactive scenes taking place within these stages, and for previewing the INSCAPE stories in a 2D or 3D performance mode. In a special area (called the Story Editor), a visual representation of the story's transition graph is visualized as a graph structure, in order to manage the overall story flow, branches etc. In addition to these basic functions, there will be specific behaviour editors, where authors can either integrate/reference predefined scripts and associate them to story objects, or to add, set, or delete properties and variables. The conditions for possible transitions between the different story situations and stages are also defined at this level. Of course, all these editors are

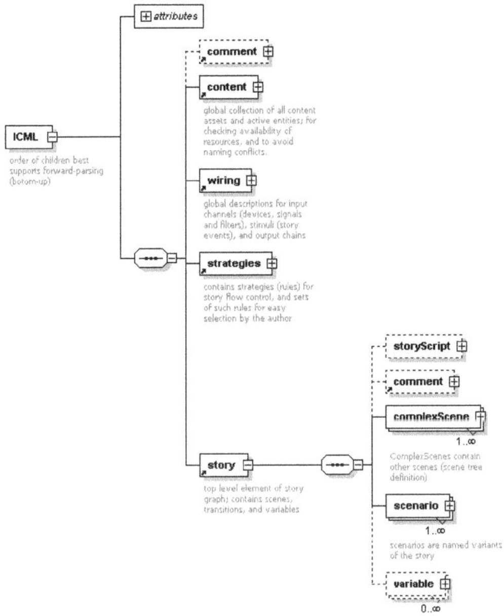

Fig. 6. ICML top level, version 2.0, preparation for INSCAPE beta

interlinked and synchronized on a system level, which is a main advantage of INSCAPE's integrated approach. A plug-in mechanism exists to add new user interfaces in the INSCAPE platform, including third party contributions.

The emotion modules described in this paper act as such additional component (optional plug-ins) of the INSCAPE system, based on the INSCAPE data model ICML (see figure 6 for an overview), and providing links to the different editors. For instance, overall strategies and variables for emotion expression and experience will be introduced via the Story Editor part (linked to the Emotion Wizard module) and placed as INSCAPE objects in the story's asset library. For instance, there might be four ICML variables (see ICML hierarchy -> story -> variable) for describing emotional states: Theta, Beta, Delta and Alpha; representing Tension, Happy, Sad and Relax. These might be further diversified in order to define more detailed emotions in the story, e.g. emotional states of specific characters. The ICML section for 'strategies' may be used to define rules and conditions for changes in emotional states.

Such emotion-related parameters, if available on the stage or scene level, may then influence the characteristics of the entire stage (e.g. light, camera, colour), as well as the visual representation of specific story objects (e.g. the mood of a virtual character, as expressed by facial animation).

5 Summary and Outlook

The described methods and concepts of authoring modules for emotion expression and experience will prototypically be implemented in form of an Emotion Wizard module, which will extend in the INSCAPE core system as an optional plug-in. This will also have some influences on the story model, as expressed through ICML, the open format developed by the INSCAPE project to describe any kind of interactive stories. Modeling emotion will extend the expressive possibilities of other INSCAPE components, such as the story, stage and behavior editors.

The Emotion Wizard will also be available during the story planning and prototyping phase, giving helpful suggestions about emotional possibilities on controlling lights and cameras, choosing colours or defining characters. Story prototyping will be made a little easier then, accordingly to the needs of the author.

The methods presented are being designed to produce a semantic intervention in the story and doesn't intend to transcend the Storyteller work. The goal is to attribute emotional meaning to the parameters that act on the virtual story-world. This intervention develops a possible pedagogical virtue permitting the learning by the story authors about potential emotional uses of specific parameters. It permits also the INSCAPE user to understand the emotional semantics canons of the interactive virtual stories.

Acknowledgements

This research is performed in the frame of the INSCAPE Integrated Project (IST-2004-004150), which is funded by the European Commission under the 6th Framework Programme. More information on that project is available at www.inscapers.com

References

1. Izard, C. E. & Ackerman, B. P. (2000), Motivational, organizational and regulatory functions of discrete emotions, In Lewis, M. & Haviland-Jones, M. (Eds.), Handbook of Emotion, New York: Guilford Press.
2. Bradley, M. M.; Codispoti, M., Cuthbert, B. N. & Lang, P.J. (2001), Emotion and Motivation I: Defensive and Appetitive Reactions in Picture Processing. Emotion, 1 (3): 276-298.
3. Lang, P. J.; Bradley, M. M. & Cuthbert, B. N. (1998), Emotion, Motivation and Anxiety: Brain Mechanisms and Psychophysiology. Biology Psychiatry, 44: 1248-1263.
4. Frijda, N. H. (1986). The emotions. Cambridge, Cambridge University Press.
5. Damasio, A. R. (1994). Descartes' error: emotion, reason, and the human brain. New York, G.P. Putnam.
6. Stern, Andrew; Creating Emotional Relationships With Virtual Characters; from: Emotions in Humans and Artifacts, eds. R. Trappl, P. Petta, and S.Payr, MIT Press, (2003),
7. Tomlinson, B., B. Blumberg, et al. (2000). Expressive autonomous cinematography for interactive virtual environments. International Conference on Autonomous Agents, Barcelona, Spain.
8. Perlin, K. (2003). Building virtual actors who can really act. 2nd International Conference on Virtual Storytelling - ICVS 2003, Toulouse, Springer Ed.
9. Ekman, P.; Universals and cultural differences in facial expressions of emotion. From: J. Cole (Ed.), Nebraska Symposium on Motivation 1971, (Vol. 19, pp. 207-283). Lincoln, NE: University of Nebraska Press (1972)
10. Half-Life 2, Gabe Newell, Valve Corporation, Vivendi Universal, (2004)
11. Mateas, M., & Stern, A. (2005). Structuring content in the façade interactive drama architecture. Paper presented at the Artificial Intelligence and Interactive Digital Entertainment (AIIDE), Los Angeles.

12. Stern, A., A. Frank, et al. (1998). Virtual Petz: A Hybrid Approach to Creating Autonomous, Lifelike Dogz and Catz. International Conference on Autonomous Agents, St. Paul, Minnepolis.
13. Gratch, J., Marsella, S., Evaluating the modeling and use of emotion in virtual humans. In: Proceedings of the Third International Joint Conference on Autonomous Agents and Multiagent Systems, New York, New York (2004)
14. Pelachaud, C. Carofiglio, V. Carolis, B.D., Rosis, F. and Poggi, I., First International Joint Conference on Autonomous Agents and Multiagent Systems, presented at Embodied Contextual Agent in Information Delivering Application, Bologna, Italy, (2002)
15. Poggi, I., Pelachaud, C., Talking faces that communicate by eyes, In: S. Santi, B. Guaitella, C. Cavé and G. Konopczynski (Eds.) "Orage'98. Oralité et gestualité, communication multimodale, interaction", Paris: L'Harmattan, (1998)
16. Klesen, M. Using Theatrical Concepts for Role-Plays with Educational Agents, Applied Artificial Intelligence special Issue Educational Agents - Beyond Virtual Tutors (2005)
17. Biswas, G., Schwartz, D., Leelawong, K., Vye, N., and TAG-V, Learning by Teaching. A New Agent Paradigm for Educational Software, Applied Artificial Intelligence Special Issue "Educational Agents - Beyond Virtual Tutors", vol. 19, (2005).
18. Mao, W., Gratch, J. Social Causality and Responsibility: Modeling and Evaluation, International Conference on Interactive Virtual Agents, Kos Greece (2005)
19. Eladhari, M. and Lindley, C. "Player Character Design Facilitating Emotional Depth in MMORPGs" Digital Games Research Conference 2003, 4-6 November 2003 University of Utrecht, The Netherlands
20. Carroll, Noel, Art and mood: preliminary notes and conjectures. (Critical Essay), The Monist, vol. 86, no. 4, 2003, pp. 521-555
21. Douglass, J. S., & Harnden, G. P. (1996). The art of technique: An aesthetic approach to film and video production.Boston, Mass.; London: Allyn and Bacon.
22. Anderson, B. F., & Anderson, J. D. (2004). Moving image theory: Ecological considerations.Carbondale: Southern Illinois University Press.
23. Grodal, T. K. (1997). Moving pictures: A new theory of film genres, feelings and cognition.Oxford: Clarendon Press.
24. Tan, E. S. (1996). Emotion and the structure of narrative film: Film as an emotion machine.Hillsdale, NJ: L. Erlbaum Associates.
25. Smith, G. M. (1999). Local emotions, global moods, and film structure. In C. R. Plantinga & G. M. Smith (Eds.), Passionate views: Film, cognition, and emotion (pp. 301). Baltimore, Md.: Johns Hopkins University Press.
26. Gross, J. J. & Levenson, R. W, (1995), Emotion Elicitation Using Films, Cognition and Emotion, 1995, 9 (1), 87 –108.
27. Niedenthal, P.M., Halberstadt, J.B., & Innes-Ker, A.H. (1999). Emotional response categorization. Psychological Review, 106, 337-361
28. Wensveen, S., Overbeeke, CJ, & Djajadiningrat, JP, (2002), Push me, shove me and I show you how you feel. Proceedings of DIS2002, London, pp. 335-340. 97
29. Zagalo N., Torres A., & Branco, V., (2005), Emotional Spectrum developed by Virtual Storytelling, 3rd International Conference on Virtual Storytelling, in Lecture Notes in Computer Science, Springer, Volume 3805/2005. (pp.105-114)
30. Asch, S. E. (1946), Forming impressions of personality, Journal of Abnormal and Social Psychology, 41, 258-290.
31. Hall, E. T. (1966). A dimensão oculta (The Hidden Dimension) (M. S. Pereira, Trans.). Lisboa: Relógio D'Água.

32. Öhman, A. (2000), "Fear and Anxiety: Evolutionary, Cognitive and Clinical Perspectives", In Lewis, M. & Haviland-Jones, J.M. (Eds), "Handbook of Emotions", New York: Guilford Press.
33. Argyle, M. (1975), Bodily Communication (2nd ED), Madison: International Universities Press.
34. Johnstone, T. & Scherer, K. R. (2000), Vocal Comunication of Emotion, In Lewis, M. & Haviland-Jones, M. (Eds.), Handbook of Emotion, New York: Guilford Press.
35. Harlow, H. F. & Harlow, M. K. (1965), The Affectional Systems, In Schrier, A. M., Harlow, H. F. & Stollnitz, F. (Eds), Behaviour of Nonhuman Primates, New York and London: Academic Press.
36. McCrae, Robert, Costa, Paul, Personality in Adulthood, h.D., New York: The Guilford Press (1990)
37. Digman, J. (1990). Personality structure: Emergence of the five-factor model. Annual Review of Psychology, 41, 417–440.

Augmenting Virtual Characters for More Natural Interaction

Markus Löckelt and Norbert Pfleger

DFKI GmbH, Stuhlsatzenhausweg 3, 66123 Saarbrücken, Germany
{pfleger, loeckelt}@dfki.de
http://www.dfki.de/~pfleger

Abstract. We describe extensions to VirtualHuman, a multimodal dialogue system. It uses an interactive game scenario to demonstrate real-time multi-party dialogue between two human users and three virtual characters. The focus is to make the interaction more natural, robust and flexible. Here, we address issues of speech recognition in noisy environments, resolution of spatial references, and enhancements in the character interactions.

1 Introduction

We report on the current version of the VirtualHuman system, a multimodal dialogue system that supports multi-party interactions between human users and virtual characters. The current demo application of our system is an interactive game where two human contestants compete. The quiz is hosted by a virtual moderator and two virtual experts are present to help the contestants with their knowledge. The two human contestants have the ability to freely interact with the virtual characters, i. e., they can answer questions, ask for advice or address a particular character.

A crucial aspect of our work is to enable naïve users to interact naturally with the characters without any need to adapt to the system. As a side-effect, we had to deal with several challenges like how to generate convincing affective behavior of the characters and how to synchronize the contributions of the human users and virtual characters (we reported on that issue in [Pfleger and Löckelt, 2005]). However, since the primary communication channel for the users is speech (in an open-microphone setting), we had to deal with another crucial aspect, namely the optimization of the input processing chain (i. e., microphones, audio-hardware, and recognizers) so that naïve users can interact with the characters without training. We successfully demonstrated the system on CeBIT 2006 under fair conditions (i. e., noisy surroundings and naïve users that changed frequently) and think that we are on a good way in solving this issue.

After an introductory scenario description and example interaction, we will first describe the setup of our system (in particular the speech processing chain) and then discuss several aspects of the system's dialogue capabilities.

S. Göbel, R. Malkewitz, and I. Iurgel (Eds.): TIDSE 2006, LNCS 4326, pp. 231–240, 2006.

2 The Scenario

The quiz is hosted by a virtual moderator. Two virtual experts are present to help the two contestants with their knowledge. The winner of the first stage proceeds to the second, where she interacts with the moderator and one of the experts to assemble a football team lineup of the German national team against one of a set of opponents with different characteristics, e. g. offensive or defensive teams. Again, the expert comments moves of the human player and can be requested to help with her expertise. The lineup game has been newly introduced in the current project phase and involves additional dialogue features over the last prototype. Since we focus here on these new features, we will only give a sample interaction of this second phase.

After completing the first stage of the game, the scenery of the game changes to the one shown in Fig. 1. The moderator and the female expert are positioned behind a 3D representation of a football field with marked positions for the players.

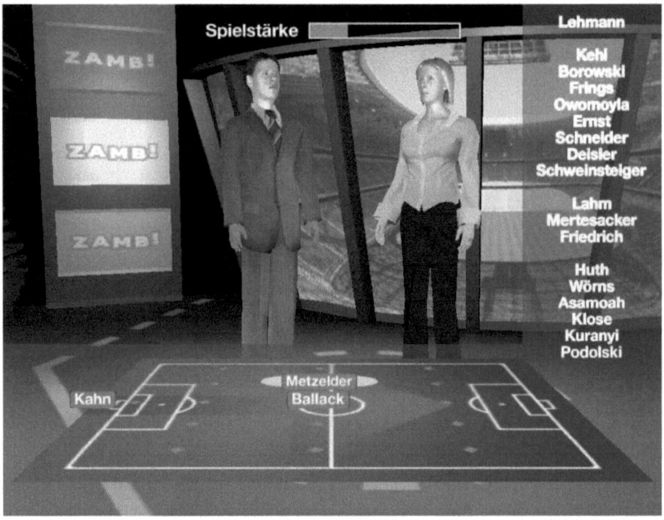

Fig. 1. The graphical representation of the second game stage

The playing field is depicted as a lying rectangle for space reasons. This introduces a first ambiguity with regard to the reference system that is used during the game. It is customary to call player positions as seen from the position of the goal. That means that a "left defender" for the team in the left half of the playing field will actually be positioned in the *upper* half of the graphics on the screen. Likewise, to move a defender "right" could mean either to put him in a midfield position, or downwards on the screen (see Sec. 4.1).

The game has a time limit after which an overall score is computed and used to rank the player. Until the time limit, the contestant can execute moves to add players to positions, remove players, and exchange players. Moves can be underspecified in that when the contestant assigns a player to the midfield without specifying the side, the game logic will look for an unoccupied position in the midfield (if there is one) and put the player there. The contestant also has the option to explicitly ask the expert or the moderator for advice (the moderator is more reluctant to help with specific moves than the expert, but rather gives general gameplay tips). Both the expert and the moderator also frequently make comments on their own, depending on the current situation. Below we give an example interaction[1]:

(1) Moderator: *Ok, let's get started.*
(2) User: *Put Oliver Kahn into the goal.*
(3) Expert Herzog: [nods] *That's an excellent move!*
(4) Moderator: [nods] *Great, Kahn in the goal position.*
(5) User: *Miss Herzog, give me a hint!*
(6) Expert Herzog: [smiles] *I would definitely put Ballack into the central midfield.*
(7) User: *Ok, let's do that.*
(8) Expert Herzog: [smiles] (nods) *You won't regret this move.*
(9) Moderator: (nods) *Great, Ballack as central midfielder.*
(10) User: ... [hesitates]
(11) Moderator: [encouraging gesture] emphDon't be shy!
(12) User: *Hhm, put Metzelder to the left of Ballack.* [...]

3 System Architecture

Viewed on an abstract level of detail the architecture of the system comprises three processing levels: (i) the narrative engine (NE) that is controls the development of the interaction so that it will follow a predetermined story-line, (ii) a set of conversational dialog engines (CDEs) representing the individual characters that participate in the interaction, and (iii) the 3D player that renders the interaction. The task of the NE is to regulate the flow of the interaction so that it will follow a predetermined story-line. To this end the NE prescribes aims for the individual CDEs. Based on these aims and the current state of the interaction the CDEs generate their individual actions that are rendered by the player.

3.1 Hardware Setup: Input Processing

The VirtualHuman demonstration system currently comprises three standard PCs (one for ASR, one for 3D rendering, and one for the dialog) and a 3D presentation system (consisting of two high-resolution video projectors). The two human users stand in front of two columns, each equipped with a microphone (Sennheiser) and a track-ball.

Figure 2 depicts the abstract setup of the input processing chain. The output of the two microphones is first routed to a standard audio mixer where

[1] The text was translated from the German original.

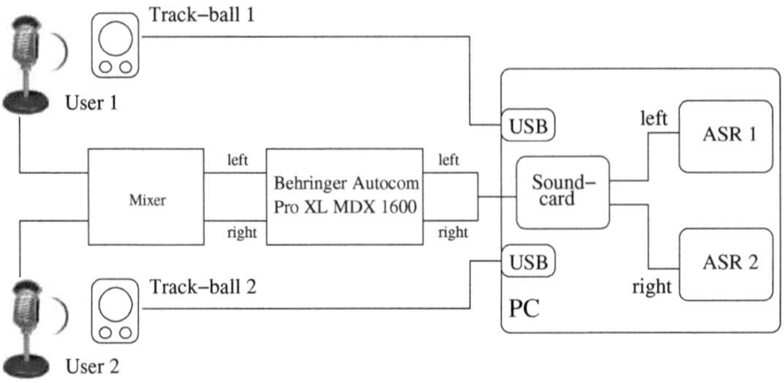

Fig. 2. Setup of the input processing chain

the two signals are assigned to different audio channels (left and right). Then the signals are routed to the Behringer Autocom device which is a 2-Channel Expander/Gate/Compressor/Peak Limiter with Integrated Dynamic Enhancer, De-Esser and Low Contour Filter. This device is usually employed for high-quality audio recordings in studios or on stage. However, we found that this device can also help a lot for conducting open-microphone speech recognition in noisy surroundings. It can be used to suppress all background noise below a certain threshold, and to limit peaks in the audio signal without corrupting the signal. Especially, the suppressed background noise drastically improves the performance of the ASRs. From our perspective, the most important features of the Behringer Autocom device for open-microphone applications are the following:

a) IGC (Interactive Gain Control) peak limiting circuitry combines a clipper and program limiter for reliable and inaudible protection against signal peaks.
b) The GATE function allows to mute signals below a certain threshold.

Finally, the output of the Behringer Autocom device (the signal of the first user is still assigned to the left channel and the signal of the second user to the right channel) is routed to the sound card of the ASR PC. Then the signal is split up and the left channel is routed to the ASR for User 1 and the right channel to the ASR of User 2. The setup provided overall good recognition results for untrained users at the CeBIT fair with the notable exception of small children who had difficulties to get over the threshold of the GATE function.

3.2 Conversational Dialog Engines

There are two different types of CDEs: (i) CDEs representing the virtual characters (*CharacterCDEs*) and (ii) CDEs representing the human users of the system (*UserCDEs*). Viewed on a more detailed level the architecture of these two types differ in several aspects. The CharacterCDEs (as depicted in Fig. 3) consist of a fusion and discourse engine (FADE; for a detailed description see

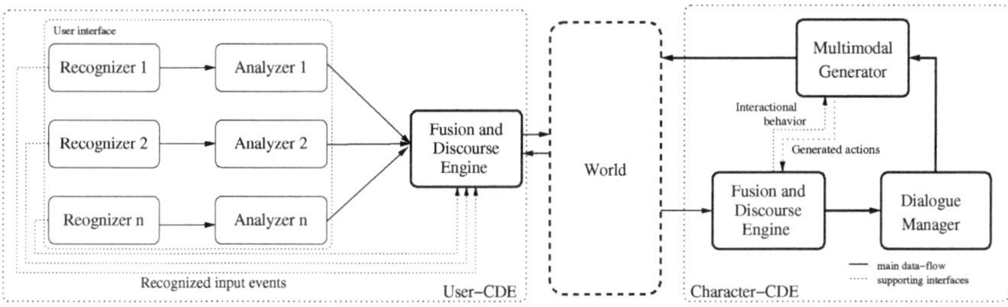

Fig. 3. Architecture of the User- and Character-CDEs

[Pfleger, 2005]), an Affect Engine, an Action Manager (for a detailed description see [Löckelt, 2005]), and a multimodal generation component.

A UserCDE comprises a speech recognizer, a natural language understanding component, a gesture recognizer and analyzer, and a fusion and discourse engine (FADE). All internal knowledge used by the CDEs is represented by means of an ontology, which provides a formal taxonomy of all objects and events that exist in the restricted world of the VirtualHuman system. Each concept comprises a set of slots that define sub-components or attributes of that concept.

4 System Improvements

In the following, we will focus on new features that were integrated into the CeBIT demonstrator. The remainder of the system is described in several other publications, e. g., [Pfleger and Löckelt, 2005, Löckelt and Pfleger, 2005]).

4.1 Resolving Spatial References

Resolving spatial references depends on the point of view the speaker takes to encode the referring expression, which is called the speaker's *frame of reference* [Levinson, 2003]. The frame of reference a speaker takes directly influences the selection of referring expressions, e. g., everything that is on my left is on the right of someone else standing in front of me. The structure and distinctions between frames of references has been a research topic in various disciplines such as philosophy, cognitive science, psychology and linguistics. Of course this led to various conceptions and terms describing different types of frames of reference. Based on a detailed review of these different notions of frames of reference [Levinson, 2003] distinguishes three main frames of reference: *intrinsic*, *relative* and *absolute*. When using an intrinsic frame of reference the speaker takes the point of view of the relatum (i. e. the object that is used to locate the target object). In a relative frame of reference the speaker takes an outside perspective (e. g., his own point of view, or that of someone else). Within an absolute frame of reference everything is located with respect to an absolute point, e. g., the geographic north. While the latter frame of reference is always unambiguous the former two might introduce some ambiguities that need to be resolved.

The resolution of spatial referring expressions involves the following aspects: (i) an up-to-date representation of the physical environment, (ii) knowledge of the currently active type of frame of reference and (iii) a mapping function that converts spatial references to locations or objects in the scene.

We organize the representation of the physical environment as follows: Each object located in the scene is represented by means of an *AbsolutePosition*. The most important features of an absolute position are:

- Feature *ontologicalInstance* – this feature contains the ontological instance representing the object that is described by an AbsolutePosition.
- Feature *coordinates* – this is an optional feature, if the perception components are able to provide two-dimensional or three-dimensional coordinates describing the location of the object with respect to a fixed coordinate system, this slot will contain that information.
- Feature *orientation* – this feature describes the current orientation of the object: *north, east, south, west*
- Feature *northOf* – this feature contains a link to the AbsolutePosition of its immediate northern neighbor (it can be empty if there is no northern neighbor)
- Feature *eastOf* ...

Moreover, a physical environment can again contain other physical environments. In our scenario the physical environment describing the virtual studio contains a closed physical environment describing the virtual football field, where the line-up is displayed. See Fig. 4 for an example configuration of the physical environment.

In oder to resolve spatial references, a receiver (i. e., a virtual character) first determines the currently activated physical environment and its corresponding active frame of reference and then maps the referring expression to an absolute location. If, for example, the user commands the system to *"Put Metzelder to the left of Ballack"*, the character first retrieves the current position of the player *Ballack* in the physical environment. Then it retrieves the current orientation of that player and then maps the referring expression to one of the absolute identifiers. At this point we assume a currently active frame of reference of type *intrinsic*, otherwise the system would need to determine the orientation of the speaker and then compute the mapping.

In any case, the mapping function takes the referring expression (*left-of*) and the orientation of the relatum (*eastern*) which would result in an offset of 1. This means, we need to go *one* neighbor feature further to get the correct neighbor given the orientation. Normally (i. e., if the player would be oriented to the north), left-of would be mapped to the western neighbor. However, in our case we need to go one neighbor further which is the northern neighbor. If the player faces westward, the mapping function would return an offset of 3 which means left-of is the southern neighbor in this context.

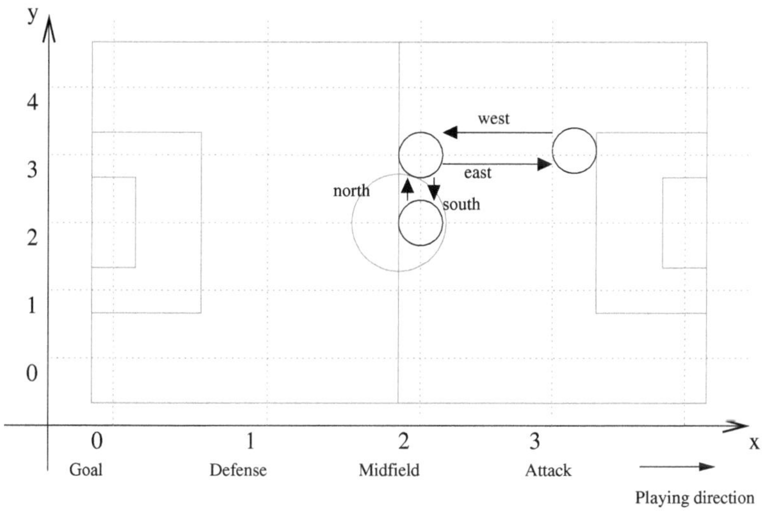

Fig. 4. Example configuration of the physical environment describing the football-field with three players placed on it

4.2 Character Interaction

In the first stage of the game, described in [Pfleger and Löckelt, 2005], the system features two experts that can comment on the user's contributions and—upon request—give their own opinion on questions posed by the moderator. Their actions are restricted to give comments on dialogue between the moderator and the human user. In the second stage, the one remaining expert takes an extended role in the interaction. She reasons over the moves occurring on the game field, and can give more substantiated advice. The experts now show more elaborate affective reactions in both phases of the game, and also occasionally take the initiative themselves.

Expert Reasoning. The character playing the expert role now contains expert knowledge that is automatically applied to the dialogue situation. The ontology provides information on each football player regarding usual playing position, fitness, and preferred side. A game logic component uses the accessible data on the football players to construct an ideal team against the given opponent, and to rate the quality of moves.

The expert perceives the actions (e. g., positioning a player on the field) of other participants and can react to them. From information such as gazing, she can infer whether she was the addressee of an utterance or just an overhearer. When the expert overhears the moderator's confirmation of a human's move (turn (4)), she determines the current configuration on the playing board, and updates her own representation of the football field.

When the user directs the moderator to make a game move (2), the expert analyzes the content of the move although she was not directly addressed. She can then make a comment on the move, e. g. if the human player places a goalie in an attack position. If the human user asks the expert for a hint (5), the game logic uses an external planner, JSHOP ([Ilghami and Nau, 2003]), to dynamically construct a plan containing the moves that would be necessary to transform the current team on the board to the expert's ideal team. The expert can then propose the first move of this plan. The moderator overhears and memorizes the proposal, and if the user accepts it, he will carry it out. The expert will show her delight about this. (example moves (5)-(9)).

The *Affect Engine* dynamically computes the affective state of all characters based on weighted emotional events. This also depends on the interrelation of the characters. For example, if the user accepts advice from the male expert in phase 1, this will trigger an event [BadActOther 0.8] for the female expert, since the experts do not like each other (the male expert will of course receive a good event). The effect is that the female expert will temporarily change her idle behavior and facial expression – she will look angry and blush, while the other will smile thankfully.

Interaction Management. Synthesizing a virtual character's utterance for the user to hear takes time. Conversely, if utterances were passed on to other characters immediately in the ontological format, this would be possible almost instantly. Since we consider dialogue acts atomic units of interaction, there is the question of when exactly such an act is considered finished, or *realized.* In natural conversation, utterances are often understood before the speaker has finished talking, and a gesture is usually recognized long before it is completed.

To account for this, we introduced *Realization Threads* that use the precomputed durations of actions to determine the start and end time point of the realization of each action unit, even if several actions are executing concurrently such as speech accompanied by gestures. Acts are passed on to other characters at realization time. It can be adjusted after which fraction of the duration of an action the semantic content is made available to the other agents. For our system, we made gestures recognizable without delay, while spoken utterances are handed over to the overhearers after two thirds of their duration.

Characters compete for the turn if they want to simultaneously make an utterance (e. g., turn (4) could also have happened before (3), if the moderator had reacted faster). If a character wants to make a contribution and somebody else is currently speaking, it will not immediately get the turn. It will then trigger a turn-grabbing gesture (e. g. raising an arm), hesitate, and try again after some time. If this repeatedly does not succeed, the character may decide to abandon its intention to say something. Figure 5 shows an example of such overlapping contributions. Also, if a contribution is expected from the user and she hesitates too long, the initiator will after some time invite the user again to answer (see example moves (10)-(11)).

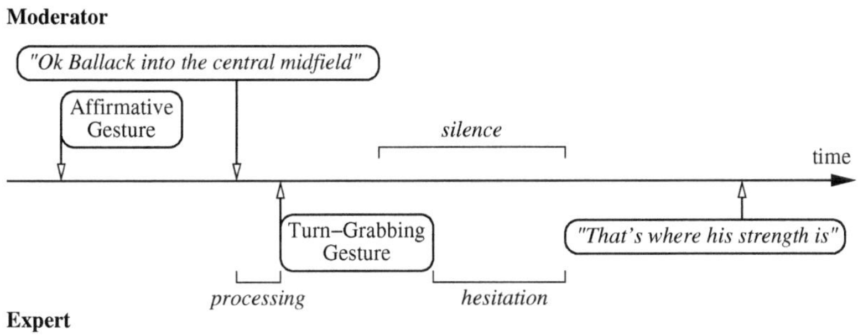

Fig. 5. Realization time points of overlapping contributions

5 Conclusion and Future Work

We gave an overview of the current VirtualHuman system, focusing on aspects that make it possible for naïve users to interact with virtual characters even in relatively noisy surroundings like fairs, and features that create a more natural interaction experience.

The reactions of visitors at the CeBIT fair were mostly positive (although the audio setup had some difficulties with recognizing the voices of children), however, the usability of the system was not quantitatively examined. To address this issue, we recently started a formal evaluation of the complete VirtualHuman system with naïve subjects. The results of this evaluation will be incorporated into the final system of the VirtualHuman project. We also plan to use the transcriptions of the sessions to further improve the coverage of the ASR's language model and the natural language interpretation. Additionally, we will integrate a 3D-camera based gesture recognition component to provide symmetric multimodality.

Acknowledgements

This research is funded by the German Ministry of Research and Technology (BMBF) under grant 01 IMB 01A. The responsibility lies with the authors.

References

[Ilghami and Nau, 2003] Ilghami, O. and Nau, D. S. (2003). A General Approach to Synthesize Problem-Specific Planners. Technical Report CS-TR-4597, UMIACS-TR-2004-40, University of Maryland.

[Levinson, 2003] Levinson, S. C. (2003). *Space in Language and Cognition.* Press Syndicate of the University of Cambridge.

[Löckelt, 2005] Löckelt, M. (2005). Action Planning for Virtual Human Performances. In *Proceedings of the International Conference on Virtual Storytelling*, Strasbourg, France.

[Löckelt and Pfleger, 2005] Löckelt, M. and Pfleger, N. (2005). Multi-Party Interaction With Self-Contained Virtual Characters. In *Proceedings of 9th Workshop on the semantics and pragmatics of dialogue (Dialor)*, Nancy, France.

[Pfleger, 2005] Pfleger, N. (2005). FADE - An Integrated Approach to Multimodal Fusion and Discourse Processing. In *Proceedings of the Doctoral Spotlight Session of the International Conference on Multimodal Interfaces (ICMI'05)*, Trento, Italy.

[Pfleger and Löckelt, 2005] Pfleger, N. and Löckelt, M. (2005). Synchronizing Dialogue Contributions of Human Users and Virtual Characters in a Virtual Reality Environment. In *Processing of Interspeech'2005 - Eurospeech 9th European Conference on Speech Communication and Technology*, pages 2773 – 2776, Lisboa, Portugal.

Automatic Customization of Non-Player Characters Using Players Temperament*

Hector Gómez-Gauchía and Federico Peinado

Depto. Ingeniería del Software e Inteligencia Artificial
Universidad Complutense de Madrid, Spain
hector@sip.ucm.es, email@federicopeinado.com

Abstract. Believability is a basic requirement for non-player characters of videogames. Players enjoy characters with personalities that reflect human behavior, specially if those personalities combine well with players' temperaments. This paper explains a model for customizing automatically non-player characters (NPC) according to the players temperament, which is obtained before the game session. The model uses Case-Based Reasoning and Ontologies to adapt the behavior of a NPC, which is the companion of a player character in the described example.

Keywords: Player Modeling, Narrative Environments, Interactive Digital Storytelling in Entertainment, Affective Computing.

1 Introduction

Videogames are pieces of procedural art. The goal of this art is evoking emotion in the player through performance of tasks in a fantasy world. There are many possible ways of evoking emotion, but it is well known that each player is emotionally affected in a particular way, depending on how the tasks of the game relate with his temperament.

In section 2 part of the state-of-art in game customization is presented. Research on game adaptability is significantly less developed than the same field of hypermedia or intelligent tutoring systems [2]. Usually current work is usually more related to the automatic adjustment of the difficulty level of action or strategy games, while this paper focus on Role-Playing Games (RPGs), characterized by strong emphasis on social interaction with Non-Player Characters (NPCs) as part of the in-game tasks instead of combat or management of resources.

NPCs are characters of the game which are controlled by the system and which are able to interact with the player's avatar interchanging items and information. The scenario of section 3 represents a short dialogue with an NPC. The model, explained in sections 4 and 5, is illustrated with this scenario because conversation is very important in the game experience of RPGs.

* Supported by the Spanish Ministry of Education and Science (TIN2005-09382-C02-01, TIN2006-15140-C03-02 and TIN2006-14433-C02-01 projects), Complutense University of Madrid and the G.D. of Universities and Research of the Community of Madrid (UCM-CAM-910494 research group grant).

S. Göbel, R. Malkewitz, and I. Iurgel (Eds.): TIDSE 2006, LNCS 4326, pp. 241–252, 2006.

Players enjoy when NPCs behave as they expect and these expectations are projections of their temperaments. We represent temperaments as a set of static values established for the current player before the game session by a questionnaire following the Keirsey's theory [6], described in section 4. The model has a knowledge base with different versions of the dialogue with an NPC related to different combinations of temperament values. Usually, each player has a new combination of those values, so a particular version of the dialogue has to be generated automatically using the knowledge base and a set of *variations* of the behavior of the NPC.

2 Current Approaches to Game Customization

Traditionally, videogames have hard-wired character behavior. Even RPGs or graphic adventures offered reasonable but simple conversation trees or state-based interaction with NPCs. New titles "sell" exciting features of their NPCs as improved intelligence, emotion or autonomy but few games are really adaptable to each particular player without some manual configuration. Blade Runner is a classical example of re-playable game whose NPCs do not act the same way each time the game is played; but the variations do not adapt the content of the game to the characteristics of the players.

A well-known example of automatically customizable game is Max Payne. Most of games have just a short number of difficulty levels that has to be manually selected by the player. In Max Pay, an auto-dynamic difficulty adjustment mechanism is implemented, allowing a more adaptable game experience to the skills of the player, but not to his temperament.

Fable uses a moral approach for the automatic customization of game content. The actions of the players can be considered good or bad by the system, and, as a consequence, their reputations change during the game, affecting the behaviour of NPCs as well. It is an interesting approach but customized only for the black-or-white fictional temperament of the player's avatar, not for the player himself.

There are many research projects trying to adapt game contents according to the feedback of the player. From the point of view of social interaction, Façade [7] is a good example. The NPCs of this interactive drama are able to speak, express emotions and even understand what the player is saying in a simplified English language. The games chooses different endings based on decisions taken by the player's avatar, but the game does not model the player's temperament.

Instead of developing an standalone system, it is becoming popular the use of middleware for the dynamic connection of external intelligent systems with commercial game engines to modify the behavior of NPCs and other game functionalities. The automatic NPC customization system could be implemented specializing some of these software platforms as Zocalo[1], based on Web Services about Planning, I-Storytelling[2], based on Hierarchical Task Networks or KIIDS[3] based on Case-Based Reasoning and Ontologies.

[1] http://zocalo.csc.ncsu.edu/
[2] http://www-scm.tees.ac.uk/users/f.charles/
[3] http://federicopeinado.com/projects/kiids/

3 The Example Scenario

The automatic NPC customization model presented here is generic, so it needs to be instantiated for a particular application involving some virtual environment, NPCs and players such as a commercial videogame.

This example scenario is an independent adventure implemented as a simple module of Neverwinter Nights[4]. The player plays the role of Drax, a knight returning home after a battle against the forces of Evil. When Drax enters his castle, one servant – a NPC – is waiting for him. The interaction with this NPC is just a short introduction to the adventure of the module that the model is trying to customize. Usually short conversations with secondary characters are not relevant for the global game experience, but this example is useful enough to show how the model works.

Servant: Welcome home, sir. [Repeating fast worship movements]
Drax: Hum, I feel so tired... Please, servant, prepare the bath.

Servant: Immediately, sir. [Running to the bathroom]

Fig. 1. Example dialogue at the 13th level of politeness

In Figure 1, we show an informal version of the scenario dialogue. Besides the canned text of dialogues, we focus on other features which change during the customization process. There are also different NPC animations in each dialogue mode. By default the servant falls to the floor and performs fast and repeated movements of worship to his lord. That is considered a funny animation for a fantasy game like this, but probably it is not the most appropriated animation from the point of view of a player with a serious temperament – this gesture could be consider grotesque or even offensive by some cultures or religions–.

[4] http://nwn.bioware.com/

4 Elements of the Automatic NPC Customization Model

Our line of work during the last years has been the research of different techniques and approaches to build Knowledge-Intensive Case-Based Reasoning (KI-CBR) systems, i.e.: integrated Knowledge Based Systems that combine case specific knowledge with models of general terminological domain knowledge [3,4]. Like in previous works we use Description Logics (DLs) based languages that are commonly used to implement ontologies, and have been proven to be useful to formalize aspects of representation and reasoning in CBR systems [8,3]. We use ontologies to represent the explicit knowledge of the model: the temperament theory, the possible variations to customize the game and the player's profile which includes his own temperament and personal data.

In Figure 2 we describe the main elements of the proposed model. There is a player playing the game, which has a standard NPCs behavior. A CBR task generates an automatic NPCs behavior customization, which consists in a set of actions performed using native commands of the game or scripts developed ad-hoc. After this customization the player finds NPCs behavior more similar to his temperament. The overall reasoning task follows this cycle: the model retrieves a case with the most similar temperament to that of the player. Inside the case there is a set of game variations to customize it to player's temperament. If the distance between the retrieved case is bigger than a specific threshold, the model adapts the variations using the distance. The player profile stores all this information to use it every time that specific player plays again. The ontologies are describen in next subsections.

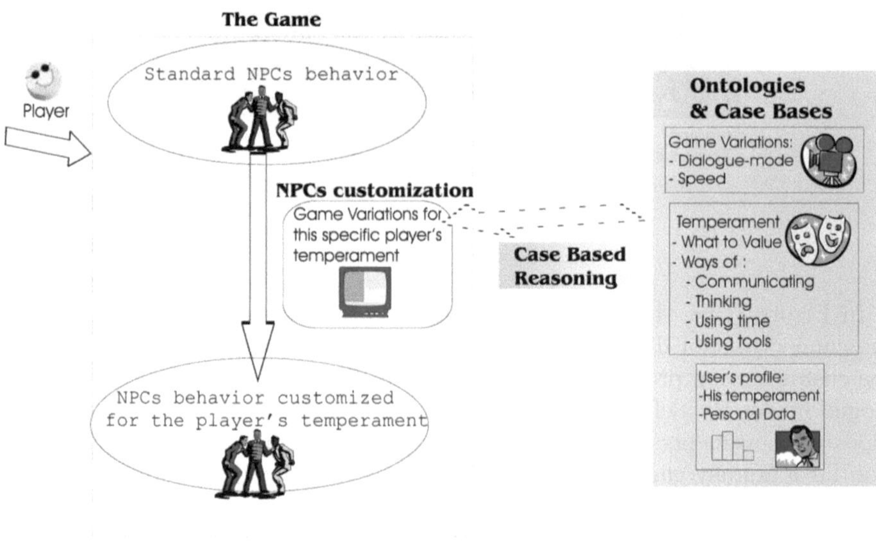

Fig. 2. Elements of the automatic NPC customization model

From a practical point of view, Neverwinter Script implements the plain interaction – without temperament-dependent modifications – using the Aurora toolset which is included in Neverwinter Nights.

The case base has cases which contain pairs of temperament-behavior change. If the temperament of the current player is exactly the same as one in the case base, the corresponding behavior change is performed; otherwise the system search for a similar temperament in the case base and the corresponding behavior is used as a basis to create a more suitable one.

This model relies heavily on ontologies. The terms of an ontology describe the static knowledge of each aspect of the design. Ontology is a term borrowed from philosophy that refers to the science of describing the kinds of entities in the world and how they relate each other. Ontologies based on DLs paradigm include definitions of concepts –classes–, roles –properties– and individuals. Given such an ontology, the formal semantics of the language that we use specifies how to derive its logical consequences, i.e. facts not literally present in the ontology, but entailed by the semantics. To formalize our ontologies we use the DL-specific part of the Ontology Web Language[5] (OWL DL). These entailments may be based on a single document or multiple distributed documents that we combine using the import OWL mechanisms. The OWL DL reasoning capabilities relies on the good computational properties of DLs.

We define cases as individuals of a concept which belongs to the ontology. A case is a complex individual that has several slots and facets represented here as properties and data type properties. Each property may contain individuals of other concepts of the same ontology or other imported ontologies. The advantage of this approach is that a reasoner may check the consistency and may classify the kind of individuals automatically. We use very narrow ontologies and cases to simplify the design and updates. This model is embedded in another model [5], and both share the ontologies and case bases.

Temperaments: TEMPOnto and the Case Base. We use temperament theory of David Keirsey [6], which is widely applied in psychology and in companies to interview job candidates. Keirsey's theory is centered in the long-term behavior patterns, i.e., what people do. It is an interpretation of the Myers-Briggs and Carl Jung's writings on personality types, more interested in what people think. We consider Keirsey's model more relevant for videogames because acting in them is usually more important than thinking. The theory defines four basic temperaments. Temperaments are not variable as emotions or feelings. Each person has a unique proportional combination of the four temperament types.

In this article we use an example where we consider an unique proportional combination as the description of a new case: *Artisan 10%, Guardian 10%, Idealist 30% and Rational 50%.*

Normally one of the temperaments is predominant, *Rational* in the example. This means that the person will behave most of the time like that temperament.

[5] http://www.w3.org/TR/owl-guide/

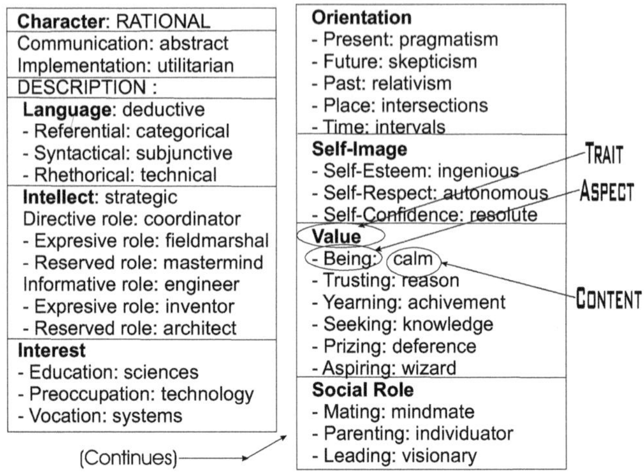

Fig. 3. The basic temperament Rational and its traits

We describe each temperament type by a set of traits composed by some aspects. In Figure 3 there is a complete set of traits for the Rational temperament. Each trait characterizes the way people behave in relation with its set of aspects.

For our example we consider the trait "value", that means what people will value most in relation with the different aspects of that trait. The aspects of the "value" trait are shown in Figure 3. One of them is *being*, that means how people appreciate to be. Rational people value being *calm*. The word "calm" is the value of the aspect "being". To represent it in the ontology, shown partially in Figure 5, we create one individual *temp:ValueBeingCalmX* as instance of *Trait*.

In contrast with the previous example, Artisan people value most being *excited*. Another example is the trait *Language* which has a *rhetorical* aspect. Rational people use a *heterodox* kind of rhetorical aspect. In contrast, Artisans prefer a *technical* kind of rhetorical aspect.

We consider that if the model may use different aspects of NPCs behavior according to the player's temperament, the player will feel more comfortable and enjoy more the videogame. We personalize the game applying variations of the game, such us the speed of movements or the language of the NPCs. Each variation may affect some traits of one specific temperament.

Variations: VARIOnto and the Case Base. We call *variations* to all the possible changes that we may execute to personalize a domain. For example, in the domain of our example scenario, we decide to customize the game by the implementation of the idea represented by one assertion: "a polite NPC with slow movements makes you feel calm". From this assertion we deduce that is important to customize two aspects, the politeness of the NPC's sentences and the speed of its movements.

To customize the NPC there are two kinds of variations depending on its relation to the virtual environment we use: *native variations*, which are direct commands to execute in the game, such as changing the speed of the animation of an NPC, or *plug-in variations*, which are embedded scripts that can be executed in the game at runtime, such as changing the dialogue mode of an NPC.

The technology we use to send commands to Neverwinter Nights is Shadow Door[6], a DLL for Neverwinter Nights Extender[7] which allows external systems to send messages by sockets to the core of the game.

These messages perform *native variations* in the game or activate *plug-in variations*. Native variations are easier to implement – just changing accordingly built-in variables of the game that controls the behaviour of NPCs –. Plug-in variations are more interesting. This is the case of the "change dialogue-mode" script in our scenario. We developed that script to maintain a variable "dialogue-mode"; its values represent possible dialogues of the NPC, i.e.: more or less polite, funny, aggressive, etc. These variations relate with the different temperaments. For each variation there are several degrees of intensity in an ordered list. For instance, the 1st level of politeness is the most polite: this variation uses a set of very polite sentences that replace the complete text of the conversation between Drax and his servant.

Figure 5 illustrates the process of implementing the assertion. In the ontology is the variation concept, which has several properties. The values of a property are individuals of other concepts. We create a variation, the NPCcalmProducer1 instance of *NPCcalmProducer*. The main properties of a variation are:

- *affectToTraits* has several traits of temperaments which are affected by the variation. Our variation example has the *temp:ValueBeingCalmX* trait.
- *hasExecutionSteps* are the necessary actions to execute the variation. In our example we have two actions, "to change the NPC dialogue mode to politeLevel-8" and "to change the NPC speed to 0.75". To implement these actions we use commands called *ExecutionSteps*.
  - `chango!#dialogue mode#politeLevel-8`, which is implemented by the individual execStepChangeDialoguePolite of the *ExecutionStep* concept.
  - `change!#speed#0.75` which is implemented by the individual execStep ChangeSpeedSlow of the same concept.

Each *ExecutionStep* individual has two main properties:

- *hasActivationCommand* has the command to execute the step, e.g.: "change!" in our example. For the speed command, "change!" corresponds to a native command of Neverwinter Script which changes the speed of the NPC behavior. For the dialogue-mode command, "change!" corresponds to a script implemented specifically by the customization developers for choosing different conversations trees.
- *hasActivationParameters* the parameters of the command. The parameters are of the ExecParam concept that is explained below.

---

[6] http://www.cs.northwestern.edu/ rob/software/shadow%20door/

[7] http://nwnx.org/

The *ExecParam* concept is specially important for the adaptation of cases. To adapt a case we need a range of flexibility. We get it by the declaration of possible ranges. Each one refers to one of the basic temperament. We continue in our example only with the ExecParamSetDialoguePolite, because execParamSetSpeedSlow is too simple to illustrate the whole adaptation mechanism. The main properties of the *ExecParam* concept are:

- *hasExecParamName* has the literal name of the parameter to be executed by the command. In the example they are "dialogue-mode" and "speed".
- *hasExecParamValue* has the value of the parameter. In the example they are "politeLevel-8" and "0.75".
- *possibleAdaptationRange* has four subproperties: idealistRange, artisan Range, rationalRange, guardianRange. It indicates how strong is the effect for each basic temperament Each one has a list of values. They describe the distance of the value to that specific temperament. The first value in the list is the "nearest" for that temperament, i.e.: with the strongest effect, and the last value is the "farthest" for that temperament, i.e.: with the weakest effect. An example of these lists is in Figure 4.
- *hasExecParamRelevancy* indicates the general relative importance in the adaptation process. It contains the corresponding four subproperties. Each subproperty is the relative importance specifically for each temperament. For example, a parameter has a very low value in guardianRelevancy because it is very little related with that temperament, e.g.: the politeness is less relevant for Guardian people than for Rational people.

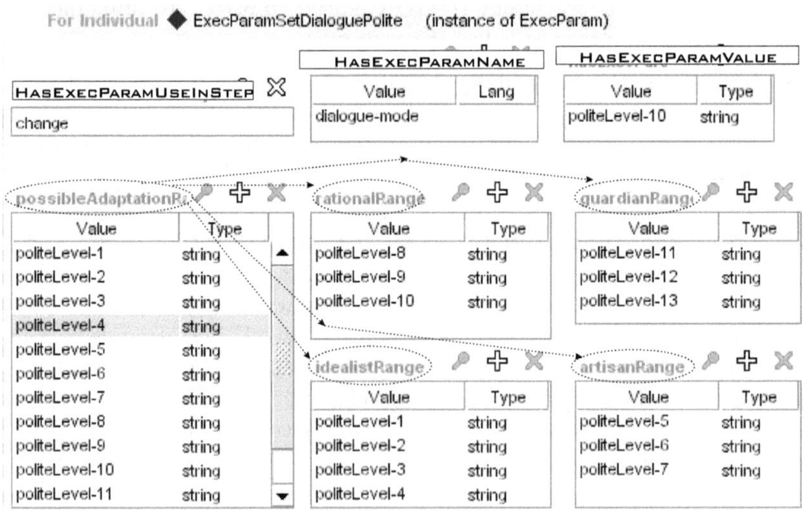

Fig. 4. ExecParam of a variation concept and ranges to be adapted

Mapping Temperaments into Variations. As we mentioned before, each variation may affect some traits of a specific temperament. In Figure 5 we depict the mechanism to represent this process: each variation is related to specific traits and values of temperaments, not just with the temperament itself. This relation is performed using affectToTraits property of *Variation* concept, which contains the affected traits of *Temperament* concept. In affectToTraits property of our example we have *ValueBeingCalmX* which is of the concept of *value* trait for Rational temperament. The way to promote this calm situation is with the execution steps: execStepChangeDialoguePolite and execStepChangeSpeedSlow.

Other important aspect to represent in the model is that each variation affects in a different way to each temperament. In our example, the dialogue mode of the NPCs affects *value* trait of Rational temperament in a very different way to the same trait of Artisan temperament. This is because the first one has "calm" as value in the *value* trait and the latter has "excited". The mechanism to represent the different effects in both temperaments is through – see Figure 4– the execution parameters contents of the execution steps belonging to the variation. We describe how we adapt the contents in section 5.

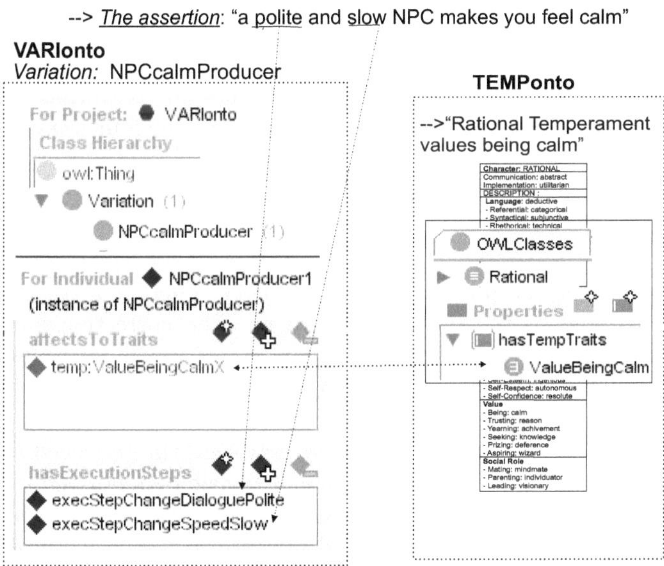

Fig. 5. An assertion as a *variation* related to a specific *trait* of a *temperament*

User Types and Users: USEROnto and the Case Base. In the USEROnto there are two kinds of cases, the UserType and the User. The *User case* describes the player knowledge needed by the model and has these main properties:

- *hasTemperamentProportions* of the four basic temperaments in %.
- *hasUserType* that is the best match of player types.
- *hasUserAdaptations* with adaptations of that UserType to the specific player.

The property *hasUserAdaptations* is empty when the UserType matches exactly or very near with the player's temperament proportions. The adaptations are obtained from the ranges of each variation explained in VARIOnto.

The *UserType case* represents the unique proportion of the four basic temperaments and the variations generated and stored for it. Each case in the case base is one of these combinations. To avoid a huge number of cases, a minimum gap between cases is defined a priori. The name of the example UserType case is *UserType-A10-G10-I30-R50*. The main properties are:

– *hasTemperamentProportions* is the same property as in the player case.
– *hasUserType* with the variations for this player type.

5 Process of the Automatic NPC Customization Model

We use the previous example to illustrate the general reasoning cycle in our model that follows the classic CBR cycle [1]. We query the CBR system with a description based on the result of the Keirsey's questionnaire. Suppose the form gives us the following player temperament proportions: Artisan 10%, Guardian 10%, Idealist 30% and Rational 50%. The reasoning cycle *retrieves* the most similar case (e.g. Artisan 10%, Guardian 30%, Idealist 30% and Rational 30%).

To measure the similarity between cases we use the following definition of distance which is a sum of the differences for each of the four temperaments:

$$\sum_{T:Artisan}^{T=Rational} (\%NewCase_T - \%retrievedCase_T) * CorrectionFactor_T$$

The *%NewCase* is the proportions of the query. There is a correction factor that is proportional to the previous difference. The correction factor is very high when the retrieved case is very far for one of the temperaments with a high percentage, because this retrieved case is not a good case even if the other percentage temperaments are similar.

The system *reuses* the retrieved case by adapting the retrieved case output slots, i.e.: a set of variations for each of the four basic temperaments. Variations are in its own case base. The adaptation actions are calculated by the difference between the proportions in the query and in the retrieved case; in our example the adaptation actions are: Artisan stays unmodified, make Guardian decreasing 20%, make Rational increasing 20% and let Idealist without modifications. After the adaptations, the system executes the modified variations. These variations represent the solved case.

The system performs the adaptation of each variation using the *possibleAdaptationRange* property that has the possible ranges for each temperament as described before. Figure 4 is our variation example; we see that the range for each temperament is a list of values, e.g.: *rationalRange*. The total number of values (e.g.: 3) is equivalent to 100%. To make the retrieved case 20% more Rational we calculate that proportion in the list and we choose the element which occupies the position corresponding to the obtained proportion. The current mood filters the adaptation, increasing or decreasing some of these adaptations.

Next tasks that are under development are *revision* of the solved case using the feedback of the player after the game session, and *remembering* of the useful cases to be reused in further iterations.

Servant: Welcome to the castle, sir! Everybody has heard about your courage in the battlefield.
Drax: I am tired because of the battle, servant. Prepare my bath.
Servant: At your command, my lord. [Saluting him] A perfumed bath is ready for you.

Fig. 6. Example dialogue at the 8th level of politeness

In Figure 6 the customized dialogue is shown. For the same scenario of Figure 1 the player obtains a different conversation because the system is aware of her temperament and therefore of the preferences on NPCs. That is the reason why the politeness of the conversation has increased from the 13th to the 8th position. The speed of the movement decreased proportionally, but it cannot be appreciated in a screenshot.

6 Conclusions

We present a model for customizing automatically NPCs according to the player's temperament. Using Ontologies and CBR the system modifies the animations of two characters and their dialogue in the context of a fantasy RPG.

The development is not mature enough for being formally evaluated, but some limitations arise from a practical point of view: e.g. an out-of-game questionnaire could not be the most comfortable way to identify the real temperament of the player. The case base of mappings between temperaments and NPC behaviors is time consuming because it has to be refined based on the experience of players; this refinement applies too to the implementation of each NPC behaviour, defined in abstract terms, for a specific platform as Neverwinter Nights or other videogame engine. Another limitation is the difficult integration with other architectures of autonomous characters whose personality may eventually contradict the behavior recommended by the system.

Besides the areas mentioned in the example, there are other areas of customization for NPC behavior, such as abilities, appearance (race, clothes, etc.), social role, etc. The same approach can be used for customizing those features. Also it can be used with any number of secondary characters as villains, partners, lovers, etc. Every element in a game is susceptible of being customized according to temperaments of players, as the weather, ambient light, camera settings, etc.

Modelling artificial temperaments of NPCs is also possible using the same theory presented here or other temperament theories. Such application could let the system customize whole groups of characters as families, troops, or even the whole cast of the game using a compatibility table of temperaments.

The process of customization according to different player temperaments is independent of the game domain and genre, except in the set of variations that have to be specifically implemented for the game (VARIOnto).

Currently the temperament is a static value in the model taken from the results of a questionnaire, but a future line of research will be to identify dynamically other values (e.g. player emotions) according to the actions of the avatar using specific heuristics.

References

1. E. Armengol and E. Plaza. A knowledge level model of knowledge based reasoning. In S. Wess, K. D. Althoff, and M. M. Richter, editors, *Proceedings of the 1st European Workshop on Topics in Case-Based Reasoning, Kaiserslautern, Germany - EWCBR'94*, pages 53–64. Springer–Verlag, Berlin, 1994.
2. P. Brusilovsky. Methods and techniques of adaptive hypermedia. *User Modeling and User Adapted Interaction: Special issue on adaptive hypertext and hypermedia*, 6(2-3):87–129, 1996.
3. B. Díaz-Agudo and P. A. González-Calero. An architecture for knowledge intensive CBR systems. In E. Blanzieri and L. Portinale, editors, *Advances in Case-Based Reasoning – (EWCBR'00)*. Springer-Verlag, Berlin Heidelberg New York, 2000.
4. B. Díaz-Agudo and P. A. González-Calero. Knowledge intensive cbr through ontologies. *Expert Update*, 2003.
5. H. Gómez-Gauchía, B. Díaz-Agudo, and P. A. González-Calero. Cobber, toward an affective conversational ki-cbr framework. In B. Prasad, editor, *B. Prasad(Ed.) Procs of the 2nd Indian International Conference on Artificial Intelligence IICAI-05*, pages 1804–1820, Pune, India, December, 20-22 2005. IICAI.
6. D. Keirsey. *Please Understand Me II.* Prometheus Nemesis Book Co Inc., 1998.
7. M. Mateas and A. Stern. Façade: An experiment in building a fully-realized interactive drama. In *Game Developer's Conference, Game Design track*, San Jose, California, USA, 2003.
8. S. Salotti and V. Ventos. Study and formalization of a case-based reasoning system using a description logic. In B. Smyth and P. Cunningham, editors, *Advances in Case-Based Reasoning – (EWCBR'98)*. Springer-Verlag, 1998.

Personalizing the Player Experience in MMORPGs

Anders Tychsen[1], Susana Tosca[2], and Thea Brolund[3]

[1] ISVR, Macquarie University, Sydney, Australia
atychsen@ics.mq.edu.au
[2] CCGS, IT University of Copenhagen, Denmark
tosca@itu.dk
[3] University of Technology, Sydney
tbrolund@yahoo.dk

Abstract. Personalizing the playing experience is a key factor in making players of computer games feel involved in the virtual world; however, current Massively Multiplayer Online Role Playing Games only to a limited degree allocate development or running resources towards facilitating a personalized experience. In Pen and Paper Role Playing Games, the player-controlled characters form a key component in facilitating the formation of a personalized experience. In these games, characters are often more than the association of stats and skills popular in online games, and several approaches towards utilizing the character-based information directly to personalize the game playing have been developed, e.g. personality systems. Some of these systems can be integrated into online games, providing a realistic and financially feasible method for improving the ability of these games to personalize the experience to the individual players.

Keywords: MMORPG, personalization, role playing game, character, personality.

1 Introduction

Personalized storytelling in Massively Multiplayer Online Role Playing Games (MMORPGs) is a much debated subject [1],[2],[3],[5],[7]. While storytelling exists in MMORPGs, it is generally tied up in quest systems [16], and player-player interactions. The virtual worlds are bound by technical, resource, format, media-related and not the least player-related limitations, which makes it inherently difficult to provide the kind of engaging, personal and emotionally meaningful storytelling, which could aid the game form in opening up to a broader audience [7].

In addressing the issue of personalizing the MMORPG experience, it is of relevance to investigate related game forms for experiences or techniques. One such game form is Pen and Paper Role Playing Games (PnP RPGs) [4],[8],[17],[18], which share a substantial number of features with MMORPGs, such as the underlying rules systems and themes. Secondly, in game forms like PnP RPGs it is possible to generate exactly the kind of personal experience that is challenging to create in the electronic

S. Göbel, R. Malkewitz, and I. Iurgel (Eds.): TIDSE 2006, LNCS 4326, pp. 253 – 264, 2006.

persistent-world equivalents[1]. This is done by combining collaborative storytelling and imagining with rules in a manner that theoretically offers complete player freedom, in-game consequence of player actions, free manipulation of time, while at the same time generating personalized stories directly tied to the motivations of the game players and their characters.

In the below, it is explored how PnP RPGs utilize PC generation to facilitate personalization, and how these techniques can be integrated into the framework of online games using the technologies currently implemented in MMORPGs. It is important to realize that the purpose of this analysis is not to advocate for the inclusion of more advanced AIs, character emotions, believable agent systems or advanced interactive storytelling systems. These approaches form highly innovate, alternative pathways that hold significant potential to improve the storytelling and immersive qualities of computer games [2],[5],[9],[11],[13],[16], however, the goal here is vastly more modest: By personalizing the gaming experience via the establishing of a series of parameters linked to the PCs and their generation at the hands of the players, which allow objects and NPCs (i.e. game agents) of MMORPG engines to recognize the characters (and possibly the players themselves) in new ways and react correspondingly; as well as allowing the players to create unique characters, jointly facilitating a more personal gaming experience than currently the norm in MMORPGs such as *World of Warcraft, Star Wars Galaxies,* and *Everquest.* In essence, the method allows for the integration of a designed narrative potential in MMORPGs [5], via the use of the narrative potential of PCs, and the utilization of this via expressive agents (mainly NPCs but also other PCs). The approach suggested here operates at a simpler and more direct level than systems utilizing e.g. advanced intelligent agents and interactive storytelling systems [e.g. 13], and the impact of implementing the PC models suggested here is also of a much smaller magnitude. The strength of the approach is that it is aimed at implementation in the technical and financial framework of existing MMORPGs.

The basic models for the character constructs presented here are drawn from pen and paper RPGs, however, it is not the direct purpose to promote PnP RPG style play in MMORPGs; nor to prevent players from creating their own vision of their PCs and role playing them (with or without the support of the game system). Rather, it is the purpose to make the game world more reactive to the specific player character. This does not implicate role playing on behalf of the player, although it certainly facilitates role playing. The core premise of this analysis is based on the hypothesis that a personalized gaming experience is better than an impersonal one - that moving around in a virtual game world that responds to your PC is more satisfactory that getting no reaction from the environment directly related to your character. This even if the responses does not provide actual ability to change the environment. This hypothesis is debateable, and it might be asked if players of MMORPGs are even interested in this kind of responsiveness to their characters, or if they would prefer "blank slates" which they can fill out to the degree they feel like it, and which the game world does

[1] One of the most important reasons for this being that PnPs RPGs are controlled by a human GM that adapts the story to the players in such an effective way that current artificial intelligence or interactive storytelling systems are challenged in emulating it [2].

not provide any special recognition of. However [19] noted that some of the main motivations for MMORPG players include: Creating background histories for, customising and role playing their PCs. Integration of their PCs into the on-going storyline of the world also features as a motivation. Furthermore, players enjoy socialising and forming relationships via their characters. These are all motivations that indicate an interest among the player base for more advanced character creation opportunities, as well as exposure to game content that allows them to take advantage of their characters. The popularity of single-player CRPGs, where the game world often reacts to the player directly (e.g. *Knights of the Old Republic*), also seems to indicate that there is an interest in MMORPGs that respond to player characters. It would seem that there is an interest among at least certain segments of the player base in more character-responsive environments. A core challenge of creating PC generation systems for use in MMORPGs that accommodate these players is to avoid alienating players who are only marginally or not at all interested in taking advantage of such a feature. Finally, if experiences from PnP RPGs are any indication of player experiences in online RPGs, a heightened degree of agency will provide better integration in the fictional universe. Additionally, while most current MMORPGs do not cater to players interested in role playing their characters, it is possible that role playing interested players would be more attracted to MMORPGs where more personalized experiences are possible [7], thus expanding the core market.

2 PnP RPGs vs. MMORPGs

In a typical PnP RPG, the player or players control one, possibly several, characters and their actions. The Game Master (GM), a specialized participant with often substantial control of the game, informs the player/-s about what other characters do and how the fictional game world responds to the actions of the characters.

A core characteristic of PnP RPGs is the magnitude of the relative freedom of the players to decide on the actions and attitudes of their characters [8], within the rules of the game and the constraints of the fictional world – in other words they have real agency (in the sense of [11]) in the fictional world, and the actions of the player characters (PCs) have direct consequences. Furthermore, the GM and the players create a shared history that constantly is developed in collaboration between the participants.

In a current MMORPG, such as *Everquest* or *World of Warcraft*, because of technical and resource limitations, as well as the basic nature of persistent, massively multiplayer games, bringing the story of the individual player to the personalized level of PnP RPGs is not currently feasible. Players of MMORPGs can thus walk into inns repeatedly, and the Non-Player Characters (NPCs – in PnP RPGs controlled by the GM, in digital games controlled by the game software and implemented e.g. as an autonomous agent [16] there will not recognize them despite their past visits. The players can drop quests and missions without any consequence from the NPCs from which they accepted them in the first place. Players can only develop a character personality as a feature outside the framework of the game, and only utilize it when interacting with other players. Finally, players cannot enter a dialogue with a NPC that is not pre-scripted or generated automatically.

3 PnP RPGs

Role Playing Games (RPGs) span a variety of formats [13], and form an important genre of both tabletop and digital gaming[2]. One of the reasons is the collaborative nature of the storytelling process in these games across media formats, which is of interest in developing interactive narratives in a digital environment [12],[17]. A core feature of PnP RPGs is the ability of these games to generate personalized stories of the type the individual player prefers. In PnP RPGs, there are a range of steps that need to be completed before the game itself can actually begin, including the creation of the PCs and their integration in the fictional world. The PCs form a primary tool in creating personalized gaming experiences in PnP RPGs. Character developed by, and personal to, the players, encourage and assist role playing and engagement. Furthermore, the integration of these characters into the game world, form a basis for anchoring the PCs in the world and give them an interest therein. PCs can have families, backgrounds, histories and previous experiences in the fictional world just like people do in the real world, and the players can define these to the extent they prefer. In the case of MMORPGs, having the virtual world react to PCs during play can only be done if the creation process is detailed enough to provide subjects for the game systems to respond to, and which provides enough variation to enable the creation of player-unique PCs.

4 PCs in MMORPGs and PnP RPGs

MMORPG character generation systems are usually limited to dealing with two factors: Avatar appearance and character stats/skills. Features that are difficult to program, model and animate such as PC personality and -background are usually de-emphasized. Some MMORPGs allow the players to enter personal information about their PCs; however, this information is rarely integrated with the game mechanics. The addition of personal information beyond name and race is usually delegated to the final stages of PC creation, and is often voluntary. The integration of the PC in the game world is minimal. E.g., in *World of Warcraft*, the integration of the PCs rests solely on the choice of race, PC class and to some degree PC level, as more content becomes available with level increases. The available content largely depends on the first two factors. Combined with NPCs recognizing the PC name, class and/or race, this is the extent that these PC features are utilized by the game.

While there is a considerable variation in the approach to PC building in PnP RPG rules systems, the process often requires the players (or the participants choose) to go through a similar set of overall phases in building their character, which broadly focus on establishing the **personality**, **stats** and **integration** of the PC in question. However, a stats-focused approach is also common, with the personality generating process occurring as a separate element of the establishment of stats/skills, with no

[2] While the design and development aspects of computer-based RPGs (CRPGs and MMORPGs) are well described in the games design literature (e.g. [1],[3],[6]), the tabletop- and physical forms of RPGs are primarily described outside design- and academic literature. While of varying quality, a substantial number of the treatments published outside the academia are very well researched and highly informative, a few examples including [4],[8].

rules or guide for this process (*Dungeons & Dragons RPG*). When constructing a character for PnP RPG play (with the exception of PnP RPGs with only formal or informal rules for the collaborative storytelling process), all three of these phases are addressed. Each of the three phases can be divided into a number of PC components, the exact detail of which can vary from player to player, system to system (Table 1).

Table 1. PnP RPG character elements

PnP RPG character components		
Personality	**Psyche**	The psyche basically defines the core of the character, covering all aspects of the character psychology, including emotions.
Personality	**Goals**	Goals are the primary tool for GMs in engaging the players, and the principle is known from quest systems in MMORPGs and CRPGs. Goals can be as simple as instructions or missions: Kill the dragon, free the princess; loot the orc lair, get to level 33 etc., but can also can be personal, e.g. maintaining a close relationship with a sister, or not letting a phobia control ones life. The latter are generallyharder to program and anticipate, and therefore rare in computer games.
Stats	**Traits, Abilities, Skills**	The stats provide the mathematical numbers associated with the character, e.g. strength and other physical or mental attributes, abilities and skills (e.g. farming, sword-fighting) and unique powers (i.e. spell casting). The stats directly affect the effect of the PC interacting with the virtual environment.
Integration	**Connec-tions**	PCs will have connections with other PCs. This could be as simple as them being a member of the same clan. Associations with other PCs ideally include what opinions the character has towards these. Associations can be with other player controlled PC or NPCs. Most characters start out with associations formed by their background, and build up increased contact networks during the running of a PnP RPG.
Integration	**Class**	While not a requirement in either PnP RPGs or computer-based RPGs, most MMORPGs define an occupation or character class for the character (*Dungeons & Dragons*-games), while others develop stats/skills based on character actions (*Morrowind*). Occupations and classes can be used to help develop the vision of the character, but at the same time can be restrictive. Occupations and classifications are generally developed via a rules system, but need not be so.
Integration	**Location**	Why is the character where he or she is? The characters – and thereby the players – need to have enough information to give them a solid hook into the game world. For example, it could be that the group comes together for the first time because they all were friends of an important person who is dead and his son called them to revenge him.
Integration	**Back-ground**	Background details where the characters come from, the events that have brought them to where they are in their lives. This includes the history of the character developed during game time.
Integration	**Contacts**	Contacts are a specific type of association, which is characterized by being a quest giver, mission provider or similar entity that progresses the game story. Contacts are the NPCs that initiate the adventures of the PCs. They exist in all forms of RPGs, digital or not (e.g. *City of Heroes*), and are one of the primary means of propelling the players forward in the game. The typical contact is a quest provider.

Due to the wide variety of PnP RPG rules systems and the inherent flexibility and modality of these systems, and perhaps more importantly the differing desires of the players in how to play these games, there is a broad variation in the character developing process. In many PnP RPGs, the players initially develop their character personality, forming an initial **vision** for the character and its integration in the game world fiction (an integration the GM typically expands upon). Character personality and integration thereby form the focus of the initial phases of the character generation.

The PnP RPG rules systems often provide rules-based systems for developing the personality, motivations and world integration of the PCs (e.g. *Generic Universal Role Playing System).* These rules-based systems assist the players in developing the vision for their character, and serves as an aid to the players and GM alike in running the game. For example, a PnP RPG system could include a system for determining the past career path of characters, which would influence which skills and abilities these have emphasized, and detail some experiences in the past of the characters (e.g. *Mutant Chronicles, Traveller).* It is important to note that the systems developed in PnP RPGs to help the players define the personality and integration features of their characters are not meant as a means to form complete psychological models – they form an aid to the players, a guiding system. For example, a player might have selected four psychological features of his or her character, from a list in a PnP RPG rule book, however, that does not prevent the player from developing more features for the character. The advantage that personality- and integration-systems in PnP RPGs provide, however, is a rules-based expression of these features. For example, a player might have chosen the "arachnophobia" personality trait, thus fighting less effectively against spiders, thereby providing a translation into quantifiable rules.

In the quest to personalize the experience of playing MMORPGs and CRPGs, character generation systems and approaches in PnP RPGs form an interesting feature, which holds a potential use beyond the current adoption of stats/skill-based character generation. Specifically, the rules systems developed to assist players of PnP RPGs developing the features of their characters that do not relate directly to the basic stats of the characters, e.g. their personality, and providing a mean of expressing some of these features as computationally usable quantifiable numbers. These systems do not override the vision the players have for their character, but assists in implementing it in the game world and the rules system. A common approach is to use point-buy systems, where players get a certain amount of point to spend on special character features, such as psychological strengths and weaknesses, in-game contacts, wealth or aptitude for various skills.

5 Personalizing the Characters in MMORPGs

Because MMORPGs are persistently-running massively multiplayer games with limited running resources, it is difficult if at all possible to personalize the story to the individual player to the degree of PnP RPGs. What MMORPGs can do, however, is adopt some of the techniques of PnP RPGs in developing characters with personality and integration components as well as stats components, and draw upon experiences from PnP RPGs in personalizing the playing experience even further during actual game play. For example, by utilizing the personality and integration components of the characters in directing game content to the player, e.g. via quests triggered by personality components of player characters. This, however, needs to be done in a fashion that conforms to the limitations of development resources (notably ensuring that redundant content is minimized), running processing resources, the virtual medium itself, player exploitation etc.

5.1 Personalizing PCs in MMORPGs

The personality component of PnP RPG characters can be subdivided into **Psyche** and **Goals** (Table 1), however, in the visual environment of MMORPGs the **Physical Appearance** of the character is also important. This feature of characters plays a more indirect role in the mind's eye-driven environment of PnP RPGs.

5.1.1 Psyche and Goals

As outlined above, some PnP RPG rule systems such as *Generic Universal Role Playing System* (*GURPS*) feature rules-based systems for character construction and profiling, working with all aspect of PCs. The approach utilized is a system of advantages and disadvantages. When creating a character, the player is provided a specific sum of character points (or experience points). These can be spent on stats and skills, and on advantages and disadvantages, the latter of which can refer to either physical of psychological benefits or problems/weaknesses. Advantages benefit the character one way or the other – the PC is strong-willed, fearless and passionate, have a large income etc. Disadvantages provide weaknesses: E.g. phobias, detrimental appearance, poverty, bad social manners, a persistent enemy etc. Taking a disadvantage provides the character with extra points that can be spent buying advantages, stats and skills. For example, a player might choose to be from a poor background and therefore sickly of health, in order to gain points to develop the character intellectually. In *GURPS* most of the advantages and disadvantages have an in-game, rules-based effect – e.g. a character with arachnophobia fights less effectively against spiders. However, personality building systems can also be used purely as a tool for the player in developing the personality and integration features of the character, without any actual rules-based effect (such as modified stats or skills, access to specific objects etc.). The model presented here operates at a fairly modest level, and more advanced options exist for virtual reality applications, e.g. emotion-based character models. Personality systems provide a programmable way for MMORPG character generation systems to go beyond skills, abilities and special powers, in fleshing out PC personalities. This provides the players a tool for role playing and immersing themselves in their characters, and the MMORPG engine a tool for gathering information it can use to personalize the gaming experience to the individual player. There are several ways these systems can be integrated into MMORPGs, largely dependent on the extent of the in-game effect of the PC personality elements:

In-game effect: In the case where the personality system has an in-game effect, as in the PnP RPG *GURPS*, there are several options for this effect. A very simple example could be that a player chooses the "*arachnophobia*" disadvantage. Because of this choice, the character would have a permanent disadvantage in combat against arachnid-classified MOBs, or when fighting in environments connected to the occurrence of arachnids in the fictional world. The effect can be extended to include context-sensitive quest presentations to the PC. For example, if the quest system or database (quest database, Fig. 1) is capable of recognizing whether or not a PC speaking with a NPC quest-provider has the "*arachnophobia*" disadvantage or not (character database, Fig. 1), it can modify the NPC conversation accordingly – the NPC (quest giver, Fig. 1) might be aware of the PCs phobia. Such an implementation of the personality system would, however, require an increased amount of text preparation in the design phase of MMORPG production. However, there is a direct benefit in terms of increased personalization. This provides the player with context-sensitive expression possibilities whenever in subterranean dungeons. Furthermore, a point-based personality system incorporated throughout a game provides a further option for expanding the experience point system, with players being able to buy new advantages or buy off disadvantages (which could be used as the subject of quest chains); i.e. to develop the personality and character during play.

Personality systems with an in-game effect need to be robustly designed in order not to be prone to player dissatisfaction and abuse. If a player of a MMORPG is twice as likely to fight orcs as spiders, players will quickly figure out to take the orc-fighting advantage and the spider-fighting disadvantage in order to maximise the fighting capacity of their character. Therefore the orc-fighting advantage has to cost more points – and the prices have to be calculated based on the fact that players might not encounter that many orcs if they choose to venture through areas of the MMORPG where orcs are rare. This is a balancing issue; however, these kinds of problems are common to MMORPG design.

No in-game effect: A character building system need not have an in-game effect directly. Players could e.g. select advantages and disadvantages purely for the purpose of building a PC personality. This is a very safe approach from a balancing perspective, and does not rule out using the personality profiles of the player characters to direct content accordingly. E.g.: A letter arrives for a player character via the in-game postal service or equivalent information-distribution function, from a NPC in a different area of the game world. The NPC has a problem with a demonic infestation, and has heard via the grapevine that the player character has a grudge against demons (chosen as the personality trait *demonic grudge*). The NPC is interested in hearing if the player character would care to help him with the infestation for a modest reward, and includes some travel money with a map of how to find him. This example is basic, however, it provides a very simple way of adding a bit of personalization to the player experience (and provides a role playing aid for the player), by making the game react to the choices the player made when generating the character. Note that the approach does not require the addition of extra content, only that content is directed to the player in a manner consistent with the choices the player made when generating the character. Furthermore, the approach allows for players to update their personality profiles as they play. The approach can be combined with a personality system with an in-game effect as described above. The approach is consistent with the logic of the fictional world as long as this features a method for communication between the players, while at the same time being a very obvious game mechanic. Players will realize that the game design attempts to respond to their characters, thus the development resource put into the system will be experienced (and hopefully appreciated) by the players.

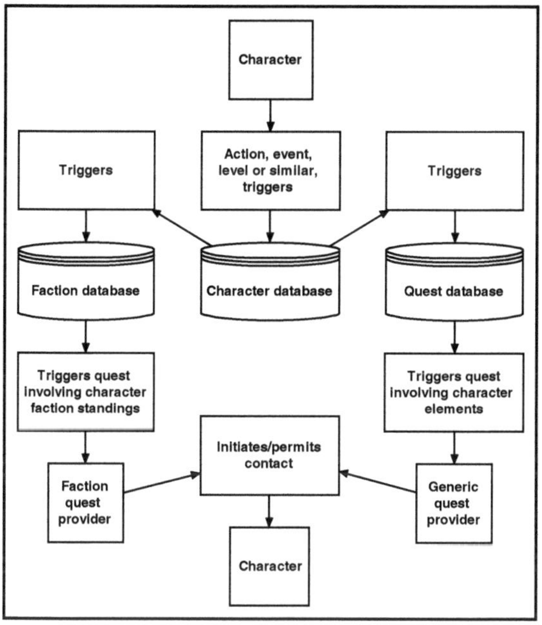

Fig. 1. Simplified implementation model of a character elements response system. Two examples provided (general and faction-triggered quests). Symbols: SSADM/IDEF0 terminology.

5.1.2 Physical Appearance

In PnP RPGs players are free to decide on the physical appearance of their PCs and what clothing they are wearing, subject to the limits of the character race and wealth. For example, a player could choose to play a fat troll with a gold cape providing the PC has the necessary funding to buy a gold cape, or acquire it via other means. In MMORPGs the options for personalizing character appearance is limited. For example, in *World of Warcraft*, the face, hair style/colour, tusks, and skin colour each has a limited number of variations; however, the basic shape of the avatar cannot be altered. While the total amount of variations using the *World of Warcraft* appearance generator is huge, the resulting characters remain similar except for the head/face and skin colour. In order to further facilitate personalization of characters in MMORPGs, appearance options could be expanded to facilitate other forms of customization, e.g. body form, which is rarely an option in MMORPGs. Virtual social worlds such as *There* and *Second Life* generally allows for advanced customization, and newer CRPGs such as *Morrowind* allows detailed customization of avatar appearance. In some PnP RPG rules systems, such customizations affect the basic stats of the character; finally, PC appearances in PnP RPGs can be modified as the game progresses, a similar system could be envisioned for MMORPGs. Appearance can even be used as the basis for quest triggers or form he basis for quest storylines. Customisation of game characters is one of the motivations of MMORPG players reported by [18], especially with female players.

5.1.3 Integration in the Fictional World

In a PnP RPG, the GM and the players can work together to achieve a high level of character integration in the world fiction. In MMORPGs, it is necessary to adopt a more limited strategy due to the relationship between development, running resources available and player number. Similarly to personality generation systems, integration and goals, associations, backgrounds etc. could be defined via a player-choice based system. In the example provided above, a quest system could be designed to react not only to personality traits, but also backgrounds and specific types of goals. For example, a PC with the background *family slain by demons* could be directed to the same quest as the PC with the personality trait *demonic grudge*. Indeed, the two PC features could be linked. As for the personality example, the quest system should ideally respond to the specific background in the way the NPC contacts and talks to the PC. In order to avoid having to deal with huge amounts of text writing and editing, a quest system could utilize a text generator or simply use a model of quest text that is easy to modify to suit different conditions (note that not all quests will need to feature texts specialized to every type of personality or background).

Goals could likewise feature in-game effects. For example, if a character has the goal to defeat a dragon in his or her lifetime, the quest system could contain a specific quest accessible by players with this goal only, however shareable with other players. Other alternatives include goal-specific rewards. Creating 30 single- or even chained quests specific to a particular character goal is not a major development issue in contemporary MMORPGs that feature quests in the hundreds. If specifically designed to include a quest chain link for specific intervals of character development, e.g. via PC level increase (the common method to advance characters in MMORPGs), and to be shareable with or requiring the assistance of other players, these goal-oriented quests remain broadly accessible content. Class-specific goal oriented quests exist in e.g. *World of Warcraft*, where each PC class has specific quests; however, these are based on character class, not the character personality itself.

A commonly used method for providing backgrounds to PCs is to associate them with specific races, factions or similar. This approach is also used in PnP RPGs (e.g. *Vampire the Masquerade, Mutant Chronicles*), and in these games PC family or clan relations can be as complex as those of the real world. While the race and clan concept exists in MMORPGs, it is possible to expand these based on PnP RPG experiences, for example in associating PCs with specific clans or families. Such families could have specific quests associated with them accessible only to PCs that are members of the family, and in order to keep the content open to PCs that e.g. perform specific tasks for the family or which are accepted as friends of the family based on their association with PC members. This would lead to a range of opportunities for quests to be tied to the different families or even between them, with any percentage of these being open quests accessible to all PCs.

6 Conclusion and Discussion

While the experiences that can be gathered from PnP RPGs to facilitate personalized experiences in MMORPGs will not revolutionize these games, they do provide relatively straight forward ideas for enhancing the character-based personalization of current MMORPGs. It remains, however, a question whether the implementation of PnP

RPG-derived PC generation and integration features are financially viable in MMORPGs, without requiring major development costs. A project aimed at developing and implementing such a system is currently being planned.

When designing personality or integration systems for MMORPGs, it is necessary to realize that players have varied ambitions with the gaming activity [19]. Just as in PnP RPGs, some players will not care about character personality, nor take any pleasure from the world responding to their character. Others will try to maximise the rules-based benefit they get from the character generation system (if relevant). An advantage of personality systems used in PnP RPGs is that they are inherently designed to be flexible to accommodate different player styles of play and ambitions.

The generation of a PC personality in MMORPGs could be completely or partly facilitated by systems constructed along similar lines as in PnP RPGs. E.g. a system which guides the player through a process of choices concerning PC background, personality traits and similar in an either selection-based or randomized system. These can include options for varying how much time the player wishes to spend on the process, to a simple auto-generation option, which provides a few keywords for the personality and background (or no background). These the player can use or ignore. Likewise, players could be allowed to refine their PC personality and integration during play, as is currently possible for stats and skills (Table 1). Neither of these features will, if designed properly, limit player access to game content, however, it will direct content based on the PC personality and world integration. Other sources of inspiration for MMORPG design include the use of role playing-based awards, contrary to the typical combat-based rewards systems. Furthermore, many PnP RPGs feature rules for "social skills", that which for example can be used to decrease item prices from vendors, quest access etc. Balancing is a central issue whenever such features are to be provided an in-game effect or similarly integrated in MMORPGs.

There are limits to how much can be achieved in terms of personalizing the gaming experience, role playing characters, creating dynamic narratives etc. when operating directly within the framework of existing mass-market gaming technologies. Work such as [9],[12],[16] point towards game formats featuring advanced user-responsiveness. PnP RPGs are investigated in developing these technologies, and will likely continue to be a source of inspiration for MMORPGs.

Acknowledgements. This study forms part of a multi-institutional research collaboration involving Australian and Scandinavian universities (Macquarie University, Sydney; The IT University, Denmark & University of Växjö, Sweden). The authors would like to thank Michael Hitchens for discussions, ideas and participation in forming the core approach of this paper, as well as manuscript editing. Anders Tychsen would like to acknowledge PhD-supervisor Manolya Kavakli and Michael Hitchens, ISVR, Department of Computing, Macquarie University.

References

1. Bartle, R.: Designing Virtual Worlds, New Riders Games, Berkeley CA (2003)
2. Combs, N.: The Intelligence in the MMOG: from scripts to stories to directorial AI. Proceedings of Other Players Conference, IT University, Copenhagen (2005).
3. Crawford, C.: Chris Crawford on Interactive Storytelling, New Riders Games, Berkeley CA, (2005)

4. Edwards, R.: GNS and Other Matters of Roleplaying Theory, Adept Press. Online publication, accessed 11th July 2006. URL: http://www.indie-rpgs.com/articles/1/ (2001)
5. Eladhari, M., Lindley, C.: Story Construction and Expressive Agents in Virtual Game Worlds. In: Proceedings of the Other Players Conference, Copenhagen, Denmark (2004)
6. Hallford, N., Hallford, J.: Swords & Circuitry: A Designer's Guide to Computer Role Playing Games. Prima Tech, Roseville, CA (2001)
7. Klug, C.: Implementing Stories in Massively Multiplayer Games. Online publication, accessed 11th July 2006. URL: http://www.gamasutra.com (2002)
8. Mackay, D.: The Fantasy Role-Playing Game: A New Performing Art. McFarland & Co., Jefferson, NC (2001)
9. Mateas, M.: Expressive AI: Games and Artificial Intelligence. DiGRA Level Up, Utrecht, Holland (2003)
10. Montola, M.: Designing Goals for Online Role-Players. Proceedings of the DiGRA Conference (2005)
11. Murray, J. H.: Hamlet on the Holodeck – The Future of Narrative in Cyberspace. The MIT Press, Cambridge MA (1997)
12. Peinado, F., Gervás, P.: Transferring GMing Laws to Interactive Digital Storytelling. In: Göbel, S., Spierling, U., Hoffmann, A., Iurgel, I., Schneider, O., Dechau, J., Feix, A. (eds.): TIDSE 2004: Springer Verlag, Darmstadt, Germany (2004) 48-54
13. Salen, K., Zimmerman, E.: Rules of Play - Game Design Fundamentals. MIT Press, London (2004)
14. Tosca, S.: Role-playing in multiplayer environments. Vampire: The Masquerade. Redemption. Computer Games & Digital Textualities, Copenhagen, Denmark (2001)
15. Tosca, S.: The Quest Problem in Computer Games. In: Göbel, S., Spierling, U., Hoffmann, A., Iurgel, I., Schneider, O., Dechau, J., Feix, A. (eds.): TIDSE 2004: Springer Verlag, Darmstadt, Germany (2004) 48-54
16. Trappl, R., Petta, P. (Eds.): Creating Personalities for Synthetic Actors: Towards Autonomous Personality Agents. Springer-Verlag, Berlin (1997)
17. Tychsen, A., Hitchens, M., Brolund, T., Kavakli, M.: The Game Master. Proceedings of the Interactive Entertainment Conference (2005) 215-222
18. Tychsen, A., Pagden, N.: Making Magic! Enhancing PnP RPGs with computing technology. Playing Roles seminar, Tampere, Finland (2006)
19. Yee, N. (in press): Motivations of Play in Online Games. CyberPsychology and Behavior

Plot Clusters – Intertwined and Re-playable Storyline Components in a Multiplayer RPG

Tony Manninen, Laura Vallius, and Tomi Kujanpää

LudoCraft Game Design Unit
University of Oulu, Finland
{tony.manninen, laura.vallius, tomi.kujanpaa}@oulu.fi

Abstract. This paper proposes and outlines a novel method for designing multiplayer computer role-playing games that revolve around procedural interactive narratives, which are further developed by the participating players. The proposed Plot Cluster system is evaluated practically during the design and construction of the experimental game *Castle of Oulu 1651*. The functionality and applicability of the approach is further validated with the empirical field experiment with 260 test subjects. Plot clusters enable the game designers to create controlled but re-playable emergent storylines that intertwine the participating players using multi-tier network structures.

Keywords: Interactive narrative, game design, LARP.

1 Introduction

Interactive narrative has been the holy grail of both the film and game industries for several years. The vision of having an open-ended and free, yet meaningful, narrative world to be explored by actively participating audiences has mainly escaped the grasp of the designers, authors and game developers. The traditional dramatic arc, increasing levels of anticipation and other coherent plot structures just do not seem to work when the players are placed in the "director's seat". Pre-defined story scripting in linear gameplay (e.g., *Half Life*), emergent gameplay (e.g., *Sim City*) and quest-based closed-loop branching game-stories (e.g., *Elder Scrolls of Morrowind IV: Oblivion*) are a far cry from the ultimate goal of having dramatically flexible but still coherent game worlds.

The aforementioned problem seems to increase even further if we think about multiplayer games. Instead of one controlling player there can be hundreds of "directors" all wanting to create and enjoy their own game stories – and many of those players want to be either the heroic protagonists or the archetypical antagonists of the play that emerges. The traditional mechanisms of auteur do not work anymore. Although the players want tension, climaxes and meaningful conflicts, they are not willing to submit themselves to be too tightly controlled by the game system.

This paper studies the issue of interactive narrative by focusing on a relatively simple yet functional implementation of a multiplayer role-playing game. Instead of tackling the overwhelming realm of the dramatic arc and other traditional concepts of narratives, we focus on intertwined and re-playable plot components that can offer partial solution

S. Göbel, R. Malkewitz, and I. Iurgel (Eds.): TIDSE 2006, LNCS 4326, pp. 265–276, 2006.

to the problematic area of multiplayer narratives. These "plot clusters" form the backbone and building blocks of collaborative play that produces meaningful narratives. The results of our design experiment and the corresponding test sessions with 260 participants provide practical design implications for multiplayer game developers.

In our approach, we are not creating stories *per se*. Plot Clusters is more like a support system that players use for creating (emergent) narratives. The emphasis in defining the plots is on the player objectives that are in conflict with the actions of other players. This follows the notion that many of the challenges players face are created by a form of conflict, which is an intrinsic element of every game [14]. The following sections outline the theoretical background of collaborative narratives and an empirical experience where the concepts and mechanisms are evaluated.

2 Collaborative Drama

The background for this paper covers two main areas: interactive narrative and collaborative play. In a way these seemingly separated concepts can be directly extracted from the slightly broadened definition of digital medium itself. According to Murray [10, p. 2], digital medium is procedural (i.e., it generates behaviour based on rules) and participatory (i.e., it allows the player as well as the creator to move things around). The procedural nature of games relates directly to the gameplay and plot components that may enable interactive narratives. When the player advances in the game – making meaningful choices in between – he or she is unfolding the story enabled by the gameplay. The meaningful choices, or the actions, engage the player in participation with the challenging and compelling world of the game. This participation, then, makes the player as a co-author of the narrative that results.

The aspects of interactive stories and drama have been studied within the context of games as well as within virtual worlds and hypertexts (cf. [1, 7, 9, 13]). The focus in the literature has mainly been on narratives provided by, or with, the systems, which follow the procedures of the users. Although the approach in this paper leaves the actual storyline development for the players to contribute, the related studies of interactive narrative offer a scaffolding with which to frame the discussion.

Despite the numerous methods in creating a good-quality cyberdrama, the non-linear nature of virtual environments makes the effective utilisation of drama and narrative difficult. If the participants are simply allowed to go about their business in an unstructured environment, there is no way to guarantee that the tension will build and the stakes will continue to rise [5]. Furthermore, in games where social scenarios between the participants play a great role, the complications in staging of the events can critically hinder the flow of the game [3]. However, the domain of Live Action Role-Playing (LARP) offers a context, where players physically and mentally step into the roles of the characters and act out an imaginary adventure [4, p. 128].

The application of narrative elements can be difficult in a highly non-deterministic multi-user virtual environment. In addition to the procedural and participatory part of the game system, there is the influence of fellow player actions to be taken into account. As a design implication, Wibroe *et al.* [16] state that the minimal requirement for narration is a conflict of intentions, which in turn makes some kind of planning mechanism necessary. The intention – both in a sense of forthcoming action and the possible executed task – is the key in functional social conflict. Of course, it could be argued that in most of the settings where several participants aim to collaborate, there are bound to be conflicts of intentions. Then, the main design issue involves creating the dramatic conflicts and implementing these in a way that enables fruitful narratives.

3 *Castle of Oulu 1651* – Multiplayer RPG with Variable Plots

An experimental computer based role-playing game *Castle of Oulu 1651* was constructed to find out how meaningful but re-playable and intertwined role-playing plots could be implemented in a computer environment. A group of up to thirty players can play the game simultaneously, while everyone aims at reaching his or her specific goal. The game was created to combine social structures, freedom of narrative creation of storylines and the immediate interaction of role-playing games. In addition, the game needed to capture the re-playability of board games and atmospheric attraction of adventure games. Figure 1 illustrates some scenes from the game.

Fig. 1. Example scenes from *Castle of Oulu 1651*

The castle environment, the people, the clothes, the names and the hierarchical occupations of the game characters, as well as, all the items in the castle area were designed to fit the 17th century theme. Each player had a unique role in the virtual world with a position in the society, a primary objective and special piece of information about the surroundings or other players. To encourage social communication, the goals were designed to enable cooperation with some players while conflicting with others.

Although *Castle of Oulu 1651* cannot be seen as narrative installation in the strictest sense, the design approach follows the plot system developed within fiction literature. The LOCK system, defined by James Scott Bell, contains a simple set of foundational principles that define the plot. LOCK stands for Lead, Objective, Confrontation and Knockout [2, p.10], and in the experiment these principles were developed into the character role (lead), primary goal (objective) and resulting conflict system (confrontation) with the additional threat explication.

3.1 LARP Design as Guideline

The LARP ideology with its conflicting player interests, social intrigues and conspiracy [6, p. 313] provided a suitable framework for the design of the multiplayer computer game. Unlike in many contemporary CPRGs, the progress of the *Castle of Oulu 1651* game is based on the existence of a group of people who agree on sharing the adventure together. Since the narrative aspects of the gameplay were left for the players to conduct, free and open ended storylines could be built. To overcome some of the technical limitations of self-expression, the players used headsets so that all verbal communication could be conducted through natural spoken dialogue.

The main objectives of the players were designed using basic ideas of conflict creation and plot developing, common both in LARP design and fiction literature. The aim of the design was to shift the task-oriented functions of contemporary CRPG to the side role and replace those with communication between the players. This way, the functional acts would be supporting the social interaction without which the gameplay would not progress.

The design was started by sketching different player characters and their relationships. The written character descriptions were soon selected as most feasible solution in presenting the necessary information to the players. This approach, however, proved to be too challenging in the case of digital games domain. Whereas in LARP the players are willing to invest heavily in learning their character, the computer game players cannot necessarily be requested to do so. Contemporary computer game design emphasises audio-visual content with minimal textual representation [11, p. 180]. While cut-scenes and other narratives have been widely used to convey the background information to the players [12, p. 220], they were not a feasible solution in the case of the re-playable, and thus, dynamic, multiplayer game. The resulting problem required further design in order to be solved.

3.2 Social Networks with Conflict Structures

The information overload and tedious preliminary reading tasks were reduced by following the principle described by Salen & Zimmerman [14, p. 95], in which the idea and the building blocks of the story are sprinkled around the magic circle of the gameplay in the form of the players' characters background stories and goals. The actual world of the gameplay, then, forms with these pieces coming together through social interaction. In addition to this modular approach, the game design was guided by social networks, which are evident in real life [15], but also applicable in online game settings [3].

These types of social networks can be taken into consideration when designing the game and the characters. The motives of the player characters (e.g., interests, goals, desires, loyalties, etc.) can be woven into a net of opposing conflicts and supportive objectives. In this way characters become part of the game's social structure naturally and they have a starting point into creating their own social networks. This approach is not very far from the basic LARP design.

The main method in the *Castle of Oulu 1651* game design followed the principles of network construction where each of the game characters formed a node with multitude of relations to other characters. For example, a small network could be formed with six characters, as illustrated on Table 1. In this case, all characters have objectives related to the rumoured musket murder that was supposed to be committed within the castle premises. These objectives could be defined, for example, as follows: 1) "Bounty hunter": Catch and imprison the person who is a primary suspect, 2) "Suspect": You are primary murder suspect. Prove your innocence, 3) "Murderer": Cover-up the murder you committed, 4) "Trickster": Frame the bounty hunter in order to improve your status, 5) "Assistant": Protect the murderer by keeping him safe from suspicions and capture, and 6) "Victim": Eliminate the murder rumour by proving that you are the supposed victim.

Table 1. Example matrix of a small social network with illustrative relationships

	B. hunter	**Suspect**	**Murderer**	**Trickster**	**Assistant**	**Victim**
Bounty hunter		Catch and imprison	Catch and imprison if suspicious	Evade and stay clean	Follow and learn more	Eliminate (threat to income)
Suspect	Escape		Find evidence	Support	Follow and spy	Form an alliance
Murderer	Avoid suspicions	Spread rumours		Assist in framing	Work together	Find more information
Trickster	Frame as murderer	Assist	Assist		Assist	Eliminate (threat to success)
Assistant	Avoid suspicions	Possible protect	Protect	Assist in framing		Assist in testimony
Victim	Provide evidence	Assist	Inform	Reveal the scheme	Inform	

The matrix illustrates interesting potential plots that emerge from the particular actions of the characters. For example, if the "Murderer" arouses suspicions while trying to cover-up his act, the "Bounty hunter" may focus his attention accordingly. Despite the numerous relationships between the players, the prototyping sessions revealed a critical design problem in terms of premature plot endings. If the objective of one player was possible to achieve before the end of the game, the results would ripple through the network. Winning – or loosing – would generally mean the end. Therefore it was noted that while the aforementioned approach enables the designers to chart even complicated relationships between the characters, it is not dynamic enough for re-playability and randomly configured multiplayer sessions. Something else was needed to support the mechanics with appropriate dynamic elements.

3.3 Board Game Metaphor as Randomiser

The answer to the aforementioned problem came in the form of board games. *Cluedo*, for example, is a game with endless potential for re-playability. The solution is simple – the players pick a required number of cards, which dictate the basic parameters of the game. The setup is always random and there is no way of knowing what others have. This card metaphor was selected as main premise in designing the information structuring and construction before and during the game.

The "cards" were used to give every player a character with a specific role. The role was constructed from knowledge of the characters 1) role in the society and the mundane task ("day job"), 2) primary objective, 3) threats and 4) special knowledge (see Figure 2).. For example, a character could be a town guard that had to find out who of the players were carrying guns. In order to spice things up a bit, the gun-controlling player was also told that in his opinion too many people were carrying weapons. He also had a permission to arrest suspicious characters. Another character could be an outlaw who has been hired by an unknown suspicious party to create chaos in the castle area by committing small offences.

The character, thus, comprised of four individual pieces of information and these were randomly distributed to the players in the beginning of the session. This added to the re-playability of the game because the combination of traits that build up the roles would change in each game. While the modular role construction looked promising, the amount of information distributed to the players had to be limited due to short preparation time for each game. The expectations of computer gamers do not include extensive reading before actually starting the game. For this reason some room for imagination was left for the players to fill in the blanks in the history and personality of the character randomly given to them. This was well in line with the theories of interactive narrative (cf. [13]).

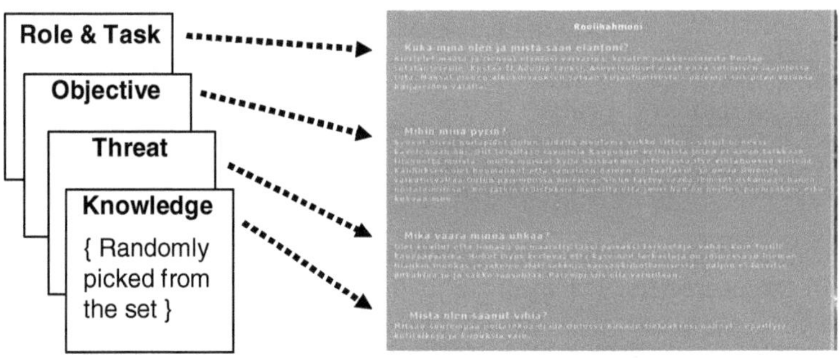

Fig. 2. Four random "cards" from four separate categories outline the character identity

The main challenge in designing a structure and components of a random game proved to be the lack of coherent plot and drama. With too random a set of cards, the resulting combinations did not necessarily create meaningful narratives. Players got confused in their mixed storylines and plot components. A method of controlling and limiting the emergence was, thus, clearly needed.

3.4 Plot Clusters as Controlled Intertwining Mechanism

The solution for enabling meaningful narratives and coherent plots is not unique within the world of storytelling. In essence, a rewarding interactive experience requires the integration of the bottom-up, partially unpredictable input of the user into the top-down designs of the storyteller [13, p. 244]. Therefore, the final step in designing the *Castle of Oulu 1651* was actually a hybrid of all the aforementioned approaches (i.e., LARP design, social networks with conflicts and board game metaphors). Since there was a need to direct the emerging plots, the game mechanics were organised in a form of plot clusters (top-down designs) that would bind a critical mass of participating players (bottom-up input) together as procedural entities.

The designed plot clusters function as a set of "cards", in which, each of the major plot themes has 6 individual points of approaches. In this approach, the original concept of social network was expanded to cover several simultaneous plot themes in all the areas of character definition (i.e., the objective, threats and special knowledge). Therefore, as a result, the game ended up having 5 groups of six cards in each of the three character traits. Furthermore, the roles and mundane tasks of the characters were divided into 6 separate groups (rich folk, merchants, guards, peasants, outlaws and travellers), each having 5 character descriptions. As a result, the game had 30 "cards" in each of the four categories (role & task, objective, threat and information), from which each participating player was randomly allocated one card per category.

The mechanics of the plot clusters were laid out in a similar manner as exemplified in the aforementioned musket murder case. However, now the players were intertwined in plot clusters by using all the components of plot system. So, for example, in the case of a musket murder, the social network design would include not only objectives, but also illustrated threats (sometimes real, sometimes only potential) and pieces of special information concerning the murder in question. In order to enhance the binding factor of these plot clusters, the role & task category was used to assign players in groups of interest and conflict. This added another layer that would support the intertwining of the players further. An example is illustrated in Figure 3.

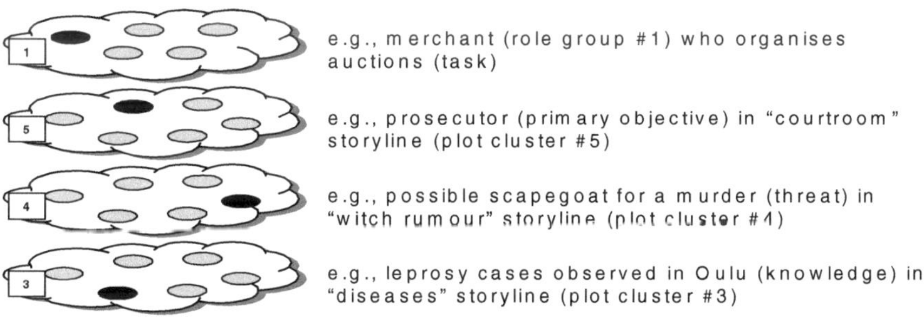

Fig. 3. An example of possible cluster combinations for one player character

As shown in this rather extreme case, an individual player could get "cards" from three out of five different plot clusters (plus an additional role & task grouping), thus, causing him or her to be part in several potential plots during the game session.

4 Field Experiment

The experimental game was commissioned by the education bureau of city of Oulu and the target player group was children from ages of 11 to 16 years. The experiment took place in a school fair and within a time of one week 260 children played the *Castle of Oulu 1651* and reported their experiences through short debriefing sessions and by filling a personal questionnaire. Each game session was observed by the researchers and findings were stored in the form of screen captures, videos and journal notes.

The game sessions were started with a short briefing where the controls of the game were introduced. After the briefing, the players sat down in front of their computers, isolated from each other with cubicle formations, and they studied their personal character information for a couple of minutes. The participants played first one practice game (10 minutes) and then the official game (1 hour) in groups of 30.

The game was configured to end when the duration of one hour was reached and the players were given scores according to their actions in the game. The scoring mechanism was relatively rudimentary and only measured the achievements that were easy to evaluate within the game logic. Role-playing and discussions were not measured because of the lack of applicable tools. However, the players were told that their role-playing performance will be monitored by the game masters and the best ones will be rewarded after the game. At the end of the session, the players were debriefed and the final score table, with corresponding group ranking, was revealed.

5 Discussion

The *Castle of Oulu 1651* offered the players a view to historical place that does not exist anymore. The authenticity of buildings, objects and roles of the characters made the feeling of travelling back in time stronger. The feeling of being in the world was strengthened by vocal communication – albeit not always in-character in nature. The size of the environment was purposefully limited to a relatively small area in order to keep the level of action high. All these features seemed to provide a fruitful ground for multiplayer cyberdrama.

However, many players had difficulties in understanding how to reach their goals, at least at the beginning of the game. Since the plot components provided only a fragment of information, the key to progressing within the mission was through interactive narrative between players, for example, talking to other players and persuading them to do something. Not all participants felt comfortable with this type of participation. Especially the more experienced players, who had a quite fixed way of seeing what computer games should be like, found this approach to be contradictory with their expectations. Most of the players, however, found this form of playing interesting and fun. Although the actual success of subjectively felt dramatic agency is difficult to measure, the heavy concentration and enthusiasm of the players indicate a level of positive results. Actually, it was noted that the natural spoken dialogue was considered as the best part of the game by majority of the participants.

In terms of design research, the iterative construction of *Castle of Oulu 1651* offers some interesting implications for future multiplayer game designers. Each of the four main methods of design that were applied during the development contributes in solving a particular area of design challenges. 1) The LARP design guidelines emphasise the character descriptions and character-driven action. Moreover, LARP-oriented games stress the role enactment and heavy participation from the players. 2) Social networks with conflict structures provide a basis for procedural and emergent storylines. If well designed, the networks reveal full-scale conflict-support continuums where character relationships are not only black-and-white in nature. 3) The board game metaphor makes it possible to create randomised characters and plot components that fully support re-playability even with the same narrative elements. Finally, 4) the plot clusters bind the players together in the form of coherent and logical storylines. The outcome is a multi-tier player intertwining system that reduces the risks caused by the lack of critical mass and varying personal levels of participation.

5.1 What About Meaningful Plots?

The most important question in evaluating the functionality of plot cluster approach is whether the emerging plots would support the development of meaningful and coherent storylines. The first test of any narrative is its clarity – if the players cannot understand what they are expected to do, they cannot progress the storylines.

In the research questionnaires 31% of the players depicted their characters according to the goals and/or roles and tasks described in the character sheet. For example, one player described his/her character as: 'A gun smuggler, whose task was to sue innocent to court.' Furthermore, the social status or a group to which the character belonged was often used to depict the character. 25% of the players used this information alone or with some additional qualities in describing their character, for example: 'An outlaw, who needed to perform crimes to get points.'

When asked what players were to do in the game, most of the answers (74%) implied that the players were clearly able to understand what was expected. However, only 47% of the players reported that they actually pursued actions presented in the character sheet. Furthermore, another 11% were describing their needs through common, and not necessarily specifically allocated, tasks taking place during the game (such as voting, trading, or point collecting). Only about six percent of the players were uncertain of their objectives in the game.

Although not exhaustive, the results indicate that majority of the players were able to interpret and execute the two primary plot components (role & task and primary objective) they received. However, only 39% of the players mentioned the threat described in the character sheet. Furthermore, up to 18% reported that they did not know or remember what was threatening them. Moreover, 39% of the players reported other actual threats they had experienced in the game (such as thieves, guards, and terrorising players). These results can be explained at least partly with the fact that most of the threats described in the "cards" were designed for other players to pursue. If the particular threatening player did not actively pursue his or her objective, the threat never concretised.

Despite the plot clusters with their pre-defined objectives, threats and information components, the instrumental interaction "stole" the attention of many players. For example, they were taking part in general trading, which turned out to be one of the main actions in the *Castle of Oulu 1651*, or, they were just exploring the environment. One explanation for this phenomenon, in addition to the core nature of instrumental computer games, is the demographics of the participants. The players generally did not have role-playing or LARP experience.

5.2 Procedural Plot Clusters and Player Participation

In order to enforce personal participation, parts of the virtual world were provided for the players only in form of textual information. So, instead of audiovisual representation, these existed only in the corresponding players' mind. This was an effective way to force the players to communicate with each other. The players were actively participating as "co-writers" [13] and they were creating parts of the story as the game progressed. However, for some participants, this aspect of imaginary world that was shared and built by the players was very difficult to understand. The conventional solutions of computer game environments tend to cater all material as ready-made. Most of the players, nevertheless, were able to use the information given to them to attain goals of gameplay.

In the experiment, the participatory role [10, p. 2] of the player was expanded to multiple simultaneous players all interacting and cooperating in the overall gameplay. Therefore, the flow and outcome of the game was not based on just the choices of one player. Instead, the group of players all affected in each others choices and resulting outcomes. In this sense, the multi-tiered intertwining of plot components was successful.

Castle of Oulu 1651 was subtle and ambiguous in its requirement of playing together. The players had separate - and oftentimes conflicting - goals, but they needed the help of other players to reach them and to progress the collaborative story. The limited virtual environment forced the players to stay near each other and encouraged them to communicate, since the environment offered very little else to do. Perhaps the clearly limited focus helped most of the players find ways to achieve their socially attainable goals through cooperation. However, as predictable in a free computer game environment, some players abandoned the goals of the game altogether and instead enjoyed the company of their friends and explored the world together. It was clearly evident that the participants should know (beforehand) that their personal enjoyment depends on a collaboratively effort to enact the narrative [13, p. 321].

The greatest challenge in procedural plot clusters is the varying levels of participation of the players. While the plot elements can be outlined using modular structures and controlled randomising, the player engagement is more difficult to manage. The findings of this paper support three specific categories of participation: 1) player as a co-author, 2) player as an active interpreter of story components and 3) player as a social entity. However, all these areas are highly vulnerable to any disturbances in the multiplayer setting. It seems that the best way to guarantee meaningful and enjoyable storylines is to both brief the players beforehand and to support the feeling of dramatic agency in as many ways as possible. For example, if several participants, after internalising their characters, were actively externalising and enacting their roles, the others seemed to follow.

The board game metaphor with its re-playability feature seemed to be successful throughout the test sessions. During the 10 individual game sessions, there combinations were unique while the overall plot clusters remained. Individual playing styles and personal levels of participation affected the outcome quite significantly. If the key characters in a particular plot cluster were not active, the remaining players tended to turn their focus elsewhere. This indicates the challenges in finding the critical mass for each cluster.

Based on the iterative construction process and the corresponding test sessions, it can be said that the plot clusters provide meaningful narrative features in multiplayer computer games. Although the development of each storyline and the outcome of the game are difficult to predict, the plot clusters offer the game designers a form of subtle control over the actions of the players while maintaining the re-playability.

Further experiments are needed in order to measure the applicability of plot clusters with different player profiles. Especially the experienced role-players (both PnP RPG and LARP) would be excellent research subjects in evaluating the approach.

6 Concluding Remarks

In this paper, the problem of how to create interactive, intertwined and re-playable plots for multiplayer role-playing games was tackled with the aid of theoretical frameworks and empirical design experiment. The design focus of *Castle of Oulu 1651* experimental game was on role-play encouragement and interaction between the players. Instead of a linear story, the game was designed as procedural system of emergent narratives that would result from the interaction and collaboration of the participating players.

The proposed design solution was iteratively constructed using LARP design guidelines, social networks with conflict structures and board game metaphors. The resulting Plot Cluster system draws from various theoretical frameworks, such as, the LOCK plot system [2], interactive narratives [7, 8, 9, 10, 13], digital media [10], and collaborative play [3]. Plot clusters enable the game designers to create controlled but re-playable emergent storylines that intertwine the participating players using multi-tier network structures. The character backgrounds, conflict-support continuum relationships, randomised characters and clustered main plots offer a new way of designing multiplayer computer role-playing games.

Plot Clusters can be applied to various multiplayer settings where there is a need to deepen the interaction and raise the stakes of social actions. In terms of implementation, the biggest challenge is in creating flexible-enough narrative elements that account for different player profiles. If purely instrumental actions are abandoned, the system can provide a simple way in designing role-playing games.

The proposed solution was validated through logically progressing iterative constructs and using extensive experiments with test subjects. Although the experimental game portrays a relatively niche concept, the results can be generalised to any multiplayer game design – despite the level of, or requirement for, narrative elements. Plot Cluster system with the proposed design methods advances the design of multiplayer role-playing games into a new territory. While social gaming and multimodal participation are the catchwords of contemporary gaming, the game industry has not yet ventured in the proposed direction.

References

1. Aarseth E (1997) Cybertext: Perspectives on Ergodic Literature. John Hopkins University Press, Baltimore.
2. Bell JS (2004) Plot & Structure. Writer's Digest Books, Cincinnati, Ohio.
3. Ducheneaut N and Moore R (2004) The Social Side of Gaming: A Study of Interaction Patterns in a Massively Multiplayer Online Game. In Proceedings of CSCW'04, November 6-10, 2004, Chicago, Illinois, USA, ACM Press, pp. 360-369.

4. Falk J and Davenport G (2004) Live Role-Playing Games: Implications for Pervasive Gaming. In Rauterberg R (ed) Proceedings of Third International Conference on Entertainment Computing - ICEC 2004. Eindhoven, The Netherlands.
5. Joiner D (1998) Real Interactivity in Interactive Entertainment. In: Dodsworth C (ed) Digital Illusion: Entertaining the Future with High Technology. ACM Press, New York, pp. 151-159.
6. Lankoski P and Heliö S (2002) Approaches to Computer Game Design – Characters and Conflict. In Mäyrä F (ed) Proceedings of Computer Games and Digital Cultures Conference. June 6-8. Tampere, Finland, Tampere University Press.
7. Laurel B (1993) Computers as Theatre. Addison-Wesley Publishing Company, Inc., Reading, MA.
8. Montfort N (2004) Interactive Fiction as "Story," "Game," "Storygame," "Novel," "World," "Literature," "Puzzle," "Problem," "Riddle," and "Machine". In Wardrip-Fruin N & Harrigan P (eds.) First Person: New Media as Story, Performance, and Game. MIT Press, pp. 310-317
9. Murray JH (1997) Hamlet on the Holodeck - The Future of Narrative in Cyberspace. The MIT Press, Cambridge, Massachusetts.
10. Murray J (2004) From Game-Story to Cyberdrama. In Wardrip-Fruin N & Harrigan P (eds.) First Person: New Media as Story, Performance, and Game. MIT Press, p. 350
11. Rollings A & Adams E (2003) Andrew Rollings and Ernest Adams on Game Design. New Riders Publishing.
12. Rouse R (2000) Game Design: Theory & Practice, Wordware Publishing, Plano, Texas
13. Ryan M-L (2001) Narrative as Virtual Reality: Immersion and Interactivity in Literature and Electronic Media. John Hopkins University Press, Baltimore, MD.
14. Salen K & Zimmerman E (2004). Rules of Play – Game Design Fundamentals. Massachusetts Institute of Technology.
15. Scott J (1991) Social Network Analysis: A Handbook. SAGE Publications Ltd, London, Great Britain.
16. Wibroe M, Nygaard KK & Bogh Andersen P (2001) Games and Stories. In: Qvortrup L (ed) Virtual Interaction: Interaction in Virtual Inhabited 3D Worlds. Springer-Verlag, London, 166-181.

Communication in Multi-player Role Playing Games – The Effect of Medium

Anders Tychsen[1], Jonas Heide Smith[2], Michael Hitchens[1], and Susana Tosca[2]

[1] Interactive Systems and Virtual Reality Research Group, Macquarie University, Sydney, Australia
{michaelh, atychsen}@ics.mq.edu.au
[2] Center for Computer Games Research, IT University of Copenhagen, Denmark
{tosca, smith}@itu.dk

Abstract. The Pen-and-Paper role-playing game is a successful example of collaborative interactive narrative. Meanwhile, computer-based role-playing games, while structurally similar, offer quite different narrative experiences. Here results are presented of an experimental study of role-playing gamers in Pen-and-Paper and computer-supported settings. Communication patterns are shown to vary significantly on measures such as the share of in-character statements and the share of dramatically motivated statements. These results are discussed in the light of differences between the two gaming forms and finally some design implications are discussed.

Keywords: Role-playing games, communication, computer-mediated communication, narrative, player behaviour.

1 Introduction

Pen-and-Paper Role-Playing Games (PnPs) are often, with good cause, heralded as one of the most successful instances of interactive narrative. PnPs have been converted to computer platforms with great structural faithfulness and yet the gaming experience is different, for instance in terms of the story development process.

Although rules and narrative settings are similar, the two game forms differ in key aspects. Computer role-playing games (CRPGs) offer a virtual representation of the fictional game world whereas PnPs do not. In PnPs, the participants must work together to uphold a shared understanding of events taking place in a shared, imagined game world. Meanwhile, in CRPGs the fictional game world is visually presented by a virtual reality engine, as witnessed by games such as *Neverwinter Nights* or *Vampire the Masquerade: Redemption*. This engine (typically) replaces the human Game Master (GM) common to most PnPs as the arbiter of rules and communicator of game state.

What would be the expected communicative effect of these differences? As the computer takes over all technical aspects of the game (processing of rules, managing and updating the game state etc.) one might expect the CRPG players to be freed of the need to communicate on non-dramatic matters. That is, one might expect them to display a higher percentage of dramatically motivated communication, i.e. more

S. Göbel, R. Malkewitz, and I. Iurgel (Eds.): TIDSE 2006, LNCS 4326, pp. 277–288, 2006.

"role-playing". As will see in the following, however, the opposite seems to be the case as the communication between CRPG players in the study was almost purely functional.

We begin by discussing the motivations for studying RPGs and briefly outline previous work. This is followed by an examination of the RPG genre and of differences between game forms. We then describe the experimental design, present results and offer a discussion of the findings.

Why Study Communication in RPGs?: Role-playing games (RPGs) provide a basis for studying the communicative structures between multiple participants in an immensely popular game form spanning different media platforms; RPGs are represented in both table-top form, physical and virtual media, as well as in forms involving from a single to thousands of players interacting simultaneously. PnPs and CRPGs present an opportunity to study directly the effect of changing the media of expression of a popular game genre on the communication between the participants and between the participants and the game world.

However, the communication which takes place in these games is under-explored. Basic data on the communicative activity of playing multi-player games in any medium, is, with certain exceptions ([2], [6], [9], [11], [12], [16], [21]), mostly absent in the academic literature. The game genre is receiving an increasing amount of attention in academia and industry alike. The main reason for this interest is that PnPs represent one of the most successful examples of interactive narratives and thus has become a core area of study in the attempt to develop interactive storytelling engines [9], [13], [19].

Furthermore, the potential benefit to the design of communication interfaces in computer games resulting from studies of multi-player communication is substantial. Results in this area hold the promise of providing an improved understanding of social gaming dynamics. Lastly, while techniques like focus groups and beta-testing have traditionally been employed by the games industry to test early-stage games in development, analysis of the communication of players engaged in the gaming activity facilitates the gathering of unbiased test data (i.e. for calculating learning curves).

Aims of This Study: This study presents a comparative quantitative analysis of the verbal communication in a PnP and a CRPG. The analysis is based on video tapes and transcriptions of verbal communication in two sets of game sessions (three PnP and three CRPG sessions). This study seeks, at a general level, to map and catalog the communication that occurs in the two game types. On a more specific level, the study aims at producing a coding system that allows for the direct comparison of the communicative statements and actions of the game players across the two game types, and thus across a media change – i.e. from a pen and paper to electronic game format.[1]

For this paper, we shall specifically direct attention to the use of dramatic additions to action and environment descriptions in the two game forms.

While RPGs have been used as the basis for the empirical experiments, the methods are likely to be relevant to the study of multi-player games outside the role-playing genre.

Previous Work: While the communicative patterns of RPG play to date have been only sporadically studied, [15] presents communication coding schemes for the study

[1] For discussions of the differences between PnPs and CRPGs see [1], [3], [5], [7], [17].

of multi-player gaming to gauge the effects of different conflict types. More generally, [8] videotaped and analyzed the behaviour of video game players in naturalistic settings. While offering observations on communicative behaviour, this study sought primarily to identify the role of emotions in video game play.

With the aim of providing applicable models, [19] reviewed the functionality of the GM and general communication patterns in RPGs across media platforms. Similarly, [7] developed models of the communication channels in multiplayer PnPs. Also, [3], [4], and [10] have developed general models of the multi-player PnP situation, including studies of communication pathways and social interactions. [20] Analysed the impact of various technologies on PnPs and other multi-player table-top games, including virtual realities. Additionally, there is a substantial amount of material viewing CRPGs from the development and design perspective, e.g. [5], [9], [13], and [14] conducted initial studies of the structure of the development of the interactive narrative in PnPs. The vast majority of publications on RPGs do not have an empirical element.

In summary, models and theoretical frameworks for the understanding of role-playing have been offered and empirical work has begun to emerge. To date, this work has been too fragmented to allow for much generalization and common methodologies have not yet been formulated.

2 Method

This study utilizes general communications terminology. A few games specific terms are defined here as their meaning varies in the literature:

Statements and utterances: In this study, the basic unit being coded is an utterance. An **utterance** is defined as consisting of: 1) A subject who performs the communication 2) The content of the communication and 3) An object or objects to whom the communication is addressed. For instance, the GM could describe an object to one of the players in a PnP. This definition of an utterance allows for application to both asynchronous and synchronous communication. In this study, all communication is synchronous. A **statement** is the entire verbally expressed communication by a participant, e.g. up to several sentences (the dialogue), before communication is initiated by another participant. A statement can contain multiple utterances.

In game and out of game: An utterance (or statement) from a participant in a multi player game can be classified as "in-game" (IG) or "out of game" (OOG). An utterance that is IG relates to the game or game content, for example a rules question, a character action description or similar; while an utterance classified as being OOG does not relate to the game or gaming activity. For example, asking what the time is; where the bathroom is etc.

In character and out of character: An utterance (or statement) from a participant can be "in character" (IC) or "out of character" (OOC). In character utterances are typical of PnPs, where the players sometime talk as if they were embodying their characters using a first person perspective, for example: "I run over to the door, and look out of it. What do I see?". Players can also describe the actions of their characters in third person, e.g.: "my character runs over to the door, looking out. What does he see?" Both of these types of utterance are in this study coded as IC, because both involve a player describing a character action or communication directly. OOC utterance could for example be rules questions, or comments about the interface with the virtual world in a CRPG. An OOC utterance can be both IG and OOG (an IC utterance cannot be OOG).

2.1 Game Selection

Initially, single-group multi-player PnPs and CRPGs were selected as the two target game types for this study. Presumably the narrative context of the chosen game scenarios will impact on the participant communication, and care was therefore taken with selecting the two scenarios. *What a Lovely War!* Produced by Sven Münthers (et al.) in 2003, was chosen as the PnP scenario. It utilizes simple rules (the *Traveller Light* D20 system). The rules concern combat and skill use, comparable to CRPGs, while the interaction with Non-Player Characters (NPCs) and overall was controlled almost exclusively by the GM (outside the rules framework). The scenario allows for a substantial player influence on the game play, and features a relatively linear storyline, thus allowing comparison with the storyline in the CRPG of the study.

The CRPG chosen for this study was the PS2 game *Champions of Norrath.* The game features elements common to the console CRPG form, e.g. action-driven gameplay, a linear storyline, and a generally collaborative environment. Although *Champions of Norrath* has a network game mode it is typically played by one to four players on a single monitor. The latter form was used in the study ensuring that all players had the same visual image of the virtual world.

Recruitment: The players for both the PnP and CRPG game sessions were recruited at the IT University of Copenhagen and the University of Copenhagen in 2004 and 2005, as well as among the Danish RPG community. Their age varied between 18-35 years (only one was below 20). For the CRPG players, almost all were university students, with a substantial amount of games experience. For the PnP RPG players, experience varied. Both sexes were represented, with about 2/3 male and 1/3 female.

Experiment procedure: In total, five PnP sessions were run with the chosen scenario (an expansion of these experiments involving over 50 players and three different RPG platforms is being conducted at Macquarie University). The participants were divided into groups of five players depending on their experience level. Two groups consisted of experienced players, two of a mixture of experienced and inexperienced players, and one group of relatively inexperienced players. All had previously played PnPs. For this study, one session of each type of group was transcribed and coded (session 1=experienced, session 2=inexperienced, session 3=mixed).

The game sessions were managed by highly experienced GMs, in two cases the primary author of the scenario. Each GM utilized the scenario as a blueprint to run the game. The scenario contains 5-10 general plot points, each describing the general properties of a particular scene. The conditions necessary to progress to the next scene were loosely defined, and substantial variation was observed between the sessions as to how the players progressed through the narrative, e.g. in jumping or altering scenes. The GMs had the freedom to alter the game narrative on the fly, however they were asked to attempt to maintain the general storyline of the scenario. This was in order to provide a similarity with the strictly linear storyline of *Champions of Norrath.*

The GMs performed exemplarily in keeping the players onto the pattern of the overall frame for the storyline, without at any time forcefully limiting player freedom.

Each game session was videotaped, and participants interviewed before and after each session in order to get feedback on the playing experience, the interests of the players in RPGs etc. Sound was recorded using a tabletop microphone. The tapes were copied to digital format and transcribed using transcription software.

Fig. 1. A PnP session (left) and a CRPG session (right) with superimposed game visuals

In the CRPG part of the experiment, six sessions were held. For this analysis, three sessions were selected based on the relative similarity of the players in terms of playing skill (and hence progress in the game in the given time). Two of these had three players, while one had four. The groups were only introduced to the game in very general terms and played it for approximately 45 minutes each. A researcher was present during the sessions not interfering but answering questions posed by players. Such questions turned out to be very rare as almost all players preferred to work out game controls etc. themselves. The sessions (Figure 1) were videotaped and the verbal communication was later transcribed and analyzed.

Coding: The basic approach towards developing a usable coding scheme was iterative. An iterative process has the advantage that it allows for testing a theoretically based scheme in practice of the coding hierarchy before the actual coding is initiated. With each iteration the system (comparable to a prototype in an Rapid Application Development process) is refined, until a saturation level is reached where no new codes appear from the testing. Initially codes were developed deductively from theory and models, and inductively from categories that arose from an initial test coding of the transcribed games sessions. The coding scheme was then tested in a pilot study, where approximately 20% of the total amount of transcription to be analysed was coded, resulting in a refinement of the system. As the system was saturated, the iterative process was stopped, and the finished coding scheme applied to the transcribed game sessions. The coding scheme is designed to specifically code utterances and to be applicable to the communication by the participants in multiplayer PnPs and CRPGs. The coding scheme was applied to the transcriptions using *nVivo*, a software package for the analysis of qualitative data. For each of the two game types, three sections of the sessions were coded as shown in Table 1.

Table 1. The scenes coded

	Scene type	What a Lovely War!	Champions of Norrath
Scene 1	Non-stressful planning and prioritizing	Players receive and don equipment	First extended shopping scene
Scene 2	Non-threatening combat scene	Players fight aliens	Players eliminate goblin invaders
Scene 3	Possibly dangerous combat scene	Players raid alien military base	Players fight goblin overlord and his pets

In both game types the length of these scenes varied somewhat. Though such detailed analysis was not conducted for this paper, the choice of sections of different type and temporal position facilitates closer subsequent examination of variation in communication patterns. Also, the coding scheme allows for tracking individual contributions meaning that communicative variations may be traced to single participants breaking the overall pattern, if that is the case.

Pros and Cons of Utterance Model: Basing the coding system on utterances generally leads to a high degree of precision and resolution of transcribed material. However, by using utterances as the basic unit of communication and by favouring relatively literal interpretations of these utterances, broader context-dependent meanings may be lost. More concretely, a player repeating a question to another player who did not hear it the first time is counted as the same type of utterance twice. Pilot testing indicated, however, that the statistical imprecision imposed thereby is of very limited magnitude in the two game forms. It is also possible to combine analysis of utterances with a context analysis, which is an approach utilized in this study. While context analysis does not reveal repetitions as in the example above, it is useful to assess general communication patterns and locate problems with an utterance-based coding hierarchy. The actual narrative progression was not measured or analyzed (this is a subject of a study currently in development).

2.2 Coding Hierarchy

Typically each utterance was given 3 codes: I) A **content code**, under one of the four general categories formed by combining the IG/OOG and IC/OOC groupings (IG+IC, IG+OOC, OOG+IC [not possible in practice], OOG+OOC). For example the utterance: "I run towards the door, readying my weapon", is spoken IC, and thereby also IG. It is furthermore a "character action description", and given the appropriate code. II) A **receiver code**, which defines to whom the utterance is directed. Utterances can either be directed at one other player (including the GM in PnPs), more than one player, or the entire group. III) A **drama code** indicating whether the speaker phrased his or her utterance in a functional or expressive manner. A statement was coded as either "purely functional", "dramatically embellished", or "purely expressive". As defined above, statements can include several utterances, thus requiring multiple codes. Similarly, utterances can have several components requiring several codes, e.g. a player describing both a character action and providing an environmental description at the same time.

2.3 Data Treatment

For all statistical evaluations of the data, care was taken to check whether a result was the result of a single aberrant game session or player. Some variation caused by individual player styles and similar was expected, however, both the CRPG and PnP sessions showed a substantial degree of internal similarity across individual coding categories, with less variation than expected.

Chi-square tests were employed to calculate the probability that the observed patterns were caused by random variation rather than an expression of dependency. In all these cases, the probability of randomness was greatly below the nominal 5% cut-off value. For example, for the content code category "Ask for Info", there was only a 8-10% variation between the PnP RPG and CRPG sessions. However, with a significance (p) = 0.00063 the statistical probability of this pattern arising randomly is extremely small. Not all content codes were used in the six investigated game sessions, and some only to a very small degree. For example, the "ask for advice" and "ask for help" categories were used from 0-3 times in the CRPG sessions and 0-4 in the PnP sessions. If the accumulated frequency of a coding category was less than 10, it was omitted from the statistical analysis because of the resulting high degree of uncertainty such an analysis would carry. For CRPGs, six content code categories had a sufficient frequency to be included in the analysis (Figure 2). For the PnP this number was ten (Figure 4). Twenty-two codes were defined during pilot test coding; however, not all of these occur in the transcription segments of the current project.

3 Results and Discussion

Due to space constraints, analysis at the level of the individual players is omitted from the data presented here, and emphasis placed on patterns at the level of the individual game sessions, with respect to: A) The content and purpose of the communication of the players in the two game forms; B) The frequency of InG/OoG utterances; C) The frequency of IC/OOC utterances, and: D) The use of dramatic embellishment.

Communication content: There is a marked difference in frequency and category of the content codes employed by the participants in the two game forms (Figures 2 & 4). The variations appear to be related to the game format and media of expression. Notably, the most frequent codes utilized by the PnP players were "environment description" and "character action description" (CAD), with "ask for info" as a close third. The two former represent specific instances of the more general "give info" codes, which explains the low frequency of these codes in the PnP. This result would seem well in line with these games being based on a shared imagined game world, which without a visual reference requires players to announce the actions of their characters to the other players, and require running updates about the game world state and the environment their characters act in.

For the CRPG sessions, the most frequent codes centre on information requests and provision: "Ask for info" rates at 25-28%, with the "give info" codes taking up even bigger chunks (Figure 2). Obviously in collaborative CRPGs, there is less need for describing character-avatar actions, and providing environment descriptions is not immediately necessary when the game world is visually provided. However, a high amount of communication still centres on keeping the players organized, reflected in the "give info" categories, with utterances warning about the presence of opponents, replies to rules questions and interface questions being very common in the CRPG sessions investigated. Many statements indicate a player drawing attention to a feature of the game space which, while visually represented by the engine, may have escaped the attention of other players (coded as "give info"). There is some variation in the distribution of the two "give info" categories. However, when the two are combined the result is very similar for the CRPG sessions (51-55%), indicating that total information provision (as well as the requests for information, varying from 25-28%), is comparable.

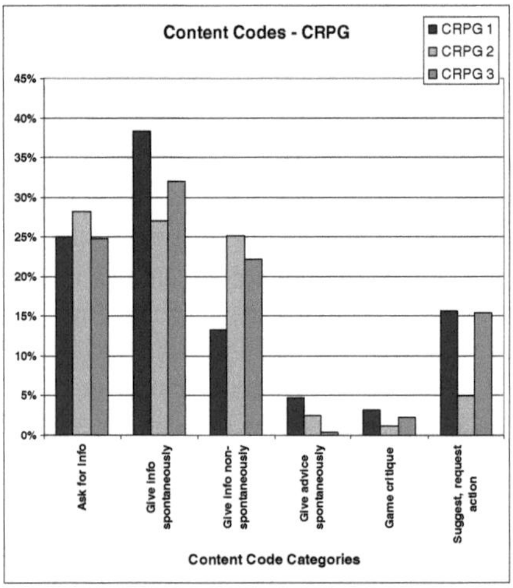

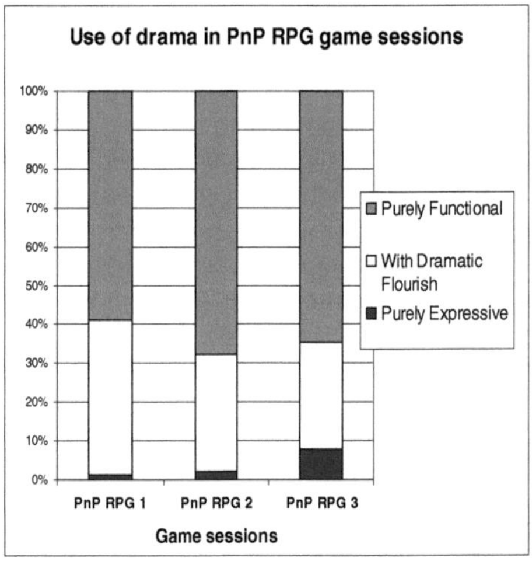

Fig. 2. and **Fig. 3.** Figure 2 content coding results of the three CRPG sessions; Figure 3 shows the variation in the use of dramatic expression[2] in the PnP sessions

In comparison, the high frequency categories of the CRPG (information related communication) has a much lower frequency in the PnP, with "Ask for info" rating 8-10% lower being the one that is closest to the CRPGs. This variation can probably be explained by the high frequency of the environment descriptions and CADs of the PnP which serve to provide information about the game world and its development (Figure 4). Unlike CRPGs, PnPs do not have interface or gameplay issues that form a substantial part of the information requesting/providing communication in CRPG sessions. Instead, the bulk of the communication in PnPs is tied up in describing the game world state and the events taking place in the game world.

In and Out of Game: The amount of OOG communication in the game sessions investigated was virtually nil, with typically 0-2 OOG utterances for each session. This indicates that there is little difference in the level of engagement of the players in the two game forms. In both circumstances, the limited amount of OOG talk points to the fact that the players are engaged in the game play. It should be noted that the

[2] In the figure, "dramatic flourish" indicates a functional statement containing at least an element of dramatic expression, i.e. "I draw my sword. The light reflects on the blade".

amount of OOG talk in the very beginning of the CRPG sessions (not included in this analysis) was substantially higher until the players figured out the basic controls. These OOG-heavy minutes of game time would not substantially alter the analysis, however. For PnPs, the amount of OOG-communication was constant throughout the game sessions. However, PnPs feature a "premise-building" phase before the actual game starts, where the players discuss rules, characters etc. This interval is comparably to the first phase of the CRPG sessions, but takes place before the game starts [18], and are thus not included in this analysis.

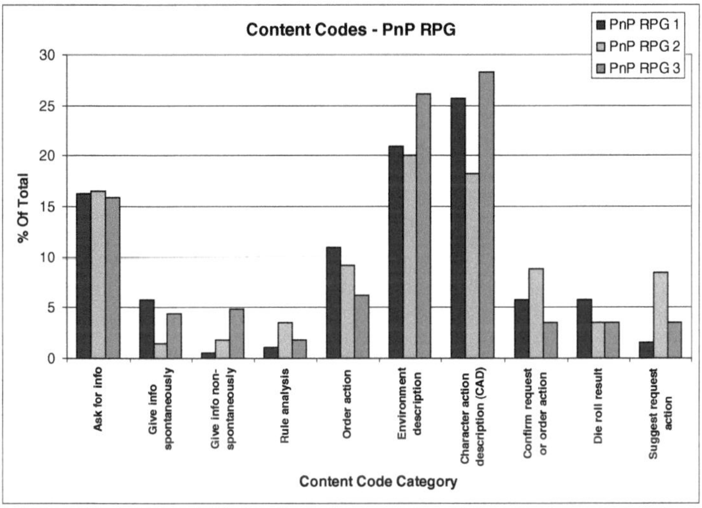

Fig. 4. Content coding results of the three PnP sessions

In and out of character: In comparison to the OOG-IG communication rates, the amount of OOC and IC communication varies substantially, with the rate of IC communication being substantially higher in the PnP (Figure 5). Likewise, internally in the game sessions there is a high degree of variety, with a rate of 39-51% (46% average) as compared to 15-33% (21% average) for CRPGs. In conclusion, players of PnPs are more prone to communicate IC although there is substantial variation, presumably related to the different player preferences. The difference is linked with the need for CADs in PnPs, which would normally rate as IC communication, and the difference between the two RPGs related to the basic format of the games. While the basic format of CRPGs do not prevent role-playing (the players are free to communicate IC), the format does not seem to encourage or facilitate it.

The use of drama: In addition to the level of IC communication, the use of dramatic flourish and expressive statements to enhance the drama can be used as a measure of the amount of actual role playing taking place in RPGs. While the purely functional statements about game rules, the actions of opponents etc. dominate in both game forms (Figure 3), the amount varies greatly between PnP and CRPG, and even between game sessions of the same type. Only three utterances with dramatic flourish were registered for the CRPG sessions, while 28-40% of all utterances in the PnP

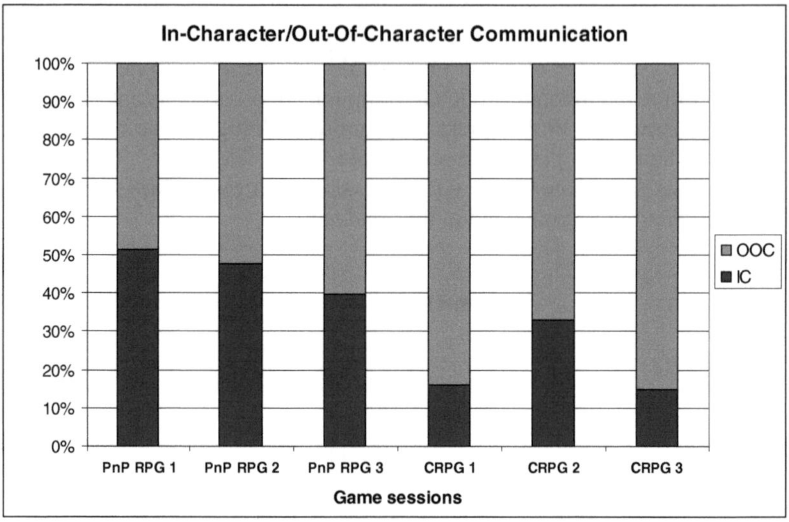

Fig. 5. In-Character (IC) and Out-of-Character (OoC) communication in the six game sessions

sessions used dramatic embellishment. However, even in the PnP sessions it was rare to see utterances which seemed to have purely dramatic purposes (that is, not *also* serving as a warning against enemies, describing a character action) (1-8%).

4 Discussion and Conclusions: Changes Across Media

In this study, a coding scheme for studying communication across media has been developed and successfully implemented in a study of a PnP and a CRPG. A communications based framework appears to be a viable approach to the study of the effect of media of expression on multi-player games.

The cross-session consistency of results indicates that the differences in communication patterns between the two investigated RPGs are not related to the players, but caused by the differences in the two investigated game forms.

CRPG communication focuses on the asking for and receiving of game-related information (Figure 2), and PnP communication focuses on describing and updating the imagined game world and the actions of the player characters in it (Figure 4). There are other differences as well, e.g. the presence of game criticism in the CRPG, and the use of "order action" statements in the PnP (almost absent in the CRPG). This latter feature of PnPs appears related to the need for managing the game flow in a game form where the players are free to act in whatever fashion allowed by their characters and the world fiction.

The results presented here lend empirical credit to certain traditional ideas of communication in PnPs and CRPGs. For example, that the amount of role playing (IC/OOC rates, the use of dramatic embellishment) in PnPs is higher than in CRPGs. The high amount of dramatic statements in PnPs is linked with a need to visualize the fictional world, which appears to encourage the use of dramatic statements. In PnPs the players are responsible for creating the drama, while in CRPGs the game to some degree takes care of this, e.g. via sweeping scenes and dramatic combat. However, this apparently also affects role-playing internally in the group – while in PnPs dramatic statements are used, this is less marked in CRPGs, where the players distance themselves from the virtual world.

When it comes to the engaging qualities of the two game forms, CRPGs do not; however, appear to be more engaging or immersive than PnPs, despite the presence of a virtual reality (OoG/IG rates).

The majority of the communication between the CRPG players concerned group management, geographic orientation and interface orientation difficulties. These would appear to be areas where the game designers of multiplayer CRPGs could focus, for instance by providing player tools for pointing out geographic locations, for assigning orders and keeping track of the status of other character-avatars. Problems were also observed with the provision of information from the game, e.g. via cutscenes and NPCs, to the players. Often information provided was to be used later in the game. As the players often asked each other questions about information provided previously in the game, it would appear that a better strategy from a design perspective is to provide information as it is needed. Of course, these conclusions are based on observations of *Champions of Norrath* play only, but the game is a fairly representative member of the multi-player console CRPG genre.

Summing up, although the two forms share structural features, the effects of switching from PNP to CRPG are substantial. A future analysis of the player level data will hopefully shed more light on detailed social dynamics and their relationships to media.

Acknowledgments. This study forms part of a multi-institutional research collaboration involving Australian and Scandinavian universities (Macquarie University, Sydney; The IT University, Copenhagen; Växjö University, Växjö). The authors would like to direct a special acknowledgement to Dr. Manolya Kavakli of Macquarie University for her support in setting up the collaboration and for hosting Jonas Heide Smith at the Interactive Systems and Virtual Reality Research Group at Macquarie University. A special thanks to the players and GMs who participated in the game sessions. Further thanks to the Macquarie ICT Innovations Centre, for providing facilities and equipment for the RPG experiments of Anders Tychsen.

References

1. Bøckman, P., Hutchison, R. (eds.): Collected papers for Knutepunkt 2005 – the 9th annual Nordic Conference on larp. Knutepunkt, Oslo (2005)
2. Ducheneaut, N., Moore, R.J.: The Social Side of Gaming: A Study of Interaction Patterns in a Massively Multiplayer Online Game. CSCW2004, Chicago (2004)
3. Edwards, R.: GNS and Other Matters of Role-playing Theory. Adept Press (2001)
4. Fine, G.A.: Shared Fantasy: Role-Playing Games as Social Worlds. University of Chicago Press, Chicago (2002)
5. Hallford, N., Hallford, J.: Swords & Circuitry: A Designer's Guide to Computer Role Playing Games. Prima Tech, Roseville, CA (2001)

6. Holmes, R.M., Pellegrini, A.D.: Children's Social Behavior During Video Game Play. In: Raessens, J., Goldstein, J. (eds.): Handbook of Computer Game Studies. The MIT Press, Cambridge, Massachusetts (2005)
7. Kim, J.: Story and Narrative Paradigms in Role-Playing Games. Vol. 2006 (2003)
8. Lazzaro, N.: Why We Play Games: Four Keys to More Emotion in Player Experiences. Game Developers Conference 2004, San Jose (2004)
9. Louchart, S., Aylett, R.: Solving the narrative paradox in VEs – lessons from RPGs. IVA 2003. Springer Verlag, Kloster Irsee, Germany (2003) 244-248
10. Mackay, D.: The Fantasy Role-Playing Game: A New Performing Art. McFarland & Co., Jefferson, N.C. (2001)
11. Manninen, T.: Virtual Team Interactions in Networked Multimedia Games - Case: "Counter-Strike" – Multi-player 3D Action Game. Proceedings of PRESENCE2001 Conference, Temple University, Philadelphia (2001)
12. Manninen, T., Kujanpää, T.: Non-Verbal Communication Forms in Multi-player Game Session. In: Faulkner, X., Finlay, J., Détienne, F. (eds.): Proceedings of HCI 2002 Conference,. Springer-Verlag (2002) 383-401
13. Peinado, F., Gervás, P.: Transferring GMing Laws to Interactive Digital Storytelling. In: Göbel, S., Spierling, U., Hoffmann, A., Iurgel, I., Schneider, O., Dechau, J., Feix, A. (eds.): TIDSE 2004: 2nd International Conference on Technologies for Interactive Digital Storytelling and Entertainment. Springer Verlag, Darmstadt, Germany (2004) 48-54
14. Salen, K., Zimmerman, E.: Rules of Play - Game Design Fundamentals. MIT Press, London (2004)
15. Smith, J.H.: Plans and Purposes: How Video Game Goals Shape Player Behaviour. PhD-Thesis. Center for Computer Games Research. IT University of Copenhagen.
16. Tosca, S.: The EverQuest Speech Community. In: Mayrä, F. (ed.): CGDC 02 Conference Proceedings. University of Tampere, Tampere (2002)
17. Tosca, S.: Role-playing in multiplayer environments. Vampire: The Masquerade. Redemption. Computer Games & Digital Textualities, Copenhagen, Denmark (2001)
18. Tychsen, A.: Role Playing Games - Comparative Analysis Across Two Media Platforms. Proceedings of the Interactive Entertainment Conference 2006, Perth, Australia (2006)
19. Tychsen, A., Hitchens, M., Brolund, T., Kavakli, M.: The Game Master. 2005 Interactive Entertainment Conference (2005) 215-222
20. Tychsen, A., Pagden, N.: Making Magic! Enhancing PnP RPGs with computing technology. Playing Roles seminar, Tampere, Finland (2006)
21. Wright, T., Boria, E., Breidenbach, P.: Creative Player Actions in FPS Online Video Games. Game Studies 2 (2002)

Experiencing Narrative Elements Through Social Communication in Computer Based Role-Playing Game – CASE: *Castle of Oulu 1651*

Laura Vallius, Tomi Kujanpää, and Tony Manninen

University of Oulu, Department of Information Processing Science,
LudoCraft Game Design and Research Unit,
P.O. Box 3000, FIN-90014 Oulun yliopisto, Finland
{laura.vallius, tony.manninen, tomi.kujanpaa}@oulu.fi

Abstract. A study on how role-play through narrative elements of social communication can be implemented in a computer-based environment. Contemporary computer role-playing games do not support playing roles in a social aspect. Play is conducted in a functional and task-oriented way due to the design of the gameplay. An experimental role-playing game, *Castle of Oulu, 1651* was constructed to test aspects of social play and elements borrowed from more traditional forms of role-play. The aim is to determine some essential elements the players need to assume a role and play towards socially structured goals.

Keywords: role-play, narrative elements, computer game.

1 Introduction

In forms of entertainment, one of the key elements is the experience of the participants. Because the time consumed playing computer games is growing, the experiences of players have become more important as a research area. Role-playing games represent one area of gaming that can offer a great variety for use of narrative elements as building blocks of gameplay. Role-playing allows the player to experience a whole new world as another person, as part of a social community. The immersion in the play through the game character can offer the player a very engaging experience. Playing a role lets the player imagine a world that does not exist and create a personality and events together with the other players. The current computer based role-playing games offer a somewhat limited amount of actual role-playing, the concentration being more on the functional and task-oriented aspects of playing. When transferring the focus of play into social structures and communication, the narrative elements can be implemented in the game to create a much deeper way of experiencing a situation. Role-playing outside computer environments offers, usually, an immediate presence and the reactions of the other players. One of the aims here is to create the same feel in a computer role-playing game. The goal is to find out how to design computer games that enable experiencing through a greater level of immersion into the character and role-play. The study was conducted as a constructive research programme and as a case study. To understand how role-playing experience forms through narrative elements, different role-playing styles were compared. The theoretical background and the background from different

S. Göbel, R. Malkewitz, and I. Iurgel (Eds.): TIDSE 2006, LNCS 4326, pp. 289–299, 2006.

role-playing styles were used concurrently with theories of experiencing to evaluate the experiences of 260 children who played the game *Castle of Oulu 1651*. The data of the experiences was collected using methods of observation and survey. Methods of phenomenography and statistics were usedto analyse the data.

2 What Is Role-Play?

To understand how experiences can be created and shaped through role-playing in a computer based environment, some elements that form the basis for role-playing need to be studied. The experimental computer based role-playing environment, *Castle of Oulu 1651*, which works as the case example for this study, was designed to support social interaction as an important element of play. This study looks into how playing a role through social interaction works in different forms of role-play. The current status of the design of computer role-playing will be compared with the design of pen'n'paper role-play (PnP RPG) and live action role-play (LARP). The aim of this study is to define elements that enable immersion in a role in those forms of role-play and to test how these elements could be used to create a basis for experiencing role-play in a computer based environment.

2.1 Defining Different Types of Role-Play

The terms used and short definitions of the three types of role-play are introduced in the following table (Table 1). The table is purposefully simplistic by nature. Due to the great differences between individual games within all the introduced types of play, the definitions are limited to explaining the differences essential for this study. The focus of this study is in experiencing social play and in playing a role. Therefore, the introduced types of role-play are considered in this perspective, even though all of these types include mechanisms and methods that are functional by nature.

Table 1. Definitions of selected types of role-play

Type of play	Definition
RPG PnP RPG	Role-playing Game Pen and paper (PnP) or tabletop role-playing. A small group of players gathered in a common space engaging in an adventure through storytelling. [4] The focus of this study is on the social and narrative elements of role-playing. Though the necessary mechanical aspects of, for example, solving a dispute with dices exists, it is seen as a supporting element to the primary element of the free narrative through which the game is played.
LARP, LRP	Live Action Role-playing Game, Live Role-playing Game Players, physically and mentally, step into the roles of the characters and act out an imaginary adventure in a physical setting. [1]

Table 1. *(continued)*

	Although LARP can be seen as an environmental and improvisational performance with little true game-like features, for the benefit of this study, LARP is classified as a game. The important area for this study is the design of social structures into the gameplay. The mechanical acts of solving conflicts play a subsidiary role.
CRPG	Computer Role-playing Game A player (or a group of players) takes part in an adventure designed to take place in a virtual environment through a game character as an interface to the action. [5] Computer environments offer various different forms of games that can be classified as role-playing games. Due to the nature of this study (to the relevance of the material bearing in mind the test environment *Castle of Oulu 1651*), the main focus is on computer adventure games where players interact with a visualised world and other players through a game character.

3 Social Play as an Element of Role-Play

One important area for this study is the role of social interaction as an element of role-play. Social play refers to social interaction between the players. Through this interaction the players can, for example, transform social relationships within the play [6]. In terms of social play, a bounded community of players forms a closed system where the play arises from the individual process of each game and the interaction between the players' [6]. For example, in a tabletop RPG the players are in the same physical space and the act of playing happens through telling the story together. The gameplay exists only in the players' imaginary space and without social communication between the players the game does not progress. This form of role-play is wholly dependent on the player's social interaction and participation [2]. In LARP, the game world and the characters exist in the physical form and the players can explore the environment of the adventure without communicating with each other. The idea and the building blocks of the story are sprinkled around the magic circle of the gameplay [6] in the form of the players' characters, background stories and goals. The actual world of the gameplay forms through these pieces coming together through social interaction. Both in RPG and LARP gaming events, the social circle is created around the roles of the participating players and everyone has a role to fulfil to carry on the game's storylines. The interaction between the players is immediate and intensive. The responses and reactions happen on an intimate and personal level through the means of communicating in "real life". The emotional state of players and means of non-verbal communication [7] are present and readable at all times.

The role of social play changes in CRPG environments due to the physical separation of the players and the design of gameplay. Unlike RPG and LARP, CRPG does not require a group of people to take part. The games are designed to support both single and multiplayer events. The communication between players is supported technically to a certain degree. It is generally possible, for example, to chat in writing with other players using in-game messaging tools. The role of communication is, however, secondary to the nature of the gameplay. The gameplay progresses according to the actions the players take through the interface, the character. Communication between the players is a secondary action that can affect the experience and create an illusion of a community. The aim of communication between players can be part of solving the problems, for example, asking for information of how to succeed in a following task or deciding on tactical moves to be used in reaching the next goal together. However, the communication does not necessarily have any effect on the progress of the game.

In CPRG environments the social interaction is also limited to a very inexpressive form. The feeling of playing together is diminished due to the technical boundaries. The immediate eloquent interaction of face to face communication cannot be reached and most of non-verbal aspects of communication are reduced to a rudimentary level. The players' means of interpreting each other's mental state and intentions lie mostly on the very limited form of reading and writing short messages.

3.1 Narrative Elements as Building Blocks of the Gameplay

The support offered by the design of the gameplay has an important role in creating social interaction. One way to encourage social interaction in CRPG environments is to design the gameplay to rely, one way or another, on communicative aspects. Narrative plot/gameplay development poses as one possibility. Traditional RPG and LARP represent game forms that use narrative elements as basis for gameplay in a very viable way. The difference is that in RPG the play progresses verbally through guided narrative whereas in LARP the physical environment and physical nature of characters offer different ways to animate the narrative frame. In both game types the players are presented with the frame of play by the game master who guides the action in the game world and solves conflicts between the players[4]. The active participation and interaction between the players through their characters form a dynamic, loosely controlled gameplay where almost anything can happen within the agreed boundaries. The imagination of the players poses as limit to the action where all the ways of free narrative are at the disposal of the players.

In a way, the gameplay in RPG and LARP is forced around social interaction by the nature of the play. The content of play can be built around socially attainable goals, for example, trying to become elected as the mayor of a city. On the other hand, the goals of a more functional nature, for example, to win a battle, do not lead to a lack of social interaction because it is the only way to make these events happen. CRPG poses a problematic environment in a sense that the content of the goals of the players can either kill almost all the interaction or support it to some level. However, the practice of the gameplay forces the mechanical tasks to be attained through mechanical interaction. Team play can be supported in a way that the mechanical goal is easier to attain through agreed tactics but the actual attaining of the goal, in other words the progress of the storylines, happens through mechanical interaction instead of social interaction. The limitations to the social interaction mostly come from the limitations of creating interactive free narrative through means of computer environments. The role-playing games exist in a way regardless of the amount of the players or the active participation of a group. The pre-designed storylines and the elements planted into the environment do not change dynamically. The computer based environments do not offer ways for free communication and the loosely guided narrative is difficult to build in a system where, for example, the computer controlled characters/avatars cannot react to the player in ways required for this sort of playing.

Table 2 shows how social play can be supported by the selected types of role-play. The narrative elements used to create social play in traditional forms of role-play can be compared with the support of narrative elements in contemporary computer based role-playing.

Table 2. Support of social play in presented types of role-play

Type of play	Forms of social play
RPG PnP RPG	- pre-created storylines and set of rules, open and dynamic imaginary environment - progress of gameplay through narrative communication between players - team creates an adventure together, players dependent on each others willingness to create the story
LARP, LRP	- pre-created storylines and set of rules, open and dynamic physical and imaginary environment - progress of gameplay through physical and narrative communication between players - team creates adventure together, players dependent on each others willingness to create the story
CRPG	- pre-created storylines, closed and mainly static represented environment - functional interaction through virtual character in virtual environment - some interaction through narrative communication between players - team can take part in adventure together, little support for co-operation or communication - players are able to experience the adventure alone

4 *Castle of Oulu 1651* – CRPG with a Social Twitch

An experimental computer based role-playing game, *Castle of Oulu 1651,* was constructed to determine how social elements of role-playing could be implemented in a computer environment and how computer players could be persuaded to play a role. *Castle of Oulu 1651* was commissioned by the city of Oulu to be a non-violent game set in a historical environment that could be used in educational purposes as well as entertainment. Using historical data of the now destroyed castle, the virtual environment was created to resemble an authentic historical setting. However, the reconstruction of the virtual setting aimed for aesthetic engagement and artistic selectivity in terms of representation. The environment, the clothes, the names and the hierarchical occupations of the characters, as well as, items in the castle area were designed to fit the 17th century theme. The environment was set up to be a logically coherent playground for the players to use as they were attempting to achieve the goals through playing the roles of their characters.

The game was designed for a target group of children aged between 11 to 16 years. A group of thirty players played the game simultaneously, while each player aimed at reaching his or her specific goal. The game was created to combine social structures, freedom of narrative creation of storylines and immediate interaction of role-playing games, the re-playability of board games, and atmospheric attraction of adventure games. The main objectives of the players were designed using basic ideas of conflict creation and developing a plot common in LARP design. The aim of the design was to replace the task-oriented functions of contemporary with the nowadays mainly secondary action of communication between the players. This way the functional acts would be supporting the social interaction without which the gameplay would not progress.

As perceived through the comparison of different types of role-play, one of the thriving forces of assuming and immersing in the role of the character in RPG and LARP is the necessity deriving from the narrative form of the gameplay. One of the challenges in creating free narrative as part of the gameplay in CRPG has been the design of games to offer single and multi-user playing. Storylines that are based on social communication place special demands on the computer-guided avatars. Providing sufficient level of free narrative for a single player game has proved challenging due to the technical limitations. In *Castle of Oulu 1651* this challenge was by-passed through designing the game to be a multiplayer game of at least six simultaneous players. This decision alone brings *Castle of Oulu 1651* closer to the other types or role-play. Unlike in many contemporary CPRGs, the progress of the game is based on an existence a group of people who agree on sharing the adventure together. Since the narrative aspects of the gameplay were left for the players to conduct, a free and open-ended storyline could be built. To overcome some of the technical limitations of communication, a headphone set with a microphone was added to the game and all communication was conducted through real-time speech.

One of the goals was to set social communication to be the central act of the gameplay. Another goal was to support and direct the players to play a role of their character in the game environment. Each player was given a role through a game character with a position in the society, a primary and a secondary goal and special piece of information of the game world or of another role distributed to another player. The character comprised of four individual pieces of the role and all the pieces of the role were randomly distributed to the players. This was designed to add to the re-playability of the game because the combination of traits that build up the roles would change at the beginning of each game. To encourage social communication, the goals were built in a way that the players needed, for example, to persuade another player to do something, give information or share their opinion about something or someone. The goals were designed to enable co-operation with some players and conflict with others. The amount of information distributed to the players had to be limited due to the preparation time for each game. Also, the expectations of computer gamers do not include extensive reading before actually starting the game. For this reason some room for imagination was left for the players to fill in the blanks in the history and personality of the character randomly given to them.

5 Player Experiences from the *Castle of Oulu 1651*

The experiment took place at a school fair. Within the period of one week 260 children played the *Castle of Oulu 1651* and reported their experiences through short debriefing sessions after each game and by filling a personal questionnaire.

5.1 Playing a Role in *Castle of Oulu 1651*

Every player was given a character with a specific role. The role was constructed from knowledge of the characters occupation, opinions, secret information, primary and secondary goals. For example, a character could be a town guard that had to find out which ones of the players were carrying guns. With the role the player was told that in his opinion too many people were carrying weapons. He also had a permission to arrest suspicious characters. Another character could have a role of a townsman who is a merchant and organises auctions to sell merchandise for the best possible price and buy other items at a cheaper price. Yet another character could be an outlaw who has been hired by an unknown suspicious party to create chaos in the castle area by committing small offences. All the roles given to the players offered information of tasks the players were supposed to do as well as a glimpse of the character's personality. In addition to the role and the position in the society with it, the players received a primary goal separately from the role. These goals could be, for example, to persuade the other characters to vote for one candidate in the election for the mayor, to reveal a person they suspected is a witch or to act as a judge at court and set free the innocent characters but sentence the guilty ones.

The players accepted the roles at varying levels. The expectations of the players towards a game played on a computer excluded many of the functions they were expected to perform in *Castle of Oulu 1651*. Thus, after realising what was expected of them, the acceptance of the style of play guided them towards playing the role. Some roles were seen as easier to appreciate, like the role of a guard due to the functional aspect of arresting other players. However, most of the players actually reported as having worked towards the goals set to them through their character. In this way the play of a role was somewhat successful. Some players clearly stepped into the role and tried to reach the goals of their character as best they could. For example, one young boy, who was set to persuade other players to vote for Kutha as mayor, continued the persuasion by shouting like a cheapjack throughout the whole one-hour gaming session. Whether or not this can be seen as an example of role-play, at least it shows a degree of dedication in the face of a social task.

Some immersion to the game character happened on the level of framing the action. On the visual level the characters were not seen as easy to immerse into. The characters were not designed to meet the concurrent visual style of game characters but to break the stereotypical look of video game characters. All characters were variations of four basic models, an older fat balding man, young rickety male, older robust wrinkled woman and a younger woman. In general, the players did appreciate the visual appearance of the characters and it made it harder for them to immerse into the character as a whole. Also the idea of a twelve year old boy to assume and immerse in the character of an older woman may have been a bit extreme, especially since the character was not his choice. In some cases the players developed personalities for their characters either through their own decision or sometimes through the influence of the other players. In describing their characters they used words like funny, easy-going, calm or annoying. This sort of immersion asks a lot of willingness on the part of the player and in this case the majority of the players were not ready or prepared for role-play on that level.

5.2 Playing Socially and Developing Storylines

Some technical solutions were used to force the players to communicate with each other. The virtual environment was limited in a way that the players could not disappear into the endless realms of the virtual world. The adventure had one main area of focus, the courtyard of the castle. The players could leave the yard in order to wander outside the castle but the area outside the castle was relevantly compact because of the level design. Some players saw the area in which the thirty players were forced to stay as quite small. They explained that they would have wanted to explore a larger world with their friends who were playing at the same time. The limiting of the space was in this light necessary more for reasons other than the disintegration of the group in general. It also prevented the disintegration of the group to parties of friends from the real world. In other words, the social structures and relationships built in the game would not have had any effect on the decision of the groups exploring the world together. The social connections from real world overrode the ones built in the game. When forced into the small area, the players were more likely to communicate with other players as well as their friends. On the other hand, the limitation of the world forced the players to use time to concentrate on the goals set for them. Since the environment did not offer the unlimited amount of mechanical computer-game-like action, the attention was brought to social communication.

The microphone and headphones -set used by the players to communicate with each other was received well. Speaking with other players was seen as one of the best aspects of the game. The goals and all action of the game were built around social interaction between the players and basically nothing would happen in the gameplay until the verbal interaction began. Where the limited space was a necessity for forming of social interaction, it was also problematic in a technical sense. The communication through speech was built in a way that the players whose characters were situated close enough in the virtual world could hear each other. The idea was that if a group of players wanted to speak in secret they could step further from the other players and speak without anyone outside the distance hearing them. The problem was then that due to the limited amount of virtual space, it forced a large amount of players into close range of each other and since everyone wanted to be heard, the general level of noise was higher than necessary. This, of course, made communicating through speech somewhat confusing. The players had difficulties hearing what was said to them and also recognising who was speaking to whom. These technical issues, however, are something that can be overcome through time and resources.

As well as through technical decisions the social communication and forming of social play was supported by the design of the gameplay of *Castle of Oulu 1651*. The aim of the design was that nearly all activities, the ones that lead to social conclusion or the ones that lead to mechanical action needed to be based on social interaction. Trading, buying or selling objects is an example of a mechanical action that needed social interaction before taking place. The players needed to verbally agree on what was being traded and for what prices before the actual trade took place. The half-social and half-mechanical function of trading made it easy for the players to take part in. Most of the players traded something during the game and in spite of the noise of the group the players enjoyed the task of negotiating prices and trading items. Also the tasks that were based on the players' will and skill to persuade other players to take a stand in some political, religious or superstitious issues was seen as fun and practised by large group of players.

Parts of storylines of the environment and the social relationships between players were left open on purpose of introducing free narrative into the gameplay. For example, although none of the characters was given a role of a witch, some players were guided to accuse others of being one. The idea was to leave the players with possibilities to fulfil the history of their character in a way they wanted to and create parts of the story of the *Castle of Oulu 1651* together. In practice this did not happen. The implications and suggestions to this form of play were not strong enough and not supported well enough. The combining of the strictly static nature of the computer games and imaginary dynamics of RPG storytelling appeared to be too difficult as an idea to work. This, however, may be heavily influenced by the test subjects' general non-role-playing backgrounds. The players were not dedicated role-players. They were a group of children merely having fun by playing a different type of computer game.

6 Discussion

Introducing free narrative into a CRPG environment as primary function does not happen without problems. The pre-designed environment and imaginary storytelling present a dilemma that complicates the understanding of what is expected in the gameplay. The players are not used to creating content into a computer environment in the same way the players of LARP and RPG are. The environment and the items, etc., are pre-designed and in that way static by nature. To use this static environment and imagine one's character in doing anything or being anything becomes problematic. For example, the player could decide to be a witch but could not decide to ride a horse, if there was no horse built into the game. The limit of what can and cannot be imagined reduces the imagination all together. The understanding of possibilities for this kind of action in a computer-based environment requires a fresh way of looking at the game. The support and guiding of the players to start telling stories as part of gameplay presents an area for further study. A balance between presented and imagined is yet to be defined in a computer based role-playing game.

Assuming of a role and playing a role were not supported sufficiently in *Castle of Oulu 1651*. Some elements needed to assume a role were implemented. The role was an important part of the goals set for players. The actual assuming of role and playing a role, however, require more. For example, the expressiveness of the game characters was not increased to enable better ways to convey emotions and feelings. Limited forms of self-expression reduced the role-playing into a form of discussion with other players. Even if the discussion itself can be seen as a relevant form of experiencing a role, the in-game discussions did not encourage out-of-character narratives that are evident in RPGs. The players did talk out-of-character, but that was generally not in favour of the role-play. In addition, the support for artificial relationships between game characters needs to be stronger in order to convince the players to override their existing relationships.

The implementation of social communication and creation of free narrative in a LARP or RPG -like manner to be the central element of gameplay proved to be partly successful. The players did enjoy the process of verbally communicating and the acts of persuading others to do something or negotiating what to trade and for what price. This suggests that goals of CRPG games can built to require social communication. In addition, this suggests that open-ended storylines can form the basis for playing on a computer as well as it can form a basis for LARP or RPG. However, computer environments present problems that need to be addressed before the forms of free narrative actually can be successfully used as sole basis for design of gameplay. For example, the measuring of success of a socially performed task is very problematic in a computer game.

While the goals and outcomes of the game were somewhat non-traditional in terms of CRPG, the basic criteria for success were, nevertheless, relatively mechanistic. The game counted, and portrayed, player scores. These, in turn, were based on certain key actions. The key action had to be something that can be measured by the computer. Naturally, this chain of design decisions leads to a more or less traditional computer game. However, the introduction of a game master (which is supported by the game) with the ability to modify attributes, could lead to a more coherent role-play.

The testing of *Castle of Oulu 1651* offered several challenges that were not only dependent on the success of the balance between social and functional actions designed for the game environment. The group of testers was not chosen through any consideration of the target group for role-playing. In this perspective one of the new challenges was to engage players who were not role-players in the role-playing like activities within the *Castle of Oulu 1651*. Some difficulties were noted in accepting the form of gameplay of *Castle of Oulu 1651*. After, in a way re-learning how to play on a computer, the general feeling of the game was positive. One downside to the playing experience of a third of the group was the lack of violence.

7 Conclusions

This study suggests that designing CRPG environments that truly support role-play is possible. *Castle of Oulu 1651* was one step towards a new way of playing on a computer. The comparison of different types of role-playing games offers valuable information of how to develop and support role-playing in CRPG environments. Important elements for experiencing the role and for assuming a role could be found from the areas of social play and narrative elements of gameplay. Implementation of some elements that support social interaction and role-play were tried out in *Castle of Oulu 1651*. For example, the implementation of narrative elements as fundamental elements of play was one effective way of emphasising social interaction. The information collected from the group of test-players can be used to study the elements of role-play further and as design tools for further constructions. The technical improvements will certainly add useful elements to support social interaction between players, but the biggest steps need to be taken in the design of the games.

Environments and games that are based on role-play, however, require another component to be successful: The willingness of players to play the roles. The idea of elaborate role-playing may be difficult to understand for players who have experience in playing on a computer. The assuming of a role and playing role-play might not be easy for players not accustomed it. Playing a role, however, is also a learning process. In other words, role-playing ability grows through role-playing experiences [3]. On the other hand, not every one wants to role-play. Through successful design of more immersive role-playing experiences, computer games can offer entertainment for new audiences. Understanding and learning how to create more rewarding experiences and demanding role-play can also open possibilities for novel ways of using computer environments in education and research.

References

1. Falk, J. and Davenport, G. (2004). *Live Role-Playing Games: Implications for Pervasive Gaming.* In Proceedings of Third International Conference on Entertainment Computing - ICEC 2004. Rauterberg, R. (eds) Eindhoven, The Netherlands, pp. 128.
2. Lankoski, P. (2004). *Character Design Fundamentals for Role-Playing Games.* In Montola, M. and Stenros, J. (eds) Beyond Role and Play: Tools, Toys and Theory for Harnessing the Imagination, The book for Solmukohta 2004. pp. 139-148
3. Mann, J.H. and Mann C.H. (1959). *The Effect of Role-Playing Experience on Role-Playing Ability.* Sociometry, Vol. 22, No. 1, pp. 64-74.
4. Pearce, C. (2002). *Emergent Authorship: The Next Interactive Revolution.* Computers & Graphics, Vol. 26, No. 1, pp. 21-29.
5. Rouse, R. (2000). *Game Design: Theory & Practice*, Wordware Publishing, Inc., Plano, Texas, pp. 558.
6. Salen, K. and Zimmerman, E. (2004). *Rules of Play - Game Design Fundamentals.* Massachusetts Institute of Technology, pp. 95, 471-475
7. Thalmann D (2001) *The Role of Virtual Humans in Virtual Environment Technology and Interfaces.* In: Earnshaw R, Guejd R, van Dam A & Vince J (eds) Frontiers of Human-Centred Computing, Online Communities and Virtual Environments. Springer-Verlag, London, 27-38.

Ghost Worlds – Time and Consequence in MMORPGs

Anders Tychsen and Michael Hitchens

Department of Computing, Macquarie University, Building E6A, 2109 North Ryde, NSW, Australia
{atychsen, mhitchens}@ics.mq.edu.au

Abstract. MMORPGs are an increasingly popular form of entertainment, yet are limited in their ability to tell stories when compared to other media. This paper analyses some of the underlying reasons for this inability, using techniques form narrative analysis. One of the basic problems identified is that the design of MMORPGs inhibits the use of techniques used in other media to create engaging stories by manipulating the presentation of time. The other issue identified is the problems MMORPGs experience in presenting stories with meaningful consequence. A means to a possible solution to these problems, in separating the personal player view point from that of the overall world view, is discussed.

Keywords: Consequence, Time, Storytelling, MMORPG, computer games.

1 Introduction

Massively Multiplayer Online Role Playing Games (MMORPGs) form a relatively young game form, it being around a decade since the launch of graphical massively multi-player games such as *Meridian 59* and *Ultima Online*. Despite being a relatively recently developed game form, MMORPGs are fast becoming a popular form of interactive entertainment. A key interest in MMORPG design is the generation of stories in these games, notably because advances in graphics appear insufficient in expanding the core market [15]. One way to achieve this is via storytelling, i.e. the provision of personalized, emotional and engaging content. Engaging narratives provide several advantages, notably: 1) Stories provide change. Players will be expecting new content and come back to experience it; 2) Emotional/personalized content. Getting players to care about their virtual characters, will in turn provide retention because players are inclined to keep playing if hooked emotionally; 3) Attract a wider audience. Currently MMORPGs are focused on conflict, however, having a non-competitive aspect will open up the market, by showing potential players that there is more to be gained from the play experience than combat [13]. The ability to include storytelling in multi-player or massively multi-player online computer games (MMOGs) is in general limited by development and running costs, as well as the general state of technological development of the electronic medium that the games inhabit as well as design challenges when accommodating thousands of players within a unified, persistent, real-time running virtual world [5]. Due to these challenges, most contemporary MMORPGs can be compared to a **ghost world** following popular western mythology: The character-avatars can interact with the physical part of the

S. Göbel, R. Malkewitz, and I. Iurgel (Eds.): TIDSE 2006, LNCS 4326, pp. 300 – 311, 2006.

virtual world, including talking to its inhabitants and each other; however, they cannot permanently affect it. When a player logs out, it is as if the character-avatar never existed in the world, and any actions performed will not have left a permanent record. In the following, MMORPGs are analysed from a literature perspective, adapting [3]'s work on interactive narrative analysis to MMORPGs. This is in an attempt to clarify the underlying theoretical causes of difficulties in incorporating storytelling within the framework of MMORPGs. Part of this difficulty arises as a function of the medium of expression itself. The purpose of this analysis is not to outline how to tell better stories in MMORPGs, but to clarify the possible solution space.

2 Related Work

During the last few decades a substantial amount of academic work has been performed on virtual worlds and environments, specifically with the purpose of exploring and improving the ability to perform storytelling in virtual environments – i.e. to combine storytelling and interactivity. The application of narrative theory to computer games is far from new, however, most work has focused on single-user experiences, not specifically been directed at the MMORPGs. A variety of approaches are currently utilized, from structural and narrative analysis [14],[17] agent-based systems [2],[21], artificial intelligence [7] to interactive storytelling management systems. The approach presented here varies from these in that the core purpose is not to create storytelling models, systems, story construction structures or similar frameworks, nor to propose direct solutions – work is already being performed along these lines [e.g. 9] – or study how players tell stories about their gaming experiences. Rather, the focus in on enhancing the current understanding of the underlying causes of the challenges related to storytelling (here defined in the broadest possible sense) in MMORPGs, based on recent methods for narrative analysis [3],[4], and how the physical format and properties of MMORPGs makes traditional literary storytelling mechanics difficult to apply.

The analysis presented here is not an attempt to comprehensively analyse MMORPGs, but to focus on the use and implications of **time** and **consequence**. MMORPGs run persistently and in real-time, preventing them from utilizing a host of narrative mechanics in creating character-based narratives. Consequence refers to the ability of players to affect the virtual world, including their characters, the environment and other players. These concepts (time, consequence) form key storytelling tools, and combined with the high number of players in these games, comprise key limiting factors for storytelling in MMORPGs.

3 Narrative Analysis of MMORPGs

From a literary perspective, because MMORPGs are based on persistently, real-time running fictional worlds, in an interactive medium, they contain inherent limitations to the traditional narrative devices they can utilize to form **stories** (or **narratives**, which is one way to understand stories – a narrative could be defined as specific telling or representation of a specific story). One method for analysing how these limitations occur is narrative analysis [3],[4]. This method basically breaks down the object of study into a specific system of elements, i.e. it is a structuralist approach. Its use here is not to meant to imply a belief that narratology is the best means of analysing MMORPGS, however: *"irrespectively of the general status of structuralist narratology within the contemporary study of narrative study, the model is very useful when applied to the analysis and design og interactive narrative and story construction systems*". [14]. There is however a problem in applying *traditional* narrative analysis to MMORPGs, namely that by being games MMORPGS inherently are non-linear with respect to stories, interactive and based on a dynamic instead of a static media.

Literature theory is traditionally concerned with static narratives, e.g. stories presented in books, films etc., where the audience does not interact with the telling of the story. This has caused considerable challenges in applying narrative theory to interactive media as vessels for storytelling [14],[17],[20], and for example [1] outlined some of the potential pitfalls in applying narratology to digital media.

The dynamic properties of games comprise a fundamental difference from the static form of traditional media, which necessitates an adaptation and evolution of narrative theory in order to deal with dynamically generated narratives [14]. A key example of an adaptation of narrative theory to an interactive situation is presented in [4], where a multi-disciplinary approach to the concept of a narrative is defined, in which a designed work implicates the reader in the enaction of a performance. This concept of narrative fits better with the participatory and performative bases of works on interactive media such as [1], and [18]. As noted by [12], the approaches of [3],[4] can with some modifications work with these theories of interactive media. Work such as [3],[4] have provided a theoretical background and the tools to – to some degree – apply a form of narrative analysis to interactive storytelling in combination with computer game design and development requirements and principles (which utilize causal relationships between e.g. agents and events to generate meaning, in a manner comparable to narrative theory), even though the concepts and methods for analysing "interactive narratives" remain debated [10] and there is a long-running conflict between narrative and interactivity [11]. Narrative analysis is not the only way to approach the subject of storytelling in games, for example, [20] utilized reader response theory, which focuses on the actual process of "reading" (experiencing) a text, and thus applicable to games. Associated theory includes the possible worlds theory of [18],[19].

A narratological approach has the benefit that it is structuralist [14]. Utilizing core principles from [3],[4], here MMORPGs are broken down into a range of components, the key ones in this study being **Fictional World, Text, Fabula** and **Story**. Other concepts (such as pre-text) can also be applied to MMORPGs. These were considered in the current study, however, they appear to be of less importance in deciphering the theoretical causes behind the storytelling challenges of MMORPGs, and are therefore due to space constraints not described here. The definition of these terms remain debated, and as it is out of scope of this paper to argue for the advantages of specific definitions, the terminology of [3],[4] has been adopted here and modified where necessary.

Fictional World: The virtual reality: The player of a MMORPG experiences the game via interacting with the game components and the other players in a virtual world, which is inherently fictional. This comprises the sum of the knowledge of the world setting – content, historical backgrounds, ecologies, developer material, fiction novels, etc. The fictional world varies with time - as more content is developed and possibly added to a MMORPG, the sum of knowledge of the fictional world, as well as the actual game code, grows in size, or changes. Players of a MMORPG may not experience the full extent of this material, but only the part of the knowledge included in the game content. This is the portion of the fictional world that the player can access via the activity of playing the specific game. Potentially, all players of MMORPGs can experience the sum of the game content. However, unless the player visits every part of the virtual world, completes every quest and examines every in-game item and so forth, the game content experienced will be less than the sum of the game content.

Text: The game and its components: In narrative theory, the text is the object being studied, and is the means by which the story is conveyed to the user. The text can be formally defined as: *"A concrete manifestation in a specific sign language"* [3].

In this case, the text could be defined as the MMORPG with all its constituent parts. This definition is purposefully kept loose – it could be argued whether e.g. the game manual should be considered part of the text. In static media the content of the story expressed in the medium will be generally similar between two people in the audience (e.g. for two readers of a book the book is unchanged). In a computer game, two players may not experience all of the same content, and not necessarily in the same order, yet the underlying game itself is identical. Therefore a number of different definitions of text are possible, of which we give three.

The first is **game text**, which is the entirety of an MMORPG, including its constituent parts and code. The second is the **playable text**, which is the part of the MMORPG text that the individual player has access to, including game manuals etc. Note that the playable text is static and unchanging in between the application of e.g. patches and content updates. This definition gets the closest to the understanding of text from a traditional narrative analysis point of view, where the text is the object of study. The third is the **player text**, which is the part of the playable text that the player actually experiences (not equalling fabula, see below). The playable text is usually the same for all players; however the player text is not.

Changes in any of these texts are introduced, at base, by changes to the game text, as all experience with game depends upon its code. However, changes in one text may not be propagated onto the next. Change in the code may be at the data structure level, not changing the playable text. An update to a MMORPG which expands the game world with new areas, MOBs or quests (i.e. new content) changes the playable text, but does not change the player text until players actually experience the new content.

Fabula: Ordering the events of a story: The fabula can be defined as a: *"series of logically and chronologically related events that are caused or experienced by actors"* [3] Here actors can be equated with the character-avatars of a MMORPG. In traditional narratology, the fabula is the chronological reconstruction of the logically related events of a possibly non-chronological story which is experienced by the character-avatars (the protagonists) of the players. It is the events covered by the Text in their full, real time, aspect within the fictional world. Because MMORPGs are played in real-time, the players will – generally speaking - experience everything their character-avatars do. It can be seen that the players are experiencing the fabula, as they experience everything there character does in the fictional world, in real-time.

However, what one character/player experiences is not the totality for that world – there are many players. This necessitates at least two levels of fabula, the sum of the events experienced by any individual player (the **personal [character] fabula**) and the sum of all players of the MMORPG (**the MMORPG fabula**). Other versions of the fabula could be defined and utilized in narrative analysis of a MMORPG, for example the fabula of a player guild. An event as used in the definition above is simply a transition from one story-state to another, for example, in MMORPG play, engaging a MOB is a transition from one story-state (non-combat) to another (combat with the MOB). Events can be defined at different scales of resolution.

It is relatively simple to describe the MMORPG fabula, if defined as the sum of the fabulas of the character-avatars of the games' players, and to order the events of the fabula chronologically, due to the unchanging nature of the game world state. For example, MMORPGs such as *World of Warcraft* have a day/night cycle, however, there is no world calendar, or changing of dates. In essence, every time the sun sets, the world is the same as it was the last time. This is also true even if the world had a calendar. An abstract date might change, however, if there is no discernible effect on world state via this passing of time, the vast majority of the fabula elements will be from the same chronological instant. Players may need to perform certain actions in order to unlock access to particular parts of the content, however, for all intents and purposes the in-game time (or game world chronology), has remained unchanged. Even if the MMORPG incorporates a night/day cycle, or even a calendar, if the passing of time in the game does not alter the game state, effectively the game world chronology remains frozen in the same instant of time.

This does not mean that MMORPGs cannot contain content from outside the chronological instant of the main world – game design does allow players to be given the opportunity to experience specific events outside the chronological instant of the MMORPG game world, i.e. in the past or the future. E.g. using **instances**: A section of a MMORPG which forms a separate unit, accessible only by individual or groups of players. Multiple iterations of the same instance can operate contemporaneously.

Story: Presentation of the fabula: In comparison to MMORPGs, a book or film can present different events taking place at different times in very different ways. For example, some actions of a protagonist can be briefly described, while another set of actions may be described in great detail. Both are fabula elements; however the presentation of them is very different. Events may be presented out of their chronological order. This transition from fabula to story forms the basis for defining story, which is the presentation of a fabula in a certain manner [3] (be it the player or game fabula). This definition varies from that of [14] who notes that: "*The game story is the total implied game world history as determined by the pre-designed potential of the game in interaction with the game play actions of the player*". The particular ordering and presentation of the events of the fabula makes one story unique from other stories. In other words, a story is a specific representation of a specific fabula. However, the presentation of the fabula is, for most MMORPGs, currently fixed in the real time-ordering of the fictional world, and thus MMORPGs use a substantial amount of the utility of using time as a narrative device. The result of this is that the mapping from fabula to story in MMORPGs is so simplistic that it could be said that for MMORPGs the **fabula is the story**. This is in marked contrast to other media, including single-player CRPGs, where the relationship between story and fabula is more sophisticated (i.e. the use of time more flexible). There are many techniques regularly used, such as summary, ellipsis, reversals, foreshadowing, etc. All of these are beyond the reach of most current MMORPGs.

There are other features of stories that are relevant. The **events** of a story concern the experiences of actors (in the terminology of [3]: Hero, villain and such-like having semantic connotations which do not apply to all stories). Actors may include subjects, who have an aim to be achieved that is central to the story, and helpers and opponents to the subjects. The fabula/story then consists of the subjects' struggles to achieve the aim. This, in traditional literature, eventually reaches some conclusion. While in some forms of literature it does not, post-modernist MMORPGs uncommon.

4 Players and Technology: The Problem of Consequence

The lack of temporal control in MMORPGs constitute a serious obstacle in the use of traditional narrative techniques, however, a similarly problematic feature of the use of the MMORPG format and the underlying technology, is the ability to add consequence to the player-focused and -driven storytelling. A substantial number of the technology, development and design challenges tie in with consequence, making it an important area to investigate.

Consequence is important to most kinds of stories. While this of course is a generalization, especially fiction novels often base their stories on conflict and the solution of the conflict/-s, be they emotional, physical etc. In causing or addressing the conflict, the actions and choices of the story protagonists have consequences. It is therefore important to the development of storytelling in computer games that the choices and actions of the player have consequences – or that the player believes they have.

Consequence should not be mistaken for **authoring rights**, although the concepts have somewhat similar in-game effects. Authoring rights [9], in the context of MMORPGs, refer to the ability of players, designers etc. to modify, delete or add content. Consequence is here used in direct relation to storytelling, e.g. in terms of the result and implications of a quest or similar story structure.

Western MMORPGs can be easily seen to derive in large part from what might be called "hero literature". Well-known examples of such literature are *Lord of the Rings* and *Star Wars*. In such stories the actions of the protagonists have large-scale consequences on the fictional world of which they are a part. The actions of the characters results in a permanent, long-term changes to the fictional world. This can also be seen in many single-player Computer Role Playing Games (CRPGs), such as *Baldur's Gate*, where the actions of the characters change the world.

There are many examples of where MMORPGs fail to provide consequences. Simple examples include delivering a parcel (an early quest in *World of Warcraft*), even after the quest is completed, the NPC is still there, asking others to deliver the parcel; and defeating individual creatures, who always respawn. Even with large and important combat scenes, such as against *Everquest* deities, not only do they not result in the permanent death of such NPCs, but they can be undertaken multiple times by the same character. In story terms, the aim becomes simply the undertaking (usually combat) itself, not some change to the world.

The core problem from a resource point-of-view relates to **story-based choice**: Every time a player is given a choice, e.g. in relation to a story development, this has to be pre-programmed (unless controlled by a good storytelling engine), and every time a decision is to have consequence on the storyline – no matter how much and the level of which the consequence applies – this has to be planned for. This leads to the situation where stories in computer games end up as continually branching trees, which quickly become unmanageable and costly. Various solutions have been sought, e.g. multiple-paths storytelling [8], story networks [8], emergent, AI-driven storytelling [7], agent-based storytelling [2],[16]. In MMORPGs, it is unrealistic to expect game content to be accessible to only a narrow percentage of the player base. Therefore the typical MMORPG quest is permanently available and the world is not changed by any one completion of it (outside of changes to the character(s) completing it, such as in level or equipment). As such, most contemporary MMORPGs are games where the actions of the players do not have any permanent consequences on the game world state. This is in contrast to some virtual worlds designed around user-generated content and development, such as *There* and *Second Life*, where the users can e.g. construct permanent objects. These are however examples of the players filling in an empty canvas, not achieving results comparable to traditional hero literature.

5 Consequence Structure in MMORPGs

While the challenge of providing story-driven consequence can be problematic in single-player computer games, the situation is even more difficult to address in MMORPGs due to the sheer number of players and the constraints on using time as a narrative device, outlined above. The type, duration and magnitude of consequences that can be utilized in character-driven storytelling are limited. For example, in a MMORPG situation where players can permanently remove MOBs or challenges from the virtual world, large amounts of content will be necessary to provide for all the players. Furthermore, players might also be frustrated that part of the game content is not accessible to them. In order to address the issue of consequence, it is first necessary to understand what types of consequence that exists in MMORPGs (and other computer games) from the perspective of the individual player (Fig. 1):

A) **Internal consequence:** Affects the character itself. Internal consequence can affect e.g. the rules-based qualities of a character (e.g. abilities, skills, stats), appearance or psychological qualities, give the character new equipment or status.
B) **External consequence:** Affects the surroundings of the character, including other character. External consequences can generally be described in terms of the effect on other player character-avatars (PvP) and those that affect the virtual environment (PvE). Consequence that affects other players can be difficult to balance properly [5].

Note that the consequence of a given action can be both internal and external. Giving one player on a MMORPG shard an incredibly powerful weapon provides internal consequence – however, the majority of the effect of the consequence is an external consequence, as the in-game balance of power is changed to favour the player with the new weapon. This example shows that the **magnitude** (Fig. 1) of the consequence is important as well. A small magnitude consequence could be a player being given a slightly improved weapon as a quest reward (as is often the case in *World of Warcraft*), or a specific MOB having a brief break between respawn times, which affects the rate at which players can kill it.

Consequence in literature is also of certain **temporal duration** (permanence; Fig. 1). Darth Vader killing the Emperor in *Star Wars* is a permanent consequence in the film narrative (such villain-slaying, arguably, has a tendency to be non-permanent). In a MMORPG, there is a substantial difference between an important quest-MOB having a respawn time of five minutes and five days. The resulting dynamics among the players is considerable. Permanence can roughly be divided into three categories: **non-permanent, limited permanence** and **permanent**. Non-permanent effects are of very limited duration – e.g. the death of a MOB in *Dark Age of Camelot* is a very short term temporary consequence of the action of attacking it, because the game engine re-spawns the MOB after a short period of time. Limited permanence effects can persist for longer, i.e. a magical weapon is useful to a character for a given period of time, or a key MOB is unavailable for several days. Choosing a character class for a character-avatar in *World of Warcraft* is an example of a choice/action with a permanent consequence (for that character-avatar). The boundaries between these categories are purposefully left loosely defined. Finally, consequence does not necessarily have to be tied to the actions of one protagonist only, or a group of players in an instance. Combined efforts of larger groups of players provide a venue for story-driven consequence that MMORPGs are in a unique position to utilize. For example, the "*War Effort*" event in *World of Warcraft* was available to all players on the various shards of the game. The goal of the event was to acquire and donate resources, and the speed with which the resources were gathered determined when a new instance would become available. Conflicts based on player guilds in *Lineage 2* are another example of consequence that operates at a level above the individual character.

In Western hero literature, the actions of the protagonists generally involve major consequences. E.g., getting half the kingdom. This kind of permanent, external, high magnitude PvP-affecting consequence is however hard to integrate in a medium where several thousand players have to operate at the same time and be given equal opportunities to affect the game world (Fig. 1). This generally means that designers have to utilize other forms of consequence in MMORPG storytelling.

It is generally external consequence that is difficult to implement to a significant degree in MMORPGs. Examples of internal permanent consequence are fairly common; however, external consequence is generally temporary. Exceptions include the building of structures in *Star Wars Galaxies* and *A Tale in the Desert*, or the production of in-game items in *Guild Wars* and *Ultima Online*. Note however how these forms of external consequence have a fairly low magnitude. Producing a magical weapon in *World of Warcraft* might be an action with an external, permanent consequence. However, it has a small magnitude (i.e impact on the game world state). As briefly outlined above, it is difficult to provide players with the ability to affect high-magnitude external consequence. This in turn places further limitations on the solution space for generating storytelling in MMORPGs. Because of the nature of MMORPGs, external consequence will affect **game balance**. Story-based consequence that affects the individual player character only – i.e. which integrates consequence in the personal text/fibula of the character without affecting other characters - is much easier to handle in terms of game balancing, however, it is difficult in a mass-medium like MMORPGs to provide character-based consequence which is not identical to every single player of the game, e.g. when relying on open-access quest systems. Another example is the use of contacts, a form of NPC that the character has a long-term relationship with, in *City of Heroes*. Relationships between characters and NPCs provide a potential for story-driven consequence, without affecting other players.

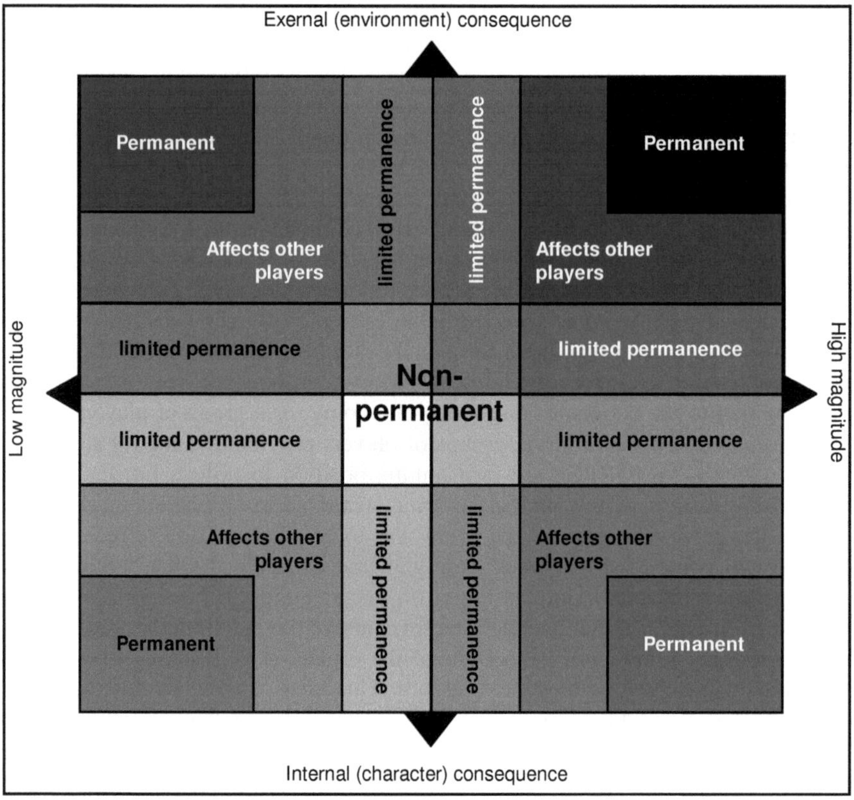

Fig. 1. A model of character-based consequence in MMORPGs. The degree of shading of a given cell indicates how hard it is to integrate in a MMORPG system.

6 Breaking the Link Between Story and Fabula

The analysis presented here is an example of a theoretical method adapted to a case-based study, and is not specifically designed to be used as a tool for MMORPG development, but clarify the underlying theoretical causes of the problems of storytelling in MMORPGs. However, as noted by [10]: "*With a secure understanding of the "how"s and the "why"s we may truly understand the limits and potentials of this thing called interactive fiction*" - in realizing the theoretical foundations behind the challenges of creating engaging and personalized storytelling in MMORPGs, it is possible to realize the operational space within which storytelling in these games must operate.

In MMORPGs the personal story equals the personal fabula – the ordering of the events in the personal fabula will always be identical to the ordering in the personal story. There is e.g. no dilation or expansion of time in MMORPGs because they run persistently in real-time, and therefore it is not possible to utilize time control in presenting the MMORPG content (i.e. to create engaging interactive stories).

This places limits on the possible stories that can be conveyed (i.e. the solution space), and restricts the employment of traditional storytelling techniques, used in traditional passive media, in the handling of time (e.g. rhythm and ellipsis), except in some limited circumstances. As a MMORPG has to cater, simultaneously, to many players, time in the game world must advance at the same rate for all players, removing most opportunities for flexibility. It cannot arbitrarily advance the time for one player or group of players from the start of a journey to the moment of an encounter along that journey, as is done for the single player of many CRPGs. This also dictates that engaging content must appear through out the entire world. It also precludes stories where large amounts of time must pass between events (for example between the childhood and maturity of a hero). Similarly, the MMORPG format to a degree prevents the application of consequence types that interfere with the gaming experience of other MMORPG-players within the same instance of the game world.

When considering storytelling in MMORPGs, the underlying technology and finance structures must be considered at the same level as the three factors of time, consequence and players. For example, with recent advances in agent-based storytelling (e.g. [2],[16],[21]), it has become possible to integrate advanced (and possibly meaningful) NPC-interaction in computer games. Similarly, interactive storytelling engines, emotion models for player characters, advanced use of game music, directorial AI etc. provide means of enhancing MMORPG storytelling. Generally these technologies aim at the individual, low-magnitude level of consequence (e.g. intelligent NPCs), which makes them highly suited to a MMORPG situation. However, the technologies remain in their relative infancy, and generally untested in the mass-market MMORPG environment. It is therefore of interest to consider the existing level of MMORPG technology and consider the solution space for storytelling within that framework.

The story-fabula relationship indicates that the solution is to create a compelling and engaging fabula, i.e. working within the restrictions of the game format. This is the strategy generally adopted in current MMORPGs, and results in rejecting a whole range of storytelling techniques (which may or may not be a problem). In trying to create a more compelling MMORPG fabula, it is important to realize that virtual game worlds are places, not stories [5] MMORPGs support the emergence of stories, but not the stories themselves – these are dependent on the players. Thus, in order for stories to emerge, the game world must contain a certain amount of content that allows stories to take place, also termed **narrative potential** by [9]. This must conform to the general boundaries of the solution space (governed by time, consequence and the players)

Narrative potential can be added to MMORPGs in a variety of ways [9], including the use of characters with a personality components and the direction of game content towards those components, personalize the delivery of content to the individual or group of players, the use of more adaptable quest systems, emergent game content (e.g. simulated environments [22], short-term content and event-driven storytelling (e.g. in-game events, either delivered via patches/live content team or via a content-delivery system that can spawn various types events), and advanced faction-based systems (e.g. as in *World of Warcraft*). There also appears to be substantial options for improving quest-based storytelling in MMORPGs by using storytelling mechanics that do not rely on external story consequence, e.g. a broader use of story elements such as betrayals and reversals (put the betrayer in a remote location and it will not matter that he respawn). Various approaches of these methods have been proposed, some of which could operate within MMORPG technological and financial limits.

There is an alternate route available to MMORPGs: Sidestepping the issue by breaking the link between story and fabula, and ignore the rules of logical consistency in narratives. The solution space dictates that this can only be done as long as it does not adversely affect other players than the individual or group of players in focus. The obvious venue for this is the instance, where alterations to the handling of time and consequence can be performed in the same way as for a single- or multiplayer CRPG.

The use of instances allows for a more directed storytelling experience, however, the result will be the loss of logical consistency of the game world. A group of players entering an instance could experience a story where time flows at a different rate than in the MMORPG. They could enter an instance, experience story content that takes a week of in-game time (game world time for the specific instance), but in terms of the time of the rest of the MMORPG world is a couple of hours. The question is whether this is a problem in ghost world MMORPGs, where time is a constant?

Given the popularity of MMORPGs that include major gaps in logical consistency (e.g. the use of instances to handle epic battles and geographic compression in *World of Warcraft*, the current flagship of the genre), in order to promote gameplay, this may not be a significant problem to MMORPG players. In a MMORPG like *Saga of Ryzom*, that actually features an evolving game world with a simple ecological system etc., this kind of time inconsistency may be more of a problem to the player base.

The ideal solution probably lies somewhere in the middle: Combining the solutions that can operate in the real-time worlds of MMORPGs, and add direct narrative potential, with directed storytelling experiences using instances. The alternative is to think outside the box of current MMORPGs. Some games, like the *Saga of Ryzom R2* project, and the *Seed* project, are exploring alternate routes to MMORPG design.

Finally, story is but one side of MMORPGs. Players have varying ambitions with their game playing, and depending on the target audience, MMORPG design face a variety of interconnected challenges of which storytelling is but one.

Acknowledgements. This study forms part of a multi-institutional research collaboration involving Australian and Scandinavian universities (Macquarie University, Syney; The IT University, Denmark & Växjö University, Sweden). Anders Tychsen also acknowledges PhD-supervisor Dr. Manolya Kavakli.

References

1. Aarseth, E.: Cybertext – Perspectives on Ergodic Literature. The Johns Hopkins University Press, London (1997)
2. Aylett, R., Louchart, S. Dias, J., Palva, A., Vala, M., Woords, S., Hall, L.: Unscripted Narrative for Affectively Driven Characters. IEEE Computer Graphics and Applications 26, 3 (2006) 42-52
3. Bal, M.: Narratology: An Introduction to the Theory of Narrative. 2nd edn. University of Toronto Press, Toronto (1997)

4. Bal, M.: Visual Narrative in The Visual-Narrative Matrix: Interdisciplinary Collision and Collusions. In: Coulter-Smith, G. (Eds.): FARC Proceedings, Southampton (2000)
5. Bartle, R.: Designing Virtual Worlds, New Riders Games, Berkeley CA (2003)
6. Castranova, E.: Synthetic Worlds: The Business and Culture of Online Games. University Of Chicago Press, Chicago, IL (2005)
7. Combs, N.: The Intelligence in the MMOG: From scripts to stories to directorial AI., Other players conference, Copenhagen, Denmark (2004)
8. Crawford, C.: Chris Crawford on Interactive Storytelling, New Riders Games, Berkeley CA, (2005)
9. Eladhari, M. and Lindley, C.: Story Construction and Expressive Agents in Virtual Game Worlds. In: Proceedings of the Other Players Conference, Copenhagen, Denmark (2004)
10. Heide-Smith, J.: The Road not Taken - The How's and Why's of Interactive Fiction. URL: http://www.game-research.com (2002)
11. Heide-Smith, J.: Stories from the sandbox. URL: http://www.game-research.com (2003)
12. Hutchison, A.: Analyzing the Performance of Interactive Narrative. Proceedings of DAC 2003, Melbourne, Australia (2003) 63-71
13. Klug, C.: Implementing Stories in Massively Multiplayer Games. URL: http://www.gamasutra.com (2002)
14. Lindley, G.: Story and Narrative Structures in Computer Games. In: Bushoff, B. (Ed.): Developing Interactive Narrative Content, High Text, Munich (2005)
15. Littlejohn, R.: Adapting the Tools of Drama to Interactive Storytelling. URL: http://www.gamasutra.com/features/20010914/littlejohn_01.htm (2001)
16. Mateas, M. 2003: Expressive AI: Games and Artificial Intelligence. DiGRA Level Up, Utrecht, Holland (2003)
17. Murray, J. H.: Hamlet on the Holodeck – The Future of Narrative in Cyberspace. The MIT Press, Cambridge, UK (1997)
18. Ryan, M.-L., Possible Worlds, Artificial Intelligence, and Narrative Theory. Indiana University Press, Bloomington, IN (1992)
19. Ryan, M.-L.: Narrative as Virtual Reality: Immersion and Interactivity in Literature and Electronic Media. John Hopkins University Press, Baltimore, MY (2003)
20. Tosca, S.: Reading Resident Evil-Code Veronica X. Proceedings of the 2003 DAC Conference, Melbourne, Australia (2003)
21. Trappl, R., Petta, P. (Eds.): Creating Personalities for Synthetic Actors: Towards Autonomous Personality Agents. Springer-Verlag, Berlin (1997)
22. Tychsen, A.: Enhancing MMOG world design with believability – Utilizing natural science principles and methods in MMOGs. Macquarie University Department of Computing Report No. C/IR06-02 (2006).

Mixed Reality Installation 'Gulliver's World': Interactive Content Creation in Nonlinear Exhibition Design

Christopher Lindinger[1], Roland Haring[1], Horst Hörtner[1], Daniela Kuka[1], and Hirokazu Kato[2]

[1] Ars Electronica Center Linz Museumsgesellschaft mbH, Ars Electronica Futurelab, Hauptstr. 2-4, 4040 Linz, Austria
{christopher.lindinger, roland.haring, horst.hoertner, daniela.kuka}@aec.at

[2] Osaka University, Machikaneyama 1-3, Toyonaka 560-8531 Japan
kato@sys.es.osaka-u.ac.jp

Abstract. 'Gulliver's World' is a Multi User Mixed Reality Environment that is part of the Ars Electronica Center Exhibition in Linz/Austria. In a public laboratory situation, the installation functions simultaneously as interactive edutainment platform as well as flexible infrastructure for the expansion of mixed reality environments via innovations in information and communication technology and media art. The installation is characterized by a nonlinear exhibition concept at the nexus of theater, digital film production and game development. At seven workstations, people of all age groups range along the reality-virtuality continuum while collaboratively creating 3D-worlds. As research project, 'Gulliver's World' features multilevel infrastructure with exemplary content: The latest insights and models to emerge from HCI research, concepts of mixed reality and virtual environments and their supporting technology are brought together and developed further. They are assembled on a multimedial platform that enables scientific development to dovetail with an educational application that is demonstrated in this paper.

Keywords: Mixed Reality, Collaborative Environment, Nonlinear Exhibition, Reality-Virtuality-Continuum, Edutainment, Haptic Interfaces.

1 Introduction

The task of designing 21st-century learning laboratories and spaces that provide a setting for futuristic experiences calls for new approaches to configuring the interface of, on one hand, digital information and simulation technologies and, on the other hand, concepts for mediating users' encounters with complex, network-linked content. In this paper, we introduce 'Gulliver's World' – a multi user mixed reality installation that is based on several conceptual approaches. Prime emphasis was placed on combining an exhibition project with a research project in a public laboratory situation. The exhibition project is characterized by a highly specific exhibition dramaturgy concept designed to achieve a nonlinear mode of mediating its content. With seven workstations on the basis of several physical-based user interfaces, 'Gulliver's World' serves as a multimedial realm of human interaction in

S. Göbel, R. Malkewitz, and I. Iurgel (Eds.): TIDSE 2006, LNCS 4326, pp. 312 – 323, 2006.

and with a virtual environment and enables users to experience and experiment with different strata of digital media production in a playful way – e.g., techniques used in contemporary filmmaking and computer game development. Thus, users in all age-groups – regardless of their previous experience with computer technology and virtual reality – can experience the interweaving of material and virtual worlds and explore it in creative ways. As heterogeneous but consistent interactive medium at the nexus of theater, digital film production and game environment, 'Gulliver's World' lets users get creative with their hand as stage designer, prop man, director, actor and spectator.

As research project, 'Gulliver's World' features multilevel infrastructure with exemplary content: The latest insights and models to emerge from HCI research, concepts of mixed reality and virtual environments and their supporting technology are brought together and developed further. One focus is the application of interaction metaphors that support a physical-based access to virtual worlds.

2 Related Work and Genesis

The presentation of 'Hidden Worlds' [1] at the 2002 Ars Electronica Festival was the first permanent exhibition based on mixed reality technology in the Ars Electronica Center (Museum of the Future). In 2003, the Ars Electronica Futurelab collaborated with Prof. Hirokazu Kato (Osaka University, Japan) to expand research focusing on this field and to develop 'Gulliver's Box' [2] - likewise a multi-user, mixed reality system - for the 2003 Ars Electronica Center exhibition. As an experimental platform, 'Gulliver's Box' served from its very inception as a means of testing new interfaces and approaches to interaction in a lab setting and as a museum exhibit being used by members of the public. The infrastructure offers artists new opportunities to convey audiovisual information, and one that ought to encourage creatives in every discipline to work with these new approaches. Performances by dancers, singers or actors can be recorded, transferred to avatars, and enhanced with any kind of computer animation. The application on display in the Ars Electronica Center also provided visitors with the opportunity to customize recordings of their own actions and subsequently to undertake a very special process of self-reflection. Portions of the installation are, in turn, reminiscent of elements of the theater. These include a stage with a set, actors and a framework plot. The scene consists of animated characters, pre-produced footage and shots of the visitors that appear by means of head mounted displays on the stage—in this case, a table. The shots are made possible by the "3DLive" system [3] developed by Cheok that computer-generates a 3-D sequence out of numerous video images.

'Gulliver's World' drew upon the conceptual approach, the technological developments and the insights regarding usability in an exhibition context gleaned from the 'Gulliver's Box' project. The installation was expanded to include multiple, interconnected media-technological levels and, above all, an open content creation concept. This meant that users at 'Gulliver's World''s seven stations would no longer have to content themselves with preset environments and prescribed characters; instead, they themselves could design, cast, script and direct the artificial world including its features and inhabitants. Users can create and manipulate social behavioural micro stories and landscape transformations in a world that is following the matter of the novel by Jonathan Swift (cf. 4.2).

In the scope of the Ars Electronica Festival 2006, the mixed reality environment was amplified with a more AI Module. ‘City Puzzle’ is an expanded spin-off of ‘Gulliver’s World’. Parts of the enhancement still are in the development phase. An interactive simulation environment visualizes technological approaches of city planning and architecting and uses a simple urban planning model. A modular software concept has been written in order to assure permanent adaptability for the installation. The ‘City Puzzle’ application features additional interaction principles (vibration sensors, wind wheel sensory) and deals with a different approach of interactive content creation.

3 Composition of the Exhibition

The ‘Gulliver’s World’ installation (fig. 1) comprises five editing stations for the creation of the dynamic content: Modeling Table (3D Scans), Extruder (extrusion objects), World Editor (Worlds), Character Editor (Character Models) and Greenbox (2dLive Video Recodings). The core of each station is composed of intuitive editors with which users can create, select and arrange the contents of the World. The AI Module behind ‘Gulliver’s World’ deliver the synchronized data for the dynamic

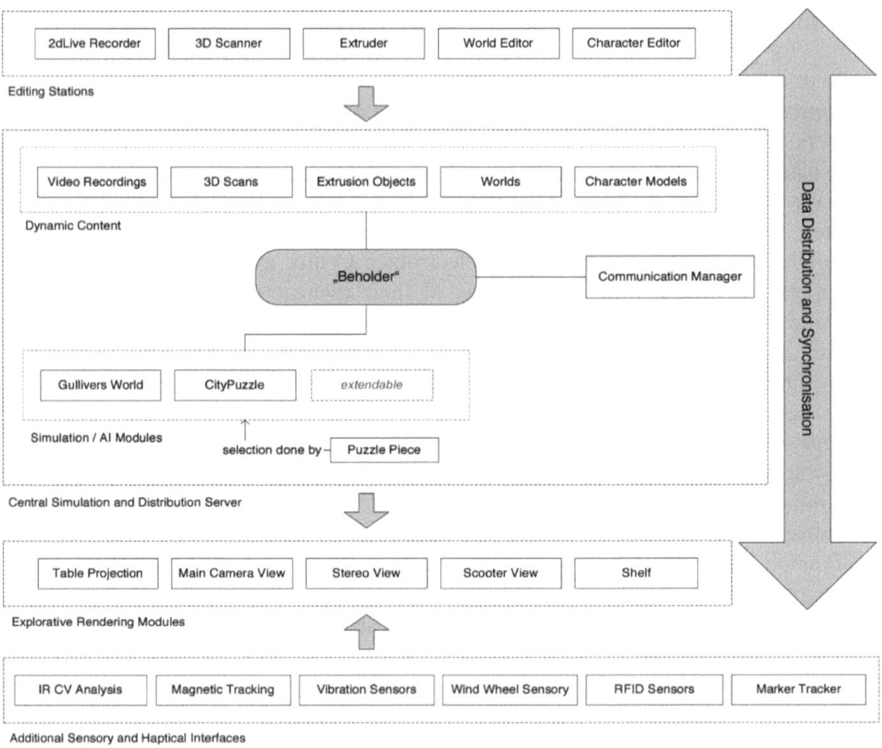

Fig. 1. Installation Overview

play that is projected at the *Gulliver's World Stage* (table projection, main camera view) and the *Virtual Expedition* (stereo view, scooter view only for 'City Puzzle', shelf).

3.1 3D-Modell Creation

Modeling Table

Consisting of a workbench complete with plastiline modeling clay (fig. 2), a photo chamber featuring a rotating stage and a 3D scanner, the Modeling Table station shows one possibility of directly transforming material objects into their virtual counterparts. At this station, objects are created by means of augmented virtuality. Real modeled objects are photographed from twelve different perspectives. The resulting texture is then transferred to a 3D model (3D scanner). RFID tags (hidden in transparent object data carriers) store the related database code under which the 3D data is saved. The data can be read again at other interfaces elsewhere on the installation.

Fig. 2. Modeling Table. 3D models from plastiline modeling clay.

Fig. 3. Extruder. 3D models from graphical inputs.

Extruder

Users can extrude three-dimensional objects from graphic inputs on a VR Flipchart by drawing simple lines on it (fig. 3). The approach to creating virtual objects by means of classical cultural techniques here is transferred due to a typical flipchart design. Users draw a number of points on the flipchart, which are then automatically linked with one another. When the pen is moved manually, ultrasound sensors track its position. It is necessary to draw half the silhouette of the mentally conceived image, which is then rotated around an axis of reflection, which is to the left of the drawing. When the silhouette is turned 360°, additional points appear that are necessary for computing the 3D object and saving it to memory.

3.2 Landscape Creation

World Editor

The station is the workshop for the stage set. A globe-like ball with a diameter of 110 cm serves as the rotatable carrier of the landscape image, which is projected onto the ball in the correct perspective (undistorted). The interface between the user's activity and the virtual landscape design has been conceived as a crossover combining the form of conventional drawing utensils and the function of digital input devices and consists of four brushes (with paint pots) and twelve stamps (with inkpads) mounted on a ring around the globe (fig. 4).

Fig. 4. Brushes and stamps as interfaces for the creation of virtual land scapes

Fig. 5. Puzzle pieces as storage media for virtual land scapes

Thus, images and symbols derived from the real world are translated into a virtual image by means of classic cultural techniques. Topographic structures can be selected, landscape textures painted and fixed as well as self-created objects added to this mixed-reality environment. The objects are positioned on the globe with the aid of a magnet-tracking system. The users' creations are added to the basic textures, so that the modified landscapes are transported from the mixed-reality station *World Editor* to the virtual environment of *Gulliver's World Stage.* Puzzle pieces, which can be placed in a specially created indent, serve as symbolic carriers of the stage setup (fig. 5) - identified by RFID.

3.3 Character Creation

Character Editor

The station consists of displays, transparent boxes and no-touch sensors (fig.6). Here, virtual characters (avatars) are selected and endowed with abilities, characteristics and moods. This is performed manually with touchless capacitive sensors. Users have at their disposal a set of designs for action figures, decorative elements and capabilities with which they can be endowed, all of which are freely combinable (fig. 7). This is the way in which the characters in animated films and computer games are created too. The created avatars are located in real Perspex boxes whose content disappears in a seemingly mysterious manner after it has been removed from the storage room and reappears only on the projection surface of *Gulliver's World Stage*. A camera tracking system using optical markers identifies both the box on the stage and its position.

Fig. 6. No-touch sensors allow to manipulate virtual characters

Fig. 7. Combinable Characters

Greenbox

Using this station, the visitor can participate as an avatar in the virtual stage action. The person is situated in a green-walled space (open at the front). With a camera (juxtaposed to the *Greenbox*) the person is recorded at one position only and filtered out in a chroma key process. With this method, body language can be used to purposefully create moods and define roles of the virtual protagonist being created here by performing specific kinds of movements. Therefore, a simple movement analysis derives behavioral patterns from attributed movement patterns: An emotion-identification program generates a motion history that metaphorically serves as indicator for a specific mood. A graph, which is generated from deviations in the pixels in two frames, triggers the emotion recognition function and interprets rapid jerky movements as aggression (negative) and slow, gentle movements as jovial behaviour (positive).[1] A projection screen set up next to the *Greenbox* displays the sequences and their transformation into a virtual character. The body images can be fed visually into the virtual world via a Plexiglas box that metaphorically serves as the data storage and transportation medium.

3.4 The 3D-World's Arrangement and Manipulation

At the workstations *Gulliver's World Stage* and *Virtual Expedition*, the collaboratively created 3D-Worlds become visible in life-size. Different interfaces enable the user to navigate through and manipulate the virtual arrangement.

[1] For Gulliver's World, the principles of the emotion-interpretation software are restricted to two kinds of motion analysis. The goal was not developing a validated emotion-recognition but to exemplify the operating mode and the scopes for designing and directing virtual scenes using simple forms of emotion identification.

Gulliver's World Stage

Here, the results of the work in the previous stations are brought together at a round table that forms part of the interface for arranging and manipulating the scenarios. The table upon which a landscape image is projected provides ample work space and has a scooped-out area in the middle in the shape of a jigsaw puzzle piece. The world that has been arranged is projected in the visual style of a 3D animation on a big screen (fig. 8).

Fig. 8. Virtual Characters at the Gulliver's World stage placed by Perspex boxes

Fig. 9. Video Recordings from the Greenbox at the Gulliver's World Stage

The digital play consists of the landscape (designed on the *World Editor* station), which supplies the set and the object-like components of the world (puzzle pieces), the animated characters from the *Character Editor*, and the *Greenbox* (Perspex boxes) (fig. 9). The displayed section can be selected and scaled by moving a hand-held camera. The camera tracking system identifies the position of the boxes and the relationship to the actors to one another and to their environment. Interventions, e.g. by moving the figures, adding new objects and characters or switching between different landscape designs, generate ever-new configurations, demonstrating the basic character of the installation as a whole, as the processes involved in making a virtual environment (as in the development of the game, for example) are rendered visible.

Virtual Expedition

Whereas *Gulliver's World Stage* allows the user to arrange and manipulate events on the stage from the outside by assigning him a superordinate position from which he can intervene in the scenario, the *Virtual Expedition* completely dissolves the transition between material and virtual reality. The user immerses himself – physically – in the virtually created environment by assuming the identity of a character in the *Character Editor.* The station essentially consists of a display surface for stereoscopic projections, a camera for image recognition purposes, as well as an illuminated quadrant positioned across from the projection wall, which captures the dark-light contrast between the user and the background for use in the image recognition process recognition (cf. the Sony Eye Toy). The carrier is identified in the silhouette as a bone structure, which allows the system to identify gestures. This way, users can interactively experience, influence and manipulate the dynamic world. To navigate in Virtual Expedition, the user intuitively steers via simple arm movements - just like in imaginary flight.

3.5 Metaphorical Interlinkage of the Installation Components

The links that connect up the installation's components are likewise metaphors that provide mobility for the content produced at the individual stations. The world created at the *World Editor* is saved to a mobile data storage medium whose form and function correspond to a jigsaw puzzle piece that, as "the world's last missing piece," is placed into the matching space at the *Gulliver's World Stage*. The media to which the object data are stored, featuring a design derived from a laboratory, combine simplicity and fascination in one. 3D data are transportable via a transparent disk featuring a knob-like handle, and the objects can be read out from a simple-to-use plug-in slot. The Plexiglas boxes in which the virtual characters are transported between the stations are imitations of a transparent container that might actually serve to accommodate such an action figure and from which it can subsequently be "unleashed" by opening the container's hatch on the *Gulliver's World Stage*.

4 Exhibition Dramaturgy

The principle of interactive content creation in 'Gulliver's World' is to independently work with different stations in an exhibition space and to collaboratively bring the results together on a central stage. Nevertheless, *Gulliver's World Stage* is not like the last element of a chain but the center of networked stations from which virtual requisites can be applied, tested and modified in every phase of the experience. The approach to breaking the rules of successive storytelling fathoms the boundaries of resigning from obvious interrelationships and exploiting complexity as a method. The secret of nonlinear exhibition design in 'Gulliver's World' lies in the discovery of individual paths through the complexity and this way in the afforded performative learning process. The story to recognize is how to get to the play, not the play itself. This way, 'Gulliver's World' is an installation to make the content to be learned a part of the mediation concept itself. An advanced approach has been realized with the 2006 application 'City Puzzle' that additionally leads to an end with the urban balance of a (virtual) city model.

4.1 Nonlinear Exhibition Approach

The exhibition concept takes advantage of insights about how people learn new things and partake of new situations, and directly translates them into action: "In contrast to the cinema, where the viewer relaxes in a comfortable seat and views a series of images and plot devices passing before him, the visitor to an exhibition moves through a space in which everything is motionless. By the very act of proceeding through it, he produces a sequence of alternating scenes. An exhibition designer has to take this into account. [...] But if an exhibition is to be designed in a way that takes these points into consideration, then it has to be kept in mind that the visitor also occasionally remains stationary, that he turns and retraces his steps and, thus, that the dramatic performance has to be effective from many different points of view." [4] Numerous exhibitions work with linear structures and programs so that the visitor proceeds from one installation to the next and follows the components of the exhibition in a linear learning process. If the model of the linear exhibition does indeed correspond at first glance to Nathan Shedroff's hypothesis that "knowledge builds [...] upon knowledge" and knowledge thus "becomes the basis for acquiring additional knowledge" [5], then it is – essentially – the contrary to that what is meant by a performative learning approach. In line with the performative learning approach, organized constructions are deconstructed and reconstructed in project-oriented tasks in the form of acquired knowledge. That activates the process of understanding complex, dynamic interrelationships. That allows the reorganization of consecutive architectures and dramaturgies and, resulting, the demolition of the self-evident process of successively partaking of exhibited content and replaces this with self-determined, attentive movement on the part of the user. The process of learning the ins and outs of the entire installation is played out in the absence of prescribed paths along which the user must proceed and without hierarchically structured sequences of actions in a universe of information fragments that the user can discover only through the process of action and interaction, and can interconnect into an individual experience. Complexity is applied as a method - in a sort of multidirectional "Easter egg hunt" as basic principle for generating knowledge and experience.

4.2 Interactive Virtual Staging

In interactive storytelling, the linearity of a classic narrative plot is replaced by multilinear brachiations and latent available scenery and plot elements. 'Gulliver's World' - in contrast to computer games - does not proceed towards an objective that is the culmination of a plot that has to be played out interactively. 'Gulliver's World' does not aim to mediate content through the instrumental use of multimedia information and communication technology; rather, these are themselves the content to be mediated in step-by-step fashion. In other words, that which is content in the classic sense -i.e. the interactively developing micro stories based on the novel by Jonathan Swift- is, in 'Gulliver's World', the instrument with which to mediate the actual content: the principle of the installation that is derived from the processes of digital media production. What has been emphasized in the conception and development is *the process* of virtual staging *itself*. This has less to do with what story is told that of how it's told; to a certain extent, the environment *is* the content. In going about this, that which is otherwise unseen is, upon partaking of the performance of the narrative, made visible, as are the techniques that enable this play to be staged.

In 'Gulliver's World', users generate micro stories that are following the experiences of Gulliver in the novel of Jonathan Swift in two cases: On the hand, it's the dimensions and the interplay of scales and relations that remind of the world of giant Brobdingnagians and tiny Lilliputians in "Gulliver's Travels". On the other hand, it's the nexus of reality and fantasy on which the micro stories are built. Virtual characters representing social stereotypes influence the play according to their typical patterns. Thus, micro stories are the specific modes of social interaction and the landscape's changes that are triggered by - for example - the get-together of two different characters.

To take a step further, the AI Module of 'City Puzzle' introduces a superordinate intention to arrange the dynamic content: having identified the ideal combination of content fragments (districts, saved in Perspex boxes), the virtual city play comes up to a level of balance.

5 Interaction Design

The design of the man-machine communication is based on customary cultural techniques and social experience in order to minimize as much as possible the barriers between physical practice (input) and virtual events (output) in the way human users work with media. Using reality-connected interface metaphors like puzzle pieces, brushes, stamps and boxes which motivate to going behind their functions affects a user-independent understanding of the installation because of relying on collective bodies of knowledge and established systems of signs. Thus, the user's explorative way from material into virtual worlds is supported by physical-based interaction principles.

5.1 Along the Reality-Virtuality Continuum

The link connecting the installation's components is the question of where exactly to position the human body within the realm at the intersection of material and virtual reality. As in Milgram's model of how to differentiate between a real and a virtual environment, the path leading through the installation also leads to the realization that real environments and virtual environments "are not to be considered simply as alternatives to each other, but rather as poles lying at opposite ends of a Reality-Virtuality (RV) continuum." [6] 'Gulliver's World' proceeds through this continuum and, in doing so, assumes intermediate positions like augmented reality (as in its precursor, 'Gulliver's Box') and augmented virtuality (*Greenbox*, *Modeling Table*) - subsidiary forms of mixed reality (*World Creator*). Users take as their starting place a real space - the exhibition area with its installation components. The new spaces that users discover finally display varying degrees of immersion until the boundaries between the materiality of the body and the virtuality of the surroundings completely vanish over the course of a Virtual Expedition.

5.2 Physical-Based Interaction Principles

For 'Gulliver's World', we consider the maintenance of the connection to the physical or haptic world -as illustrated, for example, by the ArtDeCom project [7, 8]- as essential for collaborative and constructive learning in practice: "a mixed reality environment as a collaborative and constructive learning space [...] allow children to explore concepts by interaction and with their senses and therefore allow to build and to correct mental models and a deeper understanding of the underlying domain". In concurrence with Winkler, Kritzenberger and Herczeg [8], this is supported to an especially high degree through the use of mixed reality applications: "In order not to separate the learner from their real world and their traditional tools and their senses the alternative approach with a mixed reality environment is used." In designing the workstations used in 'Gulliver's World', the effort has been made to maintain from beginning to end the connection between physical and sensory representation via physical-based interaction principles. Users, here, do *not interact in order to learn*; instead, they *learn while they are interacting*. This way they realize the interlinkage of the stations in a social sphere of creating and learning.

Our thinking here was that taking an approach often used by media artists opens up the possibility of getting computer-supported learning situations away from the desktop terminal and transferring them into a workshop situation in which objects that have a familiar significance in the material world become portals leading to and instruments for use in immaterial worlds.

6 Summary

The approach taken to designing 'Gulliver's World' - as a socio-technical field of experimentation - has established a public laboratory situation for interactive content creation used by people of all age groups. The approach was a prototypical design of an edutainment-based learning in a nonlinear interactive exhibition context. The several stations of 'Gulliver's World' enable to collaboratively create 3D worlds that include self-created 3D models, landscape textures, virtual characters, video sequences. Brought together on a virtual stage, the components merge in micro stories that show small social behavioral and environmental change scenes. The stations feature many different modes of content creation from purely real to purely virtual and enable this tightrope walk due to physical-based interfaces and navigation techniques. The concept was enhanced by a more AI Module called 'City Puzzle'.

7 Further Development and Future Prospects

Both individual components as well as the entire environment are applied a wide range of contexts. The infrastructure and the concept for mediating the encounter with content are being applied in a business context for the simulation of business procedures and to depict production sequences in industrial processes. Currently in planning are applications designed to perform simulations in the auto industry and to turn out scientific visualizations.

References

1. Hidden Worlds. In: Stocker, G., Schöpf, C. (eds): Unplugged – Art as the Scene of Global Conflicts. Ars Electronica 2002. Hatje Cantz, Ostfildern (2002) 406-410
2. Maresch, P., Lindinger, C.: Gulliver's Box. In: Stocker, G., Schöpf, C. (eds): Code – The Language of Our Time. Ars Electronica 2003. Hatje Cantz, Ostfildern (2003) 326-328
3. Prince, S.J.D., Cheok, A.D., Farbiz, F., Williamson, T., Johnson, N., Billinghurst, M., Kato, H.: 3D Live: Real time captured content for mixed reality. In: Proceedings of the IEEE and ACM. International Symposium on Mixed and Augmented Reality. IEEE CS Press, Darmstadt (ISMAR 2002) 7-14
4. Ponti, G.: Mailand 1954. In: Internationale Ausstellungsgestaltung. Haus Neuburg, Zürich (1969)

5. Shedroff, N.: Experience Design. New Riders, Indiana (2001)
6. Milgram, P., Colquhoun Jr., H.: A Taxonomy of Real and Virtual World Display Integration. In: Ohta, Y., Tamura, H. (eds): Mixed Realitiy. Merging Real and Virtual Worlds. Ohmsha, Tokyo & Springer, Wien (1999) 5-30
7. Winkler, T., Kritzenberger, H., Herczeg, M.: Mixed Reality Environments as Collaborative and Constructive Learning Spaces for Elementary School Children. In: Barker, P., Rebelsky, S. (eds): Proceedings of ED-MEDIA 2002, AACE, Norfolk, USA (2002) 1034-1039
8. Winkler, T., Kritzenberger, H., Herczeg, M.: Collaborative and Constructive Learning of Elementary School Children in Experimental Learning Spaces along the Virtuality Continuum. In: In Herczeg, M., Prinz, W., Oberquelle, H. (eds): Mensch & Computer 2002: Vom interaktiven Werkzeug zu kooperativen Arbeits- und Lernwelten. B G Teubner, Stuttgart (2002) 115-124

Navigating by Following Stories

Christian Geiger[1], Volker Paelke[2], and Ivonne Gansen[3]

[1] University of Applied Science Duesseldorf, Josef-Gockeln Str 9, 40474 Düsseldorf
geiger@fh-duesseldorf.de
[2] University of Hannover, IKG, Appelstr. 9a, 30167 Hannover
Volker.Paelke@ikg.uni-hannover.de
[3] University of Applied Science Harz, Friedrichstr 57-59, 38855 Wernigerode
ivonne.gansen@googlemail.com

Abstract. In this paper we present an approach that examines if storytelling techniques can be used to relate navigation instructions and if such a presentation improves retention of instructions. We describe the concept of a system to present geographical information as a sequence of story elements; present an initial prototype and the design of an experiment to evaluate this approach.

1 Introduction

With the proliferation of inexpensive positioning technologies navigation systems are becoming popular not only in vehicles but also for pedestrians. Due to their context of use pedestrian navigation systems place completely different demands on their user interface design than vehicle navigation systems. In vehicle navigation systems a planned route is presented primarily as a sequence of turn-by-turn instructions with distance indication, nowadays often supported by a 2D or 3D map of the immediate environment. Because pedestrians are less restricted in their movement, instructions like "turn left in 234m" can be highly ambiguous, especially as few people are trained to judge distances correctly. Current pedestrian navigation systems therefore rely heavily on maps, using "you are here" symbols and route overlays to provide navigation information. Such systems still place high cognitive demands on their users in order to translate the information provided in the map into navigation actions. In practice users therefore have to refer frequently to the navigation device to check their actions against their intentions. In many situations it would be preferable (both for convenience and security) if a significant portion of the route could be memorized (and followed) without the need for constant interaction with the navigation device.

The generation of route descriptions appropriate for pedestrians is therefore an area of active research. Previous research has found that route descriptions can be improved significantly if landmarks (significant objects) are included in addition to turn instructions. However, even with landmarks longer sequences of navigation instructions remain hard to memorize. In the "Kugerou" system we aim to examine firstly if storytelling techniques can be used to relate navigation instructions and secondly if such a presentation improves retention of instructions.

S. Göbel, R. Malkewitz, and I. Iurgel (Eds.): TIDSE 2006, LNCS 4326, pp. 324–333, 2006.

2 Related Work

Similar to car navigation, pedestrian navigation mainly uses maps combined with positioning and routing information to represent geographical knowledge. The different context of use in pedestrian navigation suggests that landmarks are well suited to identify important places of a route [9]. Experiments show that landmarks in route descriptions increase the perceived quality of maps [10]. Elias et al conclude that landmarks represent a central concept in successful route descriptions for pedestrians [2]. However, it is still difficult for most users to memorize geographical information presented in maps.

Navigational assistants on mobile devices have been implemented in many commercial projects and research prototypes. The evolution of mobile phones and PDAs allows to employ high bandwidth data transmission and exact localization techniques. Many devices are powerful enough to allow an advanced multimedia representation of geographical information, e. g., using animated 2D graphics, interactive 3D or video streaming. Baus et al presented a representative survey and comparison of map based mobile guides with references to a number of relevant projects including Tell-Maris, lol@, GUIDE, or DeepMap [13].

The combination of entertainment technology, mobile computing, and geographical information processing is not new and many approaches combine techniques from these domains. Prominent application domains are ubiquitous games, pervasive games, or trans-reality gaming experiences. Ubiquitous gaming takes advantage of ubiquitous computing environments that are concerned with embedding 'computer intelligence' in the user's environment. Sometimes this game type is also referred to as 'pervasive gaming' [14]. The integrated project on pervasive gaming is a large European project that develops new gaming experiences by tightly interweaving physical and virtual elements from our everyday life and by using references to the user's environment [15]. Craig Lindley coins the term 'trans-reality gaming' for a game type that provides fluid movement of the game experience through various physical and virtual stages [14].

Cartwright considers entertainment technologies as very helpful to deliver geographical information more efficiently. New users, who are experienced with web and game technologies, can be made 'geographically aware' of map based information. Cartright argues that the 'Nintendo generation' uses maps with a different set of skill and usually is first confronted with geographical information access in computer games. First informal experiments suggest that game like interfaces can improve the way new users interact with geographical information spaces. Geographical storytelling can thus become a new paradigm for GIS applications [4].

However, most recent projects use storytelling techniques to augment geographical information, e.g., to give more information about historic sites, tourist attraction, entertainment, etc. These projects often focus on the use of augmented reality for presenting geographical data and additional information. TouringMachine [5] and early work of Bruce Thomas [6] showed how pedestrian navigation can benefit from mobile computing and AR technology. Large projects like GEIST demonstrate the use of storytelling techniques in the context of tourist guide applications [7].

3 The Concept of "Kugerou"

Our concept is inspired by the system of "songlines" across the Australian continent, as popularized by the author Bruce Chatwin [1]. Songlines are part of the aboriginal Australian creation myth of the dreamtime. In the aboriginal creation myth the ancestors have walked across the earth and have sung everything in it into being. Thus each place has its own creation story in the form of a song. The songlines form a system of interconnected paths across the Australian continent that corresponds to the routes taken by the ancestors. Songs can be viewed as route descriptions with the strophes of a song following the linear structure of one of these paths. Strophes of the song are based on places, e.g. landscape features like rocks, mountains, springs, groups of trees, crossroads etc. Using such songs as their guidance aboriginal people can follow these songlines during their great ceremonial journeys, the so called walkabouts. From the navigation perspective the system of songlines can thus be thought of as a map with interconnected routes that is passed on from generation to generation in the oral form of songs. In the "Kugerou" system we aim to use short memorable stories as route descriptions.

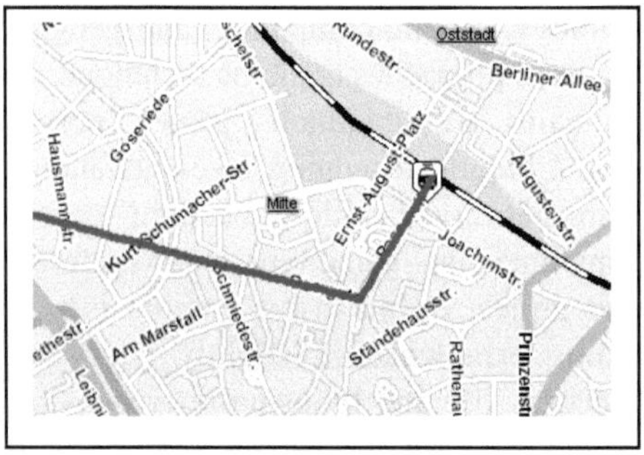

Geographical information

Landmark: H&M shop
Street name: Georgstrasse
Action: turn right
Distance: medium
Procedural instruction: After 260 meter at the H&M, shop turn right into the street Georgstraße

Story elements

Actors/objects: Fridolin (main actor); Georg, the mouse; a hat
Action: Georg meets Fridolin, gives him his hat and disappears to the right
Media: H&M logo (image), mouse/fridolin (animated 2D graphics), sound

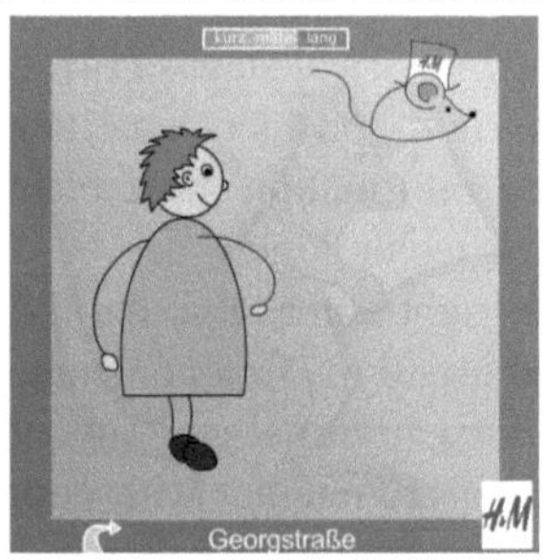

Fig. 1. Geographical Information and Illustration of a "Kugerou" Story for a Decision Point

The hypothesis is that stories related to the sequence of places that a user encounters when following a route can be used as memorable descriptions of it. The use of a story instead of a map reduces complexity for the user. While the data space of a map contains the complete network of possible routes and thus easily overwhelms the memory capacity of a user, the linear path of a route and the corresponding linear experience of following it contain far less information and should thus be easier memorize. By mapping this experience to a similarly linear story taking place at the decision points along a path we aim to create a mental representation of the route that is easier to memorize than both the complete map and abstract route descriptions. This approach can thus be thought of as the inverse of the normal location based story telling scenario. General story elements correspond to story based route descriptions: a route is a story, a decision point / landmark location is a scene, a navigation related action is a turn action, and real and virtual objects and agents in a route description refer to actors and items in a story.

Following [8], we use position information, route actions, landmarks and distances to specify critical points on a route and encode this in a data structure. A geographical information tuple consist of a landmark, a street/place name, a direction and the distance to the decision point. Instances of an information tuple for a given decision point are based on previous and following points calculated for a navigation route. For example, the generation of action values and distance values assumes the correct position and direction of the user during navigation. Additionally we store storytelling related information in a second data structure. A story tuple consists of the main actor, a set of other actors / objects, set of actions, and possible user interactions. A typical example taken from our first prototype is illustrated in figure 1.

We currently evaluate two alternative approaches to define a "Kugerou" story. In the first approach we use noncoherent scenes for each decision point. The main actor is confronted with an event at each point and new actors, objects and actions are introduced at each scene. This approach is more suitable for an automatic story generation but it may be harder to memorize the sequence of events. The second approach presents a coherent story line combining different scenes. The background story is a kidnapping / theft crime and the detective chases the suspect to different places. This follows ideas of the prominent computer game "Where in the world is Carmen Sandiego" and allows generating scenes based of geographic information. The initial prototype described in this paper only used the non-coherent story version.

Each decision point follows a simple structure of introduction, interaction, and disappearance. The main actor meets other actors/objects, interacts with them and finally disappears in a certain direction. The selection of other actors/objects and the actions performed by actors follows the concept of a minimally non-intuitive narratives as proposed Norenzayam [3]. In each scene we select an unusual aspect (object, actor or behaviour) combined with an otherwise very usual situation. We also define a number of relations between story elements and geographical information in each scene. This should help to better memorize the scene.

There are a number of ways to connect geographical information and the story content. Actor names and objects can be chosen with regards to geographical information, i.e. the mouse is called "Georg" which gives a reference to the street name "Georgstrasse". Sometime actors/objects are chosen in a similar way (apples are picked up in the Appelstraße) or we use phonetic similarities like yelling ("brüllen") statues in the "Brühlstraße". The direction described in the geographical information tuple is represented in the last action in each scene. For example, if the user should turn right at the H&M Shop in the Georgstraße, the actors in the scene disappear to the right. At the beginning of the story a short audio comment explains the scene by giving a summary of what will happen. After the story two summaries are presented.

All scenes are presented in a table like structure with the main geographical information and story elements. A map-like summary is represented that visualizes story elements and landmarks in a geographical context. The system supports user interaction. Users can switch forth and back between scenes. The final version will also enable the user to control the story but due to the simple linear storyline we only provide a limited set of interaction techniques, e. g. clicking at the correct objects, landmarks and directions. In order to test our general hypothesis that a story can be used as a route description the "Kugerou" system implements a technical test infrastructure.

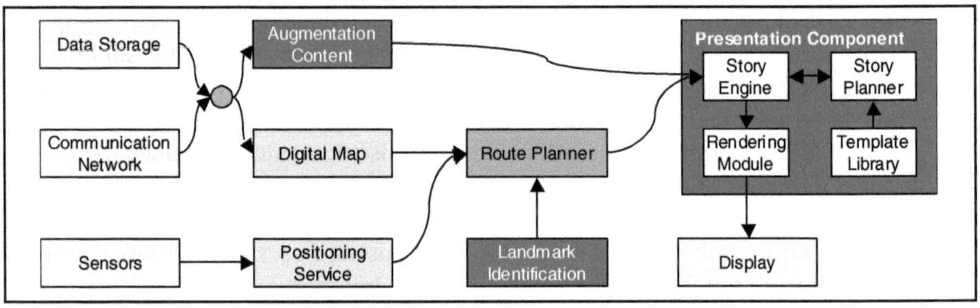

Fig. 2. Architecture of the "Kugerou" System

The principle structure of the system (figure 2) is similar to conventional navigation systems, with modifications and extensions shown in dark grey. In the first step a digital map is used by the route planner to generate a route, consisting of segments and decision points that connect them, e.g. turning instructions. In the second step landmarks along the generated route are identified using a modified ID3 data mining algorithm that operates on an object database based on cadastral data. It identifies objects with unique features that could serve as landmarks. A digital surface map (DSM) is then used to ensure the visibility of the identified potential landmarks from the user's direction of approach. Objects with limited visibility are discarded at this step. For details of the landmark identification process, see [12]. Both the landmarks and the route itself are then passed on to the presentation component. The presentation component then uses a story planner to generate a story based route description from this data. For our initial prototype we use an existing route planning systems for offline generation of the route and landmarks that is then transferred to the mobile navigation device, a PDA. Only the presentation component is currently implemented on the PDA for interactive mobile use. While interactive story generation in general is a very challenging research problem, the task in our system is significantly simpler as the stories are typically short, non-branching and are restricted to motion related storylines. In our system design we use a very simple mechanism based on pre-defined templates for the overall story structure. For each decision point a suitable story template is selected from a library, according to the instructions provided by the route planner. The template for the information tuple is then completed with pre-authored multimedia content according to the identified landmark and the turn instructions. Individual scene descriptions for decision points with the corresponding actors are stored in the augmentation content database. According to the turn instructions provided by the route planner the story planner thus identifies a suitable template and composites the corresponding scene elements accordingly. The resulting story can then be presented to the user by a story engine, using standard media formats and players for output. MobEE is a story engine for mobile entertainment computing that supports run-time presentation of content on a wide variety of mobile hardware platforms by using device-independent story structures [11]. An advantage of MobEE is the possibility to use standard tools for media creation and presentation within the system. The device-independent representation of the story structure in MobEE is implemented by hierarchical finite-state automatons that communicate by a common variable pool. This hierarchical structure is well suited to support the composition of stories from predefined elements as in our prototype. The described system structure is currently implemented as part of a thesis project. A concept for an automatic selection of story elements is also under development [16]. The selection process will be guided by a classification of landmarks, user preferences and meta-information about street names, etc. Due to its preliminary stage this is beyond the scope of this paper.

4 Initial Prototype and Evaluation

The initial prototype is intended to validate the overall viability of the "Kugerou" approach in a limited test area. As the test area we have chosen a section of the city of Hannover (Germany) for which baseline data is available from existing conventional and landmark-based pedestrian navigation systems against which the approach can be compared. We built storyboards for several scenes and manually selected some "unusual" story elements in each scene (minimally counterintuitive narrative). We provide a number of references between geographical information like names of landmarks, street names, etc and story elements like actors, objects or actions. We choose a reduced cartoon style for a multimedia representation because we found that this better supports a representation on PDA and mobile phone displays with a limited resolution (e.g. QVGA). It is easier to generate a reduced abstract illustration from data and the results look better than a photorealistic look or a hybrid mixture of photographic images and 2D animation styles. The presentation component of the initial prototype used Adobe Flash as front-end because it supports a very quick prototyping. The navigation route consists of seven decision points including start and goal (see fig. 4, bottom left image). We selected the following six minimally counterintuitive examples for the points (without goal):

Table 1. Minimally Counterintuitive Examples and Reference to Geographical Data

Minimally Counterintuitive Example	Landmark	Street name	Reference (Story Element – Geographical Element)
Main character F. rides on the roof of a locomotive	Karstadt shop	Bahnhofstraße (central station)	Locomotive – central station
F. meets Georg, the mouse with a H&M hat	H&M shop	Georgstrasse	Name of mouse – street, H&M hat – H&M shop
F. jumps from a burning tree but does not get hurt due to his health insurance	Health insurance building "Allianz"	Otto-Brenner-Strasse (burning=brennen)	Burning tree – Otto Brenner (phonetic similarities) Health insurance building

Table 1. *(Continued)*

F. meets yelling stone Statues that guide him	Stone statues	Brühlstraße (yelling=brüllen)	Yelling statues – street name (phonetic similarities)
F. is a tailor with a scissor and gets away from a crocodile	University building	Schneiderberg (tailor=Schneider)	Scissors/tailor – street name (phonetic similarities)
F. eats apples lying on the street		Appelstraße	Apples – street name (phonetic similarities)

The development of the „Kugerou" prototype was guided by frequent informal pilot evaluations. For these evaluations a route through the inner city of Hannover (Germany) was selected for which data and experiences with conventional navigation systems as well as landmark based systems specifically designed for pedestrian navigation are available as a baseline. Story-based descriptions were derived for this route, corresponding to different presentation templates, e.g. including different combinations of story-elements, landmarks, audio-snippets etc. and then evaluated with users. Figure 3 gives an overview of different parts of the prototype.

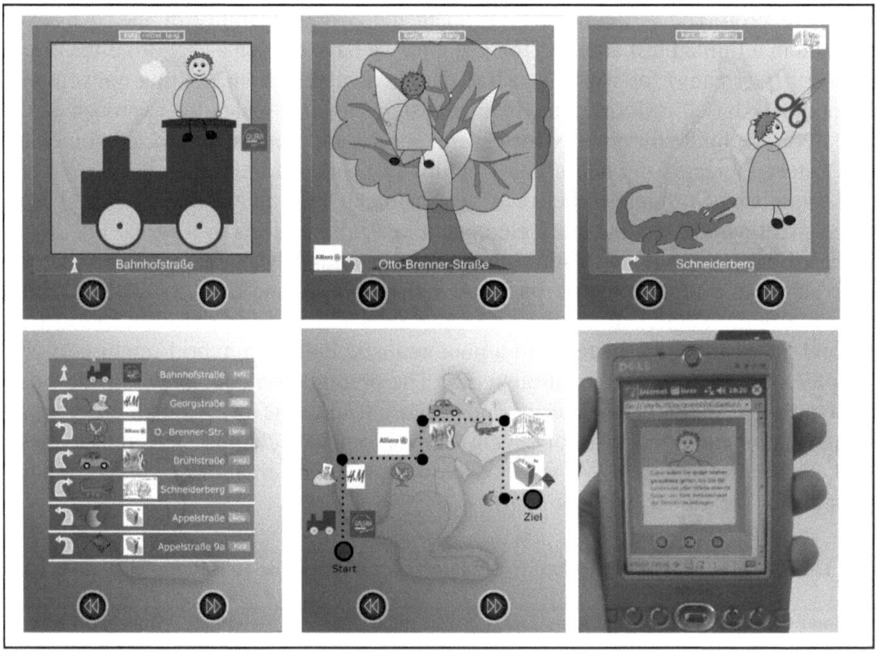

Fig. 3. Scenes from the "Kugerou" Prototype

The test approach was two-fold. The primary objective in the initial development phase was to validate that story-based descriptions aid the recall of route descriptions of significant length. The secondary objective was to ensure that our story-based approach produces viable descriptions for a concrete route. To simplify the test approach a pure recall test was used for the majority of test-users that they could complete using a PC at an arbitrary location. For this purpose a between-subject design was chosen in which users were provided either with the story-based route description or a description using conventional guidance instructions plus landmarks. In the test scenario users were asked to envision that they were travelling to Hannover by train and planning to walk to a specific university building approximately three kilometres from the station.

The instructions then asked the users to familiarize themselves with the route description (either story-based or conventional) during a five to ten minute period. Following this users had to perform a task unrelated to navigation, namely to search for a train connection, to simulate some distraction from the recall task after arrival. Users were then asked to write down what they recalled from the route description. Finally, users were asked to evaluate this against the true description and asked for further feedback on different aspects of the system. The key benefit of this approach is that it allows conducting frequent and fast evaluations with user who are unfamiliar with the real environment to guide the development process. During the iterative development of the initial prototype 22 participants were asked for feedback on different aspects of the system, with 12 completed overall evaluations and the memory recall task.

Due to the early stage of the initial prototype and the evaluation design phase no statistical significant performance of a story-based navigation was tested. The overall performance for the recall test of both groups (each with six participants) was similar, the group that tested the story-based presentation was slightly better. We found that four users with computer / media experience tend to better memorize the route if it was presented in a story-line format. On the other hand, the other two inexperienced users had problems with this type of presentation. Five of six users report that they enjoyed the multimedia presentation but two complained that it was at first difficult to accept an "unserious" story description as aid to memorize a navigation route. But all successful participants agreed that once they accepted this way of information representation, it was easy to memorize the route.

However, this test approach does not provide a real check for the suitability of the description for navigation purposes in a real urban environment. Therefore, a second test approach was used in which the suitability of the description was evaluated. Here both an expert critiquing approach was used in which six test-users who are familiar with the area were asked to critique the route description against there real-world experiences and three unfamiliar users were asked to check the use of the system in practice. Due to the prototypical state of the "Kugerou" system we did not yet conduct a formal experiment to verify our hypothesis and selected only a small number of participants. Thus, the results of this pre-test are only informal and used to refine the system and give advices for the design of the final evaluation. The six expert reviews confirmed that the idea of using stories to memorize route descriptions is very suitable for pedestrian navigation. In particular, three experts suggest that special target groups like children or older persons may benefit from this representation. However, this idea requires more research on target specific representations and a detailed evaluation. We asked three participants to check the system in practice. They reported that they found their way very easily using the story-based representation. Even if it was not possible to memorize the complete information tuple for a navigation point, landmarks or street names detected on the route helped to recall the complete information tuple. One participant reported that he usually has many problems with conventional navigation routes and was surprised the he found the correct route without any errors.

The results of these informal pre-test encouraged us to continue the design of the system and to finalize the design of a formal experiment. But we are aware that the current results can not yet be generalized to make valid conclusion on the hypothesis that a story-based description is better suited to memorize navigation routes.

5 Conclusion and Outlook

The initial results seem to warrant further investigation of the "Kugerou" concept. Obviously the development of stories for navigation purposes is still in very early stages. After a thorough test of the initial prototype several research directions seem worth pursuing to us, including:

- The systematic examination the design space of story designs (and the corresponding implications on story generation) for navigation systems. This includes an extension of the possible environment for navigation from inner-cityscapes to a wide variety of possible environments.
- The creation and implementation of different story options. The extension of the system to larger areas and more diverse content will probably require a more sophisticated story generation and management system. Existing storytelling systems should be evaluated to judge their suitability for this application context.
- The integration of route planning into the mobile system as well as dedicated authoring tools to create scene descriptions and possibly new story templates must be considered to make the inclusion of larger areas possible as a prerequisite for realistic use.

From our initial experience we think that the use of stories is an interesting and potentially relevant application area of virtual storytelling techniques. It is obvious that our initial experiments related here is only a first step in this direction, posing many new questions. The limited scope and simple structure of the required stories make this domain an interesting field for experimentation. As an example, a simplistic generator often produces absurd stories. It is however unclear if this is really problematic as it is not obvious whether users prefer simple, coherent, sense-making stories. From a mnemonic perspective absurd stories may even be preferable to some users.

Acknowledgments

We would like to thank Birgit Elias (University of Hannover) for providing the baseline navigation system, the landmark identification component and in-depth advice on pedestrian navigation. Holger Reckter and Martin Kreyßig (University of Applied Science Harz) helped us to design the look of the representation, the interface and the evaluation experiments. We would also like to thank all participants in the pre-tests.

References

1. Chatwin, B.: The Songlines, Macmillan Publishers Ltd, 1987.
2. Elias, B., Paelke, V., & Kuhnt, S.: Kartographische Visualisierung von Landmarken, in: "Aktuelle Entwicklungen in Geoinformation und Visualisierung, GEOVIS 2006, 5./6. April 2006, Potsdam", Kartographische Schriften Band 10, Kirschbaum Verlag, 2006.
3. Norenzayan, A., Atran, S., Faulkner, J., and Schaller, M. (2006): Memory and Mystery: The Cultural Selection of Minimally Counterintuitive Narratives. Cognitive Science 30 (2006), pp. 531-553.
4. Cartwright, W.E., 2004, "Using the web for focused geographical storytelling via gameplay", UPIMap 2004, The First international Joint Workshop on Ubiquitous, Pervasive and Internet Mapping, Tokyo, Japan: International Cartographic Association Commission on Ubiquitous Cartography, pp. 89 - 109.
5. Feiner, S., MacIntyre, B., and Seligmann, D. Knowledge-based augmented reality. Communications of the ACM, 36(7):53–62, July 1993.
6. Thomas, B.H., Demczuk, V., Piekarski, W., Hepworth, D., and Gunther, B. A wearable computer system with augmented reality to support terrestrial navigation. In Proc. ISWC'98, pages168–171, Pittsburgh, USA, October 19–201998. IEEE and ACM.
7. Malaka, R., Schneider, K., Kretschmer, U., Stage-based augmented edutainment, In proceedings of Smart Graphics: 4th International Symposium, SG 2004, Banff, Canada, May, 2004.
8. Daniel, M.P., Denis, M (1998): Spatial descriptions as navigational aids: a cognitive analysis of route directions. Kognitionswissenschaft 7(1), 45–52.
9. Golledge, R (1999) Human Wayfinding and Cognitive Maps. In: Wayfinding Behavior, John Hopkins Press, pp. 5–46.
10. Denis, M, Pazzaglia, F, Cornoldi, C & Bertolo, L (1999) Spatial Discourse and Navigation: An Analysis of Route Directions in the City of Venice. Applied Cognitive Psychology 13, pp. 145–174.
11. Geiger, C., Paelke, V., and Reimann, C. Mobile Entertainment Computing. Int. Conference on Techniques for Interactive Storytelling and Entertainment, TIDSE 2004, Springer LNCS.
12. Elias, B. and Brenner, C.: Automatic Generation and Application of Landmarks in Navigation Data Sets, in: Peter Fisher (Edt.): Developments in Spatial Data Handling - 11th International Symposium on Spatial Data Handling, Springer Verlag, 2004, pp. 469-480.
13. Baus, J., Cheverst, K., and Kray, C. A Survey of Map-based Mobile Guides. In Meng/Zipf (Ed.) Map-based mobile services - Theories, Methods and Implementations, Springer, pp. 197-213.
14. Lindley, C.A. Trans-Reality Gaming. Keynote Address. Proc. of the 2nd Annual International Workshop in Computer Game Design and Technology, Liverpool, John Moores University, UK, Oct. 2004.
15. European project "Integrated Pervasive Gaming (IPerG). Official web site, www.pervasive-gaming.org
16. Ivonne Gansen. Development of a Pedestrian Navigation Concept Using Storytelling Techniques, Diploma Thesis, University of Applied Science Harz (in preparation, in German).

A System for Event-Based Film Browsing

Bart Lehane, Noel E. O'Connor, Alan F. Smeaton, and Hyowon Lee

Centre for Digital Video Processing and Adaptive Information Cluster,
Dublin City University, Ireland
{lehaneb, oconnorn}@eeng.dcu.ie
{asmeaton, hlee}@computing.dcu.ie
http://www.cdvp.dcu.ie

Abstract. The recent past has seen a proliferation in the amount of digital video content being created and consumed. This is perhaps being driven by the increase in audiovisual quality, as well as the ease with which production, reproduction and consumption is now possible. The widespread use of digital video, as opposed its analogue counterpart, has opened up a plethora of previously impossible applications. This paper builds upon previous work that analysed digital video, namely movies, in order to facilitate presentation in an easily navigable manner. A film browsing interface, termed the MovieBrowser, is described, which allows users to easily locate specific portions of movies, as well as to obtain an understanding of the filming being perused. A number of experiments which assess the system's performance are also presented.

Keywords: Movie Indexing, Summarisation, Presentation, Interface.

1 Introduction

The past number of years has seen a growth in the use of digital video for creating, editing, broadcasting and viewing content. The amount of movies created each year has grown considerably since cost effective digital filming and editing equipment has become available. This digital media revolution was helped by efficient storage and transmission, while an advantageous by-product of using digital, as opposed to analogue, video and audio, is that it is possible to analyse the data automatically. Where previously video was merely stored on a reel of tape, the use of digital video means that it is possible to extract information from the video data and use it to gain knowledge about the content. Unfortunately, most, if not all, of this content is simply stored without any sort of indexing or analysis and without any associated meta-data. For videos with meta-data, then it is usually due to some manual annotation rather than any automatic indexing. Thus, locating relevant portions of video or browsing content is difficult, time consuming and generally inefficient. Automatically indexing these videos to facilitate their presentation to the user would significantly ease the retrieval process as well as allowing users to gain some higher knowledge about the video content. Films are particularly in need of indexing as their temporally long nature and varying styles make it is difficult to know where, and indeed how, to locate desired clips.

S. Göbel, R. Malkewitz, and I. Iurgel (Eds.): TIDSE 2006, LNCS 4326, pp. 334–345, 2006.

The research presented here describes a system that allows users to retrieve sought after parts of films, as well as to gain knowledge about their content. Three methods of navigation are presented, *shot-based browsing*, *event-based browsing* and *search-based browsing*. Previous work by the authors, which is summarised later, used audiovisual analysis to automatically create an event-based structure of movies as well as facilitating user initiated searching. The system described here takes the results of this and presents it as a complete system. This allows for the efficient retrieval of sought portions of a movie.

It is necessary to introduce the concept of an *event* at this point. As defined in this work, an event is something which progresses the story onward. Events are the portions of a movie which viewers remember as a semantic unit after the movie has finished. A conversation between a group of characters, for example, would be remembered as a semantic unit ahead of a single shot of a person talking in the conversation. Similarly, a car chase would be remembered as 'a car chase', not as 50 single shots of moving cars. A single shot of a car chase carries little meaning when viewed independently, it may not even be possible to deduce that a car chase is taking place from a single shot, however, when viewed in the context of the surrounding shots in the event, its meaning becomes apparent. Events are components of a single scene, and a scene may contain a number of different events. For example, a scene may contain a conversation, followed by a car chase, which would be two distinct events. Similarly, there may be three different conversations (between three sets of people) in the same scene, corresponding to three different events.

There have been a number of other approaches that aim to create a browsable index of a movie. For example, [9,1,10] aim to detect scene boundaries using a host of audiovisual features such as colour consistency, shot clustering, lighting, and ambient sound. Although scene-based indexes may be useful in certain scenarios, they have the significant drawback that no knowledge about the content is inherent in the index. A user searching for a particular point in the movie must peruse the whole movie in order to locate it, unless significant prior knowledge of the movie is available. [7] detect dialogues in video based on the common shot/reverse shot shooting technique. This approach however, is only applicable to dialogues involving two people, since if three or more people are involved the shooting structure will become unpredictable. [8] expand on this idea to detect 2-person dialogues, multi-person dialogues and hybrid events (where a hybrid event is everything that isn't a dialogue). However, only dialogues are treated as meaningful events. [2] aim to detect both dialogue and action events in a movie, however the same approach is used to detect both types of events, and the type of action events that are detected is restricted. [11] use colour, motion and audio features to classify scenes into either conversation scenes, suspense scenes or action scenes. A high classification rate is achieved. However, this approach relies on the presence of known scene breaks, and classifies a whole scene into one of the categories, while in practise an entire scene may contain a number of important events.

In general, event detection approaches are focused on detecting single events, however, previous approaches by the authors created a system which completely indexes a movie by detecting all of the relevant events present. By creating a number of event classes that represent as much of a movie as possible (dialogue events, exciting events and musical events) and then detecting all of the events in these classes, an event-based index of a movie can be created [5,6,3]. A brief overview of this technique, as well as some results presented in previous papers, are summarised later for context.

The remainder of this paper is organised as follows. Section 2 introduces the requirements for a film browsing system and presents some of the design choices made in the design process. Section 3 describes the underlying technology behind the browsing system, while Section 4 describes the user interface. Section 5 explains the set of experiments undertaken in order to assess the system. Finally, Section 6 draws a number of conclusions and indicates potential future work.

2 System Design

The aim of the system presented in this paper is to allow users to quickly and efficiently locate relevant portions of movies and also to assist in the understanding of a movie. In order to facilitate this, the system has a number of requirements. Firstly, the index should be event based so that some knowledge of the movie is inherent in the index. For example, if a user is looking at a scene-boundary based index, where each scene is presented to a user, it is quite difficult to locate relevant portions of a movie, or indeed garner any information about the movie, without actually viewing each of the scenes. Creating an event-based index, where each event belongs to a particular class, makes it easier to browse and interpret the movie as each event class is known, and therefore the browser has a better idea of what is taking place in the movie simply by viewing keyframes from the event. In order to create event-based browsing, a number of event classes must be defined. The event classes should be plentiful enough to cover all of the meaningful parts in a movie, yet generic enough so that only a low amount of event classes are required. This is to ensure that the index is as compact as possible. It may be possible to define a large number of event classes, and attempt to implement detectors for each event class. However, due to the near infinite range of possible events in movies this is an impossible task. It is proposed to create a reasonable number of event classes, some of which may encompass a number of different events. Each of the events in any event class have a common semantic thread that link the events together allowing intuitive navigation through a movie. However, the selection, and amount, of event classes is dictated by how the films themselves are created.

The first event class contains all *Dialogue* events. Dialogue constitutes a major part of any film, and the viewer usually gets most information about the plot, story, background etc. of the film from the dialogue. Dialogue events should not be constrained to a set number of characters (i.e. 2-person dialogues), so a conversation between any number of characters is classified as a dialogue event.

Dialogue events also include events such as a person addressing a crowd, or a teacher addressing a class.

The second event class is *Exciting* events (or *Action* events). These typically occur less frequently than dialogue events, but are central to many movies. Examples of exciting events include fights, car chases, battles etc. A director has a set of tools available to create excitement (such as increased editing pace, on-screen movement etc) and when these tools are used it is a good indication that an exciting event is taking place.

The final event class is a superset of a number of different events, which are all labelled as *Musical* events. The first type of event in this superset are montage events. As a montage brings a number of unrelated shots together, typically with musical accompaniment that spans all of the shots. The second event type labelled in the musical superset is an *emotional* event. Examples of this are shots of somebody crying, or a romantic sequence of shots. Emotional events and montages are strongly linked as many montages have strong emotional subtexts. The final event type in this class are *musical* events themselves. A live song, or a musician playing are examples of musical events. These typically occur quite infrequently in most movies. These three event types are linked by the common thread of having a strong musical background, or a least a non-speech audio track. All of the montage, emotional and musical events come under the common umbrella of the 'Musical' event class. Any future reference to musical events in this paper is referring to the entire set of events labelled as 'musical'.

The three event classes described aim to cover all meaningful parts of a movie. The distinction between the three event classes is quite subjective. One person may feel that a particular event belongs to a certain class, while another feels it belongs to a different class. An argument, for example, could be interpreted as an exciting event by one user, and as a dialogue event by another. Many montages events also aim to excite the viewer, and therefore could also be classified as exciting events or musical events depending on the user. Thus, when detecting events, a level of flexibility is required so that users of any system employing the event based index with differing opinions can still locate their sought events. This means classifying events into more than one event class, so that each user can easily locate the event. For example, classifying an emotional conversation into both the dialogue event class, and the musical event class counts as a multi-class event. Clearly, if manageable content is required, events should be placed into as few event classes as possible, however there is a fuzzy boundary between each class, and therefore dual classification of some events is necessary. Browsing a movie based on these three event classes is termed *event-based* browsing.

Although the event-based index aims to incorporate all relevant events in a movie, there may be occasions when a different set of events are sought. For example, a user may be interested in examining how a particular director uses editing throughout a movie and may want to locate all of the areas (or events) where fast paced editing is used. Thus, another requirement for the system is to allow users to initiate event-based searching. This allows for more specific, user defined browsing through a movie, as a user can select the features most likely to appear in the desired event. The addition of searching allows for tailored retrieval of events using audiovisual information. This is termed *search-based browsing.* Also, there may be portions of a movie that are not part of an event-based index, or cannot be located by searching. Thus, as a last resort, a method of examining all of the shots in a movie is facilitated. This is termed *shot-based browsing.*

3 System Description

Section 2 identified three methods of browsing supported by our film browsing system namely *shot-based* browsing. Previous work by the authors focused on detecting the events belonging to each event class [3] and on facilitating searching through a movie [4]. Much of the underlying mechanics of the system has been presented previously, however knowledge of some aspects of the system is required and so a summary of the most important parts is supplied here.

3.1 Shot-Based Analysis

As with many audiovisual analysis techniques, the first step in video analysis involves detecting shot boundaries. The approach employed uses colour histograms to detect large inter-frame variances in colour which can be attributed to a change in camera angle. When the approach was examined against a manually created ground truth, 97% of shot boundaries were detected. Once shot boundaries are detected, a representative frame, or keyframe, is selected for each shot. As this is the sole representation for each shot, the frame that is visually closest to the average frame in the shot is used. By combining shot boundary detection and keyframe selection, it is possible to implement shot-based browsing. The implementation of this is presented in Section 4

3.2 Event-Based Analysis

In order to detect events, film creation techniques were examined, and the features commonly used were extracted. For example, when shooting a dialogue event, a director will usually try to relax the audience so that they can interpret the words being spoken. This typically results in a relaxed shooting style which contains little camera movement, repetitive shots and clearly audible speech. When shooting an exciting event however, the aims of the filmmaker are different. Typically, fast-paced editing and high amounts of camera movement are used in order to create excitement in the audience. Finally, when filming what we term musical events, there will be a constant musical audio track, usually combined with low amounts of camera movement and slower paced editing [3].

Thus, in order to detect the events contained in these three event classes, the audiovisual features associated with each event class are extracted. The editing pace can be extracted by examining the shot boundary information and using the shot lengths. Two features which describe the motion present in each shot were extracted. The first measures the amount of *camera movement* present, while the second measures the amount of motion present within the frame (i.e. where there is a still camera but an object moving within the frame) and is termed *motion intensity*. Both of these features combine to give a complete description of the movement in each shot. In order to identify the type of audio present in each shot, a support vector machine based audio classifier was implemented which detects the amount of *speech*, *music*, *silence* and *other audio* present in each shot [6]. Finally, a measure of shot repetition is implemented which measures, for a given sequence of shots, how many repeating shots are present [6].

Once all of these features are extracted, the events themselves can be detected. The event detection approach was previously presented in [3]. Essentially, a set of finite state machines (FSMs) are used in order to detect parts of a movie where particular features are prominent, then some filtering is applied which removes incorrectly detected events. For example, in order to detect dialogue events, FSMs are used in order to detect areas which contain various combinations of speech shots, still cameras and repeating shots. The output of the FSMs is filtered, and a list of dialogue events is created. A similar process is repeated for the exciting events (where fast-paced editing and camera movement are sought) and for musical events (where, among others, shots with silence and music are sought). The output of the event detection process yields a list of dialogue, exciting and musical events present in the movie.

The results of the event detection process, which was tested on a varied collection of ten movies, are also present in [3]. It was reported that, on average, 95% of dialogue events, 94% of exciting events and 90% of musical events were detected by the system, which indicates the reliability of the event detection system. The detection of these events facilitates the use of an event-based index. Also, on average 91% of all shots in a movie were categorised into one of the event classes by the event detection system, which indicates that the three event classes cover a high percentage of the footage in a movie.

3.3 Search-Based Analysis

In order to allow users to search for particular parts of a movie, a similar approach to the event detection method is used. This can be viewed in [4]. All of the features described in Section 3.2 are also used for searching. As with event detection, searching involves two steps. Firstly, a user selects the desired FSM, and secondly selects the filtering (if any) required. So, for example, a user looking for an event that contains a moving camera and music could use the moving camera FSM to find all of the areas in the movie with a moving camera, then filter the results to only retain the parts that also contain music. Another way of searching for the same event would be to use the music FSM and then filter the results to only retain events with high amounts of moving camera shots. In another situation, a user may want to locate all of the areas with speech present, then he/she can use the speech FSM with no additional filtering and will be returned all of the areas in a movie with speech present. An implementation of this searching technique is presented in Section 4.

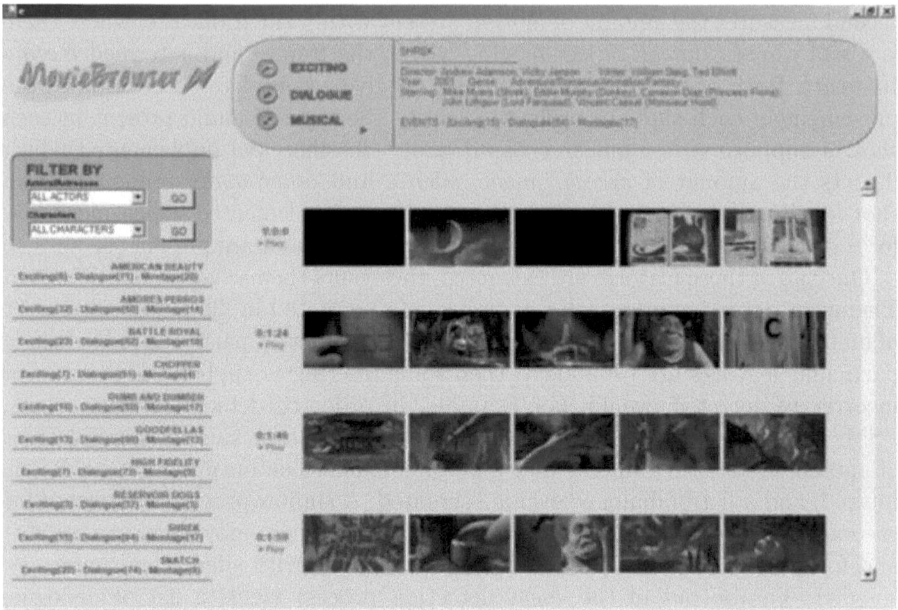

Fig. 1. Shot-based browsing using the MovieBrowser system

4 User Interface: The MovieBrowser

This section presents the user interface to the *MovieBrowser* system which implements the three methods of perusing a movie. Figures 1, 2 and 3 show the respective browsing methods. Firstly, notice that on the left hand side of the interface, each of the movies in the database are listed. By clicking on a movie, the system switches to present information (director, actors, character names, year of release, genre etc.) about the selected movie. Figure 1 shows the shot-based browsing view. In this view, the keyframe from each shot of the movie is presented in temporal order. Each row contains five shots, and a user can play the movie from any point by clicking on the respective icon. Although this is a relatively basic method of browsing a movie, it may be useful in certain scenarios where the location of a clip is known.

The event-based browsing method is shown in Figure 2. By clicking on one of the event icons in the top of the screen (i.e. exciting, dialogue or musical), each of the events in that class for the selected movie are displayed. For example, in Figure 2, all of the detected exciting events for the film 'Shrek' are displayed. Just below the information panel, a visual guide that indicates the location of the events in the movie is shown. Each event is given five keyframes in order to give the user an idea of what is taking place during the event. The event keyframes for the dialogue events are selected based on the most commonly repeating shots, as these usually correspond to the characters speaking in the event and are therefore deemed most appropriate. For the exciting and musical

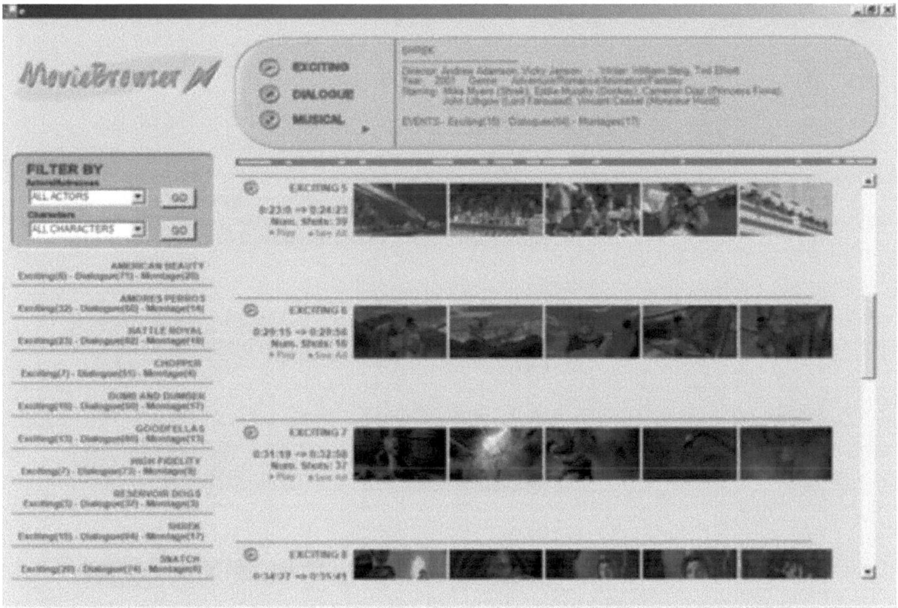

Fig. 2. Event-based browsing displaying the exciting events in the movie Shrek

events, it is more difficult to reliably select keyframes as there are many different possible activities, so they are selected at equal time increments throughout the event. For each event, the start and end time is displayed, as well as the number of shots present. It is possible to play any event by clicking on the 'Play' button.

The final method of browsing a movie, the search-based method, is presented in Figure 3. This allows users to initiate a search. By clicking on the arrow icon, the search panel is revealed. Users can then select the desired FSM on the left hand side, and the filtering on the right. For example, in Figure 3 the 'Music' FSM is selected, and only events with high amounts of 'Non-Static' camera shots are retained. This returns a set of events, which are displayed in the same manner as in the event-based approach.

5 Experiments and Testing

In order to assess the effectiveness of this system as an indexing solution, a set of browsing experiments using the MovieBrowser were devised. The purpose of the experiments is to investigate whether the system facilitates efficient retrieval and also, which method of browsing users find most useful. The process involved a number of users completing a set of tasks, which involved retrieving particular clips using the three different browsing methods. A set of thirty tasks were created. For each task, a user used one of the systems to locate a clip from a movie. An example is the task: *In the film High Fidelity, find the part where Barry sings 'Lets get it on' with his band.* The tasks were chosen in order to assess

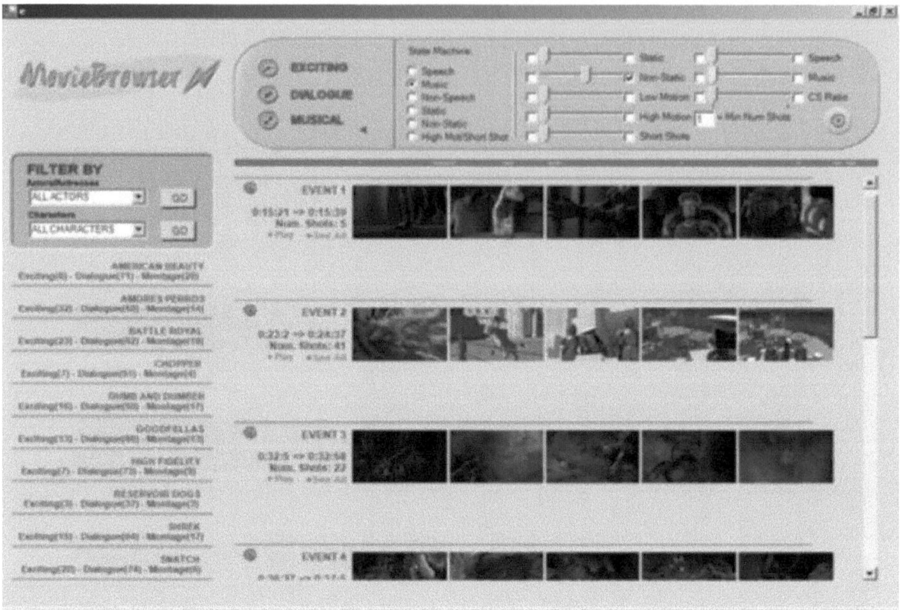

Fig. 3. Search-based browsing displaying the retrieved events after searching for events that contain high amounts of music and moving camera shots

how well the respective browsing and retrieval methods can be used in a movie database management scenario. In this scenario, retrieval of specific portions of a movie is essential, and thus the tasks were chosen based on this requirement. The complete task list is quite diverse as it incorporates many different occurrences in a wide range of movies. The tasks were created in order to challenge each of the three retrieval methods. They also aim to simulate real use cases in a video retrieval environment.

In total there were twelve volunteers, each one completing fifteen tasks, five for each method of browsing. Each task was completed by six volunteers, twice for each system. Although a brief definition of the three event classes was given to each user, no insight into the event detection methods employed in this system was provided. For example, when describing the exciting events, a number of examples were provided to each volunteer, but no insight into the features used in order to detect exciting events were given. When completing a task with one browsing method, the functionality of the other methods was removed. An automatic timing program was implemented that recorded how long it took each user to complete each task, and to check whether users have located the correct event. If a user could not complete a task, a completion time of ten minutes was assigned for the task. This heavily penalises non-completion of tasks.

The results of these tasks are presented in Figure 4. The vertical axis is the time in seconds taken to complete the task, and the horizontal axis is the task index. There are three graphs in the figure, one for each method of browsing. In

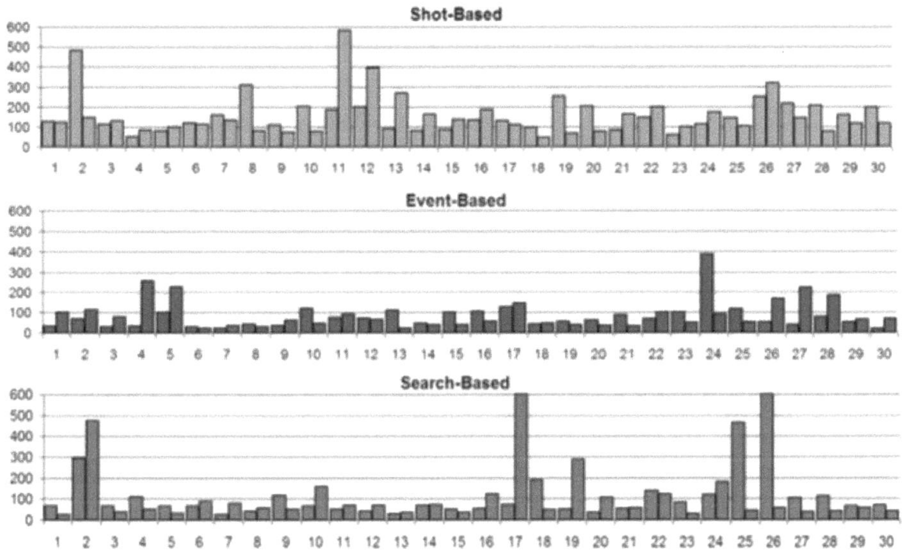

Fig. 4. Plot of time taken to locate clip for the tasks using three browsing methods

each graph, there are two results for each task (as two users completed each one). As can be seen from the graph, the shot-based system has many longer completion times than the other methods of browsing. Many of the shot-based searches take over 100 seconds, and a number take considerably longer. In contrast, most of the event-based and search-based completion times are quite low. On two occasions users gave up whilst using the search based method, thus the maximum time taken was 600 seconds. These were the only two tasks that were not completed. In both cases, although the results returned from searching contained the sought event, these were not recognised by the user. The minimum completion time was 18 seconds for user 1 in task 30 using the event-based system.

Clearly it is possible that the results could be biased depending on which films users had previously seen as he/she may know where in the movie a particular event occurs. As such, analysis of the results based on whether a person had seen the film was also undertaken. In total, 180 tasks were completed (i.e. 30 tasks completed by six people each). For 42 of these tasks, users had not seen the film before. Table 1 presents the average task completion time for tasks in which the film had, and had not, been previously viewed. As would be expected, the task completion time for each method is longer for users who have not previously viewed the movie, however in both cases the event-based method performs best, followed by the search-based method, followed by the shot-based method.

The results presented indicate that the events detected by the system correspond to the users' interpretations of the events, and are located in the correct event class. As these results show, implementing an event-based index has a number of advantages which result in reduced search time. This can be intuitively explained as when an event class is selected, users are significantly reducing the

Table 1. Average task completion times by browsing method, where the average results are shown for users that had, and had not seen the film previously

Method Used	Average Time For Unseen Movies (s)	Average Time For Seen Movies (s)
Shot method	187.5	145.11
Event method	111.47	71.27
Search method	174.3	92.7

search space of the movie. Also, as they know that the events that they are looking at belong to a particular class, this helps them to understand what is transpiring in the event. For example, looking at the representative keyframes for a dialogue event allows a browser to reach the conclusion that the characters in the keyframes are talking to each other. If the same characters were viewed in the keyframes of an exciting event, the user can infer that they are fighting or arguing. This is far more difficult to achieve when viewing the keyframes on their own with no context.

Initiating searches with the features that users feel are common to the sought events proved to be a reliable method of finding events in movies. Performance for the search-based system may be increased if the user interface of the search based method is improved, as some volunteers noted that it could be made more user friendly. Also, as the search based system requires the most user input, a larger amount of training time may help users familiarise themselves with the system and result in better search queries.

6 Conclusions

This paper described the MovieBrowser system which allows users to browse movies using a number of methods. Shot-based, event-based and search-based methods for browsing were described and the results of a number of experiments comparing their use were presented. The advantages of event-based browsing was illustrated, and proved to be highly beneficial in locating specific parts of the movie. This is demonstrated in the higher performance of both the event and search based methods over the shot based method. The combination of all three browsing methods creates a complete index of a movie. Although the experiments were focused on using the system in an event retrieval scenario, future experiments will aim to assess how much insight into the actual movie can be extracted by using this system.

The system was recently deployed in a learning environment at a University. A set of 12 movies studied as part of a film studies course were analysed and incorporated into the system, which is now used by students in order to assist in their analysis of films. Future work will focus on altering this system based on feedback from the students and faculty using it, so that it is more tailored toward this specific learning environment. For example, one user commented that in order to analyse editing pace in a movie, currently many students manually locate the shot cuts in a movie and time each individual shot length. The simple addition of an editing-pace graph using the shot boundary information would considerably reduce the effort required for this. Also, the addition of text information (obtained from the subtitle information) to the MovieBrowser may result in even more effective retrieval. Finally, additional visual analysis may yield even more contextual information from the movie. For example, face detection, detection of the camera framing etc, may enhance the system.

Acknowledgement

The research leading to this paper was partly supported by Enterprise Ireland and by Science Foundation Ireland under grant number 03/IN.3/I361

References

1. Yu Cao, Wallapak Tavanapong, Kihwan Kim, and JungHwan Oh. Audio-assisted scene segmentation for story browsing. In *Proceedings of the International Conference on Image and Video Retrieval*, 2003.
2. L. Chen, Shariq J. Rizvi, and M.T. Ötzu. Incorporating audio cues into dialog and action scene detection. In *Proceedings of SPIE Conference on Storage and Retrieval for Media Databases*, pages 252–264, 2003.
3. Bart Lehane and N. O'Connor. Movie indexing via event detection. In *Workshop on Image Analysis for Multimedia Interactive Services (WIAMIS), Incheon, Korea*, 2006.
4. Bart Lehane, N. O'Connor, and H. Lee. Searching movies based on user defined semantic events. In *International Conference of Signal Processing and Multimedia Applications (SIGMAP), Setubal, Portugal*, 2006.
5. Bart Lehane, N. O'Connor, and N. Murphy. Action sequence detection in motion pictures. In *The international Workshop on Multidisciplinary Image, Video, and Audio Retrieval and Mining*, 2004.
6. Bart Lehane, N. O'Connor, and N. Murphy. Dialogue scene detection in movies. In *International Conference on Image and Video Retrieval (CIVR), Singapore, 20-22 July 2005*, pages 286–296, 2005.
7. R. Leinhart, S. Pfeiffer, and W. Effelsberg. Scene determination based on video and audio features. In *In proceedings of IEEE Conference on Multimedia Computing and Systems*, pages 685–690, 1999.
8. Ying Li and C.-C. Jay Kou. *Video Content Analysis using Multimodal Information.* Kluwer Academic Publishers, 2003.
9. Hari Sundaram and Shih-Fu Chan. Determining computable scenes in films and their structures using audio-visual memory models. In *ACM Multimedia 2000*, 2000.
10. M. Yeung and B.-L. Yeo. Video visualisation for compact presentation and fast browsing of pictorial content. In *IEEE Transactions on Circuits and Systems for Video Technology*, pages 771–785, 1997.
11. Yun Zhai, Zeeshan Rasheed, and Mubarak Shah. A framework for semantic classification of scenes using finite state machines. In *International Conference on Image and Video Retrieval*, 2004.

Future Garden

Holger Schnädelbach[1], Jonathan Hale[2], Willi Dorner[3], Ben Bedwell[1], Steve Benford[1], and Jo Mardell[4]

[1] Mixed Reality Lab, University of Nottingham
[2] Architectural History and Theory Group, University of Nottingham
[3] Cie. Willi Dorner, Studio 70
[4] Dance4
hms@cs.nott.ac.uk, Jonathan.Hale@nottingham.ac.uk, wi.do@gmx.net, bzb@cs.nott.ac.uk, sdb@cs.nott.ac.uk, jo@dance4.co.uk

Abstract. The Eastern edge of Nottingham (UK) city centre is undergoing substantial restructuring, which will have a major impact on the people living in the area. Future Garden is an interactive story, delivered on a handheld PDA device, which explores the past, present and possible futures of Sneinton Market, one part of the area to be re-developed. This paper introduces Future Garden including its novel navigation interface based on video and self-reporting and some early results of the still ongoing evaluation.

Keywords: mobile HCI, storytelling, interactive, urban regeneration.

1 Introduction

Wide ranging changes have been proposed for the Eastern edge of Nottingham (UK) city centre [1]. A large area of land, partly occupied and partly derelict, will eventually be transformed into a mixed-use development, including commercial and leisure facilities as well as housing. Although these developments have been announced, a lot of uncertainty about the details does remain. Future Garden was developed to allow people in the area to reflect on the possible changes, focusing on Sneinton Market, a small part of the overall development, which is currently a relatively vibrant market area. Not in itself a formal part of the required public consultation, Future Garden was designed to tell the story of the Sneinton Market area, reflecting on its past, present and possible future.

Arguably, one of the most effective ways to explore a story that is tied to a particular place, is to explore it at that particular place, allowing comparisons between what is being told and the place itself. There has been a long-standing interest in developing location based content for mobile interactive storytelling and gaming. The Guide system used tablet PCs tracked through GPS as a portable tourist guide in Lancaster [2]. Can You See Me Now involved runners on the street equipped with PDAs and GPS chasing players online, who occupied a virtual copy of the physical play area [3]. Beyond using GPS, it is also possible to tag physical locations electronically for location based experiences. The Hypertag system is a product in this

S. Göbel, R. Malkewitz, and I. Iurgel (Eds.): TIDSE 2006, LNCS 4326, pp. 346–351, 2006.

area, the tags being readable via infrared and Bluetooth, technologies which are available on many mobile phones [4]. There are also a number of experiences that do not rely on technology to provide positioning. Uncle Roy All Around You mixed online and on-the-street participants in the hunt for the fictitious figure Uncle Roy. People self-reported their location in physical space, resulting in additional clues to be revealed [5]. Moving City, a tour of architectural proposals for Nottingham (UK), made use of an onscreen map but also employed a person as a guide to take people around the city and through the interactive story [6]. Finally, the current commercial interest in digital content that can be delivered easily to widely available technology platforms, is evident in the range of self-guided city tours based entirely on audio [7, 8].

Future Garden, an interactive tour deployed on the PocketPC platform, was designed to enable the public to appreciate the history of Sneinton Market in Nottingham (UK), its present use and also some possibilities for its redevelopment. For this purpose, participants were invited to embark on a self-guided tour, which included location specific digital content associated with nine stations that were marked out physically in the area and virtually onscreen.

2 Future Garden

Future Garden was authored by a multi-disciplinary team including dancers, event managers, architects and architecture students, HCI experts and film makers in a very tight time frame of around 10 weeks. The overall concept and direction was provided by a choreographer, whose interest lies in bodily movement through architectural space. The team was distributed between multiple sites in Nottingham in the UK and Vienna, Austria. The event itself was advertised and staged, during three days in May 2006, as part of the annual Nottingham dance festival nottdance. The nottdance06 festival had a number of different venues across Nottingham, including Sneinton Market, a small vibrant network of streets and Market stalls and one part of the Nottingham area to be redeveloped. A number of Market stalls were rented there, one of which being the starting point for the tour.

On arrival, visitors had a choice between different experiences. These included a treasure hunt, a dance performance, a photo exhibition, a documentary film screened in a café in the market and two interactive experiences set up on desktop PCs, in addition to Future Garden. If they decided on the latter, visitors were asked to register personal details against the particular PDA that they would take out on the tour. They were also required to leave a valuable item as security, such as their wallet or mobile phone. Participants were then handed their own PDA together with a set of headphones. A sheet of instructions was provided to helpers so that they could give a structured introduction. One of the helpers then took individual participants or groups out to the station, just outside the starting point. From then on, Future Garden took the form of a self-guided interactive tour, which will be described in more detail below (an interactive version of the on-screen interface can be found in [9]). In case of problems, there were additional helpers out in the area of a cluster of 5 stations. Helpers were ready to give additional advice and fix technical issues, such as problems with the battery or memory. Although such problems did occur, they were not frequent enough to impact on the experience a great deal.

2.1 Follow the Video

As the main form of navigation, to take people from station to station, participants were asked to follow pre-recorded video sequences that would guide them as to where to go. Each sequence began at a specific marker that was painted on the floor. The beginning of each video sequence started with a picture of the associated physical marker. On arrival, the video would end on a picture of the next physical marker in the sequence, indicating successful navigation. The following sequence of frames demonstrates the beginning of a typical navigation video (between stations 0 and 1) to guide a participant from the start position to the specific viewing position for some content. The participant would follow the movement in the video sequence until they arrived at the designated spot.

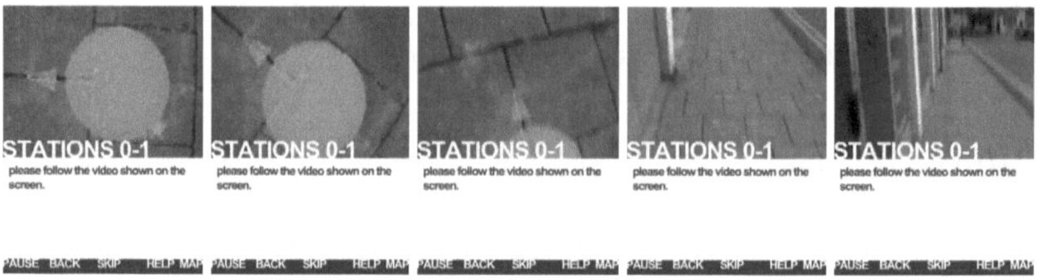

Fig. 1. A video navigation sequence

There were nine key starting positions within the environment. While these had been designed to be followed in their sequential order, participants were free to interactively select their own ordering and to skip sequences if they wished.

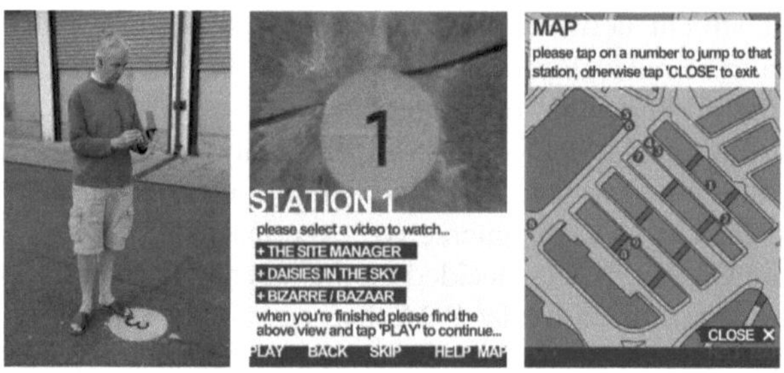

Fig. 2. A participant at one of the stations, an example of the onscreen interface at another station and the map

An interactive map was also available to assist navigation and this could be used to access the content at each station (potentially without the user having to physically go there – for example, as part of planning their tour). Tapping on any of the numbers would bring up the virtual content associated with that physical station. The facilities for selecting between different pieces of content at certain stations, the ability to skip content and the interactive map enabled non-linear exploration of an otherwise linear navigation interface.

For participants, the experience then involved following the navigational video clips from station to station. Once at a target station, participants frequently had to line up their PDA with a specific physical view shown onscreen. When they had confirmed onscreen that they were lined up, digital content was overlaid over this view (see Fig. 3 for an example). At the end of the presentation, content could be replayed or additional content associated with that station could be played. Alternatively, participants could move on to the next station, following the next video clip.

2.2 Content

At most stations, participants could select from among several pieces of location-specific content that was intended to help them appreciate different aspects of the past, present and future of Sneinton Market. This content included architectural schemes developed by architecture students who were part of the development team. The design schemes were inspired by interviews with market stall holders, but fictitious in the sense that they were not set up to become part of the actual redevelopment. These were represented on screen and participants were asked to line up the view manually to obtain an augmented-reality style view in which the projected screen could be seen against the current physical backdrop as shown in the following series of images.

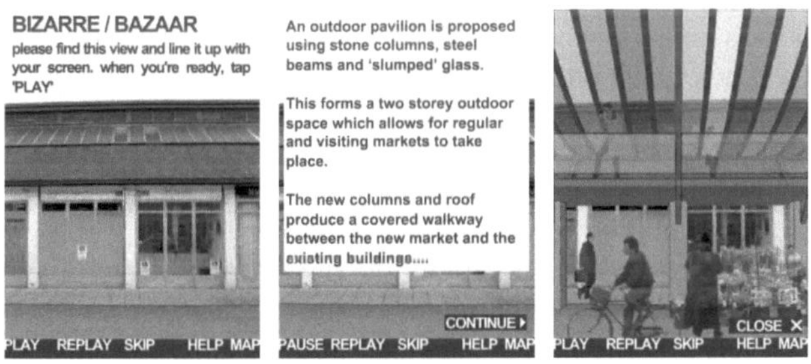

Fig. 3. Architectural projections as content at station 1 (see menu in Fig 2)

This glimpse into the possible future of Sneinton Market was accompanied by a view into its past. Station 7 provided participants with a historical photo archive showing how Sneinton Market would have appeared in the past. For this purpose, one of the stations was located on a raised platform to provide participants with a better overview. A third form of content which focused on the present was access to an interview with the current market manager, who reflects on the current use of market area, the stall holders and objections to the future re-development of Sneinton Market. This interview was shot in the office of the site manager (see Fig. 4.). One of the stations was located in front of the office and participants were asked to enter, sit down and experience the content as if they were speaking to the site manager himself. In addition, there was one station that featured a physical homeless shelter made from card board, which could be entered and a station that gave access to a video of the soup kitchen for the homeless recorded at night. Both prompted participants to consider the parallel, even invisible life that the homeless lead alongside the general population.

Fig. 4. Interview with the site manager (photo on the left: copyright Julian Hughes)

Finally, station four included Alpha60, a video of a dance performance acted and filmed within Sneinton Market as the backdrop. This dynamic virtual story prompted participants to follow the dancers shown on screen around the market streets, into one of the stalls and back to the starting point.

3 Early Results

Future Garden was experienced by 44 participants, 28 of whom completed self-administered feedback questionnaires that (beyond participant demographics) focused on the reaction of the participants to the video follow interface, the potential for non-linearity and overall reaction to the experience. Analysis of the data is still underway, but we will very briefly present some key results. Participants generally accepted and were even enthusiastic about the video navigation interface, especially for interactive storytelling. All 28 respondents agreed that the devices they were given were reliable and straightforward to use, with the majority strongly agreeing in both cases (79% and 66% respectively). Some participants had issues with following the earlier parts of some of the video clips. We believe that this was due to the fact that those clips did not provide enough context, pointing at the floor for too long instead. The tour also succeeded in getting people to take note of and memorize aspects of the content presented at the different stages. Finally, a significant minority of participants stated that they were worried about safety and security, walking around with a relatively expensive handheld device. This sometimes led to people staying in groups and even to one participant skipping a station, as they felt uncomfortable there, an indication how physical circumstances can impact on the pace of virtual stories.

4 Conclusions

Future garden was produced by a multi-disciplinary authoring team in a very short time frame. It was experienced by a substantial amount of people as part of the nottdance06 dance festival. A novel navigation interface, based on pre-recorded video clips and self-reporting, successfully guided participants along 9 stations, where digital content could be selected on screen. Future Garden proved to be a powerful combination of physical and virtual narratives. It was based on a specific area of Nottingham, with all its associated pieces of history, present uses and (controversial) plans for the future. The connection between physical space and virtual story was reinforced by physically marking out points of interest on the ground, from which virtual content could best be viewed. The virtual content was then specifically tailored to suit the chosen view points. This meant that the story became well integrated but spanned physical and virtual spaces. Early results from our on-going evaluation indicate that the video navigation interface was generally well received, but that it could clearly be further improved. Furthermore, the tour succeeded in getting participants to take note of the digital content presented on screen, tying together the physical and virtual story spaces. Finally, fears about safety concerning the use of expensive handheld devices in public, will probably have to be addressed in any future experiences that we develop.

Acknowledgements. Future Garden was developed as part of Future, which in turn was commissioned by Dance4, the national dance agency based in Nottingham, for nottdance06. Thanks to the INSCAPE Integrated Project (EU RTD contract IST-2004-004150) for its support. We would also like to thank the dance4 team as well as Suzie Firth, Satu Herrala, Sonja Pregrad, Adam Robertson, Juels Winter, James Alexander, Sheldon Brown, Sarah Elmusrati, Matthew Parr, Bhavna Solanki, James Spencer, Rafid Sulaiman, Charlotte Thornton, Elizabeth Webster, Tom Huggon and Steve the market manager.

References

1. EastsideCity, Eastside & City Developments, 2006, accessed 11/072006, available from http://www.eastside-city.com
2. Cheverst, K., et al. Developing a Context-aware Electronic Tourist Guide: Some Issues and Experiences. in CHI. 2000. The Hague, The Netherlands: ACM Press.
3. Flintham, M., et al. Where on-line meets on the streets: experiences with mobile mixed reality games. in CHI. 2003. Ft. Lauderdale, USA.
4. Hypertag Limited, Hypertag - Point, Click, Receive, 2006, accessed 12/072006, available from
5. Flintham, M., et al. Uncle Roy All Around You: Mixing games and theatre on the city streets. in Level Up: The First Intl. Conf. of the Digital Games Research Association (DIGRA). 2003: DIGRA.
6. Hale, J. and H. Schnädelbach, Moving City - The Electronic Guidebook, 2003, accessed 12/072006, available from http://www.nottingham.ac.uk/sbe/research/ahtg/Moving_City.htm
7. Soundwalk, Soundwalk - Audio Tours For People Who Don't Normally Take Audio Tours, 2006, accessed 12/072006, available from
8. Candide Media Works, I., Talking Street - Discover Where You Are, 2006, accessed 12/072006, available from http://www.talkingstreet.com/index.php
9. Dorner, W., J. Hale, and H. Schnädelbach, Future Garden - nottdance06, 2006, accessed 12072006, available from http://www.crg.cs.nott.ac.uk/~hms/future/FutureGarden.html

ARC - Towards Alternate Reality Cinema

Wendy Ann Mansilla, Andreas Schrader, and Ranjan Shetty

ISNM - International School of New Media at the University of Luebeck
Willy-Brandt Allee 31c
23554 Luebeck, Germany
{w.mansilla, andreas.schrader}@isnm.de

Abstract. Today's popular presentations of immersive digital narrative experiences commonly utilise wide screens or forms of panoramic projections to display visually realistic content. The shift of focus to other media forms that includes non-realistic and aesthetic expression using audio and small displays is a challenging step. This paper describes an interactive narrative content and design approach that explores small displays and wide perceptual audio projections to achieve an immersive experience. A mixed media content known as Autophobia was implemented as a proof of concept. Autophobia uniquely presents film, radio, and photomontage to achieve an alternate reality experience.

Keywords: Experimental Cinema, Interactive TV, iTV, Mobile Cinema, Augmented and Mixed Reality, Alternate Reality Games.

1 Narrative Avant-Garde

Stories have played a major role in the life of humans since ancient times and storytelling has been performed in a universe of media channels (e.g., oral presentations, printed novels, radio dramas, etc.) Most of the conventional media channels reduce interactivity to a minimum, e.g. the "vibration" between the presenter and the audience created by voice and gesture feedback. With the introduction of computers, networks and advanced human computer interaction technologies, this has changed dramatically during the last few decades. Especially in the domain of movies and films, a number of experimental extensions have been explored.

One of the early works in experimental cinema were by futurist brothers Ginanni-Corradini who declared their idea in the manifesto arte in 1910, claiming that colours express emotion and harmony in an expressive work [5]. This idea of image transformations or "photocinematic" gave rise to the futurist cinema, also known as abstract cinema. It is based on representational imagery that calls for a radical challenge to the "hegemony" of narrative through new structural modes [2]. Since then experimental cinema has emerged into new forms of non-linear narration employing techniques such as juxtaposition of story sequences, randomness, manipulation of montage, and image and sound analogy. Some of the recent developments include concepts, like "abstract cinema" [5], "future cinema" [9], "experimental cinema" [1], and "mobile cinema" [6], to mention only a few.

S. Göbel, R. Malkewitz, and I. Iurgel (Eds.): TIDSE 2006, LNCS 4326, pp. 352–357, 2006.

The idea of non-linear narrations based on user decisions, and context-based narrative concepts based on user location tracking has created completely new environments for experiencing stories, especially in the context of convergence between genres, like games and films [7]. Alternate reality games (ARG) grew out of the popular role playing games (RPG). ARG creates a scenario where the game's alternate reality and the real world meet. The game successfully becomes part of the world the players live in [10]. This is achieved using open-ended puzzles solved by collaborative efforts of the players. Sometimes the game requires participants to find clues or artefacts in the real world. The use of mystery-solving strategies not only contributes to the player's immersion but also extends the communication level among players using other media forms (e.g. email, chat room, or SMS).

This paper generalises the concept of ARG and introduces the notion of "alternate reality cinema" (ARC). ARC extends the alternative universe (e.g. cinema, radio, etc.) into imagined realities by exploring the real-world. An alternate reality where non-realistic elements in the expressive work and artefacts in the real-world, co-exist, collide and initiate the viewer's re-construction of the story. ARC removes the boundary of the cinema screen and allows for potentially unbounded narratives in time and space using context-aware mobile devices. Viewers can experience an expressive work interwoven with the real world, anytime, anywhere.

That is, what Jeffrey Shaw calls "... the synaesthetic convergence of all our modalities of perception in a conjoined space-time of real, surrogate und virtual formations" [8].

2 Autophobia

As a proof of ARC's concept, a mixed media content called Autophobia was developed [4]. Autophobia is an experimental story of fear or paranoia inspired by the tragic that the world is facing today. The presentation of the story evolves around series of confined spaces with self-contained episodes. Autophobia utilises three main media forms: photomontage, film, and radio. The viewer is placed inside the content's physical setting of episodes related to the physical location (see Figure 1.a).

2.1 Concept

Autophobia is experienced in four locations of the campus of the ISNM: the library, the student lounge, the project lab and the kitchen hall. All these places are located next to each other and are easy to navigate (see Fig. 1b). Autophobia uses a ubiquitous computing infrastructure named ALADIN developed at ISNM [7] that is capable of detecting the location of the viewers and streaming the respective media sequences to mobile devices (PDAs) equipped with headsets. Location beacons (IR/RFID/Bluetooth) are strategically placed in the designated location spots where story episodes could be viewed. Autophobia's four spots include library photocopier, library door, project lab phone, and student lounge phone. Approaching a location beacon will cause media content to be played on the participant's mobile device.

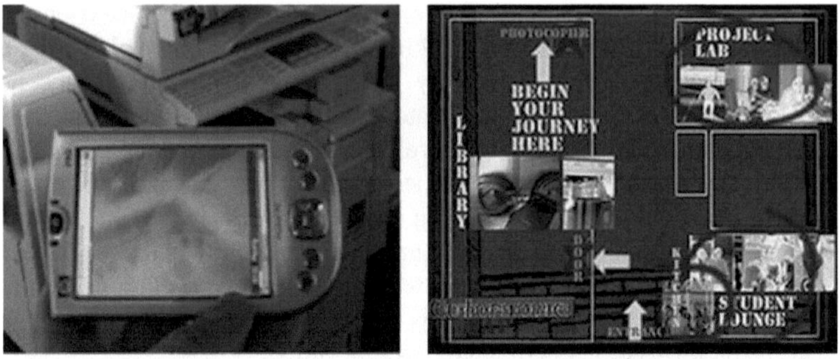

a) b)

Fig. 1. a) Library's active location spot. b) Autophobia map.

The media content played at each location tells a story of the place, invites the user to have another view at the environment. At the end of each piece the user is not explicitly told where to proceed next: they are encouraged to interpret what they just saw and heard and to use these elements to guess where to go next.

The installation works best when several users are involved simultaneously. A collaborative interpretation work – exchanging views on the media contents, on their meaning and implications – gives the Autophobia experience a unique dimension. This is encouraged by the fact that the audio sequences vary between the viewers.

2.2 Media Contents

Autophobia is inspired by experimental and silent film; there is no dialogue between characters but offscreen sounds are extensively employed. Autophobia is intended to create a perceptual collage by using self-contained contents distributed in space and time.

Three types of media contents are used in Autophobia: photomontage, film and radio. The objective of the photomontage is to immerse the user in each of the physical locations showing the inner life and real experiences in the place by various scenes from the actual spot. The film brings fiction into play: at the same location a fictional world appears, a new story unfolds. Finally, the radio drama blurs the boundary between fiction and reality: it uses sounds connected to the stories shown in the photomontage and in the movie sequence and sounds from the immediate environment to guide the user to the next location. Thus, the user is invited to actively study the environment without really leaving the fictional world.

Photomontage: The Autophobia map containing links to the collection of photomontages is shown initially to the viewer before approaching the first film episode. The collection is accessible throughout the interaction. Each photomontage is a storyteller in the form of fixed and moving images and is supported by a soundtrack. They last at most two minutes each.

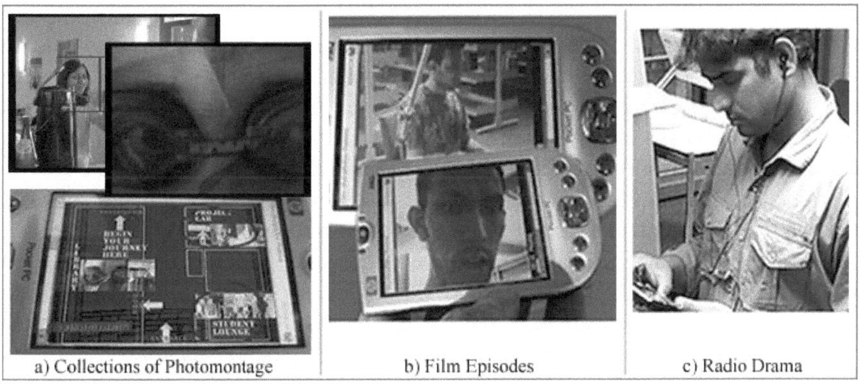

Fig. 2. Three levels of narrative experience in Autophobia

Film: A short film is shown after each photomontage. The four episodes of at least two minutes length have been shot entirely in the ISNM premises. The film starts in the library, where the first film sequence is played. Each subsequent episode is played at the location where the action takes place. Depending on the user's decision on where to proceed, a location-based film episode will be played, thus giving each user a potentially different interpretation of the action.

Radio: After each film episode, the participants receive one (random) version of a radio drama, each detailing slightly varying clues to the next location. They are termed radio drama since they use only off screen sounds to develop tension in the narrative, following the principles of acousmêtre[1] which is in itself suspense-generating [3]. Sounds such as superimposed voices, running persons or slamming doors increase this effect and utilize the viewer's imagination. Viewers are invited to listen carefully to the spatial and temporal form of the cues (action, movement, distance) in the soundtrack and to relate them to the physical environment to eventually discover the next interaction location points. The nature of the presented sound sequences builds doors for complexity, narrative construction, and mystery-solving.

3 Evaluation

The original Autophobia system (containing only video sequences) was initially demonstrated at ISNM Open House. Visitors were provided with a mobile device and could freely move around the interaction space, triggering and viewing film episodes. The viewers were advised to proceed to the library to locate the first interaction point. This initial installation was well received, although the viewers required more

[1] Acousmêtre, explored by Fritz Lang or Alfred Hitchcock in cinema is a character hidden behind a curtain; an offscreen sound that either speaks over the image or augments the sound naturally expected from the image. An offscreen sound that engages the spectator's anticipation to see the real source of the sound. Visually, it is the silent character whose imaginary voice is waiting to be heard. Thus, relative to what is shown on the screen, temporary or not, it is the offscreen character whose source is invisible [1].

assistance than anticipated. First, the visitors needed assistance on locating the interaction points despite having brightly coloured infrared beacons. Secondly, some visitors felt that further introduction to the environment would help them feel more engaged with the location and understand some cues found in the story. Interestingly, most viewers who are familiar with the campus have little problem identifying story cues. Third, the viewers preferred to ask questions and collaborate with the creators of the project rather than with other viewers. Despite receiving a favourable feedback we observed that engagement in the interaction could further be improved.

Autophobia was again exhibited in public during the second ISNM Open House with some improvements added. A map was added showing explicitly the location points to access the film sequences and images representing objects or events related to the interaction spots. This feature improved the issue on locating the film sequences and showed improvement on viewer's engagement. But, again despite this feature, collaboration among viewers was lacking.

Realising the possibility to greatly involve the viewers in the narrative, Autophobia was further improved to not only extend the drama but also to encourage the viewers to solve problems themselves. To cater to this feature, Autophobia was adapted into a three-level experience as described above (see Fig. 2). A map links to photomontages introducing the physical locations. To encourage a problem-solving task, unlike the previous installation, the map does not explicitly state the actual spots of the location beacons. The film sequences represent the metaphors of Autophobia using a fictional story. The radio dramas act as a cue to invite the user to put pieces of collected fragments together while navigating in the environment.

This new concept was tested internally with two groups of student subjects; newly arrived students were invited to use the Autophobia experience to discover the campus. They were told that some contents may vary among participants, thus they are encouraged to share experiences. The first group viewed the movie without the radio drama. The subjects find it difficult and distracting to find the next location spots. Since the film sequences shown were the same for each participant, collaboration with other viewers was reported to be not so necessary. The second group viewed the installation using the full three-level experience. The viewers were able to successfully navigate using the cues in the radio drama. The subjects reported that this navigational approach was viewed as being part of the narrative experience. Interestingly, the viewers discussed among each other about their interpretation of the story and of the cues included in the three media contents. This suggests that they were able to relate the three levels of the experience together to build a unique and consistent approach to the Autophobia story. As is typical of ARG, at the end of the experience, the participants feel that there are still more episodes to play and tasks to solve.

4 Conclusion

In this paper we presented a mixed media approach for immersive narrative experiences using a location-aware infrastructure. The system supports the presentation of multimodal sequences of photomontages, films and radio on mobile devices. Navigation in the story is realised by tracking the viewer's location. The project has been presented publicly during ISNM Open House events, and tested with students.

Through observations and gathered suggestions, the use of several media fragments in an interactive narrative installation seems to effectively increase involvement of the viewers and to enhance the guidance during the spatial navigation.

The notion of Alternate Reality Cinema (ARC) introduced in this paper goes beyond traditional immersive or mobile applications by hybrid integration of real-life and virtual elements. By blurring the border between fiction and reality, new expressive ways for creative storytelling can emerge. In the future, we plan to extend the project with tools for supporting direct collaboration of users during the experience, and a framework for content development for the system.

References

1. Chion, M.: La Voix au Cinéma. Paris: Cahiers du Cinéma (1982)
2. Le Grice, M.: Experimental Cinema in the Digital Age. London: BFI Publishing (2001)
3. Mansilla, W. A.: Interactive Dramaturgy by Generating Acousmêtre in a Virtual Environment. In: Harper R., et. al. (eds.): Proceedings of the 5th International Conference on Entertainment Computing (ICEC 2006), LNCS 4161. Berlin: Springer Verlag (2006) 90-95
4. Mansilla, W. A.: Autophobia Website. http://isnm.de/~wmansill/Autophobia/
5. Marinetti, F.T., Corra, B., Settimelli, E., Ginna, A., Balla, G., & Chiti R.: Futurist Cinema. Manifestro futurista pubblicato nel 10° numero del giornale "L'Italia Futurista, 11 settembre 1916 - 15 novembre 1916. English translation at: http://www.unknown.nu/futurism/cinema.html, retrieved: Sep. 2006
6. Pengkai, P.: Mobile Cinema. MIT Ph.D. Thesis, MIT Interactive Cinema Group (2004). http://ic.media.mit.edu, retrieved: Sep. 2006
7. Schrader, A., Carlson, D. & Busch, D.: Mobile Cinema – Context-aware Interactive Video. In: Proceedings of Workshop: Investigating new user experience challenges in iTV: mobility & sociability, Montreal, Canada, April 22, 2006
8. Shaw, J.: Movies after Film – The Digitally Expanded Cinema. In: Rieser, M., Zapp, A. (Ed.): New Screen Media – Cinema/Art/Narrative. London: British Film Institute (2002)
9. Shaw, J. & Weibel, P.: Future Cinema. Cambridge: MIT Press (2003)
10. Szulborski, D.: This Is Not A Game: A Guide to Alternate Reality Gaming. US: New Fiction Publishing, LLC (2005)

Interactive Audiobooks: Combining Narratives with Game Elements

Niklas Röber, Cornelius Huber, Knut Hartmann, Matthias Feustel, and Maic Masuch

Department of Simulation and Graphics
Otto-von-Guericke University of Magdeburg
Universitätsplatz 2, D-39106 Magdeburg, Germany
{niklas, knut, masuch}@isg.cs.uni-magdeburg.de

Abstract. The authoring and the design of immersive, non-linear plots remains one of the main challenges in interactive digital storytelling. This paper introduces the concept of *interactive audiobooks*, which combines the potential of complex (non-)linear narratives (e.g. books and radio plays) with interactive elements from computer games. The design concentrates on a flexible degree of interaction, in a way that the listener's experience ranges between a passive listening to an interactive audio-only computer game. In this paper we discuss the story-engine used in interactive audiobooks, as well as present an authoring framework along several design guidelines to create them. Finally, we demonstrate the capabilities of our system with an adaptation of a short story from Edgar Allen Poe.

Keywords: interactive storytelling, audiobooks, story authoring, audio-only games.

1 Introduction

Over the last years, audiobooks and radio plays have enjoyed a constant increase in popularity that is still on the rise. One reason is there convenient usability, as no special equipment and no continuous observation by the user are required. Audiobooks and radio plays are therefore often used by people who are committed to another (possibly boring) task, like driving or ironing, that requires visual but no continuous auditory attention. This lack of visual information requires an active participation and a focused attention of the audience in order to reconstruct the fictional universe. Oral presentations are therefore, compared to visual depictions of the same content, considered to be much more stimulant and immersive. By using linear plots and fixed story lines, the users of conventional audiobooks might detect additional details through a repeated listening, but can not experience a changed, nor influence the existing story line. This changes with the introduction of *interactive audiobooks*, in which the listener/player may and can intervene with the story at pre-defined and user-selected points using an auditory user-interface.

The idea of interactive audiobooks is simply to combine the narrative advantages of an oral storytelling with additional story-related interaction and game elements. The system is thereby designed with a varying degree of interactivity that allows anything between a passive listening to a free interaction as an auditory computer game.

S. Göbel, R. Malkewitz, and I. Iurgel (Eds.): TIDSE 2006, LNCS 4326, pp. 358–369, 2006.

The paper is organized as follows: After this introduction, Sec. 2 discusses related work ranging from audio-only computer games to the principles of interactive digital storytelling. The basic concepts of interactive audiobooks are then presented in Sec. 3. Here we also discuss the varying levels of interaction, story-dependent game elements, and the design of auditory user interface. Sec. 4 provides an overview of the system's architecture and presents details of the story- and game-engines used. The following Sec. 5 evaluates the concept by adapting a short story from Edgar Allan Poe as an example. Finally, we summarize the results and discuss possible improvements in Sec. 6.

2 Related Work

Audiobooks and radio plays build the foundation of our work and are at the same time the most prominent reference. While *audiobooks* often feature only one speaker, *radio plays* involve, depending on the plot, several actors and additional ambient-related sounds and acoustical effects. The commonality between audiobooks, radio plays, and printed literature is their underlying linear and static plot. One of the foci in digital interactive storytelling lies therefore in the design and authoring of non-linear plots and the development of techniques that integrates user interaction into the story-line.

Adventure games and audio-only computer games are the second support of our concept. Interactive audiobooks and adventure games, both focus on narration but also contain game elements to enhance the storytelling. Audio-only computer games on the other hand represent a small niche of game titles that are often developed by and for the visually impaired. Although, some of these games feature novel and intuitive sonification and interaction techniques, the majority is still rather simple and not comparable with regular computer games. Interactive audiobooks can therefore be seen as a union between auditory adventure games and radio plays; although complex narratives prevail game elements.

The available *interactive audiobooks* from digital publishing AG are language learning aids, in which translations are interactively blended over the read out text [1].

Our approach examines several challenges in interactive digital storytelling:

1. The design of intuitive authoring tools to create data structures required in story-engines and to design control mechanisms for narrative flow,
2. Mechanisms to achieve the same complexity as in real narratives, and
3. Mechanisms to maintain the coherency of plots after user interactions (i. e., to integrate the user's actions within a dynamic plot).

(1) The main focus in interactive storytelling lies in the development of formal representations to characterize actors (role, personality, and emotional status) and plot structures. Current story-engines represent plot elements with a varying level of detail: scenes, beats, or actions. The narrative flow is often controlled by simple mechanisms, such as finite state machines (FSM), but also more complex planning systems are used[1]. Although there are powerful authoring tools for FSM story-engines available, there are few approaches only that feature intuitive interfaces to design more complex internal

[1] For a more detailed discussion, we refer to the work by [2]).

formal representations, and who can also be used to control the narrative flow using inference mechanisms [3].

(2) The complexity of real narratives raises another challenge. The GEIST [4] and the Façade [5] projects impressively demonstrated how detailed narratives can be constructed by using basic elements, that are more complex then Propp's motivs or beats. These structures easily enable authors to design complex interactive narratives [6].

(3) Another difficulty is the coherency of dynamic plots, as user interactions might cause severe changes in the fictional universe. Plot structures based on automatically generated simulations contain an explicit representation of causal dependencies, which can be used to apply repair strategies in order to integrate the users interaction (see [7]). With the lack of formal representations for preconditions and the effect of actions, our system exploits manual specifications of the intended functional links between plot elements (e. g., setup & payoff [8], foreshadowing & pay-off [9]).

3 Interactive Audiobooks

The concept of interactive audiobooks aims to combine complex narratives with game elements from adventure- and audio-only computer games. Using story-dependent interactions, players can influence the development of the plot and drive it in their own direction.

3.1 Action and Interaction

Adding the right amount of action and interaction is not a trivial task. Audiogames and the therein employed sonification and interaction techniques were used as a basis for creating story-dependent mini-games. In a previous project and in a first attempt to create an interactive auditory adventure game, we adopted several sagas and myth around the cathedral of Magdeburg and integrated this into a 3D audio-only adventure game [10,11]. In here, the player, a tourist visiting the city, stumbles over several incidents and unveils a mystery surrounding the old place. The game is set in a 3D auditory environment, in which events are triggered over time and through user interaction. Although several assisting sonification and interaction techniques were used (e. g., head-tracking, spatialized sound sources, beacons, and earcons), evaluations revealed that players got lost very easily due to the possibilities of a free exploration. Therefore we restricted the user movements in interactive audiobooks. The *transportation* from one scene to another is now guided by a narrator and controlled by the story-engine, who motivates and mediates the change. Yet, some of the interactive parts require and are centered on 3D user interaction, similar to the mouse searches in classic adventure games.

3.2 Enhanced Story-Graphs

Story-graphs offer an interesting alternative to create a non-linear story design. This technique is often used by game designers to provide alternative plots and endings that are consistent with the player's performance. Our story-engine is based on such story-graph structures and further extended by *interaction nodes*. These interaction nodes contain dialogs and story-dependent mini-games and allow the user to partially control the main character. The listener now actively participates in the narration and steers the plot within a predefined range. Fig. 1 visualizes a simplified story-graph, in which *narrative nodes* (light/green) and interactive nodes (dark/blue) intertwine. The story starts at the root node atop and traverses down till it reaches an end condition (*terminal nodes*). It branches at predefined points, at which decisions and challenges in the form of interactive parts are placed. The path chosen depends on the player's actions and decisions, but also on the main characters conduct defined by the story-engine.

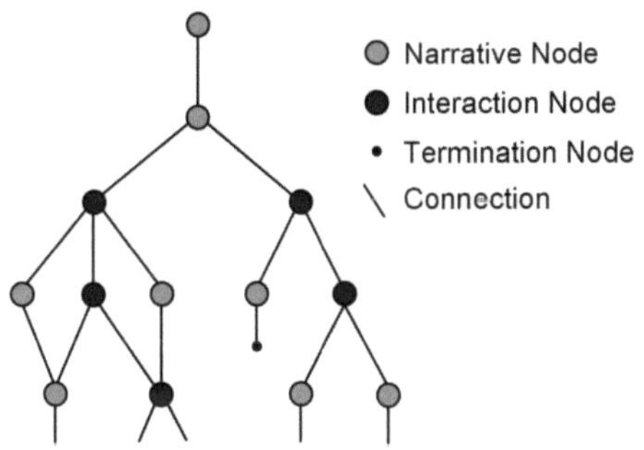

Fig. 1. Story-graph excerpt

An adaptable interpretation by a motival classification system offers here a more flexible narrative flow [12]. Appropriate narrative nodes are selected from a set of alternatives, in which plot elements can be omitted in order to jump to another more appropriate position. To maintain the plots consistency, functional dependencies between plot elements have to be considered. Therefore, payoff elements may trigger the inclusion of setup elements. Additional story correction techniques can be specified by the game designer (e. g., the player should not be able to kill one of the main characters if this is not part of the story-line).

Before jumping to the authoring tools to design interactive audiobooks (e. g., Sec. 4), we need to discuss the specifications of narrative and interactive nodes, as well as address the potentials of the internal game logic used.

Game Logic: In order to design interactive audiobooks on the basis of complex linear narratives, authors have to segment the story into chunks and determine their arrangement within the story-graph. An internal logic controls thereby the development of the plot and maintains a coherent narrative flow. It therefore integrates with the story-graph and registers the users actions and decisions. Designers and authors are able to specify a simplified behavior of the main characters using several parameters. These conduct-variables are elements of the initial design and set up as part of the authoring, but may be adjusted to incorporate the players decisions and actions during the game play. Traversing the story-graph automatically (e. g., in non-interactive mode), the system chooses the *right path* according to the designed or adapted conduct-variables.

The amount of interaction that is expected by the user can be varied smoothly and is changeable throughout the story-line. This allows the user to start the story as a regular audiobook and later change it into an *interactive* audiobook with additional gaming and interactive components. Ahead each interaction task, the user has a short time slot (a few seconds) within he must decide whether he wants to interact with the system, or let it run automatically. This time slot becomes shorter after several non-interaction decisions, and is thereafter running in automatic-mode, but can be changed back at any time. The mini-games also feature a timer component. If the correct action within a certain amount of time is not made, the mini-game is lost. The story branches now into a different path that penalizes the player opposed to the winning pathway, in which additional story details might be revealed.

Narration Nodes are the non-interactive parts and represent the basic narrative elements of the story. They contain the majority of (narrative) information (e. g., narrators voice, (internal) monologues, non-interactive dialogs, and ambient and environmental sound effects). The narrator of the story introduces the initial setting (the fictional universe), presents later advances, and drives the story-line. The (internal) monologues provide hints and guide the player, but should not dominate his decisions. Non-verbal ambient and environmental sounds effects, as well as background music denote a special group of narrative nodes. They usually contain no narrative information, but intensify the game's atmosphere, enhance the perception of the story, and deepen the player's immersion into the virtual environment.

Interaction Nodes are placed in between and sometimes in exchange of narrative nodes. They comprise story-related mini-games, dialogs, and techniques to influence the story-line or the behavior of the main character. In story-dependent mini-games, players can re-enact certain story events and therefore adding personal experiences to the story-line. These mini-games focus either on action and fast user reaction (arcade-style) or on a precise listening using a 3D interface to search for various items and hints (adventure-style). By searching for necessary items and hidden secrets, the listener/player actively participates in the story and its development. However, the mapping of some of these game elements to an auditory game play is not an easy task. For an intuitive determination of an items location, these objects are labeled with an acoustic beacon or earcon [10]. After its finding, a secret or additional information is revealed and the story proceeds. Dialogs and the interaction with other characters also provide details from the fictional universe and may influence the behavior of the main characters. The dialogs comprise pre-defined answers, but can also consider the mood of the main character to determine the right selection. Here we employ a small set of interaction primitives (e. g., *think*, *look*, *do it*, *do not*, and *exit*). These actions are custom fit to the current situation and provide the player with additional knowledge. Not all decisions lead in a different conclusion, but the selections made may influence the later story line.

3.3 Interface Design

The design of effective and intuitive user interfaces and interaction techniques are crucial aspects in the development of computer games. Moreover, the interaction should not distract the player from the game play and instead convey a feeling of being immersed into a virtual auditory world. Our interface employs therefore conventional game interaction paradigms, but also several new, more intuitive definitions.

Speech recognition would be the easiest and most convenient solution to control interactive audiobooks, but the absence of robust speech recognition technologies in mobile systems prevent such an implementation. An ideal platform are mobile gaming consoles, such as Sony's PlayStation Portable (PSP) or Nintendo's DS; but also modern Pocket PC's and PDA's offer enough power for acoustic rendering and playback. A simpler and less interactive system might also be realizable on iPod's and common MP3 players.

Our user interface is centered around a gamepad control and uses Sony's PSP game interface and design (see Fig. 4). This gamepad interface comprises a simplified joystick

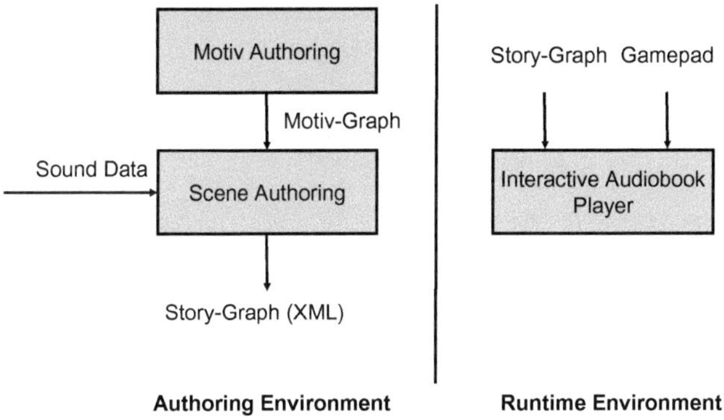

Fig. 2. Interactive audiobooks — system overview

cross (left) and several buttons (right). Currently, a gamepad is the only interaction device to control the mini-games and the plot development. Future versions might also integrate head-tracking and real-time 3D sound rendering techniques for spatialized listening, or make use of additional sensors that provide further user feedback to adjust and fine tune the experience and the main characters conduct.

Using the joystick, players can control the character and search for items and hidden objects in adventure-style mini-games. The buttons are used to control arcade-style games, in which the player has to react quickly on certain inputs, and sometimes also repeatedly over time to achieve a certain goal. Acoustic feedback through earcons and the narrators voice is provided to convey additional information. Some of these arcade-style games were inspired by the recent adventure *Fahrenheit*, who employed many action mini-games as addition besides the actual story-line [13]. The dialogs and the in-game menu system are as well controlled using the gamepad and mapped as auditory display to various buttons and the joystick. This allows an easy interaction with the games and the setup of story and audio parameters.

4 System

The interactive audiobook framework is composed out of two modules. Figure 2 visualizes an overview of the system with the authoring part on the left and the runtime system on the right hand side. The authoring is further split into two parts, and enables an easy reuse of the designed motiv-graph also for other forms of interactive narrative.

The *runtime environment* is used for the presentation of the interactive audiobooks, and responsible for mapping the user's interactions to progressions in the plot (cf. Sec. 3.3). The *authoring environment* supports a hierarchical plot design, in which in an initial step authors specify abstract properties of important motivs that are part of the story-line (*motiv authoring*; cf. Sec. 4.1). In a second step, game designers and authors specify temporal and functional dependencies between motivs in the graph structure. As these motivs often correspond to scenes, we refer to *scene authoring* as the refinement of motiv-graphs to story-graphs by the addition of interaction and termination nodes (cf. Sec. 4.2).

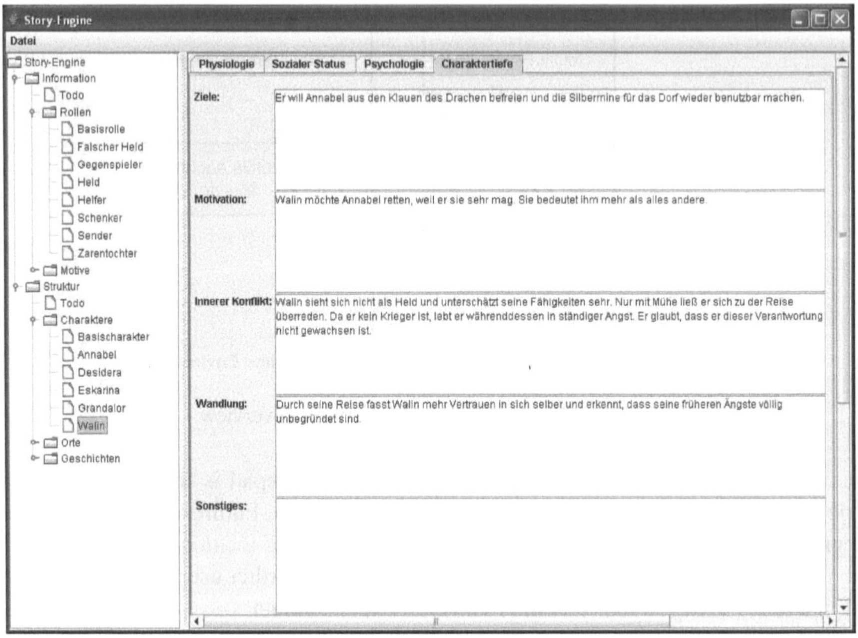

Fig. 3. Character input form

4.1 Motiv Authoring

One aim of this project is to enhance complex narrative structures that will later be combined with additional game elements. Therefore, it is crucial that professional authors and game designers can express their ideas in their own terminology. Thus, our authoring tool integrates concepts and approaches to develop and analyze the plot for complex narratives as well as for the elements of game design.

Several story analysts extracted commonalities in the plots of narratives, myths, and movies. Polti, Propp, Campbell, and Vogler [14,15,16,17], for example, proposed a small number of typical plot elements (*motivs*) and *archetypes* [18] or *dramatis personae* [15] to describe acting characters. Our system contains these motiv sets and examples of their realization in German folk tales. Moreover, our approach extends motiv-based authoring tools (e. g., [6]) by a semi-automatic classification of new plot elements according to known motivs (see [12]). But some motiv sets are not appropriate for certain genre or the iterative process of plot refinement requires more specific or more general motivs. Hence, authors can use, define, extend, and refine motiv sets to structure their plots.

Initially, authors describe the properties of all important entities of the fictional universe: characters, scenes, locations, and plot elements (motivs), which can be used for several episodes of a sequential. Moreover, they can specify temporal or causal dependencies between motivs that are visualized and represented in a *motiv-graph*. Authors have to provide as much information as possible about the dependencies between motivs, so that the story-engine can prevent an omission of plot elements required to establish them. For a more convenient visualization of motiv-graphs, authors can assign icons to motivs; the associated design principles are discussed in [12].

Fig. 3 shows a screenshot of the motiv authoring system. The navigation panel on the left hand side eases the access to dedicated input masks to characterize all story elements. The right panel presents the description of the main character in small interactive fiction. This input mask reflects Egri's model of personality [19], which considers physiological, sociological, and psychological aspects, all with up to 10 different points in any dimension. Egri's model also focuses on the goals, motivations, internal conflicts, and value changes for all characters. Hence, our framework contains a complex character data sheet that unites all these elements.

The representation of motivs contains formal and informal elements. Motivs specify the abstract structure of plot elements which can be specified by motival variants. Motivs also contain references to archetypes; these variable elements are instantiated by individual characters in different stories. Authors can select archetypes and characters from automatically generated lists (formal element) and characterize the content of motivs in natural language (informal element).

One main objective of our approach is to support the iterative plot and character development. Authors should be able to create incomplete plots and to redefine every formal specification. Therefore, plot specifications can contain gaps and inconsistencies (e. g., between the archetypes defined in a motiv and an associated scene description). Our system contains completeness and consistency checks, which generate ToDo-lists for authors as a reminder.

4.2 Scene Authoring

Inspired by authoring tools for (screen) writers (e. g., Dramatica [20]) and interactive fiction (e. g., DraMachina [21]), our system enables authors to integrate game elements in moderately adaptable narratives. The scene authoring module extends individual nodes of the motiv-graph with a more elaborated specification of narrative and interactive elements. Additionally, authors can supply auditory content for the narrative nodes (e. g., individual voices, background and ambient sounds). Finally, the game logic bridges and combines the narrative and interactive elements.

Fig. 4 displays a screenshot of the scene authoring module. It visualizes in the top left view the motiv-graph and provides in the middle display a more detailed overview of the current selected scene along the nodes and interactions possible. The larger window on the right hand side presents all information associated with the current node of the story-graph. Authors can specify acoustic realizations of narrative nodes (sound data files) or define the systems behavior at interaction nodes (actions, reaction, priorities). Action describing icons are simply dragged and added to the scene and filled with audio data and interaction details. Every icon represents here an interaction primitive (cf. Sec. 3.3) and contains the time required to later complete the task. All actions and interactions can be tested online with the integrated runtime component visualizing a PSP gamepad, or by using a regular gamepad that is connected to the computer.

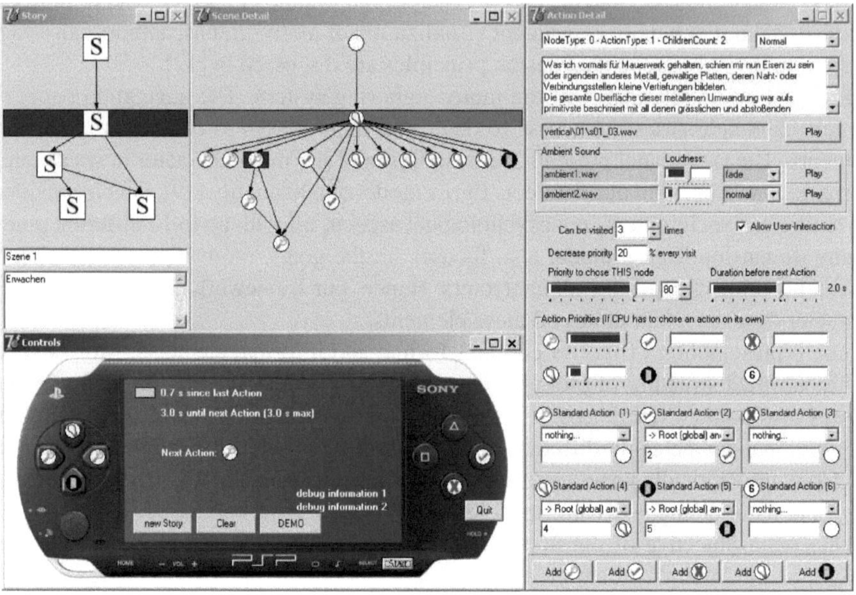

Fig. 4. Interactive audiobook authoring environment

4.3 Implementation

The system was developed on the PC platform, although it was initially planned to design the runtime component for the PlayStation Portable (PSP). Due to difficulties in obtaining a licensed developer kit for the PSP, we moved to the PocketPC platform. This also features enough processing power to handle the story- and both game- and sound-engines. The motiv-authoring system is written in Java, while the scene authoring- and runtime-components are designed with Delphi and C++. The sound rendering is handled by OpenAL, atop which we build a simple mixer system that allows a blending between several sound sources and channels. Although OpenAL supports 3D sound spatialization, we currently only employ pre-rendered 3D sounds due to simplicity. Parameters, such as gain, pitch or roll-off, are adjustable for each sound source, and can also be mapped to the users game play. Additionally, using the OpenAL Effects Extension (EAX), reverberation and environmental acoustics can be designed to further enhance the scenes auditory realism.

5 Interactive Audiobook: *"The Pit And The Pendulum"*

This section provides a more practical look at the authoring and design of interactive audiobooks using a short story by Edgar Allen Poe as an example. First, we provide a brief summary of the story and describe our adaptations while transforming the plot into an interactive audiobook. Here we discuss the entire story line as well as the placement and the selection of the mini-games and other interactions. The second paragraph looks on the authoring process itself, while the last part discusses the results achieved.

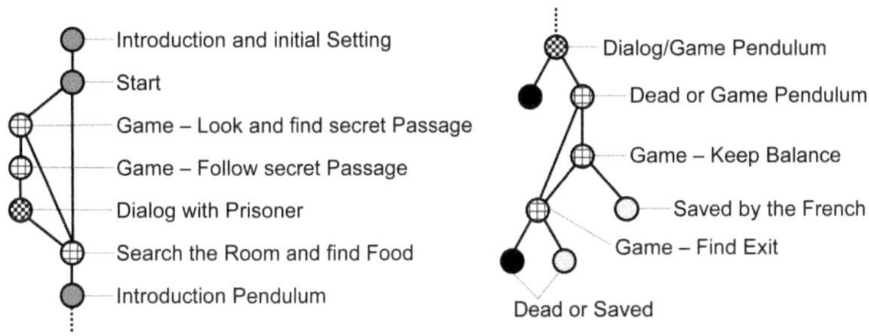

Fig. 5. Simplified story-graph from the interactive audiobook: "The Pit And The Pendulum"

Story and Adaptation: The story of "The Pit And The Pendulum" is one of the most popular works of Edgar Allen Poe and contains elements of the grotesque and arabesque. The plot is staged in a dungeon during the time of the Spanish Inquisition. The description of the hearing and the death sentence of its protagonist is very short and vaguely; the story itself centered around his endeavors to explore and escape his prison. One of the most scary parts in the story is as the hero awakens under a large pendulum with a razor sharp blade that slowly moves towards his chest. After several deadly situations, the hero is safely rescued in the last minute by French forces under the command of General Lasalle.

The plot as it appears in the original text is entirely contained in the interactive audiobook and can be experienced in the same way. Adding to this, the story has now three different endings, additional narrative to support a broader and more complex storytelling, three dialogs and several mini-games. Depending on the users selections and interaction, the story experienced can be the same as the original one, or completely different. A simplified story-graph of the interactive audiobook is presented in Fig. 5. It highlights on the key narrative components, the added narrative, the dialogs, as well as the mini-games.

Authoring and Design: The design and authoring of this example posed no major difficulties. The largest challenge hereby was the adaptation of the story-line to fit the new game play and the integration of interactions and mini-games. Here we first employed the motiv authoring tool (cf. Sec. 4.1) to integrate the additional narratives and alternative story-lines. The resulting motiv-graph was imported into the scene authoring tool (Sec. 4.2), from which we derived the final story-graph that is depicted in a summarized version in Fig. 5. The sounds, voices and music were recorded in a regular sound studio using professional voices, and after some mixing and compositing assigned to their designated nodes. A time-consuming task was the fine tuning of the individual scenes and the integration of the interactive game elements. Every scene and every scene fragment was individually set up and the time and priorities for certain interactions were specified. The resulting scene graph now connects all events and scenes and contains verifications for the user interactions. In order to achieve the right balance between narration and interaction, several tests were necessary.

Discussion: The interactive audiobook "The Pit And The Pendulum" resembles the original text and further extends it by additional narrative and interactive elements. As the default traversal of the story-graph results in the original plot, the experiences in non-interactive mode are similar to listening to an audiobook. But it can also be an interactive auditory adventure game that relies on the listeners experience and skills to complete the original story or to deviate from the genuine path to explore an alternative story-line. The choice is up to the listener/player of the interactive audiobook.

Our current implementation comprises a tutoring level to teach the user interface along the game play and interaction techniques used. The duration depends on the degree of interaction and varies between 20 to 30 minutes. A preliminary user study with 17 participants between age 20 and 59 recognized the innovative concept of interactive audiobooks. About two third found the user interface intuitive, while others had difficulties to find the mini-games and interactive parts. This proves that the concept itself is valid, yet some aspects need to be improved.

6 Conclusions and Future Work

We have introduced the concept of interactive audiobooks that unifies the potential of complex narratives with interactive elements from computer games. Therefore the experience of the listener/player can range from a non-interactive radio play to an interactive auditory adventure game. The degree of interaction can be varied smoothly during the listening, and thus bridges active and passive media. In the paper we discussed principles to design non-linear plots for interactive audiobooks, presented a hierarchical approach to author complex story-lines, and proposed a new intuitive interaction scheme for narrative games. Comparing the here described authoring environment with other related systems, shows that the design and authoring of interactive audiobooks is more similar to the design of audiobooks and radio plays, than the creation of audiogames. The authoring and the design of 3D auditory worlds is, due to the added spatiality, a more difficult and challenging task.

Future work should include a user analysis to evaluate the balance and the design of the interactive parts, as well as to measure the usability of the user interface. Additionally, future improvements should also consider the development of a mobile system that is tailored to the needs of interactive audiobooks.

Acknowledgment

The authors would like to thank Andy Hein for his invaluable help in making the recordings and for lending his voice to the project, as well as Lars Stockmann for his work on developing a portable version of the runtime system for the PocketPC platform.

References

1. Goscinny, R., Sempé, J.J.: Interaktives Hörbuch Französisch: Historires inédites du Petit Nicolas. Digital Publishing AG, München (2005)
2. Charles, F., Lozano, M., Mead, S.J., Fornes Bisquerra, A., Cavazza, M.: Planning Formalisms and Authoring in Interactive Storytelling. In: Technologies for Interactive Digital Storytelling and Entertainment. (2003) 216–225

3. Szilas, N., Marty, O., Rety, J.H.: Authoring Highly Generative Interactive Drama. In: 2nd Int. Conf. on Virtual Storytelling. (2003) 37–46
4. Spierling, U., Grasbon, D., Braun, N., Iurgel, I.: Setting the Scene: Playing Digital Director in Interactive Storytelling and Creation. Computer & Graphics **26**(1) (2002) 31–44
5. Mateas, M., Stern, A.: Integrating Plot, Character and Natural Language Processing in the Interactive Drama Façade. In: Technologies for Interactive Digital Storytelling and Entertainment. (2003) 139–151
6. Schneider, O.: Storyworld Creation: Authoring For Interactive Storytelling. In: 10th Int. Conf. in Central Europe on Computer Graphics, Visualization and Computer Vision. (2002) 405–412
7. Riedl, M.O., Saretto, C.J., Young, R.M.: Managing Interaction Between Users and Agents in a Multi-Agent Storytelling Environment. In: Int. Joint Conf. on Autonomous Agents and Multi Agent Systems. (2003) 741–748
8. McKee, R.: Story: Style, Structure, Substance, and the Principles of Screenwriting. Harper Collins, New York (1997) (dt.: *Story: Die Prinzipien des Drehbuchschreibens.* Alexander Verlag Berlin, 2001).
9. Seger, L.: Making a Good Script Great. 2nd edn. Samuel French (1994)
10. Röber, N., Masuch, M.: Playing Audio-Only Games: A Compendium of Interacting with Virtual, Auditory Worlds. In: 2nd Int. Digital Games Research Association Conf. (DIGRA). (2005)
11. Röber, N., Masuch, M.: Leaving the Screen: New Perspectives in Audio-Only Gaming. In: 11th Int. Conf. on Auditory Display (ICAD). (2005)
12. Hartmann, K., Hartmann, S., Feustel, M.: Motif Definition and Classification to Structure Non-Linear Plots and to Control the Narrative Flow in Interactive Dramas. In: 3rd Int. Conf. on Virtual Storytelling. (2005) 158–167
13. Quantic Dream and Atari Europe S.A.S.U.: Fahrenheit — Indigo Prophecy. CD-ROM (2005)
14. Polti, G.: Thirty-Six Dramatic Situations. The Writers, Inc. Publishers, Boston (1944) (Orig.: *Les Trente-Six Situations Dramatiques.* 1868).
15. Propp, V.: Morphology of the Folktale. University of Texa Press, Austin (1968) (Orig: *Morphologija Skazki.* Moskau 1928).
16. Campbell, J.: The Hero With a Thousand Faces. Princeton University Press, Princeton (1948)
17. Vogler, C.: The Writer's Journey: Mythic Structure for Writers. 2nd edn. Michael Wiese Productions (2002)
18. Jung, C.G.: Four Archetypes; Mother, Rebirth, Spirit, Trickster. Princeton University Press, Princeton (1970)
19. Egri, L.: Art of Dramatic Writing: Its Basis in the Creative Interpretation of Human Motives. Simon and Schuster, New York (1946) (dt.: *Dramatisches Schreiben*).
20. Phillips, M.A., Huntley, C.: Dramatica: A New Theory of Story. 4th edn. Screenplay Systems Incorporated (2001)
21. Donikian, S., Portugal, J.N.: Writing Interactive Fiction Scenarii with DraMachina. In: 2nd Int. Conf. on Technologies for Interactive Digital Storytelling and Entertainment. (2004) 101–112

CitizenTalk: Application of Chatbot Infotainment to E-Democracy

Cordula Boden, Jessika Fischer, Kathrin Herbig, and Ulrike Spierling

FH Erfurt, University of Applied Sciences,
Altonaer Str. 25, 99085 Erfurt, Germany
{boden, j.fischer, k.herbig, spierling}@fh-erfurt.de

Abstract. "CitizenTalk", an applied research project at FH Erfurt, investigates the potential and challenges of interactive communication using chatbots as an innovative tool for involving citizens in public planning processes. This comprises research into the state of the art in virtual planning communication, as well as the technical possibilities of chatbot communication. We present the opportunities and limitations associated with the adoption of chatbot concepts and show future prospects offered by storytelling mechanisms. An authoring tool is presented together with a new scheme to control the communication process better than current chatbot technologies and approaches allow.

Keywords: AIML, chatbot, authoring, knowledge base, virtual planning communication.

1 Introduction

The applied research project „CitizenTalk" is a joint initiative of researchers from different professional fields and communities working together at the Erfurt University of Applied Sciences, Germany. The project explores the potential of special web-based interactive communication tools in the expanding domain of virtual planning communication. In particular, information processes in spatial planning are addressed, which – as they constitute one subarea of e-democracy - aim at increased transparency and conceptual accessibility of urban planning processes. In the media part of the project, chatbots are explored as aspiring web communication features, being able to attract attention and to entertain. The focus of the project lies in the application of chatbots on Websites delivering planning information for citizens.

A chatbot simulates a human-like verbal conversation on a Web page, allowing a user to type complete questions or sentences into a text input field, and, in return, generating an answer that is printed on the screen or spoken by means of a voice synthesis. Recently, chatbots have experienced increased popularity on commercial Websites, often rendered together with the depiction of avatars[1] that represent virtual personalities (compare Figure 1). Chatbots are not only used for pure entertainment

[1] Avatar: A visual representative of a software agent (here, the chatbot) or of a real person in a virtual world.

S. Göbel, R. Malkewitz, and I. Iurgel (Eds.): TIDSE 2006, LNCS 4326, pp. 370–381, 2006.

on commercial Websites[2] but also increasingly for consulting purposes, or for information and education[3]. In the project „CitizenTalk", several functions of a possible chatbot have been explored. The example chatbot "Christian Friedrich" (compare Figure 1 in the German language) informs and consults citizens about the living conditions and development plans for the City of Gotha in Thuringia, Germany. Embedded into the main chat interaction on the left part of the screen, the bot offers links to explanatory graphics, maps and, for example, a glossary.

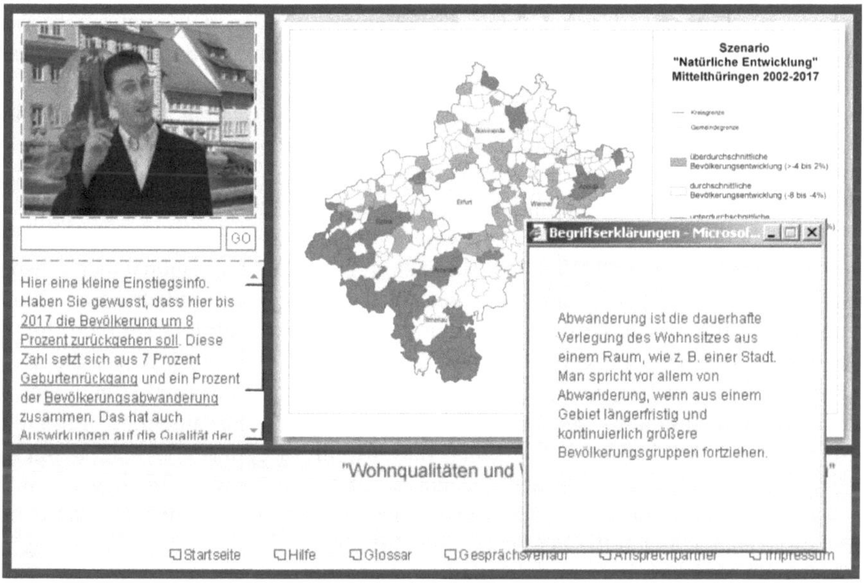

Fig. 1. CitizenTalk chatbot example, including the linked presentation of additional media

For its creation, we used AIML and ProgramD from the A.L.I.C.E. Foundation [1]. While the goal within the scope of the project was to apply state-of-the-art technology, and not to make it a technical development project, the actual research was on practical application procedures, building a bridge between two separate fields of study. This raised several difficulties, led to new insights and pointed to future work that is necessary beyond "mere" development of better chatbot technology.

This paper presents the case study of our application of chatbots to virtual planning communication. As a result, we discuss the affordances of chatbots for communication design and propose a modus operandi for their conception and development that includes storytelling aspects. We further present an authoring tool that supports

[2] Examples for commercial chatbots: "Epson Ink Devil": http://www.epson-store.de; FAQ-Bot "Mira" from Mercateo: http://www.mercateo.com; bank consultant "Max" from Sparkasse Erlangen: http://www.sparkasse-erlangen.de

[3] Examples for educational chatbots and consulting: "Horst Förster" from the „Future Wood" (Zukunftswald): http://www.zukunftswald.de; information desk bot "Stella" for the academic library: http://www.sub.uni-hamburg.de/informationen/projekte/infoass.html; military duty adviser "Stefanie" from the German Federal Armed Forces: http://mil.bundeswehr-karriere.de

the creation of structured dialogues with AIML. Finally, the practicality and the various prospects of chatbot development within the addressed domain are discussed.

2 Related Work in Applications of Chatbots

2.1 Virtual Communication in Spatial Planning

E-democracy is a collective term constituting political developments associated with varieties of electronic (mostly: Internet) communication in democratic processes, resulting in increased transparency and accountability. In this project, the emphasis is on electronic communication aiming at various levels of citizen involvement. In general, three main steps in increasing involvement can be recognized: e-information, e-participation, and e-cooperation [2]. As e-communication in democratic processes is still in its infancy, the first step of one-way information is currently the prevalent form, however, in increasing omnipresence even for small municipalities.

Within the project CitizenTalk, an exploration study has been carried out [3], analysing current electronic communication strategies in urban, regional and transport planning. It showed that in most all cases, the primary aim is still the first step of preparing the data for a Web presentation and, secondly, finding a structure for the data, leading to sufficient accessibility for end-users. This involves mainly the use of text and pictures, of late, increasingly enriched by videos and visual simulations, or even by participation tools, such as live chats and blogs. At the same time, it has to be recognized that basically for budgetary reasons, the scepticism among municipal carriers against the realisation and acceptance of further new technologies is high, often only allowing for a “simple” website. This is also the conclusion of an expert colloquium carried out at the FH Erfurt with participants from communal planning[4].

We didn´t find any other project employing chatbots with a similar goal as that of CitizenTalk – enhancing the human-machine interface for e-information, increasing the interest of new target groups through infotainment, and paving the road for future e-participation. The interviewed experts acknowledged the opportunities associated with the application of chatbots for delivering information in dialogical form, serving as FAQ substitute. Scepticism remained, however, concerning any applications of chatbots to the handling of more authoritative information.

2.2 Creation of Chatbot Content

Generally, there are several approaches to the task of designing human-computer conversations. Chatbots in their literal sense differ fundamentally from dialogue systems used in task-oriented applications, such as those designed for electronic information desks or limited-domain tutorials, since they also simulate a human being in addition to simply providing a language-based channel for the human-computer dialogue. Technically, they follow a pragmatic shallow approach that is designed to prioritize performance over deep logical structure in natural language processing, such as grammatical structure, dialogue goals, planning, or semantical inferences [4].

[4] Expert colloquium: „Zielgruppengerechte Aufbereitung online-gestützter Beteiligungsangebote in der Stadt-, Regional- und Verkehrsplanung“, FH Erfurt, 21 April 2005.

As a start, in our project, we used AIML[5], an XML dialect, for chatbot creation, for the one and only reason that it is highly accessible even for non-programmers. Both AIML and the chatbot program used are developments of the open source community A.L.I.C.E. AIML builds the so-called "knowledge base" of a chatbot [5]. It supports pattern matching following a simple "stimulus-response" principle. The simplest AIML element is a category, containing a pattern (the stimulus – any possible utterance of a user) and a template (the response – the corresponding answer of the bot). For the English language, there is a basic source for AIML categories available on the Web[6]. The predefined set mainly leads to basic small talk. For the German language, such a general knowledge base still has to be created.

The stimulus-response principle facilitates the creation of simple question-answer pairs as primitive dialogue elements. Though AIML is highly accessible as a creation language, it is hard to create a structured dialogue with it, especially when needing to avoid exact repetitions and to enable decent dialogue context. Even the creation of simple AIML is an obstacle for many media designers as persons in charge of Web communication. Therefore, recently, a number of AIML editors have been created[7]. These developments mainly focus on the reduction of the writing task for pure AIML. They also support the overview of the knowledge base, which can easily grow into a huge amount of categories. However, the currently existing AIML editors do not support any dialogue structuring.

2.3 Conclusions

In order to successfully apply chatbots to the field of e-communication for spatial planning in particular and democratic processes in general, the current state of the art in available technology and established concepts requires further developments:

- AIML follows a metaphor of a so-called "knowledge base" as a synonym for a collection of pattern-template pairs. This advances the assumption that transferring mere factual "knowledge" as questions and answers to chatbot programming is a straight-forward process. Instead, the task is rather more complex, since a chatbot dialogue has to be well-balanced with the overall appearance of its implicitly revealed personality. Thus, storytelling principles need to be applied to the design process.
- The current tools available for the creation of chatbot dialogues only simplify the XML coding of patterns and templates with a visual interface, but do not support the structuring of a dialogue for authors.

The CitizenTalk project mainly tackled the above-mentioned issues associated with the creation of a bot conversation that appears believable even in an application field far away from the entertainment business. The remaining portion of the article reports on the findings that have led to the development of example chatbot prototypes, a modus operandi and a prototype authoring tool for AIML that also supports the creation of conditional states within a conversation beyond questions and answers.

---

[5] AIML: Artificial Intelligence Markup Language.

[6] The Annotated A.L.I.C.E. AIML Files (AAA): http://www.alicebot.org/downloads/sets.html

[7] Recent AIML editors have been announced on http://www.alicebot.org/oldnews2006.html

3 Case Study: CitizenTalk

3.1 Interdisciplinary Challenges in the Creation of Chatbot Stories

As a result of looking at existing chatbots, certain expectations of the target group were prevalent that actually first had to be overcome in order to achieve better acceptance. First, a metaphor of a "know-it-all" chatbot rather reduced the appreciation of the whole application, and critical questions of trust were raised. Second, the creation of the chatbot's conversational behaviour is a function not only of a chatbot's technical development, but of the responsible design in agreement with the municipal persons in charge. There has to be a basic understanding of the limitations and possibilities of chatbots even by the non-technical knowledge providers. Instead of directly turning factual knowledge into a "knowledge base" of questions and answers in AIML, a different, practical modus operandi had to be developed, including the design of a fictional character, its personality traits and its communication goal. Figure 2 shows a schema of the process.

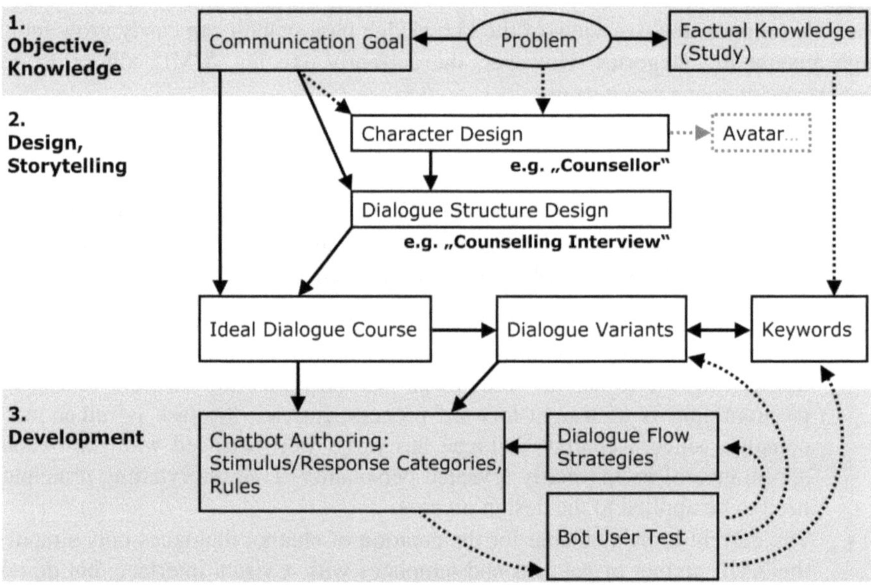

Fig. 2. Schema of the development process

Several experiences have shown that it is not effective to apply all known facts to the knowledge base of the chatbot – quite the contrary, as there are other media forms that are more reliable and trustworthy in terms of factual information. Users, as well as information providers, have been shown to believe more in traditionally presented electronic text as soon as the information concerned is crucial. Another major problem with the question-answer structure of typical contemporary chatbots is that, in order to retrieve information, users must know the specific questions that trigger the delivery of facts. In reality, this is not the case and leads to frustration.

On the path from existing knowledge to the technical knowledge base of the chatbot, the design of a virtual character is central, together with an associated dialogue structure that fits that character's role. In the case explained in Figures 1 and 2, it is a counsellor, who is actually able to explain facts on demographic trends in the region. As he has the goal to consult the Website visitor individually on suitable housing conditions in different areas of the City, his dialogue is structured around a catalogue of questions the user can answer. Another virtual character designed within the project was Martina, a private citizen concerned with urban management strategies, living in the future. She tells her personal story as an exemplary experience and is less dependent on the external information of users. Martina is quite obviously a fictional character. As an infotainment element, she entertains and informs along the way, not being assessed critically by end-users as presenting authoritative information, which could cause acceptance problems in the application domain. For each designed character, the minimum dialogue structure constitutes at least a conversation made up of a start, a main middle part and even an end – in contrast to the conventional, for the most part endless, chatbot conversations.

The design process described here involves basic storytelling strategies introduced to chatbot design, pointing in a different direction as to an abstract knowledge base of provided answers to user questions. After the story outline is generated, the technical chatbot development follows the typical workflow of iterative botmaster[8] activity, constantly testing the chatbot with users, in order to eliminate the cases where unmatched user input leads to conversational breakdowns. The botmasters, of course, have to take into account the personality of the designed character, while they also include strategies that shall lead the dialogue back on the track of the ideal course. In the experience of conducting our project, this turned out to be a complex, non-straightforward process, which makes the interdisciplinary work between the knowledge providers and the technical botmasters essential.

3.2 "Knowledge Base" Development in AIML

As mentioned in section 2, general AIML knowledge bases exist, and one initial expectation was to be able to reuse a lot of this work, since the workload of authoring a successful chatbot was considered massive. As implied by Figure 2, there is more than one type of dialogue element. Several levels of either more specific or more general AIML categories can be categorized that show differences in their reusability. They should be administrated separately in order to be easy to maintain. While some are context-dependent, as they fit into a designed course of interaction, others are more general. "Small talk" is the most general type of AIML category, which is nevertheless essential, since it is often the best strategy to overcome situations of non-matched user utterances. However, it can be stated that associated with increasingly specific story designs, reusability of existing code is decreasing.

Since a chatbot "knowledge base" needs constant administration and completion, most likely, several people have to cooperate and may even maintain the AIML base in parallel. The pure amount of code gets complex very quickly, reducing the facility of inspection for each team member.

---

[8] A botmaster is typically the programmer of a chatbot who maintains the knowledge base also during runtime while taking into account ongoing user interaction.

Finally, achieving the dialogue structure beyond simple question-answer pairs is a technical challenge in plain AIML. Stages in the course of the dialogue have to be distinguished by introducing abstract states, which, in AIML, can only be cumbersomely accomplished with the <topic> and <set> tags.

3.3 Conclusion

A result of these findings is the recognition of an existing chasm between the desirable storytelling concepts and the limitations of AIML, and the metaphor of an abstract "question-answer knowledge base". In order to support better conversational structure with AIML, and to support the creation process as an interlocking procedure between professionals of different disciplines, further achievements in the project were made with the development of an adjusted AIML authoring tool.

4 AIML Authoring Tool

The main emphasis in the development of the AIML authoring tool in the CitizenTalk project was on features for dialogue control. Further, it facilitates inspection of large AIML code bases, supporting the cooperative creation of AIML in a team.

4.1 Basic Dialogue Control

Even with the limited possibilities of AIML, some ways to implement basic dialogue flow strategies to the conversation system are possible. However, for most of the AIML chatbot creators, this is difficult to program. Examples are:

- States
- Occurrence counters
- Assembled templates

States
Using AIML elements, such as predicates (addressed by the <set> and <get> tags) and <topic>, we developed an approach to model the conversation as a basic system of states. States describe the conversation situation according to various criteria (state types), for example, dialogue stages, themes, user types, emotions, etc. According to their priority for the dialogue, state types will be defined hierarchically, so the combination of all states results in a tree structure representing various dialogue situations. Over the course of the conversation, states can be set, determining the bot responses given according to a current situation.

Occurrence Counter
In order to avoid repetitive bot answers and for triggering state transitions, we use counters to record the conversation flow. Since AIML does not support counting in any way, embedded PHP scripts are used to implement this feature.

Assembled Responses
A sort of mixed initiative dialogue can be emulated by appending state-dependent questions to answers of the bot, which are extracted from a "question pool" containing relevant prompts for every stage of conversation. This way, on the one

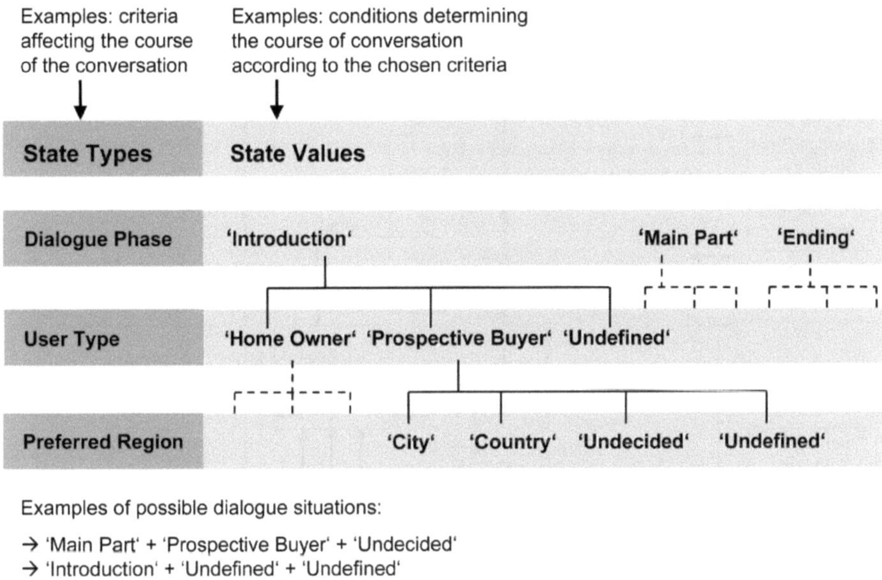

Fig. 3. System of proposed states

hand, the conversation can be kept on track by using the questions and prompts to go in a desired direction, and, on the other hand, this can be integrated in a form-filling strategy, in order to gather information about the user.

4.2 Tool Architecture

The authoring tool is a MySQL database Web application. Its front end is based on input forms written in HTML/PHP. Through two basic application views, authors may enter their dialogue concept and the stimulus/response categories without the necessity of knowing or following the exact AIML syntax. The entered data is stored in a MYSQL database, which provides the possibility to fill the knowledge base in a structured and consistent way, even by several authors at once. Then, authors are able to export stored categories into AIML files at any time and load these into any AIML-interpreting chatbot engine. For maintaining and documenting the knowledge base, search and report features are also implemented. Figure 4 not only shows the tool's architectural structure, but also illustrates the basic procedure to create a chatbot knowledge base using the authoring tool.

4.3 Using the Tool

Dialogue Structure

Starting from the chatbot's objective, a dialogue structure has to be designed in order to pursue a communication goal. Criteria for the definition of structural states (such as dialogue stages, emotional values or user criteria) have to be determined. There is no fixed guideline for how to find these criteria; this greatly depends on the goal. For a meaningful definition, a good understanding of their mode of operation is beneficial.

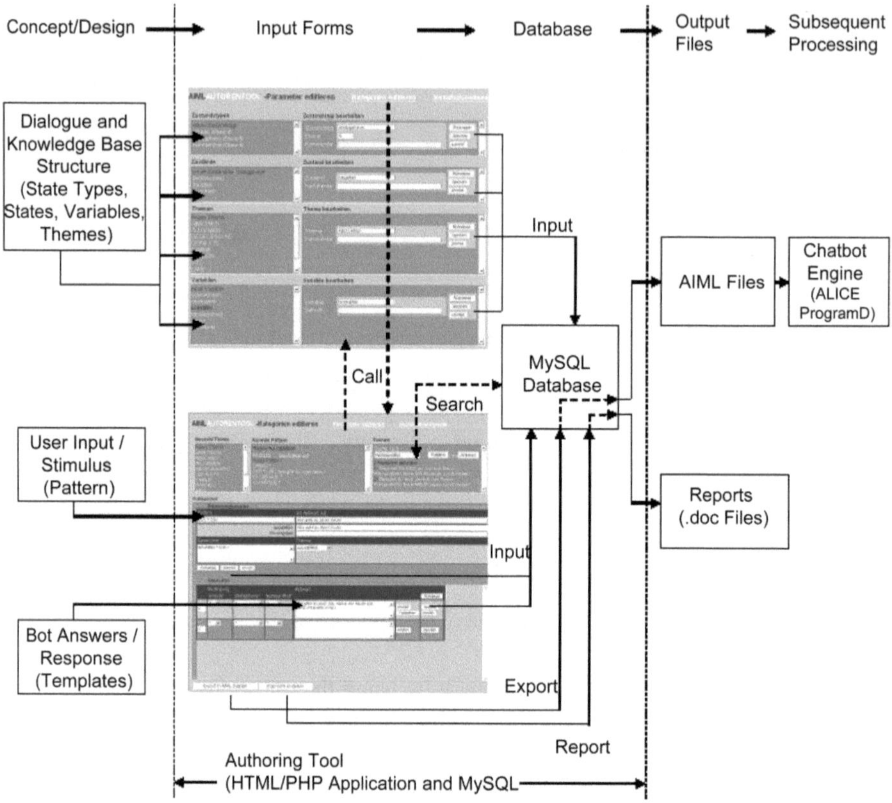

Fig. 4. Architecture of the authoring tool and process

Themes, Variables

Themes can be defined that structure the knowledge base for easier maintenance. Variables can store information extracted from the conversation course (e.g. user name, user age) to customize bot responses.

Conversation Example

An ideal dialogue course example is a good starting point. From there, dialogue variants can be derived and lists of keywords can be composed. Based on this information, first stimulus/response pairs are defined, beginning with so-called "default patterns" for each dialogue situation, matching in any event when a user's input can't be recognized otherwise.

Input Forms

Figure 5 shows the main input form. Once the dialogue structure and first stimulus response pairs are defined, the authoring tool's input forms will be used to

- enter the dialogue structure, themes and variables
- enter stimulus/response pairs considering different dialogue situations

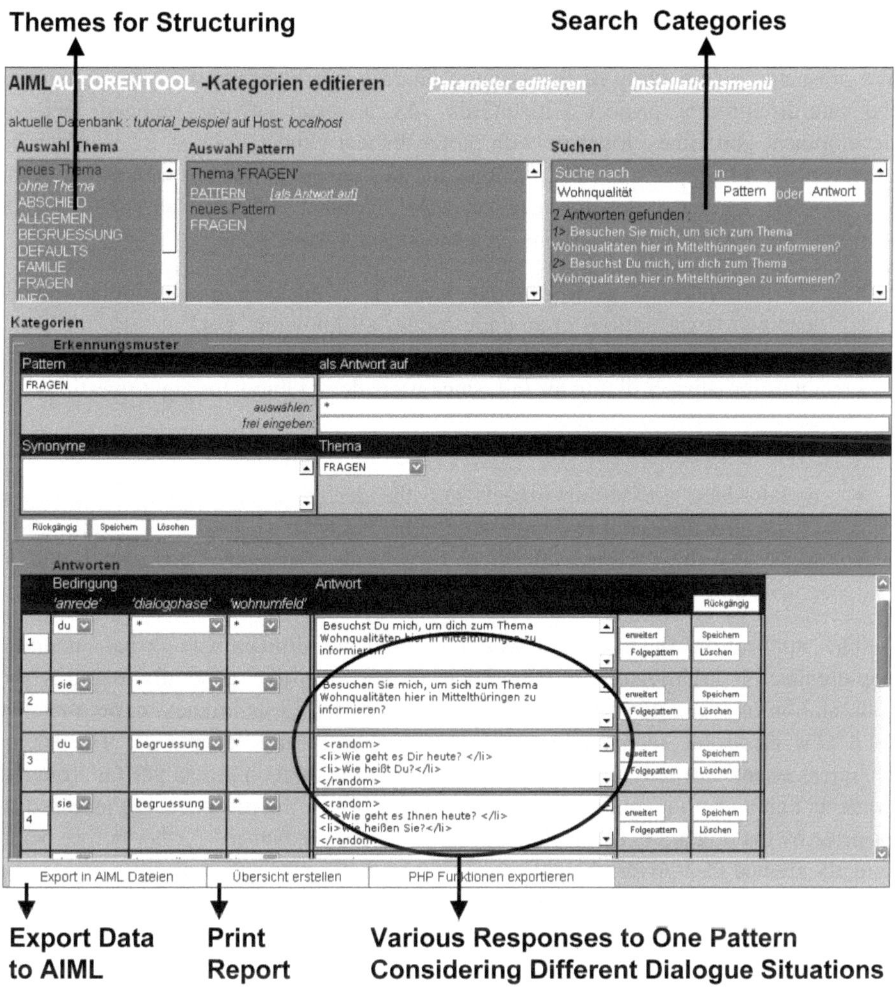

Fig. 5. Input forms of the authoring tool

- search for existing categories
- export data subdivided into themes from the database to AIML files
- print reports for documentation of the bot's knowledge base

Testing

Last but not least, generated AIML files can be loaded into any standard AIML-interpreting Chatbot engine, (e.g. Alice Programm D) where they can (and should) be tested by various prospective users repeatedly, in order to expand and advance the chatbot's ability to communicate with users.

5 Conclusions and Future Work

We presented a case study of the creation process for chatbot-based infotainment in the interdisciplinary project CitizenTalk. As a result of the realized lack of development guidelines, together with partly unclear expectations as to what can be achieved, we developed a modus operandi for the concept phases, as well as a tool for the concrete technical development of AIML content. Looking at contemporary chatbots, we learned several lessons on what does not work:

- The metaphor of a “knowledge base” is a misleading conceptual model, leading to expectations of an undesirable “all-knowing” bot;
- Reusable knowledge bases exist, but lead to simple question-answer dialogues;
- Question-answer dialogues fail, since users do not know the right questions.

As solutions to these issues, we propose

- to introduce storytelling aspects into the design process, such as creating a character with a goal in a limited domain, and having a backstory to tell;
- to avoid waiting for user questions by offering a structured dialogue, based on conversational states.

The application field of e-democracy, and the domain of virtual planning communication highlighted in this article, is an area that generally requires the presentation of accountable information, while it is still in its infancy, experimenting with new electronic media in respect to accessibility and acceptance. The socio-technical issues currently under discussion within the domain are as yet far from the contents that a chatbot could deliver believably. Though the prospects are assessed as positive by the domain experts, chatbots still need to be advanced further before being directly applied to e-governmental areas, in which still more pilot projects have to be carried out. Then, we suggest that the apparent character and the story frame of the chatbot should be designed carefully, in order to avoid possible irritations concerning its potential role as a representative.

Future conceptual work includes the creation of more design guidelines for chatbot applications. During the project, first category collections of conversational turns have been identified that build the basis of a practical “cookbook” for the creation of chatbot conversations. This work will have to be followed up, since there are numerous different conversational situations to be identified.

Acknowledgements

The project "CitizenTalk" has received funds from the German Federal State of Thuringia. Thanks to Jana Liebe and Heidi Sinning for the many fruitful discussions on aspects of virtual planning communication and for the collaboration in knowledge base creation.

References

1. A.L.I.C.E. Artificial Linguistic Internet Computer Entity, Alicebot Foundation, http://www.alicebot.org (Last accessed: 07.31.2006)
2. Boden, C., Fischer, J., Herbig, K., Liebe, J. Sinning, H., Spierling, U.: Chatbots als Instrument der Planungskommunikation – Chancen, Anforderungen und Perspektiven. In: Proceedings of Informatik 2006, Dresden (2006)
3. Richter, S. & Sinning, H.: Online-gestützte Kommunikationsformen für Handlungsfelder der Stadt-, Regional- und Verkehrsplanung. Exploration Study, Erfurt (in print, 2006)
4. Wilks, Y. & Catizone, R.: Human-Computer Conversation. Encyclopedia of Microcomputers. Dekker, New York. (2000)
5. Wallace, R.: The Elements of AIML Style. ALICE A.I. Foundation, Inc. Online: http://www.alicebot.org/documentation/ (Last accessed: 07.31.2006) (2003)

Author Index

Lecture Notes in Computer Science

For information about Vols. 1–4233

please contact your bookseller or Springer

Vol. 4337: S. Arun-Kumar, N. Garg (Eds.), FSTTCS 2006: Foundations of Software Technology and Theoretical Computer Science. XIII, 430 pages. 2006.

Vol. 4331: G. Min, B. Di Martino, L.T. Yang, M. Guo, G. Ruenger (Eds.), Frontiers of High Performance Computing and Networking – ISPA 2006 Workshops. XXVII, 1141 pages. 2006.

Vol. 4329: R. Barua, T. Lange (Eds.), Progress in Cryptology - INDOCRYPT 2006. X, 454 pages. 2006.

Vol. 4326: S. Göbel, R. Malkewitz, I. Iurgel (Eds.), Technologies for Interactive Digital Storytelling and Entertainment. X, 384 pages. 2006.

Vol. 4325: J. Cao, I. Stojmenovic, X. Jia, S.K. Das (Eds.), Mobile Ad-hoc and Sensor Networks. XIX, 887 pages. 2006.

Vol. 4318: H. Lipmaa, M. Yung, D. Lin (Eds.), Information Security and Cryptology. XI, 305 pages. 2006.

Vol. 4313: T. Margaria, B. Steffen (Eds.), Leveraging Applications of Formal Methods. IX, 197 pages. 2006.

Vol. 4312: S. Sugimoto, J. Hunter, A. Rauber, A. Morishima (Eds.), Digital Libraries: Achievements, Challenges and Opportunities. XVIII, 571 pages. 2006.

Vol. 4311: K. Cho, P. Jacquet (Eds.), Technologies for Advanced Heterogeneous Networks II. XI, 253 pages. 2006.

Vol. 4307: P. Ning, S. Qing, N. Li (Eds.), Information and Communications Security. XIV, 558 pages. 2006.

Vol. 4306: Y. Avrithis, Y. Kompatsiaris, S. Staab, N.E. O'Connor (Eds.), Semantic Multimedia. XII, 241 pages. 2006.

Vol. 4304: A. Sattar, B.-H. Kang (Eds.), AI 2006: Advances in Artificial Intelligence. XXVII, 1303 pages. 2006. (Sublibrary LNAI).

Vol. 4302: J. Domingo-Ferrer, L. Franconi (Eds.), Privacy in Statistical Databases. XI, 383 pages. 2006.

Vol. 4301: D. Pointcheval, Y. Mu, K. Chen (Eds.), Cryptology and Network Security. XIII, 381 pages. 2006.

Vol. 4300: Y.Q. Shi (Ed.), Transactions on Data Hiding and Multimedia Security I. IX, 139 pages. 2006.

Vol. 4296: M.S. Rhee, B. Lee (Eds.), Information Security and Cryptology – ICISC. XIII, 358 pages. 2006.

Vol. 4295: J.D. Carswell, T. Tezuka (Eds.), Web and Wireless Geographical Information Systems. XI, 269 pages. 2006.

Vol. 4293: A. Gelbukh, C.A. Reyes-Garcia (Eds.), MICAI 2006: Advances in Artificial Intelligence. XXVIII, 1232 pages. 2006. (Sublibrary LNAI).

Vol. 4292: G. Bebis, R. Boyle, B. Parvin, D. Koracin, P. Remagnino, A. Nefian, G. Meenakshisundaram, V. Pascucci, J. Zara, J. Molineros, H. Theisel, T. Malzbender (Eds.), Advances in Visual Computing, Part II. XXXII, 906 pages. 2006.

Vol. 4291: G. Bebis, R. Boyle, B. Parvin, D. Koracin, P. Remagnino, A. Nefian, G. Meenakshisundaram, V. Pascucci, J. Zara, J. Molineros, H. Theisel, T. Malzbender (Eds.), Advances in Visual Computing, Part I. XXXI, 916 pages. 2006.

Vol. 4290: M. van Steen, M. Henning (Eds.), Middleware 2006. XIII, 425 pages. 2006.

Vol. 4289: M. Ackermann, B. Berendt, M. Grobelnik, A. Hotho, D. Mladenič, G. Semeraro, M. Spiliopoulou, G. Stumme, V. Svatek, M. van Someren (Eds.), Semantics, Web and Mining. X, 197 pages. 2006. (Sublibrary LNAI).

Vol. 4288: T. Asano (Ed.), Algorithms and Computation. XX, 766 pages. 2006.

Vol. 4285: Y. Matsumoto, R. Sproat, K.-F. Wong, M. Zhang (Eds.), Computer Processing of Oriental Languages. XVII, 544 pages. 2006. (Sublibrary LNAI).

Vol. 4284: X. Lai, K. Chen (Eds.), Advances in Cryptology – ASIACRYPT 2006. XIV, 468 pages. 2006.

Vol. 4283: Y.Q. Shi, B. Jeon (Eds.), Digital Watermarking. XII, 474 pages. 2006.

Vol. 4282: Z. Pan, A. Cheok, M. Haller, R.W.H. Lau, H. Saito, R. Liang (Eds.), Advances in Artificial Reality and Tele-Existence. XXIII, 1347 pages. 2006.

Vol. 4281: K. Barkaoui, A. Cavalcanti, A. Cerone (Eds.), Theoretical Aspects of Computing - ICTAC 2006. XV, 371 pages. 2006.

Vol. 4280: A.K. Datta, M. Gradinariu (Eds.), Stabilization, Safety, and Security of Distributed Systems. XVII, 590 pages. 2006.

Vol. 4279: N. Kobayashi (Ed.), Programming Languages and Systems. XI, 423 pages. 2006.

Vol. 4278: R. Meersman, Z. Tari, P. Herrero (Eds.), On the Move to Meaningful Internet Systems 2006: OTM 2006 Workshops, Part II. XLV, 1004 pages. 2006.

Vol. 4277: R. Meersman, Z. Tari, P. Herrero (Eds.), On the Move to Meaningful Internet Systems 2006: OTM 2006 Workshops, Part I. XLV, 1009 pages. 2006.

Vol. 4276: R. Meersman, Z. Tari (Eds.), On the Move to Meaningful Internet Systems 2006: CoopIS, DOA, GADA, and ODBASE, Part II. XXXII, 752 pages. 2006.

Vol. 4275: R. Meersman, Z. Tari (Eds.), On the Move to Meaningful Internet Systems 2006: CoopIS, DOA, GADA, and ODBASE, Part I. XXXI, 1115 pages. 2006.

Vol. 4274: Q. Huo, B. Ma, E.-S. Chng, H. Li (Eds.), Chinese Spoken Language Processing. XXIV, 805 pages. 2006. (Sublibrary LNAI).

Vol. 4273: I. Cruz, S. Decker, D. Allemang, C. Preist, D. Schwabe, P. Mika, M. Uschold, L. Aroyo (Eds.), The Semantic Web - ISWC 2006. XXIV, 1001 pages. 2006.

Vol. 4272: P. Havinga, M. Lijding, N. Meratnia, M. Wegdam (Eds.), Smart Sensing and Context. XI, 267 pages. 2006.

Vol. 4271: F.V. Fomin (Ed.), Graph-Theoretic Concepts in Computer Science. XIII, 358 pages. 2006.

Vol. 4270: H. Zha, Z. Pan, H. Thwaites, A.C. Addison, M. Forte (Eds.), Interactive Technologies and Sociotechnical Systems. XVI, 547 pages. 2006.

Vol. 4269: R. State, S. van der Meer, D. O'Sullivan, T. Pfeifer (Eds.), Large Scale Management of Distributed Systems. XIII, 282 pages. 2006.

Vol. 4268: G. Parr, D. Malone, M. Ó Foghlú (Eds.), Autonomic Principles of IP Operations and Management. XIII, 237 pages. 2006.

Vol. 4267: A. Helmy, B. Jennings, L. Murphy, T. Pfeifer (Eds.), Autonomic Management of Mobile Multimedia Services. XIII, 257 pages. 2006.

Vol. 4266: H. Yoshiura, K. Sakurai, K. Rannenberg, Y. Murayama, S. Kawamura (Eds.), Advances in Information and Computer Security. XIII, 438 pages. 2006.

Vol. 4265: L. Todorovski, N. Lavrač, K.P. Jantke (Eds.), Discovery Science. XIV, 384 pages. 2006. (Sublibrary LNAI).

Vol. 4264: J.L. Balcázar, P.M. Long, F. Stephan (Eds.), Algorithmic Learning Theory. XIII, 393 pages. 2006. (Sublibrary LNAI).

Vol. 4263: A. Levi, E. Savas, H. Yenigün, S. Balcisoy, Y. Saygin (Eds.), Computer and Information Sciences – ISCIS 2006. XXIII, 1084 pages. 2006.

Vol. 4262: K. Havelund, M. Núñez, B. Wolff, G. Roşu, B. Wolff (Eds.), Formal Approaches to Software Testing and Runtime Verification. VIII, 255 pages. 2006.

Vol. 4261: Y. Zhuang, S. Yang, Y. Rui, Q. He (Eds.), Advances in Multimedia Information Processing - PCM 2006. XXII, 1040 pages. 2006.

Vol. 4260: Z. Liu, J. He (Eds.), Formal Methods and Software Engineering. XII, 778 pages. 2006.

Vol. 4259: S. Greco, Y. Hata, S. Hirano, M. Inuiguchi, S. Miyamoto, H.S. Nguyen, R. Słowiński (Eds.), Rough Sets and Current Trends in Computing. XXII, 951 pages. 2006. (Sublibrary LNAI).

Vol. 4257: I. Richardson, P. Runeson, R. Messnarz (Eds.), Software Process Improvement. XI, 219 pages. 2006.

Vol. 4256: L. Feng, G. Wang, C. Zeng, R. Huang (Eds.), Web Information Systems – WISE 2006 Workshops. XIV, 320 pages. 2006.

Vol. 4255: K. Aberer, Z. Peng, E.A. Rundensteiner, Y. Zhang, X. Li (Eds.), Web Information Systems – WISE 2006. XIV, 563 pages. 2006.

Vol. 4254: T. Grust, H. Höpfner, A. Illarramendi, S. Jablonski, M. Mesiti, S. Müller, P.-L. Patranjan, K.-U. Sattler, M. Spiliopoulou, J. Wijsen (Eds.), Current Trends in Database Technology – EDBT 2006. XXXI, 932 pages. 2006.

Vol. 4253: B. Gabrys, R.J. Howlett, L.C. Jain (Eds.), Knowledge-Based Intelligent Information and Engineering Systems, Part III. XXXII, 1301 pages. 2006. (Sublibrary LNAI).

Vol. 4252: B. Gabrys, R.J. Howlett, L.C. Jain (Eds.), Knowledge-Based Intelligent Information and Engineering Systems, Part II. XXXIII, 1335 pages. 2006. (Sublibrary LNAI).

Vol. 4251: B. Gabrys, R.J. Howlett, L.C. Jain (Eds.), Knowledge-Based Intelligent Information and Engineering Systems, Part I. LXVI, 1297 pages. 2006. (Sublibrary LNAI).

Vol. 4250: H.J. van den Herik, S.-C. Hsu, T.-s. Hsu, H.H.L.M. Donkers (Eds.), Advances in Computer Games. XIV, 273 pages. 2006.

Vol. 4249: L. Goubin, M. Matsui (Eds.), Cryptographic Hardware and Embedded Systems - CHES 2006. XII, 462 pages. 2006.

Vol. 4248: S. Staab, V. Svátek (Eds.), Managing Knowledge in a World of Networks. XIV, 400 pages. 2006. (Sublibrary LNAI).

Vol. 4247: T.-D. Wang, X. Li, S.-H. Chen, X. Wang, H. Abbass, H. Iba, G. Chen, X. Yao (Eds.), Simulated Evolution and Learning. XXI, 940 pages. 2006.

Vol. 4246: M. Hermann, A. Voronkov (Eds.), Logic for Programming, Artificial Intelligence, and Reasoning. XIII, 588 pages. 2006. (Sublibrary LNAI).

Vol. 4245: A. Kuba, L.G. Nyúl, K. Palágyi (Eds.), Discrete Geometry for Computer Imagery. XIII, 688 pages. 2006.

Vol. 4244: S. Spaccapietra (Ed.), Journal on Data Semantics VII. XI, 267 pages. 2006.

Vol. 4243: T. Yakhno, E.J. Neuhold (Eds.), Advances in Information Systems. XIII, 420 pages. 2006.

Vol. 4242: A. Rashid, M. Aksit (Eds.), Transactions on Aspect-Oriented Software Development II. IX, 289 pages. 2006.

Vol. 4241: R.R. Beichel, M. Sonka (Eds.), Computer Vision Approaches to Medical Image Analysis. XI, 262 pages. 2006.

Vol. 4239: H.Y. Youn, M. Kim, H. Morikawa (Eds.), Ubiquitous Computing Systems. XVI, 548 pages. 2006.

Vol. 4238: Y.-T. Kim, M. Takano (Eds.), Management of Convergence Networks and Services. XVIII, 605 pages. 2006.

Vol. 4237: H. Leitold, E. Markatos (Eds.), Communications and Multimedia Security. XII, 253 pages. 2006.

Vol. 4236: L. Breveglieri, I. Koren, D. Naccache, J.-P. Seifert (Eds.), Fault Diagnosis and Tolerance in Cryptography. XIII, 253 pages. 2006.

Vol. 4234: I. King, J. Wang, L. Chan, D. Wang (Eds.), Neural Information Processing, Part III. XXII, 1227 pages. 2006.

MIX
Papier aus verantwortungsvollen Quellen
Paper from responsible sources
FSC® C105338

If you have any concerns about our products,
you can contact us on
ProductSafety@springernature.com

In case Publisher is established outside the EU,
the EU authorized representative is:
Springer Nature Customer Service Center GmbH
Europaplatz 3, 69115 Heidelberg, Germany

Printed by Libri Plureos GmbH
in Hamburg, Germany